Using Excel

For *Principles of Econometrics, Fourth Edition*

Using Excel

For *Principles of Econometrics, Fourth Edition*

GENEVIEVE BRIAND
Washington State University

R. CARTER HILL
Louisiana State University

JOHN WILEY & SONS, INC
New York / Chichester / Weinheim / Brisbane / Singapore / Toronto

Genevieve Briand dedicates this work to Tom Trulove

Carter Hill dedicates this work to Todd and Peter

This book was set by the authors.

To order books or for customer service call 1-800-CALL-WILEY (225-5945)

ISBN-13 978-111-803210-7

10 9 8 7 6 5 4 3 2 1

Preface

This book is a supplement to *Principles of Econometrics, 4th Edition* by R. Carter Hill, William E. Griffiths and Guay C. Lim (Wiley, 2011). This book is not a substitute for the textbook, nor is it a stand alone computer manual. It is a companion to the textbook, showing how to perform the examples in the textbook using Excel 2007. This book will be useful to students taking econometrics, as well as their instructors, and others who wish to use Excel for econometric analysis.

In addition to this computer manual for Excel, there are similar manuals and support for the software packages EViews, Gretl, Shazam, and Stata. In addition, all the data for *Principles of Econometrics, 4th* in various formats, including Excel, are available at **http://www.wiley.com/college/hill**. Individual data files, as well as errata for this manual and the textbook, can also be found at **http://principlesofeconometrics.com**.

The chapters in this book parallel the chapters in *Principles of Econometrics, 4th*. Thus, if you seek help for the examples in Chapter 11 of the textbook, check Chapter 11 in this book. However within a Chapter the sections numbers in *Principles of Econometrics, 4th* do not necessarily correspond to the Excel manual sections.

This work is a revision of *Using Excel 2007 for Principles of Econometrics, 3rd Edition* by Genevieve Briand and R. Carter Hill (Wiley, 2010). Genevieve Briand is the corresponding author.

We welcome comments on this book, and suggestions for improvement. *

Genevieve Briand
School of Economic Sciences
Washington State University
Pullman, WA 99164
gbriand@wsu.edu

R. Carter Hill
Economics Department
Louisiana State University
Baton Rouge, LA 70803
eohill@lsu.edu

BRIEF CONTENTS

CONTENTS

CHAPTER 1

Introduction to Excel

CHAPTER OUTLINE

1.1 STARTING EXCEL

Find the **Excel** shortcut on your desktop. Double click on it to start Excel (left clicks).

Alternatively, left-click the **Start** menu at the bottom left corner of your computer screen.

Slide your mouse over **All programs**, **Microsoft Office**, and finally **Microsoft Office Excel 2007**. Left-click on this last one to start Excel—or better yet, if you would like to create a shortcut, right-click on it; slide your mouse over **Send to**, and then select (i.e. drag your mouse over and left-click on) **Desktop (create shortcut)**. An Excel 2007 short-cut is created on your desktop. If you right-click on your shortcut and select **Rename,** you can also type in a shorter name like Excel.

Excel opens to a new file, titled Book1. You can find the name of the open file on the very top of the Excel window, on the **Title bar**. An Excel file like Book1 contains several sheets. By default, Excel opens to Sheet1 of Book1. You can figure out which sheet is open by looking at the **Sheet tabs** found in the lower left corner of your Excel window.

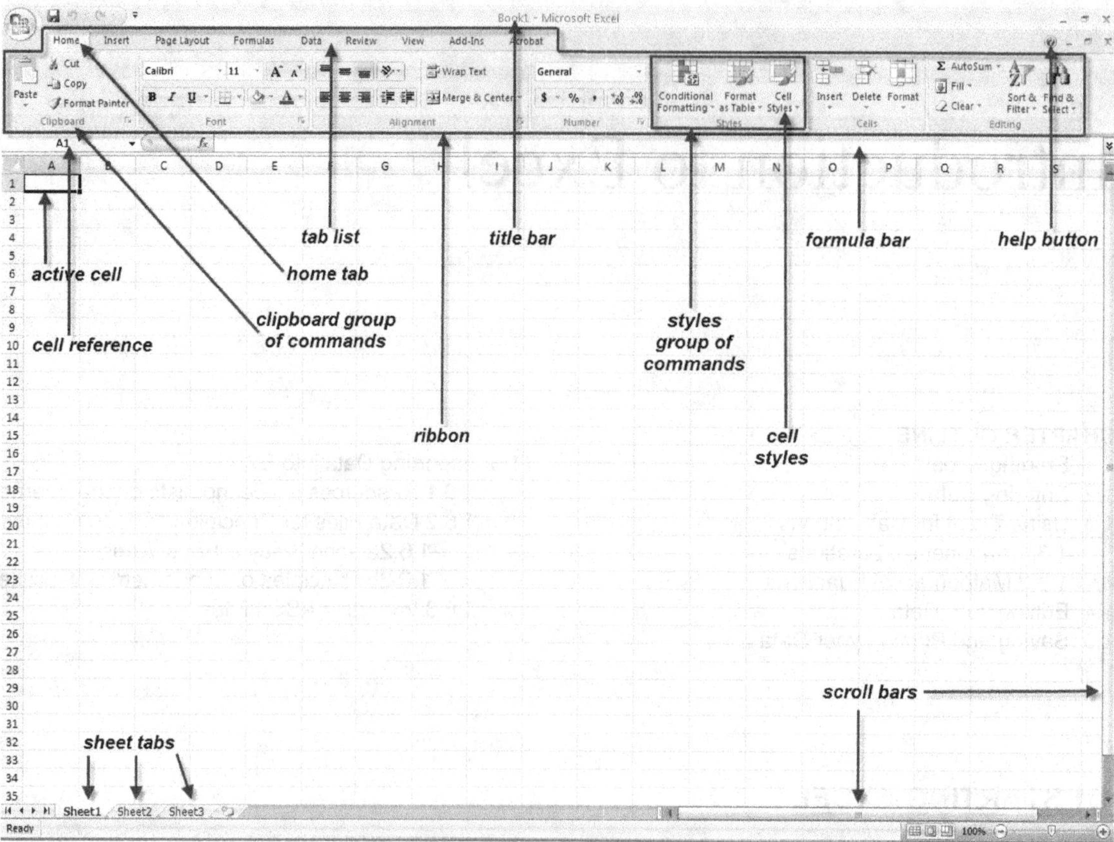

There are lots of little bits that you will become more familiar with as we go along. **The Active cell** is surrounded by a border and is in Column A and Row 1; its **Cell reference** is **A1**.

Below the title bar is a **Tab list**. The **Home tab** is the one Excel opens to. Under each tab you will find groups of commands. Under the home tab, the first one is the **Clipboard group of commands**, named after the tasks it relates to. The wide bar including the tab list *and* the groups of commands is referred to as the **Ribbon**. The content of the **Active cell** shows up in the **Formula bar** (right now, there is nothing in it). Perhaps the most important of all of this is to locate the **Help button** on the upper right corner of the Excel window. Finally, you can use the **Scroll bars** and the arrows around them to navigate up-down and right-left in your worksheet. And you have a long way to go: each worksheet in Microsoft Excel 2007 contains 1,048,576 rows and 16,384 columns!!!!

Note that your **Ribbon** might look slightly different than the one shown above. If your screen is bigger, Excel will automatically display more of its available options. For example, in the **Styles** group of command, instead of the **Cell styles** button, you might have a colorful display of cell styles.

1.2 ENTERING DATA

We will use Excel to analyze data. To enter labels and data into an Excel worksheet move the cursor to a cell and type. First type **X** in cell **A1**. Press the **Enter** key on your keyboard to get to cell **A2** or navigate by moving the cursor with the mouse, or use the **Arrow** keys (to move right, left, up or down). Fill in the rest as shown below:

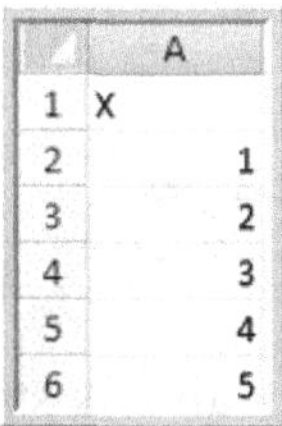

	A
1	X
2	1
3	2
4	3
5	4
6	5

1.3 USING EXCEL FOR CALCULATIONS

What is Excel good for? Its primary usefulness is to carry out repeated calculations. We can add, subtract, multiply and divide; and we can apply mathematical and statistical functions to the data in our worksheet. To illustrate, we are going to compute the squares of the numbers we just entered and then add them up. There are two main ways to perform calculations in Excel. One is to write formulas using arithmetic operators; the other is to write formulas using mathematical functions.

1.3.1 Arithmetic Operations

Select the **Excel Help** button in the upper right corner of your screen. In the window of the **Excel Help** dialog box that pops up, type **arithmetic operators** and select **Search**. In the list of results, select **Calculation operators and precedence**.

Standard arithmetic operators are defined as shown below. To close the Excel help dialog box, select the **X** button found on its upper right corner.

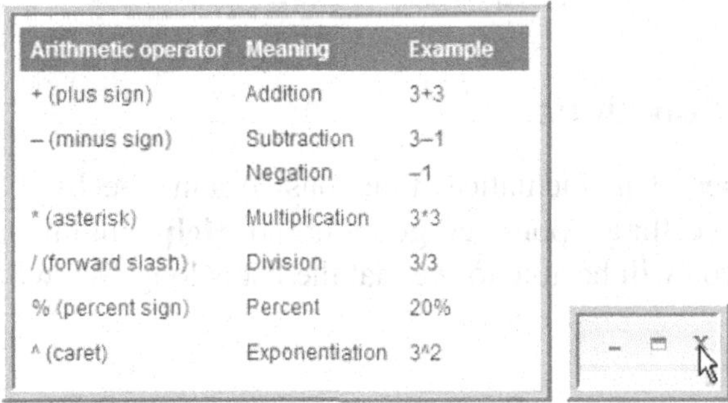

Arithmetic operator	Meaning	Example
+ (plus sign)	Addition	3+3
– (minus sign)	Subtraction Negation	3–1 –1
* (asterisk)	Multiplication	3*3
/ (forward slash)	Division	3/3
% (percent sign)	Percent	20%
^ (caret)	Exponentiation	3^2

Place your cursor in cell **B1**, and type **X-squared**. In cells **B2** through **B6** below (henceforth referred to as **B2:B6**), we are going to compute the squares of the corresponding values from cells **A2:A6**. *Let us emphasize that the trick to using Excel efficiently is NOT to re-type values already stored in the worksheet, but instead to use references of cells where the values are stored.* So, to compute the square of 1, which is the value stored in cell **A1**, instead of using the formula **=1*1**, you should use the formula **=A2*A2** or **=A2^2**. Place your cursor in cell **B2** and type the formula.

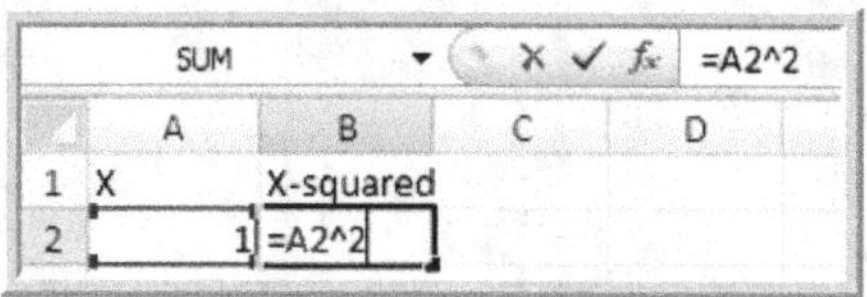

Then press **Enter**. Note that: (1) a formula always starts with an equal sign; this is how Excel recognizes *it is* a formula, and (2) formulas are not case sensitive, so you could also have typed **=a2^2** instead. Now, we want to copy this formula to cells **B3:B6**. To do that, place your cursor back into cell **B2**, and move it to the south-east corner of the cell, until the fat cross turns into a skinny one, as shown below:

	A	B	C
1	X	X-squared	
2	1	1	
3	2		

Left-click, hold it, drag it down to the next four cells below, and release!

Excel has copied the formula you typed in cell **B2** into the cells below. The way Excel understands the instructions you gave in cell **B2** is "square the value found at the address **A2**". Now, it is important to understand how Excel interprets "address **A2**". To Excel "address **A2**" means "from where you are at, go left by one cell"—because this is where **A2** is located vis-à-vis **B2**. In other words, an address gives directions: left-right, up-down, and distances: number of cells away—all in reference to the cell where the formula is entered. So, when we copied the formula we entered in cell **B2**, which instructed Excel to collect the value stored one-cell away from its left, and then square it—those exact same instructions were given in cells **B3:B6**. If you place your cursor back into **B3**, and look at the **Formula bar**, you can see that, in this cell, these same instructions translate into "**=A3^2**".

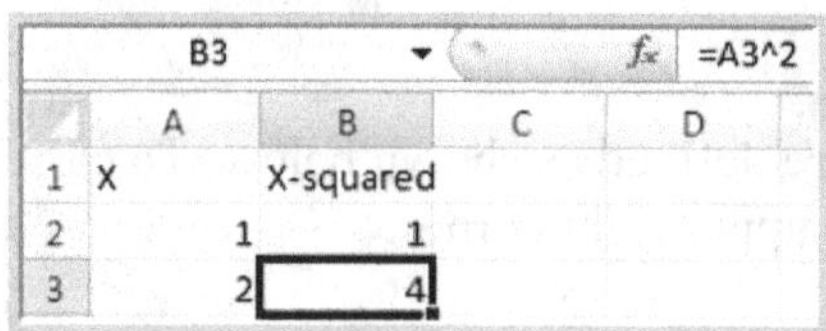

1.3.2 Mathematical Functions

There are a large number of mathematical functions. Again, the list of functions available in Excel can be found by calling upon our good friend **Help** button and type **Mathematical functions**. If you try it, you will be able to see that the list is long. We will not copy it here.

We did compute the squares of the numbers we had. Now we will add them up—the numbers, and the squares of the numbers, separately. For that, we will be using the **SUM** function.

We first need to select or highlight all the numbers from our table. There are several ways to highlight cells. For this small area the easiest way is to place your cursor in **A2**, hold down the left mouse button and drag it across the area you wish to highlight—i.e. all the way to cell **B6**. Here is how your worksheet should look like:

	A	B
1	X	X-squared
2	1	1
3	2	4
4	3	9
5	4	16
6	5	25

Next, go to the **Editing** group of command, which is found in the extreme right of the **Home** tab, and select **Σ AutoSum**.

Excel sums the numbers from each column and places the sum in the bottom cell of each column. The result is:

	A	B
1	X	X-squared
2	1	1
3	2	4
4	3	9
5	4	16
6	5	25
7	15	55

Notice that if you select the arrow found to the right of **Σ AutoSum** you can find a list of additional calculations that Excel can automatically perform for you.

Alternatively, you could have placed your cursor in cell **A7**, typed **=SUM(A2:A6)**, and pressed the **Enter** key (and then copied this formula to cell **B7**).

Note that: (1) as soon as you type the first letter of your function, a list of all the other available functions that start with the same letter pops up. This can be very useful: if you left click on any of them, Excel gives you its definition; if you double left-click on any of them, it automatically finishes typing the function name for you, and (2) once the function name and the opening parenthesis are typed, Excel reminds you of what the needed **Arguments** are, i.e. what else you need to specify in your function to use it properly.

Now, you could also have used the **Insert function** button, which you can find on the left side of the **Formula bar**.

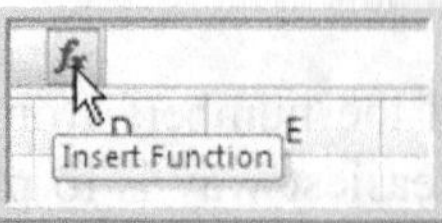

Once your cursor is placed in **A7**, select the **Insert function** button. An **Insert function** dialog box pops up. You can **Select a function** you need (highlight it, and select **OK**), or **Search for a function** first (follow the instructions given in that window).

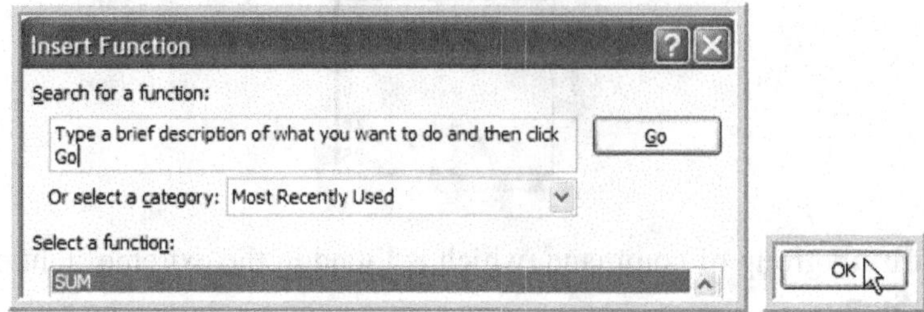

In the **Function Arguments** dialog box that pops up, you need to specify the cell references of the values you want to add. If they are not already properly specified, you can type **A2:A6** in the **Number 1** window, or place your cursor in the window, delete whatever is in it, and then select **A2:A6**. Select **OK**. Now that you have the formula in **A7**, copy it into **B7**.

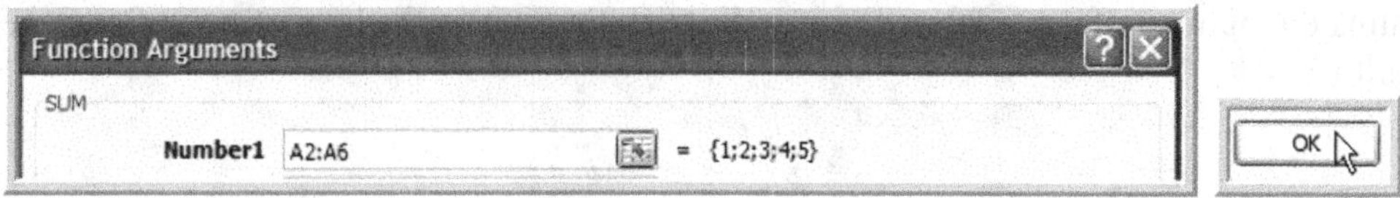

1.4 EDITING YOUR DATA

Before wrapping-up, you want to polish the presentation of your data. It actually has less to do with appearance than with organization and communication. You want to make sure that anyone can easily make sense of your table (like your instructor for example, or yourself for that matter—when you come back to it after you let it sit for a while).

We are going to add labels and color/shade to our table. Hold your cursor over cell **A** until it turns into an arrow-down; left-click to select the whole column; and select **Insert** in the **Cells** group of commands, found left to the **Editing** group of commands.

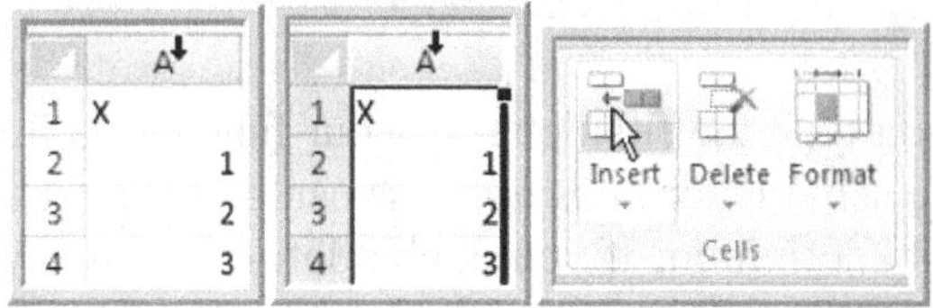

Excel adds a new column to the left of the one you selected. That's where we are going to write our labels. In the new **A1** cell, type **Variables**; in cell **A2**, type **Values**; in cell **A7** type **Sum**.

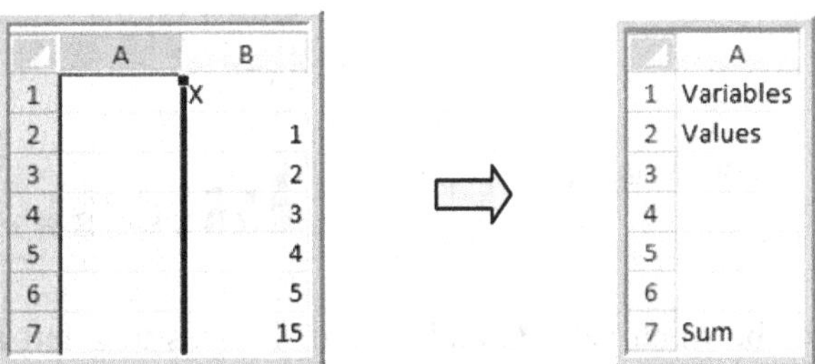

Select column **A** again, make it **Bold (Font** group of commands, right to the **Clipboard** one), and align it **Left (Alignment** group of commands, right to the **Font** one).

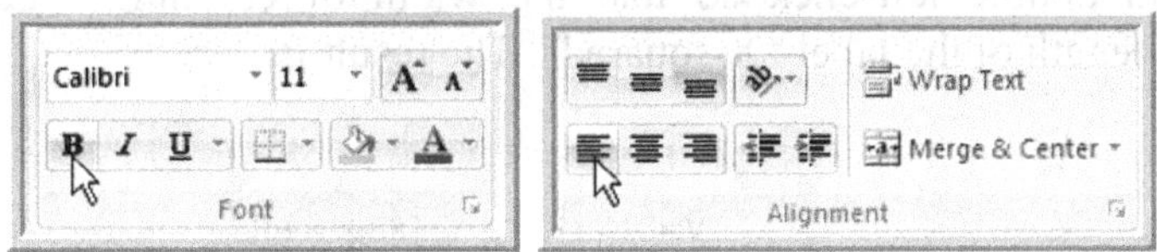

Select cells **B1** and **C1**, and make them **Bold**. Repeat with cells **B7** and **C7**. Better, but not there yet. Select row 7, make it **Italic** (next to **Bold**). Select column **B**, hold your left-click and drag your mouse over cell **C** to select column **C** too; select **Center** alignment (next to **Left**). Next, select **A2:A6**; left-click the arrow next to **Merge & Center** (on the **Alignment** group of commands), and select **Merge cells**.

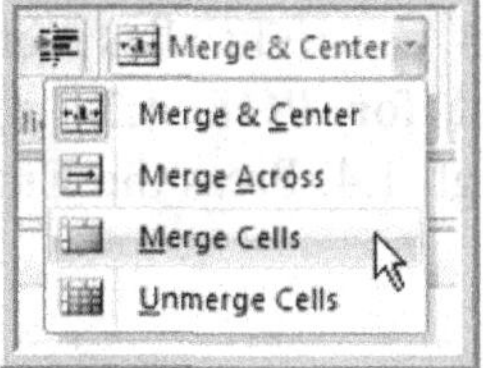

Immediately after, select **Middle Align**, which is found right above the **Center** alignment button.

Select **A1:C7**, left-click the arrow next to the **Bottom Border** button and select **All Borders**.

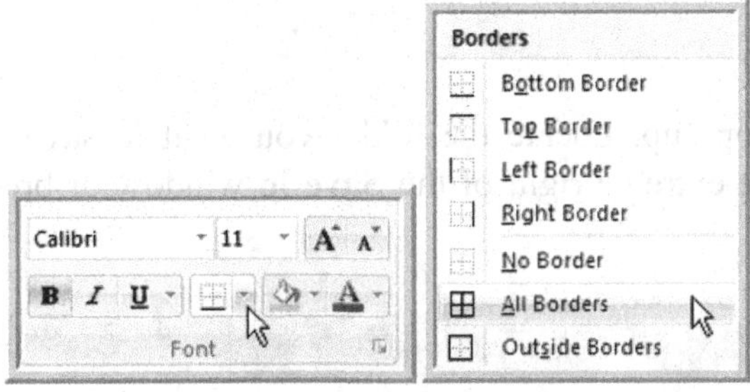

Select **A7:C7** (**A7:C7**, not **A1:C7** this time), left-click the arrow next to the **Fill Color** button, and select a grey color to fill in the cell with. Choose a different color for **A1:C1**.

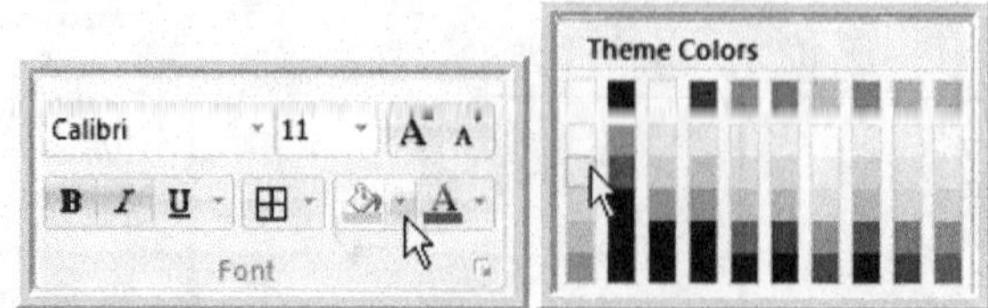

Finally, put your cursor between cells **C** and **D** until it turns to a left and right arrow as shown here:

Hold it there and double left-click so that the width of column **C** gets resized to better accommodate the length of the label "X-squared". The result is:

	A	B	C
1	Variables	X	X-squared
2		1	1
3		2	4
4	Values	3	9
5		4	16
6		5	25
7	*Sum*	*15*	*55*

Next, drag your cursor over the **Sheet1** tab, right-click, select **Rename** and type in a descriptive name for your worksheet like **Excel for POE 1.2-1.4**, for *Using Excel for Principles of Econometrics, 4e*—sections 1.2 through 1.4. Press the **Enter** key on your keyboard or left-click anywhere on your worksheet.

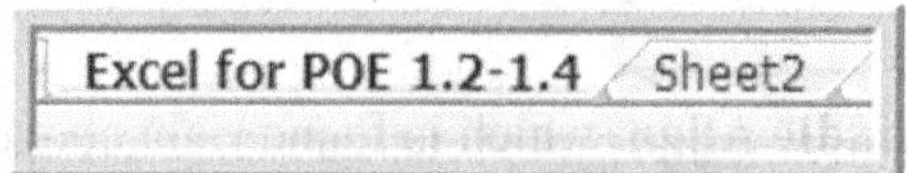

1.5 SAVING AND PRINTING YOUR DATA

All you need to do now is to save your Excel file. Select the **Save** button on the upper left corner of the Excel window.

A **Save As** dialog box pops up. Locate the folder you want to save your file in by using the arrow-down located at the extreme right of the **Save in** window or browsing through the list of folders displayed below it.

In the **File name** window, at the bottom of the **Save As** dialog box, the generic name Book1 should be outlined. Type the descriptive name you would like to give to your Excel file, like **POE Chapter 1**. Finally, select **Save**.

If you need to create a new folder, use the **Create New Folder** button found to the right of the **Save in** window.

A **New Folder** dialog box pops up; it is prompting you for the name you want to give to your new folder, **Excel for POE** for example. Type it in the **Name** window and select **OK**. Finally, select **Save**.

If you would like to print your table, select the **Office Button**, next to the **Save** button; go to **Print**, and select one of the print options.

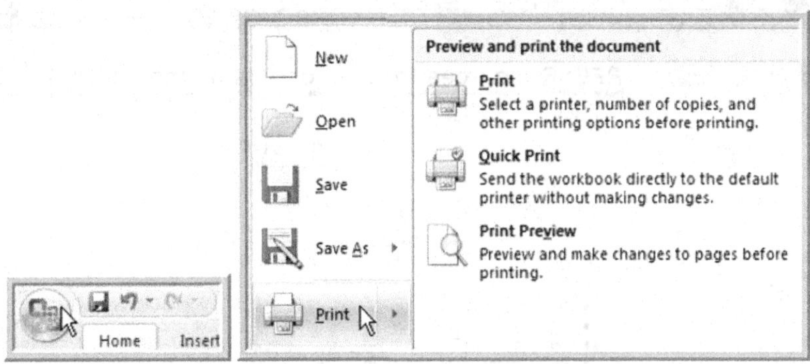

For more print options, you might want to check out the **Page Layout** tab, on the upper left of your screen, as well as the **Page Layout** button on the bottom right of your screen.

To close your file, select the **X** button on the upper right corner of your screen.

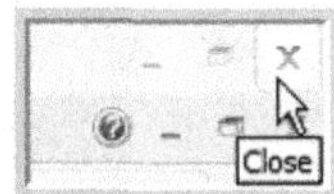

In the next section, we show you how to import data into an Excel spreadsheet. Getting data for economic research is much easier today than it was years ago. Before the Internet, hours would be spent in libraries, looking for and copying data by hand. Now we have access to rich data sources which are a few clicks away.

First we will illustrate how convenient sites that make data available in Excel format can be. Then we illustrate how to import ASCII or, text files, into Excel.

1.6 IMPORTING DATA INTO EXCEL

1.6.1 Resources for Economists on the Internet

Suppose you are interested in analyzing the GDP of the United States. The website **Resources for Economists** contains a wide variety of data, and in particular the macro data we seek. Websites are continually updated and improved. We guide you through an example, but be prepared for differences from what we show here.

First, open up the website http://rfe.org/.

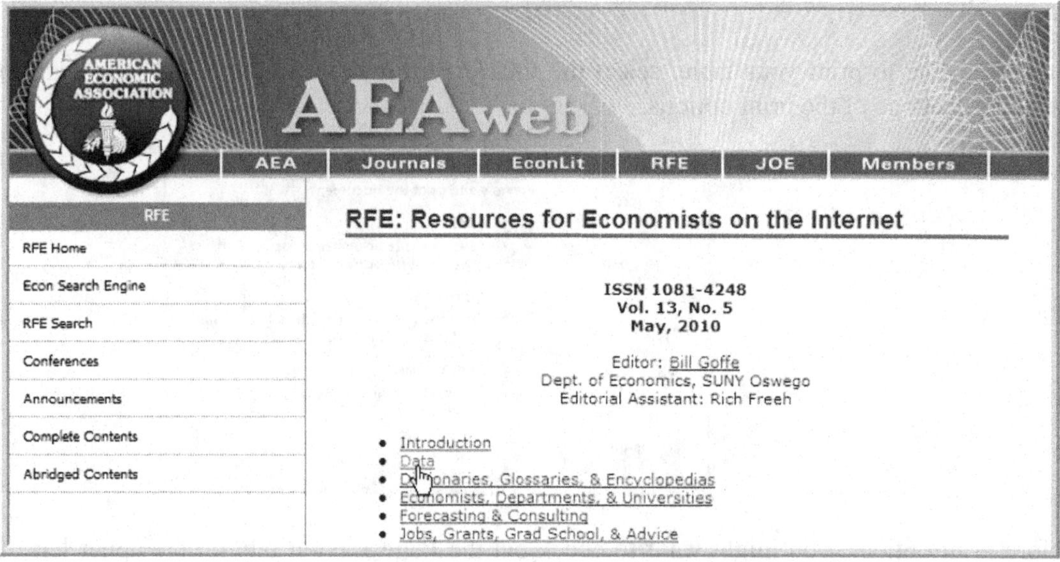

Select the **Data** link and then select **U.S. Macro and Regional Data**.

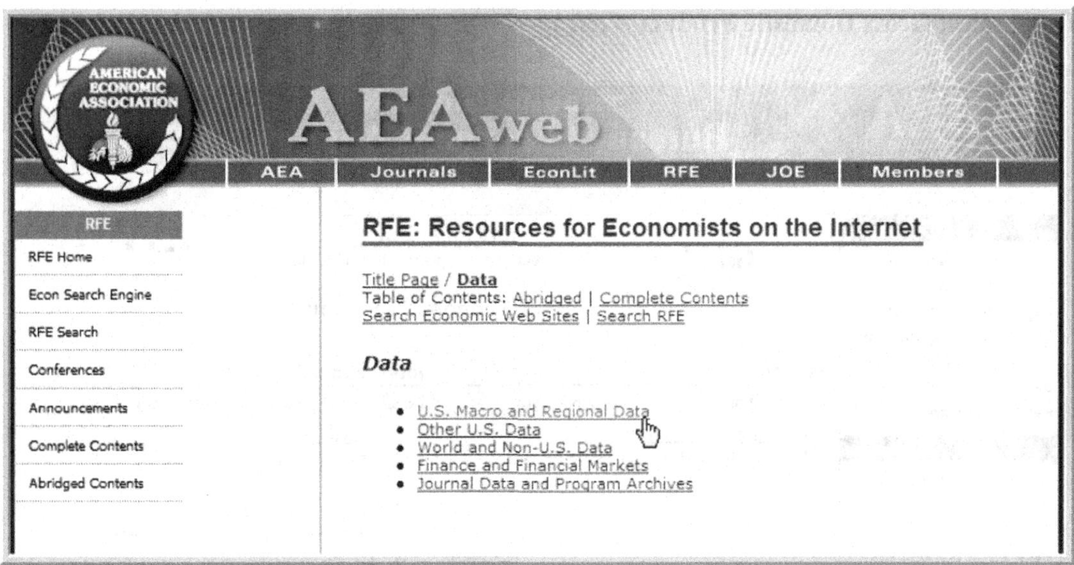

This will open up a range of sub-data categories. For the example discussed here, select the **Bureau of Economic Analysis (BEA).**

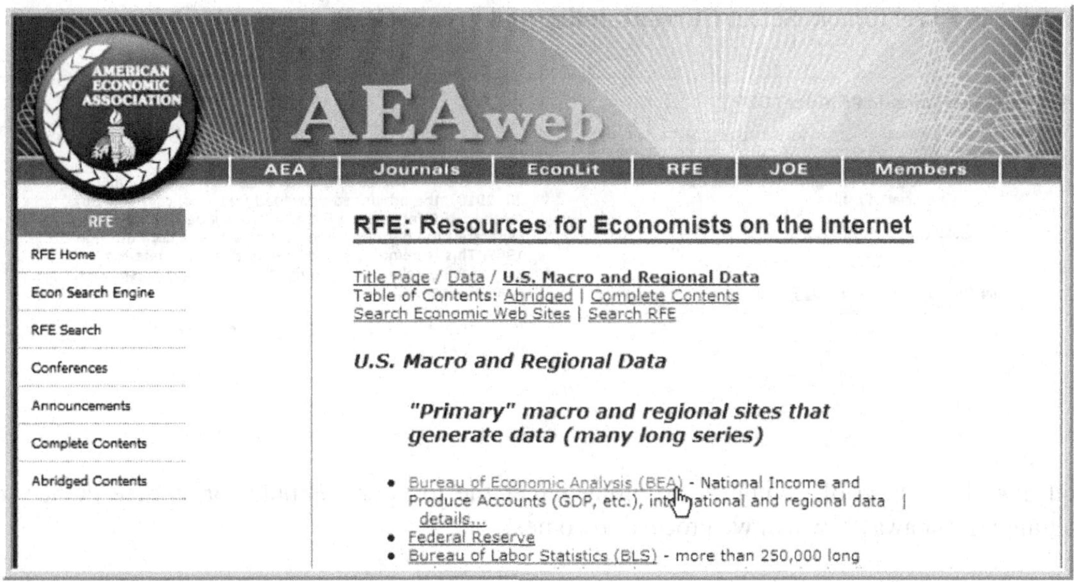

Finally, select **Gross Domestic Product (GDP).**

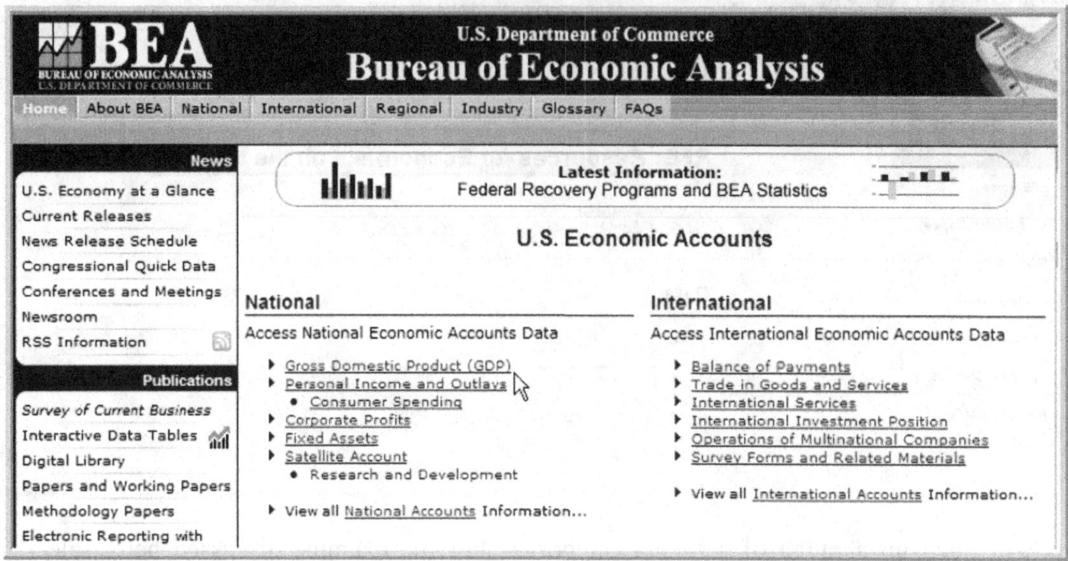

The result shows the point we are making. Many government and other web sites make data available in **Excel** format. Select **Current-dollar and "real" GDP**.

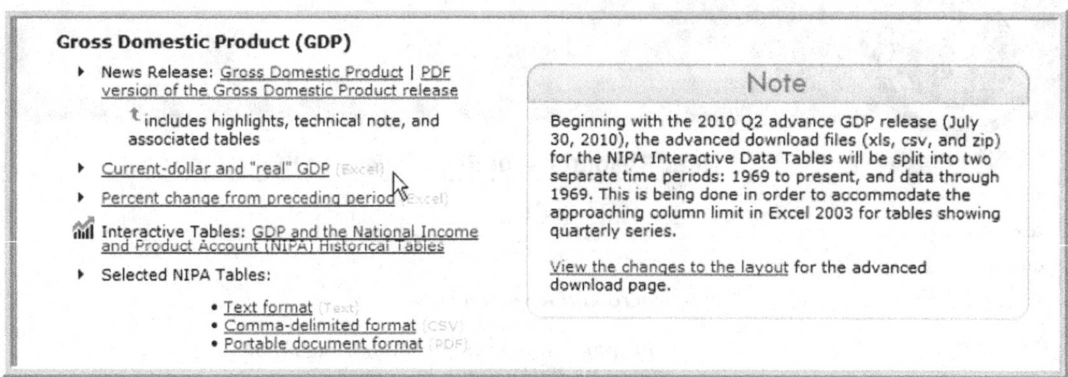

You have the option of saving the resulting Excel file to your computer or storage device, or opening it right away—which we proceed to do next.

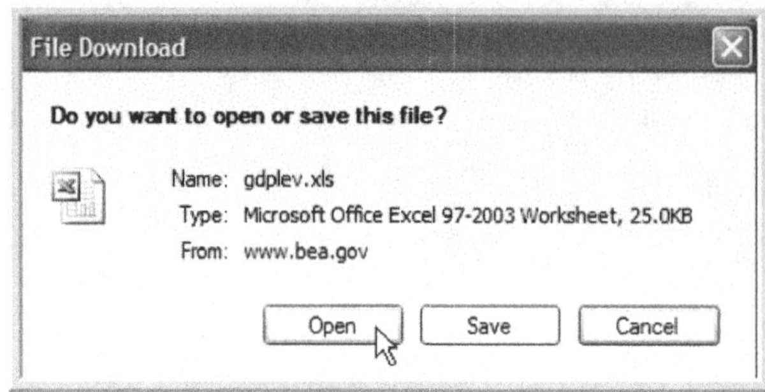

What opens is a workbook with headers explaining the variables it contained. We see that there is a series of annual data and a quarterly series.

	A	B	C	D	E	F	G
1		Current-Dollar and "Real" Gross Domestic Product					
2							
3		Annual				Quarterly	
4						(Seasonally adjusted annual rates)	
5							
6		GDP in billions of current dollars	GDP in billions of chained 2005 dollars			GDP in billions of current dollars	GDP in billions of chained 2005 dollars
7							
8							
9	1929	103.6	977.0		1947q1	237.2	1,772.2
10	1930	91.2	892.8		1947q2	240.4	1,769.5
11	1931	76.5	834.9		1947q3	244.5	1,768.0
12	1932	58.7	725.8		1947q4	254.3	1,794.8
13	1933	56.4	716.4		1948q1	260.3	1,823.4

The opened file is "Read Only" so you must save it under another name to work with it, graph, run regressions and so on.

1.6.2 Data Files for Principles of Econometrics

The book *Principles of Econometrics, 4e*, uses many examples with data. These data files have been saved as workbooks and are available for you to download to your computer. There are about 150 such files. The data files and other supplementary materials can be downloaded from two web locations: the publisher website or the book website maintained by the authors.

1.6.2a John Wiley and Sons Website

Using your web browser, enter the address www.wiley.com/college/hill. Find, among the authors named "Hill", the book *Principles of Econometrics, 4e.*

Follow the link to **Resources for Students**, and then **Student Companion Site**. There, you will find links to supplement materials, including a link to **Data Files** that will allow you to download all the data definition files and data files at once.

1.6.2b Principles of Econometrics Website

The address for the book website is www.principlesofeconometrics.com. There, you will find links to the Data definitions files, Excel spreadsheets, as well as an Errata list. You can download the data definition files and the Excel files all at once or select individual files. The data definition files contain variable names, variable definitions, and summary statistics. The Excel spreadsheets contain data only; those files were created using Excel 2003.

1.6.3 Importing ASCII Files

Sometimes data that you want to use may be provided but in ASCII or text format. To illustrate go to http://principlesofeconometrics.com. There you will find that one of the formats in which we provide data is ASCII or text files. These are used because they contain no formatting and can be used by almost every software once imported.

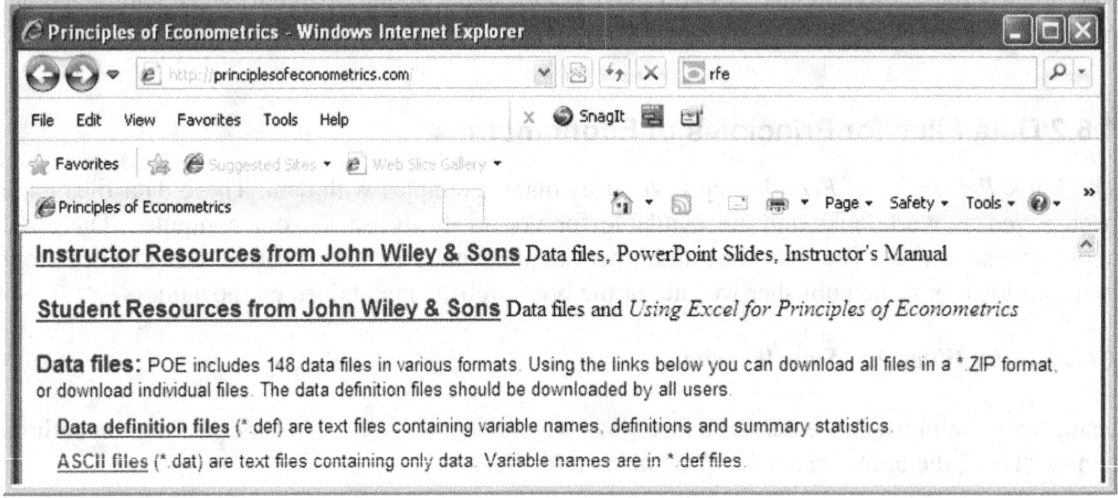

Select **ASCII files** and then go to the **food** data.

ASCII data files (*.dat) are text files containing only data.

Download all the *.dat files in (a) ZIP format or (b) a self-extracting EXE file (download and double-click)

Select individual *.dat files from the table below.

airline	cola	gold	meat	profits	tax
alcohol	cola2	golf	medical	pub	tax2
andy	commute	growth	metrics	pubexp	term
asparas	computer	grunfeld	mexico	qtm	texas
bangla	consumption	grunfeld2	mining	quizzes	theories
beer	cps	grunfeld3	money	returns	tobit
bond	cps_small	hhsurvey	monop	rice	tobitmc
br	cps1	hip	mroz	robbery	toodyay
br2	cps2	house_starts	music	salary	transport
broiler	crime	housing	nels	sales	truffles
brumm	csi	hwage	nels_small	savings	tuna
byd	demand	indpro	newbroiler	share	uk
canada	demo	inflation	nls	sheep	unit
capm2	edu_inc	insur	nls_panel	sirmans	usa
cars	euro	ivreg1	nls_panel2	sp	utown
cattle	exrate	ivreg2	oil	spurious	vacan
ces	fair	jobs	olympics	sterling	vacation
cespro	figureC-3	korea	orange	stockton	var
ch10	florida	learn	oscar	stockton2	vec
chard	food	liquor	oz	stockton96	vote
cloth	fullm[illegible]on	lon1	phillips	surplus	vote2

Right-click on the file name. Select **Save Target As**. A **Save As** dialog box pops up. Locate the folder you want to save your file in by using the arrow-down located at the extreme right of the **Save in** window or browsing through the list of folders displayed below it. Finally, select **Save**.

Once the download of the file is completed, a **Download complete** window pops up. Choose **Close**.

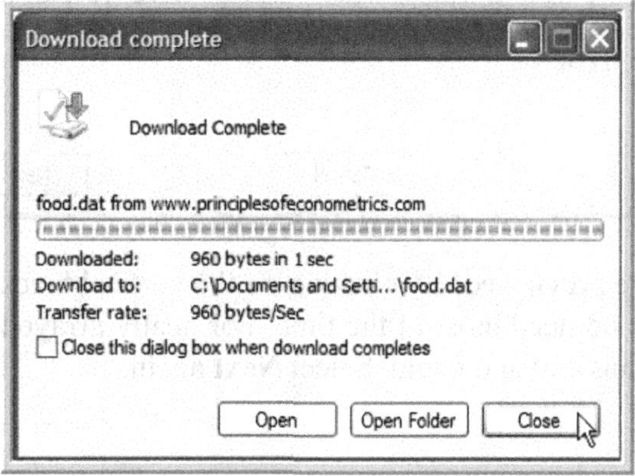

Start Excel. Select the **Office Button** on the upper left corner of the Excel window, then **Open.**

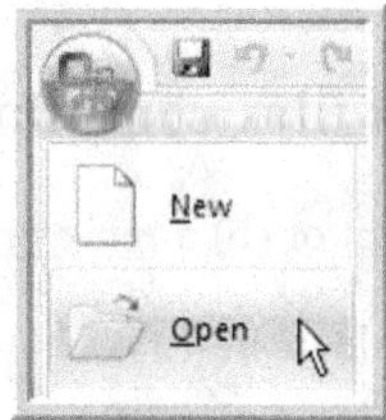

Navigate to the location of the data file. Make sure you have selected **All Files** in the **Files of Type** window. Select you **food.dat** file and then select **Open**.

What begins is a Windows "Wizard" that will take you through 3 steps to import the data into Excel. Our ASCII data files are neatly lined up in columns with no commas or anything else separating the columns. Select **Fixed width**, and then **Next**.

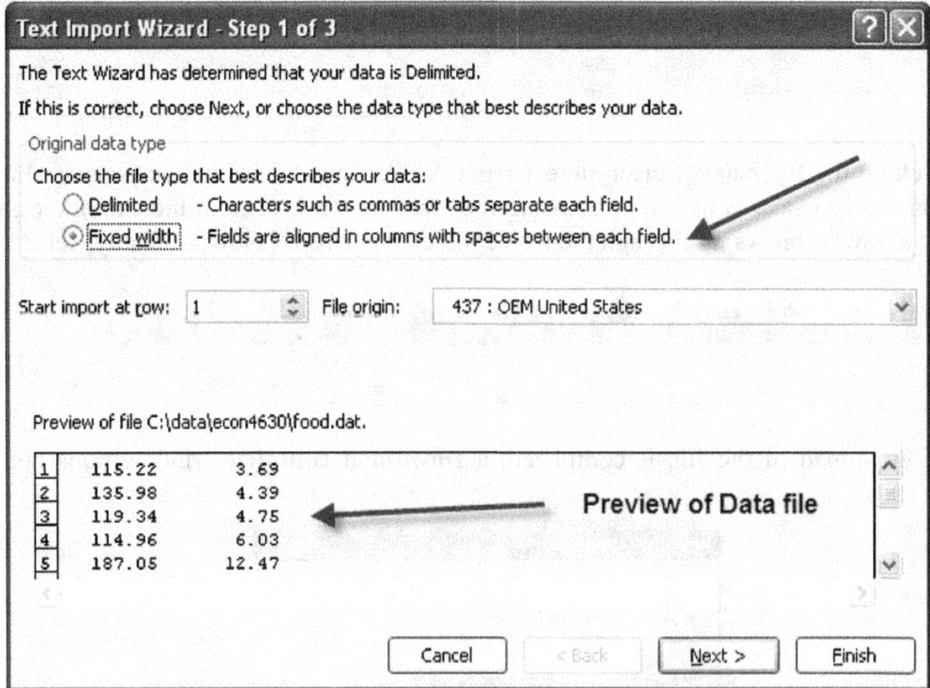

In the next step the data are previewed. By clicking on the vertical black line you could adjust the column width, but there is no need most of the time. For neatly arrayed data like ours, Excel can determine where the columns end and begin. Select **Next** again.

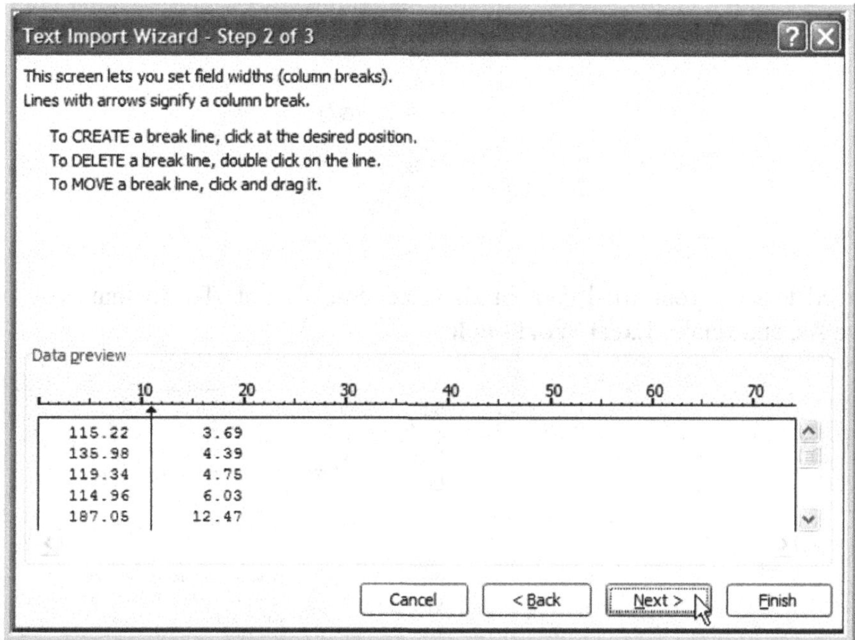

In the third and final step Excel permits you to format each column, or in fact to skip a column. In our case you can simply select **Finish**.

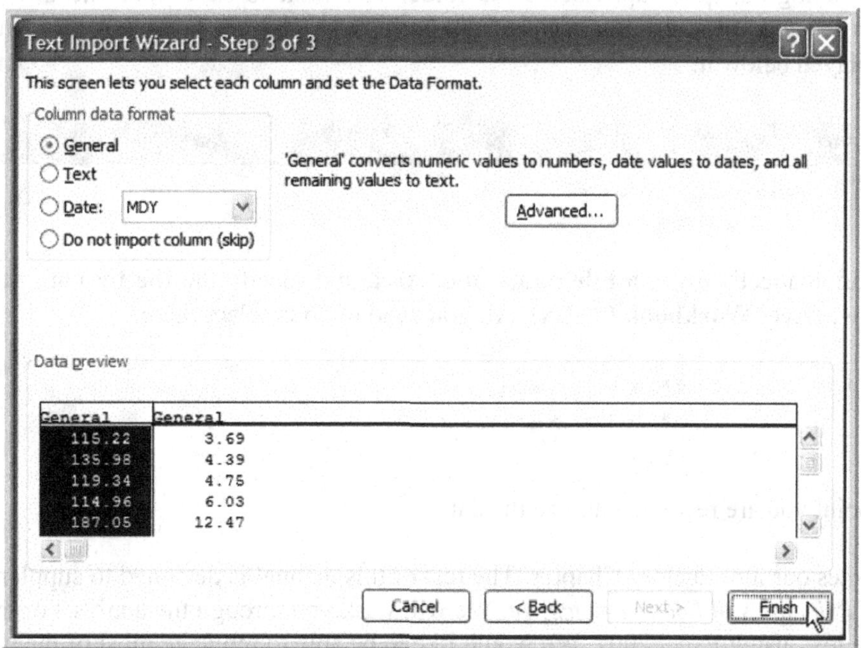

This step concludes the process and now the data is in a worksheet named **food**.

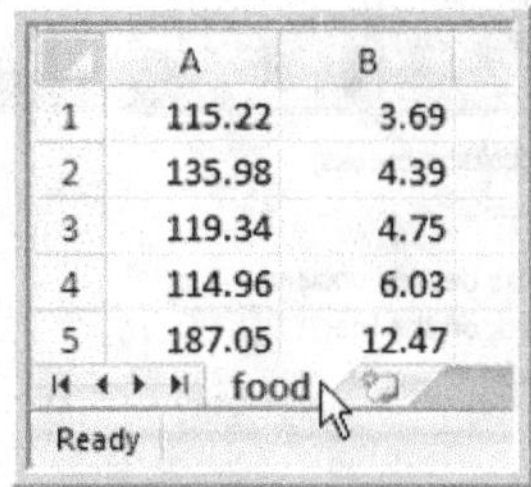

Next, you need to save your food data in an Excel File format. To do that, select the **Office Button**, **Save As**, and finally **Excel Workbook**.

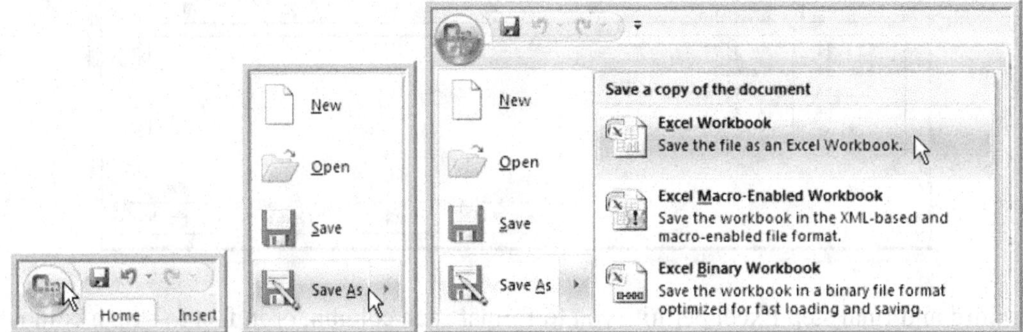

A **Save As** dialog box pops up. Locate the folder you want to save your file in by using the arrow-down located at the extreme right of the **Save in** window or browsing through the list of folders displayed below it.

Excel has automatically given a **File name**, **food.xlsx**, and specify the file format in the **Save as type** window, **Excel Workbook (*.xlsx)**. All you need to do is select **Save**.

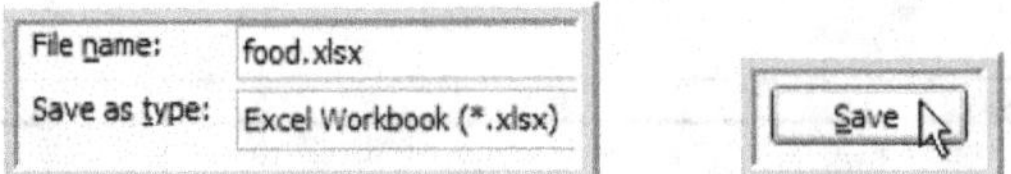

From this point you are ready to analyze the data.

This completes our introductory Chapter. The rest of this manual is designed to supplement your readings of *Principles of Econometrics*, *4e*. We will walk you through the analysis of examples found in the text, using Excel 2007. We would like to be able to replicate most of the plots of data and tables of results found in your text.

CHAPTER 2

The Simple Linear Regression Model

CHAPTER OUTLINE

In this chapter we estimate a simple linear regression model of weekly food expenditure. We also illustrate the concept of unbiased estimation. In the first section, we start by plotting the food expenditure data.

2.1 PLOTTING THE FOOD EXPENDITURE DATA

Open the Excel file ***food***. Save it as **POE Chapter 2**.

Compare the values you have in your worksheet to the ones found in Table 2.1, p. 49 of *Principles of Econometrics*, *4e*. The second part of Table 2.1 shows summary statistics. You can compute and check on those by using Excel mathematical functions introduced in Chapter 1, if you would like.

Select the **Insert** tab located next to the **Home** tab. Select **A2:B41**. In the **Charts** groups of commands select **Scatter**, and then **Scatter with only Markers**.

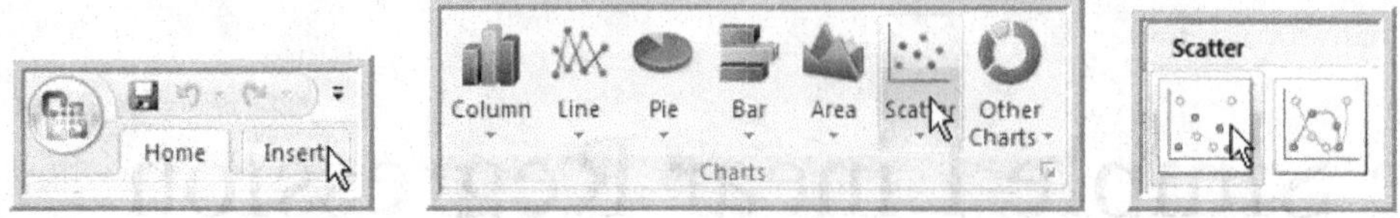

The result is:

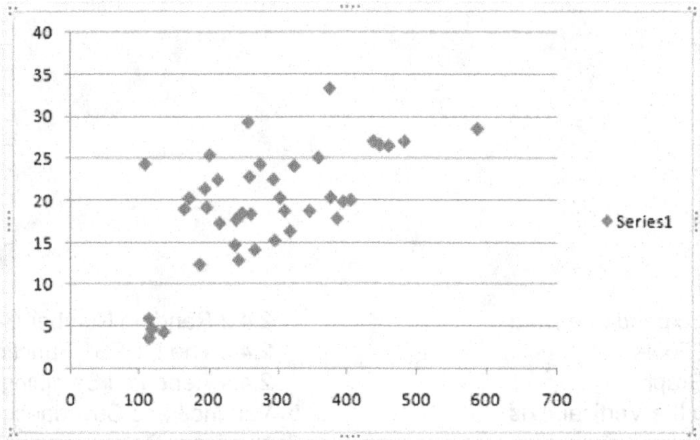

Each point on this **Scatter chart** illustrates one household for which we have recorded a pair of values: weekly food expenditure *and* weekly income. This is very important. We *chose* **Scatter chart** because we wanted to keep track of those pairs of values. For example, the point highlighted below illustrates the pair of values (187.05, 12.47) found in row 6 of your table.

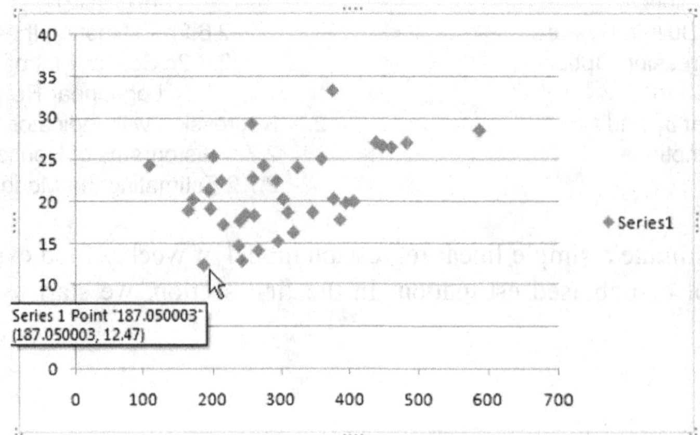

When we select two columns of values to plot on a **Scatter chart**, Excel, by default, represents values from the *first column on the horizontal axis* and values from the *second column on the vertical axis*. So, in this case, the expenditure values are illustrated on the horizontal axis and income values on the vertical axis. Indeed, you can see that the scale of the values on the horizontal axis corresponds to the one of the food expenditure values in column **A**, and the scale of the values on the vertical axis corresponds to the one of the income values in column **B**.

We actually would like to illustrate the food expenditure values on the vertical axis and the income values on the horizontal axis—opposite of what it is now. By convention, across disciplines, the variable we monitor the level of (the dependent variable) is illustrated on the vertical axis (Y-variable). And by convention, across disciplines, the variable that we think might explain the level of the dependent variable is illustrated on the horizontal axis (X-variable).

In our case, we think that the variation of levels of income across households might explain the variation of levels of food expenditure across those same households. That is why we would like to illustrate the food expenditure values on the vertical axis and the income values on the horizontal axis.

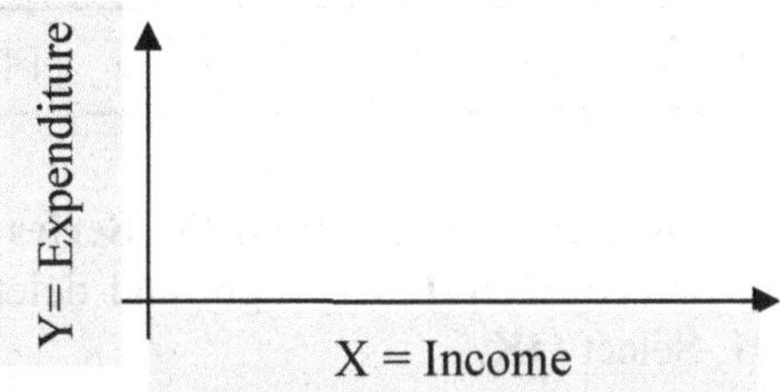

2.1.1 Using Chart Tools

If you look up on your screen, to the right end of your tab list, you should notice that **Chart Tools** are now displayed, adding the **Design**, **Layout**, and **Format** tabs to the list. The **Design** tab is open. (If, at any time, the **Chart Tools** and its tabs seem to disappear, all you need to do is to put your cursor anywhere in your Chart area, left-click, and they will be made available again.)

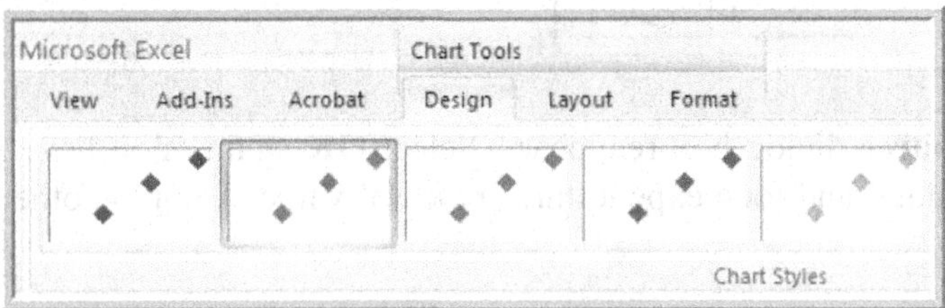

Go to the **Data** group of commands, to the left, and select the **Select Data** button.

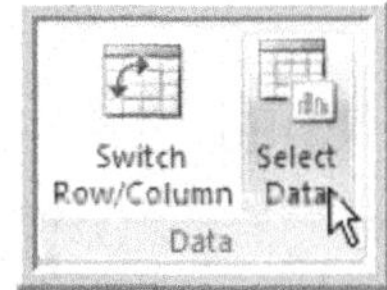

A **Select Data Source** dialog box pops up. Select **Edit.**

In the **Edit Series** dialog box, highlight the text from the **Series X values** window. Press the **Delete** key on your keyboard. Select **B2:B41**. Highlight and delete the text from the **Series Y values** window. Select **A2:A41**. Select **OK.**

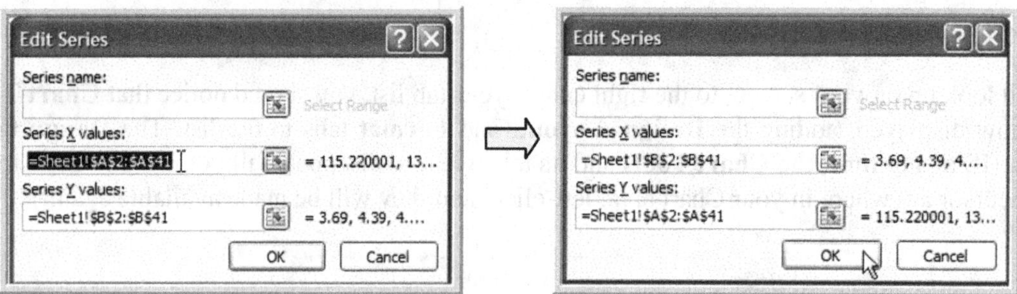

The **Select Data Source** dialog box reappears. Select **OK** again. You have just told Excel that income are the X-values, and food expenditure are the Y-values—not the other way around.

The result is:

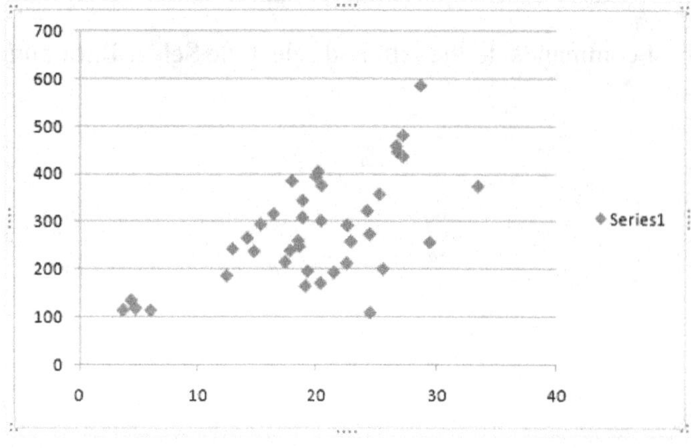

2.1.2 Editing the Graph

Now, we would like to do some editing. We do not need a **Legend**, since we have only one data series. Our expenditure values do not go over 600, so we can restrict our vertical axis scale to that. We definitely would like to label our axes. We might want to get rid of our **Gridlines**, and change the **Format** of our data series. Finally, we would like to move our chart to a new worksheet.

Select the **Layout** tab. On the **Labels** group of commands, select **Legend** and **None** to delete the legend.

2.1.2a Editing the Vertical Axis

Select the **Axes** button on the **Axes** group of commands. Go to **Primary Vertical Axis**, and select **More Primary Vertical Axis Options**.

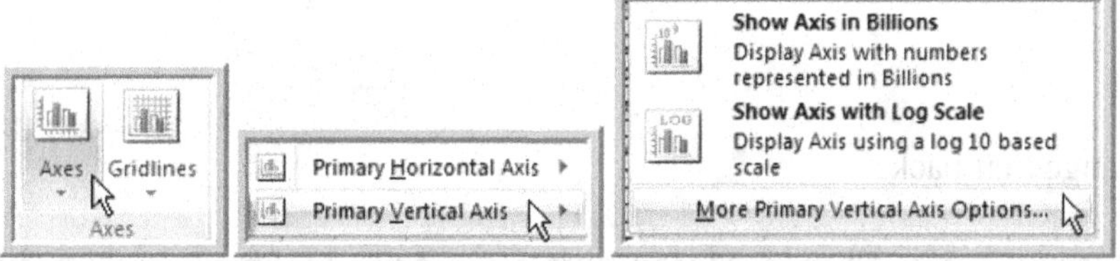

A **Format Axis** dialog box pops up. Change the **Maximum** value illustrated on the axis from **Auto** to **Fixed**, and specify **600**.

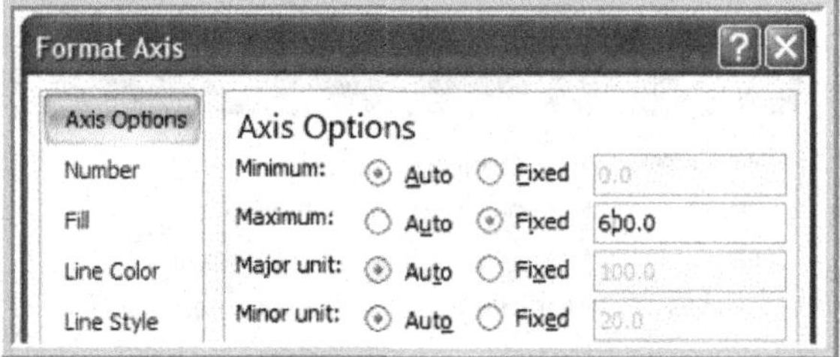

Next select **Alignment**, and use the arrow-down in the **Text direction** window to select **Rotate all text 270°**.

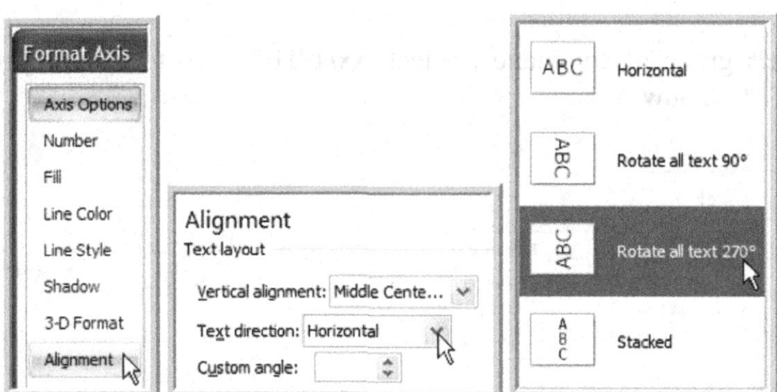

Place your cursor on the upper blue border of your **Format Axis** dialog box.

Left-click, hold it, and drag the box over so you can see your chart; release. Look at the vertical axis of your chart.

The numbers are now displayed vertically instead of horizontally, but less of them are displayed as well:

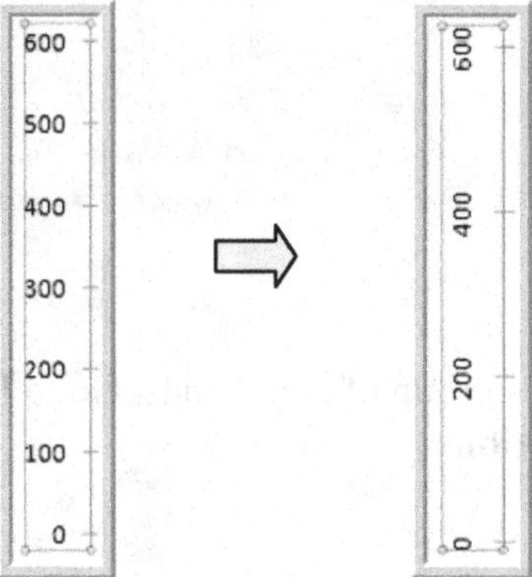

We want to change that back.

Select **Axis Options** again. Change **Major unit** from **Auto** to **Fixed**, and specify **100**. Select **Close**.

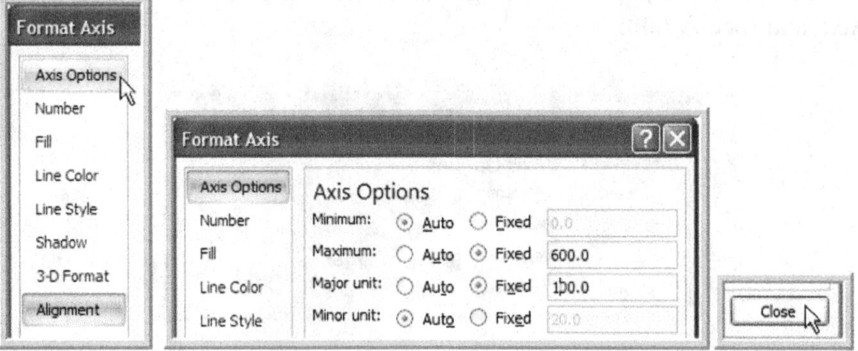

2.1.2b Axis Titles

Back to the **Labels** group of commands; select **Axis Titles**, go to **Primary Horizontal Axis Title**, and select **Title Below Axis**.

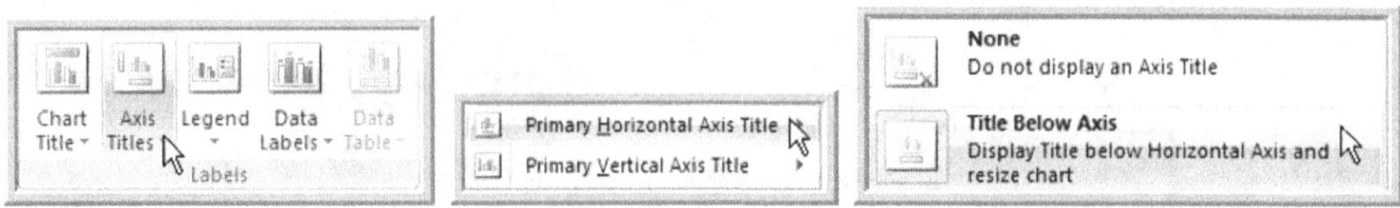

Select the generic **Axis Title** in the bottom of your chart and type in **x = weekly income in $100**.

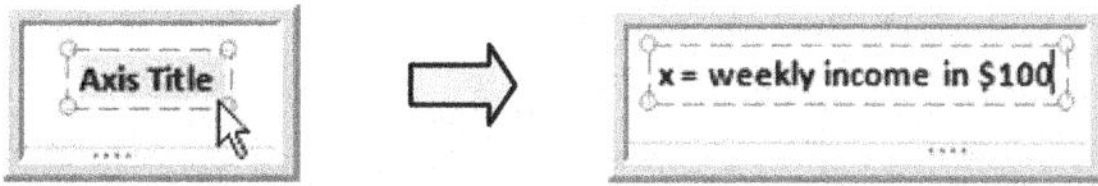

Go back to **Axis Titles**, then to **Primary Vertical Axis Title** this time. Select **Rotated Title.**

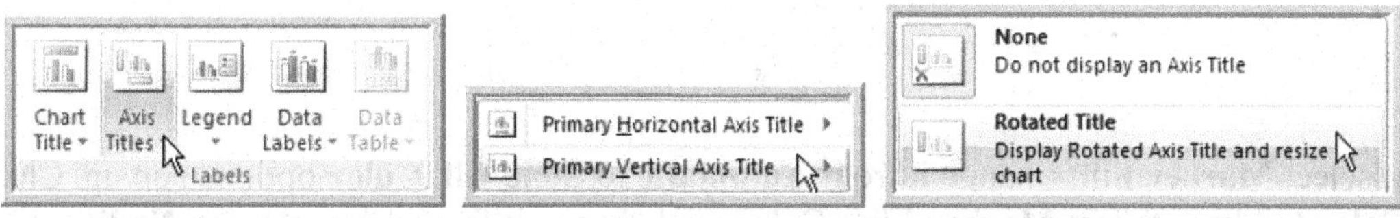

Select the generic **Axis Title** on the left of your chart and press **Delete**, or put your cursor on top of the **Axis Title** box, left-click, and press the **Backspace** key to delete the generic **Axis Title.** Type in **y = weekly food expenditure in $.**

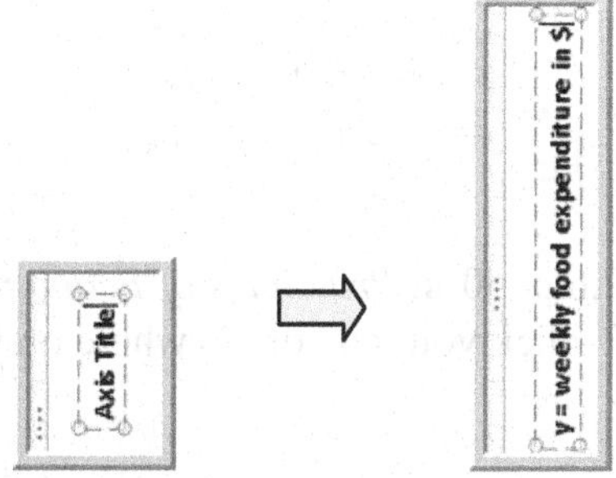

2.1.2c Gridlines and Markers

Back to the **Axes** group of commands now. Select **Gridlines**. Go to **Primary Horizontal Gridlines**, and select **None**.

Change the **Current Selection** (group of commands to the far left) to **Series 1** (use the arrow down button to the right of the window to make that selection). Select **Format Selection**.

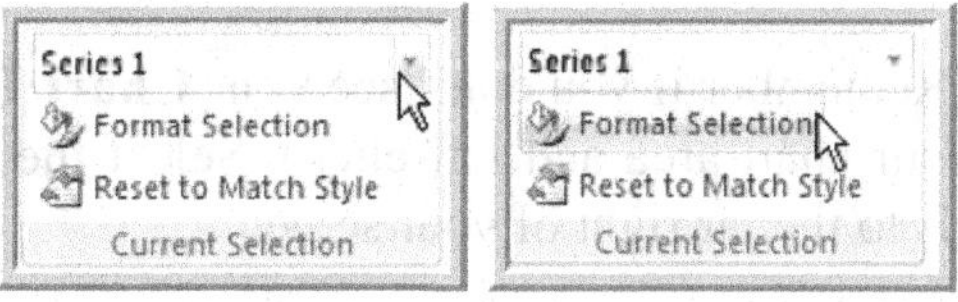

A **Format Data Series** dialog box pops up. Select **Marker Options**. Change the **Marker Type** from **Automatic** to **Built-in**. Change the **Type** and the **Size** as shown below:

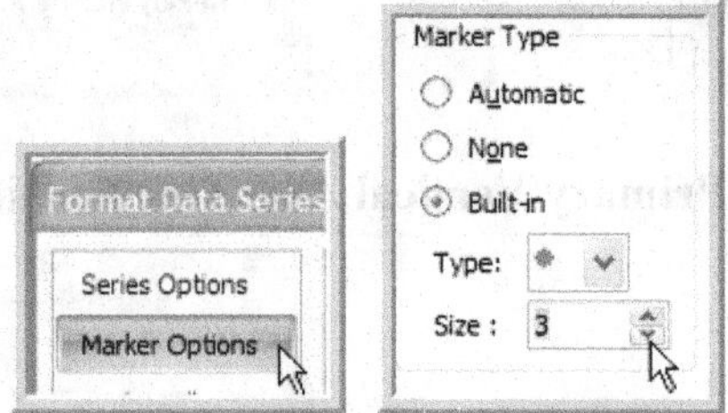

Next, select **Marker Fill**. Change it from **Automatic** to **Solid fill**. **Color** options pop up. Change the **Color** to black. Select **Marker Line Color**, and change it from **Automatic** to **No line**. Select **Close**.

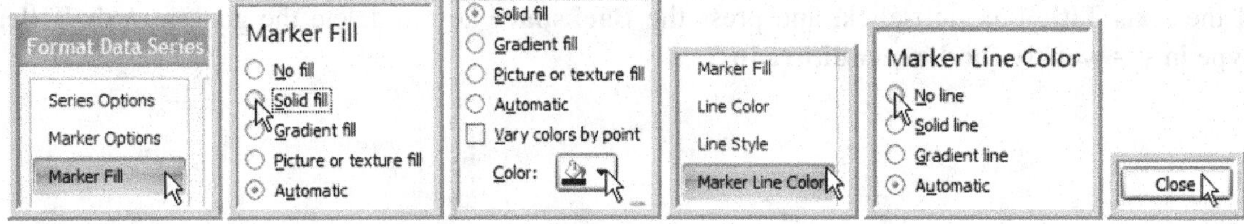

The result is a replica of Figure 2.6 p. 50 in *Principles of Econometrics, 4e*: (if it looks like some of your dots are little flowers, left–click your cursor anywhere on your screen first)

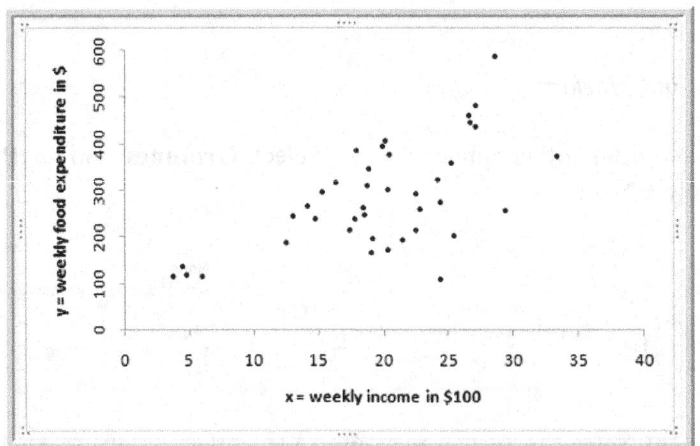

2.1.2d Moving the Chart

Go back to the **Design** tab. (Remember if you don't see your **Chart Tools** tabs, what you need to do is place your cursor in your chart area and left-click). Select the **Move Chart** button on the **Location** group of commands to the far right of your screen.

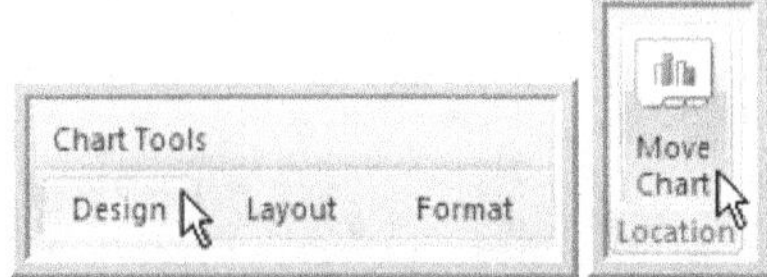

A **Move Chart** dialog box pops up. Select **New sheet** and give it a name like **Figure 2.6**. Select **OK**.

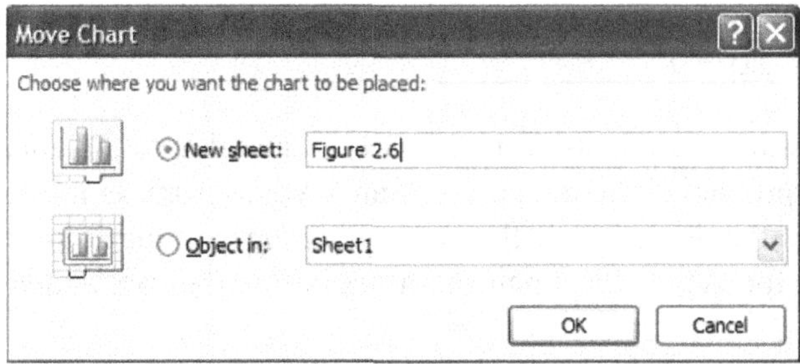

Rename Sheet 1 **Data** (if needed, see Section 1.4 of this manual on how to do that).

We have plotted our data, and edited our chart. Next, we want to estimate the regression line that best fit the data, and add this line to the chart.

2.2 ESTIMATING A SIMPLE REGRESSION

In this section, we are going to use two different methods to obtain the least squares estimates of the intercept and slope parameters β_1 and β_2. Method 1 consists of plugging in values into the b_1 and b_2 least squares estimators' formulas. Method 2 consists of making use of Excel built-in regression analysis routine.

2.2.1 Using Least Squares Estimators' Formulas

The least squares estimators are:

$$b_2 = \frac{\sum(x_i - \bar{x})(y_i - \bar{y})}{\sum(x_i - \bar{x})^2} \tag{2.1}$$

$$b_1 = \bar{y} - b_2\bar{x} \tag{2.2}$$

These formulas are telling us two things: (1) which values we need, and (2) how we need to combine them to compute b_1 and b_2.

(1) *Which values do we need?*

We need the (x_i, y_i) pairs of values—they do appear explicitly in equation (2.1). We also need $\bar{x}$ and $\bar{y}$, which are the sample means, or simple arithmetic averages of the x_i values and y_i values—those averages appear both in equation (2.1) and equation (2.2). Note that the subscript i in x_i and y_i keeps count of the x and y values. In other words, i denotes the *i*th value or *i*th pair of values. Also, $\bar{x}$ and $\bar{y}$, are referred to as "x-bar" and "y-bar".

(2) *How do we combine those values?*

Equation (2.1): $b_2 = \frac{\Sigma(x_i - \bar{x})(y_i - \bar{y})}{\Sigma(x_i - \bar{x})^2}$

The *numerator* is the sum of products; Σ is the Greek capital letter "sigma" which denotes sum. The first term of each product is the deviation of an x value from its mean $(x_i - \bar{x})$. The second term of each product is the deviation of the *corresponding* y value from its mean $(y_i - \bar{y})$. The products are computed for each (x_i, y_i) pair of values before they are added together.

The *denominator* is the sum of the squared deviations from the mean, for the x values only. In other words, each x value deviation from its mean is first squared, and then all those squared deviations values are summed.

Equation (2.2): $b_1 = \bar{y} - b_2\bar{x}$

This equation tells us to multiply b_2 by $\bar{x}$, and then subtract this product from $\bar{y}$. Note that b_2 must be computed first—before b_1 can be computed.

There is actually no magic to this. We use the food expenditure and income values we have collected from our random sample of 40 households, and perform *simple* arithmetic operations to compute the estimates the intercept and slope coefficient of our regression line.

As for the computation of b_1 and b_2 itself, there is only one trick. We need to make sure we know which values are the x's and which ones are the y's. So, we are going to start by adding labels to our columns of data.

You should be in your **Data** worksheet. If not, you can go back to it by selecting its tab on the bottom of your screen.

Figure 2.6 Data

Select **row 2** and insert a new row (see Section 1.4 of this manual if you need help on that). In the new cell **A2**, type **y**; and in the new cell **B2**, type **x. Right-align A1:B2.**

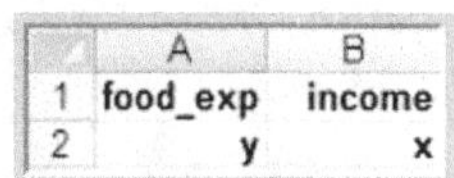

	A	B
1	food_exp	income
2	y	x

Next, we need to lay out the frame of the table where we are going to store our intermediate and final computations. Type **x_bar** = in cell **D2, y_bar** = in cell **D3, b2** = in cell **D6,** and **b1** = in cell **D7.** In cell **G2:J2,** type **x_deviation, y_deviation, (x_dev)(y_dev),** and **(x_deviation)2,** respectively. (Note that you can use your **Tab key**, instead of moving your cursor or using the **Arrow key**, to move to the next cell to your right).

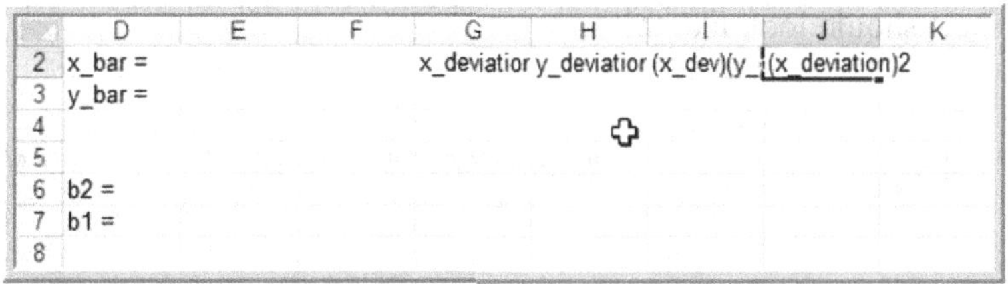

Below **x_deviation** we are going to compute and store the deviations of the x values from their mean. Below **y_deviation,** we are going to compute and store the deviations of the y values from their mean. Below **(x_dev)(y_dev)**, we are going to compute and store the products of the x deviation and the y deviation for each pair of values. Finally, below **(x_deviation)2** we are going to compute and store the x deviations squared.

To show the **2** of **(x_deviation)2** as a square, place your cursor in **J2**, if it is not already in it. Move to the **Formula bar** to select the **2**, and select the arrow to the right corner of the **Font** group of commands.

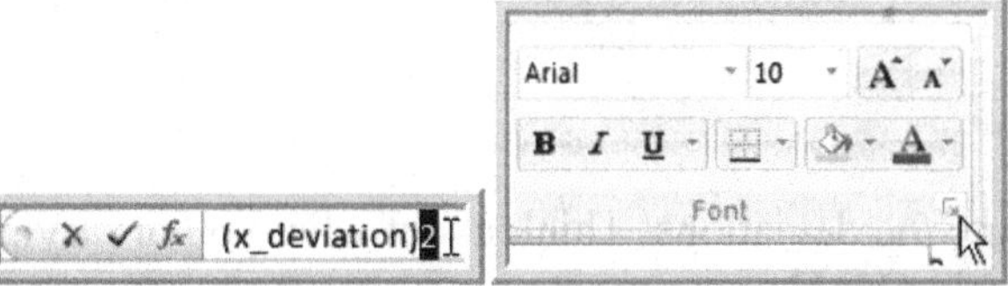

A **Format cells** dialog box pops up. Select **Superscript** and then **OK.**

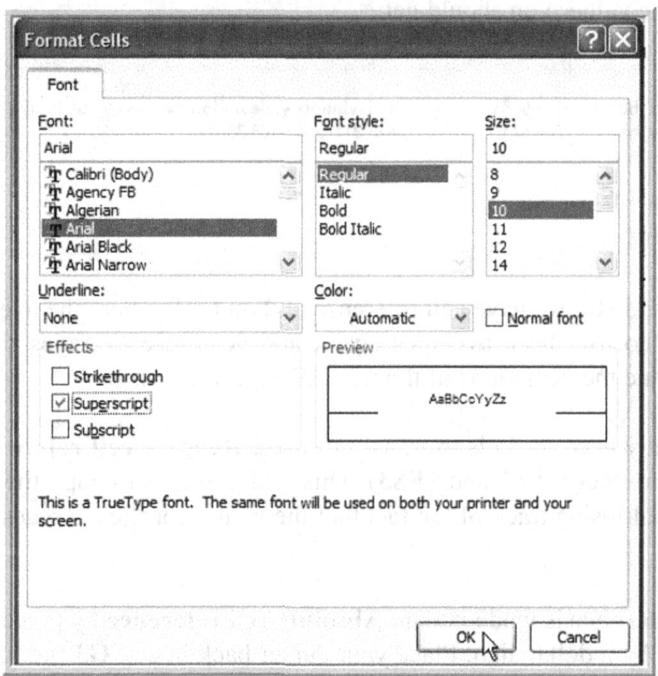

In cells **D6** and **D7** proceed to format the **2** and **1** of b_2 and b_1 as **Subscripts** instead. **Bold** all the labels you just typed, and **Align Right** the ones from **G2:J2**. Finally, resize the width of columns **G:J** to accommodate the width of its labels (see Section 1.4 of this manual if you need help on that).

Now, your worksheet should look like this one:

	D	E	F	G	H	I	J
2	x_bar =			x_deviation	y_deviation	(x_dev)(y_dev)	(x_deviation)^2
3	y_bar =						
4							
5							
6	b_2 =						
7	b_1 =						

We have computed averages before. The formula you should have in cell **E2** is **=AVERAGE(B3:B42)**, and the one in cell **E3** is **= AVERAGE(A3:A42)**. Compare the averages you get to the sample means of Table 2.1 in *Principles of Econometrics, 4e* (p. 49); they should be the same.

	D	E	F	G	H	I	J
2	x_bar =	19.60475		x_deviation	y_deviation	(x_dev)(y_dev)	(x_deviation)^2
3	y_bar =	283.5735					
4							
5							
6	b_2 =						
7	b_1 =						

Next, we want to compute the deviations. Think about what you are trying to compute. And then type the needed formulas in **G3:J3**.

You should type **=B3 – E2** in cell **G3**, **=A3 – E3** in cell **H3**, **=G3*H3** in cell **I3**, and **G23^2** in cell **J3**. Here are the values you should get:

	D	E	F	G	H	I	J
2	x_bar =	19.60475		x_deviation	y_deviation	(x_dev)(y_dev)	(x_deviation)^2
3	y_bar =	283.5735		-15.9147501	-168.353498	2679.303845	253.2792692
4							
5							
6	b_2 =						
7	b_1 =						

Now, in cells **G3** and **H3**, we gave cell references **E2** and **E3,** where the averages are stored. Note that we will need to use those averages again, and get those averages from these same exact locations, to compute the deviations of the next 39 observations.

So, what we actually need to do is to transform these **Relative cell references** (**E2** and **E3**) into **Absolute cell references** (**$E$2** and **$E$3**). This will allow us to copy the formula from **G3:H3** down below without losing track of the fact that the values for the averages are stored in cells **E2** and **E3**.

A **Relative cell reference** is made into an **Absolute cell reference** by preceding both the row and column references by a dollar sign. Place your cursor back in cell **G3** (i.e. move your mouse over and left-click); in the **Formula bar**, place your cursor before the **E** and insert a dollar sign (press the **Shift-key** and the **$ key** at the same time); move your cursor before the **2** and insert another dollar sign; place your cursor at the end of the formula and press **Enter**.

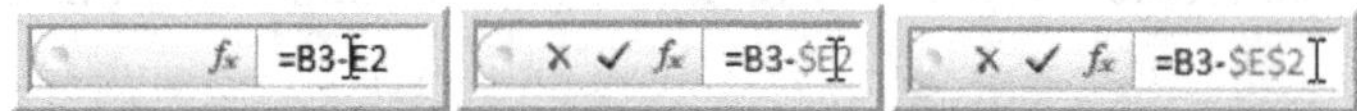

Go to cell **H3**, and add the needed dollar signs there too. Now, you can select **G3:J3**. Select **Copy** on the **Clipboard** group of command. Select **G4:J42**, and select **Paste** (next to **Copy**). You have just copied the formulas to compute the needed deviations for the rest of the (x_i, y_i) pairs.

Your worksheet should look like this:

	D	E	F	G	H	I	J
2	x_bar =	19.60475		x_deviation	y_deviation	(x_dev)(y_dev)	(x_deviation)^2
3	y_bar =	283.5735		-15.9147501	-168.353498	2679.303845	253.2792692
4				-15.2147501	-147.593503	2245.598261	231.4886191
5				-14.8547501	-164.233503	2439.647641	220.663599
6	b_2 =			-13.5747501	-168.6135	2288.886121	184.2738389
7	b_1 =			-7.13475005	-96.5234963	688.6710199	50.90465828

We have everything we need to finalize the computation of b_1 and b_2.

Place your cursor in cell **E6**, and again think about what you need to compute b_2. Recall that the least squares estimators are:

$$b_2 = \frac{\sum(x_i - \bar{x})(y_i - \bar{y})}{\sum(x_i - \bar{x})^2} \tag{2.1}$$

$$b_1 = \bar{y} - b_2\bar{x} \tag{2.2}$$

If you refer back to equation (2.1), you can see that **=SUM(I3:I42)/SUM(J3:J42)** is the formula you need in cell **E6**. The one you need in cell **E7** is **=E3 – E6*E2** for equation (2.2).

Your worksheet should look like this:

	A	B	C	D	E	F	G	H	I	J
2	y	x		x_bar =	19.60475		x_deviation	y_deviation	(x_dev)(y_dev)	(x_deviation)^2
3	115.22	3.69		y_bar =	283.5735		-15.9147501	-168.353498	2679.303845	253.2792692
4	135.98	4.39					-15.2147501	-147.593503	2245.598261	231.4886191
5	119.34	4.75					-14.8547501	-164.233503	2439.647641	220.663599
6	114.96	6.03		b_2 =	10.20964		-13.5747501	-168.6135	2288.886121	184.2738389
7	187.05	12.47		b_1 =	83.41601		-7.13475005	-96.5234963	688.6710199	50.90465828

In the table above we obtain the same exact least squares estimates as those reported on p. 53 of *Principles of Econometrics, 4e*.

That was Method 1 of obtaining the least squares estimates of the intercept and slope parameters β_1 and β_2. For Method 2, we are going to use the Excel built-in regression analysis routine.

2.2.2 Using Excel Regression Analysis Routine

Select the **Data** tab, in the middle of your tab list. On the **Analysis** group of commands to the far right of the ribbon, select **Data Analysis**.

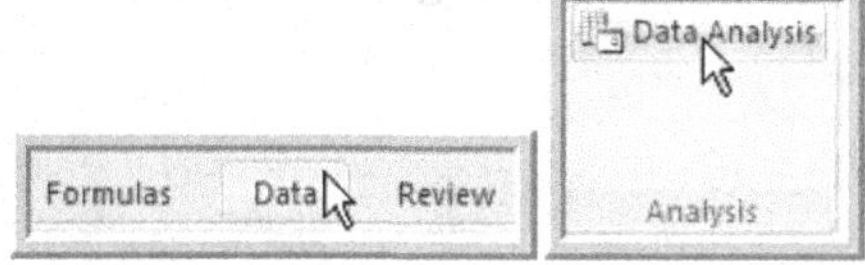

If the **Data Analysis** tool does not appear on the ribbon, you need to load it first.

Select the **Office Button** in the upper left corner of your screen, **Excel Options** on the bottom of the **Office Button** tasks panel, **Add-Ins** in the **Excel Options** dialog box, **Excel Add-ins** in the **Manage** window at the bottom of the **Excel Options** dialog box, and then **Go**.

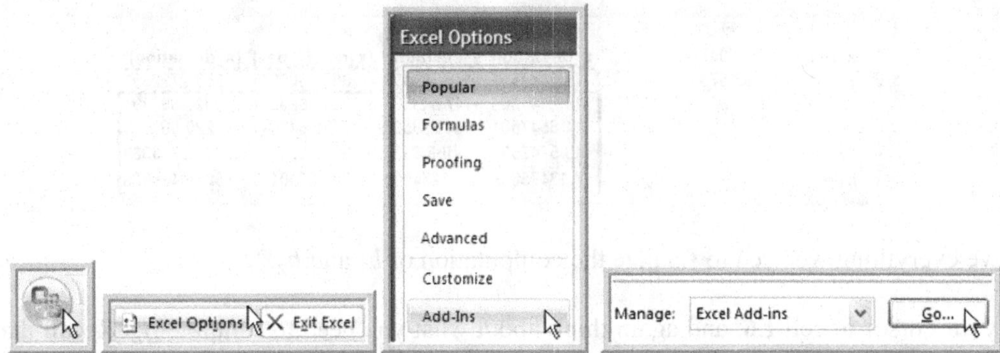

In the **Add-Ins** dialog box, check the box in front of **Analysis ToolPak**. Select **OK**.

Now **Data Analysis** should be available on the **Analysis** group of commands. Select it.

A **Data Analysis** dialog box pops up. In it, select **Regression** (you might need to use the scroll up and down bar to the right of the **Analysis Tools** window to find it), then select **OK**.

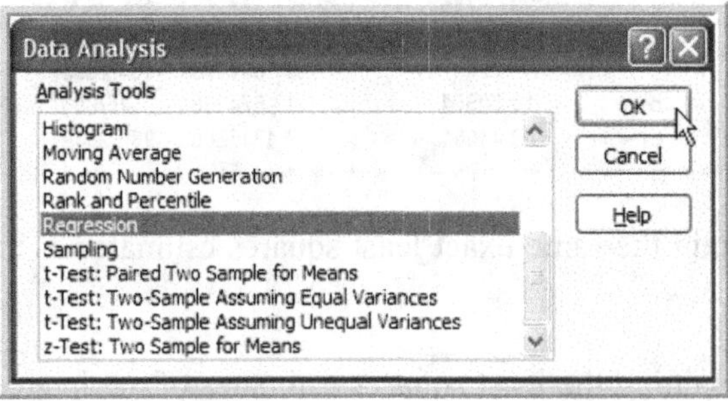

The **Regression** dialog box that pops up next is very similar to the **Edit Series** box we encountered before (see Section 2.1.1). Place your cursor in the **Input Y Range** window, and select **A3:A42** to specify the y-values you are working with. Similarly, place your cursor in the **Input X Range** window, and select **B3:B42** to specify the x-values you are working with. Next, place your cursor in the **New Worksheet Ply** window and type **Regression**—this is going to be the name of the new worksheet where Excel regression analysis results are going to be stored. Select **OK**.

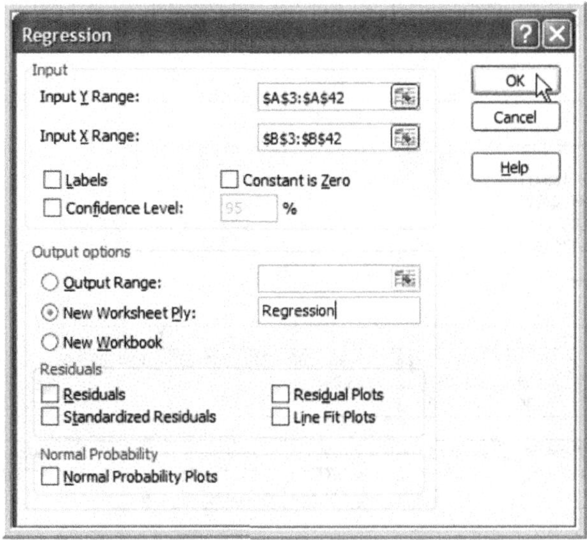

The **Summary Output** that Excel just generated should be highlighted as shown below:

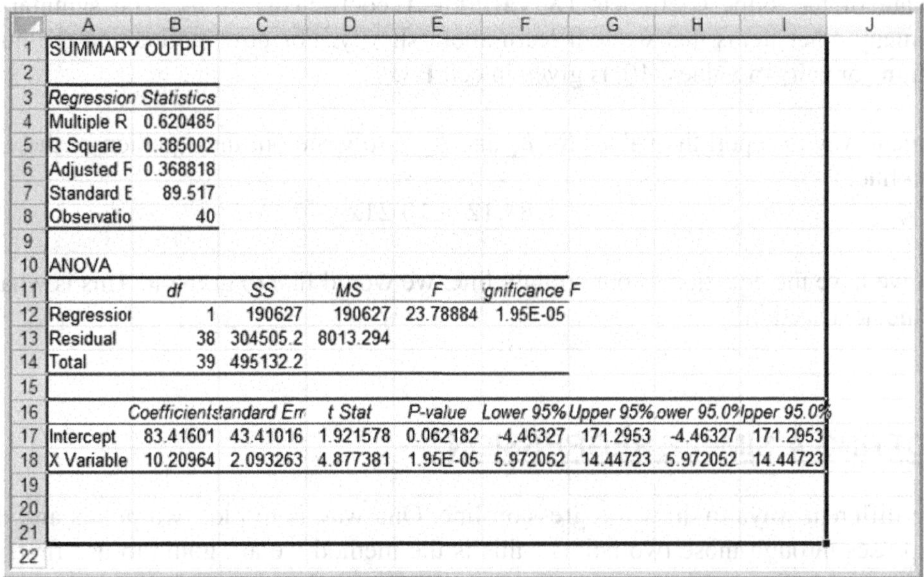

	A	B	C	D	E	F	G	H	I
1	SUMMARY OUTPUT								
2									
3	*Regression Statistics*								
4	Multiple R	0.620485							
5	R Square	0.385002							
6	Adjusted F	0.368818							
7	Standard E	89.517							
8	Observatio	40							
9									
10	ANOVA								
11		*df*	*SS*	*MS*	*F*	*gnificance F*			
12	Regressioı	1	190627	190627	23.78884	1.95E-05			
13	Residual	38	304505.2	8013.294					
14	Total	39	495132.2						
15									
16		*Coefficients*	*tandard Err*	*t Stat*	*P-value*	*Lower 95%*	*Upper 95%*	*ower 95.0%*	*lpper 95.0%*
17	Intercept	83.41601	43.41016	1.921578	0.062182	-4.46327	171.2953	-4.46327	171.2953
18	X Variable	10.20964	2.093263	4.877381	1.95E-05	5.972052	14.44723	5.972052	14.44723
19									
20									
21									
22									

Select the **Home** tab. In the **Cells** group of commands, select **Format**, and **AutoFit Column Width**; this is an alternative to adjust the width of the selected columns to fit their contents.

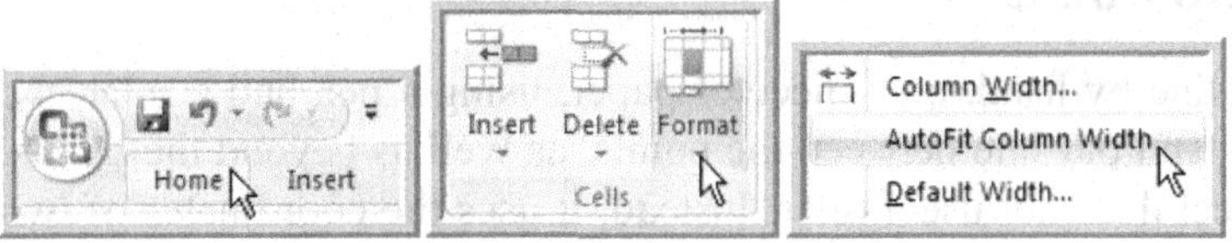

Your worksheet should now look like this:

	A	B	C	D	E	F	G	H	I
1	SUMMARY OUTPUT								
2									
3	*Regression Statistics*								
4	Multiple R	0.620485472							
5	R Square	0.385002221							
6	Adjusted R Square	0.368818069							
7	Standard Error	89.51700429							
8	Observations	40							
9									
10	ANOVA								
11		*df*	*SS*	*MS*	*F*	*Significance F*			
12	Regression	1	190626.9788	190626.9788	23.78884107	1.94586E-05			
13	Residual	38	304505.1742	8013.294058					
14	Total	39	495132.153						
15									
16		*Coefficients*	*Standard Error*	*t Stat*	*P-value*	*Lower 95%*	*Upper 95%*	*Lower 95.0%*	*Upper 95.0%*
17	Intercept	83.41600997	43.41016192	1.921577951	0.062182379	-4.463267721	171.2952877	-4.463267721	171.2952877
18	X Variable 1	10.2096425	2.093263461	4.877380554	1.94586E-05	5.972052202	14.4472328	5.972052202	14.4472328

The least squares estimates are given under the **Coefficients** column in the last table of the **Summary Output**. The estimate for the **Intercept** coefficient or b_1 is the first one; followed by the estimate of the slope coefficient (**X variable 1** coefficient) or b_2. The summary output contains many other items that we will learn about shortly. For now, notice that the number of **observations** or pairs of values, 40, is given in cell **B8**.

A convenient way to report the values for b_1 and b_2 is to write out the equation of the estimated regression line:

$$\hat{y}_i = 83.42 + 10.21x_i \tag{2.3}$$

Now that we have the equation of our straight line, we would like to graph it. This is what we are doing in the next section.

2.3 PLOTTING A SIMPLE REGRESSION

There are different ways to draw a regression line. One way is to plot two points and draw the line that passes through those two points—this is the method we are going to use first. Another way is plot many points, and then draw the line that passes through all those points—this is the method that Excel uses in its built-in features we are going to look at next.

2.3.1 Using Two Points

When we draw a line by hand, on a piece of paper, using a pen and a ruler, we can use *any* two points. We can extend our line between the points, as well as beyond the points, up and down, or right and left. Excel does not use a ruler. Instead, it uses the coordinates of two points to draw a line, and it draws the line *only* between them. So, to have Excel draw a line that spans over the whole range of data we have, we need to choose those two points a little bit more strategically than usual.

If you look back at your scatter chart (**Figure 2.6** worksheet) or back in your table (**Data** worksheet), you can see that our x values range from about 0 to 35 (from 3.69 to 33.4 exactly). So, we choose our first point to have an x value equal to 0, and our second point an x value of 35.

The point with an x value of zero is our y intercept. It is the point where the line crosses the vertical axis. Its coordinates are $x = 0$ and $y = b_1$ or $(0, 83.42)$. This is our first point.

For our second point, we let $x = 35$; plug this x value in equation (2.3), and compute its corresponding or predicted y value. We obtain:

$$\hat{y} = 83.42 + 10.21(35) = 440.77 \tag{2.4}$$

This is our second point, with coordinates $(35, 440.77)$.

Go back to your **Data** worksheet (if you are not already there). In cell **L1**, type **Points to graph regression line**. In columns **L** and **M** we are going to record the coordinates of the two points we are using to draw our regression line. In cell **L2**, type **y**; in cell **M2**, type **x**. In cell **M3**, type **0**; in cell **M4**, type **35**. In cell **L3**, we actually want to record the value for our y intercept or b_1, which we already have in cell **E7**. So, we are going to get it from there: in cell **L3**, type = **E7**, and press **Enter**. In cell **L4**, we want to have the computed predicted y value from (2.4). So we type **=E7+E6*M4**, and press **Enter**. Note that instead of typing all those cell references, you can just move your cursor to the cells of interest as if you were actually getting the needed values—this is a very good way to avoid typing errors. So, you would type the equal sign, move your cursor to **E7** and left-click to select it, type the plus sign, move your cursor to cell **E6** and left-click to select it, type the asterisk, move your cursor to sell **M4** and left-click to select it, and finally press **Enter**. Once you have done all of that, your worksheet should look like this:

	L	M	N
1	Points to graph regression line		
2	y	x	
3	83.41601	0	
4	440.7535	35	

Note that the predicted y value we obtain in the worksheet for $x = 35$ is slightly different than the one we just computed in equation (2.4) due to rounding number differences.

Now, go back to your **Figure 2.6** worksheet. The data we have plotted on the chart represent *one* set or series of data. The two new pairs of values we want to add to this chart represent a *second* set or series of data.

Select the **Design** tab, then the **Select data** button from the **Data** group of commands.

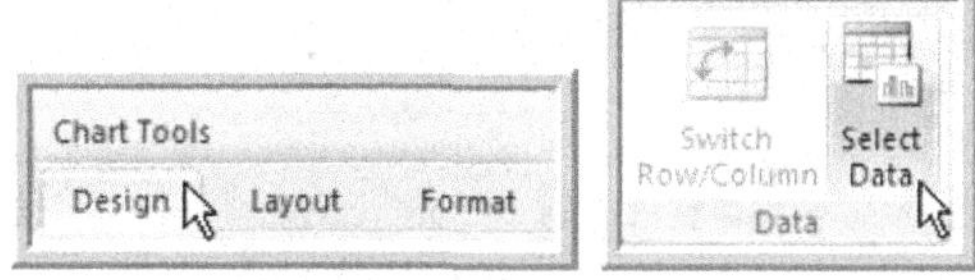

In the **Legend Entries (Series)** window of the **Select data source** dialog box, select the **Add** button.

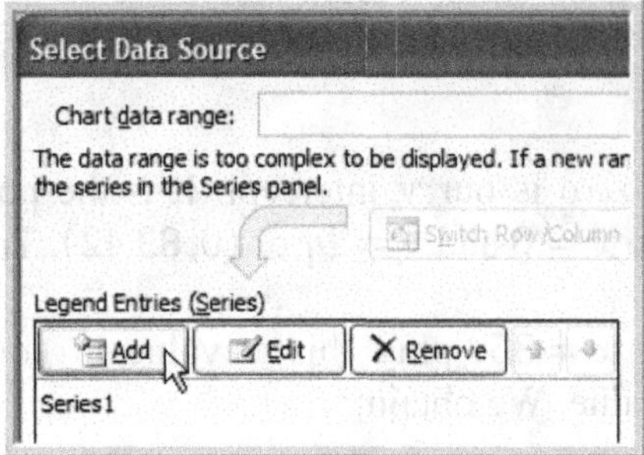

Place your cursor in the **Series X values** window of the **Edit series** dialog box, and select **M3:M4** in the **Data worksheet**. Place your cursor in the **Series Y values** window (delete whatever is in there), and select **L3:L4** in the **Data worksheet**. Select **OK**.

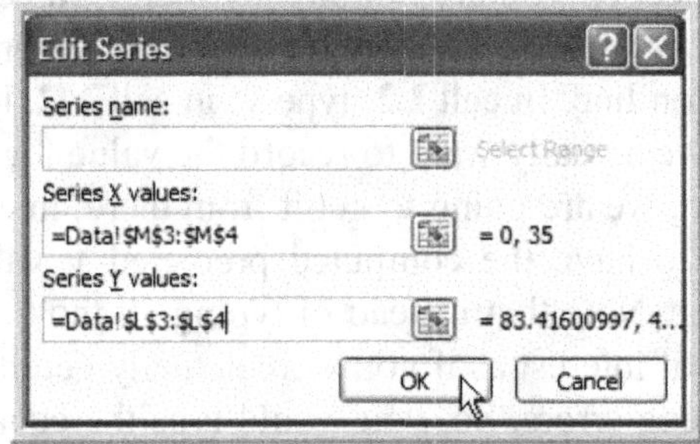

The **Select data source** dialog box reappears. A second data series, **Series2**, was created from the selection you just specified. Select **OK**.

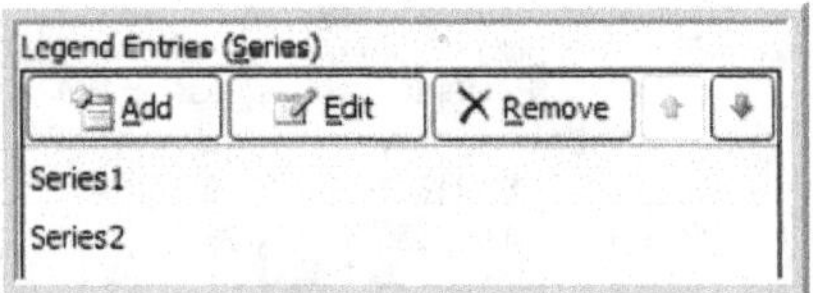

The two points from your new series are plotted on your chart (squares below):

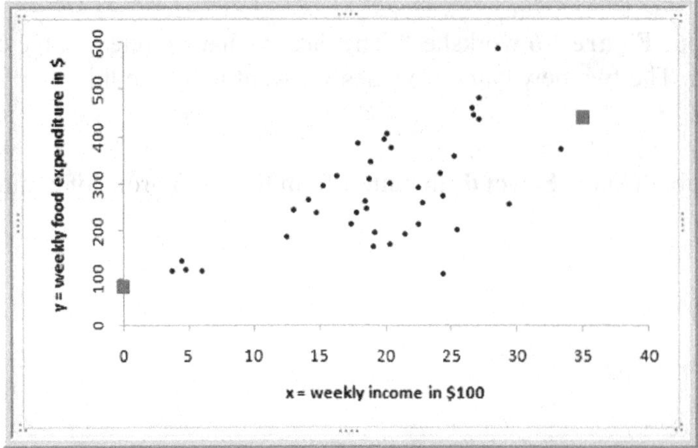

Now, we need to draw a line across those two points. Go to the **Layout** tab. Change the **Current selection** (group of command to the far left) to **Series 2** (use the arrow down button to the right of the window to make that selection). Select **Format selection**.

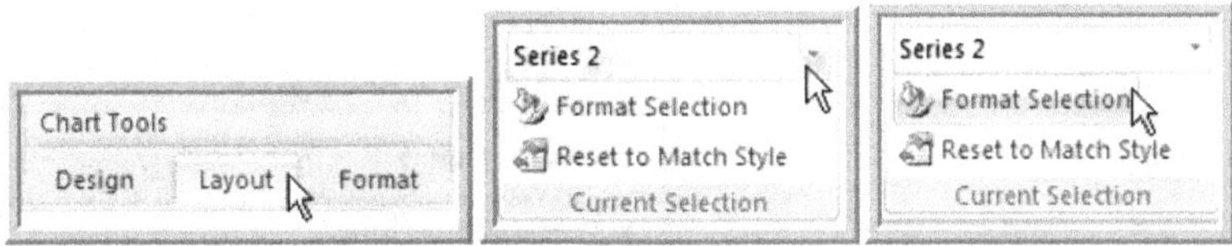

A **Format data series** dialog box pops up. Select **Line color** and change its selection from **No line** to **Solid line**. Select **Close**.

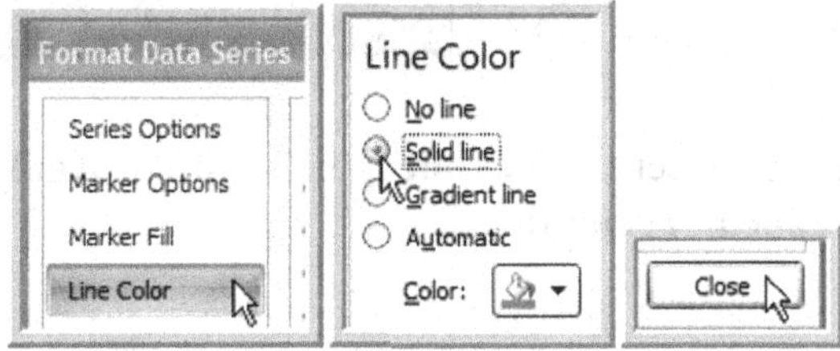

The result is:

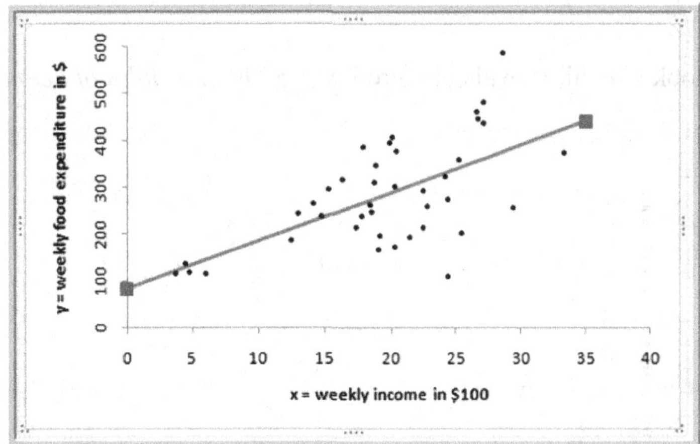

Note that while you *need* only two points to be able to draw a straight line, you *can use* more than two points. So we could have computed a predicted level of food expenditure for every level of income we have in our original data set, and use the 40 $(x_i, \hat{y}_i)$ pairs of values as our data Series 2. This is actually what Excel does when it adds a **Linear Trend Line** to a **Scatter** chart or a **Line** of best **Fit** to **Plots** of data as part of the **Regression Analysis** routine.

We are going to delete the line and two points we just added to our graph and successively look at these other two ways to plot our regression line.

2.3.2 Using Excel Built-in Feature

In the **Design** tab, go back to the **Data** group of commands, and select the **Select Data** button. In the **Select Data Source** dialog box, select **Series2** and **Remove**. Finally select **OK**.

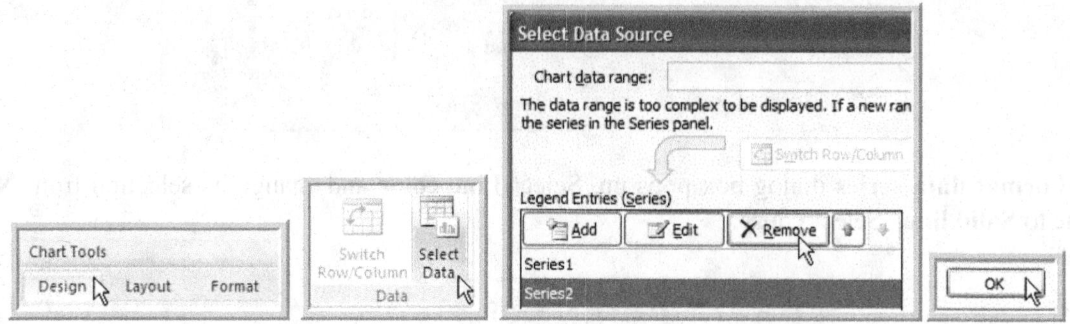

To add a **Linear Trend Line**, select the **Layout** tab. Go to the **Analysis** group of commands, select **Trendline**, and then **Linear Trendline**.

Your chart should look like this (see also Figure 2.8 p. 54 in *Principles of Econometrics, 4e*):

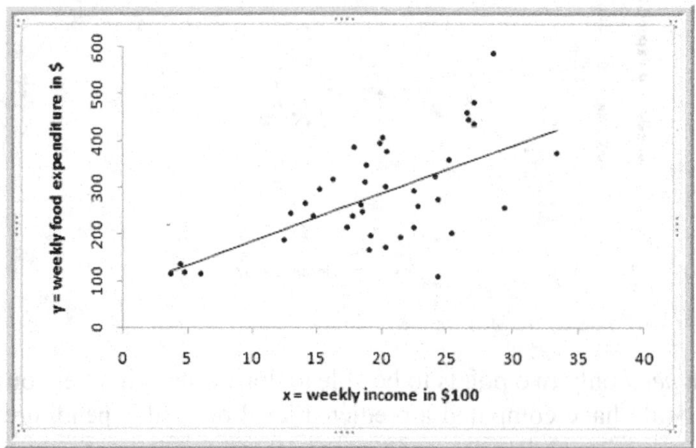

2.3.3 Using a Regression Option

You can also have Excel add the **Line** that best **Fit** your data by choosing that option on the **Regression** dialog box.

Go back to your **Data** worksheet (bottom left corner of your screen).

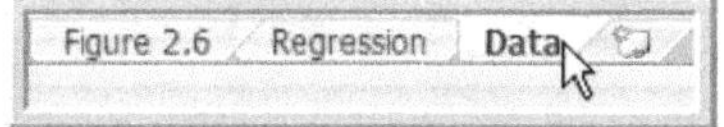

Select the **Data** tab, located in the middle of your tab list. Select **Data Analysis** on the **Analysis** group of commands to the far right of the ribbon. Select **Regression** in the **Data Analysis** dialog box, and then **OK**.

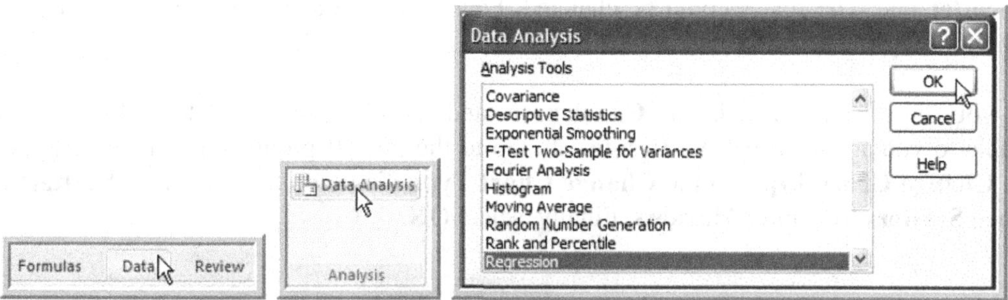

In the **Regression** dialog box, proceed as you did before, except this time, name your worksheet **Regression and Line**, and check the box in front of **Line Fit Plots**. Select **OK**.

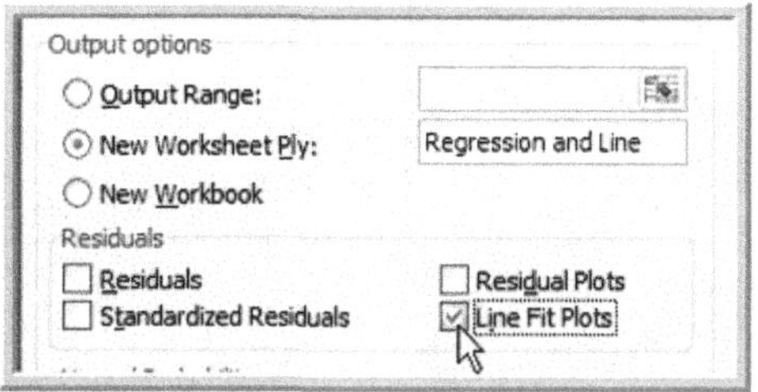

In addition to the **Summary Output** you now have a **Residual Output** table and a **Chart** in your new worksheet. The **Residual Output** table is only partially shown below, and shown after **AutoFit**ting the **Column Width** (see Section 2.2.2 for more details on that).

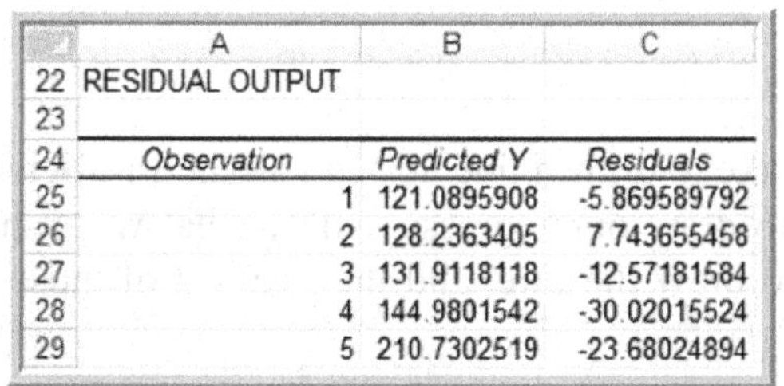

	A	B	C
22	RESIDUAL OUTPUT		
23			
24	*Observation*	*Predicted Y*	*Residuals*
25	1	121.0895908	-5.869589792
26	2	128.2363405	7.743655458
27	3	131.9118118	-12.57181584
28	4	144.9801542	-30.02015524
29	5	210.7302519	-23.68024894

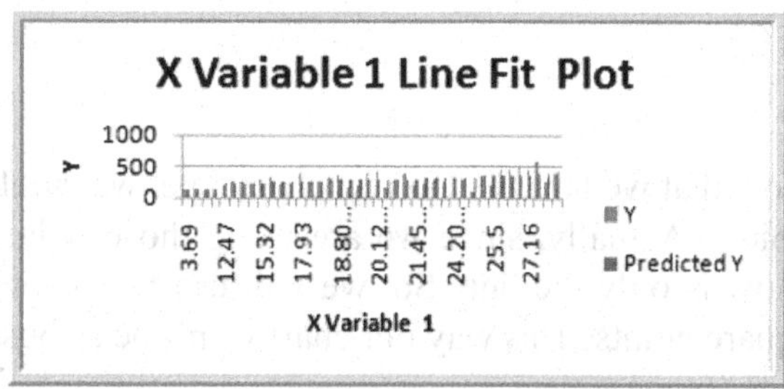

The **Predicted Y** or $\hat{y}_i$ values have been computed for all the original observed x_i values, similarly to the way we computed $\hat{y}$ for $x = 35$ (see Section 2.3.1).

The least squares **Residuals** are defined as

$$\hat{e}_i = y_i - \hat{y}_i = y_i - b_1 - b_2 x_i \tag{2.5}$$

You can compare the **Predicted Y** and **Residuals** values reported in the Excel **Residual Output** to the ones reported in Table 2.3 of *Principles of Econometrics, 4e* (p. 66). They should be the same.

2.3.4 Editing the Chart

Now, the chart needs a little bit of editing. For one it looks like it is a **Column chart** as opposed to a **Scatter** one. The scales could be changed. Finally, **Chart** and **Axis titles** are not currently very helpful.

Place your cursor anywhere in the **Chart area**, and left-click, so that **Chart Tools** are made available to you again. Select the **Design** tab. Go to the far left group of commands, **Type**, and select **Change Chart Type**. In the **Change Chart Type** dialog box, select **X Y (Scatter)** chart, and then **Scatters with only Markers**. Finally, select **OK**.

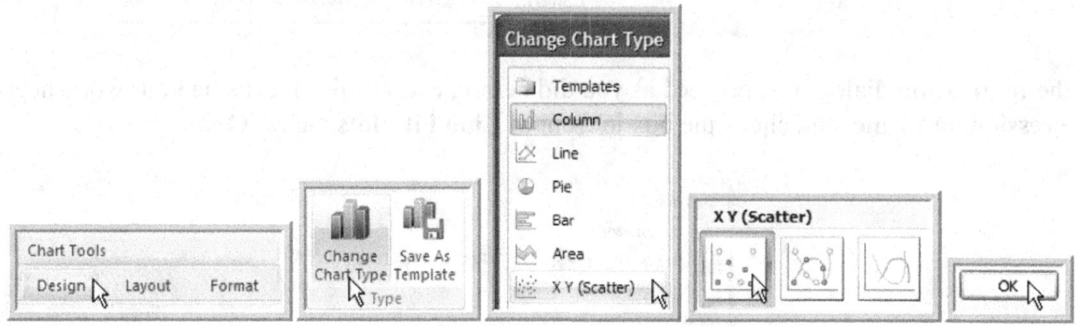

The result is:

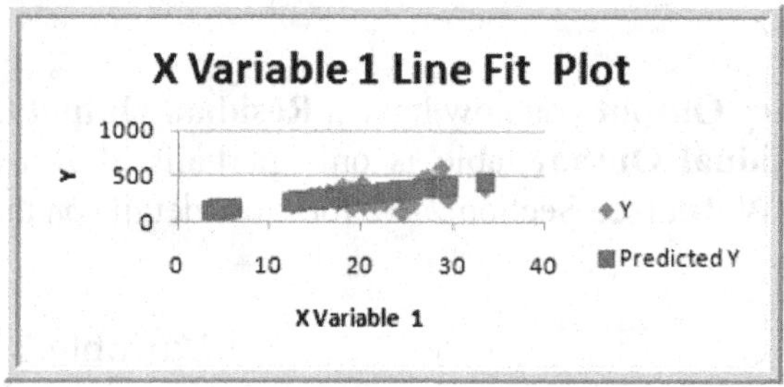

Now that we have the correct chart type, we would like to draw a line through all the **Predicted Y** points. Actually, since we are using those points to draw our regression line, what we want to show is only the line. So, we will use the points to draw the line, and then get rid of those big square points. This way our chart won't be as busy.

On your chart, select the **Predicted Y** points with your cursor. Your cursor should turn into a fat cross as shown below:

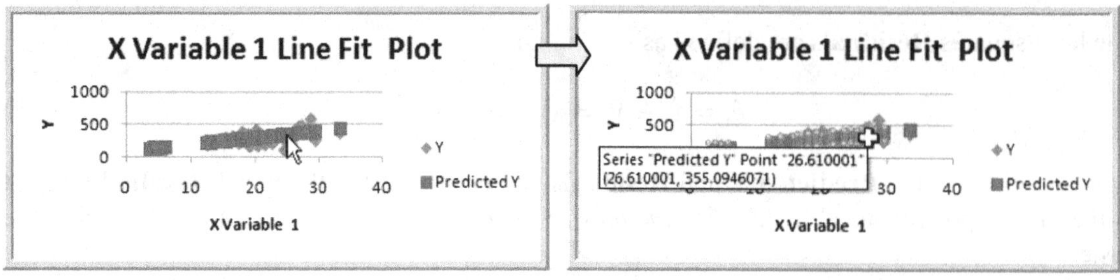

Right-click and select **Format Data Series**. A **Format Data Series** dialog box pops up. Select **Line Color** and **Solid line**. Change the line color to something different from the **Y** points. Select **Marker Options**, and change the **Marker Type** from **Automatic** to **None**. Select **Close**.

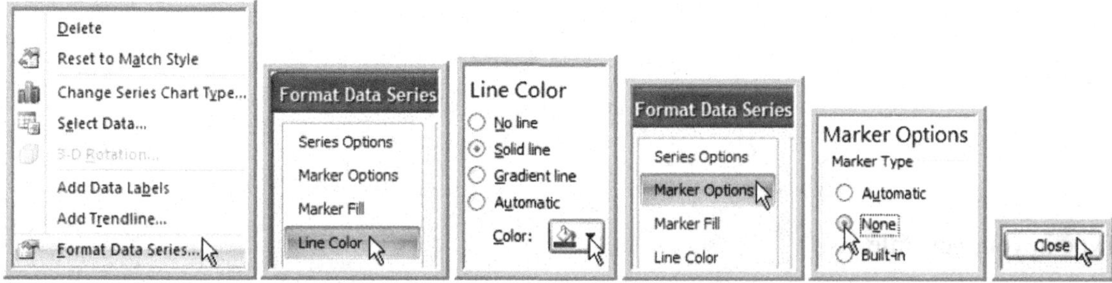

The result is:

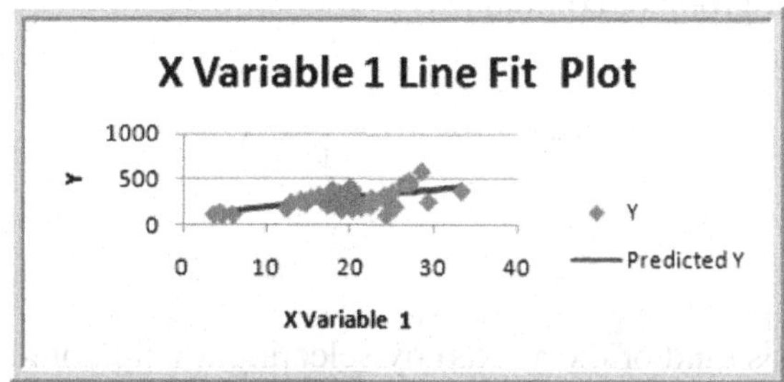

On your chart, select the **Legend** with your cursor, right-click and select **Delete**.

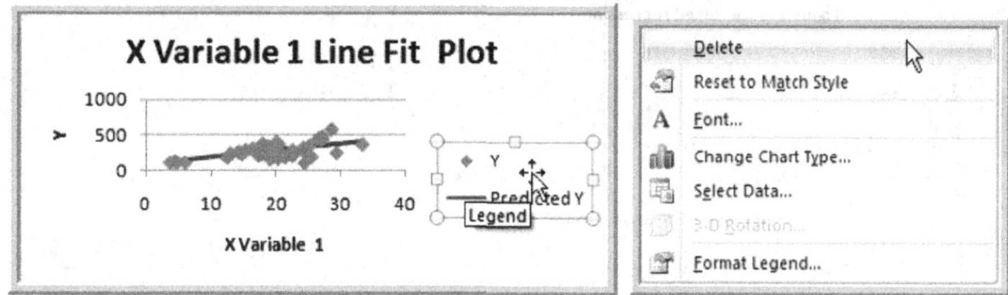

Change the **Chart** and **Axis titles** as you see fit. Below, we show you how you can change the **Chart title**. You can follow a similar process to change the **Axis titles**.

Place your cursor in the title area and left click.

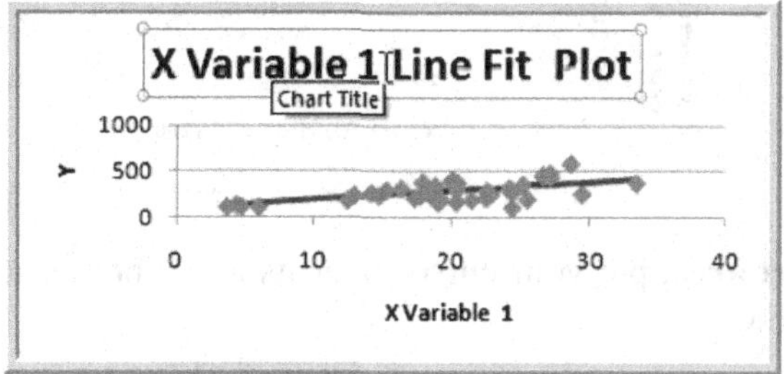

Select the generic title.

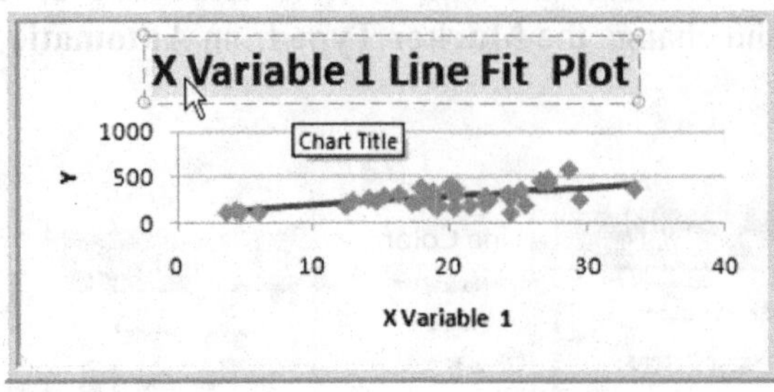

Type in your new title.

You can select any of the titles and change the **Font** size by going back to the **Home** tab. Select what you need on the **Font** group of commands.

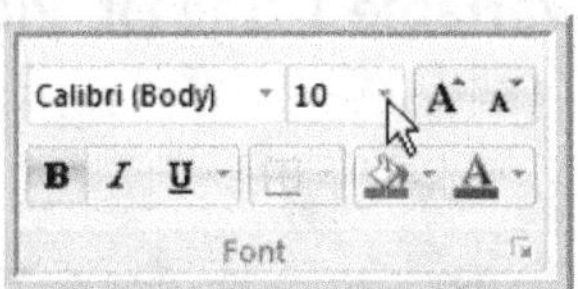

You can reformat the y-axis (and/or the x-axis) by selecting it with your cursor, right-clicking and selecting **Format Axis**.

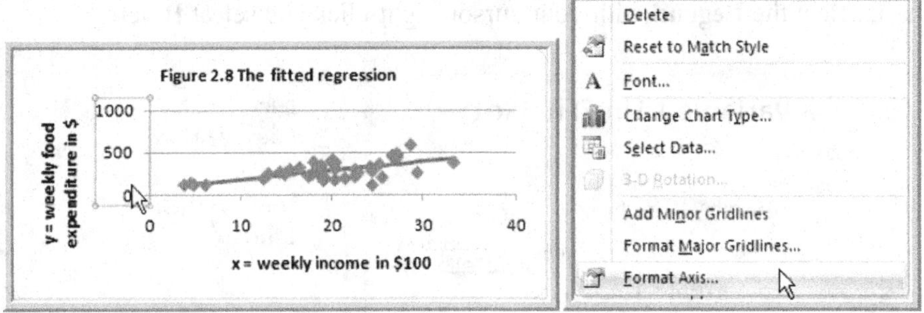

If you proceed as you did before to edit your vertical axis (see Section 2.1.2a), you should obtain the following:

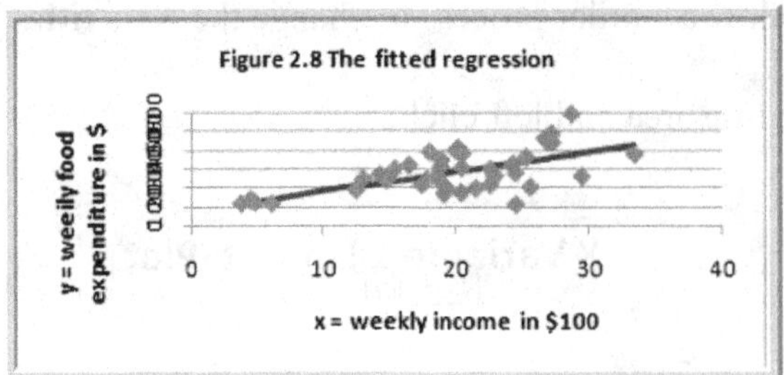

To resize the whole **Chart area**, put your cursor over its lower border until it turns into a double cross arrow as shown below.

Left click, and it should turn into a skinny cross.

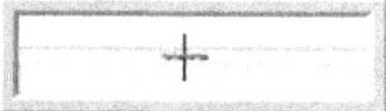

Hold it, and drag it down until you are satisfied with the way your chart looks.

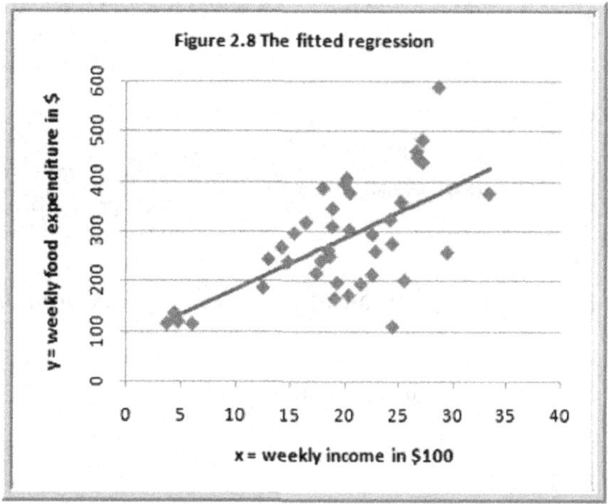

You can delete the **Gridlines** by first selecting them, right-clicking and then selecting **Delete**.

You can also reformat the **Data Series Y** by selecting the points, right-clicking and selecting **Format Data Series**. Then proceed as you did before to change your markers' options (see Section 2.1.2c).

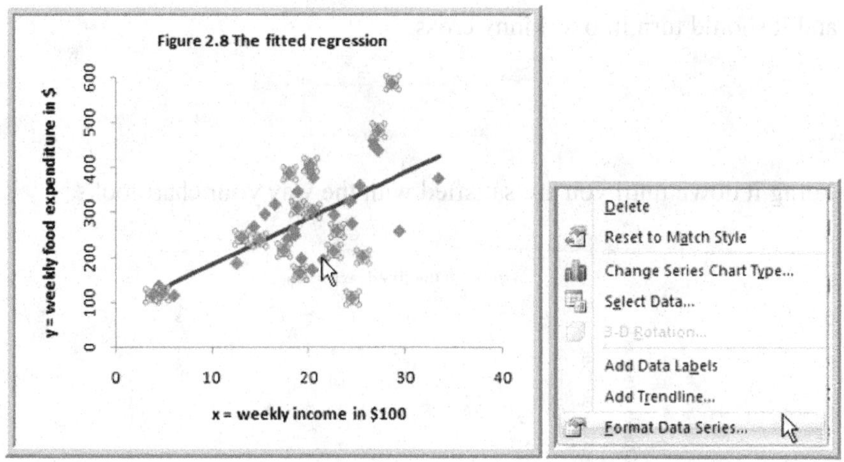

Your result might be (see also Figure 2.8 p. 54 in *Principles of Econometrics, 4e*):

In this next section we illustrate the concept of unbiased estimators.

2.4 EXPECTED VALUES OF b_1 AND b_2

To show that under the assumptions of the simple linear regression model, $E(b_1) = \beta_1$ and $E(b_2) = \beta_2$, we first put ourselves in a situation where we know our population and regression parameters (i.e. we know the truth). We then use the least squares regression technique to unveil the truth (which we already know). This allows us to check on the validity of the least squares regression technique, and specifically to check on the unbiasedness of the least squares estimators.

2.4.1 Model Assumptions

First, let us restate the assumptions of the simple linear regression model (see p. 45 of *Principles of Econometrics, 4e*):

- The mean value of y, for each value of x, is given by the linear regression function:

$$E(y|x) = \beta_1 + \beta_2 x \tag{2.6}$$

- For each value of x, the values of y are distributed about their mean value, following probability distributions that all have the same variance:

$$var(y|x) = \sigma^2 \tag{2.7}$$

- The sample values of y are all uncorrelated and have zero covariance, implying that there is no linear association among them:

$$cov(y_i, y_j) = 0 \tag{2.8}$$

- The variable x is not random and must take at least two different values.

- (*optional*) The values of y are normally distributed about their mean for each value of x:

$$y \sim N[(\beta_1 + \beta_2 x), \sigma^2] \tag{2.9}$$

In the specific and simplified case we are considering in this section, half of our hypothetical population of three person households has a weekly income of \$1000 ($x = 10$), and half of it has a weekly income of \$2000 ($x = 20$). Because we are all mighty, we know the values of our population parameters, and consequently the values of our regression parameters. Let $\mu_{y|x=10} = 200$, $\mu_{y|x=20} = 300$, and $var(y|x = 10) = var(y|x = 20) = \sigma^2 = 2500$. This implies $\beta_1 = 100$ and $\beta_2 = 10$.

The probability distribution functions of weekly food expenditure, y, given an income level $x = 10$ and an income level $x = 20$, are assumed to be Normal. They look like this:

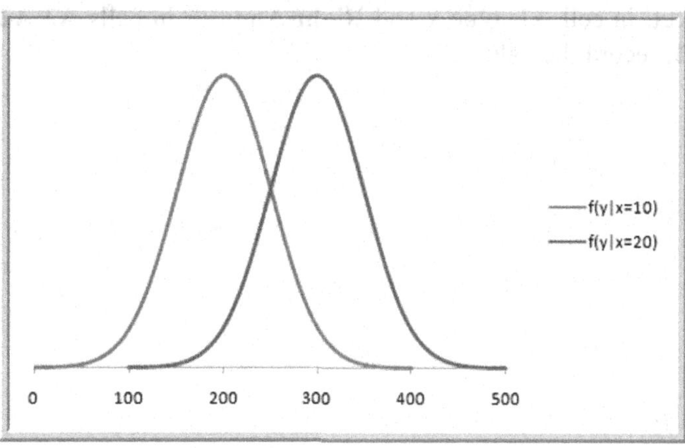

The linear relationship between weekly food expenditure and weekly income looks like the following:

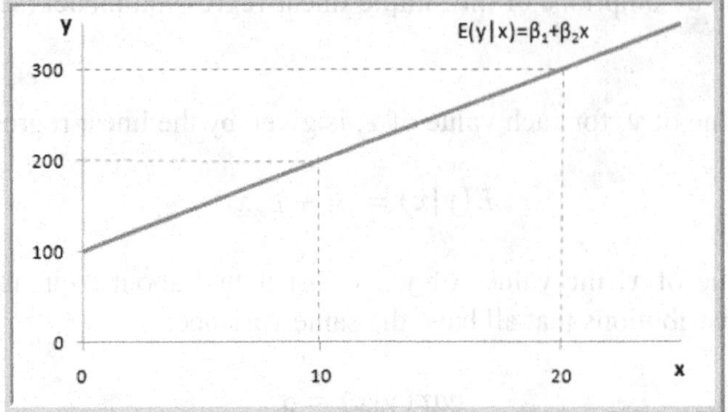

Let us emphasize the difference between this section and Chapter 2 in *Principles of Econometrics, 4e*. In this section, we do *know* the truth. In other words, we have information regarding weekly food expenditure and weekly food income on *all* three person households that constitute our population. In Chapter 2 of *Principles of Econometrics, 4e*, like it is the case in real-life, you do not have that population information. You must thus rely *solely* on your random sample information to make inferences about your population.

Now, as an exercise, and as a way to prove the unbiasedness of the least squares estimators, we are going to use the least square regression technique to unveil the truth.

Insert a new worksheet in your workbook by selecting the **Insert Worksheet** tab at the bottom of your screen (or Press the **Shift** *and* **F11** keys). Name it **Simulation**.

We are going to draw a random sample of 40 households from our population. Half of the sample is drawn from the first type of households, with weekly income $x = 10$; and half of the sample is drawn from the second type of households, with weekly income $x = 20$.

Let us keep records of the level of weekly income for our 40 households in column **A** of our **Simulation** worksheet: in cell **A1**, type **x** and **Right-Align** it; in cells **A2:A21**, record the value **10**; in cells **A22:A41**, record the value **20**.

	A
1	x
2	10
3	10
4	10
5	10
6	10
7	10
8	10
9	10
10	10
11	10
12	10
13	10
14	10
15	10
16	10
17	10
18	10
19	10
20	10
21	10

	A
22	20
23	20
24	20
25	20
26	20
27	20
28	20
29	20
30	20
31	20
32	20
33	20
34	20
35	20
36	20
37	20
38	20
39	20
40	20
41	20
42	

2.4.2 Random Number Generation

We use the **Random Number Generation** analysis tool to draw our random sample of households. We keep record of their weekly food expenditure in column **B** of our **Simulation** worksheet: type **y** in **B1**, and **Right-Align** it.

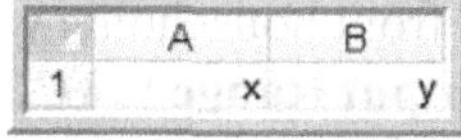

Select the **Data** tab, in the middle of your tab list. On the **Analysis** group of commands to the far right of the ribbon, select **Data Analysis.**

The **Data Analysis** dialog box pops up. In it, select **Random Number Generation** (you might need to use the scroll up and down bar to the right of the **Analysis Tools** window to find it), then select **OK.**

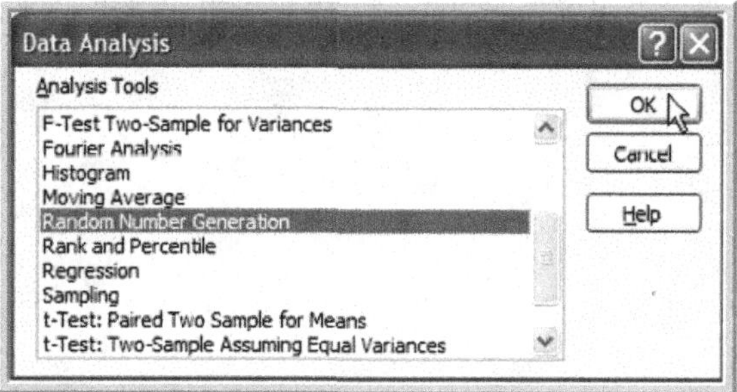

A **Random Number Generation** dialog box pops up. Since we are drawing *one* random sample, we specify **1** in the **Number of Variables** window. We first draw a random samples of 20 from households with weekly income of $x = 10$, so we specify the **Number of Random Numbers** to be **20**. For simplicity we assumed that our population of households has weekly food expenditure that is normally distributed, so this is the distribution we choose. Once you have selected **Normal** in the **Distribution** window, you will be able to specify its **Parameters**: for $x = 10$, its **Mean** is $\mu_{y|x=10} = \mathbf{200}$ and its **Standard deviation** is $\sqrt{var(y|x = 10)} = \sigma = \mathbf{50}$. Select the **Output Range** in the **Output options** section, and specify it to be **B2:B21** in your **Simulation** worksheet. Finally, select **OK**.

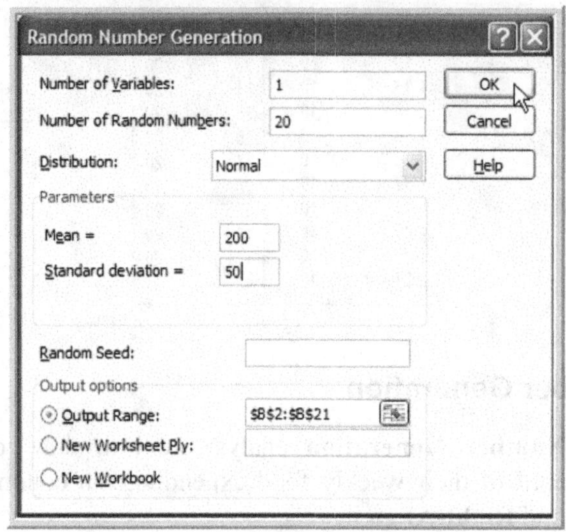

Repeat to draw a random sample of 20 from households with weekly income of $x = 20$. Change the **Mean** to $\mu_{y|x=10} = \mathbf{300}$ and the **Output Range** to **B22:B41**.

Here is the random sample that we obtained. NOTE: you will obtain a *different* random sample, due to the nature of random sampling.

	A	B
1	x	y
2	10	122.4908
3	10	163.1711
4	10	221.0102
5	10	294.1295
6	10	192.9407
7	10	228.5627
8	10	223.1013
9	10	184.7241
10	10	164.8267
11	10	125.1754
12	10	274.037
13	10	136.9209
14	10	190.4468
15	10	121.6272
16	10	202.8224
17	10	123.431
18	10	116.1414
19	10	209.413
20	10	152.0113
21	10	200.4915
22	20	274.6751
23	20	336.5785
24	20	303.5467
25	20	216.4365
26	20	358.9562
27	20	278.1513
28	20	267.9295
29	20	331.2386
30	20	328.9643
31	20	297.1585
32	20	338.727
33	20	297.3423
34	20	201.3894
35	20	309.4636
36	20	305.0402
37	20	334.5588
38	20	286.2402
39	20	273.6785
40	20	318.1071
41	20	283.9447
42		

2.4.3 The LINEST Function

Next, we use the **LINEST** function to obtain the least squares estimates for the intercept and slope parameters, based on the random sample we just drew. The **LINEST** function is an alternative to using the Least Squares Estimators' Formulas (see Section 2.2.1) or the Excel Regression Analysis Routine (see Section 2.2.2). It allows us to quickly get the least squares estimates for the intercept and slope parameters. For this purpose, the general syntax of the **LINEST** function is as follows:

= LINEST(*y*'s, *x*'s)

The first argument of the **LINEST** function specifies the y values, and the second argument specifies the x values, the least squares estimates are based on. In our case, we thus need to specify:

= LINEST(B2:B41,A2:A41)

The **LINEST** function creates a table where it stores the least squares estimates in Excel memory. It first reports the slope coefficient estimate, and then the intercept coefficient estimate. So, if we were to look into Excel memory, the estimates would be reported as shown below:

	column 1	column 2
row 1	b_2	b_1

We nest the **LINEST** function in the **INDEX** function to get the estimated coefficients, *one at a time*. The **INDEX** function returns values from within a table. In the case of a table with only one row, the **INDEX** function general syntax is as follows:

= INDEX(table of results, column_num)

The first argument of the **INDEX** function specifies which table to get the results from. In our case, this is the table of results generated by the **LINEST** function above. So, we replace "table of results" by "**LINEST(B2:B41,A2:A41)**". The second argument indicates from which column of the table to retrieve the result of interest to us. So, if we want to retrieve the estimate of the intercept coefficient, b_1, from the table above, we would indicate that it can be found in column 2 by replacing "column_num" by "**2**".

We are going to report our estimated coefficients at the bottom of our table. In cell **A43**, type **b1 =**; in cell **A44**, type **b2 =**. **Bold** those labels. In cell **B43** and **B44**, type the following equations, respectively:

	A	B
43	**b1=**	**=INDEX(LINEST(B2:B41,A2:A41),2)**
44	**b2=**	**=INDEX(LINEST(B2:B41,A2:A41),1)**

Here are the estimates that we get:

	A	B
43	**b1 =**	67.64114
44	**b2 =**	11.47326

The estimates of the intercept and slope coefficients are based on *one* random sample. Our random sample is different than yours, and each random sample yields different estimates, which may or may not be close to the true parameter values. The property of unbiasedness is about the *average* values of b_1 and b_2 if *many* samples of the same size are drawn from the same population. In the next section, we are thus going to repeat our sampling and least squares estimation exercise.

2.4.4 Repeated Sampling

Note that in Chapter 2 of *Principles of Econometrics, 4e*, the repeated samples given to you were randomly collected from a population with *unknown* parameters. In this section, we draw our samples from a population with *known* parameters.

Go back to the **Random Number Generation** dialog box. We would like to draw 9 additional random samples, so we specify **9** in the **Number of Variables** window. Again, we first draw random samples of 20 from households with weekly income of $x = 10$, so we specify the **Number of Random Numbers** to be **20**. We also select **Normal** in the **Distribution** window, and specify its **Parameters**. For $x = 10$, its **Mean** is $\mu_{y|x=10} = \mathbf{200}$ and its **Standard Deviation** is $\sqrt{var(y|x=10)} = \sigma = \mathbf{50}$. Specify the **Output Range** to be **C2:K21**. Finally, select **OK**.

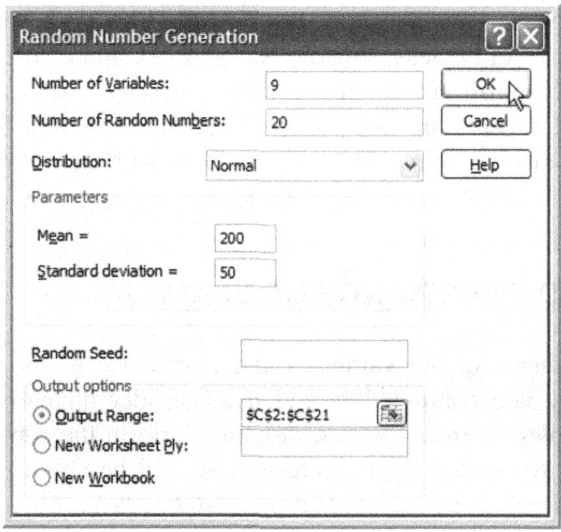

Repeat to draw a random sample of 20 from households with weekly income of $x = 20$. Change the **Mean** to $\mu_{y|x=10}$ **= 300** and the **Output Range** to **C22:K41.**

Next, before we copy the formula to get our coefficient estimates, we need to transform their **Relative cell references A2:A41** into **Absolute cell references $A$2:$A$41**, since we will be using the same *x*-values for our next 9 rounds of least squares estimates.

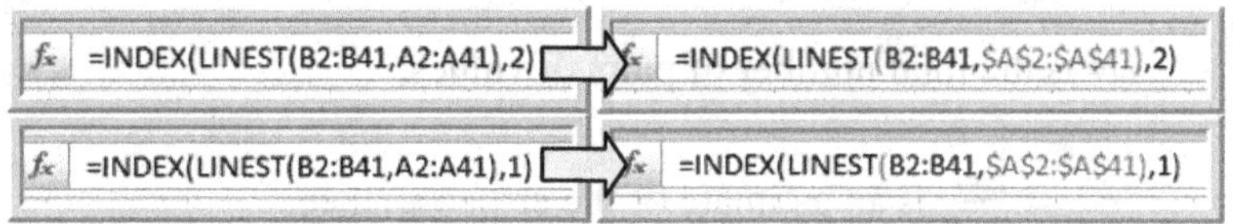

Copy the formulas from **B43:B44** into **C43:K44**. In cells **L43:L44** compute the **AVERAGE**s of your estimates from your 10 samples. In cell **L43**, you should have **=AVERAGE(B43:K43)**; in cell **L44**, you should have **=AVERAGE(B44:K44)**. The estimates and average values that we get for our 10 samples are:

	A	B	C	D	E	F	G	H	I	J	K	L
43	**b1 =**	67.64114	66.92893	110.0845	60.41892	102.9383	127.2066	68.02508	80.43498	132.2953	75.4688	**89.14425**
44	**b2 =**	11.47326	12.2687	8.813088	11.73885	10.11186	8.6169	11.5521	10.8758	8.048971	11.33003	**10.48296**

If we took the averages of estimates from many samples, these averages would approach the true parameter values β_1 and β_2. To show you that this is the case, we repeated the exercise again. Here are the average values of b_1 and b_2 that we did get as we increased the number of samples from 10, to 100, and finally to 1000:

Number of samples	**10**	**100**	**1000**	**Parameter Values**
Average value of b_1	89.14425	98.44593	99.48067	**100**
Average value of b_2	10.48296	10.08958	10.04135	**10**

The next section of this chapter is very short. It points out how you can compute an estimate of the variances and covariance of the least squares estimators b_1 and b_2 using Excel. It also outlines other numbers you can recognize in the Excel summary output. Note that for this section we are getting back to our food expenditure and income data of Sections 2.1-2.3, i.e. data from *one* sample of 40 households that was drawn from a population with *unknown* parameters.

2.5 VARIANCES AND COVARIANCE OF b_1 AND b_2

You can compute an estimate of the variances and covariance of the least squares estimators b_1 and b_2, the same way you computed b_1 and b_2. Consider their algebraic expressions (see below or p. 65 of *Principles of Econometrics, 4e*), and perform the simple arithmetic operations needed. You might want to do that as an exercise; you will be able to check on your work by comparing your estimates to the one reported on pp. 66-67 of *Principles of Econometrics, 4e.*

Estimates of the variances and covariance of the least squares estimators b_1 and b_2 are given by:

$$\widehat{var(b_1)} = \hat{\sigma}^2 \left[\frac{\sum x_i^2}{N \sum (x_i - \bar{x})^2} \right] \tag{2.10}$$

$$\widehat{var(b_2)} = \frac{\hat{\sigma}^2}{\sum (x_i - \bar{x})^2} \tag{2.11}$$

$$\widehat{cov(b_1, b_2)} = \hat{\sigma}^2 \left[\frac{-\bar{x}}{\sum (x_i - \bar{x})^2} \right] \tag{2.12}$$

where: N is the total number of pairs of values,

and $\hat{\sigma}^2 = \frac{\sum \hat{e}_i^2}{N-K}$ is an estimate of the error variance, (2.13)

where: K is the number of regression parameters, $K = 2$,

and $\hat{e}_i = y_i - \hat{y}_i = y_i - b_1 - b_2 x_i$ are the least squares residuals.

The square roots of the estimated variances are the standard errors of b_1 and b_2. They are denoted as $se(b_1)$ and $se(b_2)$.

$$se(b_1) = \sqrt{\widehat{var(b_1)}} \quad \text{and} \quad se(b_2) = \sqrt{\widehat{var(b_2)}} \tag{2.14}$$

Excel regression routine does not automatically generate estimates of the variances and covariance of the least squares estimators b_1 and b_2, but it does compute the standard errors of b_1 and b_2, as well as other intermediary results.

Specifically, the following estimates can be found in the Excel **Summary Output** you generated earlier:

$\sum \hat{e}_i^2$:	Sum of Squared Residuals (**SS Residual**)	in **C13**
$\hat{\sigma}^2$:	Mean Square Residual (**MS Residual**)	in **D13**
$\hat{\sigma}$:	**Standard Error** of the **Regression**	in **B7**
$se(b_1)$ and $se(b_2)$:	**Standard Errors** of **Intercept** and **X Variable 1**	in **C17:C18**

	A	B	C	D	E	F	G	H	I
1	SUMMARY OUTPUT								
2									
3	*Regression Statistics*								
4	Multiple R	0.620485472							
5	R Square	0.385002221							
6	Adjusted R Square	0.368818069							
7	Standard Error	89.51700429							
8	Observations	40							
9									
10	ANOVA								
11		*df*	*SS*	*MS*	*F*	*Significance F*			
12	Regression	1	190626.9788	190626.9788	23.78884107	1.94586E-05			
13	Residual	38	304505.1742	8013.294058					
14	Total	39	495132.153						
15									
16		*Coefficients*	*Standard Error*	*t Stat*	*P-value*	*Lower 95%*	*Upper 95%*	*Lower 95.0%*	*Upper 95.0%*
17	Intercept	83.41600997	43.41016192	1.921577951	0.062182379	-4.463267721	171.2952877	-4.463267721	171.2952877
18	X Variable 1	10.2096425	2.093263461	4.877380554	1.94586E-05	5.972052202	14.4472328	5.972052202	14.4472328

Note that $\sum \hat{e}_i^2$, the **Sum of Squared Residuals (SS Residual)**, is also referred to as the **Sum of Squared Errors**—hence the abbreviation **SSE** used in p. 51 of *Principles of Econometrics, 4e*.

2.6 NONLINEAR RELATIONSHIPS

2.6.1 A Quadratic Model

2.6.1a Estimating the Model

Open the Excel file ***br***. Excel opens the data set in Sheet 1 of a new Excel file. Since we would like to save all our work from Chapter 2 in one file, create a new worksheet in your **POE Chapter 2** Excel file, name it **pr data**, and in it, copy the data set you just opened.

This data set contains data on 1080 houses sold in Baton Rouge, LA during mid-2005, which we are using to estimate the following quadratic model for house prices:

$$PRICE = \alpha_1 + \alpha_2 SQFT^2 + e \tag{2.15}$$

In your **br data** worksheet, insert a column to the right of the **sqft** column **B** (see Section 1.4 for more details on how to do that). In your new cells **C1:C2**, enter the following column label and formula.

	C
1	**sqft²**
2	=B2^2

Copy the content of cells **C2** to cells **C3:C1081**. Here is how your table should look (only the first five values are shown below):

	A	B	C
1	**price**	**sqft**	**sqft²**
2	66500	741	549081
3	66000	741	549081
4	68500	790	624100
5	102000	2783	7745089
6	54000	1165	1357225

In the **Regression** dialog box, the **Input Y Range** should be **A2:A1081**, and the **Input X Range** should be **C2:C1081**. Select **New Worksheet Ply** and name it **Quadratic Model**. Finally select **OK**.

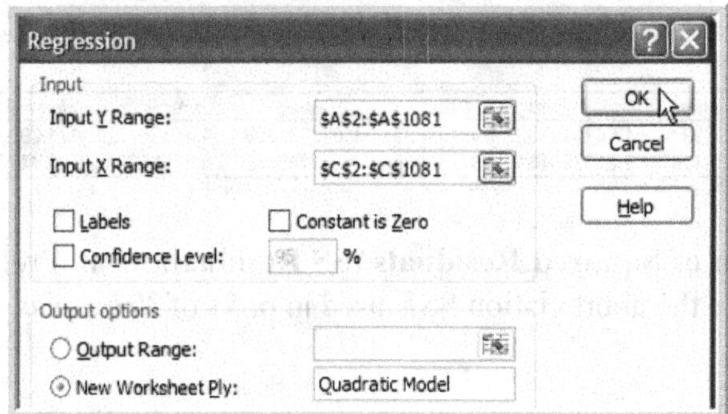

The result is (matching the one reported on p. 70 in *Principles of Econometrics, 4e*):

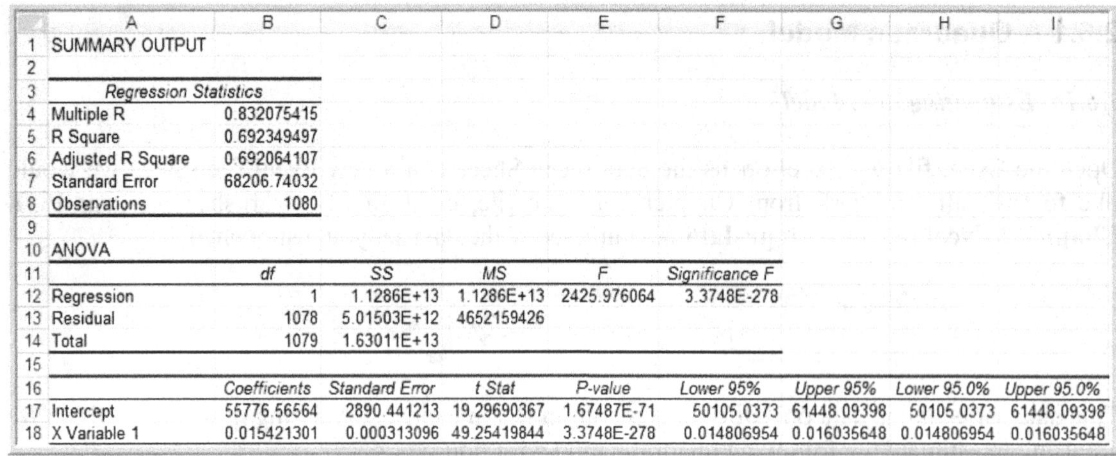

	A	B	C	D	E	F	G	H	I
1	SUMMARY OUTPUT								
2									
3	*Regression Statistics*								
4	Multiple R	0.832075415							
5	R Square	0.692349497							
6	Adjusted R Square	0.692064107							
7	Standard Error	68206.74032							
8	Observations	1080							
9									
10	ANOVA								
11		*df*	*SS*	*MS*	*F*	*Significance F*			
12	Regression	1	1.1286E+13	1.1286E+13	2425.976064	3.3748E-278			
13	Residual	1078	5.01503E+12	4652159426					
14	Total	1079	1.63011E+13						
15									
16		*Coefficients*	*Standard Error*	*t Stat*	*P-value*	*Lower 95%*	*Upper 95%*	*Lower 95.0%*	*Upper 95.0%*
17	Intercept	55776.56564	2890.441213	19.29690367	1.67487E-71	50105.0373	61448.09398	50105.0373	61448.09398
18	X Variable 1	0.015421301	0.000313096	49.25419844	3.3748E-278	0.014806954	0.016035648	0.014806954	0.016035648

2.6.1b Scatter of Data and Fitted Quadratic Relationship

Go back to your **br data** worksheet and select **A2:B1081**. Select the **Insert** tab located next to the **Home** tab. In the **Charts** group of commands select **Scatter**, and then **Scatter with only Markers**.

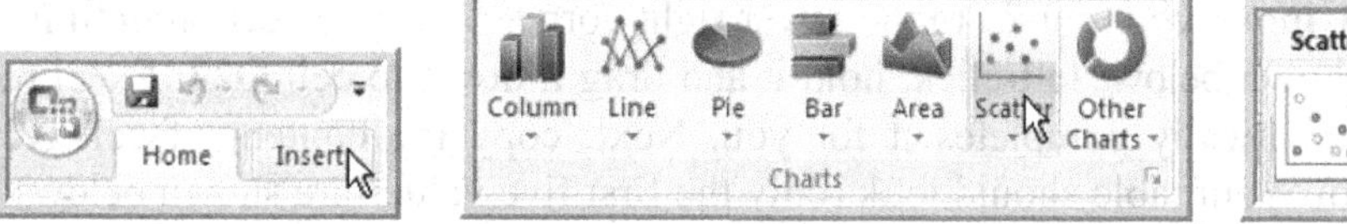

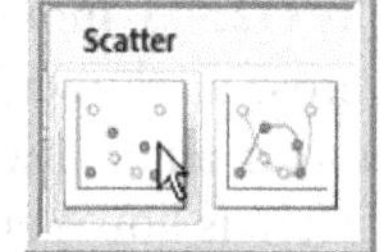

The result is:

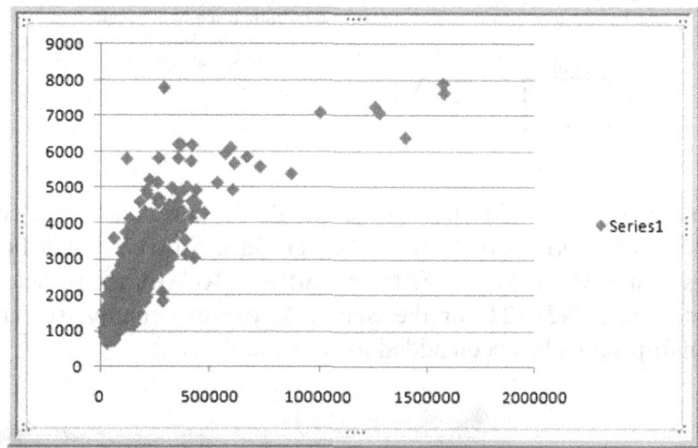

You can see that our house price values are on the horizontal axis and square footage values are on the vertical axis; we would like to change that around and edit our chart as we did in Section 2.1 with our plot of food expenditure data. The result is (see also Figure 2.14 on p. 70 in *Principles of Econometrics, 4e*):

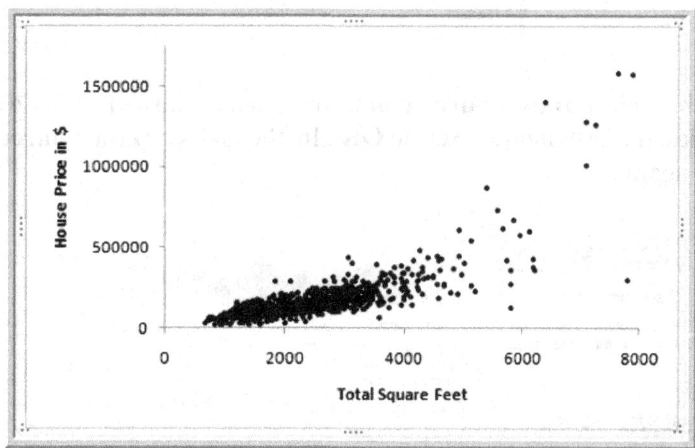

Finally, we add the fitted quadratic relationship to our scatter plot. In cells **N1:N2** and **O1:O3** of your **br data** worksheet , enter the following column label and formula.

	N	O
1	**quadratic price-hat**	**sqft**
2	='Quadratic Model'!$B$17+'Quadratic Model'!$B$18*'br data'!O2	0
3		400

Select cells **O2:O3**, move your cursor to the lower right corner of your selection until it turns into a skinny cross as shown below; left-click, hold it and drag it down to cell **O22**: Excel recognizes the series and automatically completes it for you. Next, copy the content of cell **N2** to cells **N3:N22**. Here is how your table should look (only the first five values are shown below):

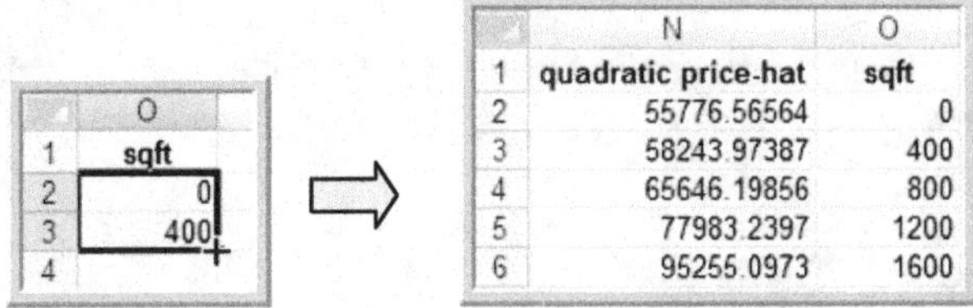

	N	O
1	**quadratic price-hat**	**sqft**
2	55776.56564	0
3	58243.97387	400
4	65646.19856	800
5	77983.2397	1200
6	95255.0973	1600

Go back to your scatter plot and right-click in the middle of your chart area. Select **Select Data**. In the **Legend Entries (Series)** window of the **Select Data Source** dialog box, select the **Add** button. In the **Series name** window, type **Fitted Quadratic Relationship**. Select **O2:O22** for the **Series X values** and select **N2:N22** for the **Series Y values**. Finally, select **OK**. The **Fitted Quadratic Relationship** series has been added to your graph.

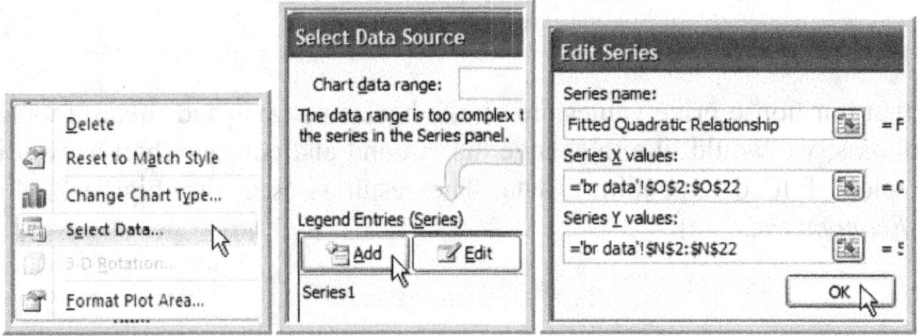

Before you close the **Select Data Source** dialog box, select **Series1** and **Edit**. Type the name **Actual** in the **Series name** window. Select **OK**. In the **Select Data Source** window that re-appears, select **OK** again.

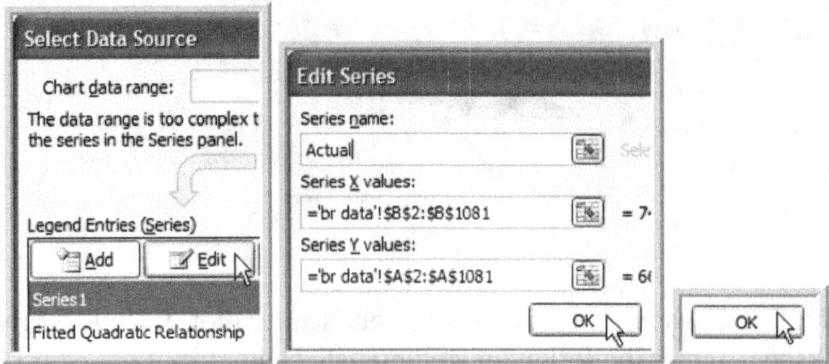

Make sure you chart is selected so that the **Chart Tools** are visible. In the **Layout** tab, go to the **Labels** group of commands. Select the **Legend** button and choose either one of the **Overlay**

Legend options. Grab your legend with your cursor and move it to the upper left corner of your chart area.

Finally, we want to reformat our **Fitted Quadratic Relationship** values series. Select the plotted series in your chart area, right-click and select **Format Data Series**. A **Format Data Series** dialog box pops up. Select **Line Color** and **Solid line**. Change the line color to something different from the **Actual** series points. Select **Marker Options**, and change the **Marker Type** from **Automatic** to **None**. Select **Close**.

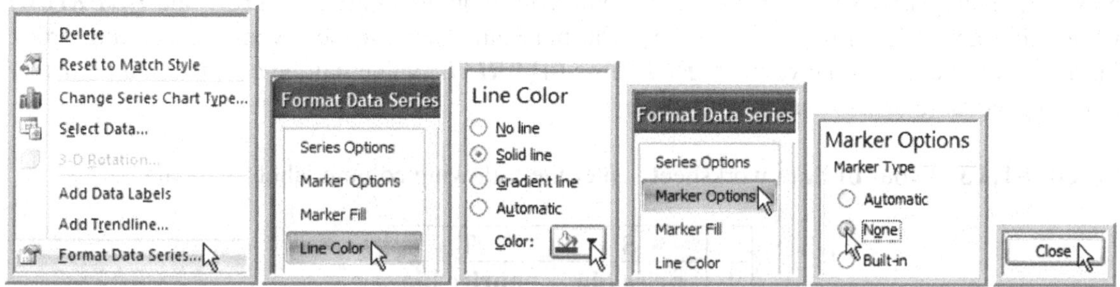

The result is (see also Figure 2.14 on p. 70 in *Principles of Econometrics, 4e*):

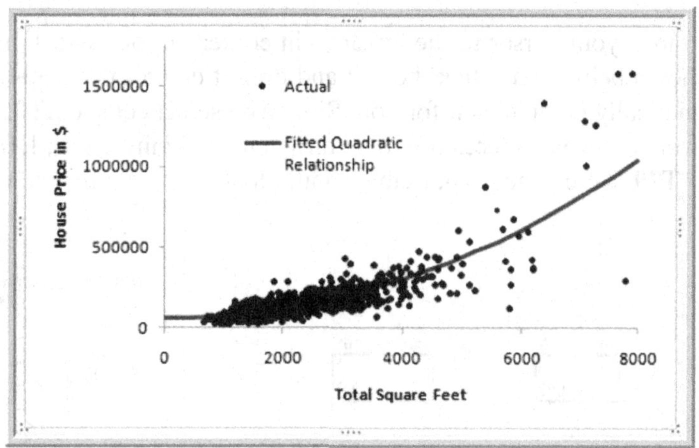

2.6.2 A Log-Linear Model

2.6.2a Histograms of PRICE and ln(PRICE)

In your **br data** worksheet, insert a column to the right of the **sqft²** column **C** (see Section 1.4 for more details on how to do that). In your new cells **D1:D2**, enter the following column label and formula.

	D
1	**ln(price)**
2	=ln(A2)

Copy the content of cells **D2** to cells **D3:D1081**. Here is how your table should look (only the first five values are shown below):

	A	B	C	D
1	**price**	**sqft**	**sqft²**	**ln(price)**
2	66500	741	549081	11.10496
3	66000	741	549081	11.09741
4	68500	790	624100	11.13459
5	102000	2783	7745089	11.53273
6	54000	1165	1357225	10.89674

Next, we specify **BIN** values. These values will determine the range of $\boldsymbol{PRICE}$ and $\boldsymbol{ln(PRICE)}$ values for each column of the histogram. The bin values have to be given in ascending order. Starting with the lowest bin value, a $\boldsymbol{PRICE}$ or $\boldsymbol{ln(PRICE)}$ value will be counted in a particular bin if it is equal to or less than the bin value.

In cells **S1:T3** of your **br data** worksheet , enter the following column labels and data.

	S	T
1	**price bin**	**lnprice bin**
2	0	9
3	50000	9.2

Select cells **S2:S3**, move your cursor to the lower right corner of your selection until it turns into a skinny cross as shown below; left-click, hold it and drag it down to cell **S34**: Excel recognizes the series and automatically completes it for you. Similarly, select cells **T2:T3**, move your cursor to the lower right corner of your selection until it turns into a skinny cross; left-click, hold it and drag it down to cell **T29**. Here is how your table should look (only the first five values are shown below):

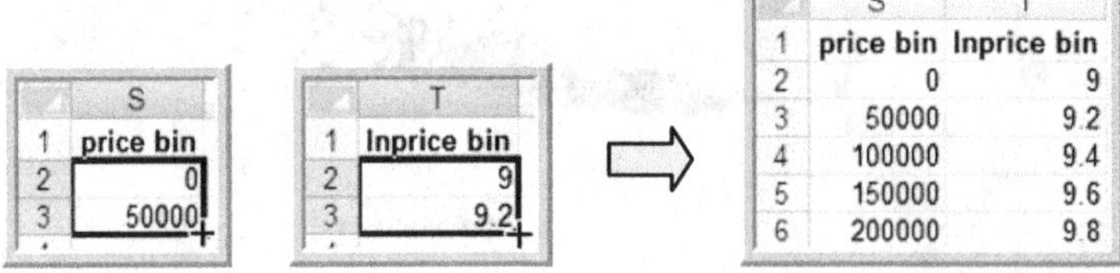

	S	T
1	**price bin**	**lnprice bin**
2	0	9
3	50000	9.2
4	100000	9.4
5	150000	9.6
6	200000	9.8

Select the **Data** tab, in the middle of your tab list. On the **Analysis** group of commands to the far right of the ribbon, select **Data Analysis**.

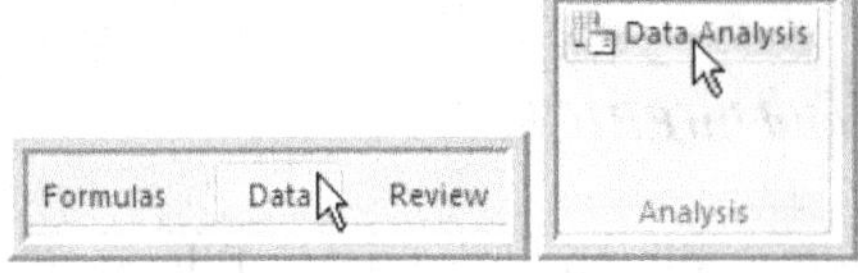

The **Data Analysis** dialog box pops up. In it, select **Histogram** (you might need to use the scroll up and down bar to the right of the **Analysis Tools** window to find it), then select **OK**.

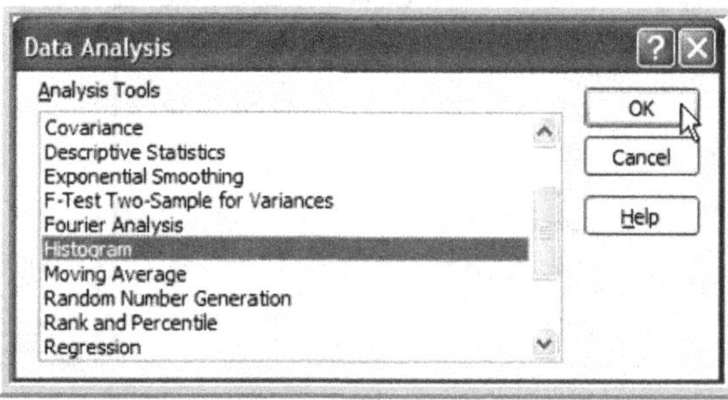

An **Histogram** dialog box pops up. For the **Input Range**, specify **A2:A1081**; for the **Bin Range**, specify **S2:S34**. The **Input Range** indicates the data set Excel will look at to determine how many values are counted in each bin of the **Bin Range**. Check the **New Worksheet Ply** option and name it **Price Histogram**; check the box next to **Chart Output**. Finally, select **OK**.

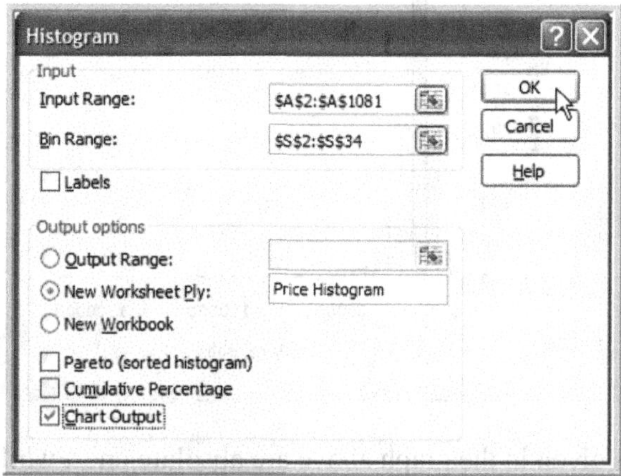

Select the columns in your chart area, right-click and select **Format Data Series**. The **Series Options** tab of the **Format Data Series** dialog box should be open. Select the **Gap Width** button and move it to the far left, towards **No Gap**.

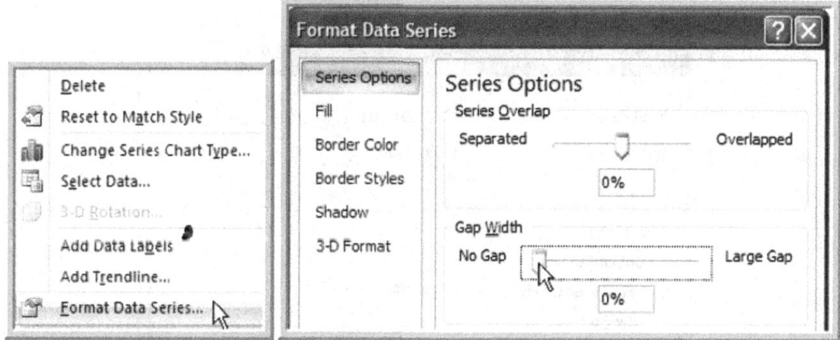

Go to the **Border Color** tab and select **Solid line**, choose a different **Color** if you would like. Select **Close**.

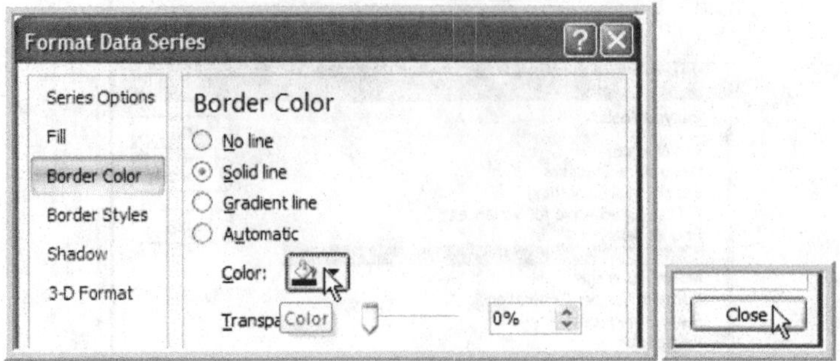

After editing our chart as we did in Section 2.1 with our plot of food expenditure data, the result is (see also Figure 2.16(a) on p. 72 in *Principles of Econometrics, 4e*):

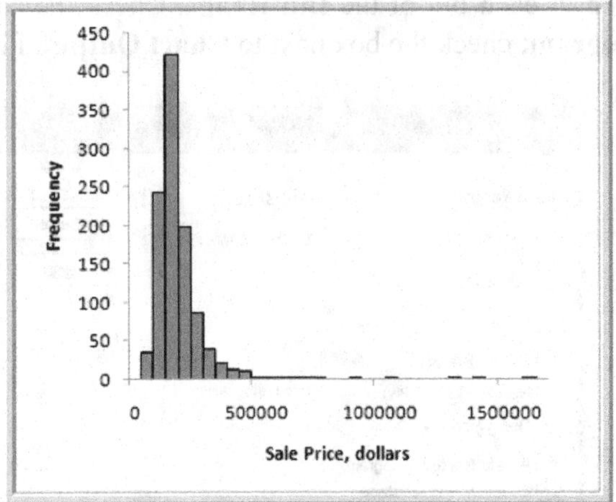

Note that the frequencies given in the graph above are absolute ones, while the frequencies given in Figure 2.16(a) of *Principles of Econometrics, 4e* are relative ones.

Go back to your **br data** worksheet. In the **Histogram** dialog box, specify **D2:D1081** for the **Input Range** and **T2:T29** for the **Bin Range**. Check the **New Worksheet Ply** option and name it **lnPrice Histogram**; check the box next to **Chart Output**. Finally, select **OK**.

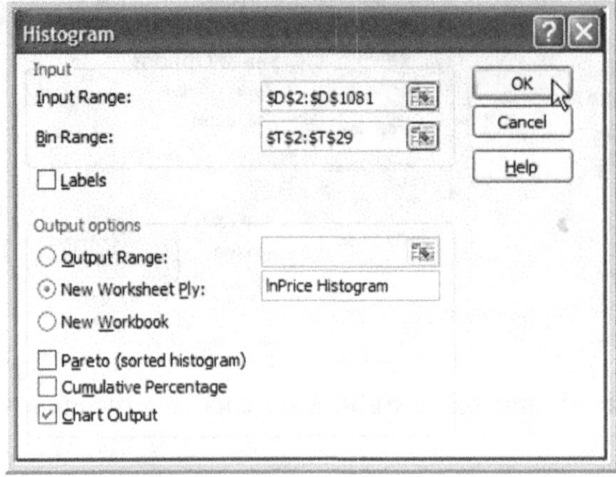

The final result is (see also Figure 2.16(b) on p. 72 in *Principles of Econometrics, 4e*):

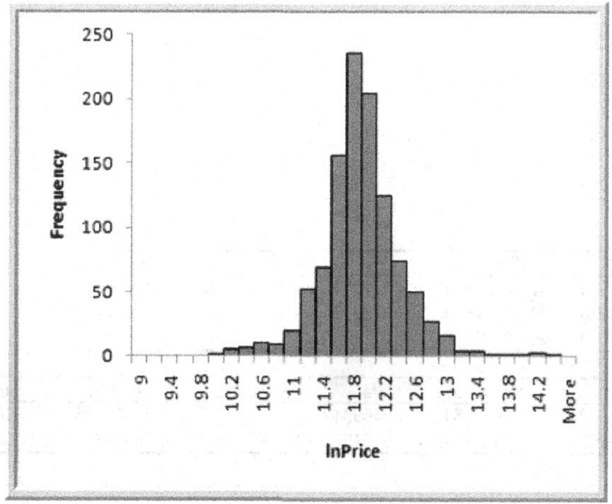

Again, note that the frequencies given in the graph above are absolute ones, while the frequencies given in Figure 2.16(b) of *Principles of Econometrics, 4e* are relative ones.

2.6.2b Estimating the Model

We estimate the following log-linear model for house prices:

$$ln(PRICE) = \gamma_1 + \gamma_2 SQFT + e \qquad (2.16)$$

In the **Regression** dialog box, the **Input Y Range** should be **D2:D1081**, and the **Input X Range** should be **B2:B1081**. Select **New Worksheet Ply** and name it **Log-Linear Model**. Finally select **OK**.

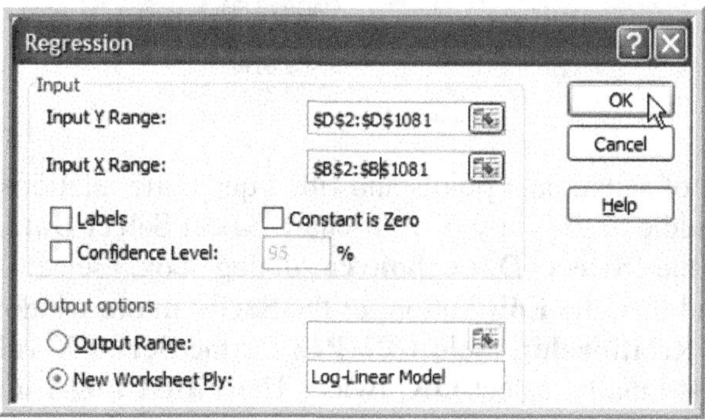

The result is (matching the one reported on p. 72 in *Principles of Econometrics, 4e*):

	A	B	C	D	E	F	G	H	I
1	SUMMARY OUTPUT								
2									
3	*Regression Statistics*								
4	Multiple R	0.790413619							
5	R Square	0.624753689							
6	Adjusted R Square	0.624405594							
7	Standard Error	0.321465013							
8	Observations	1080							
9									
10	ANOVA								
11		*df*	*SS*	*MS*	*F*	*Significance F*			
12	Regression	1	185.4720974	185.4720974	1794.779738	1.1066E-231			
13	Residual	1078	111.4002553	0.103339754					
14	Total	1079	296.8723527						
15									
16		*Coefficients*	*Standard Error*	*t Stat*	*P-value*	*Lower 95%*	*Upper 95%*	*Lower 95.0%*	*Upper 95.0%*
17	Intercept	10.83859632	0.024607484	440.459342	0	10.79031232	10.88688031	10.79031232	10.88688031
18	X Variable 1	0.000411269	9.70779E-06	42.36484082	1.1066E-231	0.000392221	0.000430317	0.000392221	0.000430317

2.6.2c Scatter of Data and Fitted Log-Linear Relationship

In cells **Q1:Q2** of your **br data** worksheet, enter the following column label and formula.

	Q
1	**log-linear price-hat**
2	=EXP('Log-Linear Model'!$B$17+'Log-Linear Model'!$B$18*'br data'!P2)

Next, copy the content of cells **Q2** to cells **Q3:Q22**. Here is how your table should look (only the first five values are shown below):

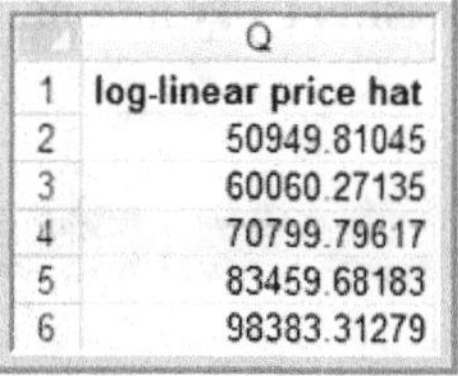

	Q
1	**log-linear price hat**
2	50949.81045
3	60060.27135
4	70799.79617
5	83459.68183
6	98383.31279

Select your scatter plot of actual data points and fitted quadratic relationship and make a copy of it. Right-click in the middle of the copy of your chart. Select **Select Data**. In the **Legend Entries (Series)** window of the **Select Data Source** dialog box, select the **Fitted Quadratic Relationship** series, and then the **Edit** button. In the **Series name** window, replace the old name by **Fitted Log-Linear Relationship**. Select **P2:P22** for the **Series X values** and select **Q2:Q22** for the **Series Y values**. Finally, select **OK**, twice. The **Fitted Log-Linear Relationship** series has been added to your graph.

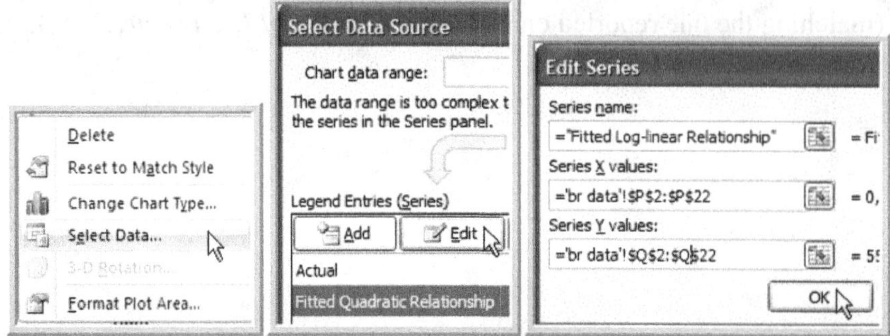

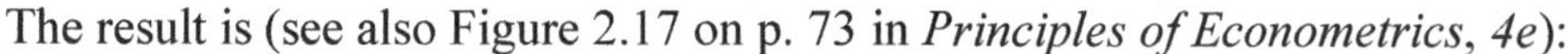

The result is (see also Figure 2.17 on p. 73 in *Principles of Econometrics, 4e*):

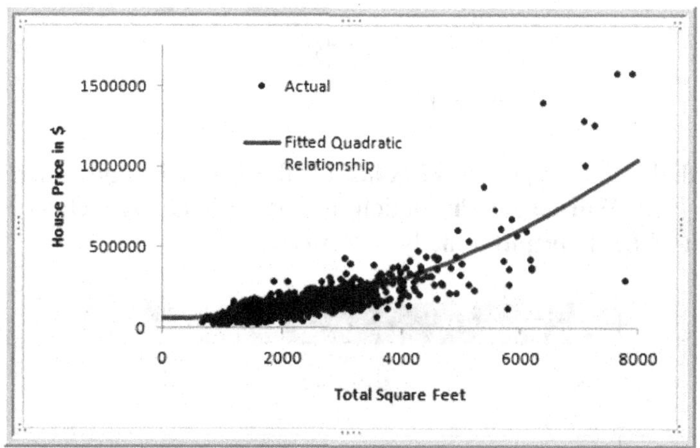

2.7 REGRESSION WITH INDICATOR VARIABLES

2.7.1 Histograms of House Prices

Open the Excel file ***utown***. Excel opens the data set in Sheet 1 of a new Excel file. Since we would like to save all our work from Chapter 2 in one file, create a new worksheet in your **POE Chapter 2** Excel file, name it **utown data**, and in it, copy the data set you just opened.

This data file contains a sample of 1000 observations on house prices in two neighborhoods. One neighborhood is near a major university and called University Town. Another similar neighborhood, called Golden Oaks, is a few miles away from the university.

In cells **H1:H3** of your **utown data** worksheet, enter the following column label and data.

	H
1	**bin**
2	125
3	137.5

Select cells **H2:H3**, move your cursor to the lower right corner of your selection until it turns into a skinny cross as shown below; left-click, hold it and drag it down to cell **H20**. Here is how your table should look (only the first five values are shown below):

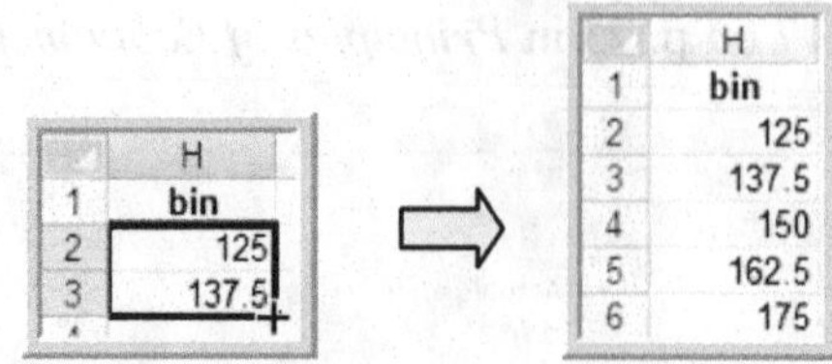

In the **Histogram** dialog box, specify **A2:A482** for the **Input Range** and **H2:H20** for the **Bin Range**. Check the **New Worksheet Ply** option and name it **Golden Oaks Prices Histogram**; check the box next to **Chart Output**. Finally, select **OK**.

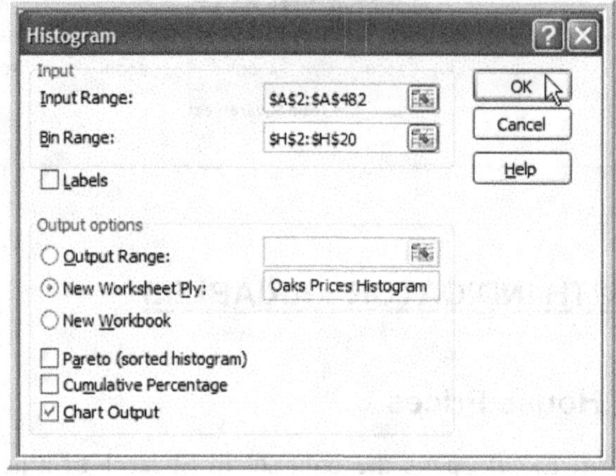

The final result is (see also Figure 2.18 on p. 74 in *Principles of Econometrics, 4e*):

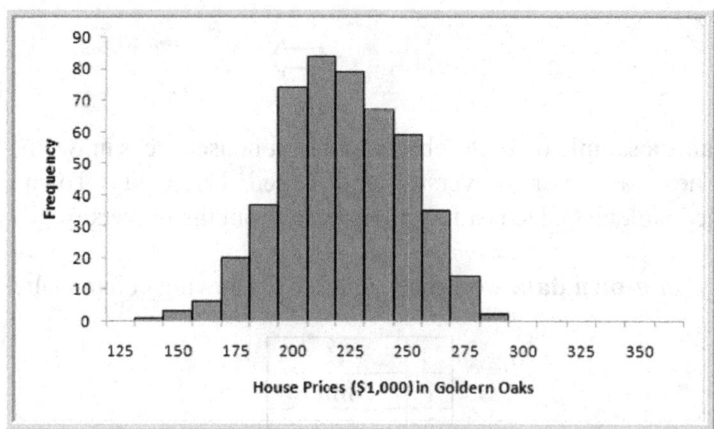

Note that the frequencies given in the graph above are absolute ones, while the frequencies given in Figure 2.18 of *Principles of Econometrics, 4e* are relative ones.

Go back to your **utown data** worksheet. In the **Histogram** dialog box, specify **A483:A1001** for the **Input Range** and **H2:H20** for the **Bin Range**. Check the **New Worksheet Ply** option and name it **U Town Prices Histogram**; check the box next to **Chart Output**. Finally, select **OK**.

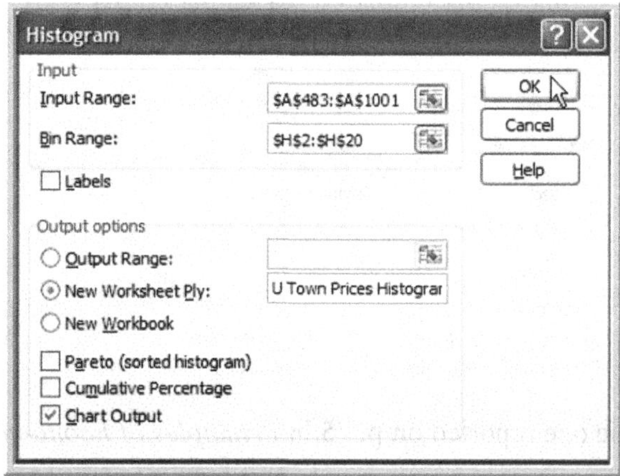

The final result is (see also Figure 2.18 on p. 74 in *Principles of Econometrics, 4e*):

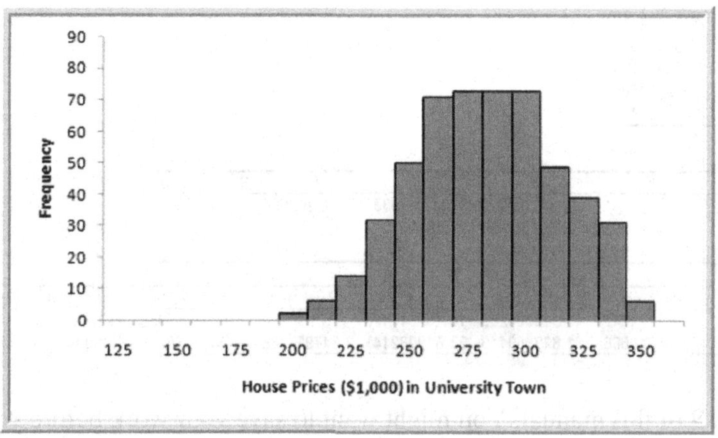

2.7.2 Estimating the Model

We estimate the following regression model for house prices

$$\boldsymbol{PRICE = \beta_1 + \beta_2 UTOWN + e} \tag{2.17}$$

The indicator variable is

$$UTOWN = \begin{cases} 0 & \text{house is in University Town} \\ 1 & \text{house is in Golden Oaks} \end{cases} \tag{2.18}$$

Go back to your **utown data** worksheet.

In the **Regression** dialog box, the **Input Y Range** should be **A2:A1001**, and the **Input X Range** should be **D2:D1001**. Select **New Worksheet Ply** and name it **Indicator Variable Model.** Finally select **OK**.

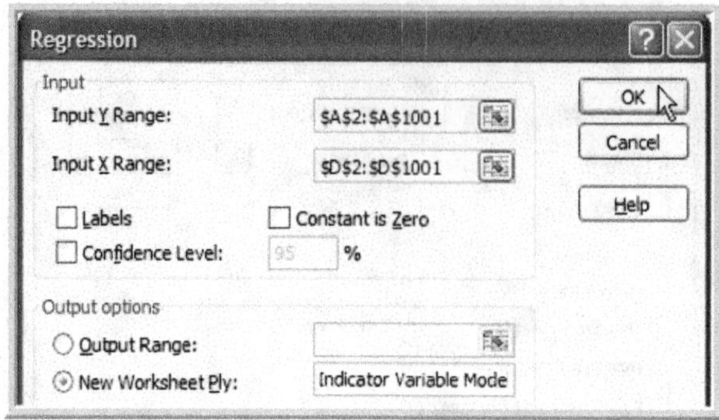

The result is (matching the one reported on p. 75 in *Principles of Econometrics, 4e*):

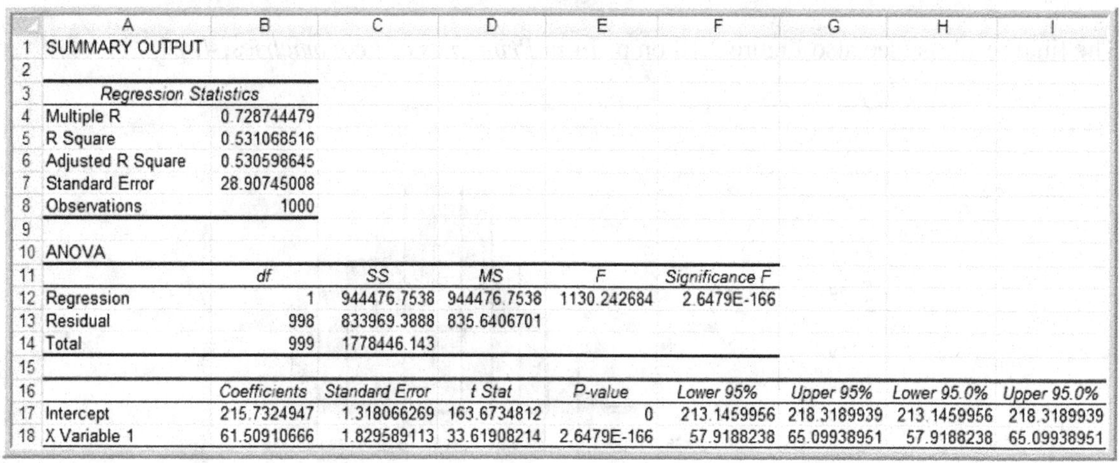

	A	B	C	D	E	F	G	H	I
1	SUMMARY OUTPUT								
2									
3	*Regression Statistics*								
4	Multiple R	0.728744479							
5	R Square	0.531068516							
6	Adjusted R Square	0.530598645							
7	Standard Error	28.90745008							
8	Observations	1000							
9									
10	ANOVA								
11		*df*	*SS*	*MS*	*F*	*Significance F*			
12	Regression	1	944476.7538	944476.7538	1130.242684	2.6479E-166			
13	Residual	998	833969.3888	835.6406701					
14	Total	999	1778446.143						
15									
16		*Coefficients*	*Standard Error*	*t Stat*	*P-value*	*Lower 95%*	*Upper 95%*	*Lower 95.0%*	*Upper 95.0%*
17	Intercept	215.7324947	1.318066269	163.6734812	0	213.1459956	218.3189939	213.1459956	218.3189939
18	X Variable 1	61.50910666	1.829589113	33.61908214	2.6479E-166	57.9188238	65.09938951	57.9188238	65.09938951

This ends Chapter 2 of this manual. You might want to save your work before you close shop.

CHAPTER 3

Interval Estimation and Hypothesis Testing

CHAPTER OUTLINE

In this chapter we will use the t-distribution to construct interval estimates and perform hypothesis tests. We continue to work with the simple linear regression model of weekly food expenditure.

3.1 INTERVAL ESTIMATION

Open the Excel file *food*. Save it as **POE Chapter 3**.

Rename Sheet 1 **Data**. Quickly re-estimate the regression parameters using Excel regression analysis routine as in Section 2.2.2. In the **Regression** dialog box, the **Input Y Range** should be **A2:A41**, and the **Input X Range** should be **B2:B41**. Select **New Worksheet Ply** and name it **Regression**; you do not need to check the box next to **Line Fit Plots**.

3.1.1 The *t*-Distribution

3.1.1a The t-Distribution versus Normal Distribution

The t-distribution is a bell-shaped curve centered and symmetric around its mean, equal to zero. It looks like the standard normal distribution, except it is more spread out, with a larger variance and thicker tails. The exact shape of the t-distribution is controlled by a single parameter called the degrees of freedom, often abbreviated as *df*. The notation $t_{(m)}$ is used to specify a t-distribution with m degrees of freedom.

Below is a graph of the t-distribution with $m = 3$ degrees of freedom and the standard normal distribution.

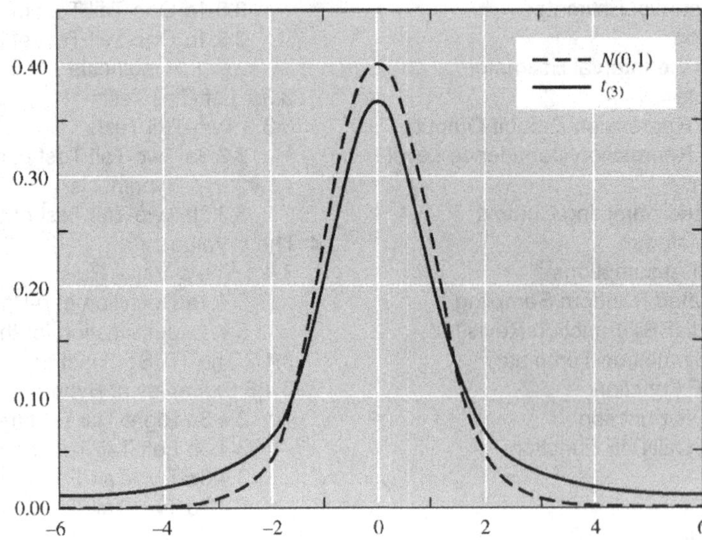

3.1.1b t-Critical Values and Interval Estimates

In order to construct interval estimates, we will need critical values of *t*-distributions with various degrees of freedom. The abbreviation used for a critical value is t_c. The values $-t_c$ and t_c are the endpoints of a closed interval around zero such that the probability of drawing a *t*-value in this interval is $(1 - \alpha)$, and the probability is α that a value is either less than $-t_c$ or greater than t_c. Since the distribution is symmetric, the probability that a *t*-value is less than $-t_c$ is $(\alpha/2)$, and the probability that a *t*-value is greater than t_c is $(\alpha/2)$.

We are usually interested in the critical value t_c such that the probability that a randomly drawn *t*-value is within the closed interval $[-t_c, t_c]$ is 0.95 or 0.99, which means that the probability of a value outside the interval, in the tails of the distribution, is only 0.05 or 0.01.

Let $\alpha = 0.05$. This leads to a closed interval $[-t_c, t_c]$ such that the probability is $(1 - \alpha) = (1 - 0.05) = 0.95$ of randomly drawing a *t*-value in this interval.

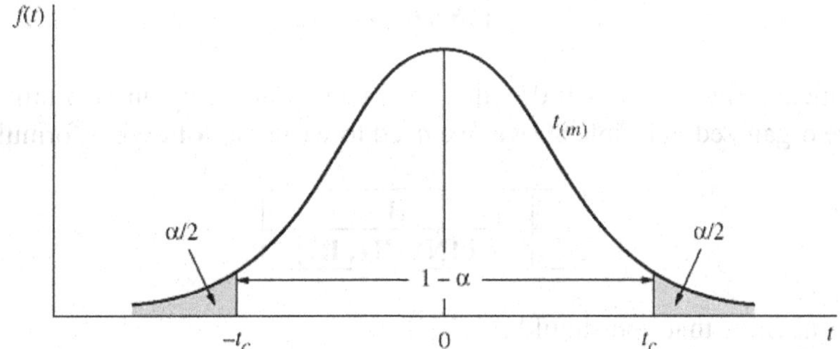

3.1.1c Percentile Values

Since the probability is $(\alpha/2)$ that a *t*-value is greater than t_c, this also means that the probability of drawing a *t*-value less than or equal to t_c is $(1 - \alpha/2)$. The critical value t_c is the $100(1 - \alpha/2)$ percentile of the *t*-distribution, denoted $t_{(1-\alpha/2,m)}$.

3.1.1d TINV Function

We will use the **TINV** function to compute *t*-critical values. First, we create a new worksheet and table where we will store our computations.

Insert a new worksheet by selecting the **Insert Worksheet** tab at the lower left corner of your screen, next to the **Data** tab. Name it **t-critical value**.

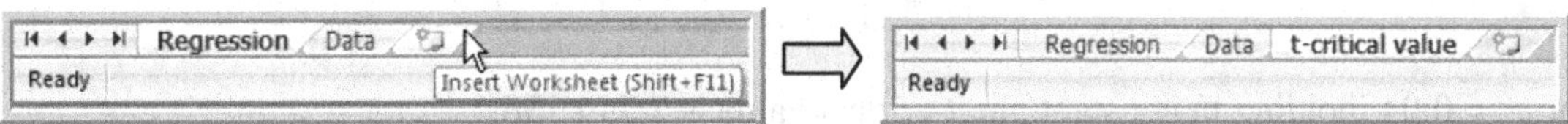

Select cell **A1**. Select the **Insert** tab located next the **Home** tab. In the **Text** group of commands select **Symbol**. In the **Symbol** dialog box, the **Symbols** tab should be open. Select **α** (you might need to use the scroll bar to move up and down the window and find this symbol). Finally, select **Insert**.

Fill in the rest as shown below:

	A	B
1	α =	0.05
2	m =	38
3	t_c =	

t-critical values are obtained in Excel by using the **TINV** function. The syntax of the **TINV** function is as follows:

=TINV(α, m)

To find the t-critical value for $\alpha = 0.05$ (the combined probability in two-tails) and $m = 38$, given the way we organized our table above, we need to write the following formula in **B3**:

	B
3	**=TINV(B1, B2)**

Here is the t-critical value that you should get:

	A	B
3	t_c =	2.024394

Although we could have directly enter the α and m values into the **TINV** function, **=TINV(0.05, 38)**, we chose instead to refer to the cells where we have stored and displayed those values. Displaying the values of the function's arguments makes our worksheet much easier to read and understand. In addition, we can compute a new t-critical value by changing one or both arguments' values.

In cell **B1**, change α from 0.05 to 0.01. Here is how your table should look like:

	A	B
1	α =	0.01
2	m =	38
3	t_c =	2.711558

For $\alpha = 0.01$, holding m constant, the t-critical value is 2.711558.

3.1.1e Appendix E: Table 2 in POE

Alternatively, we could have gotten those *t*-critical values from Table 2 at the end of *Principles of Econometrics, 4e*. Recall that the critical value t_c is also the $100(1-\alpha/2)$th percentile of the *t*-distribution, denoted $t_{(1-\alpha/2,m)}$. For $\alpha = 0.05$ and $m = 38$, the critical value t_c is the $100(1-\alpha/2) = 100(1-0.05/2) = 100(1-0.025) = 97.5$ or 97.5th percentile of the *t*-distribution, denoted $t_{(.975,38)}$. At the intersection of the column labeled "$t_{(.975,df)}$" and the row "38" degrees of freedom (*df*), $t_c = 2.024$.

For $\alpha = 0.01$, holding m constant, the critical value t_c is the $100(1-\alpha/2) = 100(1-0.01/2) = 100(1-0.005) = 99.5$ or 99.5th percentile of the *t*-distribution, $t_{(.995,38)}$. Its value is found at the intersection of the column labeled "$t_{(.955,df)}$" and the row "38" degrees of freedom (*df*): $t_c = 2.712$. Those *t*-critical values are slightly different from the ones we obtained in Excel due to rounding in Table 2.

3.1.2 Obtaining Interval Estimates

The interval estimator of β_k is defined as:

$$b_k \pm t_c se(b_k) \tag{3.1}$$

The interval $b_k \pm t_c se(b_k)$ has probability $(1-\alpha)$ of containing the true but unknown parameter β_k. When using data, we say that we have a $100(1-\alpha)\%$ interval estimate or $100(1-\alpha)\%$ confidence interval.

We are usually interested in constructing either a 95% or a 99% confidence interval, so the corresponding α values that we would use to get our *t*-critical values are $\alpha = 0.05$, and $\alpha = 0.01$.

To obtain the interval estimates, we use equation (3.1) and replace the least squares estimators b_k, the critical *t*-value t_c, and the standard errors of b_k's, $se(b_k)$, by their estimated values. The lower limit (LL) and the upper limit (UL) of the interval will be:

$$LL = b_k - t_c se(b_k) \tag{3.2}$$

$$UL = b_k + t_c se(b_k) \tag{3.3}$$

3.1.3 An Illustration

In this section, we will first illustrate how to obtain an interval estimate by plugging values into the interval estimator's formula. Next, we will go back to the Excel regression analysis tool and look at the output we already have generated, as well as look at the built-in option available to generate additional interval estimates.

3.1.3a Using the Interval Estimator Formula

We create a template to compute the interval estimates for the least squares regression parameters of the food expenditure model.

Insert a new worksheet by selecting the **Insert Worksheet** tab at the lower left corner of your screen, next to the **t-critical value** tab. Name it **Interval Estimate.**

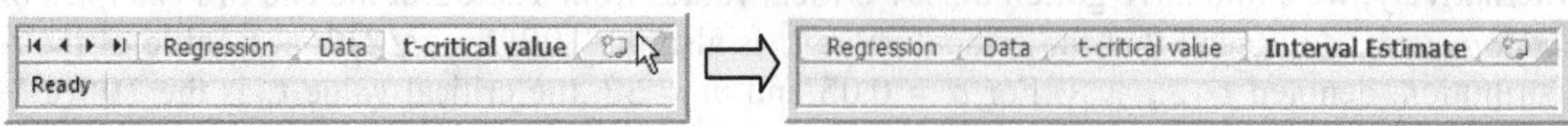

Create the following template to construct interval estimates:

	A	B	C
1	**Data Input**	Sample Size =	=Regression!B8
2		Confidence Level =	
3		Estimated b_k =	=Regression!B18
4		Standard Error of b_k =	=Regression!C18
5			
6	**Computed Values**	α =	=1-C2
7		df or m =	=C1-2
8		t_c =	=TINV(C6,C7)
9			
10	**Interval Estimate**	Lower Limit =	=C3-C8*C4
11		Upper Limit =	=C3+C8*C4

Note that we get the sample size, estimated coefficient and standard error from our **Regression** worksheet. All you have to do in cells **C1** and **C3:C4** is, first, type the equal sign, and then, go select the needed value in the **Regression** worksheet with your cursor. Finally, press **Enter**. We are computing the interval estimate for β_2, the slope parameter. Cell **C2** is left blank for now. Later, you will enter either 95 or 99 depending on whether you are constructing a 95% or a 99% confidence interval, but you could also enter any other confidence level. In cell **C6**, the α level will be computed based on the level of confidence entered in **C2**. In cell **C7**, the degrees of freedom are set equal to $N-2$, where N is the sample size, which we record in cell **C1**. Cell **C8** is where the critical t-value is computed, as shown in Section 3.1.1d. Cells **C10-C11** are where the limits of the interval estimate are computed, using equations (3.2) and (3.3).

Before we specify our level of confidence, we would like to reformat **C2** so that the level of confidence can be displayed as a percentage. In cell **C2**, right-click, and select **Format Cells** on the tasks panel that opens up. In the **Format Cells** dialog box, select **Percentage** in the **Category** window, choose **0** decimal place (use the up and down arrows for that, to the right of the **Decimal places** window). Finally, select **OK**.

Reformat cell **C6** the same way.

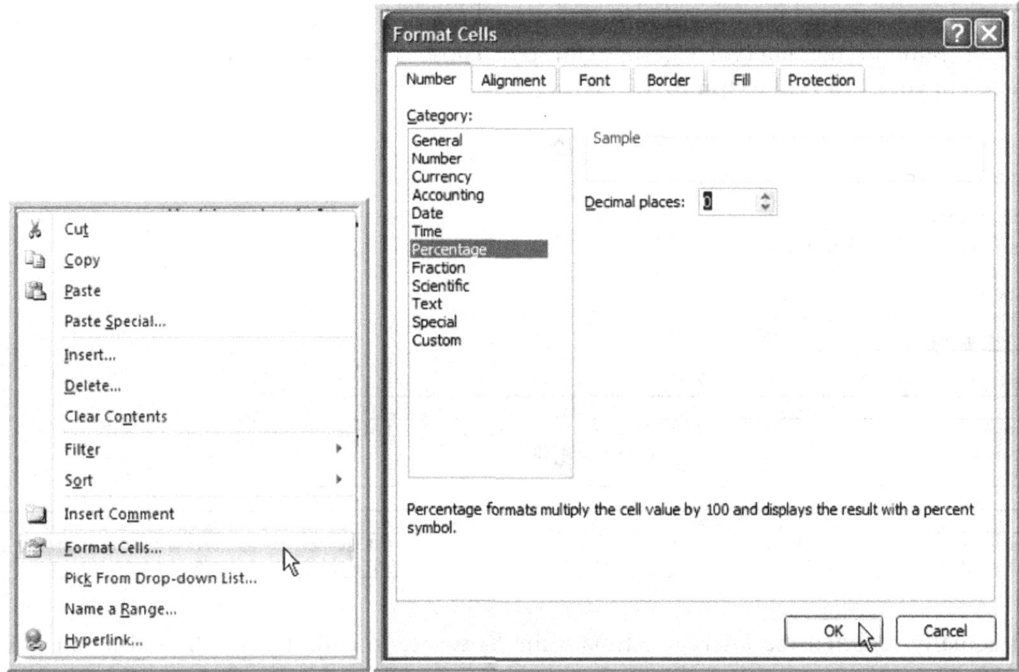

Here are the results you should get for a 95% confidence interval estimate for β_2 (make sure you type 95, and not 0.95, in **C2**):

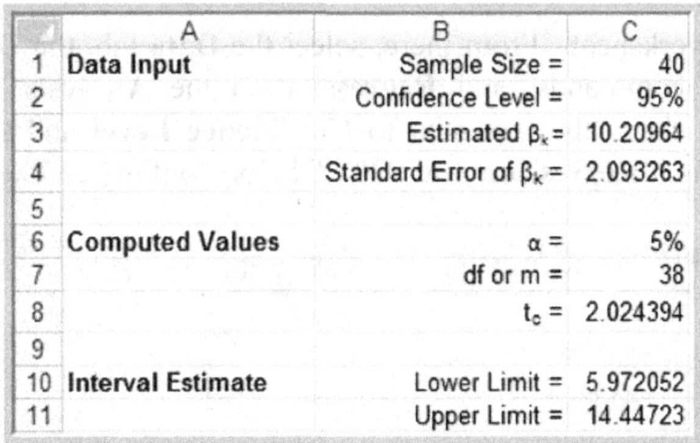

	A	B	C
1	**Data Input**	Sample Size =	40
2		Confidence Level =	95%
3		Estimated β_k =	10.20964
4		Standard Error of β_k =	2.093263
5			
6	**Computed Values**	α =	5%
7		df or m =	38
8		t_c =	2.024394
9			
10	**Interval Estimate**	Lower Limit =	5.972052
11		Upper Limit =	14.44723

The lower limit and upper limit of the interval estimate above should be the same as those reported on p. 98 of *Principles of Econometrics, 4e*.

We plugged values in equation (3.1), and built a template, to obtain interval estimates. Next, we will go to our **Regression** worksheet and look at the interval estimates Excel has already generated in the regression summary output.

3.1.3b Excel Regression Default Output

Go to your **Regression** worksheet, and look at the last table of the summary output. Columns **F** and **G** of that table present the lower limits and upper limits of the interval estimates for the intercept and slope parameters, β_1 and β_2 (shaded cells below). Excel regression analysis routine automatically generates the 95% confidence interval estimates.

In cell **F18**, you can find the lower limit of the interval estimate for β_2. In cell **G18**, you can find the upper limit of the interval estimate for β_2. Those values are identical to the ones you computed in your **Interval Estimate** worksheet.

	A	B	C	D	E	F	G	H	I
1	SUMMARY OUTPUT								
2									
3	*Regression Statistics*								
4	Multiple R	0.620485472							
5	R Square	0.385002221							
6	Adjusted R Square	0.368818069							
7	Standard Error	89.51700429							
8	Observations	40							
9									
10	ANOVA								
11		*df*	*SS*	*MS*	*F*	*Significance F*			
12	Regression	1	190626.9788	190626.9788	23.78884107	1.94586E-05			
13	Residual	38	304505.1742	8013.294058					
14	Total	39	495132.153						
15									
16		*Coefficients*	*Standard Error*	*t Stat*	*P-value*	*Lower 95%*	*Upper 95%*	*Lower 95.0%*	*Upper 95.0%*
17	Intercept	83.41600997	43.41016192	1.921577951	0.062182379	-4.463267721	171.2952877	-4.463267721	171.2952877
18	X Variable 1	10.2096425	2.093263461	4.877380554	1.94586E-05	5.972052202	14.4472328	5.972052202	14.4472328

Excel actually reported the interval estimate for β_2 twice: in cells **F18:G18**, and again in cells **H18:I18**. The table is set so that, if you choose to, Excel will be able to report confidence interval estimates, other than the 95% one.

3.1.3c Excel Regression Confidence Level Option

Go back to your **Data** worksheet. From there, select the **Data** tab, the **Data Analysis** button in the **Analysis** group of commands, and **Regression** in the **Analysis Tools** window. In the **Regression** dialog box, check the box next to **Confidence Level** and type in **99**. Select **New Worksheet Ply** and name it **Regression and 99% CI** (for Confidence Interval). Select **OK**.

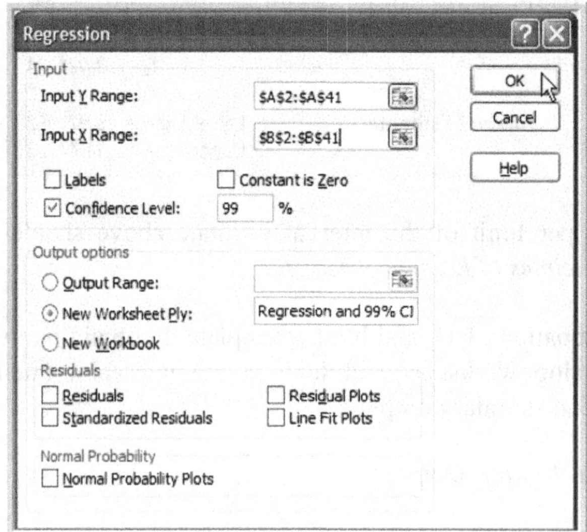

Alongside the 95% interval estimates, Excel now has also generated 99% interval estimates for β_1 and β_2 (cells **H16:I18**, shaded below):

	A	B	C	D	E	F	G	H	I
1	SUMMARY OUTPUT								
2									
3	*Regression Statistics*								
4	Multiple R	0.620485472							
5	R Square	0.385002221							
6	Adjusted R Square	0.368818069							
7	Standard Error	89.51700429							
8	Observations	40							
9									
10	ANOVA								
11		*df*	*SS*	*MS*	*F*	*Significance F*			
12	Regression	1	190626.9788	190626.9788	23.78884107	1.94586E-05			
13	Residual	38	304505.1742	8013.294058					
14	Total	39	495132.153						
15									
16		*Coefficients*	*Standard Error*	*t Stat*	*P-value*	*Lower 95%*	*Upper 95%*	*Lower 99.0%*	*Upper 99.0%*
17	Intercept	83.41600997	43.41016192	1.921577951	0.062182379	-4.463267721	171.2952877	-34.29314438	201.1251643
18	X Variable 1	10.2096425	2.093263461	4.877380554	1.94586E-05	5.972052202	14.4472328	4.533638058	15.88564694

The interpretation of confidence intervals requires a great deal of care. The true meaning of being 95% or 99% confident about our interval estimates is that, if we were to repeat this exercise of drawing a sample size of $N = 40$, estimate the least regression parameters, and construct interval estimates for those regression parameters, *many more times*, then 95% or 99% of all the interval estimates constructed this way would contain the true parameters' values. To illustrate this concept we are going back to our simulation exercise of Section 2.4.4.

3.1.4 The Repeated Sampling Context (Advanced Material)

In Section 2.4.4 we drew *many* random samples of size $N = 40$, and, based on each, estimated the corresponding least squares regression parameters. We can repeat this exercise and extend it to compute, for each sample, not only least squares estimates, but interval estimates as well.

Note that in Section 3.1.4 of *Principles of Econometrics, 4e*, 10 samples were randomly drawn from a population with *unknown* parameters, while in this section we will draw 100 samples from a population with *known* parameters.

3.1.4a Model Assumptions

In the simulation exercise we are considering in this section, half of our hypothetical population of three person households has a weekly income of \$1000 ($x = 10$), and half of it has a weekly income of \$2000 ($x = 20$). Because we know the data generation process, we know the values of population parameters for the normal distribution, and consequently the values of our regression parameters. Let $\mu_{y|x=10} = 200$, $\mu_{y|x=20} = 300$, and $var(y|x = 10) = var(y|x = 20) = \sigma^2 = 2500$. This implies $\beta_1 = 100$ and $\beta_2 = 10$.

3.1.4b Repeated Random Sampling

We will draw random samples of 40 households from our population. Half of each sample will be drawn from the first type of households, with weekly income $x = 10$; and half of each sample will be drawn from the second type of households, with weekly income $x = 20$.

First, insert a new worksheet in your workbook by selecting the **Insert Worksheet** tab at the bottom of your screen, next to the **Interval Estimate** tab. Name it **Simulation**.

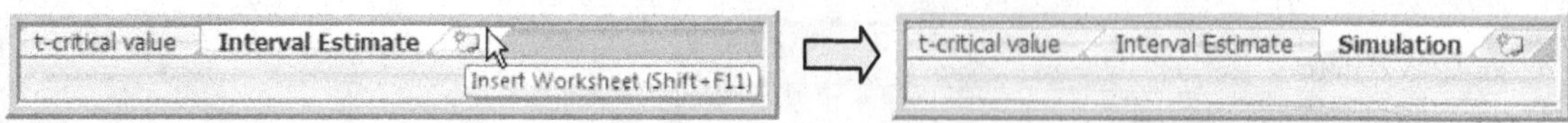

Let us keep records of the level of weekly income for our 40 households in column **A** of our **Simulation** worksheet: in cell **A1**, type **x** and **Right-Align** it; in cells **A2:A21**, record the value **10**; in cells **A22:A41**, record the value **20**.

	A
1	x
2	10
3	10
4	10
5	10
6	10
7	10
8	10
9	10
10	10
11	10
12	10
13	10
14	10
15	10
16	10
17	10
18	10
19	10
20	10
21	10

	A
22	20
23	20
24	20
25	20
26	20
27	20
28	20
29	20
30	20
31	20
32	20
33	20
34	20
35	20
36	20
37	20
38	20
39	20
40	20
41	20
42	

Next, use the **Random Number Generation** analysis tool to draw 100 random samples of households.

Select the **Data** tab, in the middle of your tab list. On the **Analysis** group of commands to the far right of the ribbon, select **Data Analysis**.

The **Data Analysis** dialog box pops up. In it, select **Random Number Generation** (you might need to use the scroll up and down bar to the right of the **Analysis Tools** window to find it), then select **OK**.

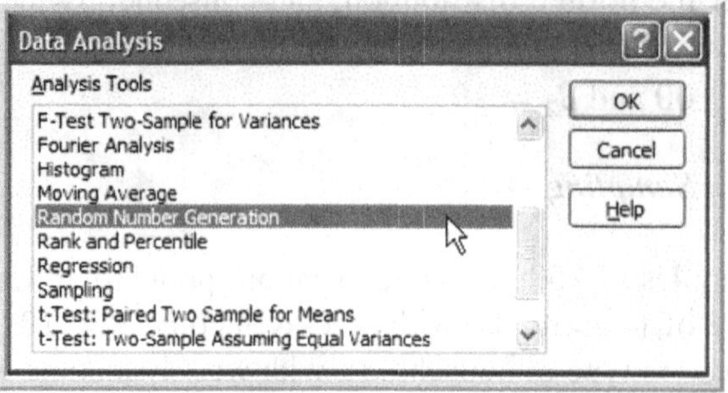

A **Random Number Generation** dialog box pops up. Since we are drawing 100 random samples, we specify **100** in the **Number of Variables** window. We first draw random samples of

20 from households with weekly income of $x = 10$, so we specify the **Number of Random Numbers** to be **20**. For simplicity we assumed that our population of households is normally distributed, so this is the distribution we choose. Once you have selected **Normal** in the **Distribution** window, you will be able to specify its **Parameters**: for $x = 10$, its **Mean** is $\mu_{y|x=10} = \mathbf{200}$ and its **Standard Deviation** is $\sqrt{var(y|x=10)} = \sigma = \mathbf{50}$. Select the **Output Range** in the **Output options** section, and specify it to be **B2:CW21**. Finally, select **OK**.

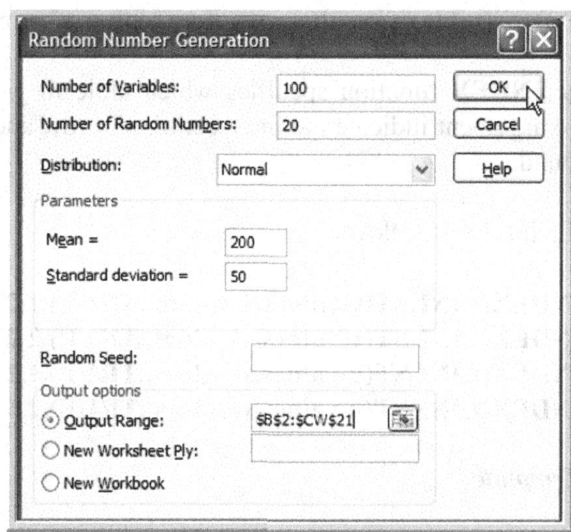

Repeat to draw a random sample of 20 from households with weekly income of $x = 20$. Change the **Mean** to $\mu_{y|x=10} = \mathbf{300}$ and the **Output Range** to **B22:CW41**.

3.1.4c The LINEST Function Revisited

This time we use the **LINEST** function to obtain the least squares estimates *and* their standard errors. The **LINEST** function can compute the latter, if you ask it to return additional regression statistics. For this purpose, the general syntax of the **LINEST** function is as follows:

= LINEST(*y*'s, *x*'s, ,TRUE)

The first argument of **LINEST** function specifies the y values; the second argument specifies the x values; we ignore the third argument by putting a *space* between the second and third commas; and the fourth argument, **TRUE**, indicates that we would like **LINEST** to return additional regression statistics.

The **LINEST** function creates a table where it stores the least squares and standard errors estimates in Excel memory. The following illustration shows the order in which they are reported:

	column 1	column 2
row 1	b_2	b_1
row 2	se(b_2)	se(b_1)

We nest the **LINEST** function in the **INDEX** function to get the estimated coefficients, *one at a time*. The **INDEX** function returns values from within a table. The **INDEX** function general syntax is as follows:

= INDEX(table of results, row_num, column_num)

The first argument of the **INDEX** function specifies which table to get the results from. The second argument and third argument indicate the intersection of a row and a column at which the result of interest can be found.

The nested commands will thus be as follows:

b_1: **=INDEX(LINEST(y-values,x-values,,TRUE),1,2)**
$se(b_1)$: **=INDEX(LINEST(y-values,x-values,,TRUE),2,2)**
b_2: **=INDEX(LINEST(y-values,x-values,,TRUE),1,1)**
$se(b_2)$: **=INDEX(LINEST(y-values,x-values,,TRUE),2,1)**

3.1.4d The Simulation Template

We will report our estimated coefficients and standard errors at the bottom of our table of random samples. We will also compute our *t*-critical value and limits of our interval estimates (Lower Limit: LL and Upper Limit: UL). Finally, we would like to count how many of our 100 interval estimates contain the true parameters' values.

We will specify cells **A42:B57** as shown below (we outlined some cells in different shades of gray only to distinguish groups of similar or related cells which we comment on shortly):

	A	B
42	**N =**	**40**
43	**α =**	**0.05**
44	**m =**	**=B42-2**
45	**t_c =**	**=TINV(B43,B44)**
46	**b_1 =**	**=INDEX(LINEST(B2:B41,$A$2:$A$41,,TRUE),1,2)**
47	**se(b_1) =**	**=INDEX(LINEST(B2:B41,$A$2:$A$41,,TRUE),2,2)**
48	**LL =**	**=B46-$B$45*B47**
49	**UL =**	**=B46+$B$45*B47**
50	**β_1 in CI**	**=IF(OR(100<B48,100>B49),"No", "Yes")**
51	**Yes'**	**=COUNTIF(B50:CW50, "Yes")**
52	**b_2 =**	**=INDEX(LINEST(B2:B41,$A$2:$A$41,,TRUE),1,1)**
53	**se(b_2) =**	**=INDEX(LINEST(B2:B41,$A$2:$A$41,,TRUE),2,1)**
54	**LL =**	**=B52-$B$45*B53**
55	**UL =**	**=B52+$B$45*B53**
56	**β_2 in CI**	**=IF(OR(10<B54,10>B55),"No", "Yes")**
57	**Yes'**	**=COUNTIF(B56:CW56, "Yes")**

In cells **A42:B43**, the N (sample size) and α values are specified so that m (degrees of freedom) and t_c (*t*-critical value) can be computed and reported in cell **A44:B45**. t_c is computed as shown in Section 3.1.1d.

Cells **A46:B47** and **A52:B53** are used to report and compute coefficient and standard error estimates, as explained in Section 3.1.4c. The **cell references** to the x values are in **Absolute** format, **$A$2:$A$41**, as opposed to **Relative** format, as we will be using the same x values for all 100 repetitions.

Cells **A48:B49** and **A54:B55** are used to report and compute interval estimates, as explained in Section 3.1.2. The value for t_c will be the same over all repetitions; its cell reference is thus in **Absolute** format, **$B$45,** in the formulas of the intervals limits.

3.1.4e The IF Function

We make use of the **IF** and **OR** logical functions to indicate, for each interval estimate, whether or not it contains the true parameter value. The general syntax for the **IF** function is as follows:

IF(logical_test,value_if_true,value_if_false)

Logical_test is any value or expression that can be evaluated to be TRUE or FALSE. In this exercise we want to determine whether or not the true parameter value, β_k, is within the estimated interval $[LL, UL]$, where $LL = b_k - t_c se(b_k)$ and $UL = b_k + t_c se(b_k)$. The logical expression we use is: if $\beta_k < LL$ or $\beta_k > UL$. If β_k is outside $[LL, UL]$, then this expression is TRUE. Otherwise, the expression is FALSE.

Value_if_true is the value that is returned if **logical_test** is TRUE. For example, if this argument is the text string "No" and the **logical_test** argument is TRUE, then the **IF** function displays the text "No".

Value_if_false is the value that is returned if **logical_test** is FALSE. For example, if this argument is the text string "Yes," and the **logical_test** argument is FALSE, then the **IF** function displays the text "Yes".

3.1.4f The OR Function

We use the **OR** function to write our **logical test**. The general syntax of the **OR** function is as follows:

OR(argument_1,argument_2)

If the first logical expression, **argument_1**, *or* the second logical expression, **argument_2**, is TRUE, then the **OR** function returns TRUE. It returns FALSE only if both arguments are FALSE.

The general syntax for the **OR** function, nested in the **IF** function, is:

IF(OR(argument_1,argument_2),value_if_true,value_if_false)

Applied to our exercise, the nested function looks like this (which is what we have in cell **B56**):

IF(OR(β$_k$ < LL, β$_k$ > UL),"No","Yes")

If β_k is outside $[LL, UL]$, then the **logical test** $\beta_k < LL$ or $\beta_k > UL$ is TRUE, and "No" is returned to indicate that β_k is not in the estimated confidence interval. Otherwise, the logical expression is FALSE, and "Yes" is returned to indicate that β_k is in the estimated confidence interval.

3.1.4g The COUNTIF Function

Finally, we use the **COUNTIF** function to count the number of times β_k is found within the estimated interval $[LL, UL]$.

The **COUNTIF** function is a statistical function that counts the number of cells within a range that meet a given criteria. Its general syntax is:

COUNTIF(cell_range,criteria)

Cell_Range is one or more cells to count. **Criteria** is the number, expression, cell reference, or text that defines which cells will be counted. Since we are interested in counting how many interval estimates, among all the ones we will construct, actually contain the true parameter value, we will count the "Yes" that are generated following the application of our **logical test** (this is what we do in cell **B57**):

COUNTIF(cell_range,"Yes")

Once you have reviewed and understood the formulas and values from **B42:B57**, you can copy the content of **B46:B50** to **C46:CW50** and copy the content of **B52:B56** to **C52:CW56**.

Here is how our worksheet looks like (only 10 out of 100 simulations results are shown below):

	A	B	C	D	E	F	G	H	I	J	K
42	**N =**	**40**									
43	**α =**	**0.05**									
44	**m =**	**38**									
45	**t_c =**	**2.024394**									
46	b_1=	63.62645	128.1579	46.82636	110.9713	135.5643	85.48465	93.69496	89.25077	117.0464	119.4847
47	se(b_1)=	28.53373	22.14145	24.00909	23.81712	27.41891	26.52329	19.24102	19.19294	27.79757	22.4184
48	LL=	5.862943	83.33492	-1.77749	62.75603	80.0576	31.79105	54.74354	50.39669	60.77321	74.10106
49	UL=	121.39	172.981	95.43022	159.1865	191.071	139.1782	132.6464	128.1049	173.3197	164.8684
50	β_1 in CI	Yes	Yes	No	Yes	Yes	Yes	Yes	Yes	Yes	Yes
51	**Yes'**	**98**									
52	b_2=	12.32048	7.215456	13.31895	9.297985	8.060182	11.07061	10.90295	10.74238	9.009011	8.548776
53	se(b_2)=	1.804631	1.400348	1.518468	1.506327	1.734124	1.67748	1.216909	1.213868	1.758073	1.417864
54	LL=	8.667196	4.380599	10.24497	6.248586	4.549631	7.674729	8.439441	8.285028	5.44998	5.678459
55	UL=	15.97377	10.05031	16.39293	12.34738	11.57073	14.46649	13.36645	13.19972	12.56804	11.41909
56	β_2 in CI	Yes	Yes	No	Yes	Yes	Yes	Yes	Yes	Yes	Yes
57	**Yes'**	**98**									

We find that 98 out of our 100 confidence intervals contain the true parameter value, both for our intercept and slope coefficient confidence intervals. Note that you will draw different random samples, obtain different interval estimates and thus obtain a different number of intervals that will contain the true parameters values.

We first extended our repetitions to 1,000 samples, and found that 959 out of 1,000 interval estimates contained β_1, and 962 out of 1,000 interval estimates contained β_2. Finally, we extended the repetitions to 10,000 samples and found that 95.08% of both the intercept and slope coefficients interval estimates contained the true parameters values.

In the next section of this chapter, we will perform hypothesis tests. To go over examples of hypothesis tests, we are getting back to our simple linear regression model of weekly food expenditure.

3.2 HYPOTHESIS TESTS

If the null hypothesis $H_0\colon \beta_k = c$ is true, then the test statistic $t = (b_k - c)/se(b_k)$ follows a t-distribution with $m = N - 2$ degrees of freedom:

$$t = \frac{b_k - c}{se(b_k)} \sim t_{(m = N-2)} \tag{3.4}$$

When we reject H_0, we accept a logical alternative hypothesis H_1. There are three possible alternative hypotheses to H_0:

$$H_1\colon \beta_k > c \tag{3.5}$$

$$H_1\colon \beta_k < c \tag{3.6}$$

$$H_1\colon \beta_k \neq c \tag{3.7}$$

3.2.1 One-Tail Tests with Alternative "Greater Than" (>)

If the alternative hypothesis (3.5) is true, then the value of the computed test statistic will tend to be unusually large. We will reject H_0 if the test statistic is in the *right-tail* of the distribution.

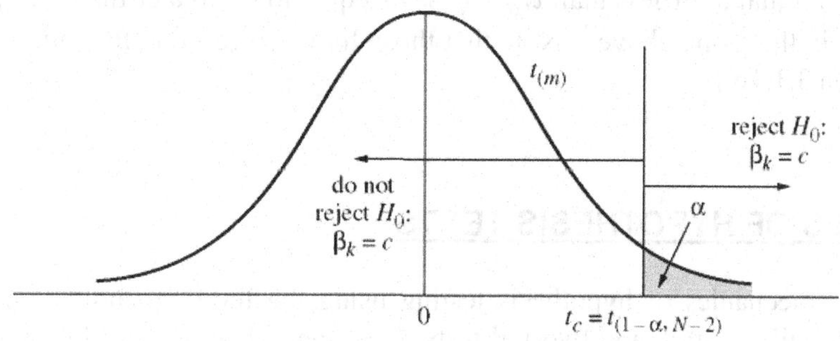

Note that in this case the probability is α that a randomly drawn t-value is equal to or greater than t_c, where t_c is defined as the lower limit of the right-tail of the distribution shown in the graph above.

3.2.2 One-Tail Tests with Alternative "Less Than" (<)

If the alternative hypothesis (3.6) is true, then the value of the computed test statistic will tend to be unusually small. We will reject H_0 if the test statistic is in the *left-tail* of the distribution.

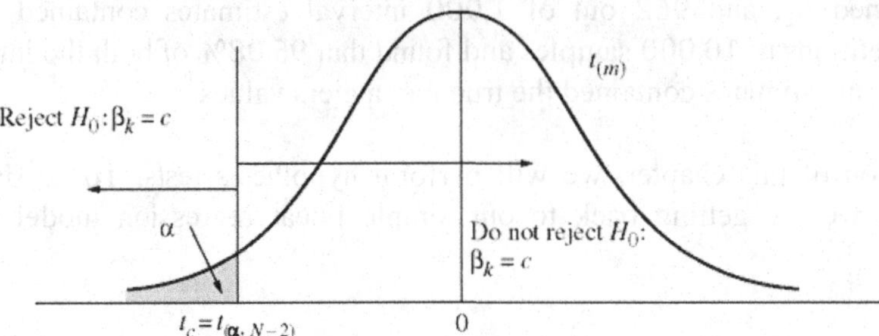

Note that in this case the probability is α that a randomly drawn t-value is equal to or less than t_c, where t_c is defined as the upper limit of the left-tail of the distribution shown in the graph above.

3.2.3 Two-Tail Tests with Alternative "Not Equal To" (≠)

If the alternative hypothesis (3.7) is true, then the value of the computed test statistic will tend to be unusually small *or* large. We will reject H_0 if the test statistic is either in the *left-tail or* the *right-tail* of the distribution.

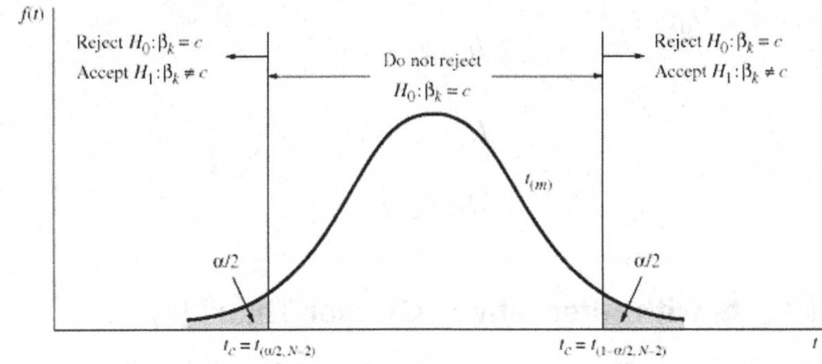

Note that in this case the probability is α that a randomly drawn t-value will fall in the tails of the distribution, either equal to or less than $t_{(\alpha/2,N-2)}$ *or* equal to or greater than $t_{(1-\alpha/2,N-2)}$. Those limits are shown in the graph above. (Note that those limits correspond to values $-t_c$ and t_c first defined in Section 3.1.1b.)

3.3 EXAMPLES OF HYPOTHESIS TESTS

We illustrate the mechanics of hypothesis testing using the food expenditure model. We give examples of right-tail, left-tail, and two-tail tests. Note that when the null hypothesis of a test is that the parameter is zero, the test is called a test of significance. We can have one-tail tests of significance or two-tail tests of significance.

Recall our estimated regression model; below the estimated values for b_1 and b_2, we report their estimated standard errors, $se(b_1)$ and $se(b_2)$:

$$\begin{array}{l} \hat{y}_i = 83.42 + 10.21x_i \\ (se)\ (43.41)\ \ (2.09) \end{array} \tag{3.8}$$

3.3.1 Right-Tail Tests

We create a template for right-tail tests.

Insert a new worksheet by selecting the **Insert Worksheet** tab at the bottom of your screen, next to the **Simulation** tab. Name it **Right-Tail Tests**.

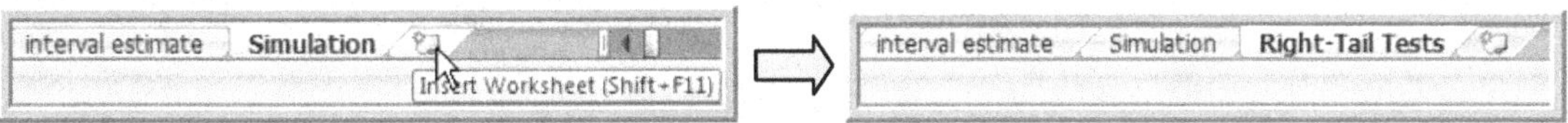

Create the following template to perform right-tail tests:

	A	B	C
1	**Data Input**	N =	=Regression!B8
2		b_k =	=Regression!B18
3		se(b_k) =	=Regression!C18
4		H_0: β_k =	
5		α =	
6			
7	**Computed Values**	df or m =	=C1-2
8		t_c =	=TINV(C5*2,C7)
9			
10	**Right-Tail Test**	t-statistic =	=(C2-C4)/C3
11		Conclusion:	=IF(C10>=C8,"Reject Ho","Do Not Reject Ho")

We get the sample size N, estimated coefficient b_2 and standard error $se(b_2)$ from our **Regression** worksheet. All you have to do in each of cells **C1:C3** is, first, type the equal sign, and then, select the needed value in the **Regression** worksheet with your cursor. Next, press **Enter**. We are performing hypothesis tests on the slope parameter, β_2. Cells **C4:C5** are left blank for now. Later, you will specify the value you hypothesize β_2 takes, as well as the level of significance of your test (α). In cell **C7**, the degrees of freedom are set equal to $N - 2$, where N is the sample size, which we record in cell **C1**.

Cell **C8** is where the critical-value for the right-tail rejection region is computed. Recall that all the probability α of rejecting H_0 is in the right tail of the distribution greater than or equal to t_c. The **TINV** function, on the other hand, gives us a t_c value such that $P(t_m > t_c) = \alpha/2$. So, what we need to do, to get the correct critical-value for the right-tail rejection region, is to multiply the specified α value by 2 in the **TINV** function (*half* of $\alpha \times 2$ is α, which is what we want).

Cell **C10** is where the test-statistic t is computed. The test statistic is computed by plugging the least squares estimate and its standard error into the equation for t in (3.4).

Finally, in cell **C11**, we use the **IF** function to determine whether or not our *t*-statistic falls into the rejection region. If it does, we reject our null hypothesis; if it does not, we do not reject it (see Section 3.1.4e for details on how the **IF** logical function works).

3.3.1a One-Tail Test of Significance

Let $\alpha = 0.05$; $H_0: \beta_2 = 0$ and $H_1: \beta_2 > 0$.

	A	B	C
1	**Data Input**	N =	40
2		b_k =	10.20964
3		se(b_k) =	2.093263
4		H_0: β_K =	0
5		α =	0.05
6			
7	**Computed Values**	df or m =	38
8		t_c =	1.685954
9			
10	**Right-Tail Test**	t-statistic =	4.877381
11		Conclusion:	Reject Ho

3.3.1b One-Tail Test of an Economic Hypothesis

Let $\alpha = 0.01$; $H_0: \beta_2 \leq 5.5$ and $H_1: \beta_2 > 5.5$.

Note that the hypothesis testing procedure for testing the null hypothesis that $H_0: \beta_2 \leq 5.5$ against the alternative hypothesis $H_1: \beta_2 > 5.5$ is *exactly the same* as testing $H_1: \beta_2 = 5.5$ against the alternative hypothesis $H_1: \beta_2 > 5.5$.

	A	B	C	D
1	**Data Input**	N =	40	
2		b_k =	10.20964	
3		se(b_k) =	2.093263	
4		H_0: β_K =	5.5	
5		α =	0.01	
6				
7	**Computed Values**	df or m =	38	
8		t_c =	2.428568	
9				
10	**Right-Tail Test**	t-statistic =	2.249904	
11		Conclusion:	Do Not Reject Ho	

3.3.2 Left-Tail Tests

We create a template for left-tail tests.

Insert a new worksheet by selecting the **Insert Worksheet** tab at the bottom of your screen, next to the **Right-Tail Tests** tab. Name it **Left-Tail Tests**.

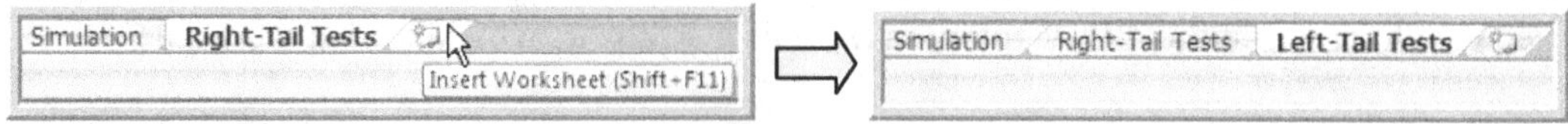

The left-tail test template will be very similar to the right-tail test template. You can copy cell **A1:C11** from the **Right-Tail Tests** worksheet to cells **A1:C11** in the **Left-Tail Tests** worksheet.

Alternatively, you can select the whole **Right-Tail Tests** worksheet by left clicking on the upper left-corner of the worksheet. Your cursor should turn into a fat cross as shown below:

Select **Copy**. Left-click in cell **A1** of the **Left-Tail Tests** worksheet, and select **Paste**.

You will need to make just a few modifications to create the following left-tail test template:

	A	B	C
1	**Data Input**	N =	=Regression!B8
2		b_k =	=Regression!B18
3		se(b_k) =	=Regression!C18
4		H_0: β_k =	
5		α =	
6			
7	**Computed Values**	df or m =	=C1-2
8		t_c =	= -TINV(C5***2**,C7)
9			
10	**Left-Tail Test**	t-statistic =	=(C2-C4)/C3
11		Conclusion:	=IF(C10<=C8,"Reject Ho","Do Not Reject Ho")

The rejection region for a left-tail test is the mirror image of the rejection region for a right-tail test; it is on the left-tail instead of the right-tail of the distribution. The critical value for a left-tail test is thus the negative of the critical value for a right-tail test: in cell **C8**, we precede the **TINV** function by a minus sign to reflect that.

In a left-tail test, we reject our null hypothesis if our *t*-statistic is less than or equal to our critical value, *not* greater than or equal to our critical value as it is the case in a right-tail test; we adjust the equation in **C11** accordingly.

Finally change the label in cell **A10** to "Left Tail Test".

Let $\alpha = 0.05$; $H_0\colon \beta_2 \geq 15$ and $H_1\colon \beta_2 < 15$.

Note that the hypothesis testing procedure for testing the null hypothesis that $H_0\colon \beta_2 \geq 15$ against the alternative hypothesis $H_1\colon \beta_2 < 15$ is *exactly the same* as testing $H_1\colon \beta_2 = 15$ against the alternative hypothesis $H_1\colon \beta_2 < 15$.

	A	B	C
1	**Data Input**	N =	40
2		b_k =	10.20964
3		se(b_k) =	2.093263
4		H_0: β_k =	15
5		α =	0.05
6			
7	**Computed Values**	df or m =	38
8		t_c =	-1.685954
9			
10	**Left-Tail Test**	t-statistic =	-2.288464
11		Conclusion:	Reject Ho

3.3.3 Two-Tail Tests

We create a template for two-tail tests.

Insert a new worksheet by selecting the **Insert Worksheet** tab at the bottom of your screen, next to the **Left-Tail Tests** tab. Name it **Two-Tail Tests.**

The two-tail test template will also be very similar to the right-tail test template. You can copy cell **A1:C11** from the **Right-Tail Tests** worksheet to cells **A1:C11** in the **Two-Tail Tests** worksheet. Alternatively, you can select the whole **Right-Tail Tests** worksheet and copy it in the **Two-Tail Tests** worksheet.

You will need to make just a few modifications to create the following two-tail test template:

	A	B	C
1	**Data Input**	N =	=Regression!B8
2		b_k =	=Regression!B18
3		se(b_k) =	=Regression!C18
4		H_0: β_k =	
5		α =	
6			
7	**Computed Values**	df or m =	=C1-2
8		t_c =	=TINV(C5,C7)
9			
10	**Two-Tail Test**	t-statistic =	=(C2-C4)/C3
11		Conclusion:	=IF(OR(C10<=-C8,C10>=C8), "Reject Ho","Do Not Reject Ho")

The rejection region for a two-tail test is split in half between the left-tail and the right-tail of the distribution: only $\alpha/2$ of the probability is in each tail of the distribution. So, we do not need to multiply α by 2 in the **TINV** function any more: delete ***2** in cell **C8**.

In a two-tail test, we reject our null hypothesis if our t-statistic is less than or equal to the left-tail critical value, *or* greater than or equal to right-tail critical value: we adjust the equation in **C11** to reflect that (see Section 3.1.4f for details on how the **OR** logical function works).

Finally we change the label in cell **A10** to "Two-Tail Test".

3.3.3a Two-Tail Test of an Economic Hypothesis

Let $\alpha = 0.05$; $H_0\colon \beta_2 = 7.5$ and $H_1\colon \beta_2 \neq 7.5$.

	A	B	C	D
1	**Data Input**	N =	40	
2		b_k =	10.20964	
3		se(b_k) =	2.093263	
4		H_0: β_K =	7.5	
5		α =	0.05	
6				
7	**Computed Values**	df or m =	38	
8		t_c =	2.024394	
9				
10	**Two-Tail Test**	t-statistic =	1.294458	
11		Conclusion:	Do Not Reject Ho	

3.3.3b Two-Tail Test of Significance

Let $\alpha = 0.05$; $H_0\colon \beta_2 = 0$ and $H_1\colon \beta_2 \neq 0$.

	A	B	C
1	**Data Input**	N =	40
2		b_k =	10.20964
3		se(b_k) =	2.093263
4		H_0: β_K =	0
5		α =	0.05
6			
7	**Computed Values**	df or m =	38
8		t_c =	2.024394
9			
10	**Two-Tail Test**	t-statistic =	4.877381
11		Conclusion:	Reject Ho

Note that the t-statistic in a two-tail test of significance is equal to the t-statistic in one-tail test of significance (compare the t-statistic value above to the one obtained in Section 3.3.1a). Also note that this t-statistic value for tests of significance is reported in the regression summary output generated by Excel.

Go back to your **Regression** worksheet. If you do not see your **Regression** tab, it is because it is hidden. Use either one of the left-arrows at the left corner of your screen so that the first worksheets you were working with can be seen again.

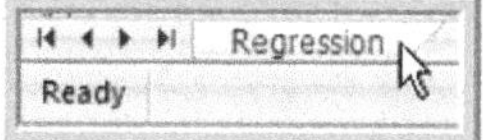

Column **D** of the last table of the summary output presents the *t*-statistic values for tests of significance of the intercept and slope parameters, β_1 and β_2 (shaded cells below).

	A	B	C	D	E	F	G	H	I
1	SUMMARY OUTPUT								
2									
3	*Regression Statistics*								
4	Multiple R	0.620485472							
5	R Square	0.385002221							
6	Adjusted R Square	0.368818069							
7	Standard Error	89.51700429							
8	Observations	40							
9									
10	ANOVA								
11		*df*	*SS*	*MS*	*F*	*Significance F*			
12	Regression	1	190626.9788	190626.9788	23.78884107	1.94586E-05			
13	Residual	38	304505.1742	8013.294058					
14	Total	39	495132.153						
15									
16		*Coefficients*	*Standard Error*	*t Stat*	*P-value*	*Lower 95%*	*Upper 95%*	*Lower 95.0%*	*Upper 95.0%*
17	Intercept	83.41600997	43.41016192	1.921577951	0.062182379	-4.463267721	171.2952877	-4.463267721	171.2952877
18	X Variable 1	10.2096425	2.093263461	4.877380554	1.94586E-05	5.972052202	14.4472328	5.972052202	14.4472328

3.4 THE *p*-VALUE

When reporting the outcome of statistical hypothesis tests, it has become standard practice to report the *p*-value (an abbreviation for probability value) of the test. If we have the *p*-value of a test, we can determine the outcome of the test by comparing p to the chosen level of significance, α. This is an alternative to comparing the test-statistic value to the critical value(s) or limit(s) of the rejection region for a test.

3.4.1 The *p*-Value Rule

In order to explain the *p*-value decision rule for hypothesis tests, we first give a definition of the *p*-value.

3.4.1a Definition of p-Value

How the *p*-value is computed depends on the alternative hypothesis of our test. If $\boldsymbol{H_1}: \boldsymbol{\beta_k} > c$, $\boldsymbol{p}$ is the probability that a *t*-value be equal to or greater than the test statistic $\boldsymbol{t}$ value.

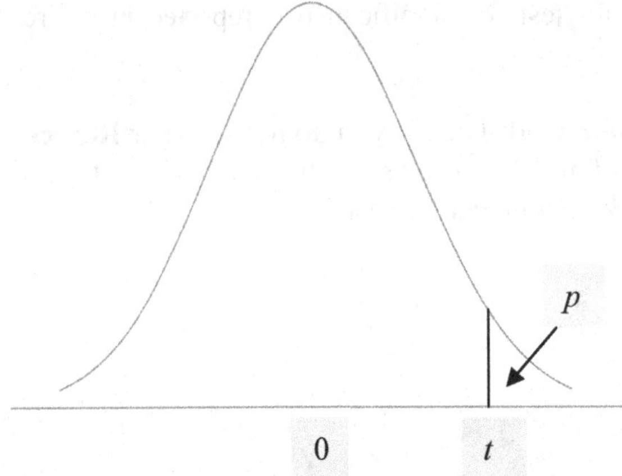

If $H_1: \beta_k < c$, p is the probability that a t-value be equal to or less than the test statistic t value.

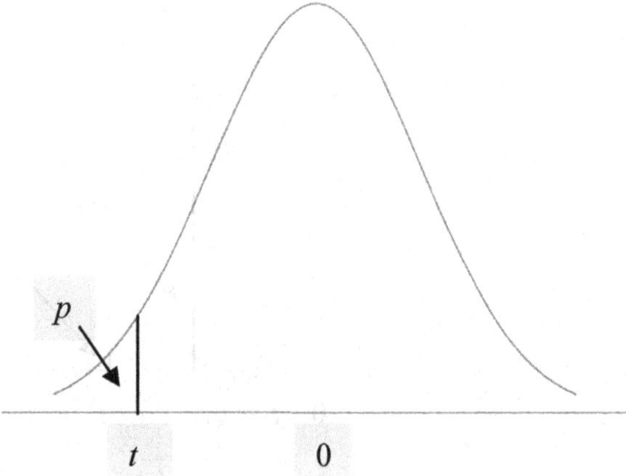

If $H_1: \beta_k \neq c$, p is the probability that a t-value be equal to or less than $-|t|$ *or* equal to or greater than $|t|$, where t is test statistic value.

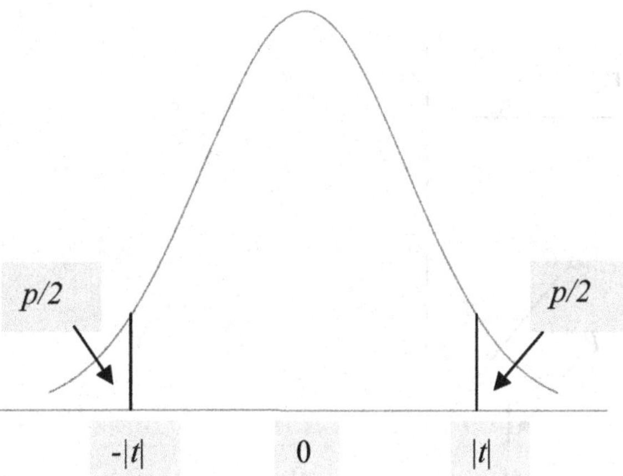

3.4.1b Justification for the p-Value Rule

We can see that when the test statistic value t falls into the rejection region, this means that its p-value is less than, or equal to, the level of significance α.

For $H_1: \beta_k > c$; if $t \geq t_c$, t is in the rejection region and $p \leq \alpha$. The case illustrated below is where $t > t_c$, and $p < \alpha$. H_0 is rejected.

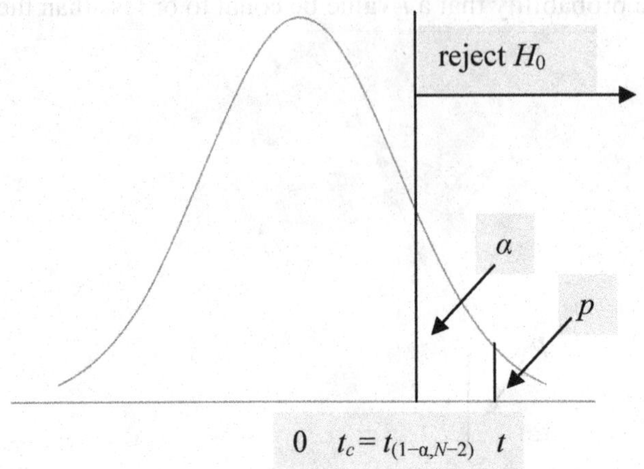

For $H_1\colon \beta_k < c$; if $t \le t_c$, t is in the rejection region and $p \le \alpha$. The case illustrated below is where $t < t_c$, and $p < \alpha$. H_0 is rejected.

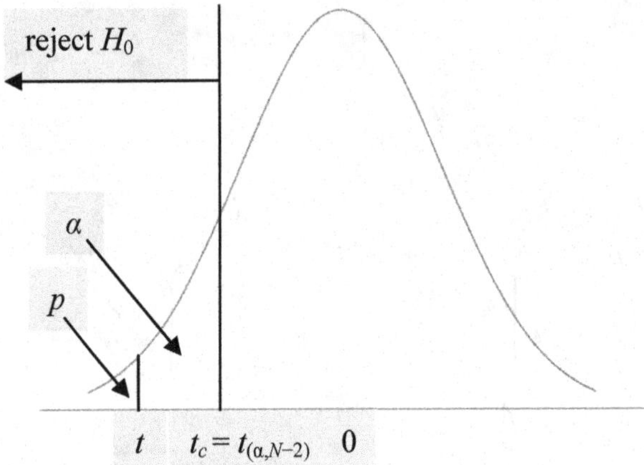

For $H_1\colon \beta_k \ne c$; if $t \le t_c$ on the left-tail of the distribution or $t \ge t_c$ on the right-tail of the distribution, t is in the rejection region and $p \le \alpha$.

The case illustrated below is where $t > t_c$ on the right-tail of the distribution, and $p < \alpha$. H_0 is rejected.

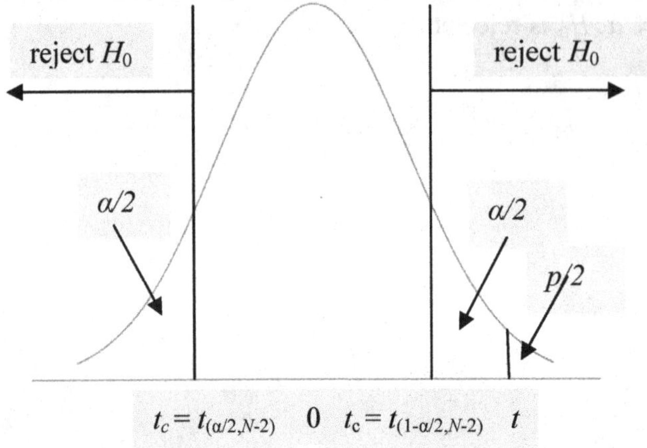

The case illustrated below is where $t < t_c$ on the left-tail of the distribution, and $p < \alpha$. H_0 is rejected.

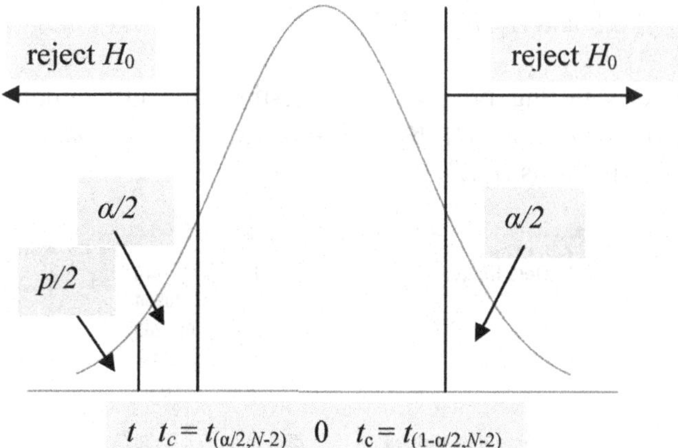

We can thus compare the *p*-value of a test, p, to the chosen level of significance, α, and determine the outcome of our hypothesis test: if $p \leq \alpha$, we reject H_0 and accept H_1; if $p > \alpha$, we do not reject H_0. This is the *p*-value rule.

3.4.2 The TDIST Function

p-values are obtained in Excel by using the **TDIST** function. For hypothesis tests purposes, the syntax of the **TDIST** function is as follows:

=TDIST(ABS(t),m,tails)

t is the value of the computed test statistic, **ABS** is a mathematical function that will return the absolute value of t, ***m*** is the degrees of freedom, and **tails** specifies whether we are seeking the *p*-value for a one-tail test or a two-tail test. Set **tails** to **1** for a one-tail test, and set **tails** to **2** for a two-tail test.

Go back to your **Right-Tail Tests** and **Left-Tail Tests** worksheets and add the following at the bottom of each template:

	A	B	C
12		p-value =	=TDIST(ABS(C10),C7,**1**)
13		Conclusion:	=IF(C12<=C5,"Reject Ho","Do Not Reject Ho")

Go back to your **Two-Tail Tests** worksheet and add the following at the bottom its template:

	A	B	C
12		p-value =	=TDIST(ABS(C10),C7,**2**)
13		Conclusion:	=IF(C12<=C5,"Reject Ho","Do Not Reject Ho")

3.4.3 Examples of Hypothesis Tests Revisited

3.4.3a Right-Tail Test of an Economic Hypothesis from Section 3.3.1b

Let $\alpha = 0.01$; $H_0: \beta_2 \leq 5.5$ and $H_1: \beta_2 > 5.5$.

Note that the hypothesis testing procedure for testing the null hypothesis that $H_0: \beta_2 \leq 5.5$ against the alternative hypothesis $H_1: \beta_2 > 5.5$ is *exactly the same* as testing $H_0: \beta_2 = 5.5$ against the alternative hypothesis $H_1: \beta_2 > 5.5$.

	A	B	C	D
1	**Data Input**	N =	40	
2		b_k =	10.20964	
3		se(b_k) =	2.093263	
4		H_0: β_k =	5.5	
5		α =	0.01	
6				
7	**Computed Values**	df or m =	38	
8		t_c =	2.428568	
9				
10	**Right-Tail Test**	t-statistic =	2.249904	
11		Conclusion:	Do Not Reject Ho	
12		p-value =	0.015163	
13		Conclusion:	Do Not Reject Ho	

Let $\alpha = 0.05$.

	A	B	C
1	**Data Input**	N =	40
2		b_k =	10.20964
3		se(b_k) =	2.093263
4		H_0: β_k =	5.5
5		α =	0.05
6			
7	**Computed Values**	df or m =	38
8		t_c =	1.685954
9			
10	**Right-Tail Test**	t-statistic =	2.249904
11		Conclusion:	Reject Ho
12		p-value =	0.015163
13		Conclusion:	Reject Ho

3.4.3b Left-Tail Test of an Economic Hypothesis from Section 3.3.2

Let $\alpha = 0.01$; $H_0: \beta_2 \geq 15$ and $H_1: \beta_2 < 15$.

Note that the hypothesis testing procedure for testing the null hypothesis that $H_0: \beta_2 \geq 15$ against the alternative hypothesis $H_1: \beta_2 < 15$ is *exactly the same* as testing $H_0: \beta_2 = 15$ against the alternative hypothesis $H_1: \beta_2 < 15$.

	A	B	C	D
1	**Data Input**	N =	40	
2		b_k =	10.20964	
3		se(b_k) =	2.093263	
4		H_0: β_k =	15	
5		α =	0.01	
6				
7	**Computed Values**	df or m =	38	
8		t_c =	-2.428568	
9				
10	**Left-Tail Test**	t-statistic =	-2.288464	
11		Conclusion:	Do Not Reject Ho	
12		p-value =	0.013881	
13		Conclusion:	Do Not Reject Ho	

Let $\alpha = 0.05$.

	A	B	C
1	**Data Input**	N =	40
2		b_k =	10.20964
3		se(b_k) =	2.093263
4		H_0: β_k =	15
5		α =	0.05
6			
7	**Computed Values**	df or m =	38
8		t_c =	-1.685954
9			
10	**Left-Tail Test**	t-statistic =	-2.288464
11		Conclusion:	Reject Ho
12		p-value =	0.013881
13		Conclusion:	Reject Ho

3.4.3c Two-Tail Test of an Economic Hypothesis from Section 3.3.3a

Let $\alpha = 0.05$; $H_0\colon \beta_2 = 7.5$ and $H_1\colon \beta_2 \neq 7.5$.

	A	B	C	D
1	**Data Input**	N =	40	
2		b_k =	10.20964	
3		se(b_k) =	2.093263	
4		H_0: β_k =	7.5	
5		α =	0.05	
6				
7	**Computed Values**	df or m =	38	
8		t_c =	2.024394	
9				
10	**Two-Tail Test**	t-statistic =	1.294458	
11		Conclusion:	Do Not Reject Ho	
12		p-value =	0.203318	
13		Conclusion:	Do Not Reject Ho	

3.4.3d Two-Tail Test of Significance from Section 3.3.3b

Let $\alpha = 0.05$; $H_0\colon \beta_2 = 0$ and $H_1\colon \beta_2 \neq 0$.

	A	B	C
1	**Data Input**	N =	40
2		b_k =	10.20964
3		se(b_k) =	2.093263
4		H_0: β_K =	0
5		α =	0.05
6			
7	**Computed Values**	df or m =	38
8		t_c =	2.024394
9			
10	**Two-Tail Test**	t-statistic =	4.877381
11		Conclusion:	Reject Ho
12		p-value =	1.95E-05
13		Conclusion:	Reject Ho

Note that the *p*-value for this test is very tiny. "1.95E-05" is a standard scientific notation which means "1.95 times 10 exponent −5":

$$\text{"1.95E-05"} \equiv 1.95 \times 10^{-5} = \frac{1.95}{10^5} = \frac{1.95}{100{,}000} = 0.0000195$$

Also note that this *p*-value for the two-tail test of significance is reported in the regression summary output generated by Excel.

Go back to your **Regression** worksheet. If you do not see your **Regression** tab, it is because it is hidden. Use either one of the left-arrows at the left corner of your screen so that the first worksheets you were working with can be seen again.

Column **E** of the last table of the summary output presents the *p*-statistic values for the two-tail test of significance for the intercept and slope parameters, β_1 and β_2 (shaded cells below).

	A	B	C	D	E	F	G	H	I
1	SUMMARY OUTPUT								
2									
3	*Regression Statistics*								
4	Multiple R	0.620485472							
5	R Square	0.385002221							
6	Adjusted R Square	0.368818069							
7	Standard Error	89.51700429							
8	Observations	40							
9									
10	ANOVA								
11		*df*	*SS*	*MS*	*F*	*Significance F*			
12	Regression	1	190626.9788	190626.9788	23.78884107	1.94586E-05			
13	Residual	38	304505.1742	8013.294058					
14	Total	39	495132.153						
15									
16		*Coefficients*	*Standard Error*	*t Stat*	*P-value*	*Lower 95%*	*Upper 95%*	*Lower 95.0%*	*Upper 95.0%*
17	Intercept	83.41600997	43.41016192	1.921577951	0.062182379	-4.463267721	171.2952877	-4.463267721	171.2952877
18	X Variable 1	10.2096425	2.093263461	4.877380554	1.94586E-05	5.972052202	14.4472328	5.972052202	14.4472328

CHAPTER 4

Prediction, Goodness-of-Fit, and Modeling Issues

CHAPTER OUTLINE

In this chapter we continue to work with the simple linear regression model of weekly food expenditure to make predictions, compute goodness-of-fit measures, and address modeling issues. We also work with additional examples.

4.1 LEAST SQUARES PREDICTION

A $100(1-\alpha)\%$ prediction interval at value x_0 of the explanatory variable is defined as:

$$\hat{y}_0 \pm t_c se(f) \tag{4.1}$$

where: $\hat{y}_0 = b_1 + b_2 x_0$ is the least squares predictor, (4.2)

t_c is the $100(1-\alpha/2)$th percentile from the t-distribution with $N-2$ degrees of freedom,

and $se(f)$ is the standard error of the forecast.

The standard error of the forecast is given by:

$$se(f) = \sqrt{\widehat{var(f)}} = \sqrt{\hat{\sigma}^2 + \frac{\hat{\sigma}^2}{N} + (x_0 - \bar{x})^2 se(b_2)} \tag{4.3}$$

where: $\hat{\sigma}^2$ is the estimate of the error variance or mean square residual (MS residual),

N is the sample size,

and $se(b_2)$ is the standard error estimate for b_2.

The lower limit (LL) and upper limit (UL) of the prediction interval are:

$$LL = \hat{y}_0 - t_c se(f) \tag{4.4}$$

$$LL = \hat{y}_0 + t_c se(f) \tag{4.5}$$

Before we create a template to compute prediction intervals, we quickly re-estimate the food expenditure model; note that this time we also want to generate the *residual output*. We are interested in the **Predicted Y** values generated in this output. Also, since we will use more than one data set and run more than one regression in this chapter, we will choose to give our data and regression worksheets more explicit names.

Open the Excel file ***food***. Save it as **POE Chapter 4**.

Rename Sheet 1 **food data**. Re-estimate the regression parameters using Excel **Regression** analysis routine as in Section 2.2.2. In the **Regression** dialog box, the **Input Y Range** should be **A2:A41**, and the **Input X Range** should be **B2:B41**. Select **New Worksheet Ply** and name it **Food Regression**; and <u>*do check the box*</u> next to **Residuals**.

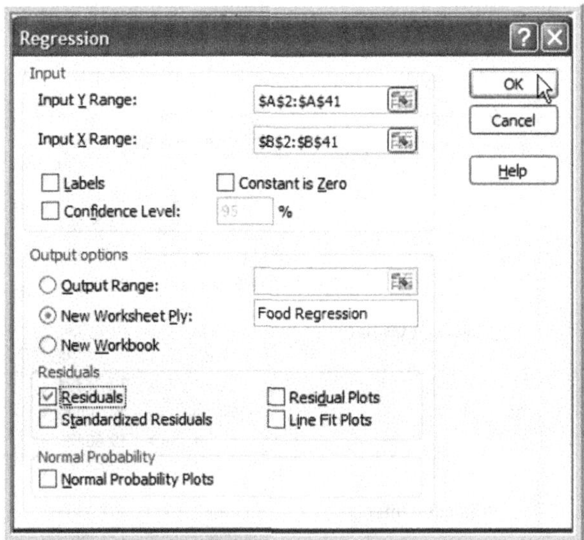

Next, insert a new worksheet by selecting the **Insert Worksheet** tab at the lower left corner of your screen. Name it **Prediction Interval**.

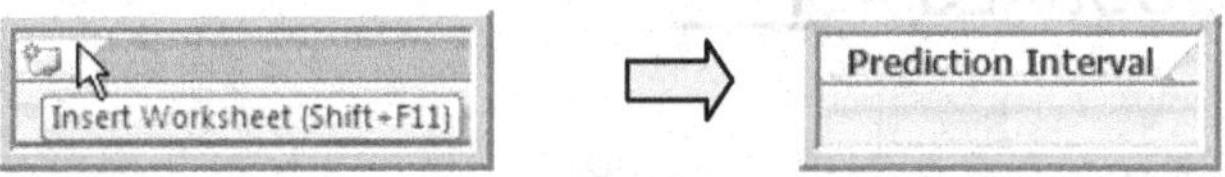

Create the following template to construct interval estimates. In the last column you will find the numbers of the equations and the formatting options used, if any, in the template.

	A	B	C	
1	**Data Input**	Sample Size =	='Food Regression'!B8	
2		Confidence Level =		*percentage* *0 decimal place*
3		x_0 =		
4		b_1 =	='Food Regression'!B17	
5		b_2 =	='Food Regression'!B18	
6		$se(b_2)$ =	='Food Regression'!C18	
7		MS residual =	='Food Regression'!D13	
8				
9	**Computed Values**	α =	=1-C2	
10		df or m =	=C1-2	
11		t_c =	=TINV(C9,C10)	
12		predicted y_0=	=C4+C5*C3	*(4.2)*
13		*x*-bar =	=AVERAGE('food data'!B2:B41)	
14		$se(f)$ =	=SQRT(C7+C7/C1+((C3-C13)^2)*C6)	*(4.3)*
15				
16	**Prediction Interval**	Lower Limit =	=C12-C11*C14	*(4.4)*
17		Upper Limit =	=C12+C11*C14	*(4.5)*

At $x_0 = 20$, the results of a 95% prediction interval for y_0 is (see also p. 134 of *Principles of Econometrics, 4e*):

	A	B	C
1	**Data Input**	Sample Size =	40
2		Confidence Level =	95%
3		x_0 =	20
4		b_1 =	83.41601
5		b_2 =	10.20964
6		$se(b_2)$ =	2.093263
7		MS residual =	8013.294
8			
9	**Computed Values**	α =	5%
10		df or m =	38
11		t_c =	2.024394
12		predicted y_0 =	287.6089
13		x-bar =	19.60475
14		$se(f)$ =	90.63086
15			
16	**Prediction Interval**	Lower Limit =	104.1363
17		Upper Limit =	471.0814

4.2 MEASURING GOODNESS-OF-FIT

4.2.1 Coefficient of Determination or R^2

The coefficient of determination, or R^2, is the proportion of variation in y explained by x within the regression model:

$$R^2 = \frac{SSR}{SST} = 1 - \frac{SSE}{SST} \tag{4.6}$$

where: SSR is the sum of squares due to the regression (**SS Regression**),

SST is the total sum of squares (**SS Total**),

and SSE is the sum of squared errors or sum of squared residuals (**SS Residual**).

4.2.2 Correlation Analysis and R^2

R^2 can be computed as the square of the sample correlation coefficient between x_i and y_i values. This result is valid only in simple regression models:

$$R^2 = r_{xy}^2 \tag{4.7}$$

R^2 can also be computed as the square of the sample correlation coefficient between y_i and $\hat{y}_i = b_1 + b_2 x_i$. This result is valid not only in simple regression models but also in multiple regression models that will be introduced in Chapter 5.

$$R^2 = r_{y\hat{y}}^2 \tag{4.8}$$

4.2.3 The Food Expenditure Example and the CORREL Function

We create a template to compute goodness-of-fit measures based on our estimated food expenditure model.

Insert a new worksheet by selecting the **Insert Worksheet** tab at the lower left corner of your screen. Name it **Correlation Analysis and R2**.

Create the following template (in the last column, you will find the numbers of the equations used in the template):

	A	B	C	
1	**Data Input**	SS Residual =	='Food Regression'!C13	
2		SS Total =	='Food Regression'!C14	
3				
4	**Computed Values**	R^2 =	=1-C1/C2	*(4.6)*
5		r_{xy} =	=CORREL('food data'!B2:B41, 'food data'!A2:A41)	
6		r^2_{xy} =	=C5^2	*(4.7)*
7		$r_{yy\text{-hat}}$ =	=CORREL('food data'!A2:A41, 'Food Regression'!B25:B64)	
8		$r^2_{yy\text{-hat}}$ =	=C7^2	*(4.8)*

The sample correlation coefficients in cells **C5** and **C7** are computed using the **CORREL** statistical function. **CORREL** returns the correlation coefficient between two data sets. The general syntax of this function is:

=CORREL(cell_range1, cell_range2)

In cell **C5**, we compute the correlation coefficient between x and y values, which we find in the **food data** worksheet. In cell **C7**, we compute the correlation coefficient between y and $\hat{y}$ values; the latter are found in the **Food Regression** worksheet, under the column labeled "Predicted Y" from the residual output.

Here are the results you should get (see also p. 138 of *Principles of Econometrics, 4e*):

	A	B	C
1	**Data Input**	SS Residual =	304505.2
2		SS Total =	495132.2
3			
4	**Computed Values**	R^2 =	0.385002
5		r_{xy} =	0.620485
6		r^2_{xy} =	0.385002
7		$r_{yy\text{-hat}}$ =	0.620485
8		$r^2_{yy\text{-hat}}$ =	0.385002

Note that $r_{y\hat{y}}$ and R^2 are actually reported in the summary output of your regression analysis: cells **B4:B5**, shaded below ($r_{y\hat{y}}$ is labeled "Multiple R" and R^2 is called by its familiar name "R Square").

	A	B
1	SUMMARY OUTPUT	
2		
3	*Regression Statistics*	
4	Multiple R	0.620485472
5	R Square	0.385002221
6	Adjusted R Square	0.368818069
7	Standard Error	89.51700429
8	Observations	40

4.3 THE EFFECTS OF SCALING THE DATA

In our **food data** worksheet, weekly food expenditure (y values) are recorded in dollars while weekly income (x values) are recorded in units of \$100.

Recall our estimated regression model. Below the estimated values for b_1 and b_2, we report their estimated standard errors, $se(b_1)$ and $se(b_2)$:

$$\begin{aligned} \hat{y}_i &= 83.42 + 10.21x_i \\ (se)\ &(43.41)\quad (2.09) \end{aligned} \tag{4.9}$$

Given the units of measurement of the data, the interpretation of the estimated slope coefficient is as follows: as weekly income increases by 1 unit, i.e. \$100, weekly food expenditure is expected to increase by 10.21 units, i.e. \$10.21. The interpretation of the estimated intercept coefficient is as follows: weekly food expenditure for a household with zero income is estimated at \$83.42.

4.3.1 Changing the Scale of *x*

Let $x^* = 100x$. We change the scale of measurement of our x values so that weekly income is now recorded in dollars.

Go back to your **food data** worksheet. In **D1**, enter the column label **x*=100x**. In cell **D2**, enter the formula **=100*B2**; copy it to cells **D3:D41**. Here is how your table should look (only the first five values are shown below):

	A	B	C	D
1	food_exp	income		x*=100x
2	115.22	3.69		369
3	135.98	4.39		439
4	119.34	4.75		475
5	114.96	6.03		603
6	187.05	12.47		1247

We want to re-estimate the food expenditure model using our original y values and our re-scaled x^* values.

In the **Regression** dialog box, the **Input Y Range** should be **A2:A41**, and the **Input X Range** should be **D2:D41**. Select **New Worksheet Ply** and name it **Food Regression 100x** (you do not need to select **Residuals**).

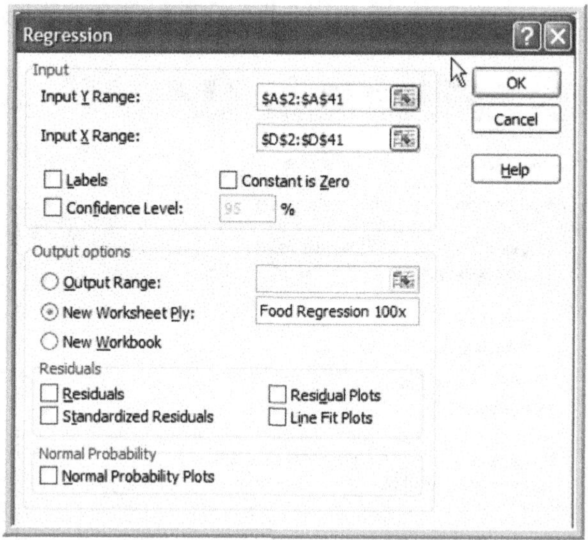

The results of your re-estimated regression model should be as reported below:

$$\hat{y}_i = 83.42 + 0.1021x_i$$
$$(se)\ \ (43.41)\ \ \ (0.0209) \tag{4.10}$$

Given the units of measurement of the data, the interpretation of the estimated slope coefficient is as follows: as weekly income increases by 1 unit, i.e. $1, weekly food expenditure is expected to increase by 0.1021 units, i.e. $0.1021 or 10.21 cents. Note that this is equivalent to saying that as weekly income increases by $100, weekly food expenditure is expected to increase by $10.21; rescaling the data does not affect the measurement of the underlying relationship.

4.3.2 Changing the Scale of *y*

Let $y^* = y/100$. We change the scale of measurement of our y values so that weekly food expenditure is now recorded in $100 units. We hold our x values at their original level of measurement, which also recorded weekly income in $100 units.

Go back to your **food data** worksheet. In **E1**, enter the column label **y*=y/100**. In cell **E2**, enter the formula **=A2/100**; copy it to cells **E3:E41**. Here is how your table should look (only the first five values are shown below):

	A	B	C	D	E
1	food_exp	income		x*=100x	y*=y/100
2	115.22	3.69		369	1.1522
3	135.98	4.39		439	1.3598
4	119.34	4.75		475	1.1934
5	114.96	6.03		603	1.1496
6	187.05	12.47		1247	1.8705

We want to re-estimate the food expenditure model using our original x values and our re-scaled y^* values.

In the **Regression** dialog box, the **Input Y Range** should be **E2:E41**, and the **Input X Range** should be **B2:B41**. Select **New Worksheet Ply** and name it **Food Regression divided by 100**.

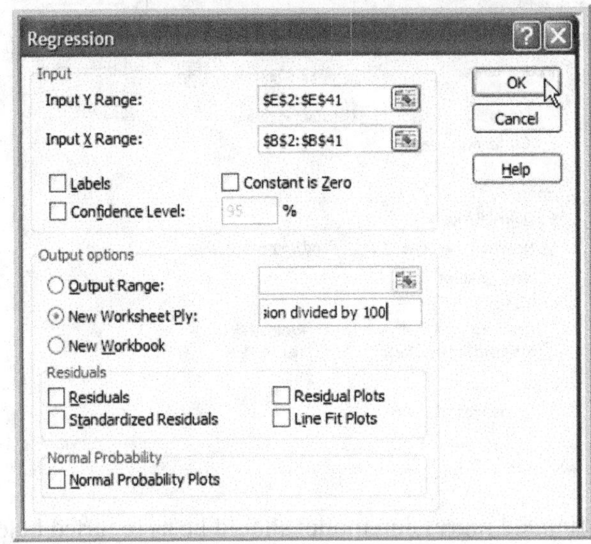

The results of your re-estimated regression model should be as reported below:

$$\begin{aligned} \hat{y}_i &= 0.8342 + 0.1021x_i \\ (se) & \quad (0.4341) \quad (0.0209) \end{aligned} \tag{4.11}$$

Given the units of measurement of the data, the interpretation of the estimated slope coefficient is as follows: as weekly income increases by 1 unit, i.e. \$100, weekly food expenditure is expected to increase by 0.1021 of a \$100 unit, i.e. \$10.21. The interpretation of the estimated intercept coefficient is as follows: weekly food expenditure for a household with zero income is estimated at 0.8342 of a \$100 unit, i.e. \$83.42. Again, note that rescaling the data does not affect the measurement of the underlying relationship.

4.3.3 Changing the Scale of *x* and *y*

Let $x^* = 4x$ and $y^* = 4y$. We change the scale of measurement of our original x values and y values so that food expenditure and income refer to a period of 4 weeks instead of 1. For simplicity we will refer to monthly food expenditure and income values. Food expenditure (y values) are still recorded in dollars while income (x values) are recorded in units of \$100.

Go back to your **food data** worksheet. In **F1**, enter the column label **x*=4x**. In **G1**, enter the column label **y*=4y**. In cell **F2**, enter the formula **=4*B2**. In cell **G2**, enter the formula **=4*A2**. Copy the content of cells **F2:G2** to cells **F3:G41**. Here is how your table should look (only the first five values are shown below):

	A	B	C	D	E	F	G
1	food_exp	income		x*=100x	y*=y/100	x*=4x	y*=4y
2	115.22	3.69		369	1.1522	14.76	460.88
3	135.98	4.39		439	1.3598	17.56	543.92
4	119.34	4.75		475	1.1934	19	477.36
5	114.96	6.03		603	1.1496	24.12	459.84
6	187.05	12.47		1247	1.8705	49.88	748.2

We want to re-estimate the food expenditure model using our newly rescaled x^* and y^* values.

In the **Regression** dialog box, the **Input Y Range** should be **G2:G41**, and the **Input X Range** should be **F2:F41**. Select **New Worksheet Ply** and name it **Regression 4x and 4y**.

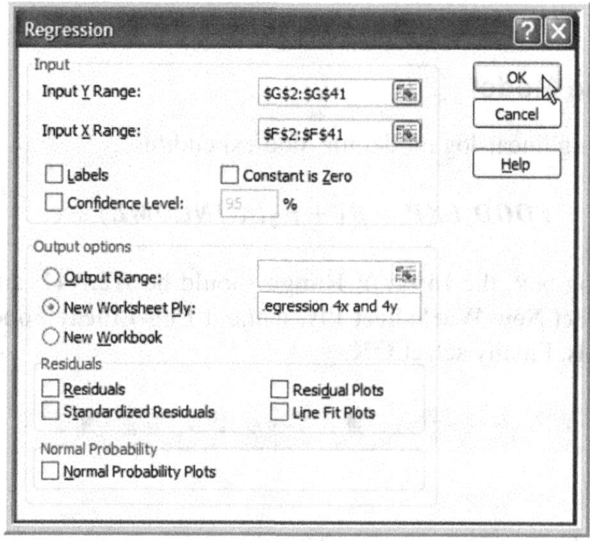

The results of your re-estimated regression model should be as reported below:

$$\hat{y}_i = 333.66 + 10.21x_i \quad (4.12)$$
$$(se) \quad (173.64) \quad (2.09)$$

Given the units of measurement of the data, the interpretation of the estimated slope coefficient is as follows: as monthly income increases by 1 unit, i.e. $100, monthly food expenditure is expected to increase by 10.21 units, i.e. $10.21. The estimated monthly food expenditure for a household with zero income is $333.41; this is 4 times the estimated weekly food expenditure for a household with zero income (see Section 4.3.1). Again, rescaling the data did not affect the measurement of the underlying relationship.

4.4 A LINEAR-LOG FOOD EXPENDITURE MODEL

In your **food data** worksheet, insert a column to the right of the **income** column **B** (see Section 1.4 for more details on how to do that). In cells **C1:C2**, enter the following column label and formula.

	C
1	**ln(income)**
2	=ln(B2)

Copy the content of cells **C2** to cells **C3:C41**. Here is how your table should look (only the first five values are shown below):

	A	B	C
1	**food_exp**	**income**	**ln(income)**
2	115.22	3.69	1.305626458
3	135.98	4.39	1.479329227
4	119.34	4.75	1.558144618
5	114.96	6.03	1.796747011
6	187.05	12.47	2.52332576

4.4.1 Estimating the Model

We estimate the following linear-log model for food expenditure:

$$FOOD\_EXP = \beta_1 + \beta_2 ln(INCOME) + e \quad (4.13)$$

In the **Regression** dialog box, the **Input Y Range** should be **A2:A41**, and the **Input X Range** should be **C2:C41**. Select **New Worksheet Ply**, name it **Log-Linear Food Model** *and do check the box next to* **Residuals**. Finally select **OK**.

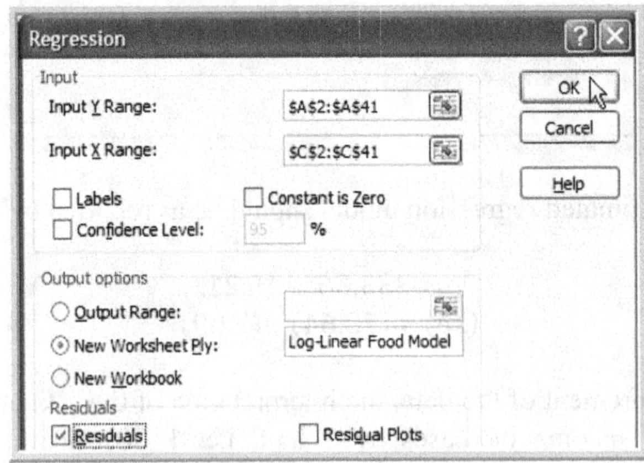

The result is (matching the one reported on p. 144 of *Principles of Econometrics, 4e*):

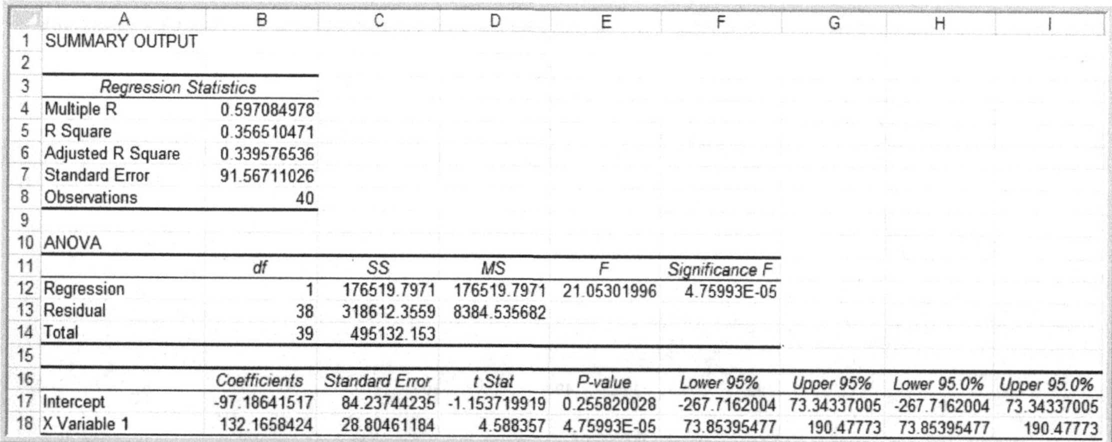

	A	B	C	D	E	F	G	H	I
1	SUMMARY OUTPUT								
2									
3	*Regression Statistics*								
4	Multiple R	0.597084978							
5	R Square	0.356510471							
6	Adjusted R Square	0.339576536							
7	Standard Error	91.56711026							
8	Observations	40							
9									
10	ANOVA								
11		*df*	*SS*	*MS*	*F*	*Significance F*			
12	Regression	1	176519.7971	176519.7971	21.05301996	4.75993E-05			
13	Residual	38	318612.3559	8384.535682					
14	Total	39	495132.153						
15									
16		*Coefficients*	*Standard Error*	*t Stat*	*P-value*	*Lower 95%*	*Upper 95%*	*Lower 95.0%*	*Upper 95.0%*
17	Intercept	-97.18641517	84.23744235	-1.153719919	0.255820028	-267.7162004	73.34337005	-267.7162004	73.34337005
18	X Variable 1	132.1658424	28.80461184	4.588357	4.75993E-05	73.85395477	190.47773	73.85395477	190.47773

Note that your ANOVA table should be followed by a RESIDUAL OUTPUT table. This last table contains a column of *Predicted Y* or fitted values and a column of *Residuals* values. We use the fitted values in the next section.

	A	B	C
22	RESIDUAL OUTPUT		
23			
24	*Observation*	*Predicted Y*	*Residuals*
25	1	75.37280548	39.84719552
26	2	98.33037827	37.64961773
27	3	108.7470808	10.59291519
28	4	140.282167	-25.32216803
29	5	236.3110594	-49.26105644

4.4.2 Scatter Plot of Data with Fitted Linear-Log Relationship

Go back to your **food data** worksheet and select **A2:B41**. Select the **Insert** tab located next to the **Home** tab. In the **Charts** group of commands select **Scatter**, and then **Scatter with only Markers**.

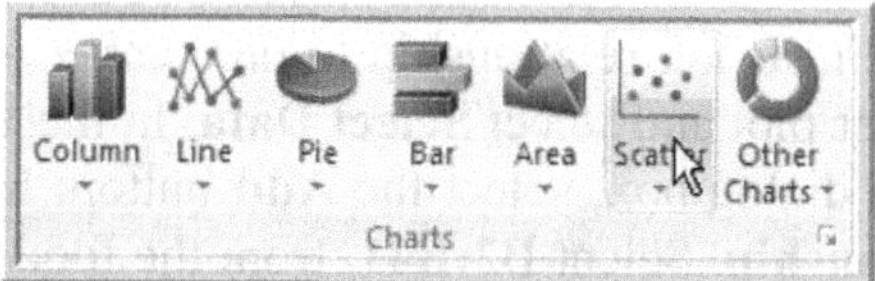

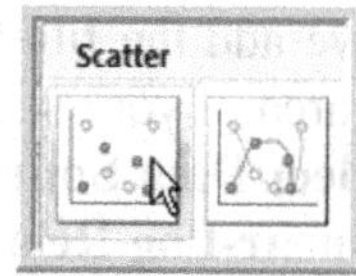

The result is:

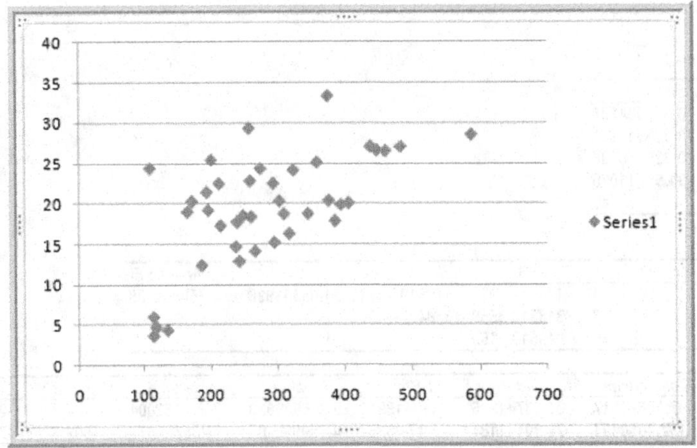

You can see that our food expenditure values are on the horizontal axis and income values are on the vertical axis; we would like to change that around and edit our chart as we did in Section 2.1. The result is (see also Figure 4.6 on p. 144 of *Principles of Econometrics, 4e*):

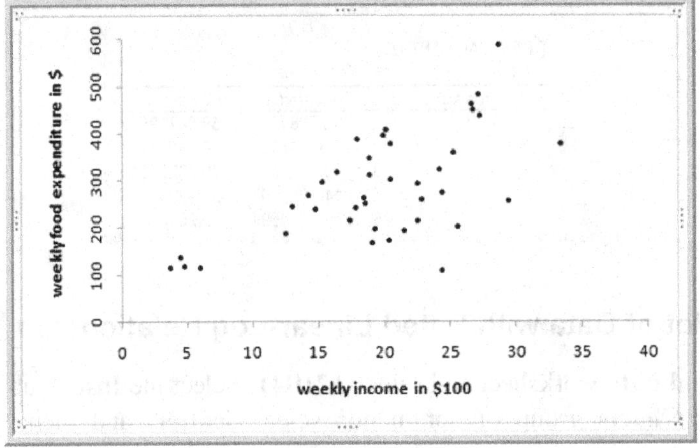

Finally, we add the fitted linear-log relationship to our scatter plot. Right-click in the middle of the chart area of your scatter plot and select **Select Data**. In the **Legend Entries (Series)** window of the **Select Data Source** dialog box, select the **Add** button. In the **Series name** window, type **Fitted Linear-Log Relationship**. Select **B2:B41**, from the food data worksheet, for the **Series X values**; select **B25:B64**, from the Log-Linear Model worksheet (*Predicted Y* values), for the **Series Y values**. Finally, select **OK**. The **Fitted Linear-log Relationship** series has been added to your graph.

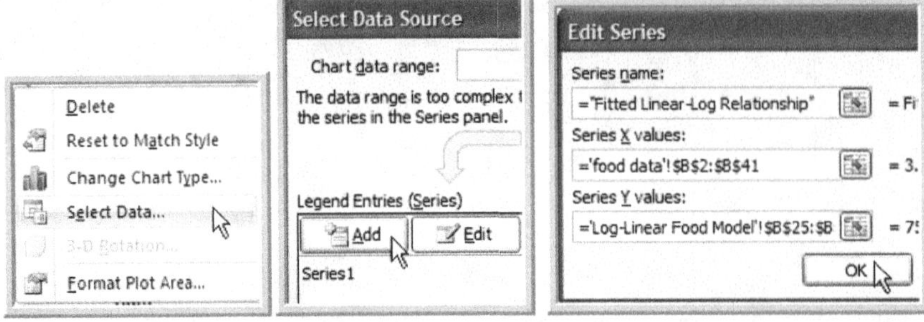

Before you close the **Select Data Source** dialog box, select **Series1** and **Edit**. Type the name **Actual** in the **Series name** window. Select **OK**. In the **Select Data Source** window that re-appears, select **OK** again.

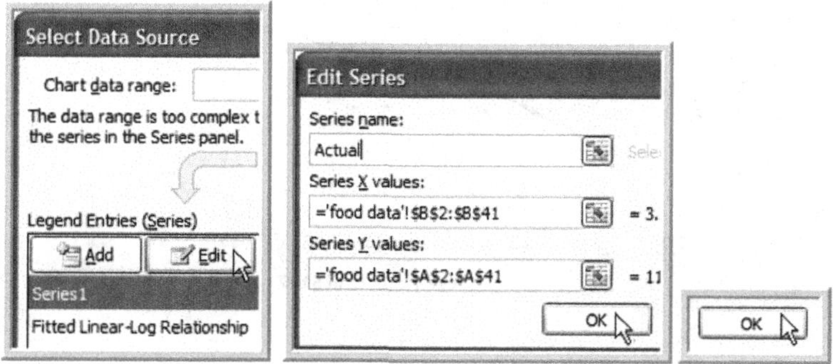

Make sure you chart is selected so that the **Chart Tools** are visible. In the **Layout** tab, go to the **Labels** group of commands. Select the **Legend** button and choose either one of the **Overlay Legend** options. Grab your legend with your cursor and move it to the upper left corner of your chart area.

Finally, we want to reformat our **Fitted Linear-Log Relationship** values series. Select the plotted series in your chart area, right-click and select **Format Data Series**. A **Format Data Series** dialog box pops up. Select **Line Color** and **Solid line**. Change the line color to something different from the **Actual** series points. Select **Marker Options**, and change the **Marker Type** from **Automatic** to **None**. Select **Close**.

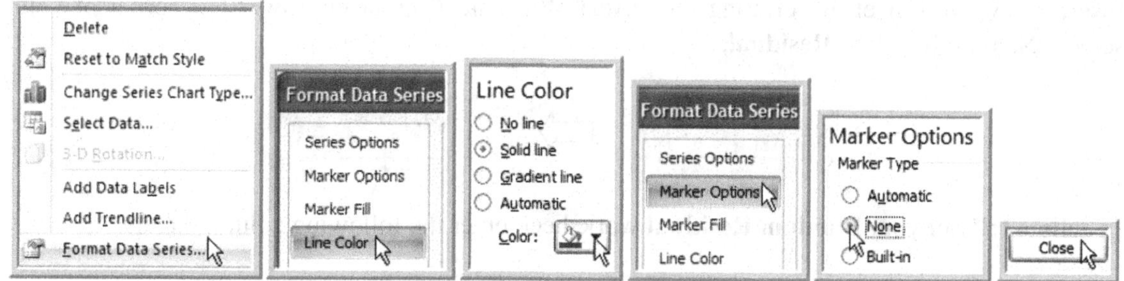

The result is (see also Figure 4.6 on p. 144 of *Principles of Econometrics, 4e*):

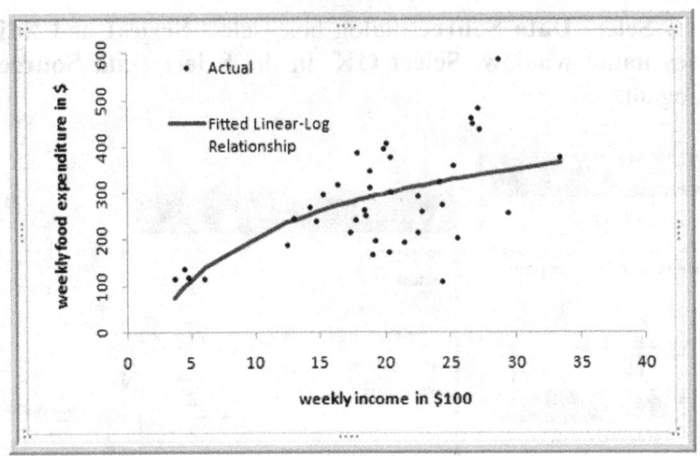

4.5 USING DIAGNOSTIC RESIDUAL PLOTS

4.5.1 Random Residual Pattern

Consider the following simple linear regression model:

$$y = 1 + x + e \tag{4.14}$$

First, 300 pairs of x_i and e_i values are created using random number generators, similarly to the way we artificially generated variables in Sections 2.4 and 3.1.4. The variable x is simulated, using a random number generator, to be evenly, or uniformly, distributed between 0 and 10. The error term e is simulated to be uncorrelated, homoskedastic, and from a standard normal distribution, or $e \sim N(0,1)$. We generate these simulated observations next.

Insert a new worksheet by selecting the **Insert Worksheet** tab at the lower left corner of your screen. Name it **Random Residual.**

In cells **A1:B1** of your **Random Residual** worksheet, enter the following column labels.

	A	B
1	**x**	**e**

Select the **Data** tab, in the middle of your tab list. On the **Analysis** group of commands to the far right of the ribbon, select **Data Analysis**.

The **Data Analysis** dialog box pops up. In it, select **Random Number Generation** (you might need to use the scroll up and down bar to the right of the **Analysis Tools** window to find it), then select **OK**.

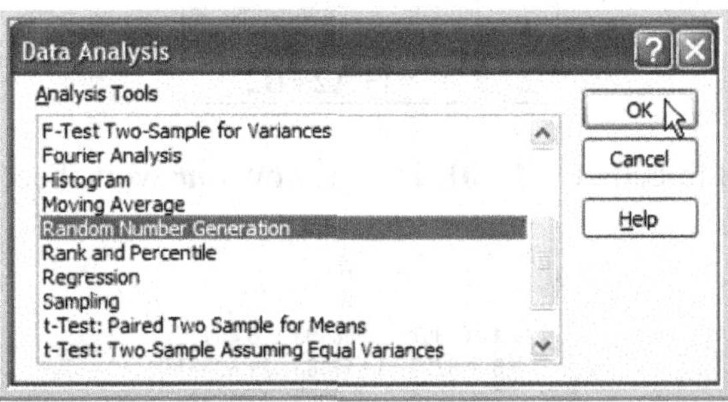

A **Random Number Generation** dialog box pops up. The **Number of Variables** simulated is **1**, and the **Number of Random Numbers** generated is **300**. The variable x is simulated to be **Uniform**ly distributed between **0** and **10**. Select the **Output Range** in the **Output options** section, and specify it to be **A2:A301** in your **Random Residual** worksheet. Finally, select **OK**.

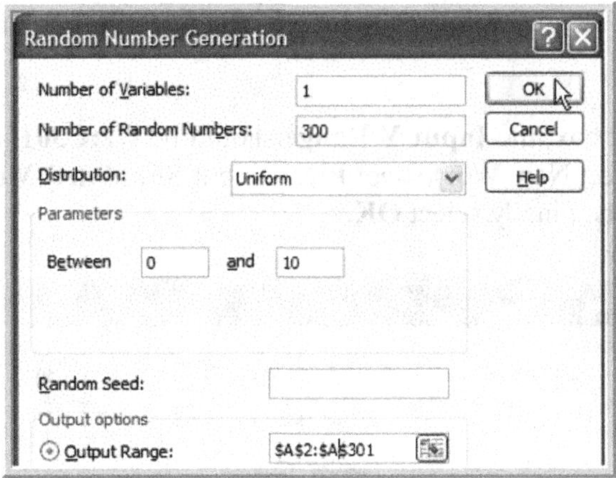

We repeat to draw a random sample of **300** error term from a standard normal distribution. Select the **Output Range** in the **Output options** section, and specify it to be **B2:B301** in your **Random Residual** worksheet. Finally, select **OK**.

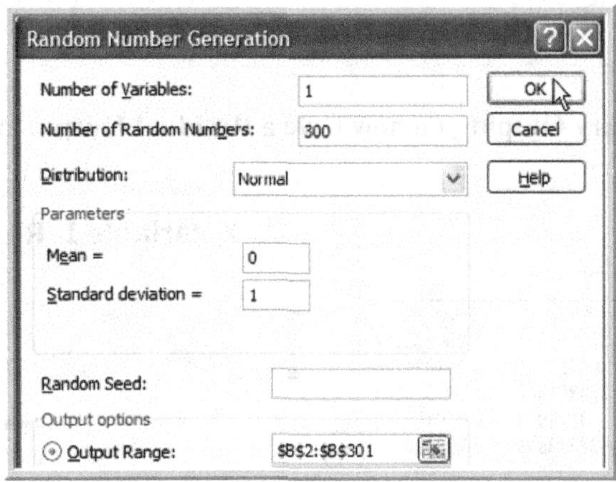

In cells **C1:C2** of your **Random Residual** worksheet, enter the following column label and formula.

	C
1	**y**
2	**=1+A2+B2**

Select cell **C2** and copy it to cells **C3:C301**. Here is how *our* worksheet looks (only the first five values are shown below):

	A	B	C
1	x	e	y
2	4.405957	0.998193	6.40415
3	9.518723	1.011883	11.53061
4	3.821223	-0.0083	4.812922
5	2.649922	-0.43201	3.217908
6	3.976562	0.25586	5.232422

Note that you will have drawn a different random samples and thus also obtained a different sample values for *y*.

Next, we apply the least squares estimator to these simulated observations and compute the least squares residuals.

In the **Regression** dialog box, the **Input Y Range** should be **C2:C301**, and the **Input X Range** should be **X2:X301**. Select **New Worksheet Ply**, name it **Simulated Model 1** *and do check the box next to* **Residual Plots**. Finally select **OK.**

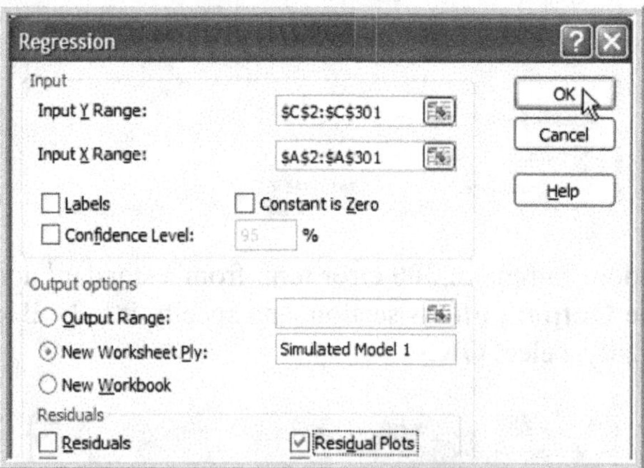

In addition to the **Summary Output** you now have a **Residual Output** table and a **Residual Plot** in your new worksheet.

	A	B	C
22	RESIDUAL OUTPUT		
23			
24	*Observation*	*Predicted Y*	*Residuals*
25	1	5.373941992	1.030208394
26	2	10.5727117	0.957894744
27	3	4.779371302	0.033550994
28	4	3.58836801	-0.370460363
29	5	4.937323536	0.295098435

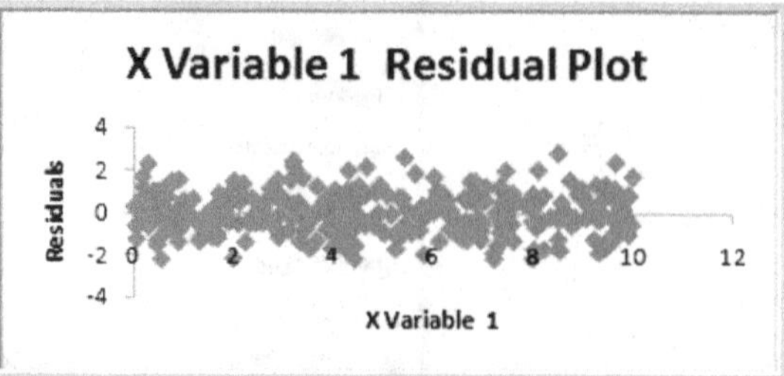

After editing the chart as we did in Section 2.1 or Section 2.3.4, the result is (see also Figure 4.7 p. 146 of *Principles of Econometrics, 4e*):

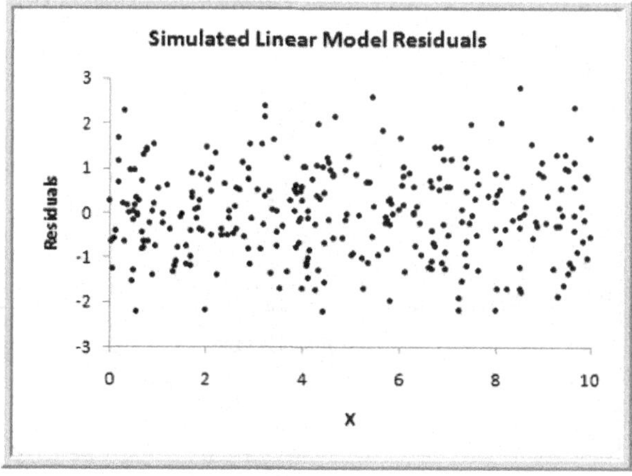

4.5.2 Heteroskedastic Residual Pattern

Go back to your **food data** worksheet, select your scatter plot of food expenditure-income data points and fitted linear-log relationship and make a copy of it. Right-click in the middle of the copy of your chart. Select **Select Data.** In the **Legend Entries (Series)** window of the **Select Data Source** dialog box, select the **Fitted Linear-Log Relationship** series, and then the **Remove** button.

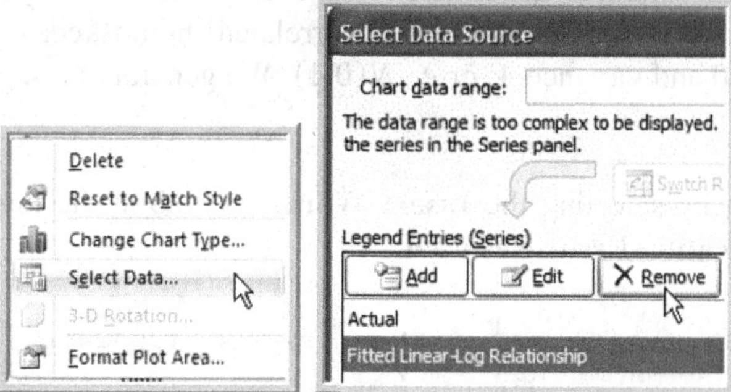

Next, select the **Actual** series, and then the **Edit** button. In the **Edit Series** window, replace delete the old **Series name** and re-specify r the **Series Y values** to be **C25:C64**, from the **Log-Linear Food Model** worksheet. Finally, select **OK**, twice.

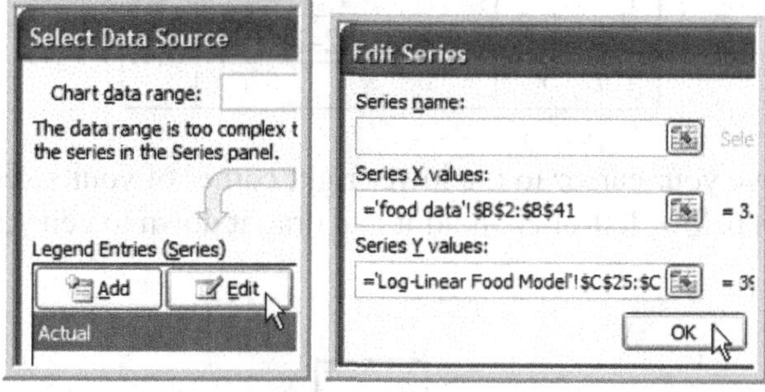

The result is (see also Figure 4.8 p. 146 of *Principles of Econometrics, 4e*):

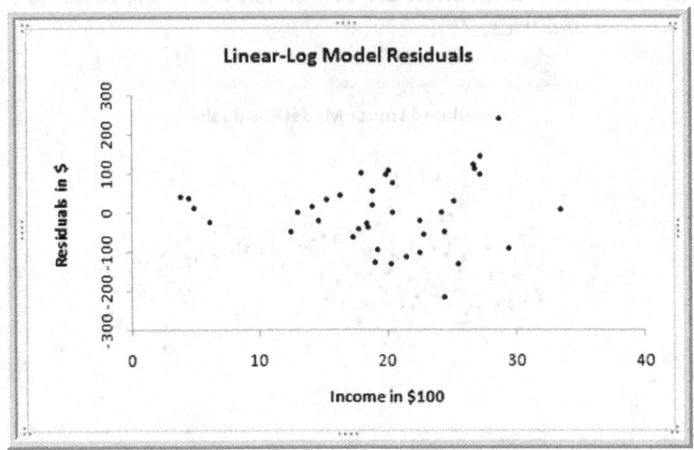

4.5.3 Detecting Model Specification Errors

Consider the following quadratic relationship:

$$y = 15 - 4x^2 + e \tag{4.15}$$

First, 50 pairs of x_i and e_i values are created using random number generators, similarly to the way we artificially generated variables in Sections 2.4, 3.1.4 and 4.5.1. The variable x is simulated, using a random number generator, to be evenly, or uniformly, distributed between 0 and 10. The error term e is simulated to be uncorrelated, homoskedastic, and from a normal distribution with mean 0 and variance 4, or $e \sim N(0,4)$. We generate these simulated observations next.

Insert a new worksheet by selecting the **Insert Worksheet** tab at the lower left corner of your screen. Name it **Specification Error Residual.**

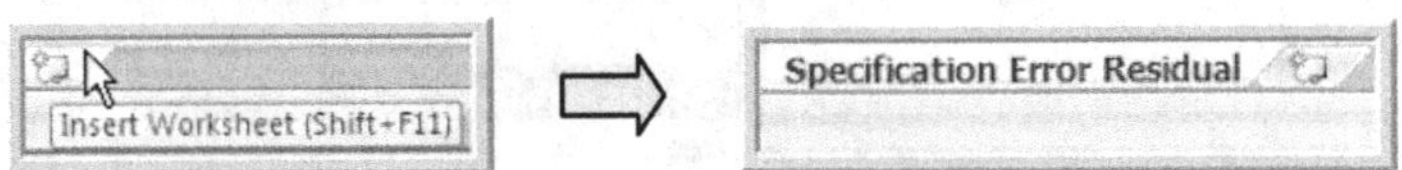

In cells **A1:C2** of your **Random Residual** worksheet, enter the following column labels and formula.

	A	B	C
1		x	e
2	1	=2.5-((A2-1)/10)	
3	2		

Select cells **A2:A3,** move your cursor to the lower right corner of your selection until it turns into a skinny cross as shown below, left-click, hold it and drag it down to cell **A52**.

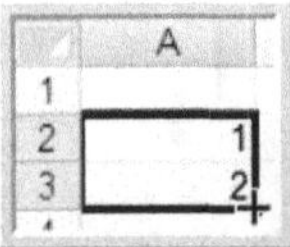

Copy cell **B2** to cells **B3:B52**. Your table should look as the one below (only the first five values are shown).

	A	B	C
1		x	e
2	1	2.5	
3	2	2.4	
4	3	2.3	
5	4	2.2	
6	5	2.1	

Select the **Data** tab, in the middle of your tab list. On the **Analysis** group of commands to the far right of the ribbon, select **Data Analysis.**

The **Data Analysis** dialog box pops up. In it, select **Random Number Generation** (you might need to use the scroll up and down bar to the right of the **Analysis Tools** window to find it), then select **OK**.

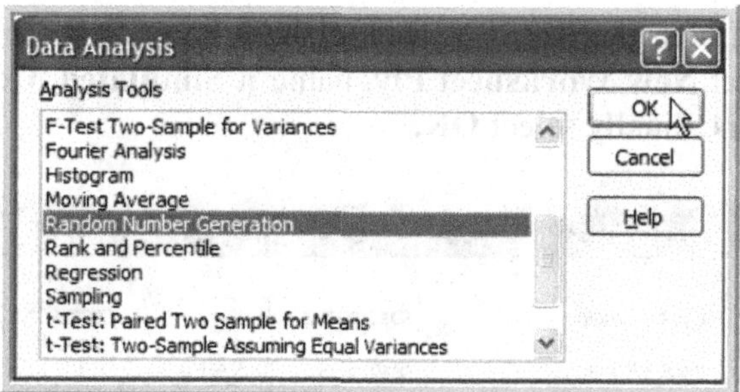

We draw **1** random sample of **51** error terms from a normal distribution with **Mean 0** and **Standard Deviation 2**. Select the **Output Range** in the **Output options** section, and specify it to be **C2:C52** in your **Random Residual** worksheet. Finally, select **OK**.

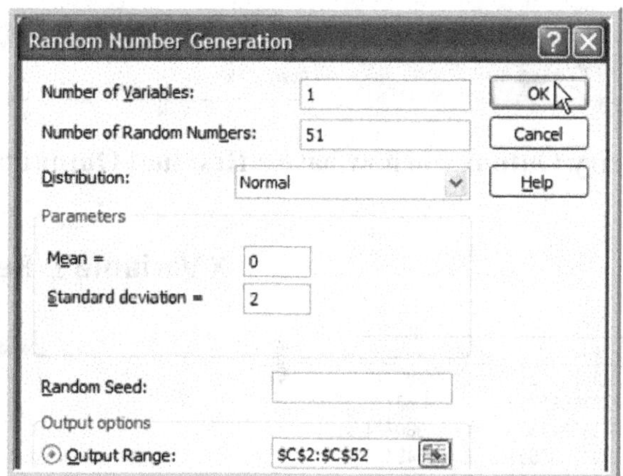

In cells **D1:D2** of your **Specification Error Residual** worksheet, enter the following column label and formula.

	D
1	**y**
2	**=15-4*(A2^2) +B2**

Select cell **D2** and copy it to cells **D3:D52**. Here is how *our* worksheet looks (only the first five values are shown below):

	A	B	C	D
1		x	e	y
2	1	2.5	2.723068	-7.27693
3	2	2.4	-0.50477	-8.54477
4	3	2.3	1.115236	-5.04476
5	4	2.2	2.916886	-1.44311
6	5	2.1	2.982706	0.342706

Note that you will have drawn a different random samples and thus also obtained a different sample values for y.

Next, we apply the least squares estimator to these simulated observations and compute the least squares residuals.

In the **Regression** dialog box, the **Input Y Range** should be **C2:C52**, and the **Input X Range** should be **A2:A52**. Select **New Worksheet Ply**, name it **Simulated Model 2** *and do check the box next to* **Residual Plots**. Finally select **OK.**

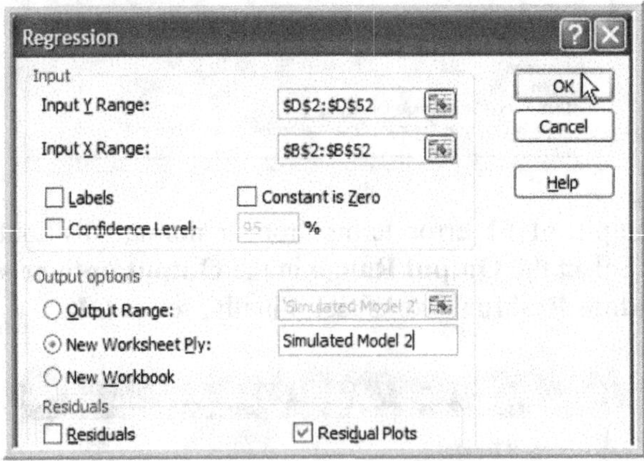

In addition to the **Summary Output** you now have a **Residual Output** table and a **Residual Plot** in your new worksheet.

	A	B	C
22	RESIDUAL OUTPUT		
23			
24	*Observation*	*Predicted Y*	*Residuals*
25	1	5.957061537	-13.23399347
26	2	5.976552712	-14.52132
27	3	5.996043887	-11.04080784
28	4	6.015535062	-7.458649129
29	5	6.035026236	-5.692320172

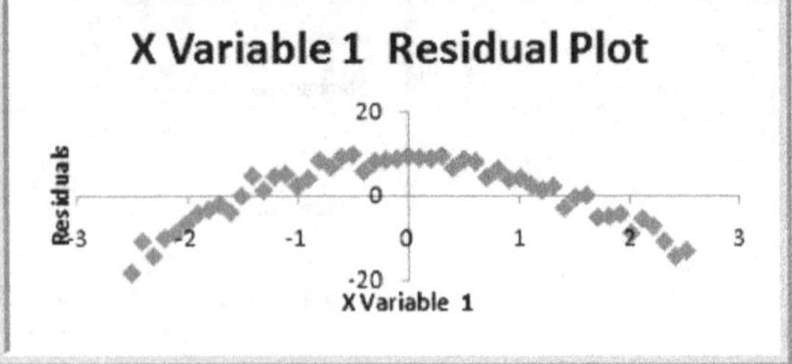

After editing the chart as we did in Section 2.1 or Section 2.3.4, the result is (see also Figure 4.9 on p. 147 of *Principles of Econometrics, 4e*):

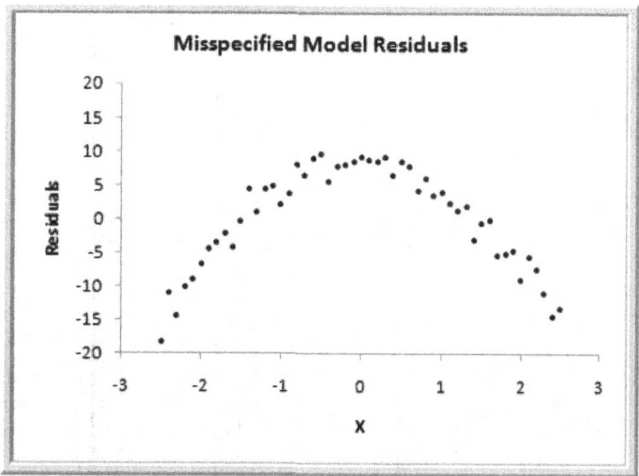

4.6 ARE THE REGRESSION ERRORS NORMALLY DISTRIBUTED?

Our analysis of normality of the regression errors will include a histogram of the residuals and the Jarque-Bera test for normality.

4.6.1 Histogram of the Residuals

Go back to your **Food Regression** worksheet. If you do not see your **Food Regression** tab, it is because it is hidden. Use either one of the left-arrows at the left corner of your screen so that the first worksheets you were working with can be seen again. (If the worksheet you need to go back to is a recently created one, use the right-arrows.)

Next to the columns of **Residuals** in the residual output section of the worksheet, we will create a **BIN** column. In cell **D24**, type **BIN**. The bin values will determine the range of residual values for each column of the histogram. The bin values have to be given in ascending order. Starting with the lowest bin value, a residual value will be counted in a particular bin if it is equal to or less than the bin value.

Fill in the bin values as shown below. Note that all you need to do is enter the first two values: **-225** and **-200**, select cells **D25:D26**, move your cursor to the lower right corner of your selection until it turns into a skinny cross as shown below, left-click, hold it and drag it down to cell **D43**: Excel recognizes the series and automatically completes it for you.

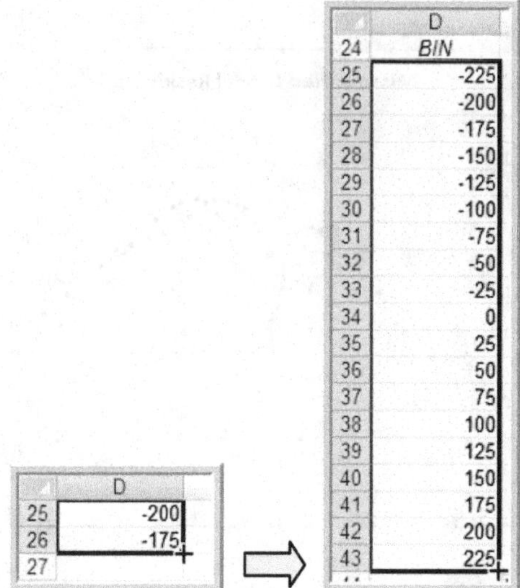

Select the **Data** tab, in the middle of your tab list. On the **Analysis** group of commands to the far right of the ribbon, select **Data Analysis**.

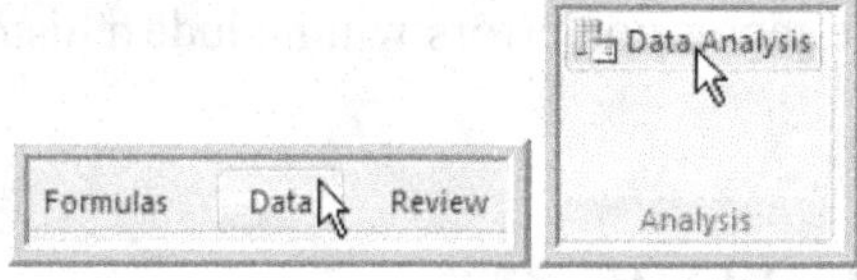

The **Data Analysis** dialog box pops up. In it, select **Histogram** (you might need to use the scroll up and down bar to the right of the **Analysis Tools** window to find it), then select **OK**.

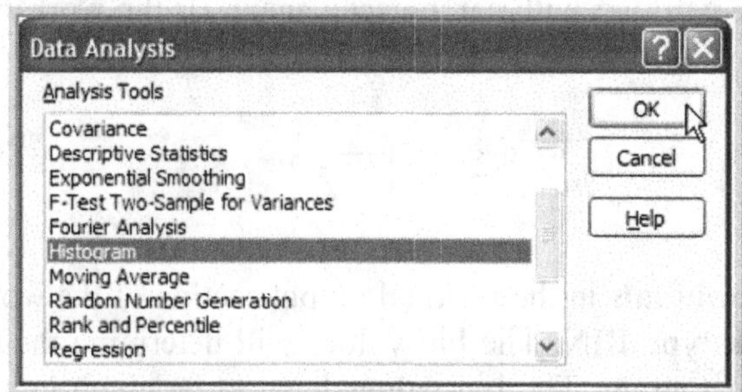

An **Histogram** dialog box pops up. For the **Input Range**, specify **C25:C64**; for the **Bin Range**, specify **D25:D43**. The **Input Range** indicates the data set Excel will look at to determine how many values are counted in each bin of the **Bin Range**. Check the **New Worksheet Ply** option and name it **Residuals Histogram**; check the box next to **Chart Output**. Finally, select **OK**.

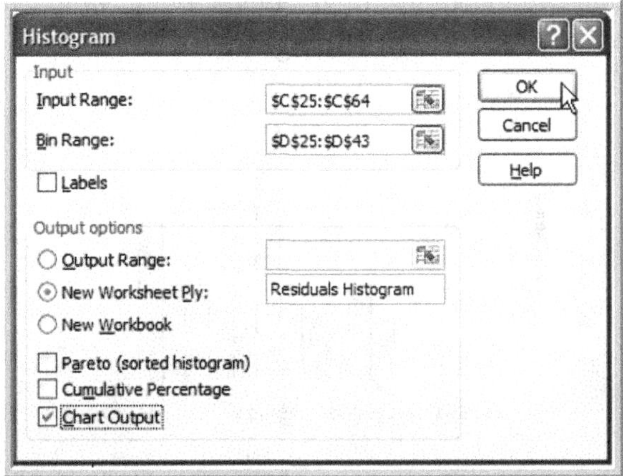

Select the columns in your chart area, right-click and select **Format Data Series**. The **Series Options** tab of the **Format Data Series** dialog box should be open. Select the **Gap Width** button and move it to the far left, towards **No Gap**.

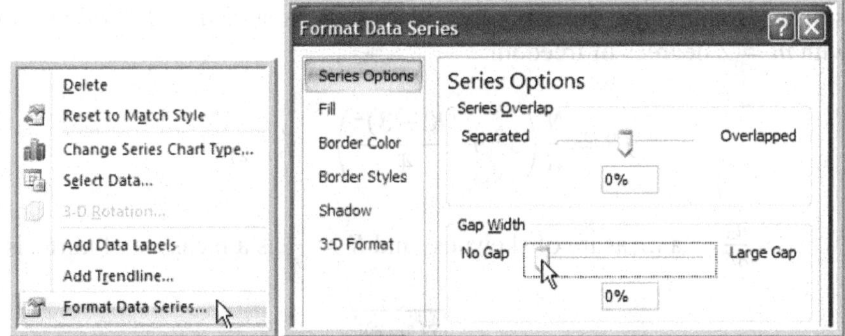

Go to the **Border Color** tab and select **Solid line**, choose a different **Color** if you would like. Select **Close**.

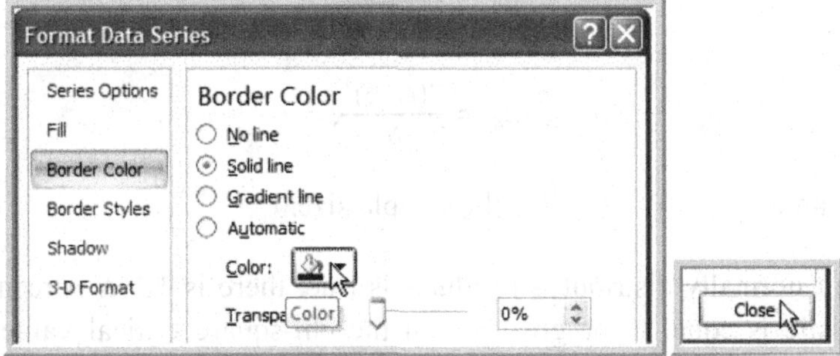

Finally, delete the **Legend**, and increase the size of the **Chart area** (see Section 2.3.4 for more details on that). The result should be very similar to Figure 4.10 on p. 148 of *Principles of Econometrics, 4e*:

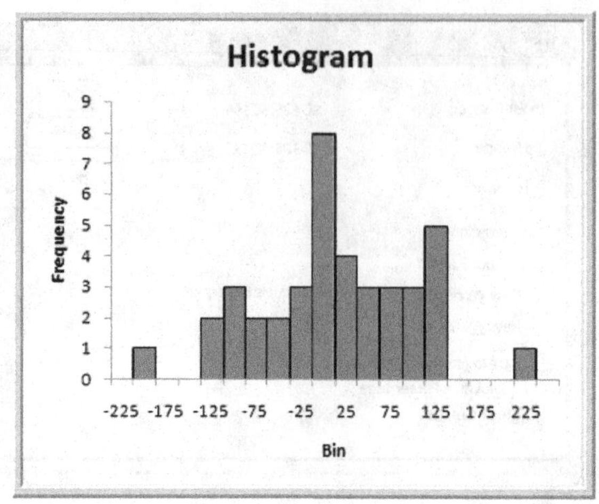

4.6.2 The Jarque-Bera Test for Normality using the CHIINV and CHIDIST Functions

When the residuals are normally distributed, the Jarque-Bera statistic (JB) follows a chi-squared distribution with $m = 2$ degrees of freedom:

$$JB = \frac{N}{6}\left(S^2 + \frac{(K-3)^2}{4}\right) \sim \chi^2_{(m=2)} \tag{4.16}$$

where $S = \frac{\tilde{\mu}_3}{\tilde{\sigma}^3}$ is a measure of skewness and $K = \frac{\tilde{\mu}_4}{\tilde{\sigma}^4}$ is a measure of kurtosis,

where

$$\tilde{\sigma} = \sqrt{\frac{\Sigma(\hat{e}_i - \bar{\hat{e}})^2}{N}}, \tag{4.17}$$

$$\tilde{\mu}_3 = \frac{\Sigma(\hat{e}_i - \bar{\hat{e}})^3}{N}, \tag{4.18}$$

$$\tilde{\mu}_4 = \frac{\Sigma(\hat{e}_i - \bar{\hat{e}})^4}{N}, \tag{4.19}$$

and N is the sample size.

If the hypothesis of normally distributed residuals is true, there is 100α percent chance that the computed JB statistic is equal to or greater than the chi-square critical value $\chi^2_{(1-\alpha,m)}$. If the computed JB statistic is equal to or greater than the chi-square critical value $\chi^2_{(1-\alpha,m)}$, then this presents us with evidence that our hypothesis of normally distributed errors is false; we thus reject it.

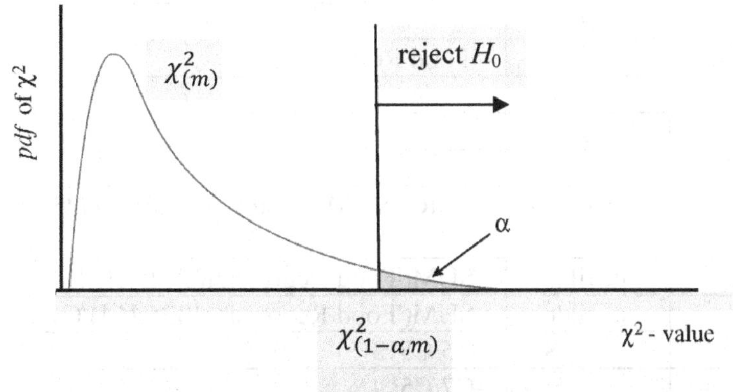

We will create a template for the Jarque-Bera test for normality. But before we do that, we need to go back to our **Food Regression** worksheet to perform intermediate calculations.

Before we compute the measure of skewness S and the measure of kurtosis K, note that since $\bar{\hat{e}} = 0$, the numerators of equations (4.17)-(4.19): $\sum(\hat{e}_i - \bar{\hat{e}})^2$, $\sum(\hat{e}_i - \bar{\hat{e}})^3$, and $\sum(\hat{e}_i - \bar{\hat{e}})^4$, can simplify to: $\sum \hat{e}_i^2$, $\sum \hat{e}_i^3$ and $\sum \hat{e}_i^4$.

To the right of the residual output section, create the following table:

	F	G	H
24	**residuals²**	**residuals³**	**residuals⁴**
25	=C25^2	=C25^3	=C25^4

Copy cells **F25:H25** to cells **F26:H64**. Your worksheet should now look like the one below (only partly shown):

	F	G	H
24	**Residuals²**	**Residuals³**	**Residuals⁴**
25	34.45208433	-202.219603	1186.946115
26	59.96419985	464.3421034	3595.705263
27	158.0505536	-1986.98245	24979.97748
28	901.2097207	-27054.4557	812178.9608
29	560.7541899	-13278.7988	314445.2614

Now, we are ready to create our Jarque-Bera test template.

Insert a new worksheet by selecting the **Insert Worksheet** tab at the bottom of your screen. Name it **Jarque-Bera Tests**.

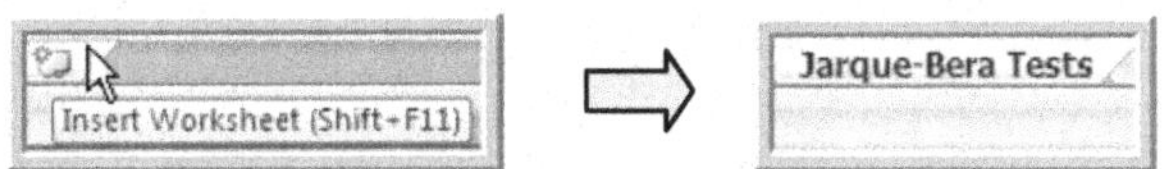

Create the following template to perform Jarque-Bera tests:

	A	B	C	
1	**Data Input**	N =	='Food Regression'!B8	
2		α =		
3		df or m =	2	
4				
5	**Computed Values**	σ-tilde =	=SQRT(SUM('Food Regression'!G25:G64)/C1)	*(4.17)*
6		μ_3-tilde =	=SUM('Food Regression'!H25:H64)/C1	*(4.18)*
7		μ_4-tilde =	=SUM('Food Regression'!I25:I64)/C1	*(4.19)*
8		S =	=C6/C5^3	
9		K =	=C7/C5^4	
10		χ^2-critical value =	=CHIINV(C2,C3)	
11				
12	**Jarque-Bera Test**	JB =	=(C1/6)*(C8^2+((C9-3)^2)/4)	*(4.16)*
13		Conclusion:	=IF(C12>=C10,"Reject the hypothesis of normally distributed errors","Do not reject the hypothesis of normally distributed errors")	
14		*p*-value =	=CHIDIST(C12,C3)	
15		Conclusion:	=IF(C14<=C2,"Reject the hypothesis of normally distributed errors","Do not reject the hypothesis of normally distributed errors")	

The χ^2-critical value is computed using the **CHIINV** statistical function. For our purpose, this function syntax is:

=CHIINV(α,m)

where **α** is the level of significance of the Jarque-Bera test, and **m** is the degree of freedom of the chi-squared distribution.

The *p*-value is computed using the **CHIDIST** statistical function. For our purpose, this function syntax is:

=CHIDIST(χ^2-value,m)

where **χ^2-value** is the χ^2-critical value for which we are computing the *p*-value, and **m** is the degree of freedom of the chi-squared distribution.

At $\alpha = 0.05$, the results of the Jarque-Bera test are (see p. 148 of *Principles of Econometrics, 4e*):

	A	B	C	D	E	F	G
1	**Data Input**	N =	40				
2		α =	0.05				
3		df or m =	2				
4							
5	**Computed Values**	σ-tilde =	87.250383				
6		μ_3-tilde =	-64639.66				
7		μ_4-tilde =	173220834				
8		S =	-0.097319				
9		K =	2.9890333				
10		χ^2-critical value =	5.9914645				
11							
12	**Jarque-Bera Test**	JB =	0.0633402				
13		Conclusion =	Do not reject the hypothesis of normally distributed errrors				
14		*p*-value =	0.9688262				
15		Conclusion =	Do not reject the hypothesis of normally distributed errrors				

4.6.3 The Jarque-Bera Test for Normality for the Linear-Log Food Expenditure Model

We first go back to our **Log-Linear Food Model** worksheet to perform intermediate calculations.

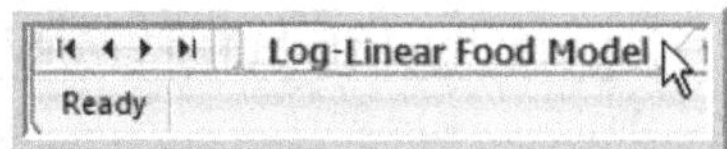

To the right of the residual output section, create the following table:

	F	G	H
24	**residuals^2**	**residuals^3**	**residuals^4**
25	=C25^2	=C25^3	=C25^4

Copy cells **F25:H25** to cells **F26:H64**. Your worksheet should now look like the one below (only partly shown):

	F	G	H
24	**Residuals^2**	**Residuals^3**	**Residuals^4**
25	1587.798991	63269.33684	2521105.635
26	1417.493715	53368.09651	2009288.432
27	112.2098522	1188.629448	12591.05094
28	641.2121938	-16236.8829	411153.0775
29	2426.651681	-119539.425	5888638.382

Now, we are ready to modify a few cell references in our Jarque-Bera test template.

Go to the **Jarque-Bera Tests** worksheet.

Replace all references to the **Food Regression** worksheet to the **Log-Linear Food Model** worksheet (see outlined below in bold).

	A	B	C
1	Data Input	N =	='**Log-Linear Food Model**'!B8
2		α =	
3		df or m =	2

	A	B	C
5	Computed Values	σ-tilde =	=SQRT(SUM('**Log-Linear Food Model**'!G25:G64)/C1)
6		μ_3-tilde =	=SUM('**Log-Linear Food Model**'!H25:H64)/C1
7		μ_4-tilde =	=SUM('**Log-Linear Food Model**'!I25:I64)/C1
8		S =	=C6/C5^3
9		K =	=C7/C5^4
10		χ^2-critical value =	=CHIINV(C2,C3)
11			
12	Jarque-Bera Test	JB =	=(C1/6)*(C8^2+((C9-3)^2)/4)
13		Conclusion:	=IF(C12>=C10,"Reject the hypothesis of normally distributed errors","Do not reject the hypothesis of normally distributed errors")
14		*p*-value =	=CHIDIST(C12,C3)
15		Conclusion:	=IF(C14<=C2,"Reject the hypothesis of normally distributed errors","Do not reject the hypothesis of normally distributed errors")

At $\alpha = 0.05$, the results of the Jarque-Bera test are (see p. 149 of *Principles of Econometrics, 4e*):

	A	B	C	D	E	F	G
1	**Data Input**	N =	40				
2		α =	0.05				
3		df or m =	2				
4							
5	**Computed Values**	σ-tilde =	89.248579				
6		μ_3-tilde =	99251.00				
7		μ_4-tilde =	203335377				
8		S =	0.1396146				
9		K =	3.2048499				
10		χ^2-critical value =	5.9914645				
11							
12	**Jarque-Bera Test**	JB =	0.1998875				
13		Conclusion =	Do not reject the hypothesis of normally distributed errrors				
14		*p*-value =	0.9048883				
15		Conclusion =	Do not reject the hypothesis of normally distributed errrors				

4.7 POLYNOMIAL MODELS: AN EMPIRICAL EXAMPLE

Open the Excel file ***wa-wheat***. Excel opens the data set in Sheet 1 of a new Excel file. Since we would like to save all our work from Chapter 4 in one file, create a new worksheet in your **POE Chapter 4** Excel file, name it **wa-wheat data**, and in it, copy the data set you just opened.

This data set gives average wheat yield for different regions of Australia for the period 1950-1997. **Time** is measured using the values 1, 2, …, 48 in column **E**. We would like to plot the yield data for the Greenough Shire area, reported in column **D**.

4.7.1 Scatter Plot of Wheat Yield over Time

Select the **Insert** tab located next to the **Home** tab. Select **D2:E49**. In the **Charts** group of commands select **Scatter**, and then **Scatter with only Markers**.

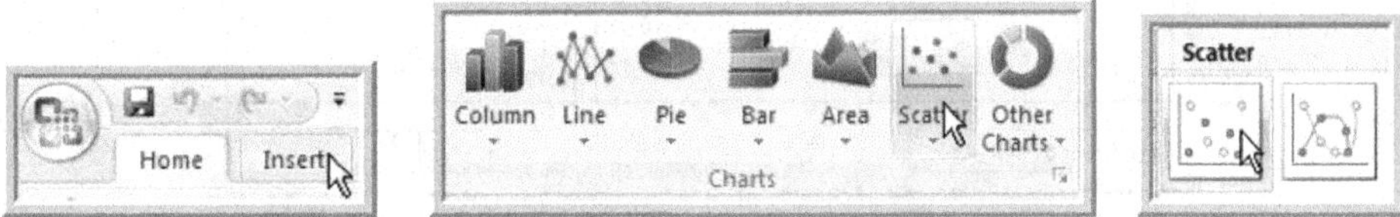

The result is:

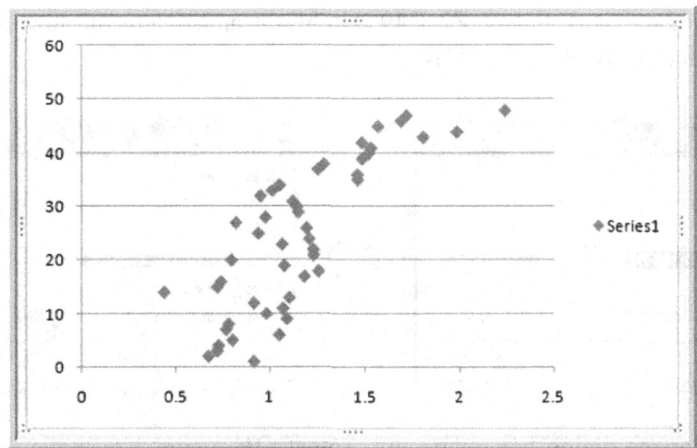

You can see that our yield values are on the horizontal axis and our time values are on the vertical axis; we would like to change that around as we did in Chapter 2 with our plot of food expenditure data. Select the points on your plot, right-click and select **Select Data**.

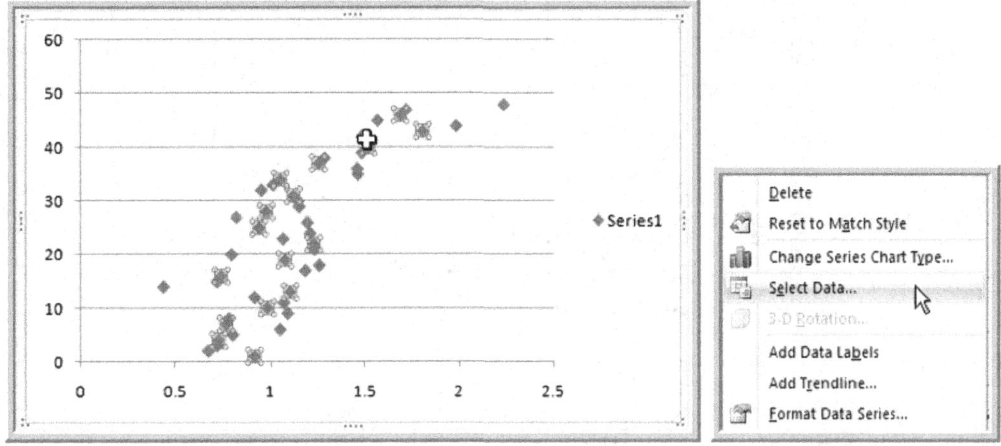

A **Select Data Source** dialog box pops up. Select **Edit**.

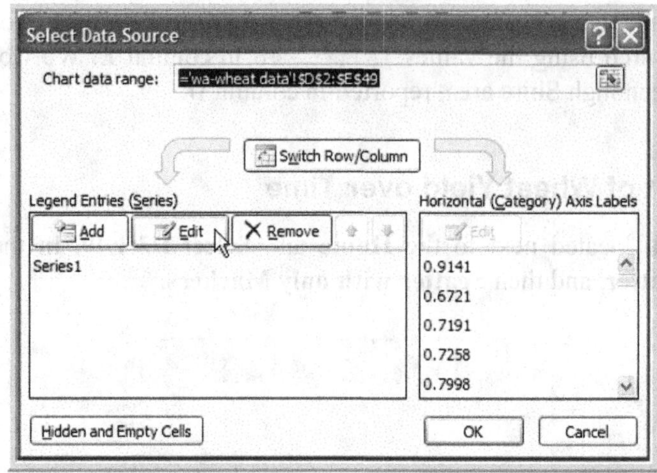

In the **Edit Series** dialog box, highlight the text from the **Series X values** window. Press the **Delete** key on your keyboard. Select **E2:E49**. Highlight and delete the text from the **Series Y values** window. Select **D2:D49**. Select **OK**.

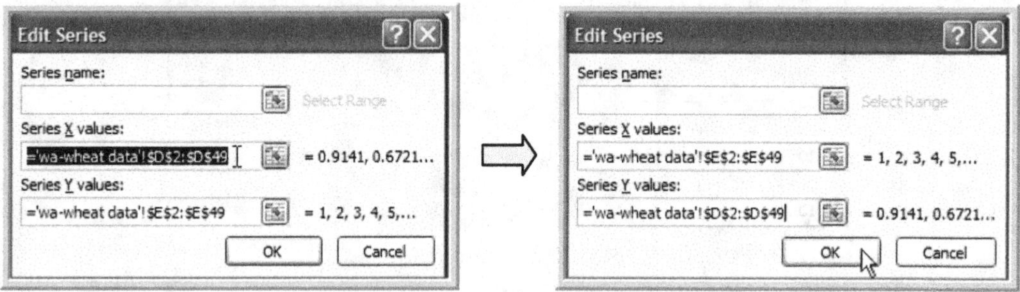

The **Select Data Source** dialog box reappears. Select **OK** again. You have just told Excel that time are the X-values, and yield are the Y-values – not the other way around.

After editing your chart like you did in Sections 2.1.2a-2.1.2c, the result is (see also Figure 4.11 p. 150 of *Principles of Econometrics, 4e*):

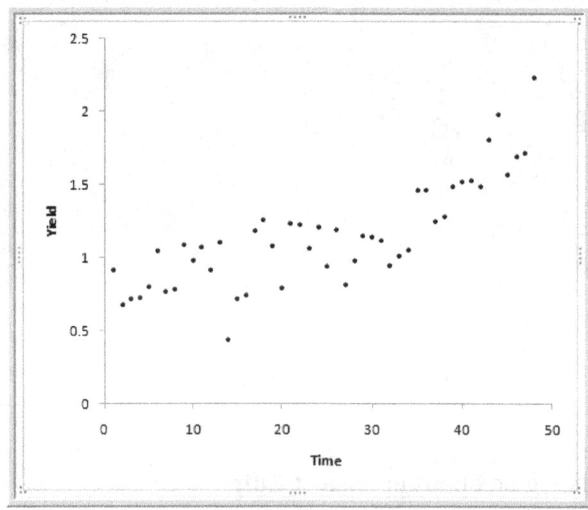

4.7.2 The Linear Equation Model

4.7.2a Estimating the Model

We start by estimating the following linear equation model:

$$YIELD_t = \beta_1 + \beta_2 TIME_t + e_t \tag{4.20}$$

In the **Regression** dialog box, the **Input Y Range** should be **D2:D49**, the **Input X Range** should be **E2:E49**. Select **New Worksheet Ply** and name it **Linear Equation Model**; and *do check the box* next to **Residual Plots**.

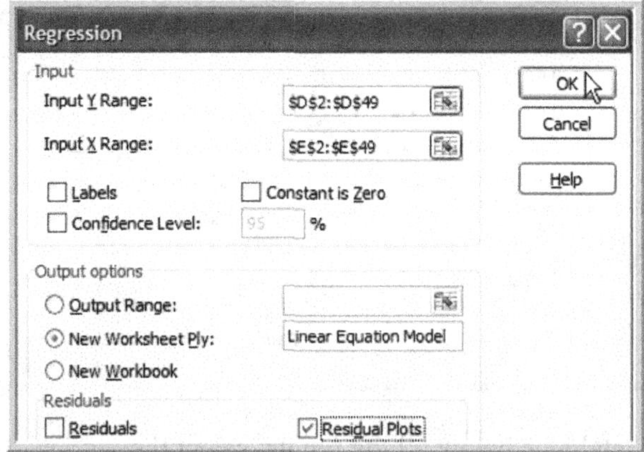

The results are (only part of the residual output section is shown below; the residual plot is not shown at all):

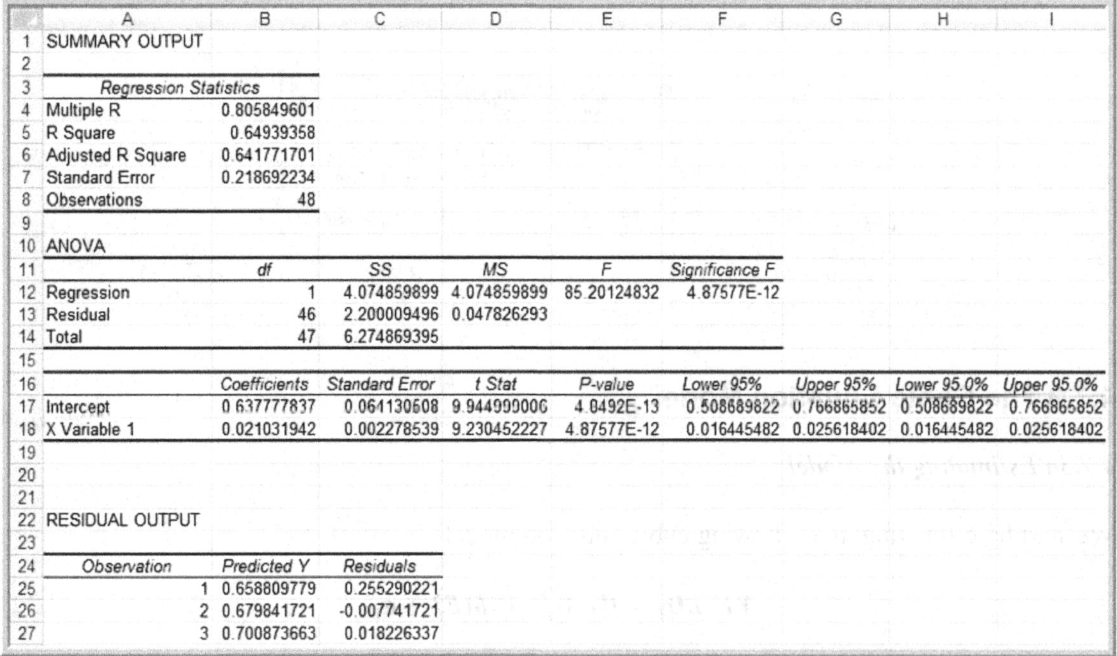

	A	B	C	D	E	F	G	H	I
1	SUMMARY OUTPUT								
2									
3	*Regression Statistics*								
4	Multiple R	0.805849601							
5	R Square	0.64939358							
6	Adjusted R Square	0.641771701							
7	Standard Error	0.218692234							
8	Observations	48							
9									
10	ANOVA								
11		*df*	*SS*	*MS*	*F*	*Significance F*			
12	Regression	1	4.074859899	4.074859899	85.20124832	4.87577E-12			
13	Residual	46	2.200009496	0.047826293					
14	Total	47	6.274869395						
15									
16		*Coefficients*	*Standard Error*	*t Stat*	*P-value*	*Lower 95%*	*Upper 95%*	*Lower 95.0%*	*Upper 95.0%*
17	Intercept	0.637777837	0.064130608	9.944990006	4.0492E-13	0.508689822	0.766865852	0.508689822	0.766865852
18	X Variable 1	0.021031942	0.002278539	9.230452227	4.87577E-12	0.016445482	0.025618402	0.016445482	0.025618402
19									
20									
21									
22	RESIDUAL OUTPUT								
23									
24	*Observation*	*Predicted Y*	*Residuals*						
25	1	0.658809779	0.255290221						
26	2	0.679841721	-0.007741721						
27	3	0.700873663	0.018226337						

The estimated linear equation model is (see also p. 150 of *Principles of Econometrics, 4e*):

$$\begin{array}{lll} \widehat{YIELD}_t = 0.638 + 0.021TIME_t \\ (se) \quad\quad (0.064) \quad (0.002) \end{array} \tag{4.21}$$

4.7.2b Residuals Plot

After editing the chart as we did in Section 2.1 or Section 2.3.4, the result is (see also Figure 4.12 on p. 150 of *Principles of Econometrics, 4e*):

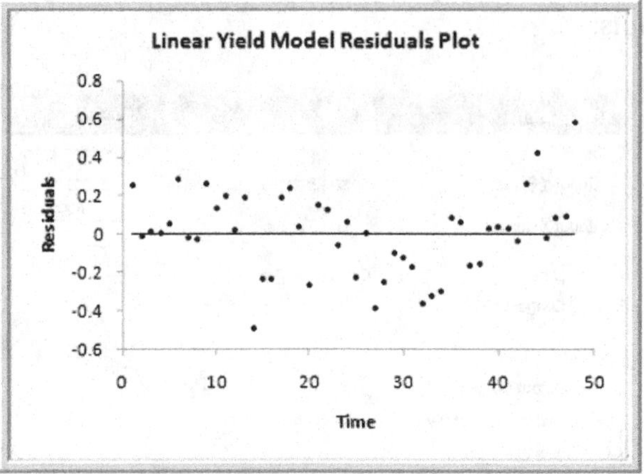

Note: to draw the horizontal axis below all the points, select the vertical axis on your chart, right-click, and select **Format Axis**. In the **Format Axis** dialog box, under the **Axis options** panel, select the **Horizontal axis crosses** at the **Axis value -6.0**. To draw an horizontal line at level 0 of the residuals values, select the plot of residuals on your chart, right-click and select **Add Trendline**. Choose the **Linear** option, and **Close**.

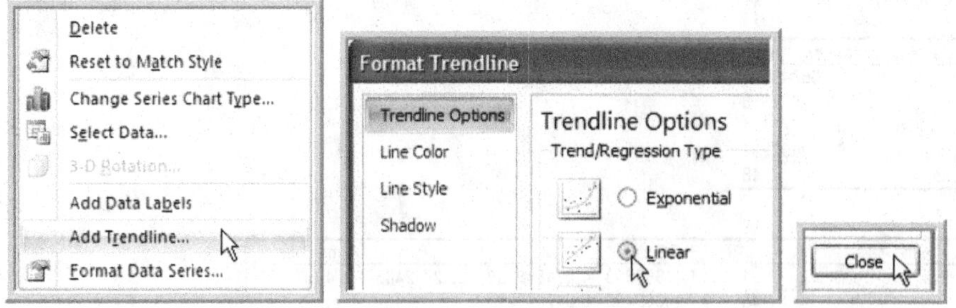

4.7.3 The Cubic Equation Model

4.7.3a Estimating the Model

We start by estimating the following cubic equation model:

$$YIELD_t = \beta_1 + \beta_2 TIME_t^3 + e_t \tag{4.22}$$

Let $TIMECUBE_t = TIME_t^3/1{,}000{,}000$: our explanatory variable is redefined as our original explanatory variable, cubed; *and* it is also rescaled before the equation above is estimated.

Go back to your **wa-wheat data** worksheet. In **F1**, enter the column label **time³**. In cell **F2**, enter the formula **=(E2^3)/1000000**; copy it to cells **F3:F49**. Here is how your table should look (only the first five values are shown below):

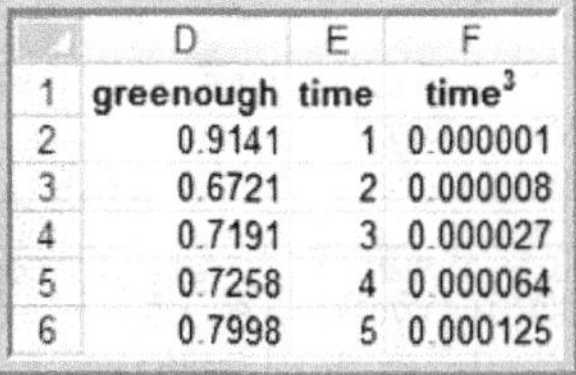

	D	E	F
1	greenough	time	time³
2	0.9141	1	0.000001
3	0.6721	2	0.000008
4	0.7191	3	0.000027
5	0.7258	4	0.000064
6	0.7998	5	0.000125

We want to re-estimate our wheat yield model using our original y values and our re-defined and re-scaled x values.

In the **Regression** dialog box, the **Input Y Range** should be **D2:D49**, the **Input X Range** should be **F2:F49**. Select **New Worksheet Ply** and name it **Cubic Equation Model**; and do check the box next to **Residuals Plots**.

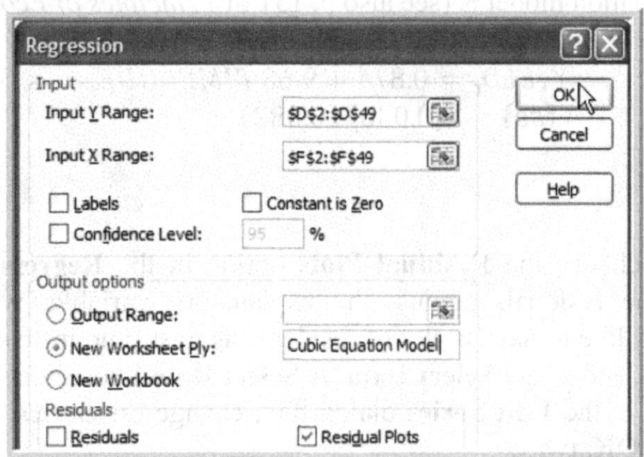

The results are (only part of the residual output section is shown below):

	A	B	C	D	E	F	G	H	I
1	SUMMARY OUTPUT								
2									
3	*Regression Statistics*								
4	Multiple R	0.866495734							
5	R Square	0.750814858							
6	Adjusted R Square	0.745397789							
7	Standard Error	0.184367557							
8	Observations	48							
9									
10	ANOVA								
11		*df*	*SS*	*MS*	*F*	*Significance F*			
12	Regression	1	4.711265172	4.711265172	138.6016965	1.76803E-15			
13	Residual	46	1.563604223	0.033991396					
14	Total	47	6.274869395						
15									
16		*Coefficients*	*Standard Error*	*t Stat*	*P-value*	*Lower 95%*	*Upper 95%*	*Lower 95.0%*	*Upper 95.0%*
17	Intercept	0.874116582	0.035630668	24.53270271	4.60223E-28	0.802395769	0.945837396	0.802395769	0.945837396
18	X Variable 1	9.68151584	0.822354527	11.77292217	1.76803E-15	8.026202058	11.33682962	8.026202058	11.33682962
19									
20									
21									
22	RESIDUAL OUTPUT								
23									
24	*Observation*	*Predicted Y*	*Residuals*						
25	1	0.874126264	0.039973736						
26	2	0.874194034	-0.202094034						
27	3	0.874377983	-0.155277983						

The estimated cubic equation model is (see also p. 151 of *Principles of Econometrics, 4e*):

$$\begin{aligned} \widehat{YIELD}_t &= 0.874 + 9.68\,TIMECUBE_t \\ (se) \quad & \quad (0.036)\ (0.082) \end{aligned} \tag{4.23}$$

4.7.3b Residuals Plot

Notice that when you choose the **Residual Plots** option in the **Regression** dialog box, Excel generates a plot of the residuals against the explanatory variable, which, in this case, is $TIMECUBE$. We would like to have a plot of residuals against time instead. Select the data point in your chart, right click and select **Select Data**. A **Select Data** Source dialog box pops up. Select **Series1** and then **Edit**. In the **Edit Series** dialog box, change the **Series X values** references to **E2:E49**. Finally, select **OK**, twice.

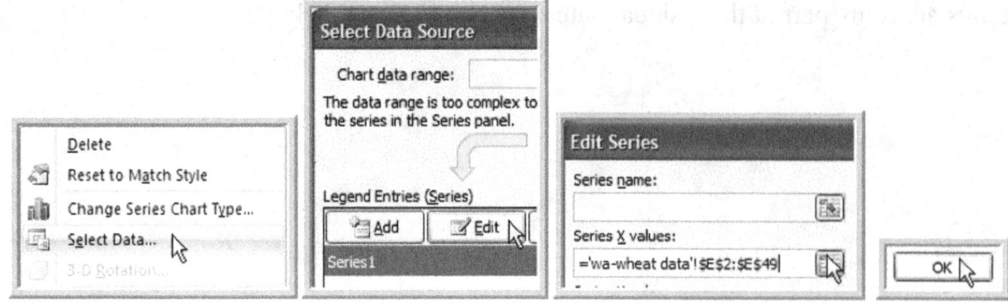

After editing the chart as we did in Section 2.1 or Section 2.3.4, the result is (see also Figure 4.13 on p. 151 of *Principles of Econometrics, 4e*):

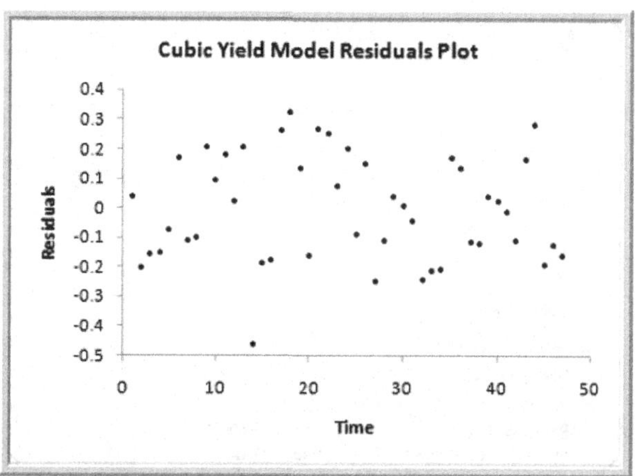

4.8 LOG-LINEAR MODELS

4.8.1 A Growth Model

We would like to estimate the following growth model:

$$ln(YIELD_t) = \beta_1 + \beta_2 TIME_t + e_t \tag{4.24}$$

where $y_t^* = ln(YIELD_t)$; i.e our dependent variable is redefined as the natural logarithm of our original dependent variable.

In your **wa-wheat data** worksheet, move your charts to the right a little bit if you would like. In cell **G1**, enter the column label **ln(greenough)**; resize the width of your column so it fits the new label. In cell **G2**, enter the formula **=ln(D2)**; copy it to cells **G3:G49**. Here is how your table should look (only the first five values are shown below):

	D	E	F	G
1	greenough	time	time³	ln(greenough)
2	0.9141	1	1E-06	-0.089815304
3	0.6721	2	8E-06	-0.39734814
4	0.7191	3	3E-05	-0.329754849
5	0.7258	4	6E-05	-0.320480784
6	0.7998	5	1E-04	-0.223393583

We want to re-estimate our wheat yield model using our original x values and our re-defined y values.

In the **Regression** dialog box, the **Input Y Range** should be **G2:G49**, the **Input X Range** should be **E2:E49**. Select **New Worksheet Ply** and name it **Growth Model**.

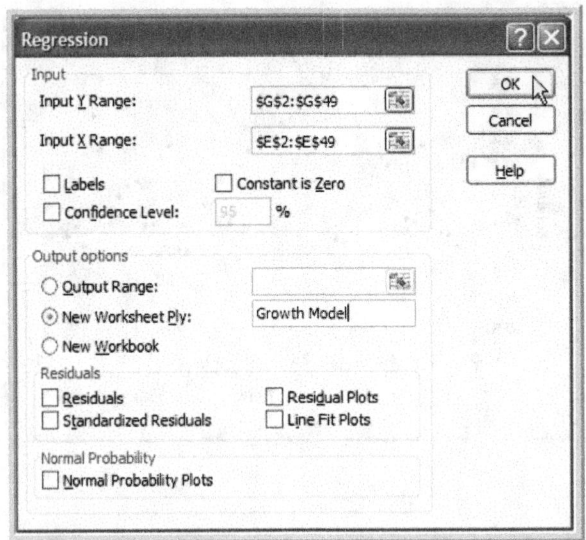

The result is:

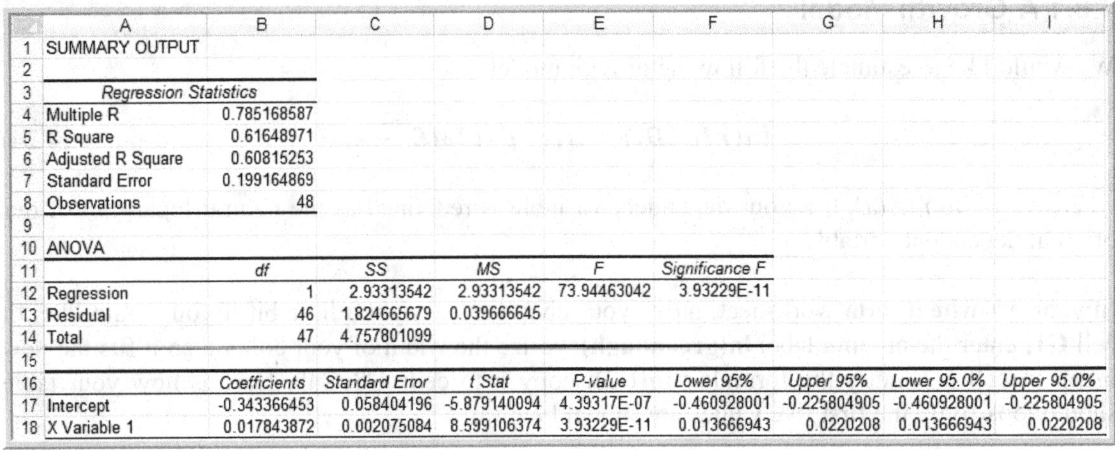

	A	B	C	D	E	F	G	H	I
1	SUMMARY OUTPUT								
2									
3	*Regression Statistics*								
4	Multiple R	0.785168587							
5	R Square	0.61648971							
6	Adjusted R Square	0.60815253							
7	Standard Error	0.199164869							
8	Observations	48							
9									
10	ANOVA								
11		*df*	*SS*	*MS*	*F*	*Significance F*			
12	Regression	1	2.93313542	2.93313542	73.94463042	3.93229E-11			
13	Residual	46	1.824665679	0.039666645					
14	Total	47	4.757801099						
15									
16		*Coefficients*	*Standard Error*	*t Stat*	*P-value*	*Lower 95%*	*Upper 95%*	*Lower 95.0%*	*Upper 95.0%*
17	Intercept	-0.343366453	0.058404196	-5.879140094	4.39317E-07	-0.460928001	-0.225804905	-0.460928001	-0.225804905
18	X Variable 1	0.017843872	0.002075084	8.599106374	3.93229E-11	0.013666943	0.0220208	0.013666943	0.0220208

The estimated growth model is (see also p. 153 of *Principles of Econometrics, 4e*):

$$\begin{aligned} ln(\widehat{YIELD_t}) &= -0.3434 + 0.0178\, TIME_t \\ (se) \quad & \quad (0.0584) \quad (0.0021) \end{aligned} \qquad (4.25)$$

4.8.2 A Wage Equation

Open the Excel file ***cps4_small***. Excel opens the data set in Sheet 1 of a new Excel file. Since we would like to save all our work from Chapter 4 in one file, create a new worksheet in your **POE Chapter 4** Excel file, name it **cps4_small data**, and in it, copy the data set you just opened.

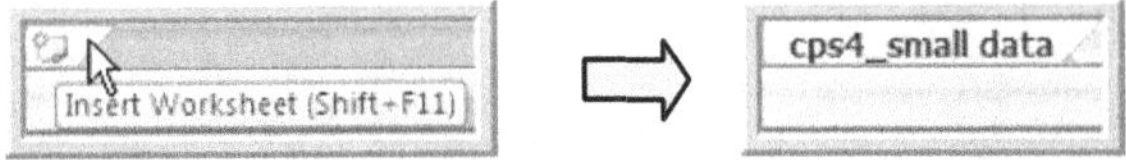

This data set gives information on hourly wages, years of education and other variables. Based on this data, we would like to estimate the following wage equation:

$$\boldsymbol{ln(WAGE_i) = \beta_1 + \beta_2 EDUC_i + e_i} \tag{4.26}$$

where $y_i^* = ln(WAGE_i)$; i.e our dependent variable is defined as the natural logarithm of the variable $WAGE$.

In cell **M1** of the **cps_small data** worksheet, enter the column label **ln(wage)**. In cell **M2**, enter the formula **=ln(A2)**; copy it to cells **M3:M1001**. Here is how your table should look (only the first five values are shown below):

	A	B	C	D	E	F	G	H	I	J	K	L	M
1	**wage**	**educ**	**exper**	**hrswk**	**married**	**female**	**metro**	**midwest**	**south**	**west**	**black**	**asian**	**ln(wage)**
2	18.7	16	39	37	1	1	1	0	1	0	0	0	2.92852352
3	11.5	12	16	62	0	0	0	1	0	0	0	0	2.44234704
4	15.04	16	13	40	1	0	1	0	0	1	1	0	2.71071332
5	25.95	14	11	40	0	1	1	0	1	0	1	0	3.25617161
6	24.03	12	51	40	1	0	1	0	0	0	0	0	3.17930305

We want to estimate our wage equation using our original x values and our re-defined y values.

In the **Regression** dialog box, the **Input Y Range** should be **M2:M1001**, the **Input X Range** should be **B2:B1001**. Select **New Worksheet Ply** and name it **Wage Equation**.

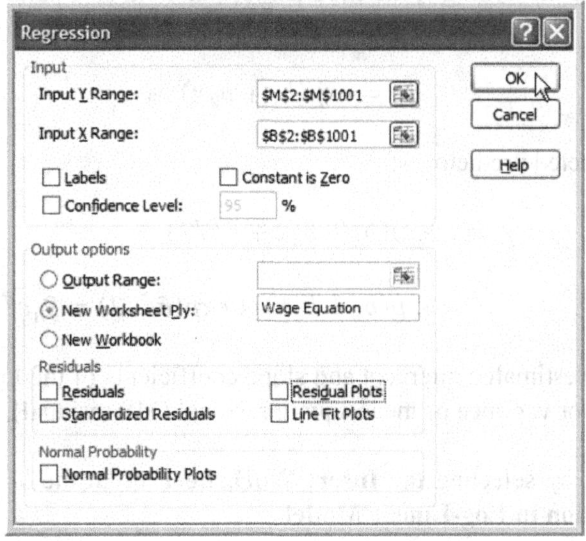

The result is:

	A	B	C	D	E	F	G	H	I
1	SUMMARY OUTPUT								
2									
3	*Regression Statistics*								
4	Multiple R	0.422142751							
5	R Square	0.178204502							
6	Adjusted R Square	0.17738106							
7	Standard Error	0.526611364							
8	Observations	1000							
9									
10	ANOVA								
11		*df*	*SS*	*MS*	*F*	*Significance F*			
12	Regression	1	60.01584269	60.01584269	216.4140511	1.74559E-44			
13	Residual	998	276.7648898	0.277319529					
14	Total	999	336.7807325						
15									
16		*Coefficients*	*Standard Error*	*t Stat*	*P-value*	*Lower 95%*	*Upper 95%*	*Lower 95.0%*	*Upper 95.0%*
17	Intercept	1.609444466	0.086422944	18.622884	1.14645E-66	1.439852937	1.779035995	1.439852937	1.779035995
18	X Variable 1	0.090408247	0.006145615	14.71101802	1.74559E-44	0.078348438	0.102468056	0.078348438	0.102468056

The estimated wage equation is (see also p. 153 of *Principles of Econometrics, 4e*):

$$\begin{aligned} \widehat{ln(WAGE_i)} &= 1.6094 + 0.0904\ EDUC_i \\ (se) \quad & \quad (0.0864) \quad (0.0061) \end{aligned} \tag{4.27}$$

4.8.3 Prediction

For the natural logarithm the antilog is the exponential function, so a natural choice for prediction in a log-linear model is:

$$\hat{y}_n = exp(b_1 + b_2 x) \tag{4.28}$$

An alternative and corrected predictor is:

$$\begin{aligned} \hat{y}_c &= exp(b_1 + b_2 x + \hat{\sigma}^2/2) \\ &= exp(b_1 + b_2 x) \times exp(\hat{\sigma}^2/2) = \hat{y}_n e^{\hat{\sigma}^2/2}, \end{aligned} \tag{4.29}$$

where b_1 and b_2 are the estimated intercept and slope coefficients of the log-linear model, and $\hat{\sigma}^2$ is the estimate of the error variance or mean square residual (MS residual).

Insert a new worksheet by selecting the **Insert Worksheet** tab at the lower left corner of your screen. Name it **Prediction in Log-Linear Model**.

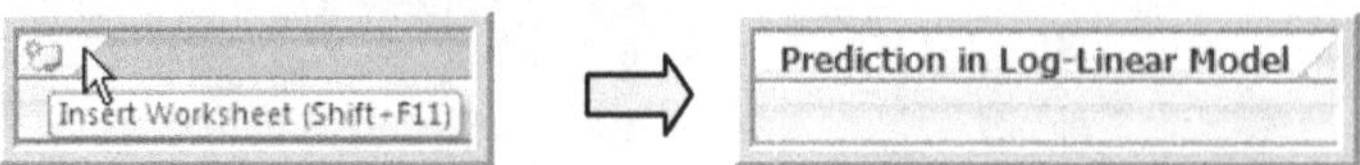

Create the following template to make prediction (in the last column below you will find the numbers of the equations used in the template):

	A	B	C	
1	**Data Input**	$x_0 =$	12	
2		$b_1 =$	='Wage Equation'!B17	
3		$b_2 =$	='Wage Equation'!B18	
4		MS residual =	='Wage Equation'!D13	
5				
6	**Computed Values**	natural predicted y_0=	=EXP(C2+C3*C1)	*(4.28)*
7		corrected predicted y_0=	=C6*EXP(C4/2)	*(4.29)*

Here are the results you should get (see also p. 154 of *Principles of Econometrics, 4e*):

	A	B	C
1	**Data Input**	$x_0 =$	12
2		$b_1 =$	1.609444
3		$b_2 =$	0.090408
4		MS residual =	0.27732
5			
6	**Computed Values**	natural predicted $y_0 =$	14.7958
7		corrected predicted $y_0 =$	16.99643

Next, we want to show graphically how the correction affects our prediction. Go to your **cps4_small data** worksheet. Here are the formulas and labels you should enter (in the last row of each of the tables below, you will find the numbers of the equations used):

	N	O
1	**educ**	**Yhatn**
2	0	=EXP('Wage Equation'!$B$17 + 'Wage Equation'!$B$18 * N2)
3	1	*(4.28)*

	P
1	**Yhatc**
2	=O2*EXP('Wage Equation'!$D$13/2)
3	*(4.29)*

Select cells **N2:N3,** move your cursor to the lower right corner of your selection until it turns into a skinny cross as shown below, left-click, hold it and drag it down to cell **N23**.

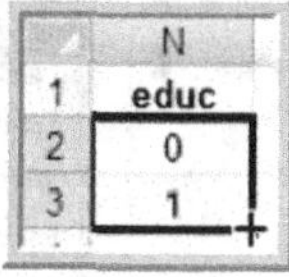

	N
1	**educ**
2	0
3	1

Select **O2:P2** and copy their content to **O3:P23**. Here is how your table should look (only the first five values are shown below):

	N	O	P
1	educ	yhatn	yhatc
2	0	5.000032769	24.40129449
3	1	5.473141211	16.99642785
4	2	5.99101568	24.40129449
5	3	6.557891984	20.36503968
6	4	7.17840673	16.99642785

Select the **Insert** tab located next to the **Home** tab. Select **N1:P23**. In the **Charts** group of commands select **Scatter**, and then **Scatter with only Markers**.

The result is:

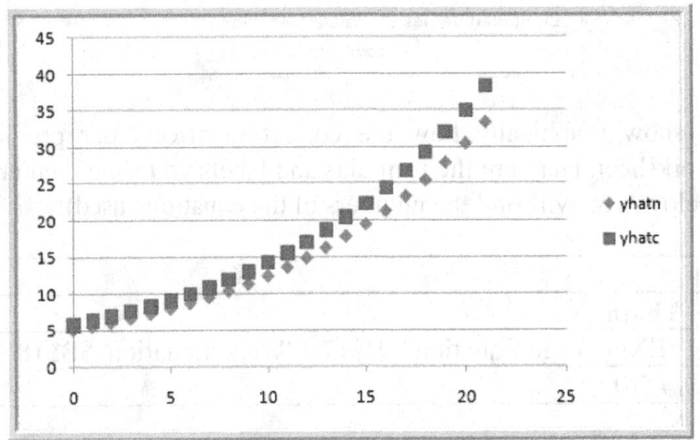

Next, we would like to plot the actual values on the same chart. Select the points on your plot, right-click and select **Select Data**. A **Select Data Source** dialog box pops up. Select **Add**. In the **Edit Series** dialog box, specify **earnings per hour** for the **Series name**, select **B2:B1001** for the **Series X values** and **A2:A1001** for the **Series Y values**—all from the **cps4_small data** worksheet. Select **OK**, and then **OK** again in the **Select Data Source** dialog box.

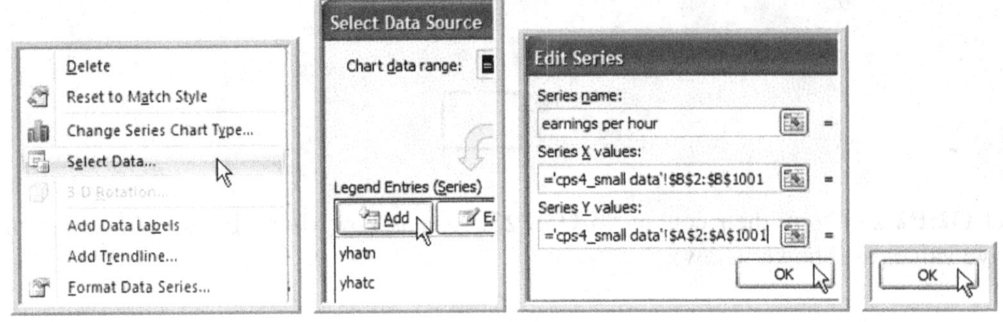

After editing your chart like you did in Sections 2.1.2a-2.1.2c, the result is (see also Figure 4.14 p. 155 of *Principles of Econometrics, 4e*):

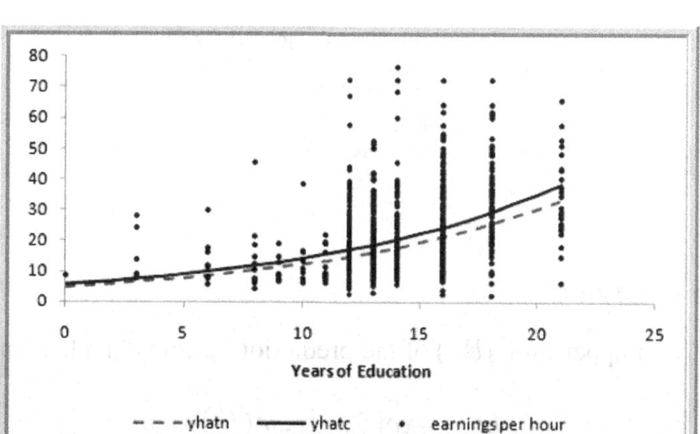

4.8.4 A Generalized R^2 Measure

A generalized R^2 measure can be computed as the square of the sample correlation coefficient between y and $\hat{y}_c$, where $\hat{y}_c$ are the *corrected* predicted y values:

$$R^2 = r^2_{y\hat{y}_c} \tag{4.30}$$

Make sure you are in your **cps4_small data** worksheet. We will compute the corrected predicted y values in column **Q**, and next to it, we will compute the generalized R^2.

Here are the formulas and labels you should enter (in the last row of each of the tables below, you will find the numbers of the equations used):

	Q
1	**corrected predicted y**
2	=EXP('Wage Equation'!$B$17 + 'Wage Equation'!$B$18 * B2) *EXP('Wage Equation'!$D$13/2)
3	*(4.29)*

Copy the content of cell **Q2** to cell **Q3:N1001.**

	R
1	**generalized R²**
2	=(CORREL(A2:A1001,Q2:Q1001))^2
3	*(4.30)*

The result is (see also p. 155 of *Principles of Econometrics, 4e*):

	Q	R
1	**corrected predicted y**	**generalized R^2**
2	24.40129449	0.185930705
3	16.99642785	
4	24.40129449	
5	20.36503968	
6	16.99642785	

4.8.5 Prediction Intervals

The lower limit (LL) and upper limit (UL) of the prediction interval in a log-linear model are:

$$LL = exp(\hat{y}_n - t_c se(f)) \tag{4.31}$$

$$UL = exp(\hat{y}_n + t_c se(f)) \tag{4.32}$$

Insert a new worksheet by selecting the **Insert Worksheet** tab at the lower left corner of your screen. Name it **PI in Log-Linear Model.**

Copy the template from the **Prediction Interval** worksheet (if you cannot see it, it is because it is hidden further to the left of your visible worksheets) to the **PI in Log-Linear Model** worksheet.

You just need to make a few modifications to it: (1) get your regression results from the **Wage Equation** worksheet instead of the **Food Regression** worksheet, (2) change x_0 to **12**, (3) compute $\bar{x}$ from the **cps4_small data** worksheet instead of the **food data** worksheet, and (4) take the anti-logs of the interval limits using the **EXP** function. Those modifications are outlined in the table below.

	A	B	C	
1	**Data Input**	Sample Size =	='**Wage Equation**'!B8	
2		Confidence Level =		*percentage* *0 decimal place*
3		x_0 =	**12**	
4		b_1 =	='**Wage Equation**'!B17	
5		b_2 =	='**Wage Equation**'!B18	
6		$se(b_2)$ =	='**Wage Equation**'!C18	
7		MS residual =	='**Wage Equation**'!D13	
9	**Computed Values**	α =	=1-C2	
10		df or m =	=C1-2	
11		t_c =	=TINV(C9,C10)	
12		predicted y_0=	=C4+C5*C3	*(4.2)*
13		*x*-bar =	=AVERAGE('**cps4_small data**'!**B2:B1001**)	

	A	B	C	
14		*se(f)* =	=SQRT(C7+C7/C1+((C3-C13)^2)*C6)	*(4.3)*
15				
16	**Prediction Interval**	Lower Limit =	=**EXP**(C12-C11*C14)	*(4.31)*
17		Upper Limit =	=**EXP**(C12+C11*C14)	*(4.32)*

Here are the results you should get (see also p. 155 of *Principles of Econometrics, 4e*):

	A	B	C
1	**Data Input**	Sample Size =	1000
2		Confidence Level =	95%
3		x_0 =	12
4		b_1 =	1.609444
5		b_2 =	0.090408
6		$se(b_2)$ =	0.006146
7		MS residual =	0.27732

	A	B	C
9	**Computed Values**	α =	5%
10		df or m =	998
11		t_c =	1.962344
12		predicted y_0 =	2.694343
13		*x*-bar =	13.85
14		*se(f)* =	0.546471
15			
16	**Prediction Interval**	Lower Limit =	5.063106
17		Upper Limit =	43.23744

Note that the results above and the ones from your textbook might differ slightly due to rounding number differences.

Next, we want to show graphically how our prediction interval changes over the range of years of education. Go to your **cps4_small data** worksheet. Here are the formulas and labels you should enter (in the last row of each of the tables below, you will find the numbers of the equations used in the template):

	S
1	**lb_wage**
2	=O2* EXP(-'PI in Log-Linear Model'!$C$11*'PI in Log-Linear Model'!$C$14)
3	*(4.31)*

	T
1	**ub_wage**
2	=O2* EXP('PI in Log-Linear Model'!$C$11*'PI in Log-Linear Model'!$C$14)
3	*(4.32)*

Select **S2:T2** and copy their content to **S3:T23**. Here is how your table should look (only the first five values are shown below):

	S	T
1	**lb_wage**	**ub_wage**
2	1.711005	14.61148
3	1.872902	15.99404
4	2.050118	17.50741
5	2.244103	19.16398
6	2.456442	20.9773

Select the whole plot area you completed in Section 4.8.3, which compares the natural and corrected predictors of wage (replica of Figure 4.14 p. 155 of *Principles of Econometrics, 4e*). Select **Copy** and then **Paste**. You should have two identical charts. Below we will work with one of them. On that chart, we want to remove the **yhatc** series and add the **lb_wage** and **ub_wage** series instead.

Select the points on the chart, right-click and select **Select Data**. A **Select Data Source** dialog box pops up. Select the **yhatc** series, and then **Remove**. Then select **Add**. In the **Edit Series** dialog box, specify **lb_wage** for the **Series name**, select **N2:N23** for the **Series X values** and **S2:S23** for the **Series Y values**—all from the **cps4_small data** worksheet. Select **OK**.

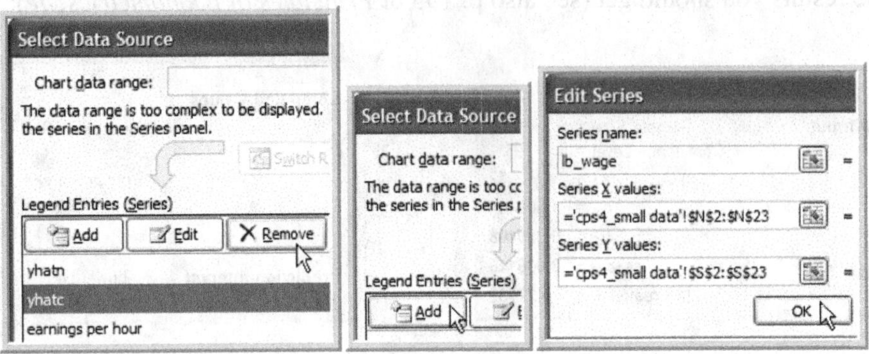

Select **Add**. In the **Edit Series** dialog box, specify **ub_wage** for the **Series name,** select **N2:N23** for the **Series X values** and **T2:T23** for the **Series Y values**—all from the **cps4_small data** worksheet. Select **OK**, and then **OK** again in the **Select Data Source** dialog box.

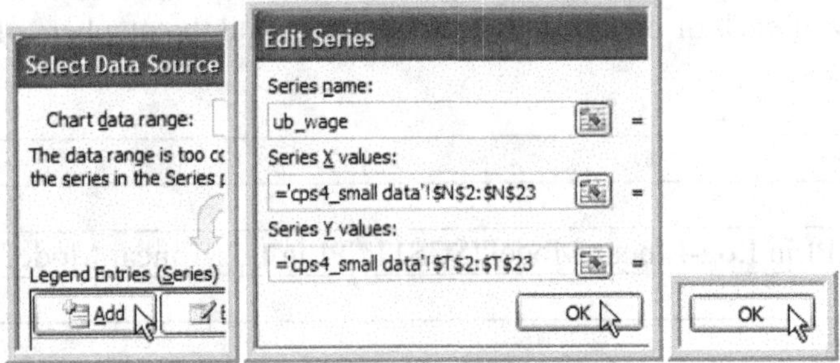

After editing your chart like you did in Sections 2.1.2a-2.1.2c, the result is (see also Figure 4.15 p. 156 of *Principles of Econometrics, 4e*):

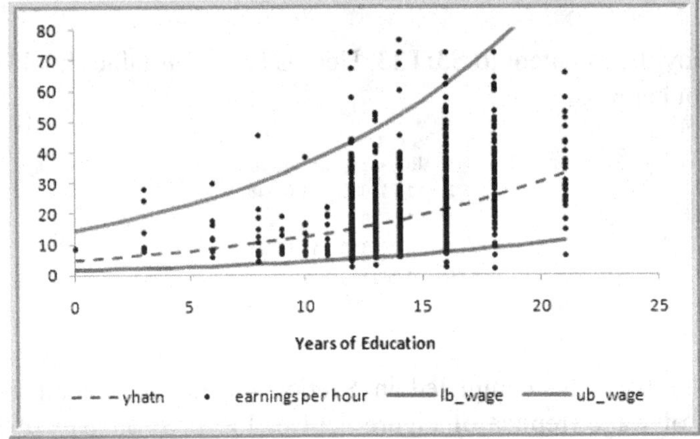

4.9 A LOG-LOG MODEL: POULTRY DEMAND EQUATION

Open the Excel file ***newbroiler***. Excel opens the data set in Sheet 1 of a new Excel file. Since we would like to save all our work from Chapter 2 in one file, create a new worksheet in your **POE Chapter 4** Excel file, name it **newbroiler data**, and in it, copy the data set you just opened.

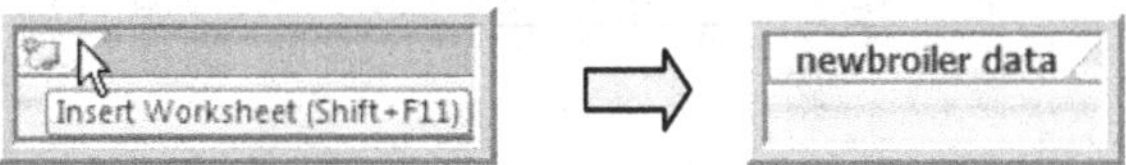

4.9.1 Estimating the Model

We estimate the following log-log model for poultry demand:

$$\boldsymbol{ln(Q) = \beta_1 + \beta_2 ln(P) + e} \tag{4.33}$$

where **Q** is the U.S. per capita consumption of chicken, in pounds and **P** is the real price of chicken, for annual observations over the period 1950 – 2001.

In cells **K1:L2** of your **newbroiler data** worksheet, enter the following column labels and formulas.

	K	L
1	**ln(q)**	**ln(p)**
2	= ln(B2)	= ln(D2)

Select **K2:L2** and copy their content to **K3: L53.** Here is how your table should look (only the first five values are shown below):

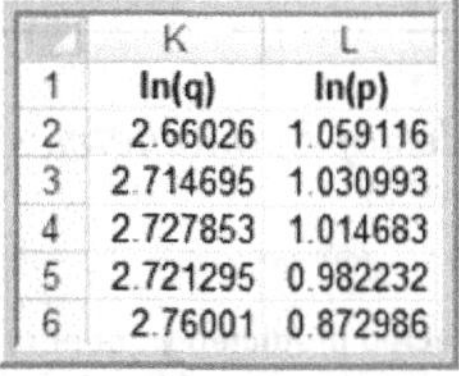

	K	L
1	ln(q)	ln(p)
2	2.66026	1.059116
3	2.714695	1.030993
4	2.727853	1.014683
5	2.721295	0.982232
6	2.76001	0.872986

In the **Regression** dialog box, the **Input Y Range** should be **K2:K53**, and the **Input X Range** should be **L2:L53**. Select **New Worksheet Ply** and name it **Log-Log Model**. Finally select **OK**.

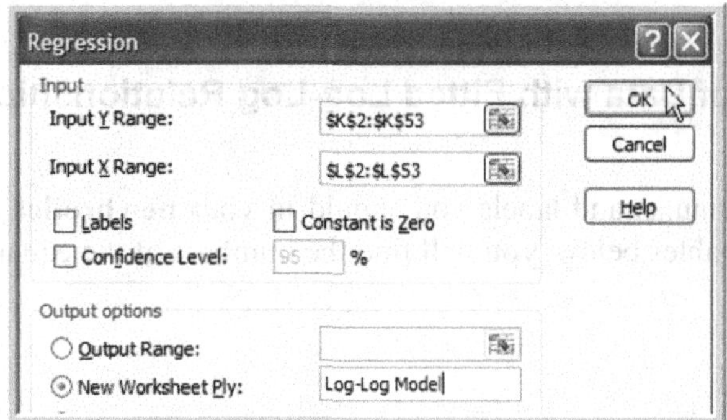

The result is (matching the one reported on p. 157 of *Principles of Econometrics, 4e*):

	A	B	C	D	E	F	G	H	I
1	SUMMARY OUTPUT								
2									
16		*Coefficients*	*Standard Error*	*t Stat*	*P-value*	*Lower 95%*	*Upper 95%*	*Lower 95.0%*	*Upper 95.0%*
17	Intercept	3.716943882	0.022359414	166.2361915	2.94446E-70	3.672033677	3.761854086	3.672033677	3.761854086
18	X Variable 1	-1.121358001	0.048756431	-22.99918135	2.99987E-28	-1.219288174	-1.023427829	-1.219288174	-1.023427829

4.9.2 A Generalized R^2 Measure

Make sure you are in your **newbroiler data** worksheet. We will compute the corrected predicted y values in column **M**, and next to it, we will compute the generalized R^2.

Here are the formulas and labels you should enter (in the last row of each of the tables below, you will find the numbers of the equations used):

	M
1	**corrected predicted y**
2	=EXP('Log-Log Model'!$B$17 + 'Log-Log Model'!$B$18 *L2) *EXP('Log-Log Model'!$D$13/2)
3	*(4.29)*

Copy the content of cell **M2** to cell **M3:M53.**

	N
1	**generalized R²**
2	=(CORREL(B2:B53,M2:M53))^2
3	*(4.30)*

The result is (see also p. 157 of *Principles of Econometrics, 4e*):

	M	N
1	**corrected predicted y**	**generalized R²**
2	12.63229707	0.881775776
3	13.03700687	
4	13.27763969	
5	13.76970711	
6	15.56421528	

4.9.3 Scatter Plot of Data with Fitted Log-Log Relationship

Enter the following formulas and labels you should in your **newbroiler data** worksheet (in the last row of each of the tables below, you will find the numbers of the equations used):

	O	P
1	P	**Yhatc**
2	0.9	=EXP('Log-Log Model'!$B$17 + 'Log-Log Model'!$B$18 * ln(O2)) * EXP('Log-Log Model'!$D$13/2)
3	1.0	*(4.29)*

Select cells **P2:P3,** move your cursor to the lower right corner of your selection until it turns into a skinny cross as shown below, left-click, hold it and drag it down to cell **P22**.

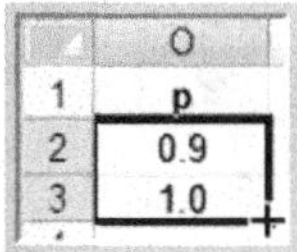

Select **P2** and copy its content to **P3:P22**. Here is how your table should look (only the first five values are shown below):

	O	P
1	p	yhatc
2	0.9	46.62103
3	1.0	41.42584
4	1.1	37.22676
5	1.2	33.76609
6	1.3	30.8674

Select the **Insert** tab located next to the **Home** tab. Select **O1:P22**. In the **Charts** group of commands select **Scatter**, and then **Scatter with only Markers.**

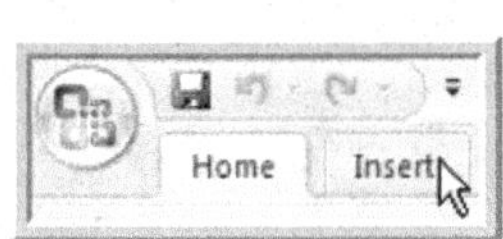

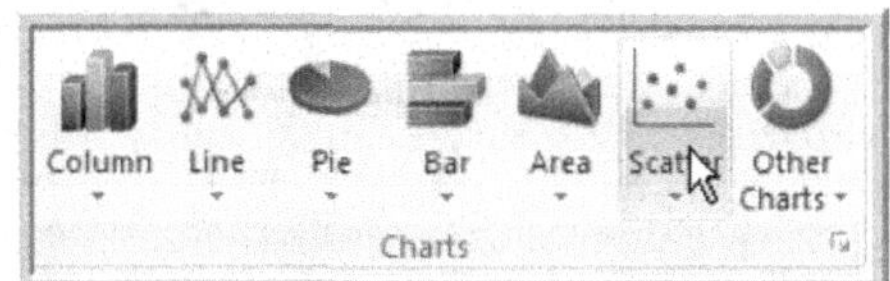

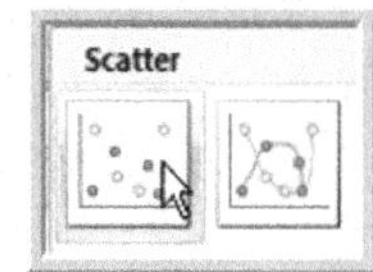

The result is:

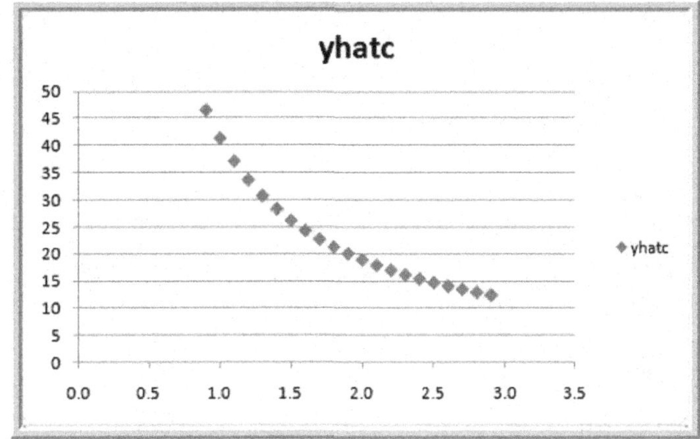

Next, we would like to plot the actual values on the same chart. Select the points on your plot, right-click and select **Select Data**. A **Select Data Source** dialog box pops up. Select **Add**. In the

Edit Series dialog box, specify **actual values** for the **Series name**, select **D2:D53** for the **Series X values** and **B2:B53** for the **Series Y values**—all from the **newbroiler data** worksheet. Select **OK**, and then **OK** again in the **Select Data Source** dialog box.

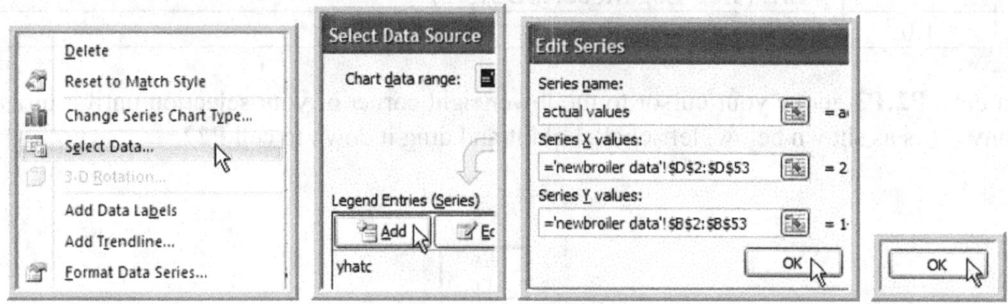

After editing your chart like you did in Sections 2.1.2a-2.1.2c, the result is (see also Figure 4.16 p. 157 of *Principles of Econometrics, 4e*):

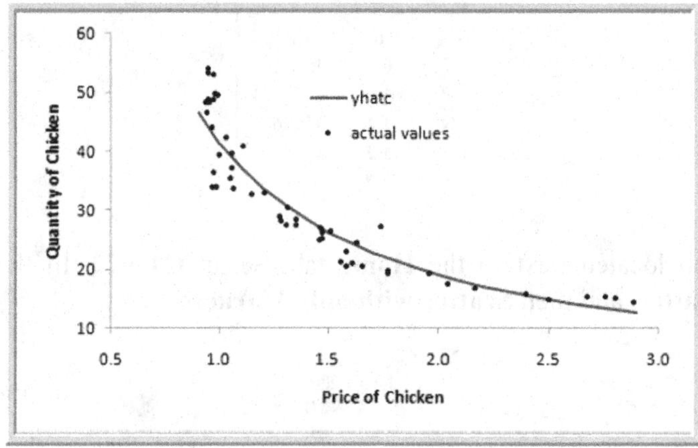

CHAPTER 5

The Multiple Linear Regression

CHAPTER OUTLINE

This chapter is a simple extension of the material covered in Chapters 2-4. Instead of only one explanatory variable in the simple linear regression model, two or more explanatory variables will be used in the multiple linear regression model.

5.1 LEAST SQUARES ESTIMATES USING THE HAMBURGER CHAIN DATA

Open the Excel file ***andy***. Save your file as **POE Chapter 5**. Rename Sheet 1 **data**.

We would like to estimate the following multiple linear regression model for Big Andy's Burger Barn hamburger chain:

$$SALES_i = \beta_1 + \beta_2 PRICE_i + \beta_3 ADVERT_i + e_i \tag{5.1}$$

where $SALES$ represents monthly sales revenue in a given city (in \$1000), $PRICE$ represents a price index in that city (in \$), and $ADVERT$ is monthly advertising expenditure in that city (in \$1000).

As we have done before, we will use the Excel **Regression** analysis tool. There are only two things to note.

- First, because we have more than one explanatory variable, we will include the labels of the variables in the input ranges we specify. Those labels will then be reported in the summary output Excel produces, and we will be able to distinguish the different estimated slope coefficients.
- Second, as long as the data on the explanatory variables are stored in adjacent columns, all we have to do is select the whole range of data and Excel will recognize each column of data as separate observations on separate explanatory variables.

In the **Regression** dialog box, the **Input Y Range** should be **A1:A76**, and the **Input X Range** should be **B1:C76**; <u>*do check the box*</u> next to **Labels**. Finally, select **New Worksheet Ply** and name it **Regression**.

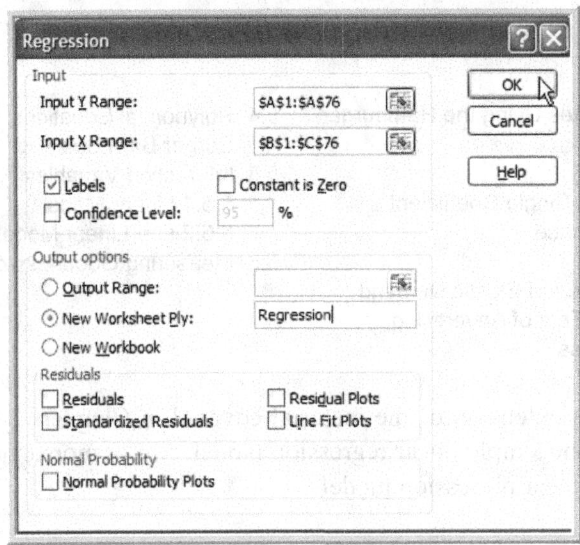

The result is (see also p. 175 in *Principles of Econometrics, 4e*):

	A	B	C	D	E	F	G	H	I
1	SUMMARY OUTPUT								
2									
3	*Regression Statistics*								
4	Multiple R	0.66952055							
5	R Square	0.448257766							
6	Adjusted R Square	0.432931593							
7	Standard Error	4.886124039							
8	Observations	75							
9									
10	ANOVA								
11		*df*	*SS*	*MS*	*F*	*Significance F*			
12	Regression	2	1396.538993	698.2694963	29.24785998	5.04086E-10			
13	Residual	72	1718.942985	23.87420813					
14	Total	74	3115.481978						
15									
16		*Coefficients*	*Standard Error*	*t Stat*	*P-value*	*Lower 95%*	*Upper 95%*	*Lower 95.0%*	*Upper 95.0%*
17	Intercept	118.9136131	6.351637595	18.72172512	2.21429E-29	106.2518552	131.5753711	106.2518552	131.5753711
18	PRICE	-7.907854804	1.095993037	-7.215241826	4.42399E-10	-10.09267696	-5.723032645	-10.09267696	-5.723032645
19	ADVERT	1.862583787	0.683195483	2.726282349	0.008038199	0.500658501	3.224509073	0.500658501	3.224509073

5.2 INTERVAL ESTIMATION

Recall from Chapter 3 that the interval estimator of β_k is defined as:

$$b_k \pm t_c se(b_k) \tag{5.2}$$

The *one* important thing to notice is that, in the case of the multiple linear regression model, the critical value t_c is from a *t*-distribution with $m = N - K$ degrees of freedoms, where K is the number of parameters in the multiple linear regression model.

To compute interval estimates, we could use the template we created in Chapter 3 and make sure we specify the degree of freedom correctly.

Instead, we use the interval estimates Excel has already generated in the regression summary output.

The results of interest to us, reported on pp. 182-183 of *Principles of Econometrics, 4e* are highlighted below:

	A	B	C	D	E	F	G
16		*Coefficients*	*Standard Error*	*t Stat*	*P-value*	*Lower 95%*	*Upper 95%*
17	Intercept	118.9136131	6.351637595	18.72172512	2.21429E-29	106.2518552	131.5753711
18	PRICE	-7.907854804	1.095993037	-7.215241826	4.42399E-10	-10.09267696	-5.723032645
19	ADVERT	1.862583787	0.683195483	2.726282349	0.008038199	0.500658501	3.224509073

Recall that to obtain interval estimates other than the 95% ones, all we have to do is to specify a different **Confidence Level** in the **Regression** dialog box (see Section 3.1.3c).

5.3 HYPOTHESIS TESTS FOR A SINGLE COEFFICIENT

Similarly to results from Chapter 3, we have the following: if the null hypothesis $H_0: \beta_k = c$ is true, then the test statistic $t = (b_k - c)/se(b_k)$ follows a *t*-distribution with $m = N - K$ degrees of freedom:

$$t = \frac{b_k - c}{se(b_k)} \sim t_{(m = N - K)} \tag{5.3}$$

Again, note that in the case of the multiple linear regression model, the *t*-distribution of interest has $m = N - K$ degrees of freedom, where K is the number of parameters in the multiple linear regression model.

5.3.1 Tests of Significance

Recall that when the null hypothesis of a test is that the parameter is zero, the test is called a test of significance. Results of two-tail test of significance are reported in the Excel summary output and highlighted below (see also pp. 185-186 of *Principles of Econometrics, 4e*):

	A	B	C	D	E	F	G
16		*Coefficients*	*Standard Error*	*t Stat*	*P-value*	*Lower 95%*	*Upper 95%*
17	Intercept	118.9136131	6.351637595	18.72172512	2.21429E-29	106.2518552	131.5753711
18	PRICE	-7.907854804	1.095993037	-7.215241826	4.42399E-10	-10.09267696	-5.723032645
19	ADVERT	1.862583787	0.683195483	2.726282349	0.008038199	0.500658501	3.224509073

Note: you could also have used the **Two-Tail Tests** template you created in Chapter 3.

5.3.2 One-Tail Tests

5.3.2a Left-Tail Test of Elastic Demand

Insert a new worksheet by selecting the **Insert Worksheet** tab at the lower left corner of your screen, next to the **data** tab. Name it **Left-Tail Tests**.

Open your **POE Chapter 3** Excel file and go to the **Left-Tail Tests** worksheet. Copy its content to the **Left-Tail Tests** worksheet you just created in your **POE Chapter 5** Excel file.

You will need to make just a few modifications to create the left-tail test template shown below. First, go back to each formula and delete the references to **POE Chapter 3** Excel file: **[POE Chapter 3.xlsx]**; this way the interval estimate will be computed based on the regression results of your current Excel file: **POE Chapter 5**. Next, insert a new row, underneath the first one, for **K**. Finally, modify the degrees of freedom formula. All needed changes are highlighted below:

	A	B	C
1	**Data Input**	N =	=**Regression!**B8
2		**K =**	**=Regression!B12+1**
3		b_k =	=**Regression!**B18
4		se(b_k) =	=**Regression!**C18
5		H_0: β_k =	
6		α =	
7			
8	**Computed Values**	df or m =	=C1-**C2**
9		t_c =	= -TINV(C6*2,C8)
10			
11	**Left-Tail Test**	t-statistic =	=(C3-C5)/C4
12		Conclusion:	=IF(C11<=C9,"Reject Ho","Do Not Reject Ho")
13		p-value =	=TDIST(ABS(C11),C8,1)
14		Conclusion:	=IF(C13<=C6,"Reject Ho","Do Not Reject Ho")

Let $\alpha = 0.05$; $H_0: \beta_3 \geq 0$ and $H_1: \beta_3 < 0$. The result is (p. 187 of *Principles of Econometrics, 4e*):

	A	B	C
1	**Data Input**	N =	75
2		K =	3
3		b_k =	-7.9078548
4		$se(b_k)$ =	1.095993
5		H_0: β_k =	0
6		α =	0.05
7			
8	**Computed Values**	df or m =	72
9		t_c =	-1.6662937
10			
11	**Left-Tail Test**	t-statistic =	-7.2152418
12		Conclusion:	Reject Ho
13		p-value =	2.212E-10
14		Conclusion:	Reject Ho

5.3.2b Right-Tail Test of Advertising Effectiveness

Insert a new worksheet by selecting the **Insert Worksheet** tab at the lower left corner of your screen, next to the **Left-Tail Tests** tab. Name it **Right-Tail Tests.**

In your **POE Chapter 3** Excel file, go to the **Right-Tail Tests** worksheet. Copy its content to the **Right-Tail Tests** worksheet you just created in your **POE Chapter 5** Excel file.

You will need to make just a few modifications to create the right-tail test template shown below. First, go back to each formula and delete the references to **POE Chapter 3** Excel file: **[POE Chapter 3.xlsx]**; this way the interval estimate will be computed based on the regression results of your current Excel file: **POE Chapter 5**. Next, change the reference to b_k and $se(b_k)$ to the *ADVERT* coefficient estimates instead of the *PRICE* coefficient estimates. Also, insert a new row, underneath the first one, for **K**. Finally, modify the degrees of freedom formula. All needed changes are highlighted below:

	A	B	C
1	**Data Input**	N =	=**Regression!B8**
2		**K =**	**=Regression!B12+1**
3		b_k =	**=Regression!B19**
4		$se(b_k)$ =	**=Regression!C19**
5		H_0: β_k =	
6		α =	
8	**Computed Values**	df or m =	=C1-**C2**
9		t_c =	=TINV(C6*2,C8)
11	**Right-Tail Test**	t-statistic =	=(C3-C5)/C4
12		Conclusion:	=IF(C11>=C9,"Reject Ho","Do Not Reject Ho")
13		p-value =	=TDIST(ABS(C11),C8,1)
14		Conclusion:	=IF(C13<=C6,"Reject Ho","Do Not Reject Ho")

Let $\alpha = 0.05$; $H_0\colon \beta_3 \leq 1$ and $H_1\colon \beta_3 > 1$. The result is (see also p. 188 of *Principles of Econometrics, 4e*):

	A	B	C	D
1	**Data Input**	N =	75	
2		K =	3	
3		b_k =	1.862583787	
4		se(b_k) =	0.683195483	
5		H_0: β_k =	1	
6		α =	0.05	
7				
8	**Computed Values**	df or m =	72	
9		t_c =	1.666293697	
10				
11	**Right-Tail Test**	t-statistic =	1.262572438	
12		Conclusion:	Do Not Reject Ho	
13		p-value =	0.105408444	
14		Conclusion:	Do Not Reject Ho	

5.4 POLYNOMIAL EQUATIONS: EXTENDING THE MODEL FOR BURGER BARN SALES

We estimate the following extended model for Big Andy's Burger Barn hamburger chain.

$$SALES_i = \beta_1 + \beta_2 PRICE_i + \beta_3 ADVERT_i + \beta_4 ADVERT_i^2 + e_i \tag{5.4}$$

Go back to your **data** worksheet. In **D1**, enter the column label **ADVERT^2**. In cell **D2**, enter the formula **=C2^2**; copy it to cells **D3:D76**. Here is how your table should look (only the first five values are shown below):

	A	B	C	D
1	SALES	PRICE	ADVERT	ADVERT^2
2	73.2	5.69	1.3	1.69
3	71.8	6.49	2.9	8.41
4	62.4	5.63	0.8	0.64
5	67.4	6.22	0.7	0.49
6	89.3	5.02	1.5	2.25

In the **Regression** dialog box, the **Input Y Range** should be **A1:A76**, and the **Input X Range** should be **B1:D76**. Check the box next to **Labels**. Select **New Worksheet Ply** and name it **Extended Model**. Finally, select **OK**.

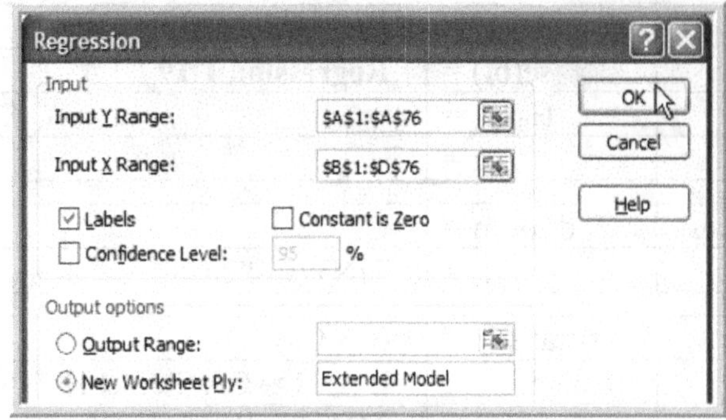

The result is (see also p. 193 in *Principles of Econometrics, 4e*):

	A	B	C	D	E	F	G	H	I
1	SUMMARY OUTPUT								
2									
3	*Regression Statistics*								
4	Multiple R	0.712906125							
5	R Square	0.508235142							
6	Adjusted R Square	0.487456346							
7	Standard Error	4.645283161							
8	Observations	75							
9									
10	ANOVA								
11		*df*	*SS*	*MS*	*F*	*Significance F*			
12	Regression	3	1583.397427	527.7991422	24.4593153	5.59997E-11			
13	Residual	71	1532.084551	21.57865565					
14	Total	74	3115.481978						
15									
16		*Coefficients*	*Standard Error*	*t Stat*	*P-value*	*Lower 95%*	*Upper 95%*	*Lower 95.0%*	*Upper 95.0%*
17	Intercept	109.7190398	6.79904566	16.1374177	1.87037E-25	96.16212798	123.2759516	96.16212798	123.2759516
18	PRICE	-7.640000543	1.045938915	-7.304442384	3.23648E-10	-9.725543479	-5.554457608	-9.725543479	-5.554457608
19	ADVERT	12.15123398	3.556164048	3.416949784	0.0010516	5.060444353	19.2420236	5.060444353	19.2420236
20	ADVERT2	-2.767962762	0.940624059	-2.942687607	0.004392671	-4.643513842	-0.892411683	-4.643513842	-0.892411683

5.5 INTERACTION VARIABLES

5.5.1 Linear Models

Consider the following life-cycle model:

$$PIZZA = \beta_1 + \beta_2 AGE + \beta_3 INCOME + e \tag{5.5}$$

where $PIZZA$ is annual expenditure on pizza, AGE is age, and $INCOME$ is income of a random sample of 40 individuals, age 18 and older.

Open the Excel file ***pizza4***. Excel opens the data set in Sheet 1 of a new Excel file. Since we would like to save all our work from Chapter 5 in one file, create a new worksheet in your **POE Chapter 5** Excel file, rename it **pizza4 data**, and in it, copy the data set you just opened.

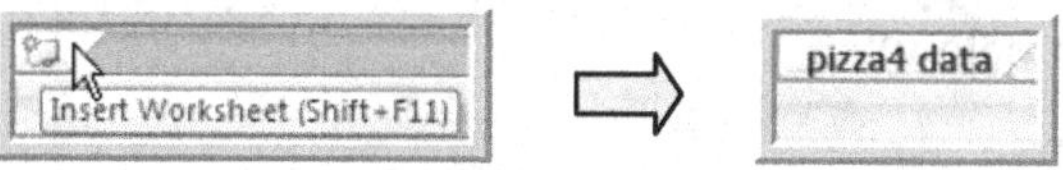

In the **Regression** dialog box, the **Input Y Range** should be **A1:A41**, and the **Input X Range** should be **F1:G41**. Check the box next to **Labels**. Select **New Worksheet Ply** and name it **Life-Cycle Model 1**. Finally select **OK**.

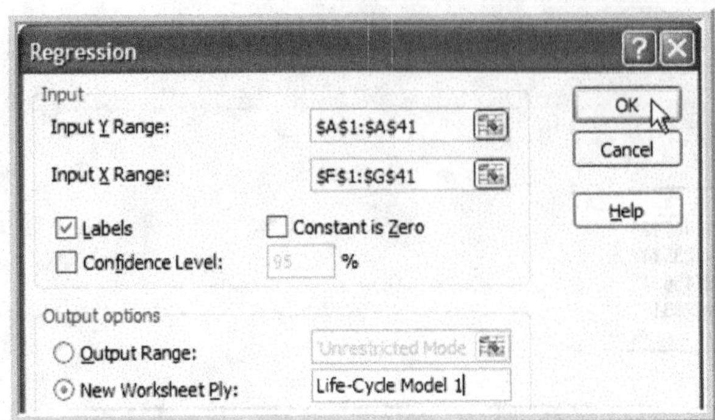

The result is (see also p. 196 in *Principles of Econometrics, 4e*):

	A	B	C	D	E	F	G	H	I
1	SUMMARY OUTPUT								
2									
3	*Regression Statistics*								
4	Multiple R	0.573803829							
5	R Square	0.329250834							
6	Adjusted R Square	0.292994123							
7	Standard Error	131.070099							
8	Observations	40							
9									
10	ANOVA								
11		*df*	*SS*	*MS*	*F*	*Significance F*			
12	Regression	2	312015.1787	156007.5894	9.081100278	0.000618533			
13	Residual	37	635636.7213	17179.37085					
14	Total	39	947651.9						
15									
16		*Coefficients*	*Standard Error*	*t Stat*	*P-value*	*Lower 95%*	*Upper 95%*	*Lower 95.0%*	*Upper 95.0%*
17	Intercept	342.8848279	72.34341966	4.73968233	3.14373E-05	196.3031373	489.4665184	196.3031373	489.4665184
18	income	1.832478934	0.464300741	3.946749963	0.000340943	0.891716278	2.773241589	0.891716278	2.773241589
19	age	-7.575555894	2.316987583	-3.269571209	0.002332607	-12.27021864	-2.880893153	-12.27021864	-2.880893153

To account for an effect of income that depends on the age of the individual, we add the interaction variable $(AGE \times INCOME)$ to the life-cycle model:

$$PIZZA = \beta_1 + \beta_2 AGE + \beta_3 INCOME + \beta_4(AGE \times INCOME) + e \tag{5.6}$$

Go back to your **pizza4 data** worksheet. In **H1**, enter the column label **age x income**. In cell **H2**, enter the formula **=F2*G2**; copy it to cells **H3:H41**. Here is how your table should look (only the first five values are shown below):

	H
1	**age x income**
2	487.5
3	1755
4	312
5	728
6	487.5

In the **Regression** dialog box, the **Input Y Range** should be **A1:A41**, and the **Input X Range** should be **F1:H41**. Check the box next to **Labels**. Select **New Worksheet Ply** and name it **Life-Cycle Model 2**. Finally select **OK**.

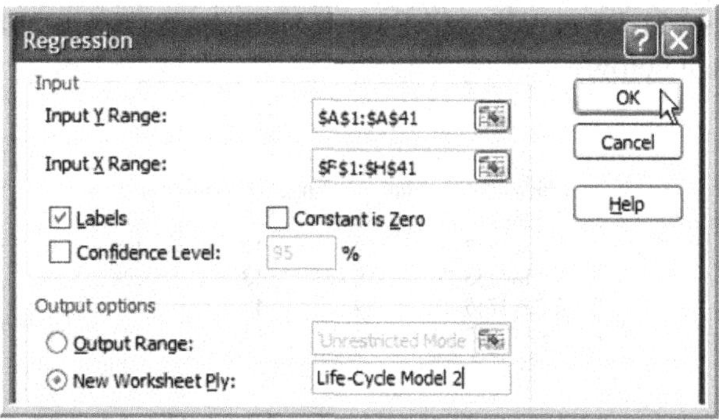

The result is (see also p. 196 in *Principles of Econometrics, 4e*):

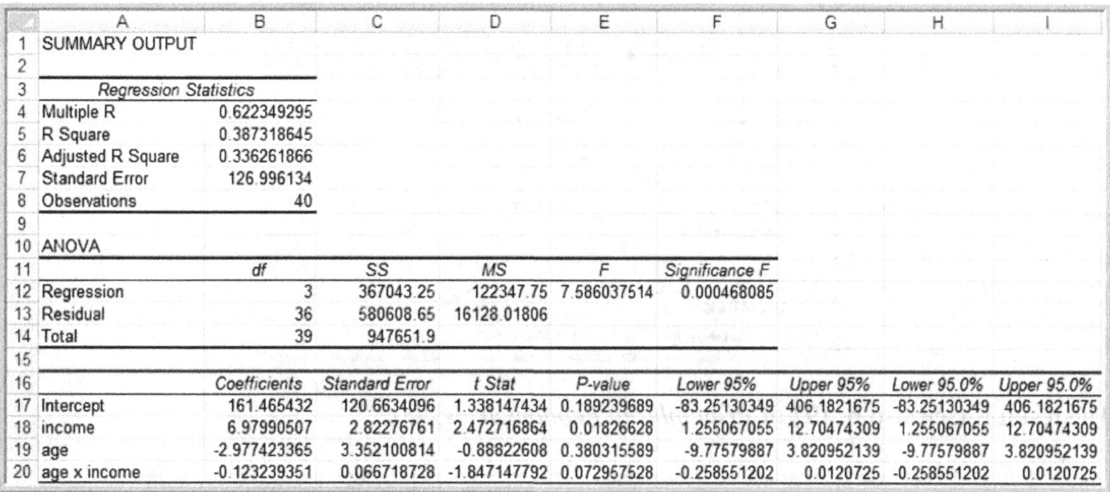

	A	B	C	D	E	F	G	H	I
1	SUMMARY OUTPUT								
2									
3	*Regression Statistics*								
4	Multiple R	0.622349295							
5	R Square	0.387318645							
6	Adjusted R Square	0.336261866							
7	Standard Error	126.996134							
8	Observations	40							
9									
10	ANOVA								
11		*df*	*SS*	*MS*	*F*	*Significance F*			
12	Regression	3	367043.25	122347.75	7.586037514	0.000468085			
13	Residual	36	580608.65	16128.01806					
14	Total	39	947651.9						
15									
16		*Coefficients*	*Standard Error*	*t Stat*	*P-value*	*Lower 95%*	*Upper 95%*	*Lower 95.0%*	*Upper 95.0%*
17	Intercept	161.465432	120.6634096	1.338147434	0.189239689	-83.25130349	406.1821675	-83.25130349	406.1821675
18	income	6.97990507	2.82276761	2.472716864	0.01826628	1.255067055	12.70474309	1.255067055	12.70474309
19	age	-2.977423365	3.352100814	-0.88822608	0.380315589	-9.77579887	3.820952139	-9.77579887	3.820952139
20	age x income	-0.123239351	0.066718728	-1.847147792	0.072957528	-0.258551202	0.0120725	-0.258551202	0.0120725

5.5.2 Log-Linear Models

Open the Excel file ***cps4_small***. Excel opens the data set in Sheet 1 of a new Excel file. Since we would like to save all our work from Chapter 5 in one file, create a new worksheet in your **POE Chapter 5** Excel file, rename it **cps4_small data**, and in it, copy the data set you just opened.

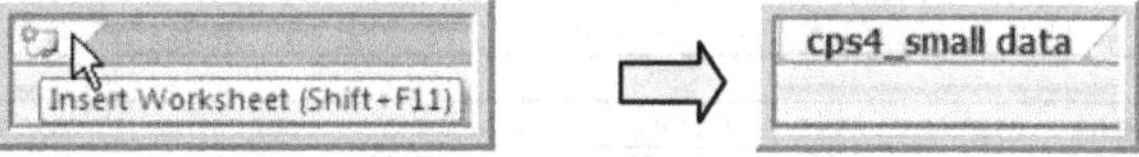

Consider the following wage equation:

$$ln(WAGE) = \beta_1 + \beta_2 EDUC + \beta_3 EXPER + \gamma\ (EDUC \times EXPER) + e \quad (5.7)$$

Go back to your **cps4_small data** worksheet. In cells **M1:O2**, enter the following column labels and formulas.

	M	N	O	P
1	**ln(wage)**	**educ**	**exper**	**educ x exper**
2	=ln(A2)	=B2	=C2	=M2*N2

Copy the content of cells **M2:P2** to cells **M3:P1001**. Here is how your table should look (only the first five values are shown below):

	M	N	O	P
1	**ln(wage)**	**educ**	**exp**	**educ x exp**
2	2.9285235	16	39	624
3	2.442347	12	16	192
4	2.7107133	16	13	208
5	3.2561716	14	11	154
6	3.179303	12	51	612

In the **Regression** dialog box, the **Input Y Range** should be **M1:M1001**, and the **Input X Range** should be **N1:P1001**. Check the box next to **Labels**. Select **New Worksheet Ply** and name it **Log-Linear Model w Interaction**. Finally select **OK**.

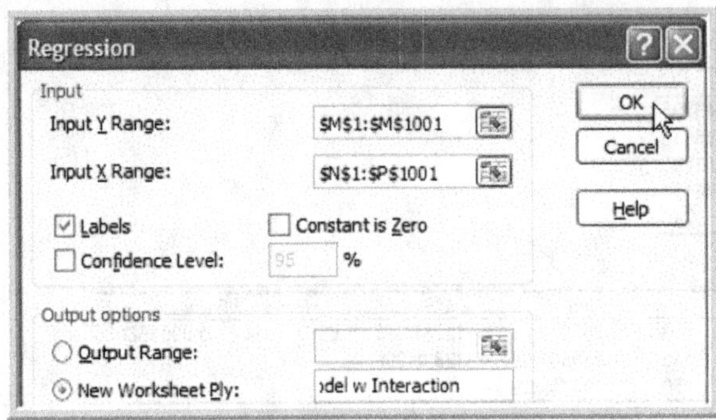

The result is (see also p. 197 of *Principles of Econometrics, 4e*):

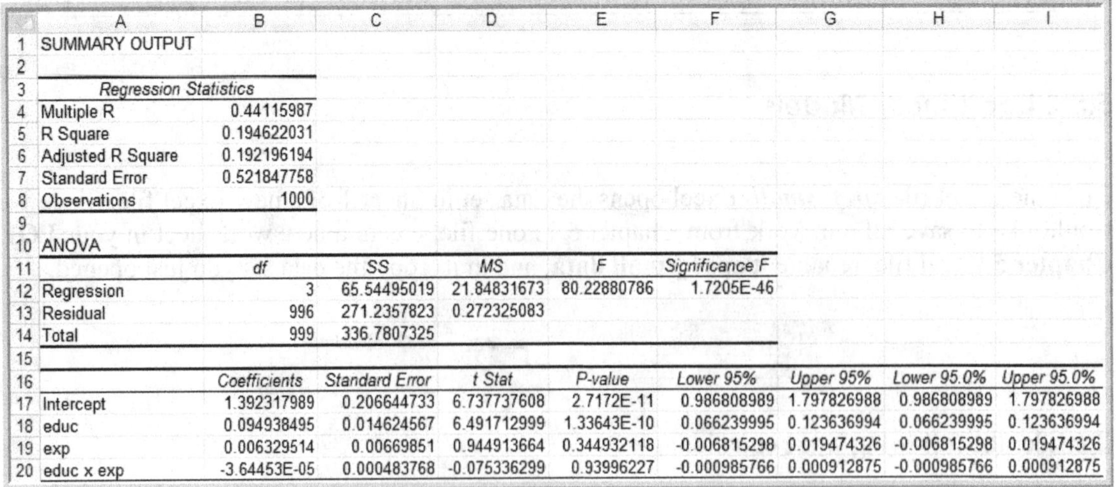

	A	B	C	D	E	F	G	H	I
1	SUMMARY OUTPUT								
2									
3	*Regression Statistics*								
4	Multiple R	0.44115987							
5	R Square	0.194622031							
6	Adjusted R Square	0.192196194							
7	Standard Error	0.521847758							
8	Observations	1000							
9									
10	ANOVA								
11		*df*	*SS*	*MS*	*F*	*Significance F*			
12	Regression	3	65.54495019	21.84831673	80.22880786	1.7205E-46			
13	Residual	996	271.2357823	0.272325083					
14	Total	999	336.7807325						
15									
16		*Coefficients*	*Standard Error*	*t Stat*	*P-value*	*Lower 95%*	*Upper 95%*	*Lower 95.0%*	*Upper 95.0%*
17	Intercept	1.392317989	0.206644733	6.737737608	2.7172E-11	0.986808989	1.797826988	0.986808989	1.797826988
18	educ	0.094938495	0.014624567	6.491712999	1.33643E-10	0.066239995	0.123636994	0.066239995	0.123636994
19	exp	0.006329514	0.00669851	0.944913664	0.344932118	-0.006815298	0.019474326	-0.006815298	0.019474326
20	educ x exp	-3.64453E-05	0.000483768	-0.075336299	0.93996227	-0.000985766	0.000912875	-0.000985766	0.000912875

5.6 MEASURING GOODNESS-OF-FIT

The coefficient of determination R^2 is reported in the Excel regression summary output. For Big Andy's Burger Barn multiple linear regression model of Section 5.1, it is highlighted below:

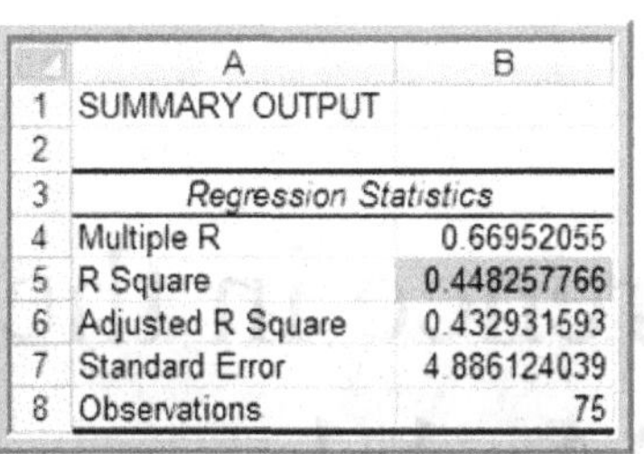

	A	B
1	SUMMARY OUTPUT	
2		
3	*Regression Statistics*	
4	Multiple R	0.66952055
5	R Square	0.448257766
6	Adjusted R Square	0.432931593
7	Standard Error	4.886124039
8	Observations	75

CHAPTER 6

Further Inference in the Multiple Regression Model

CHAPTER OUTLINE

In this chapter we continue to work with the multiple linear regression model of Big Andy's Burger Barn hamburger chain to illustrate the *F*-test procedure. We also work with additional examples to address nonsample information, model specification and collinearity issues.

6.1 TESTING THE EFFECT OF ADVERTISING: THE *F*-TEST

6.1.1 The Logic of the Test

In Chapters 3 and 5 we worked with *t*-tests for null hypotheses consisting of a single restriction on one parameter β_k. An *F*-test will be used when a null hypothesis consists of a single or more restrictions, each regarding two or more parameters.

An F-test is based on a comparison of the sum of squared errors from the original, unrestricted model, with the sum of squared errors from the model in which the null hypothesis is assumed to be true and in which the restriction(s) implied by it has(have) been imposed—this latter model is referred to as the restricted model.

If the null hypothesis is true, then the following F-statistic follows an F-distribution with $m_1 = J$ numerator degrees of freedom and $m_2 = N - K$ denominator degrees of freedom:

$$F = \frac{(SSE_R - SSE_U)/J}{SSE_U/(N-K)} \sim F_{(m_1=J, m_2=N-K)} \tag{6.1}$$

where SSE_R is the sum of squared errors from the restricted model,

SSE_U is the sum of squared errors from the unrestricted model,

J is the number of restrictions in the null hypothesis,

N is the sample size,

and K is the number of parameters in the unrestricted model.

If the null hypothesis is *not* true, then the value of the computed F-statistic will tend to be unusually large. We will reject the null hypothesis if $F \geq F_c$, where F_c is the critical value shown below.

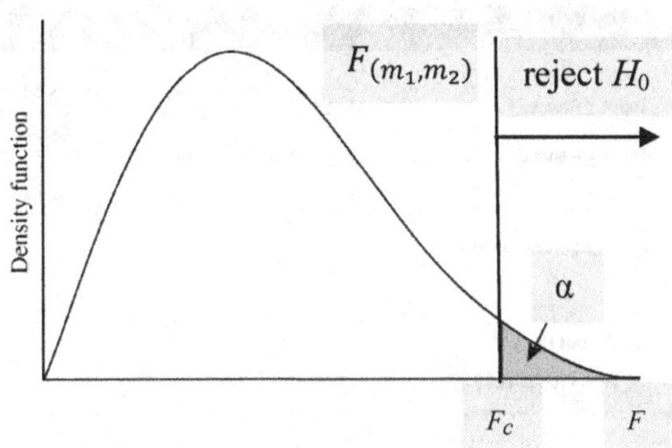

6.1.2 The Unrestricted and Restricted Models

We will use the Big Andy's Burger Barn model to illustrate the F-test procedure. We start by specifying and estimating the unrestricted and restricted models.

Recall from Chapter 5, the following multiple linear regression model for Big Andy's Burger Barn hamburger chain. This is the *unrestricted* model.

$$SALES_i = \beta_1 + \beta_2 PRICE_i + \beta_3 ADVERT_i + \beta_4 ADVERT_i^2 + e_i \tag{6.2}$$

where $SALES$ represents monthly sales revenue in a given city (in \$1000), $PRICE$ represents a price index in that city (in \$), and $ADVERT$ is monthly advertising expenditure in that city (in \$1000).

Suppose we wish to test the hypothesis that changes in price have no effect on sales revenue against the alternative that changes in price do have an effect. The null and alternative hypotheses are $H_0: \beta_3 = 0, \beta_4 = 0$ and $H_1: \beta_3 \neq 0$ or $\beta_4 \neq 0$ or both are nonzero. If we impose our null hypothesis or restriction to equation (6.2), we obtain the following *restricted* model:

$$SALES_i = \beta_1 + \beta_2 PRICE_i + e_i \quad (6.3)$$

We would like to successively estimate the unrestricted model (6.2) and the restricted model (6.3). First, open your Excel file ***andy***. Save your file as **POE Chapter 6**. Rename Sheet 1 **andy's hamburger chain data**.

In **D1**, enter the column label **ADVERT²**. In cell **D2**, enter the formula **=C2^2**; copy it to cells **D3:D76**. Here is how your table should look (only the first five values are shown below):

	A	B	C	D
1	SALES	PRICE	ADVERT	ADVERT²
2	73.2	5.69	1.3	1.69
3	71.8	6.49	2.9	8.41
4	62.4	5.63	0.8	0.64
5	67.4	6.22	0.7	0.49
6	89.3	5.02	1.5	2.25

For the unrestricted model (6.2), the **Input Y Range** should be **A1:A76**, and the **Input X Range** should be **B1:D76**. Check the box next to **Labels**. Select **New Worksheet Ply** and name it **Unrestricted Model**. Finally select **OK**.

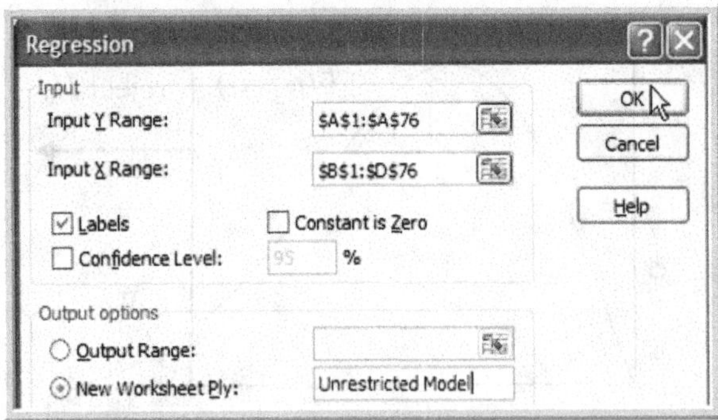

The result is what you already obtained in Chapter 5:

	A	B	C	D	E	F	G	H	I
1	SUMMARY OUTPUT								
2									
3	*Regression Statistics*								
4	Multiple R	0.712906133							
5	R Square	0.508235155							
6	Adjusted R Square	0.487456358							
7	Standard Error	4.645283021							
8	Observations	75							
9									
10	ANOVA								
11		*df*	*SS*	*MS*	*F*	*Significance F*			
12	Regression	3	1583.397408	527.799136	24.45931648	5.59996E-11			
13	Residual	71	1532.084459	21.57865435					
14	Total	74	3115.481867						
15									
16		*Coefficients*	*Standard Error*	*t Stat*	*P-value*	*Lower 95%*	*Upper 95%*	*Lower 95.0%*	*Upper 95.0%*
17	Intercept	109.719036	6.799045455	16.13741763	1.87037E-25	96.16212457	123.2759474	96.16212457	123.2759474
18	price	-7.640000035	1.045938884	-7.304442117	3.23648E-10	-9.725542907	-5.554457162	-9.725542907	-5.554457162
19	advert	12.15123567	3.556163941	3.416950364	0.001051598	5.060446263	19.24202509	5.060446263	19.24202509
20	advert2	-2.767963089	0.940624031	-2.942688043	0.004392666	-4.643514112	-0.892412066	-4.643514112	-0.892412066

Go back to your **andy's hamburger chain data** worksheet. For the restricted model (6.3), the **Input Y Range** should be **A1:A76**, and the **Input X Range** should be *only the PRICE data* **B1:B76**. Check the box next to **Labels**. Select **New Worksheet Ply** and name it **Restricted Model**. Finally, select **OK**.

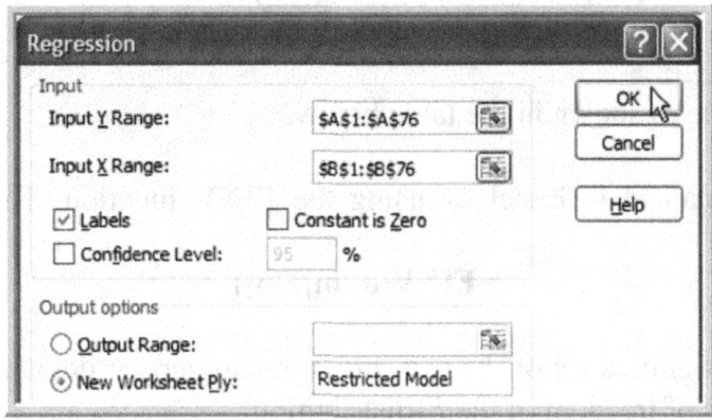

The result is:

	A	B	C	D	E	F	G	H	I
1	SUMMARY OUTPUT								
2									
3	*Regression Statistics*								
4	Multiple R	0.62554053							
5	R Square	0.391300955							
6	Adjusted R Square	0.382962612							
7	Standard Error	5.096857529							
8	Observations	75							
9									
10	ANOVA								
11		*df*	*SS*	*MS*	*F*	*Significance F*			
12	Regression	1	1219.09103	1219.09103	46.92790295	1.97078E-09			
13	Residual	73	1896.390837	25.97795667					
14	Total	74	3115.481867						
15									
16		*Coefficients*	*Standard Error*	*t Stat*	*P-value*	*Lower 95%*	*Upper 95%*	*Lower 95.0%*	*Upper 95.0%*
17	Intercept	121.9001736	6.526290698	18.67832421	1.5876E-29	108.8932951	134.907052	108.8932951	134.907052
18	price	-7.829073515	1.142864644	-6.850394365	1.97078E-09	-10.10679943	-5.551347597	-10.10679943	-5.551347597

6.1.3 Test Template

Insert a new worksheet by selecting the **Insert Worksheet** tab at the lower left corner of your screen. Name it **F-test**.

Create the F-test template as shown in the table below.

F-critical values are obtained in Excel by using the **FINV** function. The syntax of the **FINV** function is as follows:

$$\textbf{=FINV}(\alpha, m_1, m_2)$$

where α is the level of significance of the test, m_1 is the numerator degrees of freedom and m_2 is the denominator degrees of freedom of the *F*-distribution.

p-values for *F*-statistics are obtained in Excel by using the **FDIST** function. For hypothesis tests purposes, the syntax of the **FDIST** function is as follows:

$$\textbf{=FDIST}(F\textbf{-statistic}, m_1, m_2)$$

	A	B	C
1	**Data Input**	J =	
2		N =	='Unrestricted Model'!B8
3		K =	='Unrestricted Model'!B12+1
4		SSE_U =	='Unrestricted Model'!C13
5		SSE_R =	='Restricted Model'!C13
6		α =	

	A	B	C
8	**Computed Values**	m_1 =	=C1
9		m_2 =	=C2-C3
10		F_c=	=FINV(C6,C8,C9)
11			
12	**F-test**	F-statistic=	=((C5-C4)/C8)/(C4/C9)
13		Conclusion =	=IF(C12>=C10,"Reject Ho","Do Not Reject Ho")
14		p-value =	=FDIST(C12,C8,C9)
15		Conclusion =	=IF(C14<=C6,"Reject Ho","Do Not Reject Ho")

Note that the number of parameters K is equal to the Excel regression degrees of freedom plus one (see cell **C3** above).

With 2 restrictions in the null hypothesis $H_0: \beta_3 = 0, \beta_4 = 0$, and at $\alpha = 0.05$, the results of the F-test are (see also p. 225 of *Principles of Econometrics, 4e*):

	A	B	C
1	**Data Input**	J =	2
2		N =	75
3		K =	4
4		SSE_U =	1532.084
5		SSE_R =	1896.391
6		α =	0.05

	A	B	C
8	**Computed Values**	m_1 =	2
9		m_2 =	71
10		Fc =	3.125764
11			
12	**F-test**	F-statistic =	8.44136
13		Conclusion =	Reject Ho
14		p-value =	0.000514
15		Conclusion =	Reject Ho

6.2 TESTING THE SIGNIFICANCE OF THE MODEL

6.2.1 Null and Alternative Hypotheses

For a general *unrestricted* multiple regression model with $K - 1$ explanatory variables and K unknown coefficients: $y_i = \beta_1 + \beta_2 x_{i2} + \beta_3 x_{i3} + \cdots + \beta_K x_{iK} + e_i$, the null and alternative hypotheses of a test of significance of the model are:

$$H_0: \beta_2 = 0, \beta_3 = 0, \ldots, \beta_k = 0$$

$$H_1\text{: At least one of the } \beta_k \text{ is nonzero for } k = 2, 3, \ldots, K$$

Note that, in this one case, in which we are testing the null hypothesis that all the model parameters are zero, except the intercept, the sum of squared errors from the restricted model is equal to the total sum of squares from the unrestricted model: $SSE_R = SST_U$.

6.2.2 Test Template

Insert a new worksheet by selecting the **Insert Worksheet** tab at the bottom of your screen. Name it **Test of Significance of Model**.

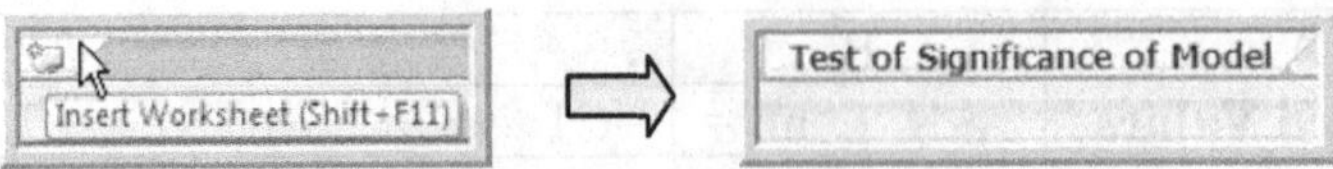

Copy the template from your **F-test** worksheet into your new worksheet. You just need to modify the reference in cell **C5**, as highlighted below, to obtain a template for a test of the overall significance of the regression model.

	A	B	C
1	**Data Input**	J =	
2		N =	='Unrestricted Model'!B8
3		K =	='Unrestricted Model'!B12+1
4		SSE_U =	='Unrestricted Model'!C13
5		SSE_R =	**='Unrestricted Model'!C14**
6		α =	
8	**Computed Values**	m_1 =	=C1
9		m_2 =	=C2-C3
10		F_c=	=FINV(C6,C8,C9)
12	**F-test**	F-statistic=	=((C5-C4)/C8)/(C4/C9)
13		Conclusion =	=IF(C12>=C10,"Reject Ho","Do Not Reject Ho")
14		p-value =	=FDIST(C12,C8,C9)
15		Conclusion =	=IF(C14<=C6,"Reject Ho","Do Not Reject Ho")

For the *unrestricted* model (6.2), $SALES_i = \beta_1 + \beta_2 PRICE_i + \beta_3 ADVERT_i + \beta_4 ADVERT_i^2 + e_i$, the null and alternative hypotheses of a test of significance of the model are:

$$H_0: \beta_2 = 0, \beta_3 = 0, \beta_4 = 0$$

$$H_1: \text{At least one of } \beta_2 \text{ or } \beta_3 \text{or } \beta_4 \text{ is nonzero}$$

The null hypothesis above contains two restrictions. With 3 restrictions, at $\alpha = 0.05$, the results of the test of significance of model (6.2) are (see also pp. 226-227 of *Principles of Econometrics, 4e*):

	A	B	C
1	Data Input	J =	3
2		N =	75
3		K =	4
4		SSE_U =	1532.084
5		SSE_R =	3115.482
6		α =	0.05

	A	B	C
8	Computed Values	m_1 =	3
9		m_2 =	71
10		Fc =	2.733647
11			
12	F-test	F-statistic =	24.45932
13		Conclusion =	Reject Ho
14		p-value =	5.6E-11
15		Conclusion =	Reject Ho

6.2.3 Excel Regression Output

For the test of significance of a model, since $SSE_R = SST_U$, there is no need to estimate a restricted model—all the information needed to compute the F-statistic is available from the regression analysis of the unrestricted model. This is why the *F*-statistic of the test of significance of a model and its p-value are found in the Excel summary output (see your **Unrestricted Model** worksheet):

	A	B	C	D	E	F
11		*df*	*SS*	*MS*	*F*	*Significance F*
12	Regression	2	1396.538993	698.2694963	29.24785998	5.04086E-10
13	Residual	72	1718.942985	23.87420813		
14	Total	74	3115.481978			

6.3 THE RELATIONSHIP BETWEEN *t*- AND *F*-TESTS

Reconsider the following multiple linear regression model for Big Andy's Burger Barn hamburger chain. This is the *unrestricted* model.

$$SALES_i = \beta_1 + \beta_2 PRICE_i + \beta_3 ADVERT_i + \beta_4 ADVERT_i^2 + e_i \tag{6.2}$$

Suppose we wish to test the hypothesis that changes in price have no effect on sales revenue against the alternative that changes in price do have an effect. The null and alternative hypotheses are $H_0: \beta_2 = 0$ and $H_1: \beta_2 \neq 0$. If we impose our null hypothesis or restriction to equation (6.2), we obtain the following *restricted* model:

$$SALES_i = \beta_1 + \beta_3 ADVERT_i + \beta_4 ADVERT_i^2 + e_i \tag{6.4}$$

Go back to your **andy's hamburger chain data** worksheet. In the **Regression** dialog box, the **Input Y Range** should be **A1:A76**, and the **Input X Range** should be **C1:D76**. Check the box next to **Labels**. Select **Output Range** and specify it to be cell **A1** in your **Unrestricted Model** worksheet: you can place your cursor in the **Output Range** window and move it to that cell to do that, or type **'Restricted Model'!A1** in **the Output Range** window. Finally, select **OK**.

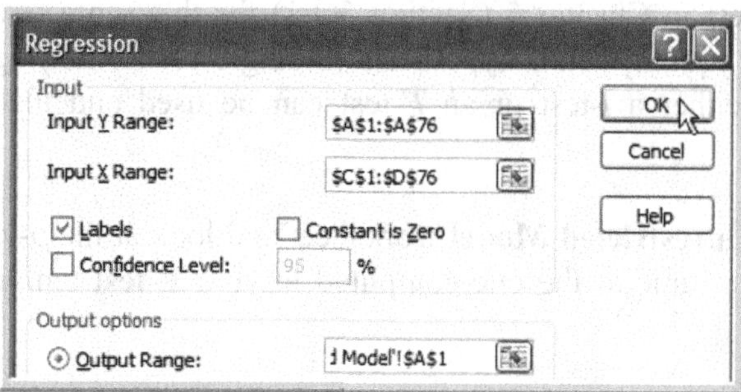

Excel informs you that the output range will overwrite existing data. Do select **OK** to overwrite the data in the specified range.

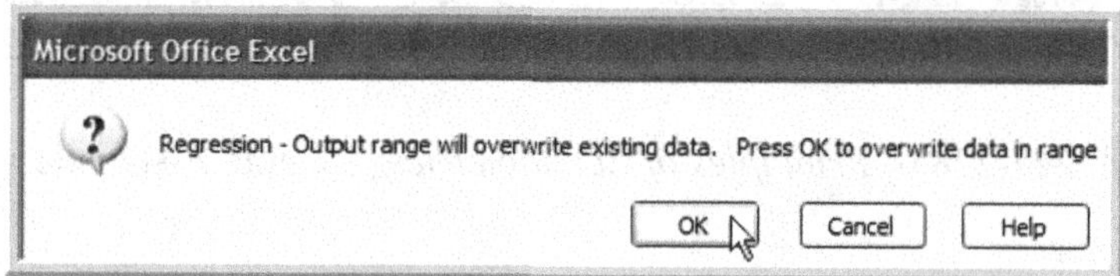

The result is:

	A	B	C	D	E	F	G	H	I
1	SUMMARY OUTPUT								
2									
3	*Regression Statistics*								
4	Multiple R	0.372404526							
5	R Square	0.138685131							
6	Adjusted R Square	0.114759718							
7	Standard Error	6.1048829							
8	Observations	75							
9									
10	ANOVA								
11		*df*	*SS*	*MS*	*F*	*Significance F*			
12	Regression	2	432.0710103	216.0355051	5.796561616	0.004632656			
13	Residual	72	2683.410856	37.26959523					
14	Total	74	3115.481867						
15									
16		*Coefficients*	*Standard Error*	*t Stat*	*P-value*	*Lower 95%*	*Upper 95%*	*Lower 95.0%*	*Upper 95.0%*
17	Intercept	64.84148981	3.827012492	16.943109	7.87896E-27	57.21247994	72.47049968	57.21247994	72.47049968
18	advert	14.24915942	4.6582829	3.058886659	0.003118901	4.963042303	23.53527653	4.963042303	23.53527653
19	advert2	-3.365894266	1.231488631	-2.733191507	0.007887268	-5.82082195	-0.910966582	-5.82082195	-0.910966582

Go back to your **F-test** worksheet. With 1 restrictions, at $\alpha = 0.05$, the result is (see also p. 227 in *Principles of Econometrics, 4e*):

	A	B	C
1	**Data Input**	J =	1
2		N =	75
3		K =	4
4		SSE_U =	1532.084
5		SSE_R =	2683.411
6		α =	0.05

	A	B	C
8	**Computed Values**	m_1 =	1
9		m_2 =	71
10		Fc =	3.97581
11			
12	**F-test**	F-statistic =	53.35487
13		Conclusion =	Reject Ho
14		p-value =	3.24E-10
15		Conclusion =	Reject Ho

Note that we used a t-test in Chapter 5 (Section 5.3.1) for this same test of significance of β_2. When testing a single "equality" null hypothesis (a single restriction) against a "not equal to" alternative hypothesis, either a t-test or an F-test can be used and the test outcomes will be identical.

If you go back to your **Unrestricted Model** worksheet and look at the p-value for b_2, you should find that it is exactly the same as the one computed in your **F-test** template. We highlight both results below:

	A	B	C
12	**F-test**	F-statistic =	53.35487
13		Conclusion =	Reject Ho
14		p-value =	**3.24E-10**
15		Conclusion =	Reject Ho

	A	B	C	D	E
16		*Coefficients*	*Standard Error*	*t Stat*	*P-value*
17	Intercept	109.719036	6.799045455	16.13741763	1.87037E-25
18	price	-7.640000035	1.045938884	-7.304442117	**3.23648E-10**
19	advert	12.15123567	3.556163941	3.416950364	0.001051598
20	advert2	-2.767963089	0.940624031	-2.942688043	0.004392666

As explained in pp. 227-228 of *Principles of Econometrics, 4e*, note F-statistic $= 53.355 = t^2 = (-7.3044)^2$.

6.4 TESTING SOME ECONOMIC HYPOTHESES

6.4.1 The Optimal Level of Advertising

For this test, as explained on p. 229 of *Principles of Econometrics, 4e*, the *restricted* model is:

$$(SALES - ADVERT)_i = \beta_1 + \beta_2 PRICE_i + \beta_4 (ADVERT^2 - 3.8\, ADVERT)_i + e_i \quad (6.5)$$

Go back to your **andy's hamburger chain data** worksheet. Because explanatory variables must be adjacent, insert a new column to the right of the **PRICE** data column. In **C1**, enter the column label **x***. In **C2**, enter the formula **=E2-3.8*D2**; copy it to cells **C3:C76**. In **F1**, enter the column label **y***. In **F2**, enter the formula **=A2-D2**; copy it to cells **F3:F76**.

Here is how your table should look (only the first five values are shown below):

	A	B	C	D	E	F
1	SALES	PRICE	x*	ADVERT	ADVERT²	y*
2	73.2	5.69	-3.25	1.3	1.69	71.9
3	71.8	6.49	-2.61	2.9	8.41	68.9
4	62.4	5.63	-2.4	0.8	0.64	61.6
5	67.4	6.22	-2.17	0.7	0.49	66.7
6	89.3	5.02	-3.45	1.5	2.25	87.8

For the restricted model (6.5), the **Input Y Range** should be **F1:F76**, and the **Input X Range** should be **B1:C76**. Check the box next to **Labels**. Select **Output Range** and specify it to be cell **A1** in your **Restricted Model** worksheet: you can place your cursor in the **Output Range** window and move it to that cell to do that, or type **'Restricted Model'!A1** in **the Output Range** window. Finally, select **OK**.

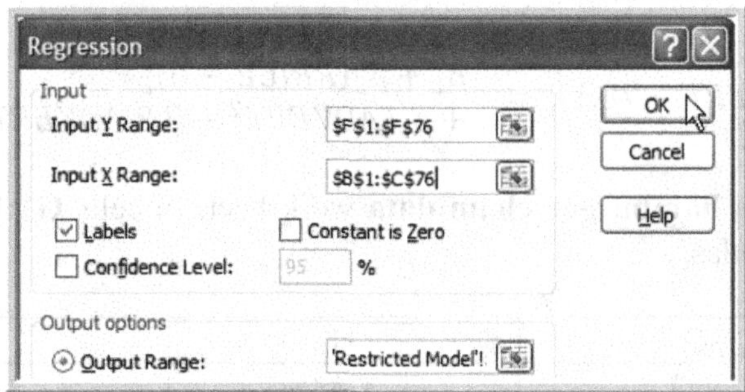

Excel informs you that the output range will overwrite existing data. Do press **OK** to overwrite the data in the specified range. The result is:

	A	B	C	D	E	F	G	H	I
1	SUMMARY OUTPUT								
2									
3	*Regression Statistics*								
4	Multiple R	0.693339057							
5	R Square	0.480719048							
6	Adjusted R Square	0.466294577							
7	Standard Error	4.64322439							
8	Observations	75							
9									
10	ANOVA								
11		*df*	*SS*	*MS*	*F*	*Significance F*			
12	Regression	2	1437.013271	718.5066356	33.32663303	5.6818E-11			
13	Residual	72	1552.286357	21.55953273					
14	Total	74	2989.299628						
15									
16		*Coefficients*	*Standard Error*	*t Stat*	*P-value*	*Lower 95%*	*Upper 95%*	*Lower 95.0%*	*Upper 95.0%*
17	Intercept	110.3589599	6.763803393	16.31610996	6.84193E-26	96.87556446	123.8423554	96.87556446	123.8423554
18	PRICE	-7.60310422	1.044780309	-7.27722771	3.39617E-10	-9.685835675	-5.52037277	-9.685835675	-5.520372768
19	x*	-2.87651491	0.93349559	-3.08144457	0.002917717	-4.737404337	-1.01562549	-4.737404337	-1.015625493

Go back to your **F-test** worksheet. With 1 restriction, at $\alpha = 0.05$, the result is (see also p. 229 in *Principles of Econometrics, 4e*):

	A	B	C
1	**Data Input**	J =	1
2		N =	75
3		K =	4
4		SSE_U =	1532.085
5		SSE_R =	1552.286
6		α =	0.05

	A	B	C	D
8	**Computed Values**	m_1 =	1	
9		m_2 =	71	
10		Fc =	3.97581	
11				
12	**F-test**	F-statistic =	0.936194	
13		Conclusion =	Do Not Reject Ho	
14		p-value =	0.336543	
15		Conclusion =	Do Not Reject Ho	

6.4.2 The Optimal Level of Advertising and Price

For this test, the *restricted* model is:

$$(SALES - ADVERT - 78.1)_i = \begin{array}{l} \beta_1 + \beta_2(PRICE - 6)_i \\ + \beta_4(ADVERT^2 - 3.8\,ADVERT + 3.61)_i + e_i \end{array} \quad (6.6)$$

Go back to your **andy's hamburger chain data** worksheet. In cells **G1:I2**, enter the following column labels and formulas.

	G	H	I
1	**y****	**x_1****	**x_2****
2	=A2-D2-78.1	=B2-6	=E2-3.8*D2+3.61

Copy the content of cells **G2:I2** to cells **G3:I76**. Here is how your table should look (only the first five values are shown below):

	G	H	I
1	y**	x_1*	x_2*
2	-6.2	-0.31	0.36
3	-9.2	0.49	1
4	-16.5	-0.37	1.21
5	-11.4	0.22	1.44
6	9.7	-0.98	0.16

For the restricted model (6.6), notice that there is *no intercept*; so you will need to select the **Constant is Zero** option in the **Regression** dialog box. The **Input Y Range** should be **G1:G76**, and the **Input X Range** should be **H1:I76**. Check the box next to **Labels** *and* **Constant is Zero**. Select **Output Range** and specify it to be cell **A1** in your **Restricted Model** worksheet: you can place your cursor in the **Output Range** window and move it to that cell to do that, or type **'Restricted Model'!A1** in **the Output Range** window. Finally, select **OK**.

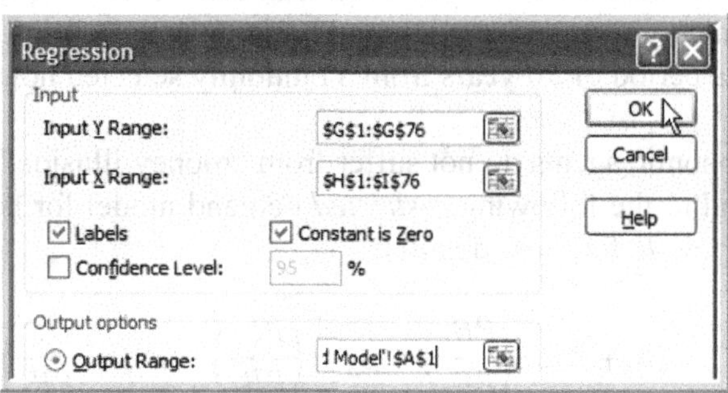

Excel informs you that the output range will overwrite existing data. Do press **OK** to overwrite the data in the specified range. The result is:

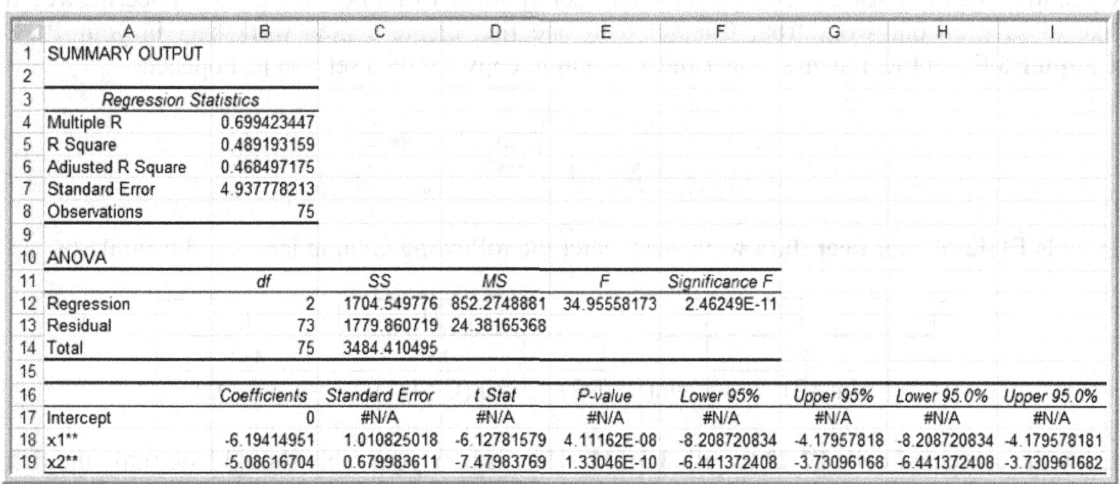

	A	B	C	D	E	F	G	H	I
1	SUMMARY OUTPUT								
2									
3	*Regression Statistics*								
4	Multiple R	0.699423447							
5	R Square	0.489193159							
6	Adjusted R Square	0.468497175							
7	Standard Error	4.937778213							
8	Observations	75							
9									
10	ANOVA								
11		*df*	*SS*	*MS*	*F*	*Significance F*			
12	Regression	2	1704.549776	852.2748881	34.95558173	2.46249E-11			
13	Residual	73	1779.860719	24.38165368					
14	Total	75	3484.410495						
15									
16		*Coefficients*	*Standard Error*	*t Stat*	*P-value*	*Lower 95%*	*Upper 95%*	*Lower 95.0%*	*Upper 95.0%*
17	Intercept	0	#N/A	#N/A	#N/A	#N/A	#N/A	#N/A	#N/A
18	x1**	-6.19414951	1.010825018	-6.12781579	4.11162E-08	-8.208720834	-4.17957818	-8.208720834	-4.179578181
19	x2**	-5.08616704	0.679983611	-7.47983769	1.33046E-10	-6.441372408	-3.73096168	-6.441372408	-3.730961682

Go back to your **F-test** worksheet. With 2 restrictions, at $\alpha = 0.05$, the result is (see also p. 231 in *Principles of Econometrics, 4e*):

	A	B	C
1	**Data Input**	J =	2
2		N =	75
3		K =	4
4		SSE_U =	1532.085
5		SSE_R =	1779.861
6		α =	0.05

	A	B	C
8	**Computed Values**	m_1 =	2
9		m_2 =	71
10		Fc =	3.125764
11			
12	**F-test**	F-statistic =	5.741233
13		Conclusion =	Reject Ho
14		p-value =	0.004885
15		Conclusion =	Reject Ho

6.5 THE USE OF NONSAMPLE INFORMATION

Consider the following *unrestricted* demand model for beer:

$$ln(Q_t) = \beta_1 + \beta_2 ln(PB_t) + \beta_3 ln(PL_t) + \beta_4 ln(PR_t) + \beta_5 ln(I_t) + e_t \quad (6.7)$$

where Q is the quantity demanded, PB is the price of beer, PL is the price of liquor, PR is the price of all other remaining goods and services, and I is income. All information for this model has been collected over a period of 30 years from a randomly selected household.

The assumption that economic agents do not suffer from "money illusion" can be imposed on the demand model. This lead to the following *restricted* demand model for beer (see pp. 231-232 in *Principles of Econometrics, 4e* for more details):

$$ln(Q_t) = \beta_1 + \beta_2 ln\left(\frac{PB_t}{PR_t}\right) + \beta_3 ln\left(\frac{PL_t}{PR_t}\right) + \beta_5 ln\left(\frac{I_t}{PR_t}\right) + e_t \quad (6.8)$$

Below we estimate the restricted model (6.8).

Open the Excel file ***beer***. Excel opens the data set in Sheet 1 of a new Excel file. Since we would like to save all our work from Chapter 6 in one file, create a new worksheet in your **POE Chapter 6** Excel file, rename it **beer data**, and in it, copy the data set you just opened.

In cells **F1:I2** of your **beer data** worksheet, enter the following column labels and formulas.

	F	G	H	I
1	y*	x_1*	x_2*	x_3*
2	=ln(A2)	=ln(B2/D2)	=ln(C2/D2)	=ln(E2/D2)

Copy the content of cells **F2:I2** to cells **F3:I31**. Here is how your table should look (only the first five values are shown below):

	F	G	H	I
1	y*	x_1*	x_2*	x_3*
2	4.403054	0.472253	1.834382	10.02578
3	4.041295	1.220257	2.391088	10.58768
4	4.160444	0.979322	2.126509	10.33316
5	4.180522	1.05315	2.258981	10.49711
6	4.160444	0.757096	1.951287	10.15131

In the **Regression** dialog box, the **Input Y Range** should be **F1:F31**, and the **Input X Range** should be **G1:I31**. Check the box next to **Labels**. Select **new Worksheet Ply** and name it **Restricted Beer Demand Model**. Finally, select **OK**.

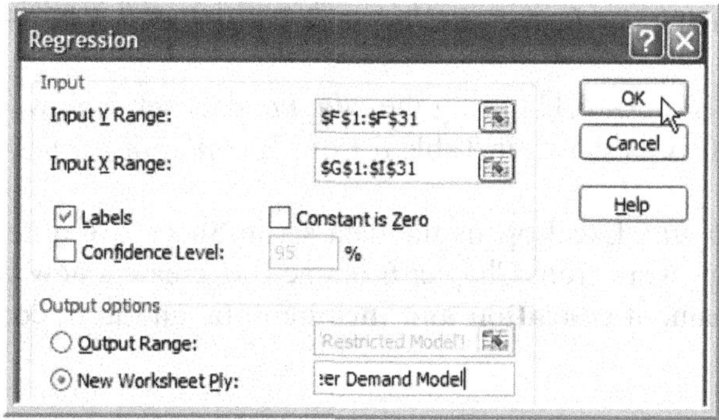

The result is (see also p. 232 in *Principles of Econometrics, 4e*):

	A	B	C	D	E	F	G	H	I
1	SUMMARY OUTPUT								
2									
3	*Regression Statistics*								
4	Multiple R	0.898859761							
5	R Square	0.80794887							
6	Adjusted R Square	0.785789124							
7	Standard Error	0.061675593							
8	Observations	30							
9									
10	ANOVA								
11		*df*	*SS*	*MS*	*F*	*Significance F*			
12	Regression	3	0.416070592	0.138690197	36.46020488	1.83399E-09			
13	Residual	26	0.098900847	0.003803879					
14	Total	29	0.514971439						
15									
16		*Coefficients*	*Standard Error*	*t Stat*	*P-value*	*Lower 95%*	*Upper 95%*	*Lower 95.0%*	*Upper 95.0%*
17	Intercept	-4.797797376	3.71390504	-1.291847079	0.207775913	-12.43183844	2.836243691	-12.43183844	2.836243691
18	x1*	-1.299386484	0.165737623	-7.840021241	2.57799E-08	-1.640065044	-0.958707925	-1.640065044	-0.958707925
19	x2*	0.186815879	0.284383258	0.656915882	0.517008126	-0.397742275	0.771374032	-0.397742275	0.771374032
20	x3*	0.945828579	0.427046831	2.214812313	0.035742225	0.068021255	1.823635904	0.068021255	1.823635904

6.6 MODEL SPECIFICATION

6.6.1 Omitted Variables

Consider the following family income model:

$$FAMINC_i = \beta_1 + \beta_2 HEDU_i + \beta_3 WEDU_i + e_i \quad (6.9)$$

where $FAMINC$ is the annual family income of married couples where both husbands and wives work; $HEDU$ is the years of education of the husband and $WEDU$ is the years of education of the wife.

If we incorrectly omit the relevant variable $WEDU$ (wife's education) from the family income model, it becomes:

$$FAMINC_i = \beta_1 + \beta_2 HEDU_i + e_i \quad (6.10)$$

If we add the omitted relevant variable $KL6$ (number of children less than 6 years old) to the family income model, it becomes:

$$FAMINC_i = \beta_1 + \beta_2 HEDU_i + \beta_3 WEDU_i + \beta_4 KL6_i + e_i \tag{6.11}$$

You can estimate models (6.9)-(6.11) using the ***edu_inc*** data set. Below, we will show you how to get the correlation matrix as shown in Table 6.1 of *Principles of Econometrics, 4e* (p. 235).

Open the Excel file ***edu_inc***. Excel opens the data set in Sheet 1 of a new Excel file. Since we would like to save all our work from Chapter 6 in one file, create a new worksheet in your **POE Chapter 6** Excel file, name it **education and income data**, and in it, copy the data set you just opened.

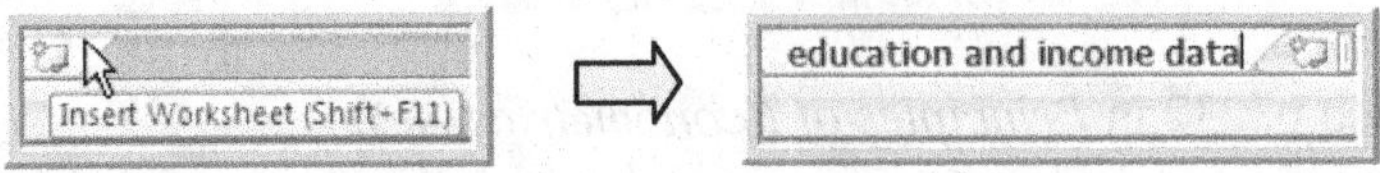

Select the **Data** tab, in the middle of your tab list located on top of your screen. On the **Analysis** group of commands, to the far right, select **Data Analysis**.

The **Data Analysis** dialog box pops up. In it, select **Correlation** (you might need to use the scroll up and down bar to the right of the **Analysis Tools** window to find it), then select **OK**.

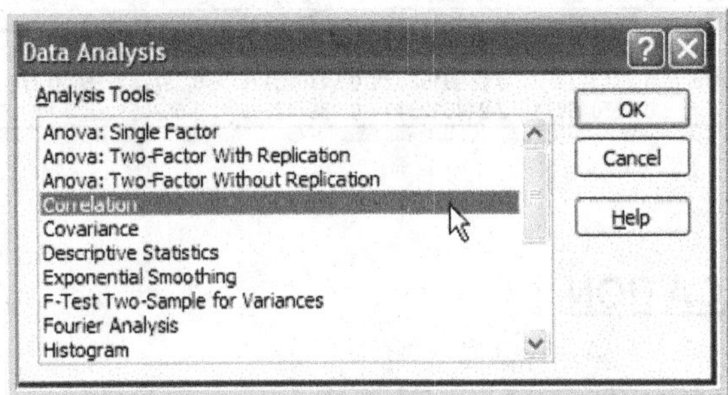

A **Correlation** dialog box pops up. Specify the **Input Range** to be **A1:F429**. Select **Grouped by Columns**, as this is the way the data on each variable are stored. Check the box next to **Labels in first row**. Select **New Worksheet Ply** and name it **Correlation Matrix**. Finally, select **OK**.

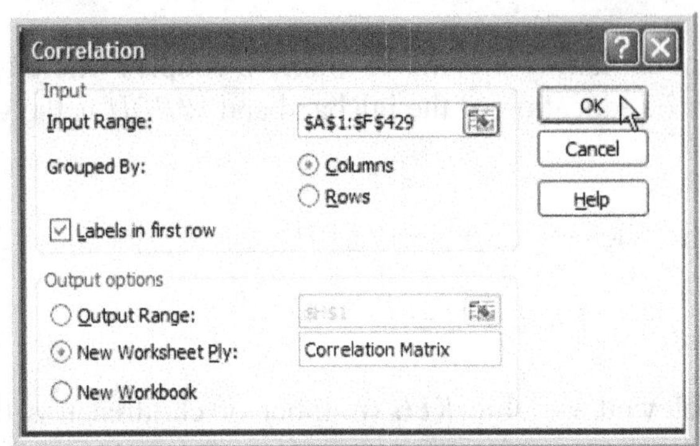

The result is:

	A	B	C	D	E	F	G
1		FAMINC	HE	WE	KL6	XTRA_X5	XTRA_X6
2	FAMINC	1					
3	HE	0.354684	1				
4	WE	0.362328	0.594343	1			
5	KL6	-0.07196	0.104877	0.12934	1		
6	XTRA_X5	0.289817	0.836168	0.517798	0.148742	1	
7	XTRA_X6	0.351366	0.820563	0.799306	0.159522	0.900206	1

6.6.2 Irrelevant Variables

To see the effect of irrelevant variables, we can add two artificially generated variables X_5 and X_6 to the family income model (6.11):

$$FAMINC_i = \beta_1 + \beta_2 HEDU_i + \beta_3 WEDU_i + \beta_4 KL6_i + \beta_5 X_{5i} + \beta_6 X_{6i} + e_i \tag{6.12}$$

You can estimate model (6.12) using the ***edu_inc.xls*** data set. Below, we will show you how the variables X_5 and X_6 were generated.

Variables X_5 and X_6 were constructed so that they are correlated with $HEDU$ and $WEDU$, but they are not expected to influence family income. Specifically, they were defined as follows:

$$X_{5i} = HEDU_i + 2N(0,1) \tag{6.13}$$

$$X_{6i} = X_{5i} + WEDU_i + N(0,1) \tag{6.14}$$

where $N(0,1)$ are random numbers from a normal distribution with mean 0 and standard deviation 1, generated the way we generated our random samples in Section 2.4.4 and Section 3.1.4.

Go back to your **education and income data** worksheet. In cells **H1:N2** enter the following column labels and formulas. In the last row of the table you will find the numbers of the equations used in the formulas.

	H	I	J	K	L	M	N
1	**N(0,1) for x_5**	**N(0,1) for x_6**	**HEDU**	**WEDU**	**KL6**	**X_5**	**X_6**
2			=B2	=C2	=D2	=J2+2*H2	=M2+K2+I2
						(6.14)	*(6.15)*

Note that we copy the values of the $HEDU$, $WEDU$ and $KL6$ variables in columns **J-L**. The reason we are doing this is that we need to have the columns of explanatory variables next to one another to be able to use the Excel regression analysis tool.

In columns **H-I**, we will generate samples of random numbers from a normal distribution with mean 0 and standard deviation 1.

Select the **Data** tab, in the middle of your tab list located on top of your screen. On the **Analysis** group of commands, to the far right, select **Data Analysis**.

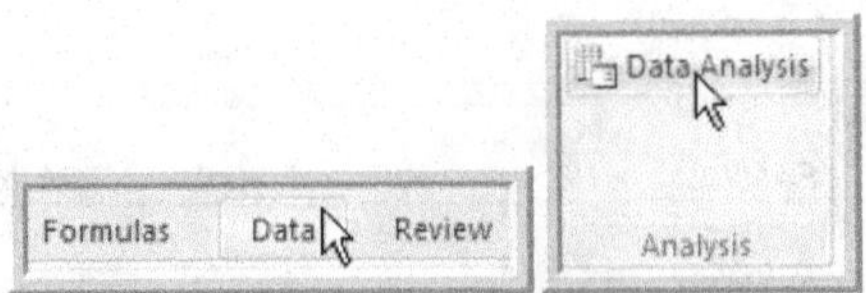

The **Data Analysis** dialog box pops up. In it, select **Random Number Generation** (you might need to use the scroll up and down bar to the right of the **Analysis Tools** window to find it), then select **OK.**

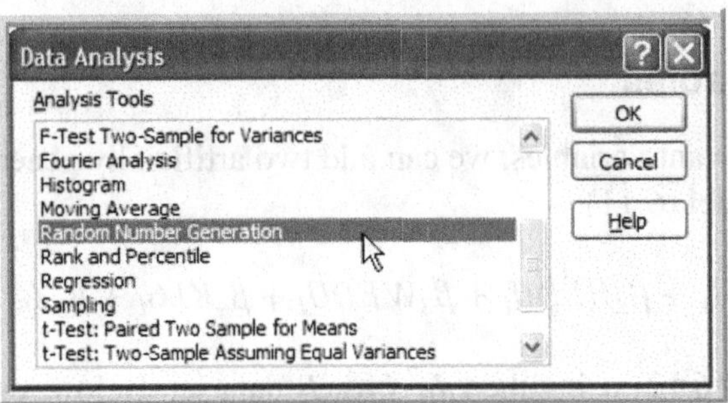

A **Random Number Generation** dialog box pops up. We need to generate two sets of random numbers: one for our X_5 variable and one for our X_6 variable, so we specify **2** in the **Number of Variables** window. We would like to generate as many data points as we have in the data set we are working with, so we specify **428** in the **Number of Random Numbers** window. We select **Normal** in the **Distribution** window; the selected **Parameters** should be **Mean** equal to **0**, and **Standard deviation** equal to **1**. Select **Output Range** and specify it to be **H2:I429**. Finally, we select **OK.**

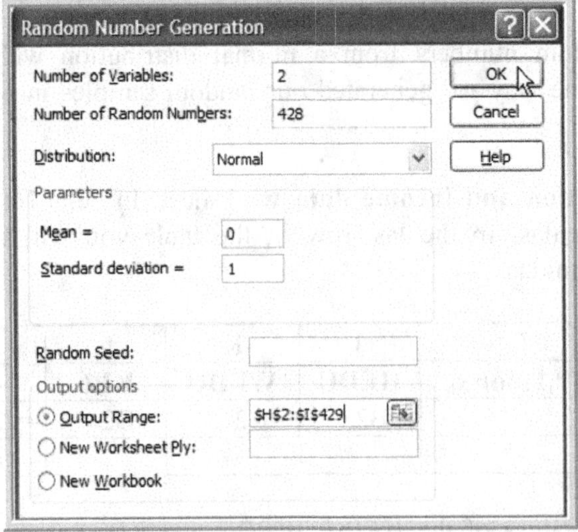

After you copy the content of cells **J2:N2** to cells **J3:N429,** your table should look like the one below (only the first five values are shown below):

	H	I	J	K	L	M	N
1	**N(0,1) for x_5**	**N(0,1) for x_6**	**HE**	**WE**	**KL6**	**x_5**	**x_6**
2	1.167550181	0.20471589	12	12	1	14.3351	26.53982
3	0.241263933	0.08421011	9	12	0	9.482528	21.56674
4	-0.723794074	0.54994871	12	12	1	10.55241	23.10236
5	0.469443648	0.53153258	10	12	0	10.93889	23.47042
6	1.790540409	-0.5618233	12	14	1	15.58108	29.01926

In the **Regression** dialog box, the **Input Y Range** should be **A1:A429**, and the **Input X Range** should be **J1:N429**. Check the box next to **Labels**. Select **new Worksheet Ply** and name it **Irrelevant Variable Model**. Finally, select **OK**.

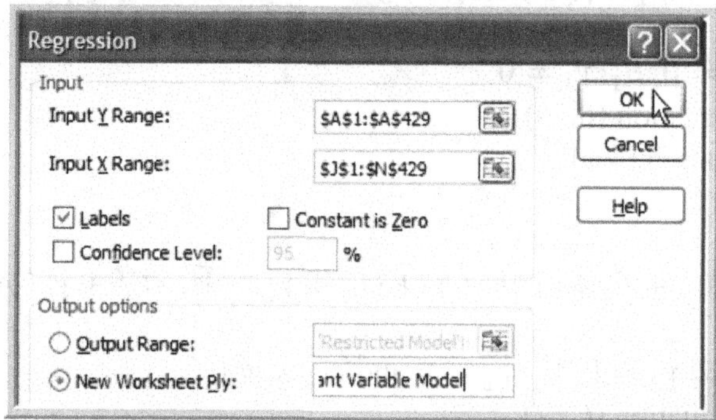

Note: we obtained different random samples than the ones recorded in the ***edu_inc*** data set, this is why our resulting estimated equation will also differ from the one reported on p. 236 of *Principles of Econometrics, 4e*. You will also obtain different parameters estimates for equation (6.12) because your random numbers will differ from those above.

Our regression analysis results are:

	A	B	C	D	E	F	G	H	I
1	SUMMARY OUTPUT								
2									
3	*Regression Statistics*								
4	Multiple R	0.421302759							
5	R Square	0.177496015							
6	Adjusted R Square	0.167750707							
7	Standard Error	40247.24063							
8	Observations	428							
9									
10	ANOVA								
11		*df*	*SS*	*MS*	*F*	*Significance F*			
12	Regression	5	1.47515E+11	29502937711	18.21348455	2.23201E-16			
13	Residual	422	6.83573E+11	1619840378					
14	Total	427	8.31087E+11						
15									
16		*Coefficients*	*Standard Error*	*t Stat*	*P-value*	*Lower 95%*	*Upper 95%*	*Lower 95.0%*	*Upper 95.0%*
17	Intercept	-7682.625152	11189.32823	-0.686602894	0.492710098	-29676.38312	14311.13281	-29676.38312	14311.13281
18	HE	3035.184489	1234.183829	2.45926451	0.014322508	609.2711683	5461.09781	609.2711683	5461.09781
19	WE	4097.602729	2248.859881	1.822080052	0.069150476	-322.7591451	8517.964604	-322.7591451	8517.964604
20	KL6	-14275.19941	5016.721707	-2.84552348	0.004649863	-24136.07405	-4414.324769	-24136.07405	-4414.324769
21	x5	-487.0440338	2234.009772	-0.218013386	0.827524063	-4878.216514	3904.128447	-4878.216514	3904.128447
22	x6	665.267784	1945.482493	0.341955164	0.732554863	-3158.775105	4489.310673	-3158.775105	4489.310673

6.6.3 The RESET Test

Let (b_1, b_2, b_3, b_4) be the least squares estimates of the family income model (6.11); the predicted values of family income are:

$$\widehat{FAMINC}_i = b_1 + b_2 HEDU_i + b_3 WEDU_i + b_4 KL6_i \tag{6.15}$$

Consider further the following two artificial models and their associated test for misspecification. We will use an *F*-test for both even though a *t*-test could be used for the RESET test 1.

$$FAMINC_i = \beta_1 + \beta_2 HEDU_i + \beta_3 WEDU_i + \beta_4 KL6_i + \gamma_1 \widehat{FAMINC}_i^2 + e_i \tag{6.16}$$

RESET test 1: $H_0: \gamma_1 = 0, H_1: \gamma_1 \neq 0$
Unrestricted model: equation (6.16)
Restricted model: equation (6.11)

$$FAMINC_i = \beta_1 + \beta_2 HEDU_i + \beta_3 WEDU_i + \beta_4 KL6_i + \gamma_1 \widehat{FAMINC}_i^2 + \gamma_2 \widehat{FAMINC}_i^3 + e_i \tag{6.17}$$

RESET test 2: $H_0: \gamma_1 = \gamma_2 = 0, H_1: \gamma_1 \neq 0$ and/or $\gamma_2 \neq 0$
Unrestricted model: equation (6.17)
Restricted model: equation (6.11)

Go back to your **education and income data** worksheet, from where we will first estimate the restricted model (6.12). In the **Regression** dialog box, the **Input Y Range** should be **A1:A429**, and the **Input X Range** should be **B1:D429**. Check the box next to **Labels**. Select **Output Range** and specify it to be cell **A1** in your **restricted Model** worksheet: you can place your cursor in the **Output Range** window and move it to that cell to do that, or type **'Restricted Model'!A1** in **the Output Range** window. Finally select **OK**.

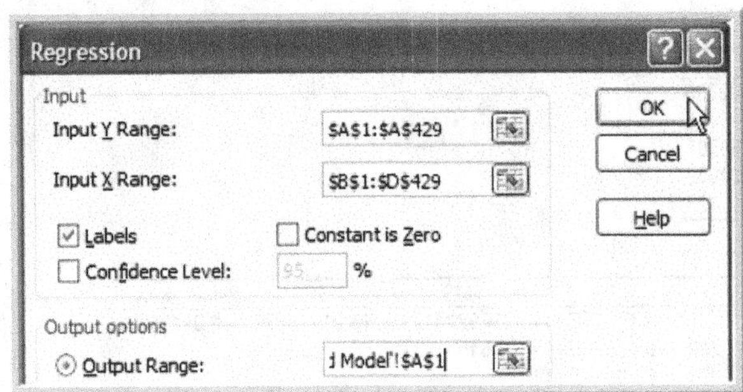

Excel informs you that the output range will overwrite existing data. Do press **OK** to overwrite the data in the specified range. The result is:

	A	B	C	D	E	F	G	H	I
1	SUMMARY OUTPUT								
2									
3	*Regression Statistics*								
4	Multiple R	0.420919613							
5	R Square	0.177173321							
6	Adjusted R Square	0.171351434							
7	Standard Error	40160.0814							
8	Observations	428							
9									
10	ANOVA								
11		*df*	*SS*	*MS*	*F*	*Significance F*			
12	Regression	3	1.47247E+11	49082167249	30.43228498	7.7736E-18			
13	Residual	424	6.83841E+11	1612832138					
14	Total	427	8.31087E+11						
15									
16		*Coefficients*	*Standard Error*	*t Stat*	*P-value*	*Lower 95%*	*Upper 95%*	*Lower 95.0%*	*Upper 95.0%*
17	Intercept	-7755.33133	11162.93447	-0.69473948	0.487599098	-29696.912	14186.24934	-29696.912	14186.24934
18	HE	3211.525676	796.7026365	4.031021775	6.58407E-05	1645.547195	4777.504158	1645.547195	4777.504158
19	WE	4776.907489	1061.16372	4.501574447	8.72703E-06	2691.111012	6862.703965	2691.111012	6862.703965
20	KL6	-14310.9203	5003.928369	-2.85993709	0.004446558	-24146.51492	-4475.32572	-24146.51492	-4475.325719

Go back to your **education and income data** worksheet. In cells **P1:W2** enter column labels and formulas as shown in the tables below.

	P	Q
1	**b1=**	='Restricted Model'!B17
2	**b2=**	='Restricted Model'!B18
3	**b3=**	='Restricted Model'!B19
4	**b4=**	='Restricted Model'!B20

In the last row of the table you will find the numbers of the equations used in the formulas, if any.

	R	S	T	U	V	W
1	**yhat**	**HEDU**	**WEDU**	**KL6**	**yhat^2**	**yhat^3**
2	=($Q$1+$Q$2*J2+$Q$3*K2+$Q$4*L2)/10000	=J2	=K2	=L2	=R2^2	=R2^3
	(6.16)					

Again note that we copy the values of the *HEDU*, *WEDU* and *KL*6 variables in columns **S-U** because we need adjacent columns of explanatory variables. Also, in cell **R2**, the division by 10,000 is there to re-scale the *y* values.

Copy the content of cells **R2:W2** to cells **R3:W429**. Here is how your table should look (only the first five values are shown below):

	P	Q	R	S	T	U	V	W
1	**b1 =**	-7755.33	**yhat**	**HEDU**	**WEDU**	**KL6**	**yhat^2**	**yhat^3**
2	**b2 =**	3211.526	7.379495	12	12	1	54.456941	401.8647041
3	**b3 =**	4776.907	7.847129	9	12	0	61.5774329	483.2060575
4	**b4 =**	-14310.9	7.379495	12	12	1	54.456941	401.8647041
5			8.168282	10	12	0	66.7208231	544.9944674
6			8.334876	12	14	1	69.4701601	579.0251793

We are now ready to estimate equation (6.16) and subsequently run the RESET test 1.

In the **Regression** dialog box, the **Input Y Range** should be **A1:A429**, and the **Input X Range** should be **S1:V429**. Check the box next to **Labels**. Select **Output Range** and specify it to be cell **A1** in your **Unrestricted Model** worksheet: you can place your cursor in the **Output Range** window and move it to that cell to do that, or type **'Unrestricted Model'!A1** in **the Output Range** window. Finally, select **OK**.

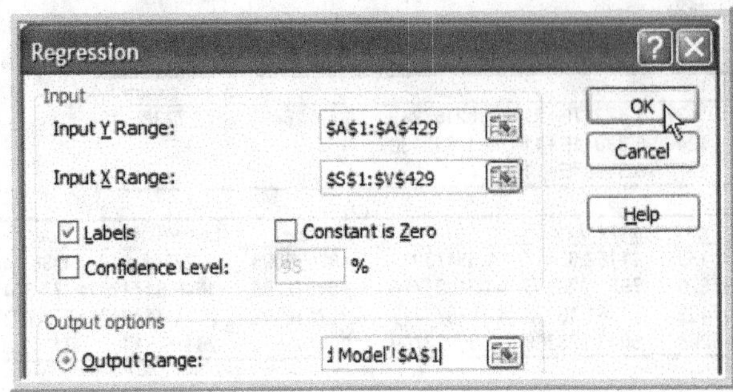

Excel informs you that the output range will overwrite existing data. Do press **OK** to overwrite the data in the specified range. The result is:

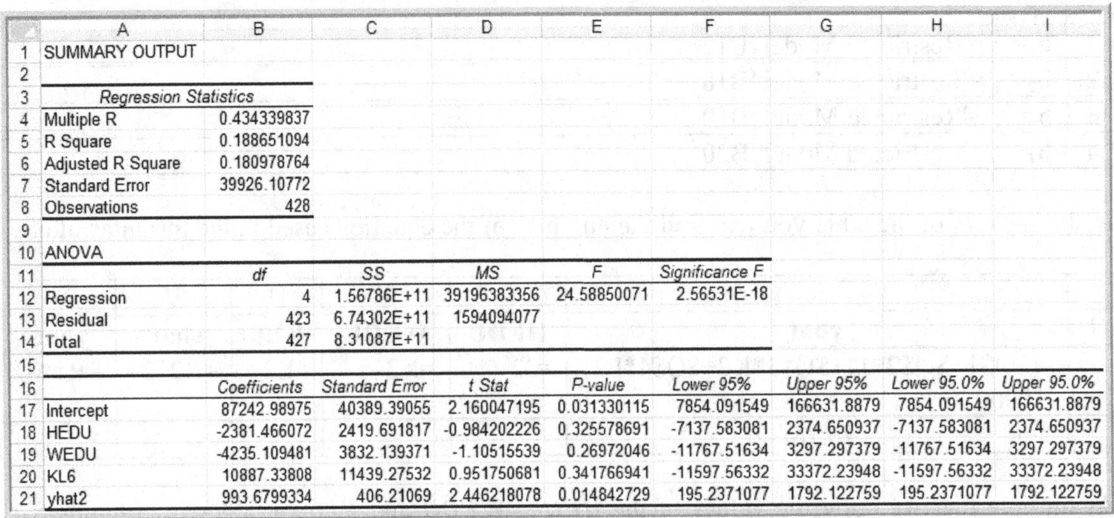

	A	B	C	D	E	F	G	H	I
1	SUMMARY OUTPUT								
2									
3	*Regression Statistics*								
4	Multiple R	0.434339837							
5	R Square	0.188651094							
6	Adjusted R Square	0.180978764							
7	Standard Error	39926.10772							
8	Observations	428							
9									
10	ANOVA								
11		*df*	*SS*	*MS*	*F*	*Significance F*			
12	Regression	4	1.56786E+11	39196383356	24.58850071	2.56531E-18			
13	Residual	423	6.74302E+11	1594094077					
14	Total	427	8.31087E+11						
15									
16		*Coefficients*	*Standard Error*	*t Stat*	*P-value*	*Lower 95%*	*Upper 95%*	*Lower 95.0%*	*Upper 95.0%*
17	Intercept	87242.98975	40389.39055	2.160047195	0.031330115	7854.091549	166631.8879	7854.091549	166631.8879
18	HEDU	-2381.466072	2419.691817	-0.984202226	0.325578691	-7137.583081	2374.650937	-7137.583081	2374.650937
19	WEDU	-4235.109481	3832.139371	-1.10515539	0.26972046	-11767.51634	3297.297379	-11767.51634	3297.297379
20	KL6	10887.33808	11439.27532	0.951750681	0.341766941	-11597.56332	33372.23948	-11597.56332	33372.23948
21	yhat2	993.6799334	406.21069	2.446218078	0.014842729	195.2371077	1792.122759	195.2371077	1792.122759

Go back to your **F-test** worksheet. With 1 restriction, at $\alpha = 0.05$, the results of RESET test 1 is (see also p. 239 of *Principles of Econometrics, 4e*):

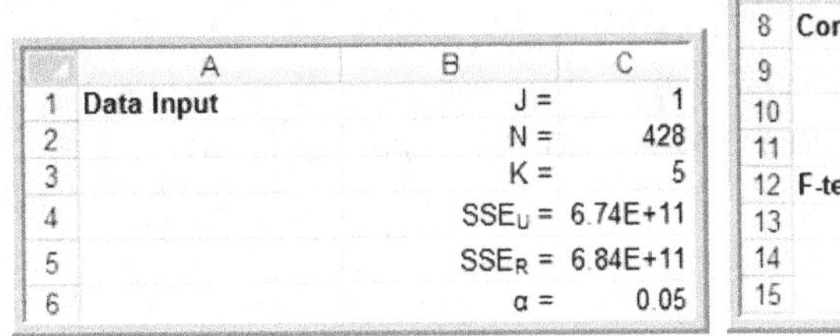

	A	B	C
1	**Data Input**	J =	1
2		N =	428
3		K =	5
4		SSE_U =	6.74E+11
5		SSE_R =	6.84E+11
6		α =	0.05

	A	B	C
8	**Computed Values**	m_1 =	1
9		m_2 =	423
10		Fc =	3.863536
11			
12	F-test	F-statistic =	5.983983
13		Conclusion =	Reject Ho
14		p-value =	0.014843
15		Conclusion =	Reject Ho

Next, we estimate equation (6.17) and subsequently run the RESET test 2.

Go back to your **education and income data** worksheet. From there, go to the **Regression** dialog box. The **Input Y Range** should be **A1:A429**, and the **Input X Range** should be **S1:W429**. Check the box next to **Labels**. Select **Output Range** and specify it to be cell **A1** in your **Unrestricted Model** worksheet: you can place your cursor in the **Output Range** window and move it to that cell to do that, or type **'Unrestricted Model'!A1** in **the Output Range** window. Finally, select **OK**.

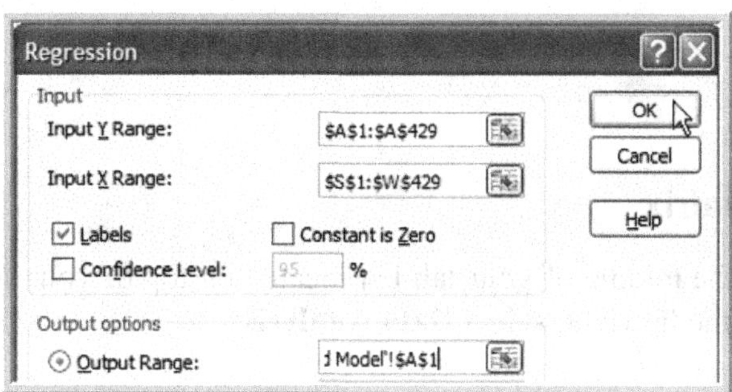

Excel informs you that the output range will overwrite existing data. Do press **OK** to overwrite the data in the specified range. The result is:

	A	B	C	D	E	F	G	H	I
1	SUMMARY OUTPUT								
2									
3	*Regression Statistics*								
4	Multiple R	0.434939912							
5	R Square	0.189172727							
6	Adjusted R Square	0.179565768							
7	Standard Error	39960.53362							
8	Observations	428							
9									
10	ANOVA								
11		*df*	*SS*	*MS*	*F*	*Significance F*			
12	Regression	5	1.57219E+11	31443811188	19.69121988	1.19924E-17			
13	Residual	422	6.73868E+11	1596844247					
14	Total	427	8.31087E+11						
15									
16		*Coefficients*	*Standard Error*	*t Stat*	*P-value*	*Lower 95%*	*Upper 95%*	*Lower 95.0%*	*Upper 95.0%*
17	Intercept	150186.5287	127386.8411	1.178979927	0.239070463	-100205.2101	400578.2674	-100205.2101	400578.2674
18	HEDU	-8451.558269	11898.91874	-0.710279518	0.477923139	-31840.08825	14936.97172	-31840.08825	14936.97172
19	WEDU	-13016.36262	17284.10885	-0.753082657	0.451820157	-46990.0292	20957.30396	-46990.0292	20957.30396
20	KL6	37410.41301	52175.36886	0.717012909	0.473762789	-65145.55912	139966.3851	-65145.55912	139966.3851
21	yhat2	3234.757008	4320.298985	0.748734525	0.454434339	-5257.228233	11726.74225	-5257.228233	11726.74225
22	yhat3	-85.69352811	164.4649942	-0.52104418	0.602609294	-408.9661322	237.579076	-408.9661322	237.579076

With 2 restrictions, at $\alpha = 0.05$, the results of RESET test 2 is (see also p. 239 of *Principles of Econometrics, 4e*):

	A	B	C
1	**Data Input**	J =	2
2		N =	428
3		K =	6
4		SSE_U =	6.74E+11
5		SSE_R =	6.84E+11
6		α =	0.05

	A	B	C
8	**Computed Values**	m_1 =	2
9		m_2 =	422
10		Fc =	3.0171
11			
12	**F-test**	F-statistic =	3.122582
13		Conclusion =	Reject Ho
14		p-value =	0.045063
15		Conclusion =	Reject Ho

6.7 POOR DATA, COLLINEARITY, AND INSIGNIFICANCE

Open the Excel file ***car***. Excel opens the data set in Sheet 1 of a new Excel file. Since we would like to save all our work from Chapter 6 in one file, create a new worksheet in your **POE Chapter 6** Excel file, name it **cars data**, and in it, copy the data set you just opened.

6.7.1 Correlation Matrix

Select the **Data** tab, in the middle of your tab list located on top of your screen. On the **Analysis** group of commands, to the far right, select **Data Analysis**.

The **Data Analysis** dialog box pops up. In it, select **Correlation** (you might need to use the scroll up and down bar to the right of the **Analysis Tools** window to find it), then select **OK**.

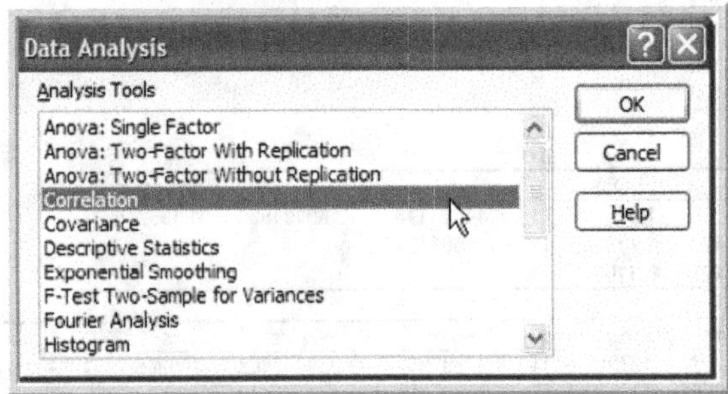

A **Correlation** dialog box pops up. Specify the **Input Range** to be **A1:D393**. Select **Grouped by Columns**, as this is how the data are stored. Check the box next to **Labels in first row**. Select **Output Range** and specify it to be **F1**. Finally, select **OK**.

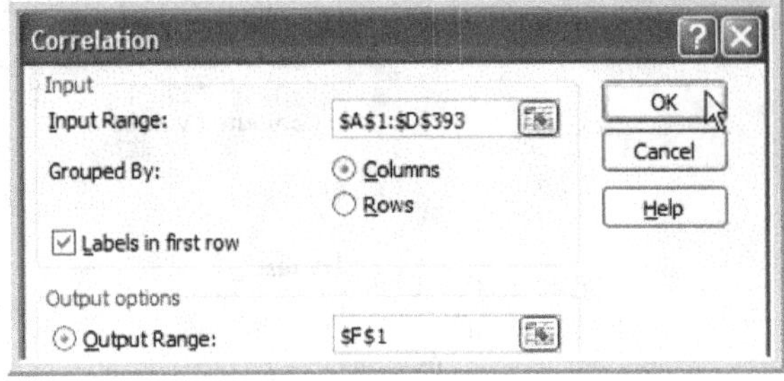

The result is:

	F	G	H	I	J
1		*MPG*	*CYL*	*ENG*	*WGT*
2	MPG	1			
3	CYL	-0.77762	1		
4	ENG	-0.80513	0.950823	1	
5	WGT	-0.83224	0.897527	0.932994	1

6.7.2 The Car Mileage Model Example

We first consider the following car mileage model.

$$MPG_i = \beta_1 + \beta_2 CYL_i + e_i \tag{6.18}$$

where MPG is miles per gallon and CYL is number of cylinders.

In the **Regression** dialog box, the **Input Y Range** should be **A1:A393**, and the **Input X Range** should be **B1:B393**. Check the box next to **Labels**. Select **New Worksheet Ply** and name it **Car Mileage Model**. Finally select **OK**.

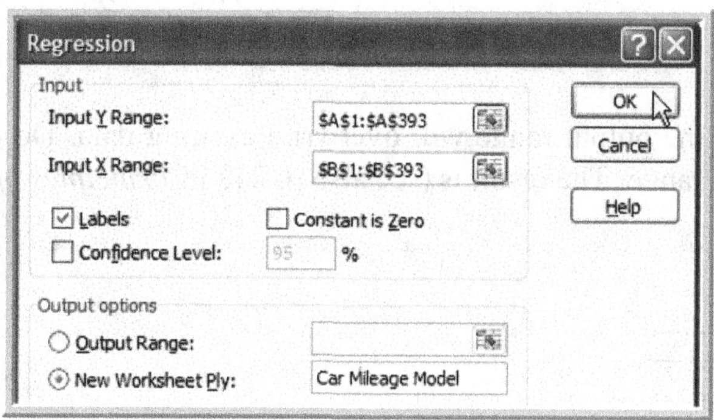

The result is (see also p. 242 in *Principles of Econometrics, 4e*):

	A	B	C	D	E	F	G	H	I
1	SUMMARY OUTPUT								
2									
3	*Regression Statistics*								
4	Multiple R	0.777617509							
5	R Square	0.60468899							
6	Adjusted R Square	0.603675372							
7	Standard Error	4.913589267							
8	Observations	392							
9									
10	ANOVA								
11		*df*	*SS*	*MS*	*F*	*Significance F*			
12	Regression	1	14403.08286	14403.08286	596.5649839	1.31138E-80			
13	Residual	390	9415.910199	24.14335948					
14	Total	391	23818.99306						
15									
16		*Coefficients*	*Standard Error*	*t Stat*	*P-value*	*Lower 95%*	*Upper 95%*	*Lower 95.0%*	*Upper 95.0%*
17	Intercept	42.9155052	0.834866841	51.4040121	8.828E-176	41.27410251	44.55690789	41.27410251	44.55690789
18	CYL	-3.558078341	0.145675537	-24.42467981	1.31138E-80	-3.844485952	-3.271670729	-3.844485952	-3.271670729

Now, consider the following *unrestricted* model:

$$MPG_i = \beta_1 + \beta_2 CYL_i + \beta_3 ENG_i + \beta_4 WGT_i + e_i \tag{6.19}$$

where ENG is the engine displacement in cubic inches and WGT is vehicle weight in pounds.

In the **Regression** dialog box, the **Input Y Range** should be **A1:A393**, and the **Input X Range** should be **B1:D393**. Check the box next to **Labels.** Select **Output Range** and specify it to be cell **A1** in your **Unrestricted Model** worksheet: you can place your cursor in the **Output Range** window and move it to that cell to do that, or type **'Unrestricted Model'!A1** in **the Output Range** window. Finally select **OK.**

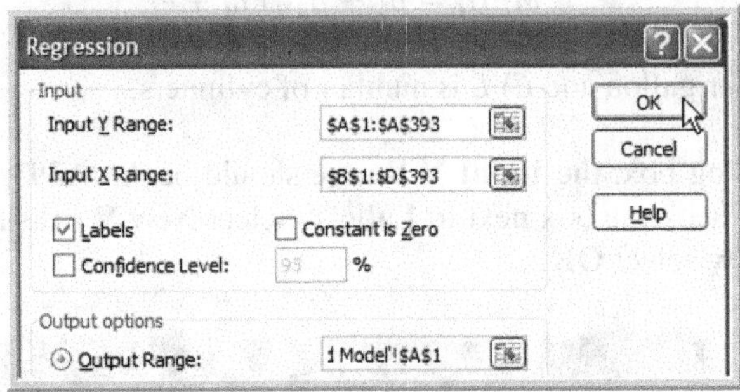

Excel informs you that the output range will overwrite existing data. Do press **OK** to overwrite the data in the specified range. The result is (see also p. 242 in *Principles of Econometrics, 4e*):

	A	B	C	D	E	F	G	H	I
1	SUMMARY OUTPUT								
2									
3	*Regression Statistics*								
4	Multiple R	0.836237128							
5	R Square	0.699292534							
6	Adjusted R Square	0.696967476							
7	Standard Error	4.296530924							
8	Observations	392							
9									
10	ANOVA								
11		*df*	*SS*	*MS*	*F*	*Significance F*			
12	Regression	3	16656.444	5552.148001	300.7635141	7.5854E-101			
13	Residual	388	7162.549057	18.46017798					
14	Total	391	23818.99306						
15									
16		*Coefficients*	*Standard Error*	*t Stat*	*P-value*	*Lower 95%*	*Upper 95%*	*Lower 95.0%*	*Upper 95.0%*
17	Intercept	44.37096115	1.480685053	29.96650844	5.3199E-103	41.459791	47.2821313	41.459791	47.2821313
18	CYL	-0.267796747	0.413067325	-0.648312588	0.517166276	-1.079927094	0.544333601	-1.079927094	0.544333601
19	ENG	-0.01267396	0.008250068	-1.536224886	0.125298269	-0.028894392	0.003546473	-0.028894392	0.003546473
20	WGT	-0.005707884	0.000713919	-7.995142549	1.50112E-14	-0.007111518	-0.00430425	-0.007111518	-0.00430425

To test the null hypothesis $H_0: \beta_2 = \beta_3 = 0$ against the alternative $H_1: \beta_2 \neq 0$ and/or $\beta_3 \neq 0$, we need to run the following *restricted* model:

$$MPG_i = \beta_1 + \beta_2 WGT_i + e_i \tag{6.20}$$

Go back to your **cars data** worksheet, and then to the **Regression** dialog box. For the restricted model (6.20), the **Input Y Range** should be **A1:A393**, and the **Input X Range** should be **B1:B393**. Check the box next to **Labels**. Select **Output Range** and specify it to be cell **A1** in your **Restricted Model** worksheet: you can place your cursor in the **Output Range** window and move it to that cell to do that, or type **'Restricted Model'!A1** in **the Output Range** window. Finally select **OK**.

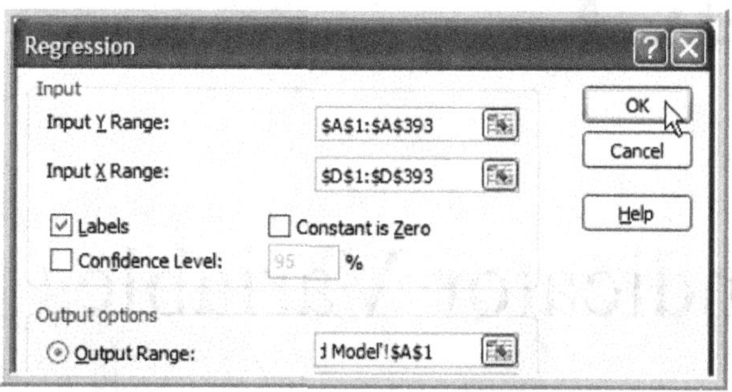

Excel informs you that the output range will overwrite existing data. Do press **OK** to overwrite the data in the specified range. With 2 restrictions in the null hypothesis $H_0\colon \beta_2 = \beta_3 = 0$, and at $\alpha = 0.05$, the results of the *F*-test are (see also p. 242 of *Principles of Econometrics, 4e*):

	A	B	C
1	**Data Input**	J =	2
2		N =	392
3		K =	4
4		SSE_U =	7162.549
5		SSE_R =	7321.234
6		α =	0.05
7			
8	**Computed Values**	m_1 =	2
9		m_2 =	388
10		Fc =	3.018982
11			
12	**F-test**	F-statistic =	4.298024
13		Conclusion =	Reject Ho
14		p-value =	0.014248
15		Conclusion =	Reject Ho

CHAPTER 7

Using Indicator Variables

CHAPTER OUTLINE

This chapter considers the use of indicator variables to add more flexibility to the regression model. We work with different examples to illustrate the use of this tool.

7.1 INDICATOR VARIABLES: THE UNIVERSITY EFFECT ON HOUSE PRICES EXAMPLE

Consider the following house price equation:

$$PRICE = \begin{array}{l} \beta_1 + \delta_1 UTOWN + \beta_2 SQFT + \gamma(SQFT \times UTOWN) \\ + \beta_3 AGE + \delta_2 POOL + \delta_3 FPLACE + e \end{array} \tag{7.1}$$

where $PRICE$ is house price in \$1000, $SQFT$ is number of hundreds of square feet of living area, and AGE is the age of the house in years. Three dummy variables are used to indicate the house location ($UTOWN = 1$ for homes near the university, 0 otherwise), whether the house has a pool ($POOL = 1$ if a pool is present, 0 otherwise) and whether the house has a fireplace ($FPLACE = 1$ if a fireplace is present, 0 otherwise).

Open the Excel file ***utown***. Save your file as **POE Chapter** 7. Rename sheet 1 **utown data**. In cell **G1** of your **utown data** worksheet, enter the column label **sqft x utown**. In cell **G2**, enter the formula **=B2*D2**; copy it to cells **G3:G1001**. Here is how your table should look (only the first five values are shown below):

	A	B	C	D	E	F	G
1	**price**	**sqft**	**age**	**utown**	**pool**	**fplace**	**sqft x utown**
2	205.452	23.46	6	0	0	1	0
3	185.328	20.03	5	0	0	1	0
4	248.422	27.77	6	0	0	0	0
5	154.69	20.17	1	0	0	0	0
6	221.801	26.45	0	0	0	1	0

In the **Regression** dialog box, the **Input Y Range** should be **A1:A1001**, and the **Input X Range** should be **B1:G1001**. Check the box next to **Labels**. Select **New Worksheet Ply** and name it **house price equation**. Finally select **OK**.

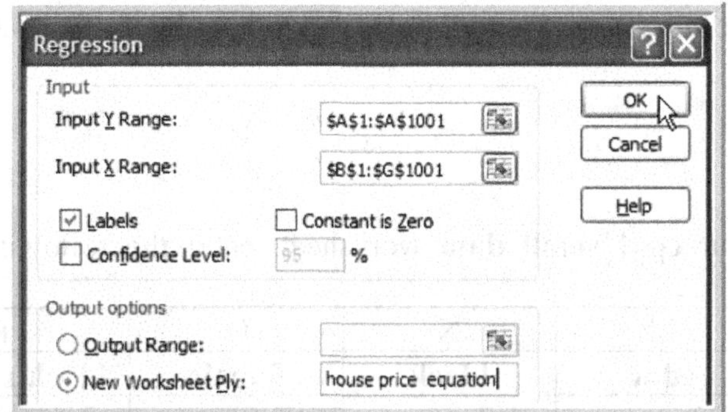

The result is (see also Table 7.2 on p. 264 of *Principles of Econometrics, 4e*):

	A	B	C	D	E	F	G	H	I
1	SUMMARY OUTPUT								
2									
3	*Regression Statistics*								
4	Multiple R	0.933043369							
5	R Square	0.870569928							
6	Adjusted R Square	0.869787873							
7	Standard Error	15.22521141							
8	Observations	1000							
9									
10	ANOVA								
11		*df*	*SS*	*MS*	*F*	*Significance F*			
12	Regression	6	1548261.73	258043.6216	1113.182743	0			
13	Residual	993	230184.413	231.8070624					
14	Total	999	1778446.143						
15									
16		*Coefficients*	*Standard Error*	*t Stat*	*P-value*	*Lower 95%*	*Upper 95%*	*Lower 95.0%*	*Upper 95.0%*
17	Intercept	24.49998329	6.191721216	3.956893801	8.13332E-05	12.34962326	36.65034333	12.34962326	36.65034333
18	sqft	7.612176612	0.245176458	31.04774691	1.8674E-148	7.131053169	8.093300056	7.131053169	8.093300056
19	age	-0.190086388	0.051204606	-3.712290812	0.000216812	-0.290568043	-0.089604732	-0.290568043	-0.089604732
20	utown	27.45295601	8.42258204	3.259446555	0.001154208	10.9248533	43.98105872	10.9248533	43.98105872
21	pool	4.377164078	1.196691609	3.65772104	0.000267836	2.028829359	6.725498798	2.028829359	6.725498798
22	fplace	1.64917557	0.971956791	1.696758113	0.090055792	-0.258149475	3.556500614	-0.258149475	3.556500614
23	sqft x utown	1.29940476	0.332047741	3.913307036	9.72454E-05	0.647808951	1.95100057	0.647808951	1.95100057

7.2 APPLYING INDICATOR VARIABLES

7.2.1 Interactions Between Qualitative Factors

Consider the following *unrestricted* wage equation:

$$WAGE = \beta_1 + \beta_2 EDUC + \delta_1 BLACK + \delta_2 FEMALE + \gamma(BLACK \times FEMALE) + e \qquad (7.2)$$

where $WAGE$ is hourly wage and $EDUC$ is years of education. $BLACK$ and $FEMALE$ are dummy variables for race and gender.

Open the Excel file ***cps4_small***. Excel opens the data set in Sheet 1 of a new Excel file. Since we would like to save all our work from Chapter 7 in one file, create a new worksheet in your **POE Chapter 7** Excel file, rename it **cps4_small data**, and in it, copy the data set you just opened.

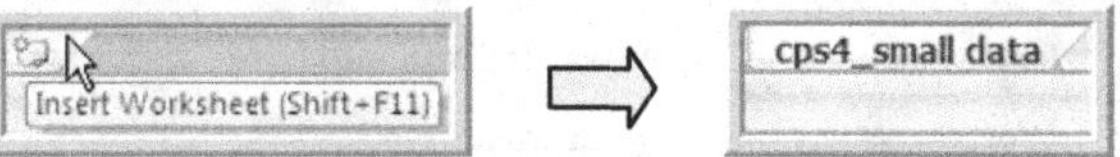

In cells **M1:P2** of your **cps4_small data** worksheet, enter the following column labels and formulas.

	M	N	O	P
1	**educ**	**black**	**female**	**black x female**
2	=B2	=K2	=F2	=N2*O2

Note that we first copy the values of $EDUC$, $BLACK$ and $FEMALE$ in columns **M-O**. Next, we create our interaction variable in column **P**; this way we end up with contiguous columns of explanatory variables.

Copy the content of cells **M2:P2** to cells **M3:P1001**. Here is how your table should look (only the first five values are shown below):

	M	N	O	P
1	**educ**	**black**	**female**	**black x female**
2	16	0	1	0
3	12	0	0	0
4	16	1	0	0
5	14	1	1	1
6	12	0	0	0

In the **Regression** dialog box, the **Input Y Range** should be **A1:A1001**, and the **Input X Range** should be **M1:P1001**. Check the box next to **Labels**. Select **New Worksheet Ply** and name it **Unrestricted Model**. Finally select **OK**.

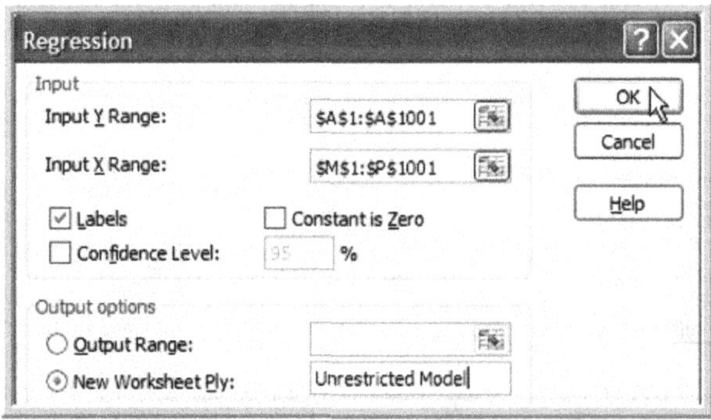

The result is (see also Table 7.3 on p. 265 of *Principles of Econometrics, 4e*):

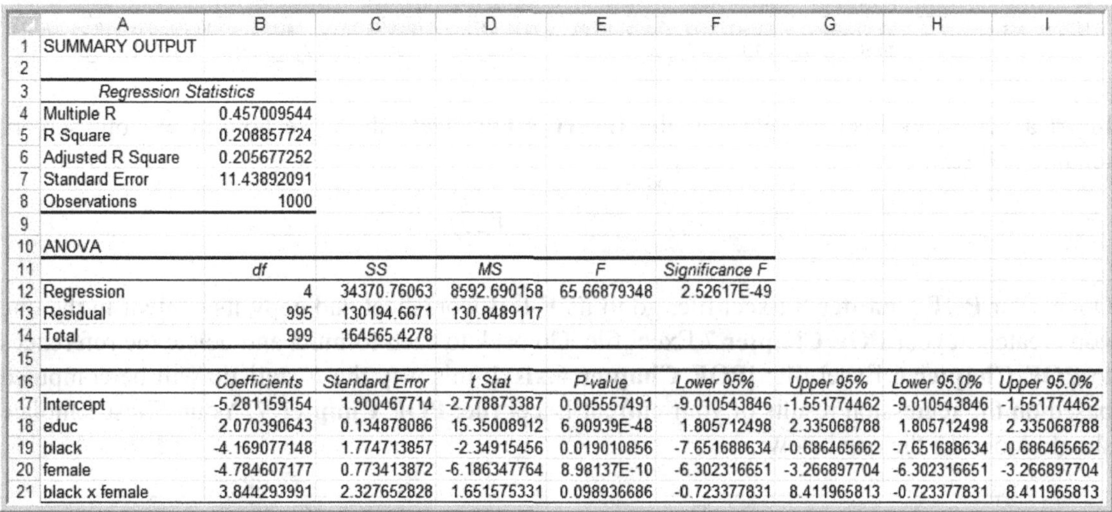

	A	B	C	D	E	F	G	H	I
1	SUMMARY OUTPUT								
2									
3	*Regression Statistics*								
4	Multiple R	0.457009544							
5	R Square	0.208857724							
6	Adjusted R Square	0.205677252							
7	Standard Error	11.43892091							
8	Observations	1000							
9									
10	ANOVA								
11		*df*	*SS*	*MS*	*F*	*Significance F*			
12	Regression	4	34370.76063	8592.690158	65.66879348	2.52617E-49			
13	Residual	995	130194.6671	130.8489117					
14	Total	999	164565.4278						
15									
16		*Coefficients*	*Standard Error*	*t Stat*	*P-value*	*Lower 95%*	*Upper 95%*	*Lower 95.0%*	*Upper 95.0%*
17	Intercept	-5.281159154	1.900467714	-2.778873387	0.005557491	-9.010543846	-1.551774462	-9.010543846	-1.551774462
18	educ	2.070390643	0.134878086	15.35008912	6.90939E-48	1.805712498	2.335068788	1.805712498	2.335068788
19	black	-4.169077148	1.774713857	-2.34915456	0.019010856	-7.651688634	-0.686465662	-7.651688634	-0.686465662
20	female	-4.784607177	0.773413872	-6.186347764	8.98137E-10	-6.302316651	-3.266897704	-6.302316651	-3.266897704
21	black x female	3.844293991	2.327652828	1.651575331	0.098936686	-0.723377831	8.411965813	-0.723377831	8.411965813

To test the hypothesis that neither race nor gender affects wages ($H_0: \delta_1 = 0, \delta_2 = 0, \gamma = 0$), the *restricted* model is:

$$WAGE = \beta_1 + \beta_2 EDUC + e \tag{7.3}$$

Go back to your **cps4_small data** worksheet. From there, go to the **Regression** dialog box. The **Input Y Range** should be **A1:A1001**, and the **Input X Range** should be **B1:B1001**. Check the box next to **Labels**. Select **New Worksheet Ply** and name it **Restricted Model**. Finally select **OK**.

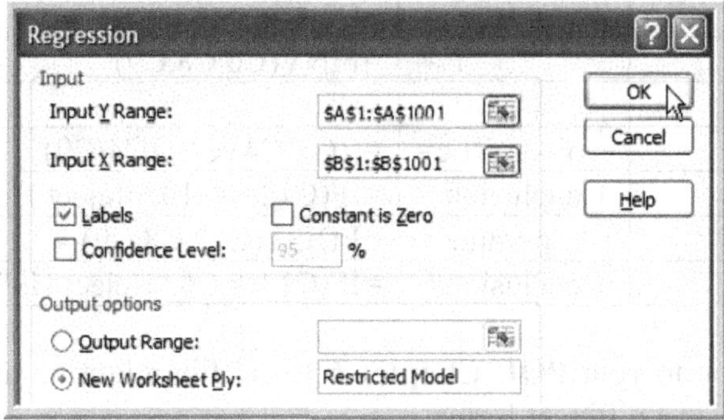

The result is (see also p. 266 of *Principles of Econometrics, 4e*):

	A	B	C	D	E	F	G	H	I
1	SUMMARY OUTPUT								
2									
3	*Regression Statistics*								
4	Multiple R	0.418296152							
5	R Square	0.174971671							
6	Adjusted R Square	0.174144989							
7	Standard Error	11.66375696							
8	Observations	1000							
9									
10	ANOVA								
11		*df*	*SS*	*MS*	*F*	*Significance F*			
12	Regression	1	28794.28782	28794.28782	211.6554318	1.24945E-43			
13	Residual	998	135771.1399	136.0432264					
14	Total	999	164565.4278						
15									
16		*Coefficients*	*Standard Error*	*t Stat*	*P-value*	*Lower 95%*	*Upper 95%*	*Lower 95.0%*	*Upper 95.0%*
17	Intercept	-6.71032842	1.914155839	-3.505633284	0.000475773	-10.46656027	-2.954096574	-10.46656027	-2.954096574
18	educ	1.980287588	0.136117372	14.54838244	1.24945E-43	1.713178506	2.247396669	1.713178506	2.247396669

Insert a new worksheet by selecting the **Insert Worksheet** tab at the bottom of your screen, rename it **F-test**.

Open your **POE Chapter 6** Excel file, go to its **F-test** worksheet and copy its content in the one you created in your **POE Chapter 7** Excel file. Go back to each formula and delete the references to **POE Chapter 6** Excel file: **[POE Chapter 6.xlsx]**; this way the *F*-statistic will be computed based on the regression results of your current Excel file: **POE Chapter 7**. Your *F*-test template should look like the one below:

	A	B	C
1	**Data Input**	J =	
2		N =	='Unrestricted Model'!B8
3		K =	='Unrestricted Model'!B12+1
4		SSE_U =	='Unrestricted Model'!C13
5		SSE_R =	='Restricted Model'!C13
6		α =	
7			
8	**Computed Values**	m_1 =	=C1
9		m_2 =	=C2-C3
10		F_c=	=FINV(C6,C8,C9)
11			
12	**F-test**	F-statistic=	=((C5-C4)/C8)/(C4/C9)
13		Conclusion =	=IF(C12>=C10,"Reject Ho","Do Not Reject Ho")
14		p-value =	=FDIST(C12,C8,C9)
15		Conclusion =	=IF(C14<=C6,"Reject Ho","Do Not Reject Ho")

Note that the extension to your **POE Chapter 6** Excel file might be different than **.xlsx** if you chose to save your file in a different format.

With 3 restrictions, at $\alpha = 0.01$, the results of the F-test are (see also p. 266 in *Principles of Econometrics, 4e*):

	A	B	C
1	Data Input	J =	3
2		N =	1000
3		K =	5
4		SSE_U =	130194.6671
5		SSE_R =	135771.1399
6		α =	0.01

	A	B	C
8	Computed Values	m_1 =	3
9		m_2 =	995
10		Fc =	3.80134471
11			
12	F-test	F-statistic =	14.20588255
13		Conclusion =	Reject Ho
14		p-value =	4.53097E-09
15		Conclusion =	Reject Ho

7.2.2 Qualitative Factors with Several Categories

Consider the following *unrestricted* wage equation:

$$WAGE = \begin{array}{l}\beta_1 + \beta_2 EDUC + \delta_1 BLACK + \delta_2 FEMALE + \gamma(BLACK \times FEMALE) \\ + \delta_3 SOUTH + \delta_4 MIDWEST + \delta_5 WEST + e\end{array} \tag{7.4}$$

where $SOUTH$, $MIDWEST$ and $WEST$ are region dummy variables.

Go back to your **cps4_small data** worksheet. In cells **Q1:S2**, enter the following column labels and formulas.

	Q	R	S
1	**south**	**midwest**	**west**
2	=I2	=H2	=J2

Note that all we are doing is copying the values of $SOUTH$, $MIDWEST$ and $WEST$ in columns **Q-S** so as to create columns of explanatory variables next to one another.

Copy the content of cells **Q2:S2** to cells **Q3:S1001**. Here is how your table should look (only the first five values are shown below):

	Q	R	S
1	south	midwest	west
2	1	0	0
3	0	1	0
4	0	0	1
5	1	0	0
6	0	0	0

In the **Regression** dialog box, the **Input Y Range** should be **A1:A1001**, and the **Input X Range** should be **M1:S1001**. Check the box next to **Labels**. Select **Output Range** and specify it to be cell **A1** in your **Unrestricted Model** worksheet: you can place your cursor in the **Output Range** window and move it to that cell to do that, or type **'Unrestricted Model'!A1** in **the Output Range** window. Finally, select **OK**.

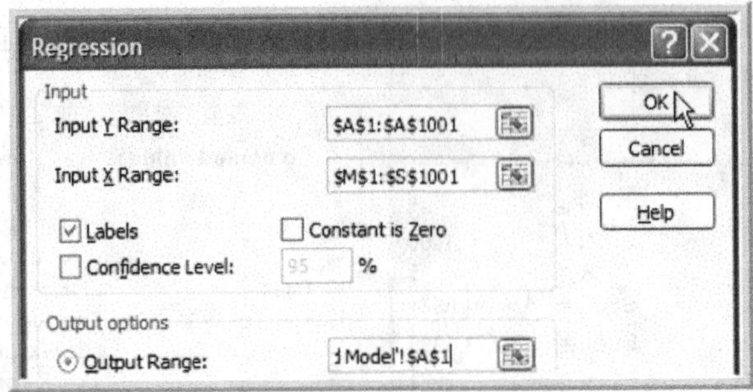

Excel informs you that the output range will overwrite existing data. Do select **OK** to overwrite the data in the specified range.

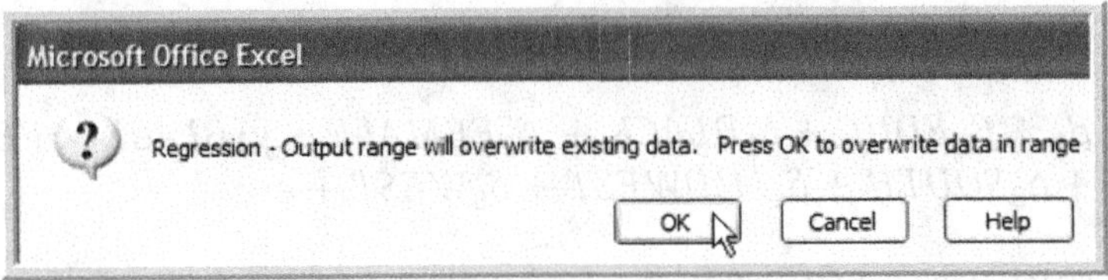

The result is (see also Table 7.4 on p. 267 of *Principles of Econometrics, 4e*):

	A	B	C	D	E	F	G	H	I
1	SUMMARY OUTPUT								
2									
3	*Regression Statistics*								
4	Multiple R	0.467853351							
5	R Square	0.218886758							
6	Adjusted R Square	0.213374871							
7	Standard Error	11.38335986							
8	Observations	1000							
9									
10	ANOVA								
11		*df*	*SS*	*MS*	*F*	*Significance F*			
12	Regression	7	36021.19302	5145.884717	39.71175875	2.31981E-49			
13	Residual	992	128544.2347	129.5808818					
14	Total	999	164565.4278						
15									
16		*Coefficients*	*Standard Error*	*t Stat*	*P-value*	*Lower 95%*	*Upper 95%*	*Lower 95.0%*	*Upper 95.0%*
17	Intercept	-4.806209986	2.028691142	-2.369118634	0.018021216	-8.78722871	-0.825191262	-8.78722871	-0.825191262
18	educ	2.071230565	0.13446871	15.40306709	3.685E-48	1.807354788	2.335106343	1.807354788	2.335106343
19	black	-3.905465125	1.786257824	-2.186394972	0.029019773	-7.410742837	-0.400187414	-7.410742837	-0.400187414
20	female	-4.744129209	0.769838107	-6.162502431	1.03977E-09	-6.254827342	-3.233431076	-6.254827342	-3.233431076
21	black x female	3.625020988	2.318375246	1.563604077	0.118229512	-0.924461718	8.174503693	-0.924461718	8.174503693
22	south	-0.449905574	1.025023817	-0.438922069	0.660813586	-2.461369479	1.561558331	-2.461369479	1.561558331
23	midwest	-2.608405756	1.059643866	-2.461587181	0.014001631	-4.687806599	-0.529004913	-4.687806599	-0.529004913
24	west	0.986633193	1.05981507	0.930948447	0.35210673	-1.093103614	3.066370001	-1.093103614	3.066370001

To test the hypothesis that there are no regional differences ($H_0: \delta_3 = 0,\ \delta_4 = 0,\ \delta_5 = 0$), the *restricted* model is our old unrestricted model (7.2).

Go back to your **cps4_small data** worksheet. From there, go to the **Regression** dialog box. The **Input Y Range** should be **A1:A1001**, and the **Input X Range** should be **M1:P1001**. Check the box next to **Labels**. Select **Output Range** and specify it to be cell **A1** in your **Restricted Model** worksheet: you can place your cursor in the **Output Range** window and move it to that cell to do that, or type **'Restricted Model'!A1** in **the Output Range** window. Finally, select **OK**.

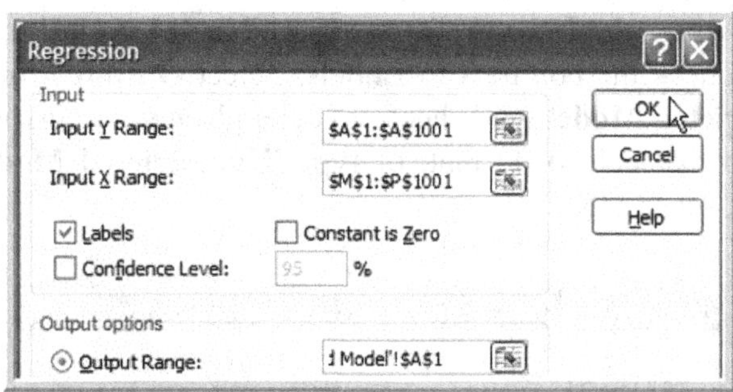

Excel informs you that the output range will overwrite existing data. Do select **OK** to overwrite the data in the specified range. With 3 restrictions, at $\alpha = 0.01$, the results of the *F*-test are (see also p. 268 in *Principles of Econometrics, 4e*):

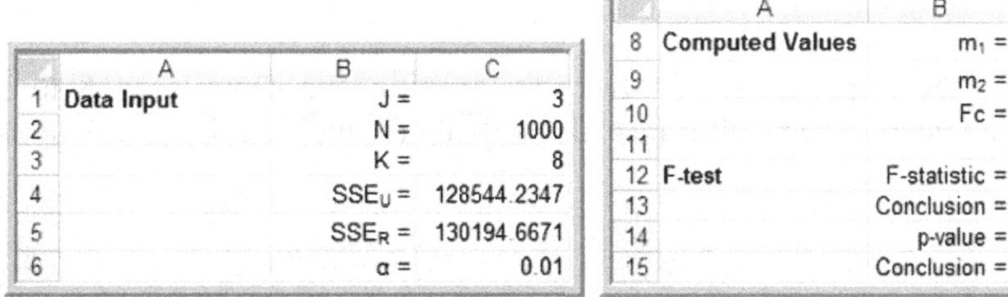

	A	B	C
1	**Data Input**	J =	3
2		N =	1000
3		K =	8
4		SSE_U =	128544.2347
5		SSE_R =	130194.6671
6		α =	0.01

	A	B	C
8	**Computed Values**	m_1 =	3
9		m_2 =	992
10		Fc =	3.801404549
11			
12	**F-test**	F-statistic =	4.24556555
13		Conclusion =	Reject Ho
14		p-value =	0.005427617
15		Conclusion =	Reject Ho

7.2.3 Testing the Equivalence of Two Regressions

Consider the following *unrestricted* wage equation:

$$
\begin{aligned}
WAGE = \ & \beta_1 + \beta_2 EDUC + \delta_1 BLACK + \delta_2 FEMALE + \gamma(BLACK \times FEMALE) \\
& + \theta_1 SOUTH + \theta_2(EDUC \times SOUTH) + \theta_3(BLACK \times SOUTH) \\
& + \theta_4(FEMALE \times SOUTH) + \theta_5(BLACK \times FEMALE \times SOUTH) + e
\end{aligned} \tag{7.5}
$$

Go back to your **cps4_small data** worksheet. Insert four columns to the left of the **midwest** column **R** (see Section 1.4 for more details on how to do that). In your new cells **R1:U2**, enter the following column labels and formulas.

	R	S	T	U
1	**educ x south**	**black x south**	**female x south**	**black x female x south**
2	=M2*Q2	=N2*Q2	=O2*Q2	=P2*Q2

Copy the content of cells **R2:U2** to cells **R3:U1001**. Here is how your table should look (only the first five values are shown below):

	R	S	T	U
1	**educ x south**	**black x south**	**female x south**	**black x female x south**
2	16	0	1	0
3	0	0	0	0
4	0	0	0	0
5	14	1	1	1
6	0	0	0	0

In the **Regression** dialog box, the **Input Y Range** should be **A1:A1001**, and the **Input X Range** should be **M1:U1001**. Check the box next to **Labels**. Select **Output Range** and specify it to be cell **A1** in your **Unrestricted Model** worksheet: you can place your cursor in the **Output Range** window and move it to that cell to do that, or type **'Unrestricted Model'!A1** in **the Output Range** window. Finally, select **OK**.

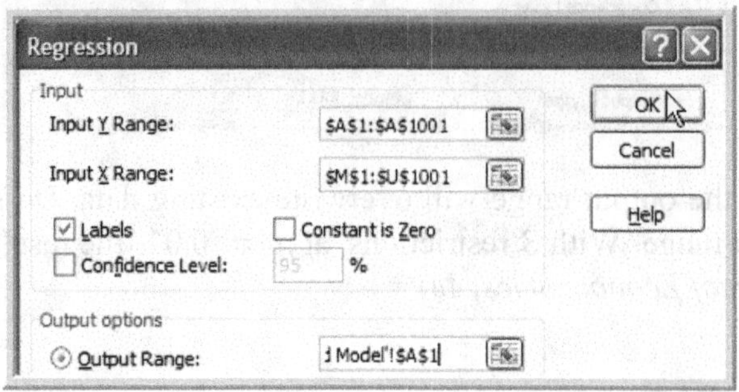

Excel informs you that the output range will overwrite existing data. Do select **OK** to overwrite the data in the specified range. The result is (see also column (1) in Table 7.5 p. 269 of *Principles of Econometrics, 4e*):

	A	B	C	D	E	F	G	H	I
1	SUMMARY OUTPUT								
2									
3	*Regression Statistics*								
4	Multiple R	0.458405258							
5	R Square	0.210135381							
6	Adjusted R Square	0.202954794							
7	Standard Error	11.458507							
8	Observations	1000							
9									
10	ANOVA								
11		*df*	*SS*	*MS*	*F*	*Significance F*			
12	Regression	9	34581.01886	3842.335429	29.26437183	2.00107E-45			
13	Residual	990	129984.4089	131.2973827					
14	Total	999	164565.4278						
15									
16		*Coefficients*	*Standard Error*	*t Stat*	*P-value*	*Lower 95%*	*Upper 95%*	*Lower 95.0%*	*Upper 95.0%*
17	Intercept	-6.605572133	2.336627655	-2.826968225	0.004793752	-11.19088392	-2.020260348	-11.19088392	-2.020260348
18	educ	2.172553705	0.166463888	13.05120126	4.88652E-36	1.845891121	2.499216289	1.845891121	2.499216289
19	black	-5.089359916	2.643060109	-1.925555873	0.054446013	-10.27600343	0.097283596	-10.27600343	0.097283596
20	female	-5.005077886	0.899007421	-5.567337678	3.33081E-08	-6.769256836	-3.240898937	-6.769256836	-3.240898937
21	black x female	5.305574257	3.497266824	1.517063045	0.129570005	-1.557332955	12.16848147	-1.557332955	12.16848147
22	south	3.943910383	4.048453462	0.974177033	0.330206612	-4.000625124	11.88844589	-4.000625124	11.88844589
23	educ x south	-0.30854104	0.285734274	-1.079818099	0.280486184	-0.869255423	0.252173342	-0.869255423	0.252173342
24	black x south	1.704395981	3.633326787	0.469100656	0.639100976	-5.425510276	8.834302238	-5.425510276	8.834302238
25	female x south	0.901119838	1.772664962	0.508341879	0.611326856	-2.577492394	4.379732069	-2.577492394	4.379732069
26	black x female x south	-2.935833839	4.787647047	-0.613210166	0.539878232	-12.33093553	6.459267852	-12.33093553	6.459267852

To test the hypothesis that there is no difference in the wage equation between the southern region and the rest of the country ($H_0: \theta_1 = \theta_2 = \theta_3 = \theta_4 = \theta_5 = 0$), the *restricted* model is our old unrestricted model (7.3). With 5 restrictions, at $\alpha = 0.1$, the results of the *F*-test are (see also p. 270 in *Principles of Econometrics, 4e*):

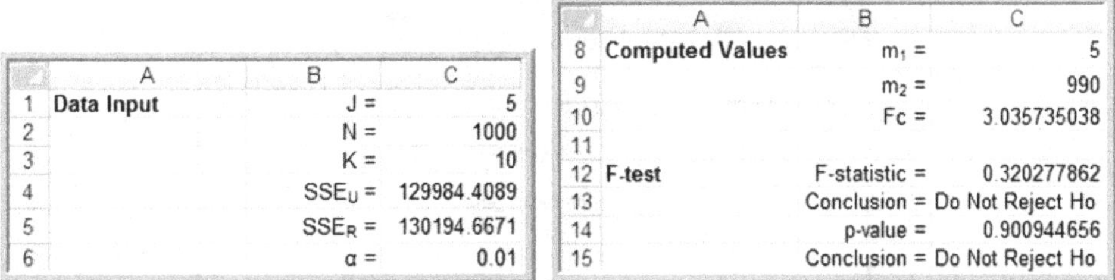

	A	B	C
1	Data Input	J =	5
2		N =	1000
3		K =	10
4		SSE_U =	129984.4089
5		SSE_R =	130194.6671
6		α =	0.01

	A	B	C
8	Computed Values	m_1 =	5
9		m_2 =	990
10		Fc =	3.035735038
11			
12	F-test	F-statistic =	0.320277862
13		Conclusion =	Do Not Reject Ho
14		p-value =	0.900944656
15		Conclusion =	Do Not Reject Ho

Note that as explained on pp. 268-269 of *Principles of Econometrics, 4e*, estimating (7.5) is equivalent to estimating (7.2) twice—once for the southern workers and again for workers in the rest of the country.

We first sort our data according to the region of origin of the workers. Go back to your **cps4_small data** worksheet. Go to the **Data** tab in the middle of your tab list on top of your screen. On the **Sort & Filter** group of commands, select the **Sort** button.

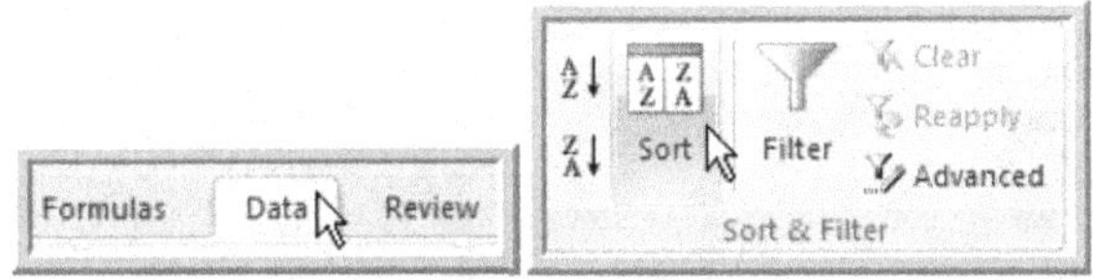

Note, alternatively you can select the **Sort & Filter** button in the **Editing** group of commands on the **Home** tab. On the drop down menu, select **Custom Sort.**

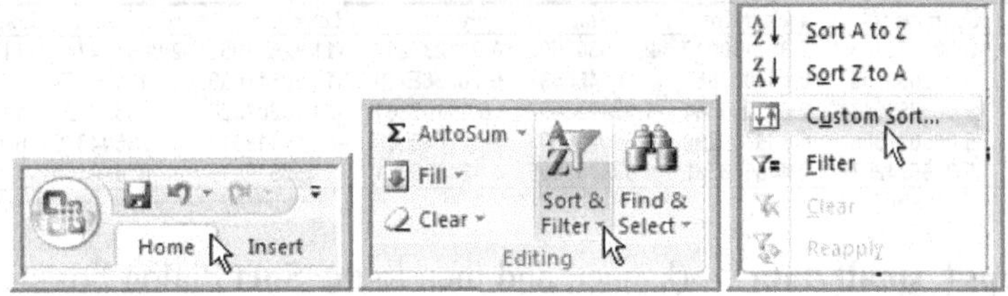

A **Sort** dialog box opens. Select the box next to **My data has headers**. Select the **south** dummy variable column in the **Sort by** window. **Values** should be selected in the **Sort On** window and **Smallest to Largest** in the **Order** window. Finally, select **OK.**

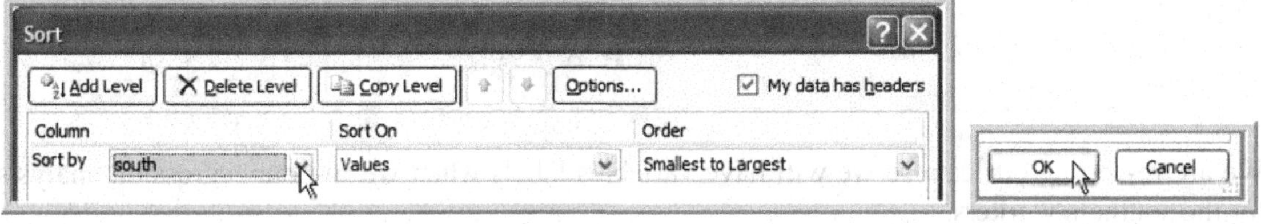

In the **Regression** dialog box, <u>*for the non-southern workers wage equation*</u>, the **Input Y Range** should be **A1:A705**, and the **Input X Range** should be **M1:P705**. Check the box next to **Labels.** Select **New Worksheet Ply** and name it **Non-South Wage Equation**. Finally select **OK.**

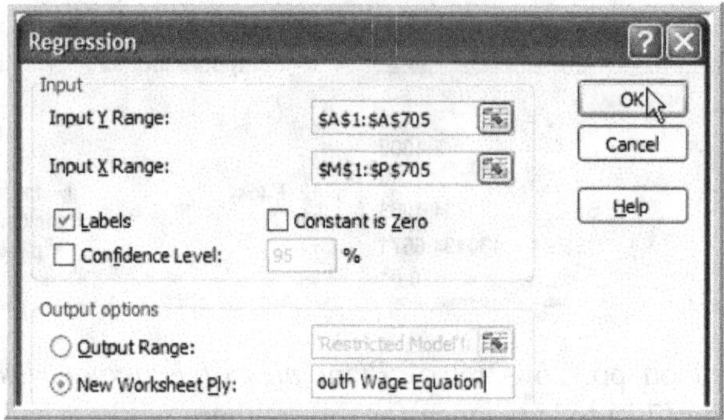

The result is (see also column (2) in Table 7.5 p. 269 of *Principles of Econometrics, 4e*):

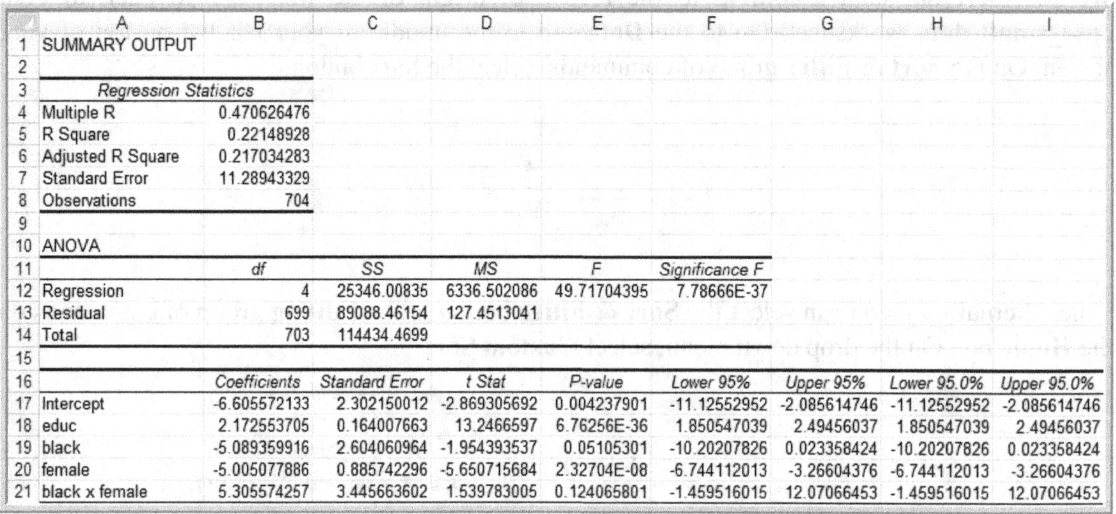

	A	B	C	D	E	F	G	H	I
1	SUMMARY OUTPUT								
2									
3	*Regression Statistics*								
4	Multiple R	0.470626476							
5	R Square	0.22148928							
6	Adjusted R Square	0.217034283							
7	Standard Error	11.28943329							
8	Observations	704							
9									
10	ANOVA								
11		*df*	*SS*	*MS*	*F*	*Significance F*			
12	Regression	4	25346.00835	6336.502086	49.71704395	7.78666E-37			
13	Residual	699	89088.46154	127.4513041					
14	Total	703	114434.4699						
15									
16		*Coefficients*	*Standard Error*	*t Stat*	*P-value*	*Lower 95%*	*Upper 95%*	*Lower 95.0%*	*Upper 95.0%*
17	Intercept	-6.605572133	2.302150012	-2.869305692	0.004237901	-11.12552952	-2.085614746	-11.12552952	-2.085614746
18	educ	2.172553705	0.164007663	13.2466597	6.76256E-36	1.850547039	2.49456037	1.850547039	2.49456037
19	black	-5.089359916	2.604060964	-1.954393537	0.05105301	-10.20207826	0.023358424	-10.20207826	0.023358424
20	female	-5.005077886	0.885742296	-5.650715684	2.32704E-08	-6.744112013	-3.26604376	-6.744112013	-3.26604376
21	black x female	5.305574257	3.445663602	1.539783005	0.124065801	-1.459516015	12.07066453	-1.459516015	12.07066453

Go back to your **cps4_small data** worksheet, and then to the **Sort** dialog box. Change the **Order** to **Largest to Smallest**, and select **OK**.

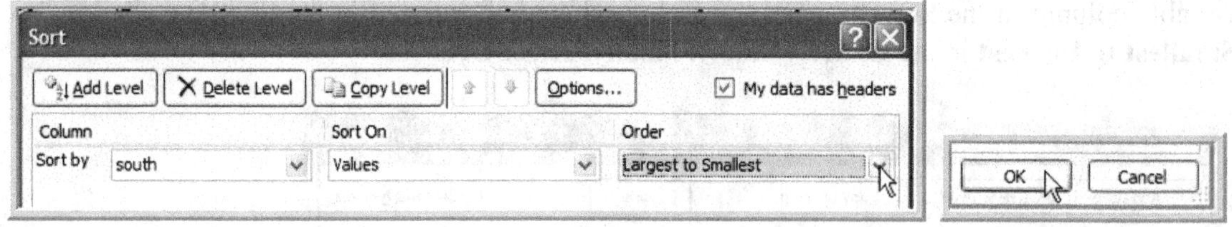

We are re-sorting our data so we will have variables labels when we run our regression analysis for the southern workers.

In the **Regression** dialog box, *<u>for the southern workers wage equation</u>*, the **Input Y Range** should be **A1:A297**, and the **Input X Range** should be **M1:P297**. Check the box next to **Labels**. Select **New Worksheet Ply** and name it **South Wage Equation**. Finally select **OK**.

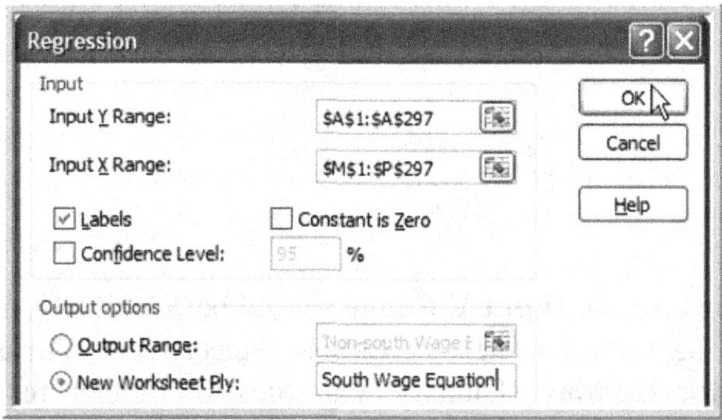

The result is (see also column (3) in Table 7.5 p. 269 of *Principles of Econometrics, 4e*):

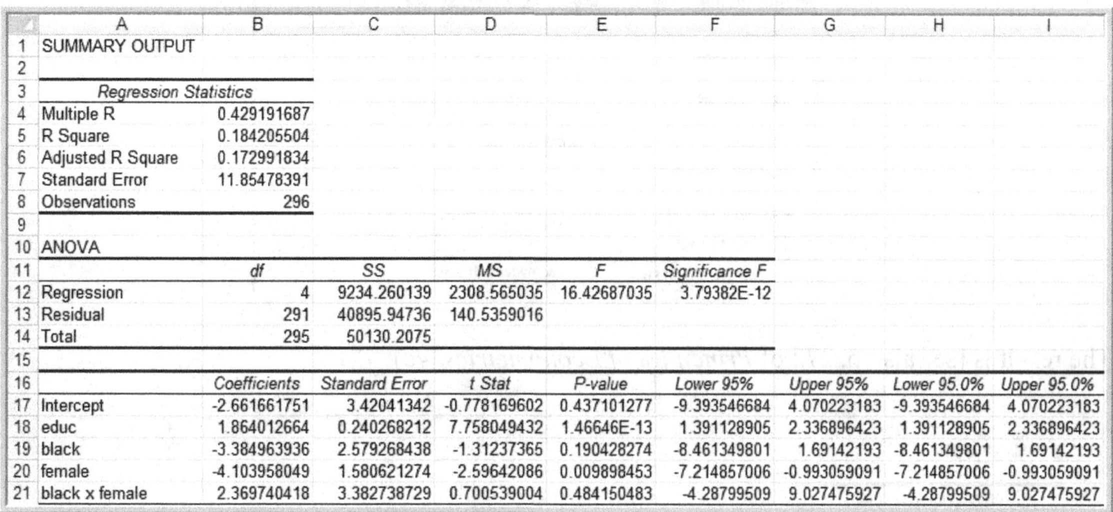

	A	B	C	D	E	F	G	H	I
1	SUMMARY OUTPUT								
2									
3	*Regression Statistics*								
4	Multiple R	0.429191687							
5	R Square	0.184205504							
6	Adjusted R Square	0.172991834							
7	Standard Error	11.85478391							
8	Observations	296							
9									
10	ANOVA								
11		*df*	*SS*	*MS*	*F*	*Significance F*			
12	Regression	4	9234.260139	2308.565035	16.42687035	3.79382E-12			
13	Residual	291	40895.94736	140.5359016					
14	Total	295	50130.2075						
15									
16		*Coefficients*	*Standard Error*	*t Stat*	*P-value*	*Lower 95%*	*Upper 95%*	*Lower 95.0%*	*Upper 95.0%*
17	Intercept	-2.661661751	3.42041342	-0.778169602	0.437101277	-9.393546684	4.070223183	-9.393546684	4.070223183
18	educ	1.864012664	0.240268212	7.758049432	1.46646E-13	1.391128905	2.336896423	1.391128905	2.336896423
19	black	-3.384963936	2.579268438	-1.31237365	0.190428274	-8.461349801	1.69142193	-8.461349801	1.69142193
20	female	-4.103958049	1.580621274	-2.59642086	0.009898453	-7.214857006	-0.993059091	-7.214857006	-0.993059091
21	black x female	2.369740418	3.382738729	0.700539004	0.484150483	-4.28799509	9.027475927	-4.28799509	9.027475927

7.3 LOG-LINEAR MODELS: A WAGE EQUATION EXAMPLE

Consider the following wage equation:

$$ln(WAGE) = \beta_1 + \beta_2 EDUC + \delta\, FEMALE + e \tag{7.6}$$

Go back to your **cps4_small data** worksheet. In cells **X1:Z2**, enter the following column labels and formulas.

	X	Y	Z
1	**ln(wage)**	**educ**	**female**
2	=ln(A2)	=M2	=O2

Copy the content of cells **X2:Z2** to cells **X3:Z1001**. Here is how your table should look (only the first five values are shown below):

	X	Y	Z
1	ln(wage)	educ	female
2	2.928524	16	1
3	3.256172	14	1
4	3.766997	16	1
5	2.956472	12	0
6	2.639057	14	1

In the **Regression** dialog box, the **Input Y Range** should be **X1:X1001**, and the **Input X Range** should be **Y1:Z1001**. Check the box next to **Labels**. Select **New Worksheet Ply** and name it **Log-Linear Model with Dummy** (Dummy Variables is another name used for Indicator Variables). Finally select **OK**.

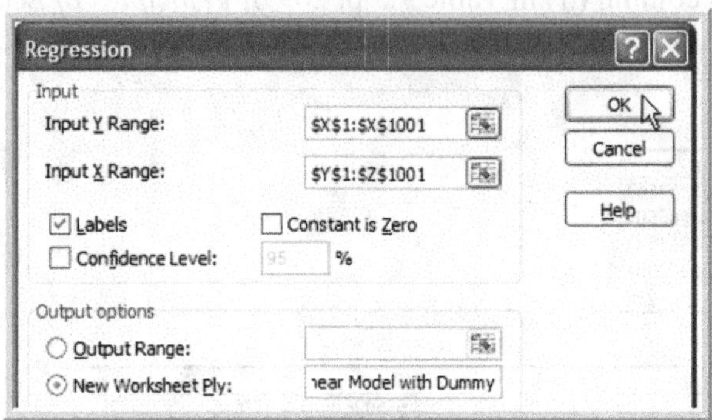

The result is (see also p. 272 of *Principles of Econometrics, 4e*):

	A	B	C	D	E	F	G	H	I
1	SUMMARY OUTPUT								
2									
3	*Regression Statistics*								
4	Multiple R	0.470464761							
5	R Square	0.221337091							
6	Adjusted R Square	0.219775079							
7	Standard Error	0.512862309							
8	Observations	1000							
9									
10	ANOVA								
11		*df*	*SS*	*MS*	*F*	*Significance F*			
12	Regression	2	74.54206772	37.27103386	141.7000075	6.88208E-55			
13	Residual	997	262.2386647	0.263027748					
14	Total	999	336.7807325						
15									
16		*Coefficients*	*Standard Error*	*t Stat*	*P-value*	*Lower 95%*	*Upper 95%*	*Lower 95.0%*	*Upper 95.0%*
17	Intercept	1.653867936	0.084378578	19.60056664	1.2991E-72	1.488287955	1.819447917	1.488287955	1.819447917
18	educ	0.096248417	0.006036534	15.94431669	3.76132E-51	0.084402647	0.108094187	0.084402647	0.108094187
19	female	-0.243213958	0.032727505	-7.431484915	2.30636E-13	-0.307436652	-0.178991264	-0.307436652	-0.178991264

7.4 THE LINEAR PROBABILITY MODEL: A MARKETING EXAMPLE

Consider the following equation:

$$COKE = \beta_1 + \beta_2 PRATIO + \beta_3 DISP\_COKE + \beta_4 DISP\_PEPSI + e \tag{7.7}$$

where
$$COKE = \begin{cases} 1 \text{ if Coke is chosen} \\ 0 \text{ if Pepsi is chosen} \end{cases}$$

$$DISP\_COKE = \begin{cases} 1 \text{ if store display is present for Coke} \\ 0 \text{ if store dispaly is absent for Coke} \end{cases}$$

$$DISP\_PEPSI = \begin{cases} 1 \text{ if store display is present for Pepsi} \\ 0 \text{ if store display is absent for Pepsi} \end{cases}$$

and $PRATIO$ is the relative price of Coke to Pepsi.

Open the Excel file ***coke***. Excel opens the data set in Sheet 1 of a new Excel file. Since we would like to save all our work from Chapter 7 in one file, create a new worksheet in your **POE Chapter 7** Excel file, rename it **coke data**, and in it, copy the data set you just opened.

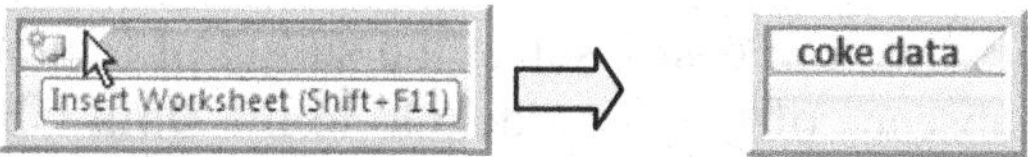

In the **Regression** dialog box, the **Input Y Range** should be **A1:A1141**, and the **Input X Range** should be **D1:F1141**. Check the box next to **Labels**. Select **New Worksheet Ply** and name it **Marketing Model**. Finally select **OK**.

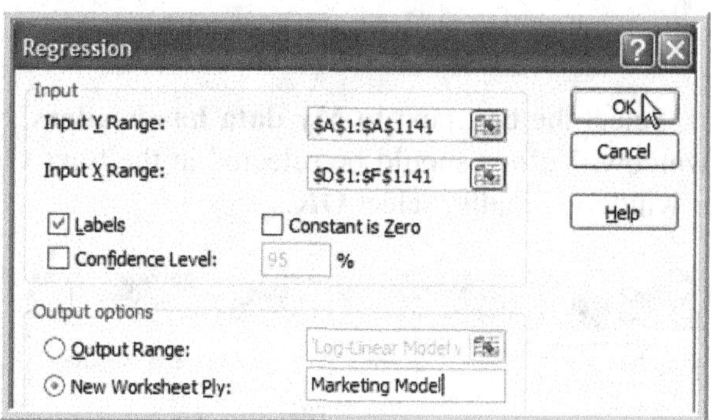

The result is (see also p. 275 of *Principles of Econometrics, 4e*):

	A	B	C	D	E	F	G	H	I
16		Coefficients	Standard Error	t Stat	P-value	Lower 95%	Upper 95%	Lower 95.0%	Upper 95.0%
17	Intercept	0.890215056	0.065484883	13.59420692	4.14847E-39	0.761730152	1.018699959	0.761730152	1.018699959
18	disp_pepsi	-0.165663685	0.035599674	-4.653516882	3.64699E-06	-0.235512182	-0.095815187	-0.235512182	-0.095815187
19	disp_coke	0.077174455	0.034391933	2.243969687	0.025026335	0.009695612	0.144653298	0.009695612	0.144653298
20	pratio	-0.400861399	0.061349448	-6.534066944	9.64113E-11	-0.521232352	-0.280490445	-0.521232352	-0.280490445

7.5 THE DIFFERENCE ESTIMATOR: THE PROJECT STAR EXAMPLE

Consider the following equations:

$$TOTALSCORE_i = \beta_1 + \beta_2 SMALL_i + e_i \tag{7.8}$$

$$TOTALSCORE_i = \beta_1 + \beta_2 SMALL_i + \beta_3 TCHEXPER_i + e_i \qquad (7.9)$$

where $SMALL = \begin{cases} 1 \text{ if the student was assigned to a small class} \\ 0 \text{ otherwise} \end{cases}$

and $TOTALSCORE$ is the combined reading and math achievement scores; $TCHEXPER$ is the teacher years of experience.

Open the Excel file ***star***. Excel opens the data set in Sheet 1 of a new Excel file. Since we would like to save all our work from Chapter 7 in one file, create a new worksheet in your **POE Chapter 7** Excel file, rename it **star data**, and in it, copy the data set you just opened.

We first sort our **star data** so we can easily select the subset of regular and small classes only-- those characterized by the absence of teacher aide. Go to the **Data** tab in the middle of your tab list on top of your screen. Select all **star data**. On the **Sort & Filter** group of commands, select the **Sort** button.

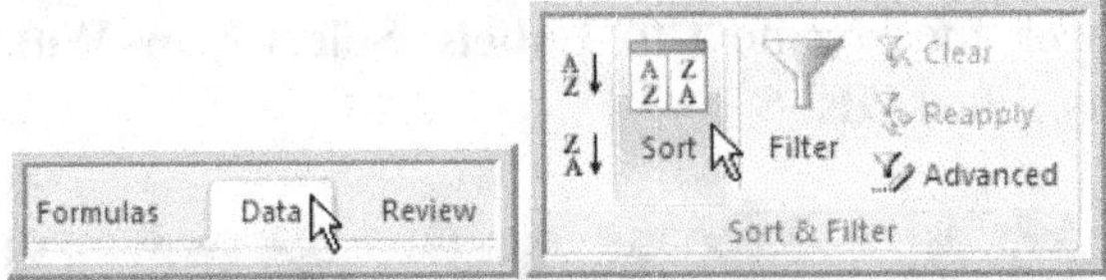

A **Sort** dialog box opens. Select the box next to **My data has headers**. Select the **aide** variable column in the **Sort by** window. **Values** should be selected in the **Sort On** window and **Largest to Smallest** in the **Order** window. Finally, select **OK**.

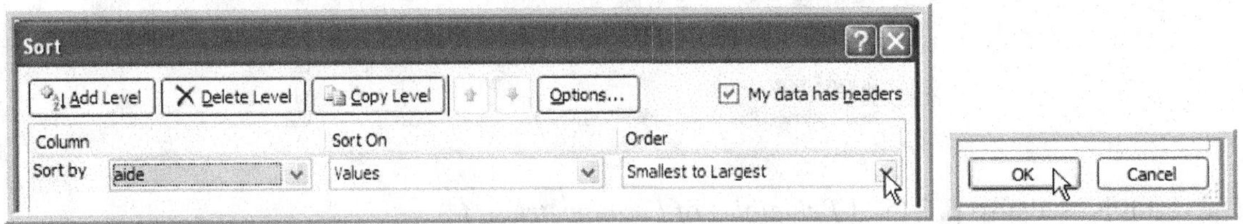

For model (7.8), the **Input Y Range** should be **H1:H3744**, and the **Input X Range** should be **Q1:Q3744**. Check the box next to **Labels**. Select **New Worksheet Ply** and name it **Star Model 1**. Finally select **OK**.

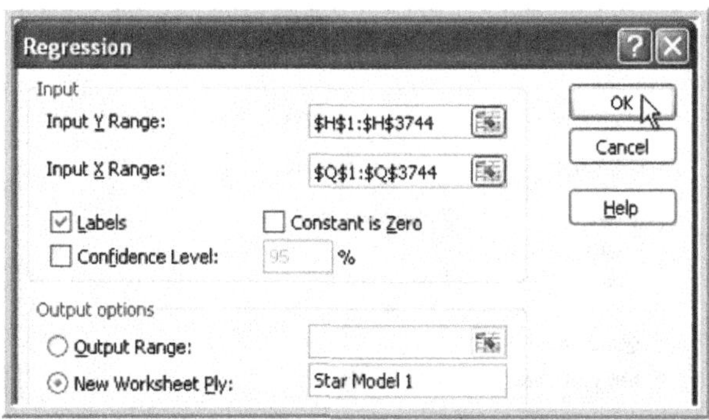

The result is (see also column (1) in Table 7.7 p. 280 of *Principles of Econometrics, 4e*):

	A	B	C	D	E	F	G	H	I
1	SUMMARY OUTPUT								
2									
3	*Regression Statistics*								
4	Multiple R	0.092483176							
5	R Square	0.008553138							
6	Adjusted R Square	0.008288116							
7	Standard Error	74.65066365							
8	Observations	3743							
9									
10	ANOVA								
11		*df*	*SS*	*MS*	*F*	*Significance F*			
12	Regression	1	179850.2664	179850.2664	32.27332709	1.44147E-08			
13	Residual	3741	20847551.44	5572.721583					
14	Total	3742	21027401.71						
15									
16		*Coefficients*	*Standard Error*	*t Stat*	*P-value*	*Lower 95%*	*Upper 95%*	*Lower 95.0%*	*Upper 95.0%*
17	Intercept	918.0428928	1.667156939	550.6637504	0	914.7742678	921.3115178	914.7742678	921.3115178
18	small	13.89899446	2.446591778	5.68096181	1.44147E-08	9.102210873	18.69577804	9.102210873	18.69577804

Go back to your sorted **star data** worksheet. In cells **T1:U2**, enter the following column labels and formulas.

	T	U
1	**small**	**tchexper**
2	=Q2	=D2

Note that all we are doing is copying the values of *SMALL* and *TCHEXPER* in columns **T-U** so as to create columns of explanatory variables next to one another.

Copy the content of cells **T2:U2** to cells **T3:U5787**. Here is how your table should look (only the first five values are shown below):

	T	U
1	**small**	**tchexper**
2	1	3
3	0	12
4	1	7
5	1	4
6	0	6

For model (7.9), the **Input Y Range** should be **H1:H3744**, and the **Input X Range** should be **T1:U3744**. Check the box next to **Labels**. Select **New Worksheet Ply** and name it **Star Model 2**. Finally select **OK**.

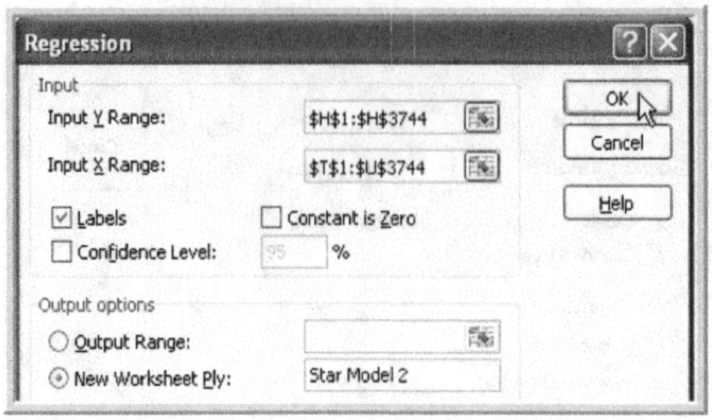

Regression

Input

Input Y Range: $H$1:$H$3744

Input X Range: $T$1:$U$3744

☑ Labels ☐ Constant is Zero

☐ Confidence Level: 95 %

Output options

○ Output Range:

◉ New Worksheet Ply: Star Model 2

OK | Cancel | Help

The result is (see also column (2) in Table 7.7 p. 280 of *Principles of Econometrics, 4e*):

	A	B	C	D	E	F	G	H	I
1	SUMMARY OUTPUT								
2									
3	*Regression Statistics*								
4	Multiple R	0.127852993							
5	R Square	0.016346388							
6	Adjusted R Square	0.01582037							
7	Standard Error	74.36662979							
8	Observations	3743							
9									
10	ANOVA								
11		*df*	*SS*	*MS*	*F*	*Significance F*			
12	Regression	2	343722.0648	171861.0324	31.07572116	4.12E-14			
13	Residual	3740	20683679.64	5530.395627					
14	Total	3742	21027401.71						
15									
16		*Coefficients*	*Standard Error*	*t Stat*	*P-value*	*Lower 95%*	*Upper 95%*	*Lower 95.0%*	*Upper 95.0%*
17	Intercept	907.5643429	2.542413485	356.9696072	0	902.579691	912.5489948	902.579691	912.5489948
18	small	13.98326835	2.437332057	5.737120762	1.03937E-08	9.204638942	18.76189775	9.204638942	18.76189775
19	tchexper	1.155510532	0.212275513	5.443447136	5.56172E-08	0.739323495	1.571697569	0.739323495	1.571697569

Next, consider the following equation (7.10):

$$SMALL_i = \beta_1 + \beta_2 BOY_i + \beta_3 WHITE\_ASIAN_i + \beta_4 TCHEXPER_i + \beta_5 FREELUNCH_i + e_i$$

where

$$BOY = \begin{cases} 1 \text{ if the student is male} \\ 0 \text{ if the student is female} \end{cases}$$

$$WHITE\_ASIAN = \begin{cases} 1 \text{ if the student is white or asian} \\ 0 \text{ otherwise} \end{cases}$$

$$FREELUNCH = \begin{cases} 1 \text{ if free lunch is provided} \\ 0 \text{ if free lunch is } \textit{not} \text{ provide} \end{cases}$$

Go back to your sorted **star data** worksheet. In cells **V1:Y2**, enter the following column labels and formulas.

	V	W	X	Y
1	**boy**	**white_asian**	**tchexper**	**Freelunch**
2	=I2	=J2	=D2	=N2

Note that all we are doing is copying the values of our explanatory variables in columns **V-Y** that are next to one another.

Copy the content of cells **V2:Y2** to cells **V3:Y5787**. Here is how your table should look (only the first five values are shown below):

	V	W	X	Y
1	boy	white_asian	tchexper	freelunch
2	0	0	3	1
3	1	1	12	0
4	1	1	7	0
5	0	1	4	1
6	1	1	6	0

For model (7.10), the **Input Y Range** should be **Q1:Q5787**, and the **Input X Range** should be **V1:Y5787**. Check the box next to **Labels**. Select **New Worksheet Ply** and name it **Check Random Assignment Model**. Finally select **OK**.

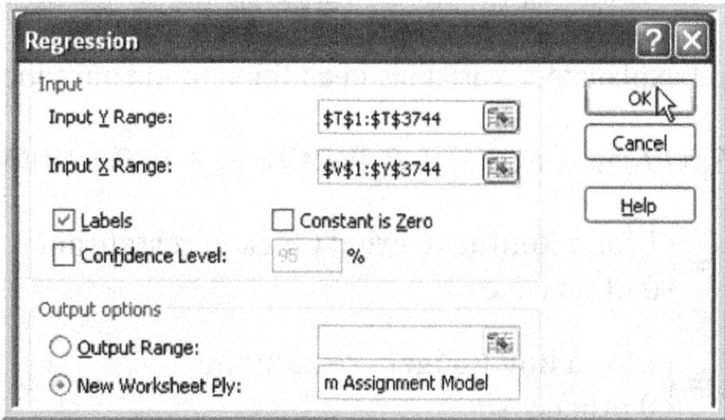

The result is (see also p. 281 of *Principles of Econometrics, 4e*):

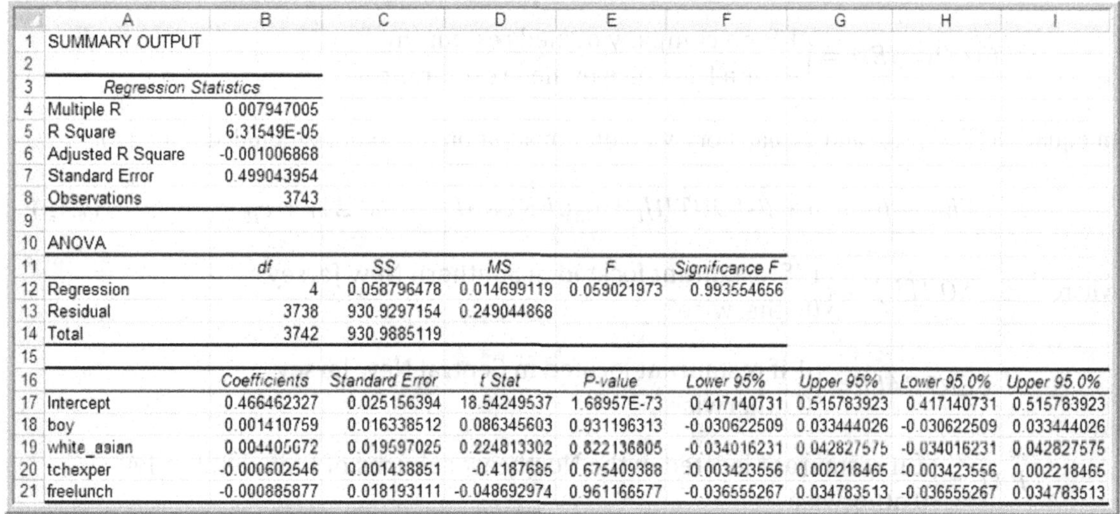

	A	B	C	D	E	F	G	H	I
1	SUMMARY OUTPUT								
2									
3	*Regression Statistics*								
4	Multiple R	0.007947005							
5	R Square	6.31549E-05							
6	Adjusted R Square	-0.001006868							
7	Standard Error	0.499043954							
8	Observations	3743							
9									
10	ANOVA								
11		*df*	*SS*	*MS*	*F*	*Significance F*			
12	Regression	4	0.058796478	0.014699119	0.059021973	0.993554656			
13	Residual	3738	930.9297154	0.249044868					
14	Total	3742	930.9885119						
15									
16		*Coefficients*	*Standard Error*	*t Stat*	*P-value*	*Lower 95%*	*Upper 95%*	*Lower 95.0%*	*Upper 95.0%*
17	Intercept	0.466462327	0.025156394	18.54249537	1.68957E-73	0.417140731	0.515783923	0.417140731	0.515783923
18	boy	0.001410759	0.016338512	0.086345603	0.931196313	-0.030622509	0.033444026	-0.030622509	0.033444026
19	white_asian	0.004405072	0.019597025	0.224813302	0.822136805	-0.034016231	0.042827575	-0.034016231	0.042827575
20	tchexper	-0.000602546	0.001438851	-0.4187685	0.675409388	-0.003423556	0.002218465	-0.003423556	0.002218465
21	freelunch	-0.000885877	0.018193111	-0.048692974	0.961166577	-0.036555267	0.034783513	-0.036555267	0.034783513

7.6 THE DIFFERENCES-IN-DIFFERENCES ESTIMATOR: THE EFFECT OF MINIMUM WAGE CHANGE EXAMPLE

Consider the following equation:

$$FTE_{it} = \beta_1 + \beta_2 NJ_i + \beta_3 D_t + \delta(NJ_i \times D_t) + e_{it} \tag{7.11}$$

where $NJ = \begin{cases} 1 \text{ if the observation is from New Jersey} \\ 0 \text{ if the observation is from Pennsylvania} \end{cases}$

$$D = \begin{cases} 1 \text{ if the observation is from November} \\ 0 \text{ if the observation is from February} \end{cases}$$

and FTE is the number of full-time-equivalent employees.

In equation (7.12), we add explanatory variables in addition to the ones included in (7.11):

$$FTE_{it} = \beta_1 + \cdots + \beta_4 KFC_i + \beta_5 ROYS_i + \beta_6 WENDYS_i + \beta_6 CO\_OWNED_i + e_{it} \tag{7.12}$$

where $KFC = \begin{cases} 1 \text{ for a Kentucky Fried Chicken restaurant} \\ 0 \text{ otherwise} \end{cases}$

$$ROYS = \begin{cases} 1 \text{ for a Roy Rodgers restaurant} \\ 0 \text{ otherwise} \end{cases}$$

$$WENDYS = \begin{cases} 1 \text{ for a Wendys restaurant} \\ 0 \text{ otherwise} \end{cases}$$

$$CO\_OWNED = \begin{cases} 1 \text{ for a company owned restaurant} \\ 0 \text{ for a franchise owned restaurant} \end{cases}$$

In equation (7.13), we add explanatory variables in addition to the ones included in (7.12):

$$FTE_{it} = \beta_1 + \cdots + \beta_7 SOUTHJ_i + \beta_8 CENTRALJ_i + \beta_9 PA1_i + e_{it} \tag{7.13}$$

where $SOUTHJ = \begin{cases} 1 \text{ if restaurant located in Southern New Jersey} \\ 0 \text{ otherwise} \end{cases}$

$$CENTRALJ = \begin{cases} 1 \text{ if restaurant located in Central New Jersey} \\ 0 \text{ otherwise} \end{cases}$$

$$PA1 = \begin{cases} 1 \text{ if restaurant located in the Northeast suburbs of Philadelphia, PA} \\ 0 \text{ otherwise} \end{cases}$$

Open the Excel file ***njmin3***. Excel opens the data set in Sheet 1 of a new Excel file. Since we would like to save all our work from Chapter 7 in one file, create a new worksheet in your **POE Chapter 7** Excel file, rename it **njmin3 data**, and in it, copy the data set you just opened.

In cells **O1:X2**, enter the following column labels and formulas.

	O	P	Q	R	S	T	U	V	W	X
1	**nj**	**d**	**d_nj**	**kfc**	**roys**	**wendys**	**co-owned**	**southj**	**centralj**	**pa1**
2	=G2	=L2	=M2	=I2	=J2	=K2	=A2	=B2	=C2	=D2

Note that all we are doing is copying the values of our explanatory variables in columns **O-Q** that are next to one another.

Copy the content of cells **O2:X2** to cells **O3:X821**. Here is how your table should look (only the first five values are shown below):

	O	P	Q	R	S	T	U	V	W	X
1	**nj**	**d**	**d_nj**	**kfc**	**roys**	**wendys**	**co-owned**	**southj**	**centralj**	**pa1**
2	1	0	0	0	0	0	0	0	1	0
3	1	0	0	0	0	0	0	0	1	0
4	1	0	0	0	1	0	0	0	1	0
5	1	0	0	0	1	0	1	0	0	0
6	1	0	0	0	0	0	0	0	0	0

We first sort our data according to **fte** because we have missing values, which means we cannot use the corresponding observations to estimate our regression model. Go to the **Data** tab in the middle of your tab list on top of your screen. Select all **your njmin3 data**. On the **Sort & Filter** group of commands, select the **Sort** button.

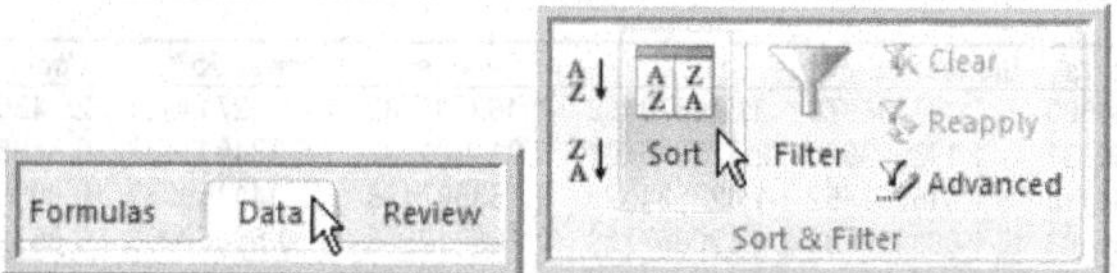

A **Sort** dialog box opens. Select the box next to **My data has headers**. Select the **fte** variable column in the **Sort by** window. **Values** should be selected in the **Sort On** window and **Largest to Smallest** in the **Order** window. Finally, select **OK**.

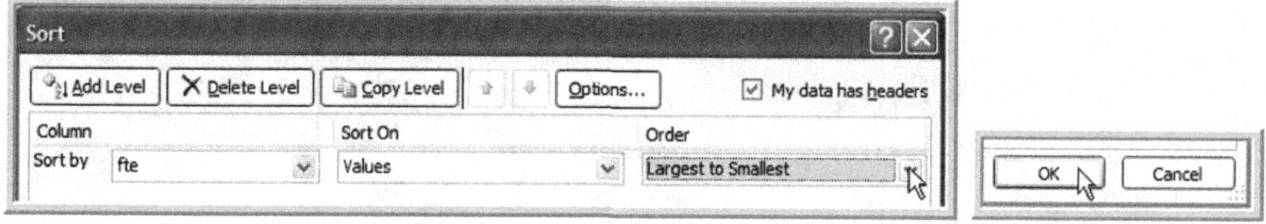

For model (7.11), the **Input Y Range** should be **N1:N795**, and the **Input X Range** should be **O1:Q795**. Check the box next to **Labels**. Select **New Worksheet Ply** and name it **Minimum Wage Model 1**. Finally select **OK**.

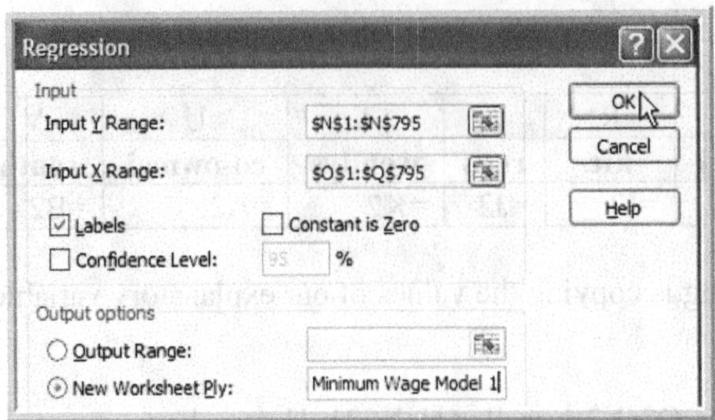

The result is (see also column (1) in Table 7.9 p. 285 of *Principles of Econometrics, 4e*):

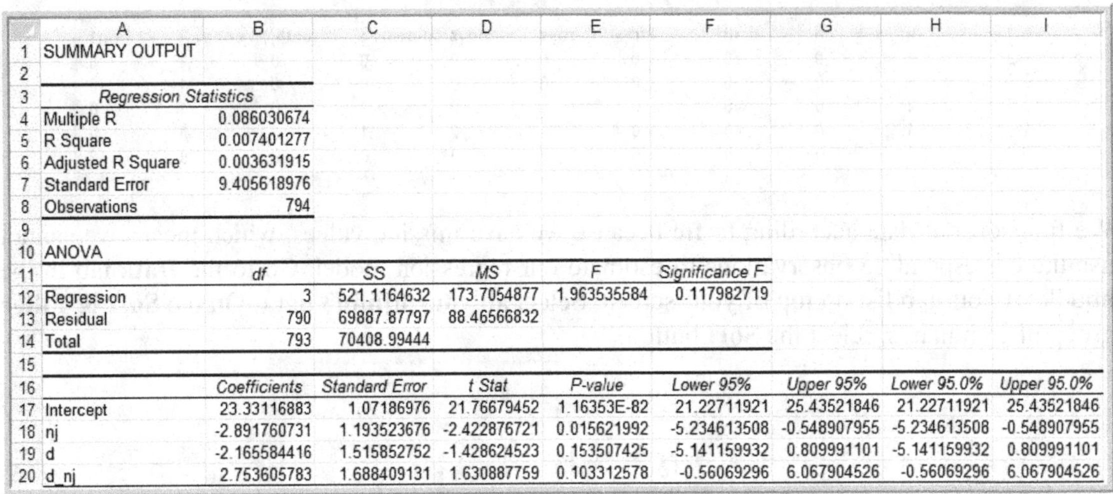

	A	B	C	D	E	F	G	H	I
1	SUMMARY OUTPUT								
2									
3	*Regression Statistics*								
4	Multiple R	0.086030674							
5	R Square	0.007401277							
6	Adjusted R Square	0.003631915							
7	Standard Error	9.405618976							
8	Observations	794							
9									
10	ANOVA								
11		*df*	*SS*	*MS*	*F*	*Significance F*			
12	Regression	3	521.1164632	173.7054877	1.963535584	0.117982719			
13	Residual	790	69887.87797	88.46566832					
14	Total	793	70408.99444						
15									
16		*Coefficients*	*Standard Error*	*t Stat*	*P-value*	*Lower 95%*	*Upper 95%*	*Lower 95.0%*	*Upper 95.0%*
17	Intercept	23.33116883	1.07186976	21.76679452	1.16353E-82	21.22711921	25.43521846	21.22711921	25.43521846
18	nj	-2.891760731	1.193523676	-2.422876721	0.015621992	-5.234613508	-0.548907955	-5.234613508	-0.548907955
19	d	-2.165584416	1.515852752	-1.428624523	0.153507425	-5.141159932	0.809991101	-5.141159932	0.809991101
20	d_nj	2.753605783	1.688409131	1.630887759	0.103312578	-0.56069296	6.067904526	-0.56069296	6.067904526

Go back to your **njmin3 data** worksheet. For model (7.12), the **Input Y Range** should be **N1:N795**, and the **Input X Range** should be **O1:U795**. Check the box next to **Labels**. Select **New Worksheet Ply** and name it **Minimum Wage Model 2**. Finally select **OK**.

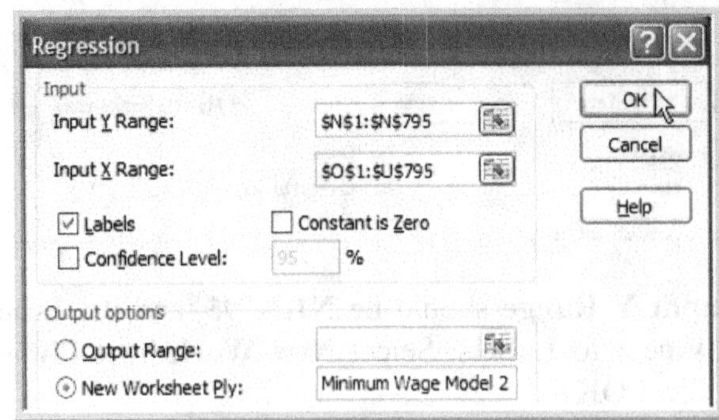

The result is (see also column (2) in Table 7.9 p. 285 of *Principles of Econometrics, 4e*):

	A	B	C	D	E	F	G	H	I
1	SUMMARY OUTPUT								
2									
3	*Regression Statistics*								
4	Multiple R	0.443204145							
5	R Square	0.196429914							
6	Adjusted R Square	0.189273438							
7	Standard Error	8.484273858							
8	Observations	794							
9									
10	ANOVA								
11		*df*	*SS*	*MS*	*F*	*Significance F*			
12	Regression	7	13830.43275	1975.776108	27.44785259	7.72477E-34			
13	Residual	786	56578.56168	71.9829029					
14	Total	793	70408.99444						
15									
16		*Coefficients*	*Standard Error*	*t Stat*	*P-value*	*Lower 95%*	*Upper 95%*	*Lower 95.0%*	*Upper 95.0%*
17	Intercept	25.95117614	1.038223461	24.99575199	6.2073E-102	23.91315732	27.98919496	23.91315732	27.98919496
18	nj	-2.376608094	1.079192119	-2.202210388	0.027940139	-4.49504784	-0.258168347	-4.49504784	-0.258168347
19	d	-2.223565041	1.367692339	-1.625778677	0.104397595	-4.908326875	0.461196793	-4.908326875	0.461196793
20	d_nj	2.845066555	1.523338497	1.867652239	0.062182504	-0.145226613	5.835359724	-0.145226613	5.835359724
21	kfc	-10.45338971	0.848956906	-12.31321593	5.52435E-32	-12.1198808	-8.786898614	-12.1198808	-8.786898614
22	roys	-1.624999072	0.859797951	-1.889977836	0.059128621	-3.312770992	0.062772848	-3.312770992	0.062772848
23	wendys	-1.063708623	0.92915025	-1.144818745	0.252632729	-2.887618181	0.760200934	-2.887618181	0.760200934
24	co-owned	-1.16854545	0.716166246	-1.631667866	0.103150035	-2.574370247	0.237279347	-2.574370247	0.237279347

Go back to your **njmin3 data** worksheet. For model (7.13), the **Input Y Range** should be **N1:N795**, and the **Input X Range** should be **O1:X795**. Check the box next to **Labels**. Select **New Worksheet Ply** and name it **Minimum Wage Model 3**. Finally select **OK**.

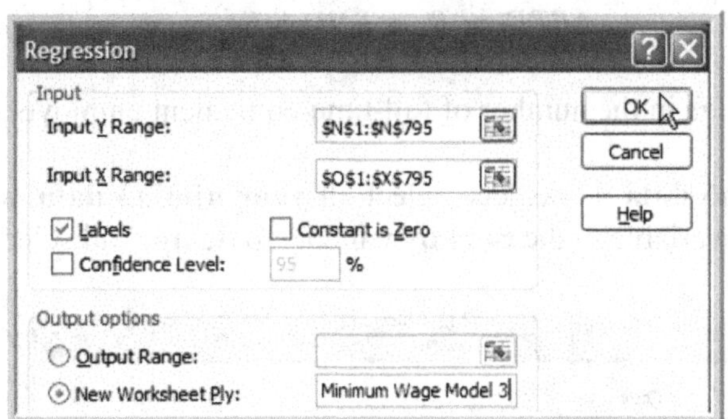

The result is (see also column (3) in Table 7.9 p. 285 of *Principles of Econometrics, 4e*):

	A	B	C	D	E	F	G	H	I
1	SUMMARY OUTPUT								
2									
3	*Regression Statistics*								
4	Multiple R	0.470527732							
5	R Square	0.221396346							
6	Adjusted R Square	0.211452494							
7	Standard Error	8.367416913							
8	Observations	794							
9									
10	ANOVA								
11		*df*	*SS*	*MS*	*F*	*Significance F*			
12	Regression	10	15588.29412	1558.829412	22.26464497	7.05564E-37			
13	Residual	783	54820.70032	70.0136658					
14	Total	793	70408.99444						
15									
16		*Coefficients*	*Standard Error*	*t Stat*	*P-value*	*Lower 95%*	*Upper 95%*	*Lower 95.0%*	*Upper 95.0%*
17	Intercept	25.3205127	1.210903135	20.91043617	1.7391E-77	22.94351194	27.69751346	22.94351194	27.69751346
18	nj	-0.907963605	1.271741824	-0.713952776	0.475469143	-3.404390609	1.588463399	-3.404390609	1.588463399
19	d	-2.211850952	1.348859584	-1.639793333	0.101449806	-4.859659985	0.43595808	-4.859659985	0.43595808
20	d_nj	2.81490803	1.50238165	1.873630464	0.061353627	-0.134264555	5.764080614	-0.134264555	5.764080614
21	kfc	-10.05800173	0.844671089	-11.90759558	3.63754E-30	-11.71608962	-8.399913837	-11.71608962	-8.399913837
22	roys	-1.693392595	0.85918373	-1.97093187	0.049083476	-3.379968772	-0.006816418	-3.379968772	-0.006816418
23	wendys	-1.064951933	0.920638473	-1.156753672	0.247725799	-2.872163664	0.742259798	-2.872163664	0.742259798
24	co-owned	-0.716309731	0.718990484	-0.996271505	0.319426023	-2.127686808	0.695067346	-2.127686808	0.695067346
25	southj	-3.701760689	0.779953191	-4.746131859	2.46482E-06	-5.232807456	-2.170713923	-5.232807456	-2.170713923
26	centralj	0.007883354	0.897493557	0.008783744	0.992993914	-1.753894947	1.769661655	-1.753894947	1.769661655
27	pa1	0.923861954	1.384927728	0.667083152	0.504915554	-1.794748784	3.642472692	-1.794748784	3.642472692

Finally, consider the following equation:

$$\Delta FTE_i = \beta_3 + \delta NJ_i + \Delta e_i \tag{7.14}$$

where ΔFTE is the change in the number of full-time-equivalent employees.

Go back to your **njmin3 data** worksheet, select all **your njmin3 data**. and then go to the **Sort** dialog box. Change the variable in the **Sort by** window to **demp**, and select **OK**.

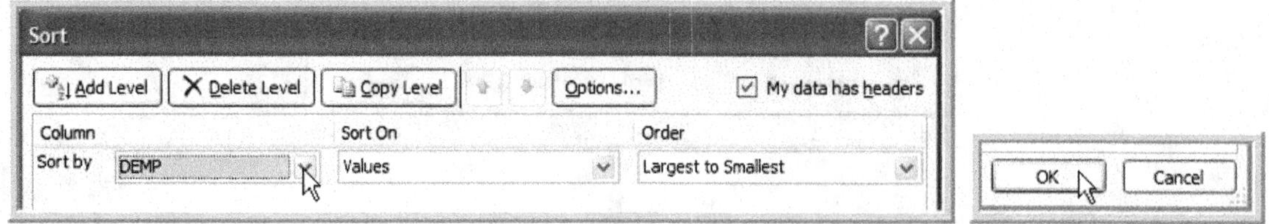

For model (7.11), the **Input Y Range** should be **F1:F769**, and the **Input X Range** should be **G1:G769**. Check the box next to **Labels**. Select **New Worksheet Ply** and name it **Minimum Wage Model 4**. Finally select **OK**.

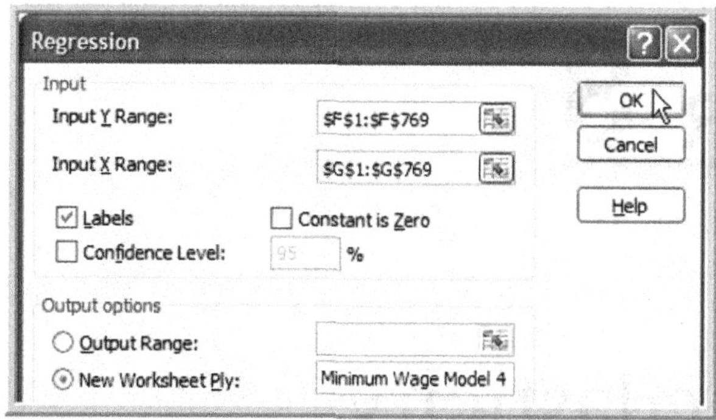

The result is (see p. 287 of *Principles of Econometrics, 4e*):

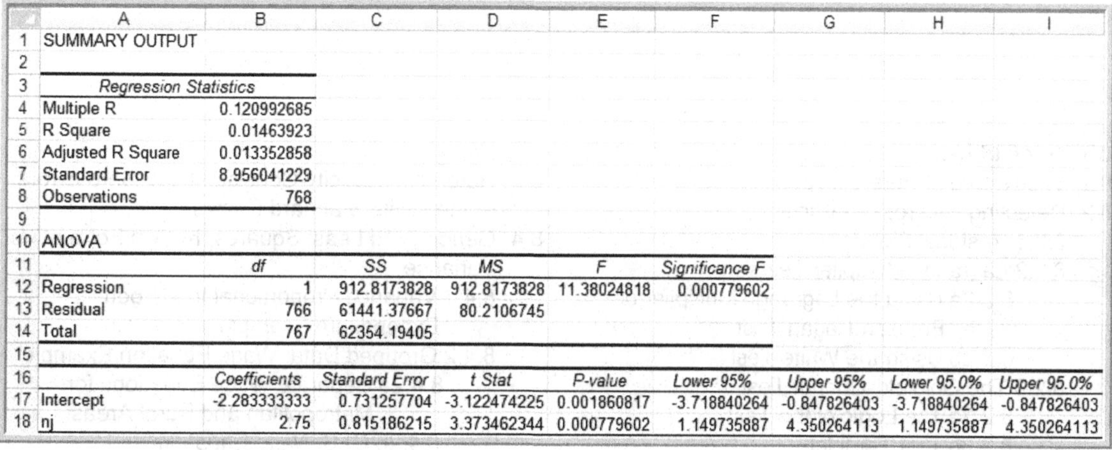

	A	B	C	D	E	F	G	H	I
1	SUMMARY OUTPUT								
2									
3	*Regression Statistics*								
4	Multiple R	0.120992685							
5	R Square	0.01463923							
6	Adjusted R Square	0.013352858							
7	Standard Error	8.956041229							
8	Observations	768							
9									
10	ANOVA								
11		*df*	*SS*	*MS*	*F*	*Significance F*			
12	Regression	1	912.8173828	912.8173828	11.38024818	0.000779602			
13	Residual	766	61441.37667	80.2106745					
14	Total	767	62354.19405						
15									
16		*Coefficients*	*Standard Error*	*t Stat*	*P-value*	*Lower 95%*	*Upper 95%*	*Lower 95.0%*	*Upper 95.0%*
17	Intercept	-2.283333333	0.731257704	-3.122474225	0.001860817	-3.718840264	-0.847826403	-3.718840264	-0.847826403
18	nj	2.75	0.815186215	3.373462344	0.000779602	1.149735887	4.350264113	1.149735887	4.350264113

CHAPTER 8

Heteroskedasticity

Chapter Outline

This chapter is concerned with the nature of heteroskedasticity, tests for heteroskedasticity, as well as generalized least squares estimation for heteroskedastic models.

8.1 THE NATURE OF HETEROSKEDASTICITY

Let us re-consider our food expenditure model first introduced in Chapter 2:

$$y_i = \beta_1 + \beta_2 x_i + e_i \tag{8.1}$$

where y is weekly food expenditure in dollars and x is weekly income in units of \$100 for a random sample of 40 three-person households.

Open the Excel file *food*. Save your file as **POE Chapter 8**. Rename sheet 1 **food data**.

In this section we illustrate the nature of heteroskedasticity by re-estimating (8.1) and plotting the estimated regression line along with the food expenditure data.

In the **Regression** dialog box, the **Input Y Range** should be **A1:A41**, and the **Input X Range** should be **B1:B41**. Check the box next to **Labels**. Select **New Worksheet Ply** and name it **Food Expenditure Equation**. Check the boxes next to **Residual Plots** and **Line Fit Plots**. Finally select **OK**.

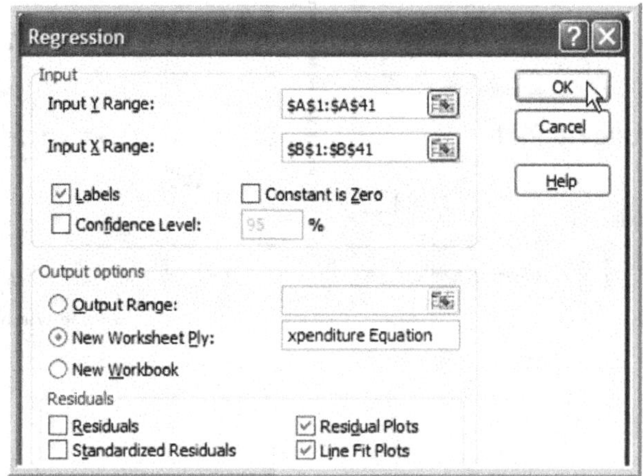

The regression analysis results are (see also p. 300 in *Principles of Econometrics, 4e*):

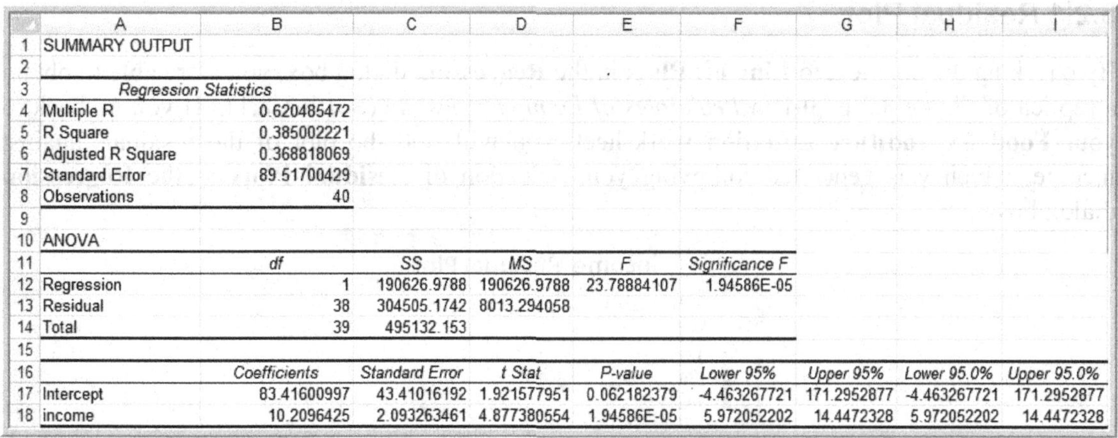

	A	B	C	D	E	F	G	H	I
1	SUMMARY OUTPUT								
2									
3	*Regression Statistics*								
4	Multiple R	0.620485472							
5	R Square	0.385002221							
6	Adjusted R Square	0.368818069							
7	Standard Error	89.51700429							
8	Observations	40							
9									
10	ANOVA								
11		*df*	*SS*	*MS*	*F*	*Significance F*			
12	Regression	1	190626.9788	190626.9788	23.78884107	1.94586E-05			
13	Residual	38	304505.1742	8013.294058					
14	Total	39	495132.153						
15									
16		*Coefficients*	*Standard Error*	*t Stat*	*P-value*	*Lower 95%*	*Upper 95%*	*Lower 95.0%*	*Upper 95.0%*
17	Intercept	83.41600997	43.41016192	1.921577951	0.062182379	-4.463267721	171.2952877	-4.463267721	171.2952877
18	income	10.2096425	2.093263461	4.877380554	1.94586E-05	5.972052202	14.4472328	5.972052202	14.4472328

After editing the **income Line Fit Plot** (see Section 2.3.4 for more details on how to do that), you should obtain a replica of Figure 8.2 p. 301 in *Principles of Econometrics, 4e*:

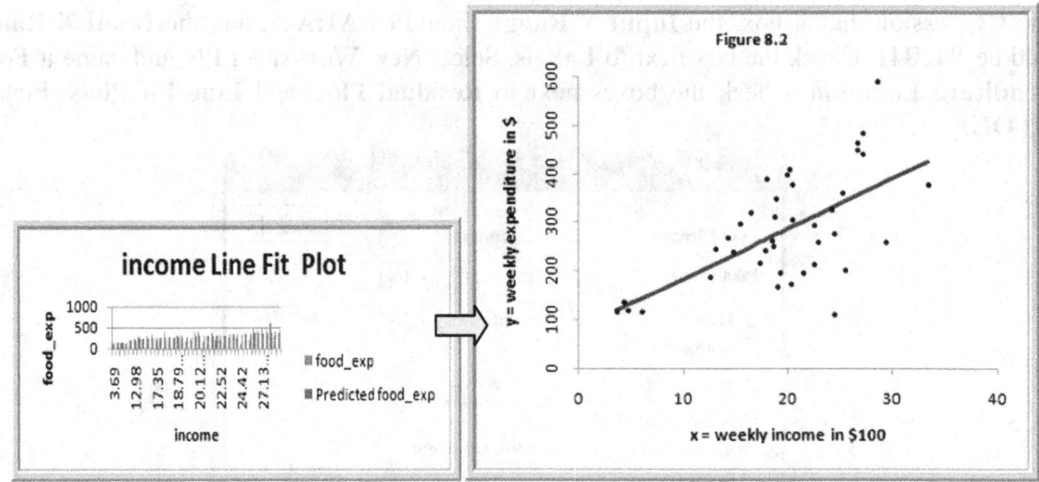

8.2 DETECTING HETEROSKEDASTICITY

8.2.1 Residual Plots

By checking the box next to **Line Fit Plots** in the **Regression** dialog box, you were able to obtain a replica of Figure 8.2 p. 301 in *Principles of Econometrics, 4e* (Section 8.1). If you go back to your **Food Expenditure Equation** worksheet, you will find the plot of the residuals against income, which was generated following your selection of **Residual Plots** in the **Regression** dialog box.

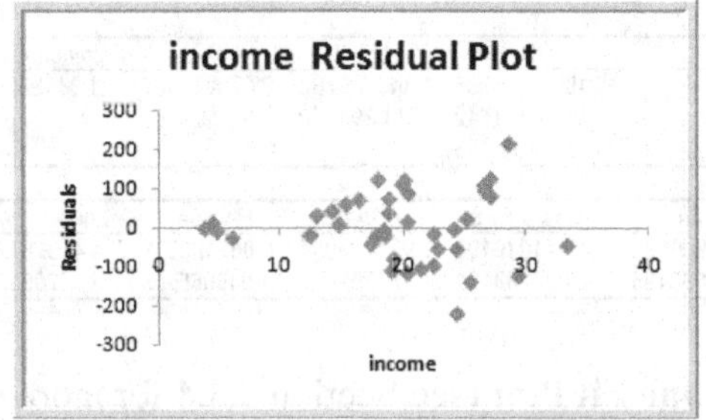

8.2.2 Lagrange Multiplier Tests

8.2.2a Using the Lagrange Multiplier or Breusch-Pagan Test

Logic of the Test:

Consider the following general heteroskedasticity assumption for the food expenditure model:

$$var(e_i) = \sigma_i^2 = h(\alpha_1 + \alpha_2 x_i) \tag{8.2}$$

Consequently, the null and alternative hypotheses for a test for heteroskedasticity based on the variance function (8.2) are: $H_0: \alpha_2 = 0$ and $H_1: \alpha_2 \neq 0$.

To obtain a test statistic we consider the linear variance function in (8.3):

$$\hat{e}_i^2 = \alpha_1 + \alpha_2 x_i + v_i \tag{8.3}$$

where $\hat{e}_i^2$ are the squares of the least squares residuals from model (8.1).

When H_0 is true, then the sample size N multiplied by the R^2 goodness-of-fit statistic from (8.3) has a chi-square distribution with $m = S - 1$ degrees of freedom, where S is the number of parameters in (8.3):

$$\chi^2 = N \times R^2 \sim \chi^2_{(m=S-1)} \tag{8.4}$$

Because a large R^2 value provides evidence against the null hypothesis, the rejection region for the statistic in (8.4) is the right tail of the distribution. Thus for a $\alpha\%$ significance level, we reject H_0 and conclude that heteroskedasticity exists when the computed χ^2-statistic is greater than the chi-square critical value $\chi^2_{(1-\alpha,m=S-1)}$.

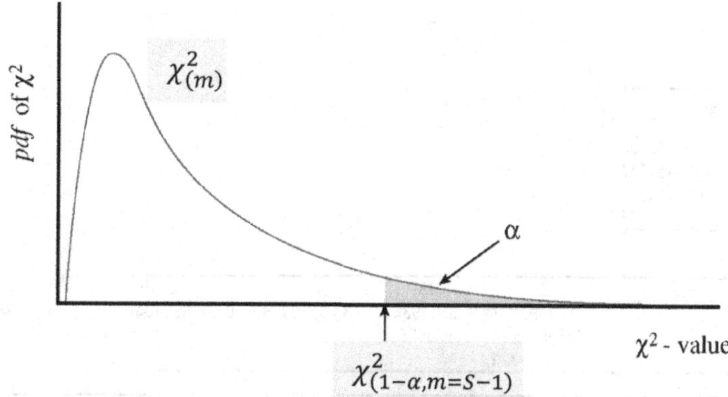

Note that we have used a test based on a chi-square distribution before, in Section 4.6.2 (for the Jarque-Bera test for Normality).

Estimating the Linear Variance Function:

Go back to your **food expenditure equation** worksheet, if you are not there already. In cells **D24:D25** enter the following column label and formula.

	D
24	**residuals²**
25	=C25^2

Copy the content of cell **D25** to cells **D26:D64**. Here is how your table should look (only the first five values are shown below):

	D
24	*residuals²*
25	34.45208433
26	59.96419985
27	158.0505536
28	901.2097207
29	560.7541899

In the **Regression** dialog box, the **Input Y Range** should be **D24:D64**, from your **food expenditure equation** worksheet, and the **Input X Range** should be **B1:B41**, from your **food data** worksheet. Check the box next to **Labels**. Select **New Worksheet Ply** and name it **Variance Function**. Finally select **OK**.

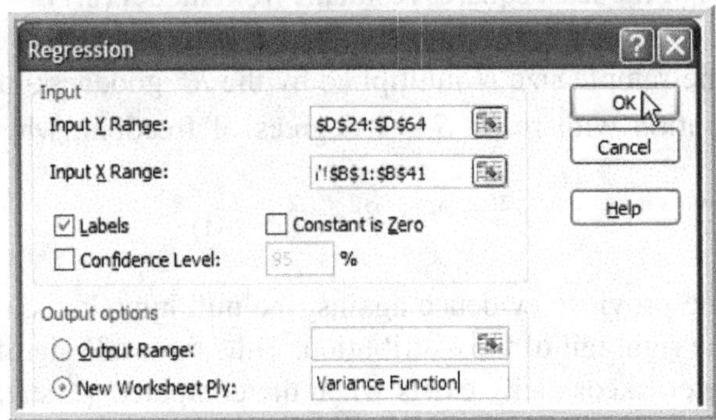

The result is:

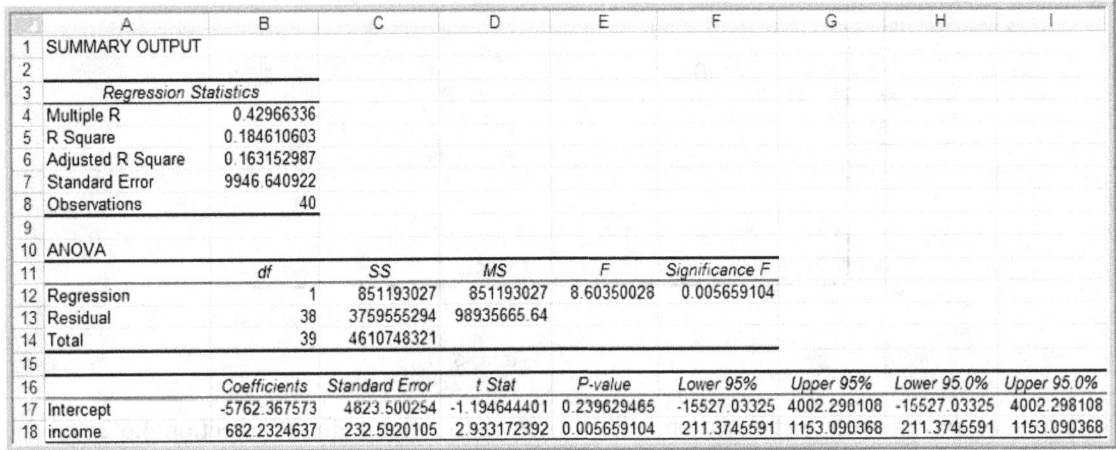

	A	B	C	D	E	F	G	H	I
1	SUMMARY OUTPUT								
2									
3	*Regression Statistics*								
4	Multiple R	0.42966336							
5	R Square	0.184610603							
6	Adjusted R Square	0.163152987							
7	Standard Error	9946.640922							
8	Observations	40							
9									
10	ANOVA								
11		*df*	*SS*	*MS*	*F*	*Significance F*			
12	Regression	1	851193027	851193027	8.60350028	0.005659104			
13	Residual	38	3759555294	98935665.64					
14	Total	39	4610748321						
15									
16		*Coefficients*	*Standard Error*	*t Stat*	*P-value*	*Lower 95%*	*Upper 95%*	*Lower 95.0%*	*Upper 95.0%*
17	Intercept	-5762.367573	4823.500254	-1.194644401	0.239629465	-15527.03325	4002.298108	-15527.03325	4002.298108
18	income	682.2324637	232.5920105	2.933172392	0.005659104	211.3745591	1153.090368	211.3745591	1153.090368

Test Template:

Insert a new worksheet by selecting the **Insert Worksheet** tab at the bottom of your screen. Name it **Lagrange Multiplier Test**.

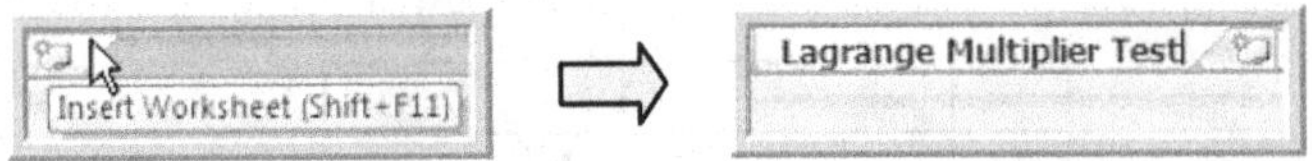

Create the following template for Lagrange multiplier tests:

	A	B	C
1	**Data Input**	N =	='Variance Function'!B8
2		S =	='Variance Function'!B12+1
3		R^2 =	='Variance Function'!B5
4		α =	

	A	B	C
6	**Computed Values**	m =	=C2-1
7		χ^2-critical value =	=CHIINV(C4,C6)
8			
9	**Lagrange Multiplier Test**	χ^2 =	=C1*C3
10		Conclusion =	=IF(C9>=C7,"Reject Ho","Do Not Reject Ho")
11		*p*-value =	=CHIDIST(C9,C6)
12		Conclusion =	=IF(C11<=C4,"Reject Ho","Do Not Reject Ho")

At $\alpha = 0.05$, the result of the test is (see also p. 306 in *Principles of Econometrics, 4e*):

	A	B	C
1	Data Input	N =	40
2		S =	2
3		R^2 =	0.184611
4		α =	0.05
5			
6	Computed Values	m =	1
7		χ^2-critical value =	3.841459
8			
9	Lagrange Multiplier Test	χ^2 =	7.384424
10		Conclusion =	Reject Ho
11		p-value =	0.006579
12		Conclusion =	Reject Ho

8.2.2b Using the White Test

For the White version of the test, we base the test statistic on the following variance function:

$$\hat{e}_i^2 = \alpha_1 + \alpha_2 x_i + \alpha_3 x_i^2 + v_i \tag{8.5}$$

where $\hat{e}_i^2$ are the squares of the least squares residuals from model (8.1).

Go back to your **food data** worksheet. In cell **C1**, enter the column label **x²**. In cell **C2** type the formula **=B2^2**; copy it to cells **C3:C41**. Here is how your table should look (only the first five values are shown below):

	C
1	x^2
2	13.6161
3	19.2721
4	22.5625
5	36.3609
6	155.5009

In the **Regression** dialog box, the **Input Y Range** should be **D24:D64**, from your **food expenditure equation** worksheet, and the **Input X Range** should be **B1:C41**, from your **food data** worksheet. Check the box next to **Labels**. Select **Output Range** and specify it to be cell **A1** in your **Variance Function** worksheet: you can place your cursor in the **Output Range** window and move it to that cell to do that, or type **'Variance Function'!A1** in **the Output Range** window. Finally, select **OK**.

Regression

Input

Input Y Range: $D$24:$D$64

Input X Range: '!$B$1:$C$41

☑ Labels ☐ Constant is Zero

☐ Confidence Level: 95 %

Output options

⊙ Output Range: unction'!$A$1

OK

Cancel

Help

Excel informs you that the output range will overwrite existing data. Do select **OK** to overwrite the data in the specified range. The result is:

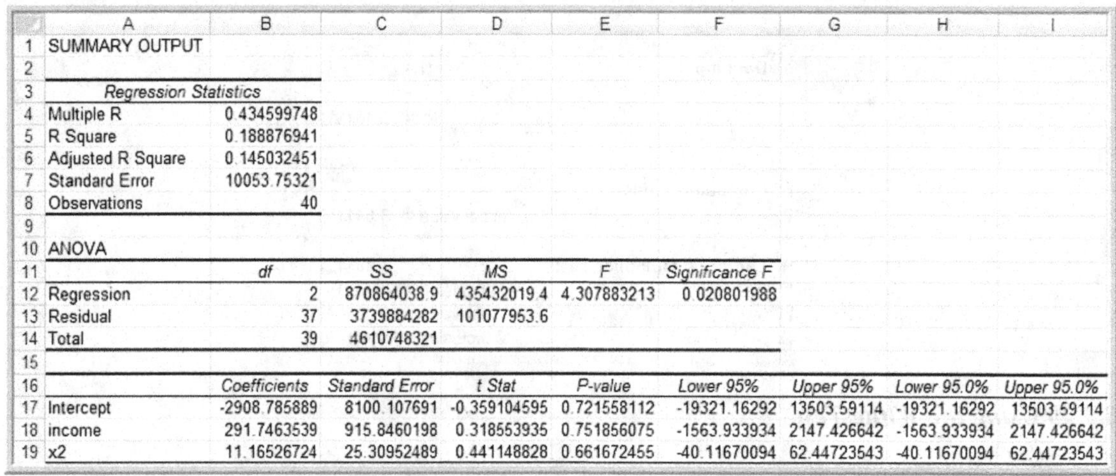

	A	B	C	D	E	F	G	H	I
1	SUMMARY OUTPUT								
2									
3	*Regression Statistics*								
4	Multiple R	0.434599748							
5	R Square	0.188876941							
6	Adjusted R Square	0.145032451							
7	Standard Error	10053.75321							
8	Observations	40							
9									
10	ANOVA								
11		*df*	*SS*	*MS*	*F*	*Significance F*			
12	Regression	2	870864038.9	435432019.4	4.307883213	0.020801988			
13	Residual	37	3739884282	101077953.6					
14	Total	39	4610748321						
15									
16		*Coefficients*	*Standard Error*	*t Stat*	*P-value*	*Lower 95%*	*Upper 95%*	*Lower 95.0%*	*Upper 95.0%*
17	Intercept	-2908.785889	8100.107691	-0.359104595	0.721558112	-19321.16292	13503.59114	-19321.16292	13503.59114
18	income	291.7463539	915.8460198	0.318553935	0.751856075	-1563.933934	2147.426642	-1563.933934	2147.426642
19	x2	11.16526724	25.30952489	0.441148828	0.661672455	-40.11670094	62.44723543	-40.11670094	62.44723543

At $\alpha = 0.05$, the result of the test is (see also p. 306 in *Principles of Econometrics, 4e*):

	A	B	C
1	**Data Input**	N =	40
2		S =	3
3		R^2 =	0.188877
4		α =	0.05
5			
6	**Computed Values**	m =	2
7		χ^2-critical value =	5.991465
8			
9	**Lagrange Multiplier Test**	χ^2 =	7.555078
10		Conclusion =	Reject Ho
11		*p*-value =	0.022879
12		Conclusion =	Reject Ho

8.2.3 The Goldfeld-Quandt Test

8.2.3a The Logic of the Test

Consider the *right-tail* hypothesis test: $H_0: \sigma_1^2 = \sigma_2^2$ against $H_1: \sigma_1^2 > \sigma_2^2$, where σ_1^2 is the error variance of subsample 1 model and σ_2^2 is the error variance of subsample 2 model. If H_0 is true, then the following F-statistic follows an F-distribution with $m_1 = N_1 - K_1$ numerator degrees of freedom and $m_2 = N_2 - K_2$ denominator degrees of freedom:

$$F = \frac{\hat{\sigma}_1^2}{\hat{\sigma}_2^2} \sim F_{(m_1 = N_1 - K_1, m_2 = N_2 - K_2)} \tag{8.6}$$

where $\hat{\sigma}_1^2$ is the estimated error variance from subsample 1 model with K_1 parameters and N_1 observations; $\hat{\sigma}_2^2$ is the estimated error variance from subsample 2 model with K_2 parameters and N_2 observations.

If H_0 is *not* true, then the value of the computed F-statistic will tend to be unusually large. We will reject the null hypothesis if $F > F_c$, where F_c is the critical value shown below.

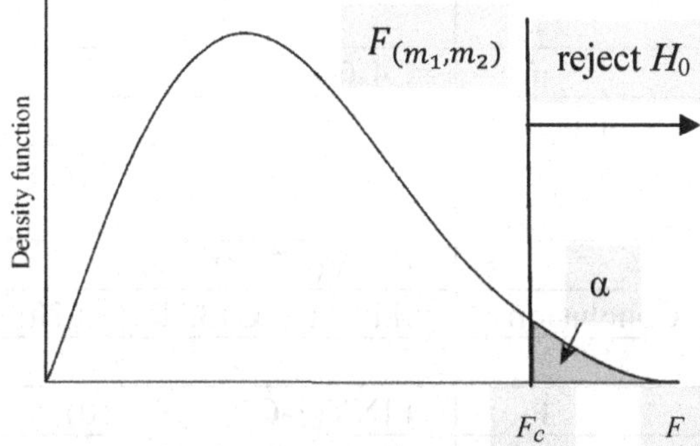

The right-tail Goldfeld-Quandt Test is similar to the F-test from Section 6.1.

For a *two-tail* hypothesis test: $H_1: \sigma_1^2 \neq \sigma_2^2$. If H_0 is *not* true, then the value of the computed F-statistic will tend to be unusually large *or* unusually small. We will reject the null hypothesis if $F < F_{Lc}$ or $F > F_{Uc}$ where F_{Lc} and F_{Uc} are the lower and upper critical values shown below. Note that in this case, $\alpha/2$ of the probability is in each tail of the distribution.

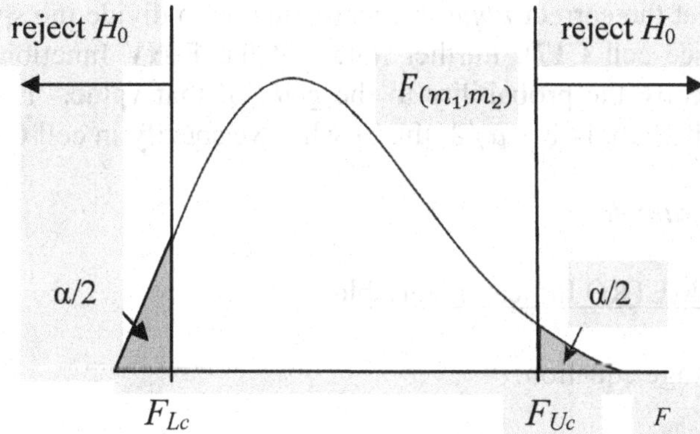

8.2.3b Test Template

Insert a new worksheet by selecting the **Insert Worksheet** tab at the bottom of your screen. Rename it **Goldfeld-Quandt Test**.

Create the Goldfeld-Quandt test template as shown in the table below.

	A	B	C
1	**Data Input**	N_1 =	='Subsample 1 Model'!B8
2		K_1=	='Subsample 1 Model'!B12+1
	A	B	C
3		MS Residual 1 =	='Subsample 1 Model'!D13
4		N_2 =	='Subsample 2 Model'!B8
5		K_2=	='Subsample 2 Model'!B12+1
6		MS Residual 2 =	='Subsample 2 Model'!D13
7		α =	
8			
9	**Computed Values**	m_1 =	=C1-C2
10		m_2 =	=C4-C5
11		F-statistic =	=C3/C6
12	**Goldfeld-Quandt test**		
13	**Right-tail**	F_c=	=FINV(C7,C9,C10)
14		Conclusion =	=IF(C11>=C13,"Reject Ho","Do Not Reject Ho")
15			
16	**Two-tail**	F_{Lc}=	=FINV(1-C7/2,C9,C10)
17		F_{Uc}=	=FINV(C7/2,C9,C10)
18		Conclusion =	=IF(OR(C11<=C16,C11>=C17),"Reject Ho", "Do Not Reject Ho")

Cells **C16:C17** are where the lower and upper critical values of the two-tail Goldfeld-Quandt test are computed. Recall that, in this case, $\alpha/2$ of the probability is in each tail of the distribution. The **FINV** function, on the other hand, gives us a F_c value such that $P\left(F_{(m_1,m_2)} > F_c\right) = \alpha$. So, what we need to do, to get the correct *upper* critical-value, is to divide the specified α value by 2 in the **FINV** function (see cell **C17**). Further note that the **FINV** function returns a *F*-critical value, once we have specify the probability to the ***right*** of that value. For our *lower* critical-value, the probability to its right is $1 - \alpha/2$; that is what we specify in cell **C16**.

8.2.3c Wage Equation Example

Wage Equation with the METRO Indicator Variable:

Consider the following wage equation:

$$WAGE = \beta_1 + \beta_2 EDUC + \beta_3 EXPER + \beta_4 METRO + e \tag{8.7}$$

where $WAGE$ is hourly wage, $EDUC$ is years of education, $EXPER$ is years of experience, and $METRO$ is an indicator variable equal to 1 for workers who live in a metropolitan area and 0 for workers who live in a rural area.

Open the Excel file ***cps2***. Excel opens the data set in Sheet 1 of a new Excel file. Since we would like to save all our work from Chapter 8 in one file, create a new worksheet in your **POE Chapter 8** Excel file, rename it **cps2 data**, and in it, copy the data set you just opened.

Insert a column to the left of the **female** column **D** (see Section 1.4 for more details on how to do that). In your new cell **D1**, enter the column label **metro**. In cell **D2**, enter the formula **=K2**; copy it to cells **K3:K1001**. Now we have a table where the explanatory variables of interest to us are in columns next to each other.

	A	B	C	D
1	wage	educ	exper	metro
2	2.03	13	2	0
3	2.07	12	7	1
4	2.12	12	35	1
5	2.54	16	20	1
6	2.68	12	24	1

In the **Regression** dialog box, the **Input Y Range** should be **A1:A1001**, and the **Input X Range** should be **B1:D1001**. Check the box next to **Labels**. Select **New Worksheet Ply** and name it **Wage Equation**. Finally select **OK**.

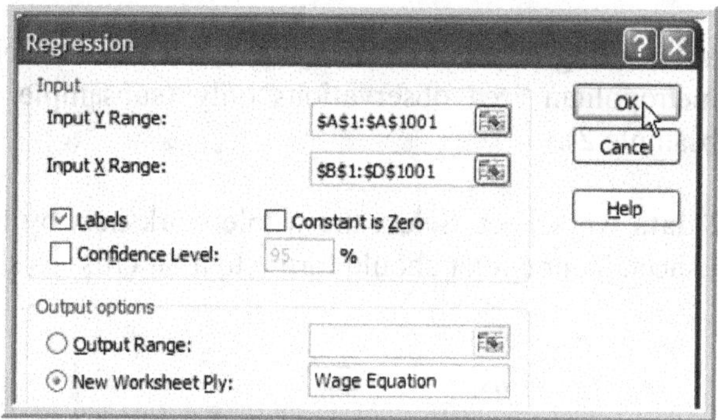

The result is (see also p. 307 in *Principles of Econometrics, 4e*):

	A	B	C	D	E	F	G	H	I
1	SUMMARY OUTPUT								
2									
3	*Regression Statistics*								
4	Multiple R	0.516626677							
5	R Square	0.266903124							
6	Adjusted R Square	0.264695001							
7	Standard Error	5.3564897							
8	Observations	1000							
9									
10	ANOVA								
11		*df*	*SS*	*MS*	*F*	*Significance F*			
12	Regression	3	10404.28343	3468.094475	120.8732979	9.24965E-67			
13	Residual	996	28577.21397	28.6919819					
14	Total	999	38981.4974						
15									
16		*Coefficients*	*Standard Error*	*t Stat*	*P-value*	*Lower 95%*	*Upper 95%*	*Lower 95.0%*	*Upper 95.0%*
17	Intercept	-9.913984218	1.075662517	-9.216630734	1.77326E-19	-12.02480904	-7.803159397	-12.02480904	-7.803159397
18	educ	1.233963998	0.069961261	17.63781812	8.42574E-61	1.096675616	1.37125238	1.096675616	1.37125238
19	exper	0.133243681	0.015231619	8.747834543	9.13789E-18	0.103353935	0.163133426	0.103353935	0.163133426
20	metro	1.524104206	0.431090949	3.535458611	0.000425795	0.678153493	2.37005492	0.678153493	2.37005492

Separate Wage Equations for Metropolitan and Rural Areas:

We estimate the following equation (8.8) twice—once for workers living in a metropolitan area and again for workers living in a rural area.

$$WAGE = \beta_1 + \beta_2 EDUC + \beta_3 EXPER + e \tag{8.8}$$

We first sort our data according to the area of residence of the workers and then successively estimate (8.8) with metropolitan area observations only (subsample 1), and with rural area observations only (subsample 2).

Go back to your **cps2 data** worksheet. Select the whole worksheet by left clicking on the upper left-corner of the worksheet. Your cursor should turn into a fat cross as shown below:

Select the **Sort & Filter** button in the **Editing** group of commands on the **Home** tab. On the drop down menu, select **Custom Sort**.

A **Sort** dialog box opens. Select the box next to **My data has headers**. Select the **metro** indicator variable column in the **Sort by** window. **Values** should be selected in the **Sort on** window. Select **Largest to Smallest** in the **Order** window. Finally, select **OK**.

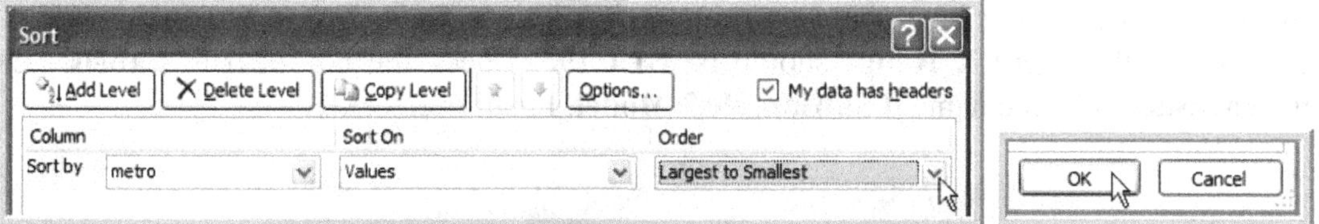

In the **Regression** dialog box, _for the metropolitan area wage equation_, the **Input Y Range** should be **A1:A809**, and the **Input X Range** should be **B1:C809**. Check the box next to **Labels**. Select **New Worksheet Ply** and name it **Subsample 1 Model**. Finally select **OK**.

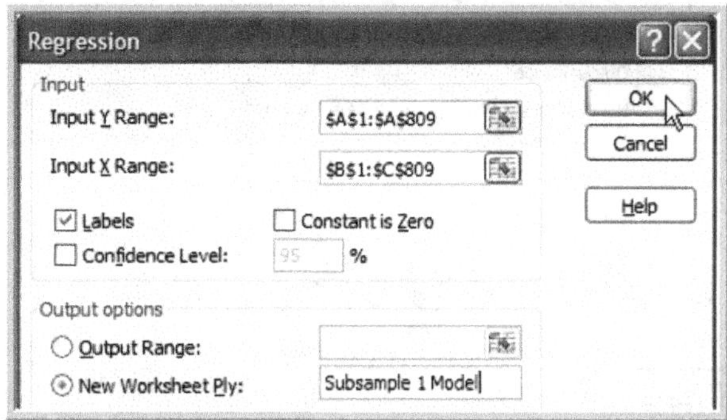

The result is:

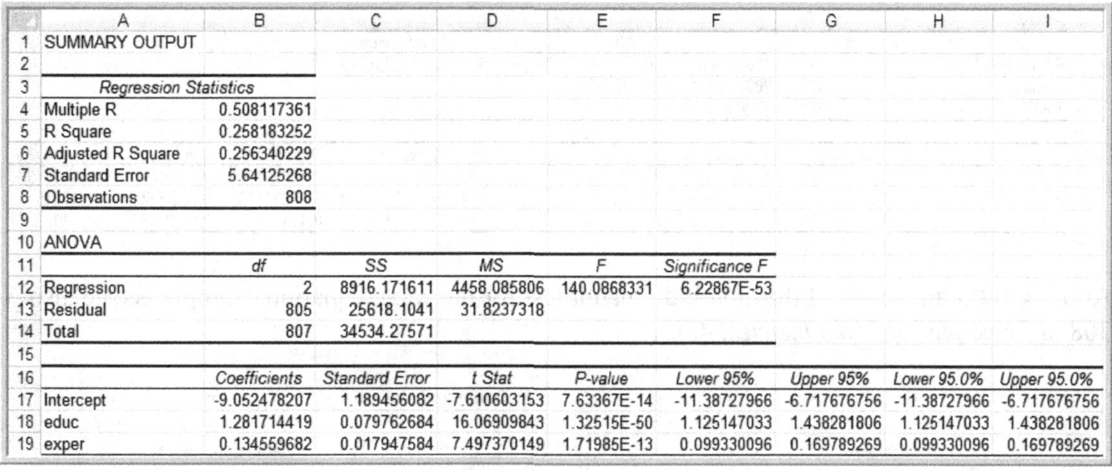

	A	B	C	D	E	F	G	H	I
1	SUMMARY OUTPUT								
2									
3	*Regression Statistics*								
4	Multiple R	0.508117361							
5	R Square	0.258183252							
6	Adjusted R Square	0.256340229							
7	Standard Error	5.64125268							
8	Observations	808							
9									
10	ANOVA								
11		*df*	*SS*	*MS*	*F*	*Significance F*			
12	Regression	2	8916.171611	4458.085806	140.0868331	6.22867E-53			
13	Residual	805	25618.1041	31.8237318					
14	Total	807	34534.27571						
15									
16		*Coefficients*	*Standard Error*	*t Stat*	*P-value*	*Lower 95%*	*Upper 95%*	*Lower 95.0%*	*Upper 95.0%*
17	Intercept	-9.052478207	1.189456082	-7.610603153	7.63367E-14	-11.38727966	-6.717676756	-11.38727966	-6.717676756
18	educ	1.281714419	0.079762684	16.06909843	1.32515E-50	1.125147033	1.438281806	1.125147033	1.438281806
19	exper	0.134559682	0.017947584	7.497370149	1.71985E-13	0.099330096	0.169789269	0.099330096	0.169789269

Go back to your **cps2 data** worksheet, and then to the **Sort** dialog box. Change the **Order** to **Smallest to Largest**, and select **OK**.

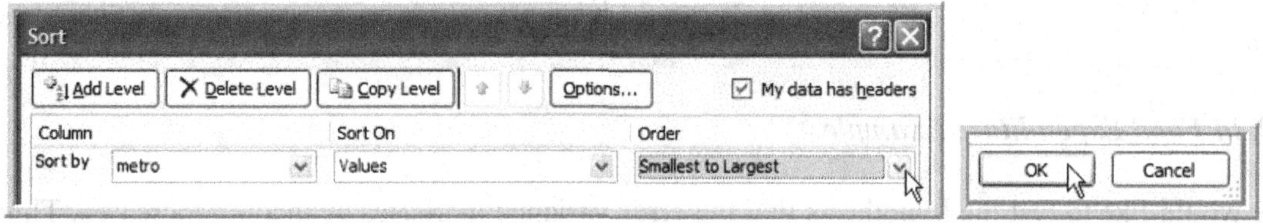

In the **Regression** dialog box, *for rural area wage equation*, the **Input Y Range** should be **A1:A193**, and the **Input X Range** should be **B1:C193**. Check the box next to **Labels.** Select **New Worksheet Ply** and name it **Subsample 2 Model**. Finally select **OK**.

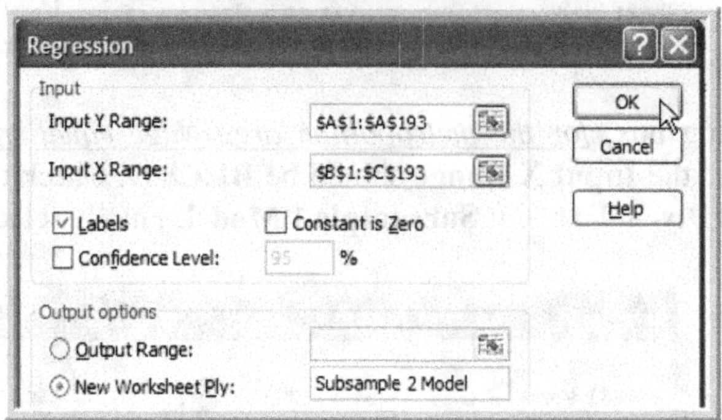

The result is:

	A	B	C	D	E	F	G	H	I
1	SUMMARY OUTPUT								
2									
3	*Regression Statistics*								
4	Multiple R	0.508673076							
5	R Square	0.258748298							
6	Adjusted R Square	0.250904365							
7	Standard Error	3.90422676							
8	Observations	192							
9									
10	ANOVA								
11		*df*	*SS*	*MS*	*F*	*Significance F*			
12	Regression	2	1005.642618	502.8213091	32.98705973	5.14943E-13			
13	Residual	189	2880.924466	15.24298659					
14	Total	191	3886.567084						
15									
16		*Coefficients*	*Standard Error*	*t Stat*	*P-value*	*Lower 95%*	*Upper 95%*	*Lower 95.0%*	*Upper 95.0%*
17	Intercept	-6.165854725	1.898510693	-3.247732418	0.001376545	-9.910847494	-2.420861956	-9.910847494	-2.420861956
18	educ	0.955585383	0.133189909	7.174607953	1.6011E-11	0.692855629	1.218315137	0.692855629	1.218315137
19	exper	0.125973719	0.02477097	5.085538445	8.79069E-07	0.077110627	0.174836811	0.077110627	0.174836811

At $\alpha = 0.05$, the result of the Godfeld-Quandt test for the wage equation example is (see also p. 308 in *Principles of Econometrics, 4e*):

	A	B	C
1	**Data Input**	N_1 =	808
2		K_1 =	3
3		MS Residual 1 =	31.82373
4		N_2 =	192
5		K_2 =	3
6		MS Residual 2 =	15.24299
7		α =	0.05

	A	B	C
9	**Computed Values**	m_1 =	805
10		m_2 =	189
11		F-statistic =	2.087762
12	**Goldfeld-Quandt test**		
13	**Right-tail**	F_c =	1.215033
14		Conclusion =	Reject Ho
15			
16	**Two-tail**	F_{Lc} =	0.805198
17		F_{Uc} =	1.26173
18		Conclusion =	Reject Ho

8.2.3d Food Expenditure Example

We would like to test the hypothesis that the error variance increases as income increases. This is a *right-tail* hypothesis test where: $H_0: \sigma_1^2 = \sigma_2^2$ and $H_1: \sigma_1^2 > \sigma_2^2$. To get the estimated error variances and test this hypothesis, we will split our sample into two equal subsamples of 20 observations each, and successively estimate (8.1) with higher income observations only (subsample 1), and with lower income observations only (subsample 2).

Go back to your **food data** worksheet. Place your cursor in any cell of the **income** data column **B**. Go to the **Data** tab in the middle of your tab list. In the **Sort & Filter** group of commands select the **Sort Largest to Smallest** button. Your data set should be sorted by descending order of income values as shown below.

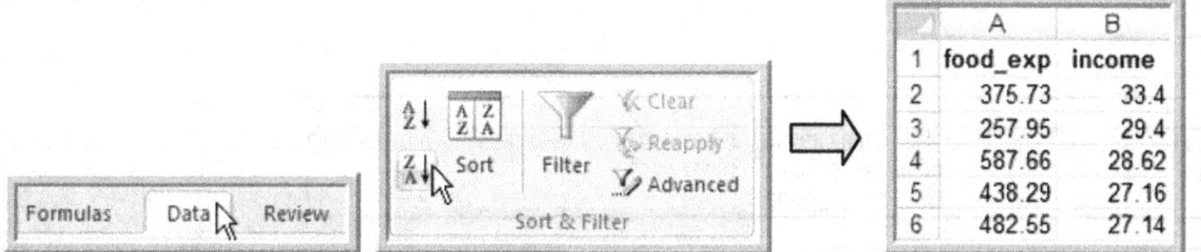

	A	B
1	food_exp	income
2	375.73	33.4
3	257.95	29.4
4	587.66	28.62
5	438.29	27.16
6	482.55	27.14

In the **Regression** dialog box, *for the higher income food expenditure model*, the **Input Y Range** should be **A1:A21**, and the **Input X Range** should be **B1:B21**. Check the box next to **Labels**. *Uncheck* the box next to **Constant is Zero**. Select **Output Range** and specify it to be cell **A1** in your **Subsample 1 Model** worksheet: you can place your cursor in the **Output Range** window and move it to that cell to do that, or type **'Subsample 1 Model'!A1** in **the Output Range** window. Finally, select **OK**.

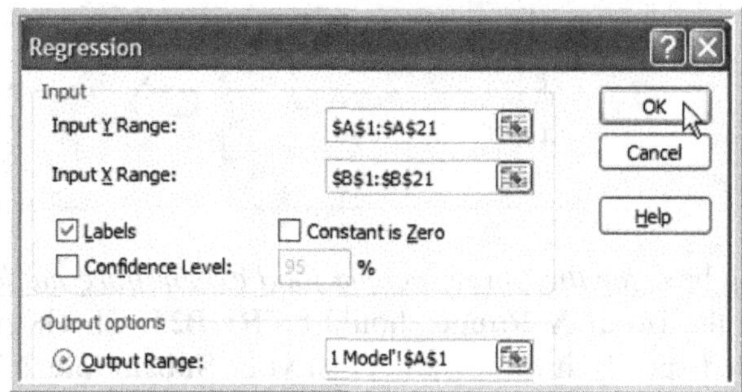

Excel informs you that the output range will overwrite existing data. Do select **OK** to overwrite the data in the specified range.

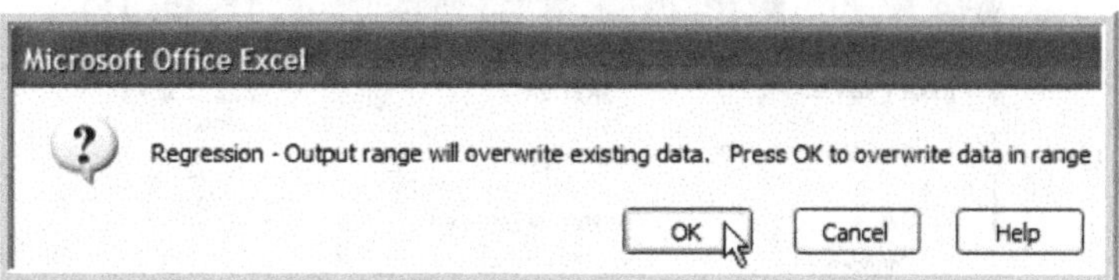

The result is:

	A	B	C	D	E	F	G	H	I
1	SUMMARY OUTPUT								
2									
3	*Regression Statistics*								
4	Multiple R	0.41248222							
5	R Square	0.170141582							
6	Adjusted R Square	0.124038337							
7	Standard Error	113.6746495							
8	Observations	20							
9									
10	ANOVA								
11		*df*	*SS*	*MS*	*F*	*Significance F*			
12	Regression	1	47687.68234	47687.68234	3.690446964	0.070707092			
13	Residual	18	232594.6668	12921.92593					
14	Total	19	280282.3492						
15									
16		*Coefficients*	*Standard Error*	*t Stat*	*P-value*	*Lower 95%*	*Upper 95%*	*Lower 95.0%*	*Upper 95.0%*
17	Intercept	-24.91462294	184.924846	-0.134728369	0.894321737	-413.4273071	363.5980612	-413.4273071	363.5980612
18	income	14.26400003	7.425092131	1.921053608	0.070707092	-1.335539657	29.86353971	-1.335539657	29.86353971

Go back to your **food data** worksheet. Place your cursor in any cell of the **income** data column **B**. Go to the **Data** tab in the middle of your tab list. In the **Sort & Filter** group of command select the **Smallest Sort to Largest** button. Your data set should be sorted by <u>*ascending*</u> order of income values as shown below.

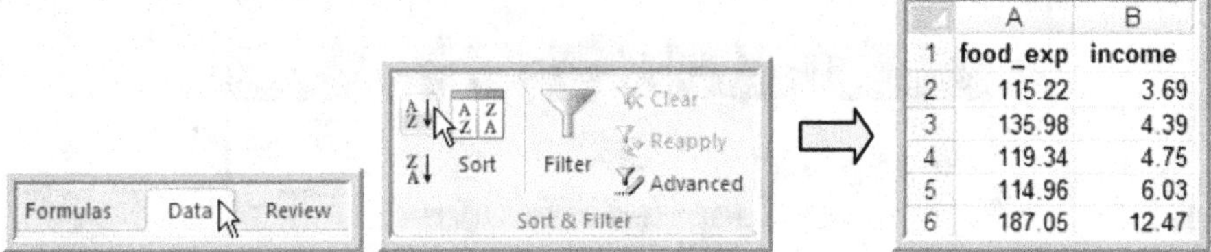

In the **Regression** dialog box, <u>*for the lower income food expenditure model*</u>, the **Input Y Range** should be **A1:A21**, and the **Input X Range** should be **B1:B21**. Check the box next to **Labels**. Select **Output Range** and specify it to be cell **A1** in your **Subsample 2 Model** worksheet: you can place your cursor in the **Output Range** window and move it to that cell to do that, or type **'Subsample 2 Model'!A1** in **the Output Range** window. Finally, select **OK**.

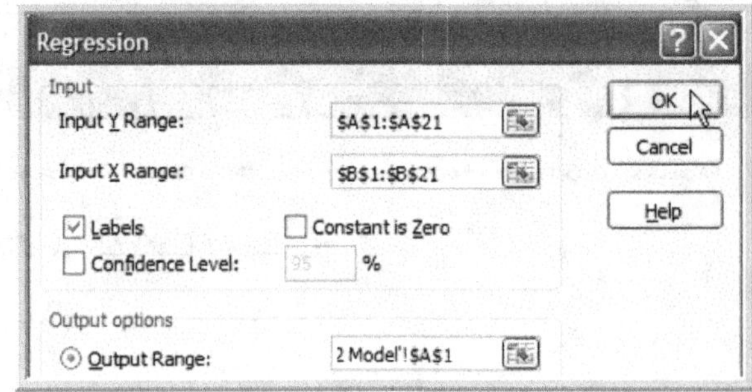

Excel informs you that the output range will overwrite existing data. Do select **OK** to overwrite the data in the specified range. The result is:

	A	B	C	D	E	F	G	H	I
1	SUMMARY OUTPUT								
2									
3	*Regression Statistics*								
4	Multiple R	0.734079402							
5	R Square	0.538872568							
6	Adjusted R Square	0.513254378							
7	Standard Error	59.78939939							
8	Observations	20							
9									
10	ANOVA								
11		*df*	*SS*	*MS*	*F*	*Significance F*			
12	Regression	1	75194.48762	75194.48762	21.03476298	0.000229013			
13	Residual	18	64345.90103	3574.77228					
14	Total	19	139540.3887						
15									
16		*Coefficients*	*Standard Error*	*t Stat*	*P-value*	*Lower 95%*	*Upper 95%*	*Lower 95.0%*	*Upper 95.0%*
17	Intercept	72.96173971	38.83435406	1.878793699	0.076566246	-8.626210517	154.5496899	-8.626210517	154.5496899
18	income	11.50037916	2.50751389	4.586367079	0.000229013	6.232287967	16.76847035	6.232287967	16.76847035

At $\alpha = 0.05$, the result of the Goldfeld-Quandt test for the food expenditure example is (see also p. 309 in *Principles of Econometrics, 4e*):

	A	B	C
1	**Data Input**	N_1 =	20
2		K_1 =	2
3		MS Residual 1 =	12921.93
4		N_2 =	20
5		K_2 =	2
6		MS Residual 2 =	3574.772
7		α =	0.05

	A	B	C
9	**Computed Values**	m_1 =	18
10		m_2 =	18
11		F-statistic =	3.614755
12	**Goldfeld-Quandt test**		
13	**Right-tail**	F_c =	2.217197
14		Conclusion =	Reject Ho

8.3 HETEROSKEDASTICITY-CONSISTENT STANDARD ERRORS OR THE WHITE STANDARD ERRORS

The White standard error estimator is given by:

$$\text{White se} = \sqrt{\widehat{var(b_2)}} = \sqrt{\frac{\sum_{i=1}^{N}[(x_i-\bar{x})^2\hat{e}_i^2]}{\left[\sum_{i=1}^{N}(x_i-\bar{x})^2\right]^2}} \tag{8.9}$$

Go back to your **food data** worksheet, if you are not there already. In cells **D1:E2**, and **G1:H2**, enter the following column labels and formulas.

	D	E
1	**x-bar =**	=AVERAGE(B2:B41)
2	**White se(b_2) =**	=SQRT(SUMPRODUCT(G2:G41,H2:H41)/SUM(G2:G41)^2)

	G	H
1	**(x_i – x-bar)^2**	**residuals^2**
2	=(B2-$E$1)^2	='Food Expenditure Equation'!C25^2

Note that we are using the **SUMPRODUCT** mathematical function to compute the White standard error. The general syntax of the **SUMPRODUCT** function is as follows:

=SUMPRODUCT(cell_range_in_column1,cell_range_in_column2)

where the cell range in both column 1 and column 2 must specify an identical number of rows. For each row, the value from column 1 is multiplied by the value from column 2, and all products are then summed.

Copy the content of cells **G2:H2** to cells **G3:H41**. Here is how your table should look (only the first five values are shown below):

	D	E	F	G	H
1	x-bar =	19.60475		(xᵢ - x-bar)²	residuals²
2	White se(b₂) =	1.76327		253.279269	34.452084
3				231.488619	59.9642
4				220.663599	158.05055
5				184.273839	901.20972
6				50.9046583	560.75419

The estimated White $se(b_2)$ above differs slightly from the value reported on p. 310 of *Principles of Econometrics, 4e*. The reason for this is the value reported in *Principles of Econometrics, 4e* was computed using the following *modified* White standard error estimator:

$$\text{modified White se} = \sqrt{\widehat{var(b_2)}} = \sqrt{\frac{N}{N-2}\frac{\sum_{i=1}^{N}[(x_i-\bar{x})^2\hat{e}_i^2]}{\left[\sum_{i=1}^{N}(x_i-\bar{x})^2\right]^2}} \tag{8.10}$$

The source of this adjustment follows from the discussion on pp. 64-65 of *Principles of Econometrics, 4e*. Namely, the expected value of the sum of squared regression errors is $E\left[\sum e_i^2\right] = N\sigma^2$. However the expected value of the sum of the squared least squares residuals is $E\left[\sum \hat{e}_i^2\right] = (N-2)\sigma^2$. The squared least squares residuals are smaller, on average, than the true regression errors. The adjustment is to offset this fact.

In cells **D3:E4** of your **food data** worksheet, add the following column labels and formulas.

	D	E
3	**N =**	=COUNT(B2:B41)
4	**Modified White se(b_2) =**	=SQRT((SUMPRODUCT(G2:G41,H2:H41)/SUM(G2:G41)^2)*(E3/(E3-2)))

The estimated *modified* White $se(b_2)$ should be equal to the value reported on p. 310 of *Principles of Econometrics, 4e*:

	D	E
3	N =	40
4	Modified White se(b₂) =	1.809077

8.4 GENERALIZED LEAST SQUARES: KNOWN FORM OF VARIANCE

8.4.1 Variance Proportional to x: Food Expenditure Example

Consider the following heteroskedasticity assumption for the food expenditure model:

$$var(e_i) = \sigma_i^2 = \sigma^2 x_i \quad (8.11)$$

Given assumption (8.12), the following food expenditure model has homoskedastic errors:

$$y_i^* = \beta_1 x_{i1}^* + \beta_2 x_{i2}^* + e_i^* \quad (8.12)$$

where the transformed dependent and explanatory variables are defined as $y_i^* = \frac{y_i}{\sqrt{x_i}}$, $x_{i1}^* = \frac{1}{\sqrt{x_i}}$, and $x_{i2}^* = \sqrt{x_i}$.

Note that model (8.12) *does not have an intercept.*

Below, we first calculate the transformed dependent and explanatory variables, and then use Excel regression analysis tool to get the generalized least squares estimate of model (8.12).

Go back to your **food data** worksheet. In cells **J1:L2** enter the following column labels and formulas.

	J	K	L
1	**y***	**x_1***	**x_2***
2	=A2/SQRT(B2)	=1/SQRT(B2)	=SQRT(B2)

Copy the content of cells **J2:L2** to cells **J3:L41**. Here is how your table should look (only the first five values are shown below):

	J	K	L
1	y*	x_1*	x_2*
2	59.98114	0.520579	1.920937
3	64.89971	0.477274	2.095233
4	54.75695	0.458831	2.179449
5	46.81533	0.407231	2.455606
6	52.96933	0.283183	3.531289

In the **Regression** dialog box, the **Input Y Range** should be **J1:J41**, and the **Input X Range** should be **K1:L41**. Check the box next to **Labels** *and* next to **Constant is Zero**. Select **New Worksheet Ply** and name it **GLS Food Expenditure Equation**. Finally select **OK**.

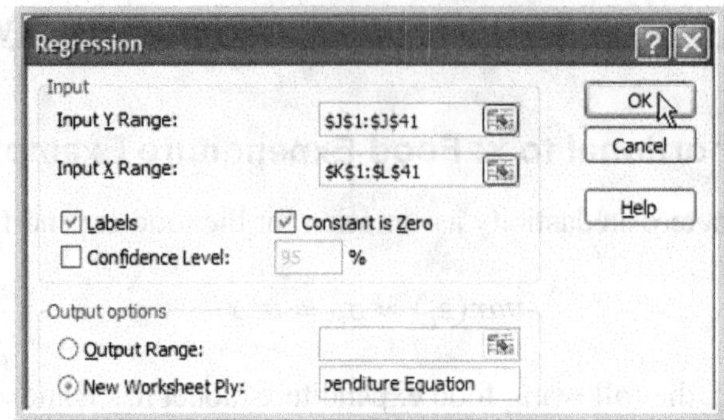

The result is (see also p. 313 in *Principles of Econometrics, 4e*):

	A	B	C	D	E	F	G	H	I
1	SUMMARY OUTPUT								
2									
3	*Regression Statistics*								
4	Multiple R	0.962446484							
5	R Square	0.926303234							
6	Adjusted R Square	0.898048056							
7	Standard Error	18.75005582							
8	Observations	40							
9									
10	ANOVA								
11		*df*	*SS*	*MS*	*F*	*Significance F*			
12	Regression	2	167916.5405	83958.27027	238.8132136	7.06526E-22			
13	Residual	38	13359.45454	351.5645932					
14	Total	40	181275.9951						
15									
16		*Coefficients*	*Standard Error*	*t Stat*	*P-value*	*Lower 95%*	*Upper 95%*	*Lower 95.0%*	*Upper 95.0%*
17	Intercept	0	#N/A	#N/A	#N/A	#N/A	#N/A	#N/A	#N/A
18	x1*	78.68408203	23.78872165	3.307621283	0.00206413	30.52633316	126.8418309	30.52633316	126.8418309
19	x2*	10.4510089	1.385891227	7.541002276	4.61376E-09	7.645418811	13.25659899	7.645418811	13.25659899

8.4.2 Grouped Data: Wage Equation Example

8.4.2a Separate Wage Equations for Metropolitan and Rural Areas

If we assume that the error variances in the metropolitan and rural areas are different, instead of estimating equation (8.7), we can estimate the following equation (8.13) twice—once for workers living in a metropolitan area and again for workers living in a rural area.

$$WAGE = \beta_1 + \beta_2 EDUC + \beta_3 EXPER + e \tag{8.13}$$

We already have done this in Section 8.2.3c.

Now, if the assumption that the effect of education and experience on wages is the same for metropolitan and rural areas is true, then better estimates can be obtained by combining both subsets of data and applying a generalized least squares estimator to the complete set of data, with recognition given to the existence of heteroskedasticity. That is what we do next.

8.4.2b GLS Wage Equation

Given the assumption that the error variances in the metropolitan and rural areas are different, the following wage model has homoskedastic errors:

$$\left(\frac{WAGE_I}{\hat{\sigma}_i}\right) = \beta_1\left(\frac{1}{\hat{\sigma}_i}\right) + \beta_2\left(\frac{EDUC_i}{\hat{\sigma}_i}\right) + \beta_3\left(\frac{EXPER_i}{\hat{\sigma}_i}\right) + \delta\left(\frac{METRO_i}{\hat{\sigma}_i}\right) + v_i \qquad (8.14)$$

where $\hat{\sigma}_i = \hat{\sigma}_M$ for metropolitan areas observations, and $\hat{\sigma}_i = \hat{\sigma}_R$ for rural area observations; $\hat{\sigma}_M$ is the estimated standard error from (8.8) using metropolitan area observations only (subsample 1 model), and $\hat{\sigma}_R$ is the estimated standard error from (8.8) using rural area observations only (subsample 2 model).

Note that model (8.14) *does not have an intercept*.

Go back to your **cps2 data** worksheet. In cells **M1:N2**, and **P1:T2**, enter the following column labels and formulas.

	M	N	P	Q
1	**σ-hat metro =**	='Subsample 1 Model'!B7	**y***	**x1***
2	**σ-hat rural =**	='Subsample 2 Model'!B7	=A2/IF(D2=1,$N$1,$N$2)	=1/IF(D2=1,$N$1,$N$2)

	R	S	T
1	**x2***	**x3***	**x4***
2	=B2/IF(D2=1,$N$1,$N$2)	=C2/IF(D2=1,$N$1,$N$2)	=D2/IF(D2=1,$N$1,$N$2)

Copy the content of cells **P2:T2** to cells **P3:T1001**. Here is how your table should look (only the first five values are shown below):

	M	N	O	P	Q	R	S	T
1	**σ-hat metro =**	5.641253		**y***	**x1***	**x2***	**x3***	**x4***
2	**σ-hat rural =**	3.904227		0.519949	0.256133	3.329725	0.512265	0
3				0.809379	0.256133	3.329725	0.256133	0
4				0.86829	0.256133	3.073592	3.84199	0
5				0.86829	0.256133	3.073592	8.196245	0
6				0.942568	0.256133	3.073592	1.280663	0

In the **Regression** dialog box, the **Input Y Range** should be **P1:P1001**, and the **Input X Range** should be **Q1:T1001**. Check the boxes next to **Labels** *and* **Constant is Zero**. Select **New Worksheet Ply** and name it **GLS Wage Equation**. Finally select **OK**.

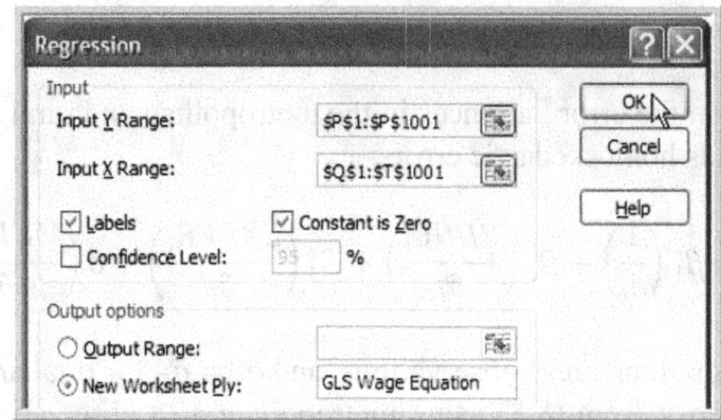

The result is (see also p. 315 of *Principles of Econometrics, 4e*):

	A	B	C	D	E	F	G	H	I
1	SUMMARY OUTPUT								
2									
3	*Regression Statistics*								
4	Multiple R	0.897416094							
5	R Square	0.805355646							
6	Adjusted R Square	0.803765352							
7	Standard Error	1.001216522							
8	Observations	1000							
9									
10	ANOVA								
11		*df*	*SS*	*MS*	*F*	*Significance F*			
12	Regression	4	4131.057618	1032.764404	1030.25622	0			
13	Residual	996	998.4247867	1.002434525					
14	Total	1000	5129.482405						
15									
16		*Coefficients*	*Standard Error*	*t Stat*	*P-value*	*Lower 95%*	*Upper 95%*	*Lower 95.0%*	*Upper 95.0%*
17	Intercept	0	#N/A	#N/A	#N/A	#N/A	#N/A	#N/A	#N/A
18	x1*	-9.398361661	1.019672608	-9.217038477	1.76706E-19	-11.39931476	-7.39740856	-11.39931476	-7.39740856
19	x2*	1.195720589	0.068507954	17.45374844	1.00115E-59	1.061284103	1.330157075	1.061284103	1.330157075
20	x3*	0.132208766	0.014548502	9.087448443	5.34461E-19	0.103659533	0.160758	0.103659533	0.160758
21	x4*	1.538803242	0.346285576	4.443740504	9.83178E-06	0.859270231	2.218336253	0.859270231	2.218336253

8.5 GENERALIZED LEAST SQUARES: UNKNOWN FORM OF VARIANCE

Consider the following *more general* heteroskedasticity assumption for the food expenditure model:

$$var(e_i) = \sigma_i^2 = exp(\alpha_1 + \alpha_2 z_i) \tag{8.15}$$

Given assumption (8.15), the following food expenditure model has homoskedastic errors:

$$y_i^* = \beta_1 x_{i1}^* + \beta_2 x_{i2}^* + e_i^* \tag{8.16}$$

where the transformed dependent and explanatory variables are defined as $y_i^* = \frac{y_i}{\hat{\sigma}_i}$, $x_{i1}^* = \frac{1}{\hat{\sigma}_i}$, and $x_{i2}^* = \frac{x_i}{\hat{\sigma}_i}$.

Note that $\hat{\sigma}_i = \sqrt{exp\left(\hat{\alpha}_1 + \hat{\alpha}_2 ln(x_i)\right)}$, where $\hat{\alpha}_1$ and $\hat{\alpha}_2$ are the least squares estimates of (8.17):

$$ln(\hat{e}_i^2) = \alpha_1 + \alpha_2 ln(x_i) + v_i \tag{8.17}$$

and $\hat{e}_i^2$ are the squares of the least squares residuals from model (8.1).

Below, we first estimate (8.17). We will then calculate the transformed dependent and explanatory variables and use Excel regression analysis tool to get the *more* generalized least squares estimate of model (8.16).

Again, note that model (8.16) <u>*does not have an intercept*</u>.

Go back to your **food data** worksheet. In cells **N1:O2** enter the following column labels and formulas.

	N	O
1	**ln(e-hat$_i^2$)**	**ln(x)**
2	=LN(H2)	=LN(B2)

Copy the content of cells **N2:O2** to cells **N3:O41**. Here is how your table should look (only the first five values are shown below):

	N	O
1	ln(e-hat$_i^2$)	ln(x)
2	3.539569	1.305626
3	4.093748	1.479329
4	5.062915	1.558145
5	6.803738	1.796747
6	6.329283	2.523326

In the **Regression** dialog box, the **Input Y Range** should be **N1:N41**, and the **Input X Range** should be **O1:O41**. Check the box next to **Labels**. Make sure the box next to **Constant is Zero** is <u>*not checked*</u>. Select **New Worksheet Ply** and name it **Log-Log Variance Function**. Finally select **OK**.

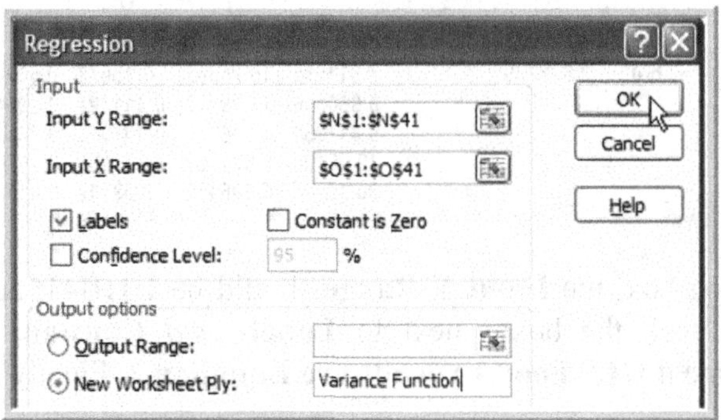

The result is (see also p. 317 in *Principles of Econometrics, 4e*):

	A	B	C	D	E	F	G	H	I
1	SUMMARY OUTPUT								
2									
3	*Regression Statistics*								
4	Multiple R	0.572361254							
5	R Square	0.327597405							
6	Adjusted R Square	0.3099026							
7	Standard Error	1.720854391							
8	Observations	40							
9									
10	ANOVA								
11		*df*	*SS*	*MS*	*F*	*Significance F*			
12	Regression	1	54.82554	54.82554	18.51376169	0.000113872			
13	Residual	38	112.5309137	2.961339835					
14	Total	39	167.3564537						
15									
16		*Coefficients*	*Standard Error*	*t Stat*	*P-value*	*Lower 95%*	*Upper 95%*	*Lower 95.0%*	*Upper 95.0%*
17	Intercept	0.93779654	1.583105245	0.592377887	0.557106301	-2.267032452	4.142625532	-2.267032452	4.142625532
18	ln(x)	2.329238594	0.541335668	4.302762101	0.000113872	1.233361837	3.425115351	1.233361837	3.425115351

Go back to your **food data** worksheet. In cells **Q1:R2**, and **T1:W2**, enter the following column labels and formulas.

	Q	R
1	**α_1-hat =**	='Log-Log Variance Function'!B17
2	**α_2-hat =**	='Log-Log Variance Function'!B18

	T	U	V	W
1	**σ-hat**	**y***	**x_1***	**x_2***
2	=SQRT(EXP($R$1+$R$2*O2))	=A2/T2	=1/T2	=B2/T2

Copy the content of cells **T2:W2** to cells **T3:W41**. Here is how your table should look (only the first five values are shown below):

	Q	R	S	T	U	V	W
1	α_1-hat =	0.937797		σ-hat	y*	x_1*	x_2*
2	α_2-hat =	2.329239		7.311555	15.75862	0.13677	0.504681
3				8.950896	15.19177	0.111721	0.490454
4				9.811386	12.16342	0.101922	0.484131
5				12.95426	8.874302	0.077195	0.465484
6				30.19306	6.195132	0.03312	0.413009

In the **Regression** dialog box, the **Input Y Range** should be **U1:U41**, and the **Input X Range** should be **V1:W41**. Check the boxes next to **Labels** *and* **Constant is Zero**. Select **New Worksheet Ply** and name it **GLS Food Expenditure Equation 2**. Finally select **OK**.

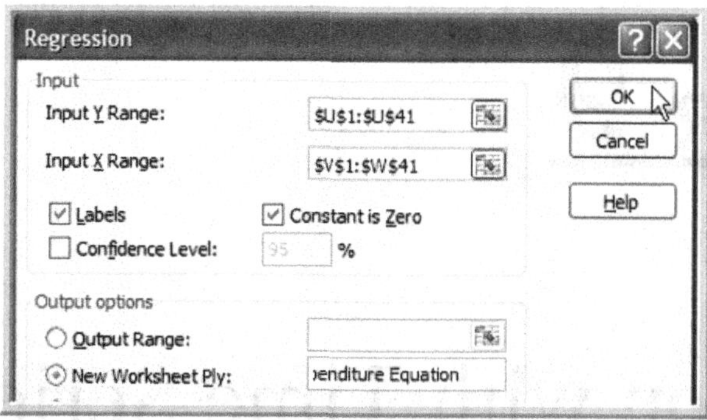

The result is (see also p. 318 in *Principles of Econometrics, 4e*):

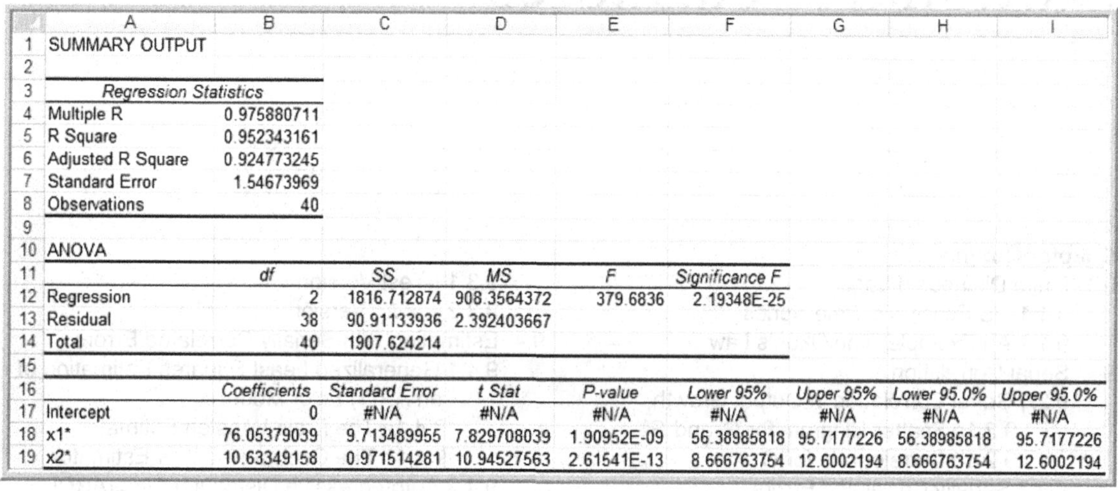

	A	B	C	D	E	F	G	H	I
1	SUMMARY OUTPUT								
2									
3	*Regression Statistics*								
4	Multiple R	0.975880711							
5	R Square	0.952343161							
6	Adjusted R Square	0.924773245							
7	Standard Error	1.54673969							
8	Observations	40							
9									
10	ANOVA								
11		*df*	*SS*	*MS*	*F*	*Significance F*			
12	Regression	2	1816.712874	908.3564372	379.6836	2.19348E-25			
13	Residual	38	90.91133936	2.392403667					
14	Total	40	1907.624214						
15									
16		*Coefficients*	*Standard Error*	*t Stat*	*P-value*	*Lower 95%*	*Upper 95%*	*Lower 95.0%*	*Upper 95.0%*
17	Intercept	0	#N/A	#N/A	#N/A	#N/A	#N/A	#N/A	#N/A
18	x1*	76.05379039	9.713489955	7.829708039	1.90952E-09	56.38985818	95.7177226	56.38985818	95.7177226
19	x2*	10.63349158	0.971514281	10.94527563	2.61541E-13	8.666763754	12.6002194	8.666763754	12.6002194

CHAPTER 9

Regression with Time Series Data: Stationary Variables

Chapter Outline

This chapter is concerned with the nature of autocorrelation, generalized least squares estimation of AR(1) models, and tests for autocorrelation. Forecasting, finite distributed lags models, and autoregressive distributed lags models, are also introduced.

9.1 FINITE DISTRIBUTED LAGS

9.1.1 US Economic Time Series

Open the Excel file ***okun***. Save your file as **POE Chapter 9**. Rename sheet 1 **okun data**.

Below we plot the time series of some important economic variables for the US economy as in Figure 9.4 on p. 345 of *Principles of Econometrics, 4e*.

In cells **C2:C3**, enter the following labels and formulas.

	C
2	**Du**
3	=B3-B2

Copy the content of cell **C3** to cells **C4:C99**. Here is how your table should look (only the first five values are shown below):

	C
2	du
3	-0.1
4	-0.2
5	0
6	0.2
7	-0.2

Select the **Insert** tab located next to the **Home** tab. Select **C3:C99**. In the **Charts** group of commands select **Line**, and **Line with Markers**.

After editing, the result is (see also Figure 9.4(a) p. 345 in *Principles of Econometrics, 4e*):

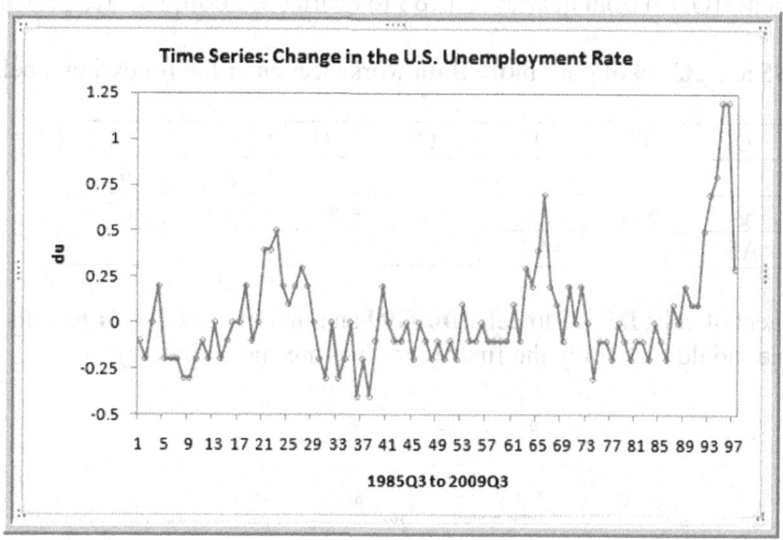

To plot the change in the US GDP series select cells **A3:A99**. After editing, the result is (see also Figure 9.4(b) p. 345 in *Principles of Econometrics, 4e*):

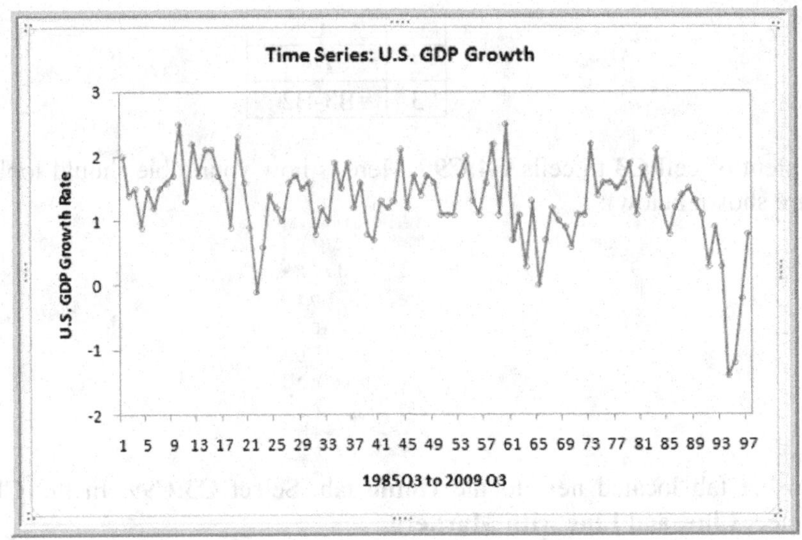

9.1.2 An Example: Okun's Law

Consider the following finite distributed lag model:

$$DU_t = \alpha + \beta_0 G_t + \beta_1 G_{t-1} + \beta_2 G_{t-2} + \cdots + \beta_q G_{t-q} + e_t \tag{9.1}$$

where DU is the change in the U.S. unemployment rate and G is the percentage change in Gross Domestic Product (GDP) from quarter 2, 1985 to quarter 3, 2009; $t = 1,..,T$ where $T = 98$.

In cells **D4:G5** and **H3:J4** of your **okun data** worksheet enter the following labels and formulas.

	D	E	F	G	H	I	J
3					g	g_{t-1}	g_{t-2}
4	g	g_{t-1}	g_{t-2}	g_{t-3}	=A4	=A3	=A2
5	=A5	=A4	=A3	=A2			

Copy the content of cells **D5:G5** to cells **D6:G99** and that of cells **H4:J4** to cells **H5:J99**. Here is how your table should look (only the first five values are shown below):

	D	E	F	G	H	I	J
3					g	g_{t-1}	g_{t-2}
4	g	g_{t-1}	g_{t-2}	g_{t-3}	1.4	2	1.4
5	1.5	1.4	2	1.4	1.5	1.4	2
6	0.9	1.5	1.4	2	0.9	1.5	1.4
7	1.5	0.9	1.5	1.4	1.5	0.9	1.5
8	1.2	1.5	0.9	1.5	1.2	1.5	0.9
9	1.5	1.2	1.5	0.9	1.5	1.2	1.5

In the **Regression** dialog box, the **Input Y Range** should be **C4:C99**, and the **Input X Range** should be **D4:G99**. Check the box next to **Labels**. Select **New Worksheet Ply** and name it **Okun's Law Lag Model q=3**. Finally select **OK**.

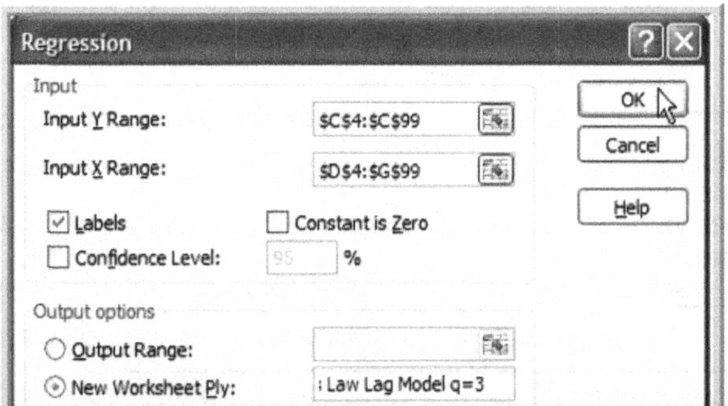

The result is (see also Table 9.2 p. 346 in *Principles of Econometrics, 4e*, for Lag Length $q = 3$):

	A	B	C	D	E	F	G	H	I
1	SUMMARY OUTPUT								
2									
3	*Regression Statistics*								
4	Multiple R	0.807716384							
5	R Square	0.652405757							
6	Adjusted R Square	0.636957124							
7	Standard Error	0.174329325							
8	Observations	95							
9									
10	ANOVA								
11		*df*	*SS*	*MS*	*F*	*Significance F*			
12	Regression	4	5.133677887	1.283419472	42.23064622	6.76928E-20			
13	Residual	90	2.735164218	0.030390714					
14	Total	94	7.868842105						
15									
16		*Coefficients*	*Standard Error*	*t Stat*	*P-value*	*Lower 95%*	*Upper 95%*	*Lower 95.0%*	*Upper 95.0%*
17	Intercept	0.580974603	0.053889266	10.78089658	6.91581E-18	0.473914173	0.688035034	0.473914173	0.688035034
18	g	-0.202052639	0.033013144	-6.120369474	2.38823E-08	-0.26763901	-0.136466267	-0.26763901	-0.136466267
19	gt-1	-0.164535169	0.03581752	-4.5937064	1.41082E-05	-0.235692922	-0.093377416	-0.235692922	-0.093377416
20	gt-2	-0.071555993	0.035304286	-2.026835881	0.045638315	-0.141694117	-0.001417869	-0.141694117	-0.001417869
21	gt-3	0.003303021	0.036260343	0.09109184	0.927622053	-0.068734477	0.07534052	-0.068734477	0.07534052

Go back to your **okun data** worksheet. In the **Regression** dialog box, the **Input Y Range** should be **C3:C99**, and the **Input X Range** should be **H3:J99**. Check the boxes next to **Labels**. Select **New Worksheet Ply** and name it **Okun's Law Lag Model q = 2**. Finally select **OK**.

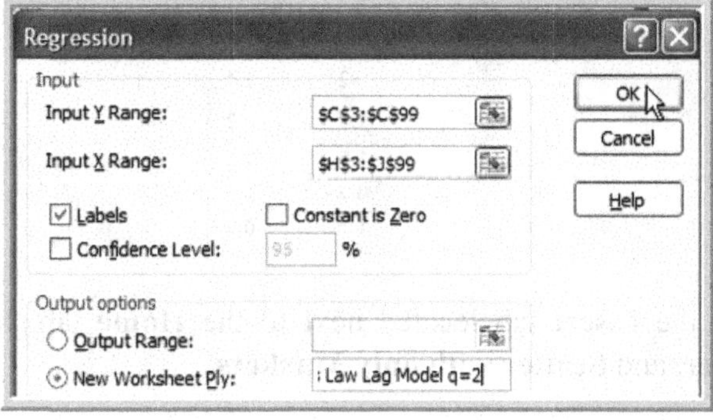

The result is (see also Table 9.2 p. 346 in *Principles of Econometrics, 4e*, for Lag Length $q = 2$):

	A	B	C	D	E	F	G	H	I
1	SUMMARY OUTPUT								
2									
3	*Regression Statistics*								
4	Multiple R	0.808669257							
5	R Square	0.653945967							
6	Adjusted R Square	0.642661596							
7	Standard Error	0.172599938							
8	Observations	96							
9									
10	ANOVA								
11		*df*	*SS*	*MS*	*F*	*Significance F*			
12	Regression	3	5.179252056	1.726417352	57.95147879	3.96428E-21			
13	Residual	92	2.740747944	0.029790739					
14	Total	95	7.92						
15									
16		*Coefficients*	*Standard Error*	*t Stat*	*P-value*	*Lower 95%*	*Upper 95%*	*Lower 95.0%*	*Upper 95.0%*
17	Intercept	0.583556112	0.047211917	12.36035632	2.9455E-21	0.489789173	0.677323052	0.489789173	0.677323052
18	g	-0.202021646	0.032383181	-6.238474373	1.33092E-08	-0.266337437	-0.137705854	-0.266337437	-0.137705854
19	gt-1	-0.16532688	0.033536844	-4.929708945	3.63103E-06	-0.231933946	-0.098719815	-0.231933946	-0.098719815
20	gt-2	-0.070013485	0.03309997	-2.115212962	0.037114442	-0.135752881	-0.00427409	-0.135752881	-0.00427409

9.2 SERIAL CORRELATION

9.2.1 Serial Correlation in Output Growth

9.2.1a Scatter Diagram for G_t and G_{t-1}

Go back to your **okun data** worksheet.

In cells **K2:L3** enter the following labels and formulas.

	K	L
2	**g**	**g_{t-1}**
3	=A3	=A2

Copy the content of cells **K3:L3** to cells **K4:L99**. Here is how your table should look (only the first five values are shown below):

	K	L
2	g	g_{t-1}
3	2	1.4
4	1.4	2
5	1.5	1.4
6	0.9	1.5
7	1.5	0.9

Select **K2:L99**. Select the **Insert** tab located next to the **Home** tab. In the **Charts** group of commands select **Scatter**, and **Scatter with only Markers**.

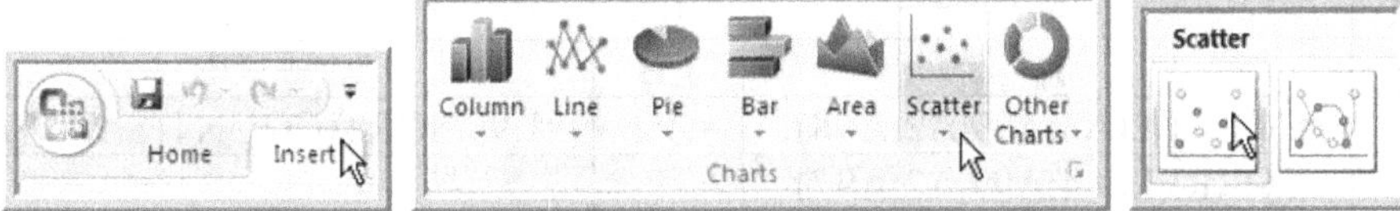

After editing, the result is (see also Figure 9.5 p. 348 in *Principles of Econometrics, 4e*):

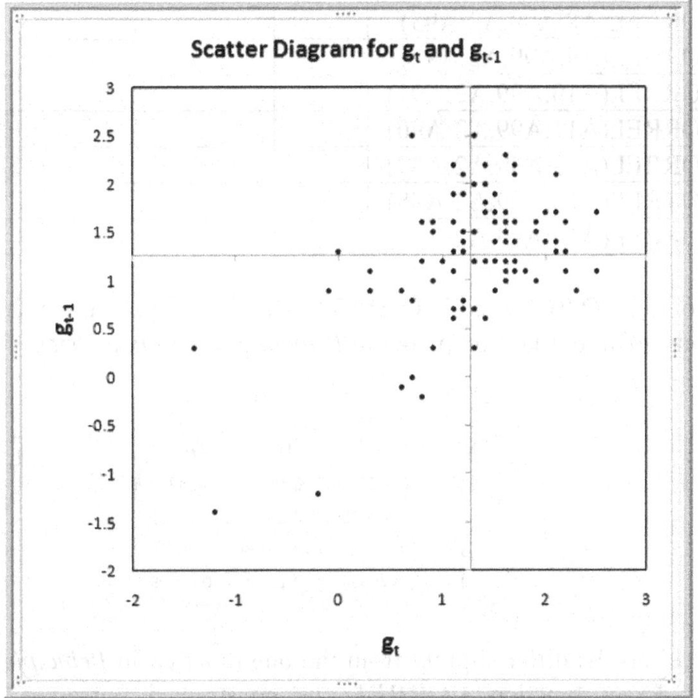

9.2.1b Correlogram for G

Let r_k be the correlation between G_t and G_{t-k}; in other words, it is the correlation between growth rates that are k periods apart. The null and alternative hypotheses for a test of autocorrelation are: $H_0{:}\,\rho_k = 0$ and $H_1{:}\,\rho_k \neq 0$. When H_0 is true, the product of the square root of the sample size and the estimated correlation r_k has an approximate standard normal distribution:

$$Z = \sqrt{T}r_k \sim N(0,1) \tag{9.2}$$

Consequently, r_k is significantly different from zero at a 5% significance level if $\sqrt{T}r_k \geq 1.96$ or $\sqrt{T}r_k \leq -1.96$, . Alternatively, we can say that r_k if significantly different from zero at a 5% significance level if $r_k \geq 1.96/\sqrt{T}$ or $r_k \leq -1.96/\sqrt{T}$. By drawing the values $\leq \pm 1.96/\sqrt{T}$ as bounds on a graph that illustrates the magnitude of each of the r_k, we can see at a glance which correlations are significant.

In cells **M1:N13** and **O1:P2** of your **okun data** worksheet enter the following column labels and formulas.

	M	N	O	P
1	**lag**	$\mathbf{r_k}$	**LB**	**UB**
2	**1**	=CORREL(A3:A99,A2:A98)	=-P2	=1.96/SQRT(COUNT($A$2:$A$99))
3	**2**	=CORREL(A4:A99,A2:A97)		
4	**3**	=CORREL(A5:A99,A2:A96)		
5	**4**	=CORREL(A6:A99,A2:A95)		
6	**5**	=CORREL(A7:A99,A2:A94)		
7	**6**	=CORREL(A8:A99,A2:A93)		
8	**7**	=CORREL(A9:A99,A2:A92)		
9	**8**	=CORREL(A10:A99,A2:A91)		
10	**9**	=CORREL(A11:A99,A2:A90)		
11	**10**	=CORREL(A12:A99,A2:A89)		
12	**11**	=CORREL(A13:A99,A2:A88)		
13	**12**	=CORREL(A14:A99,A2:A87)		

Copy the content of cells **O2:P2** to cells **O3:P13**. Here is how your table should look (see also reported correlations up to four lags on p. 349 in *Principles of Econometrics, 4e*):

	M	N	O	P
1	**lag**	r_k	**LB**	**UB**
2	**1**	0.495768	-0.19799	0.19799
3	2	0.426994	-0.19799	0.19799
4	3	0.176831	-0.19799	0.19799
5	4	0.263669	-0.19799	0.19799

Note that your Excel results differ slightly from the one reported in *Principles of Econometrics, 4e*. By using the Excel function **CORREL** we constrained ourselves to computing the autocorrelations by using $(T - k)$ observations in the numerator *and* the denominator of the correlation coefficient—an alternative, mentioned on p. 349 of your textbook, that leads to larger estimates in finite samples and is given by

$$r_k = \frac{\sum_{t=k+1}^{T}(g_t - \bar{g})(g_{t-k} - \bar{g})}{\sum_{t=k+1}^{T}(g_t - \bar{g})^2} \quad (9.3)$$

Select cells **O1:O13**. Go to the **Insert** tab, select **Line** in the **Charts** group of commands, and **Line** again in the **Line** options list.

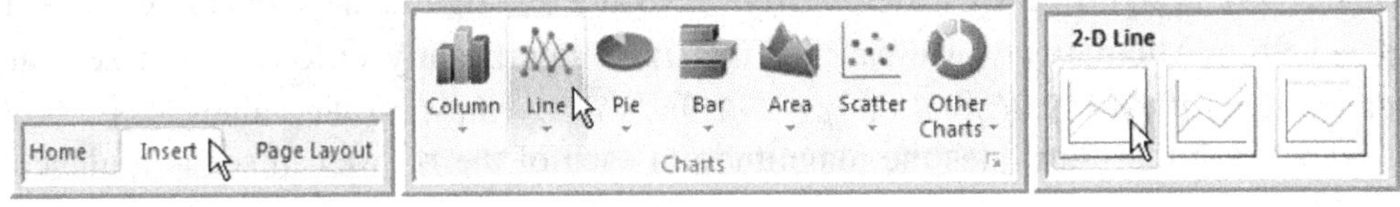

You should get the following chart:

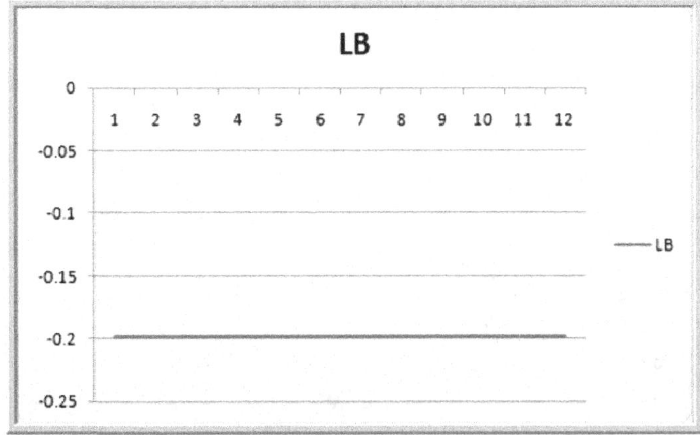

We would like to add to it, our upper bound values, and our correlation coefficient values. Right click anywhere in your chart area and choose **Select Data** on the list of options that pops up. In the **Select Data Source** dialog box, select **Add**. In the **Edit Series** dialog box, the **Series name** is the one found in cell **P1** and the **Series X values** are from **P2:P13**. Select **OK.**

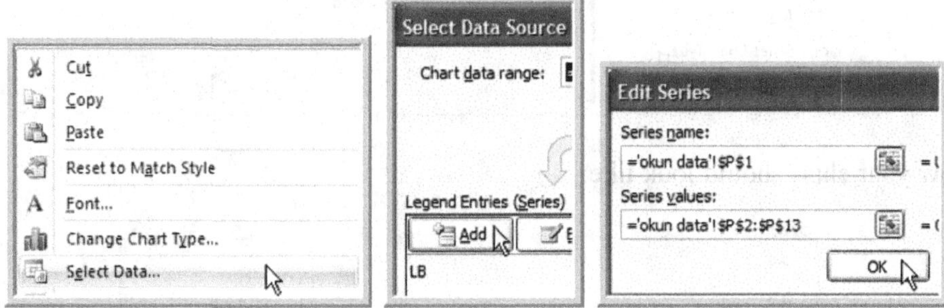

The **Select Data Source** dialog box reappears. Select **Add** again. Type **Correlation** for the **Series name**. In the **Edit Series** dialog box, the **Series X values** are from **N2:N13**. Select **OK.** The **Select Data Source** dialog box reappears again. Select **OK** one more time.

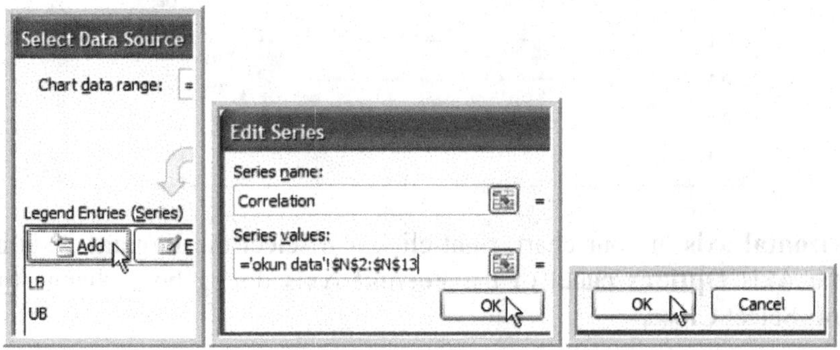

The result is:

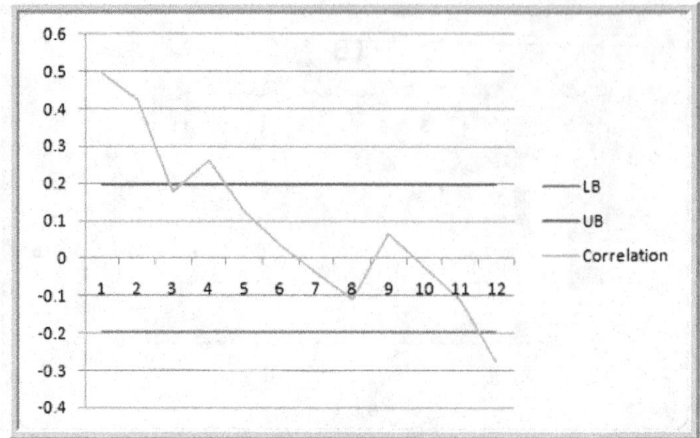

On your chart, select the **Correlation** series, right-click and select **Change Series Chart Type** in the menu of options. Select **Clustered Column** in the **Column** group of chart type. Select **OK.**

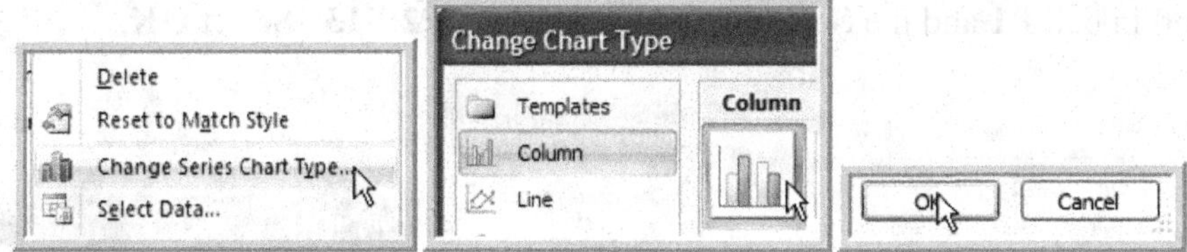

Here is how your chart should look like:

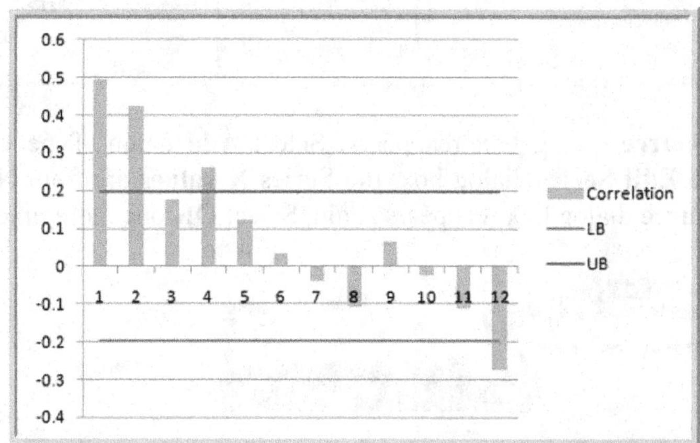

Select the **horizontal axis** in your chart, right-click and select the **Format Axis** in the menu of options. In the **Axis Options** panel of the **Format Axis** dialog box, change the **Axis labels** location to **Low**. Select **Close**.

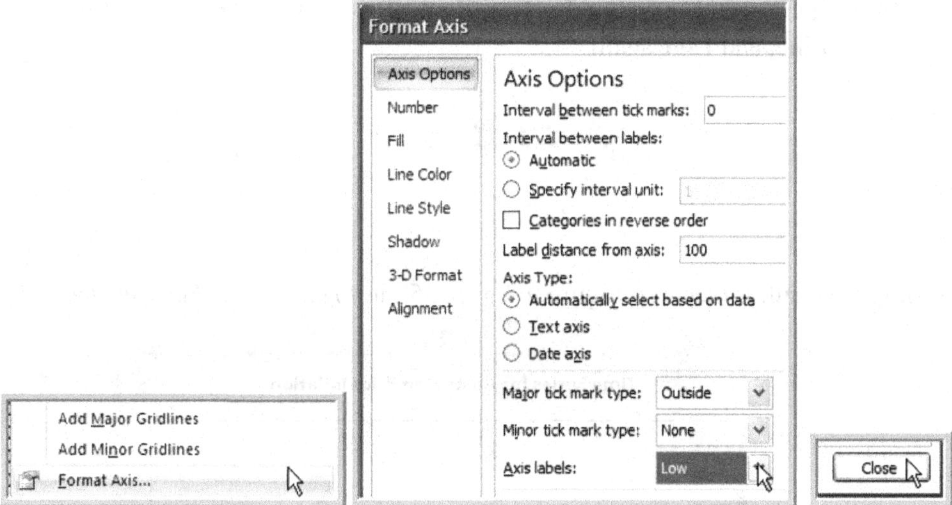

After your add axis titles and delete the legend, your chart should look similar to Figure 9.6 on p. 350 of *Principles of Econometrics, 4e*:

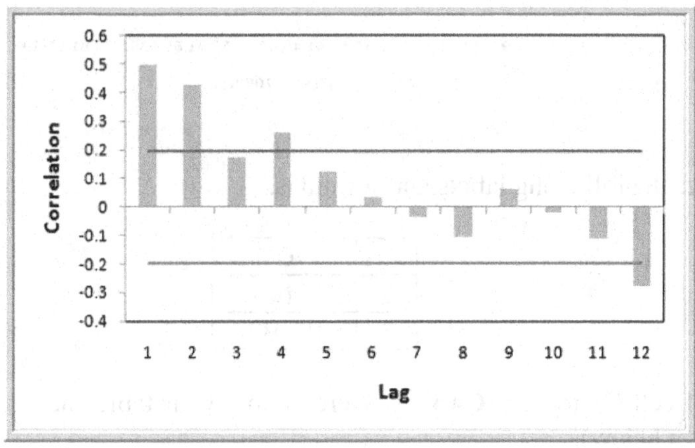

9.2.2 Serially Correlated Errors

9.2.2a Australian Economic Time Series

Open the Excel file ***phillips_aus***. Excel opens the data set in Sheet 1 of a new Excel file. Since we would like to save all our work from Chapter 9 in one file, create a new worksheet in your **POE Chapter 9** Excel file, rename it **phillips_aus data**, and in it, copy the data set you just opened.

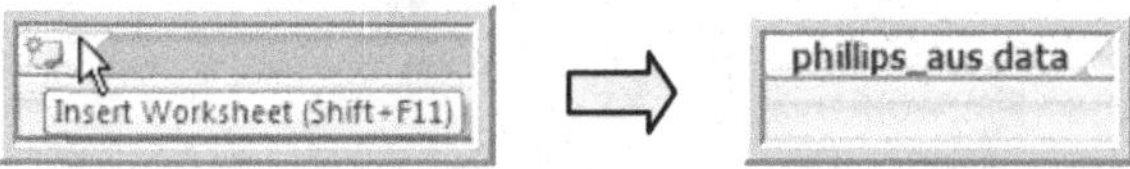

Below we plot the time series of some important economic variables for the Australian economy as in Figure 9.7 on p. 352 of *Principles of Econometrics, 4e*.

Select the **Insert** tab located next to the **Home** tab. Select **A1:A92**. In the **Charts** group of commands select **Line**, and **Line** again.

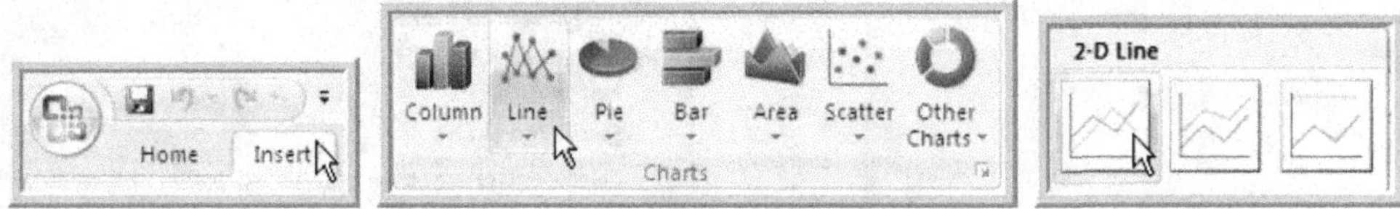

After editing, the result is (see also Figure 9.7(a) p. 352 in *Principles of Econometrics, 4e*):

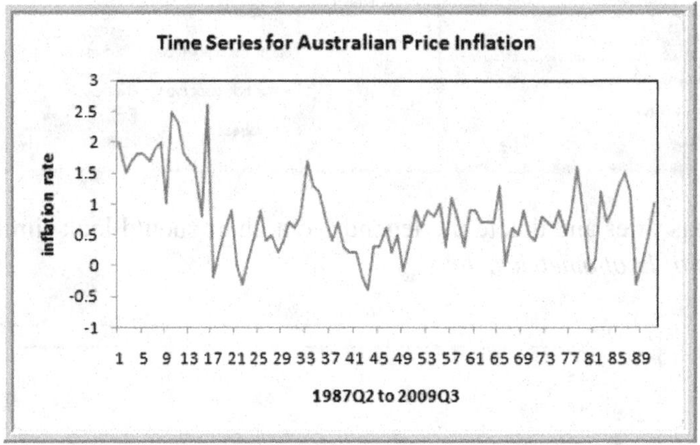

In cells **C2:C3**, enter the following labels and formulas.

	C
2	**du**
3	=B3-B2

Copy the content of cell **C3** to cells **C4:C92**. Here is how your table should look (only the first five values are shown below):

	C
2	du
3	-0.1
4	-0.2
5	-0.1
6	-0.4
7	0

To plot the time series for the quarterly change in the Australian unemployment rate select cells C2:C92. After editing, the result is (see also Figure 9.7(b) p. 352 in *Principles of Econometrics, 4e*):

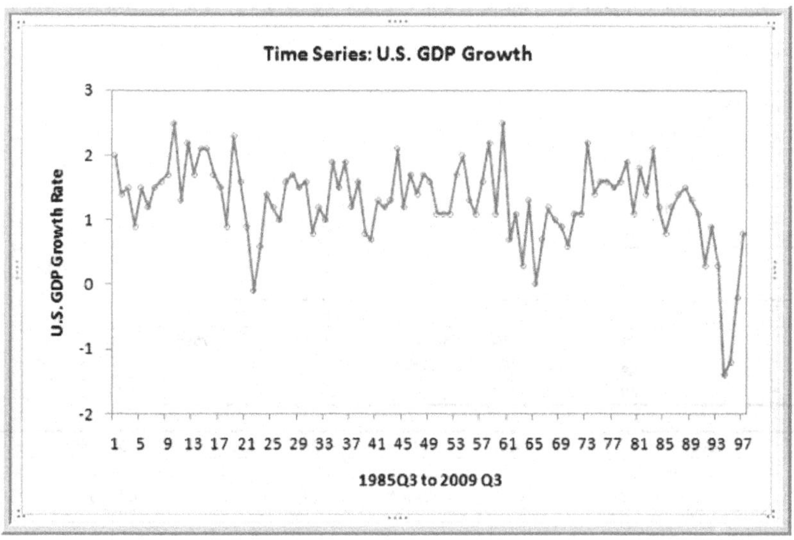

9.2.2b A Phillips Curve

Consider the following Phillips curve model:

$$INF_t = \beta_1 + \beta_2 DU_t + e_t \tag{9.4}$$

where DU is the change in the Australia unemployment rate and $INFL$ is the inflation rate from quarter 2, 1987 to quarter 3, 2009; $t = 1,..,T$ where $T = 90$ observations.

In the **Regression** dialog box, the **Input Y Range** should be **A2:A92**, and the **Input X Range** should be **C2:C92**. Check the boxes next to **Label** *and* **Residuals**. Select **New Worksheet Ply** and name it **Phillips Curve Model**. Finally select **OK**.

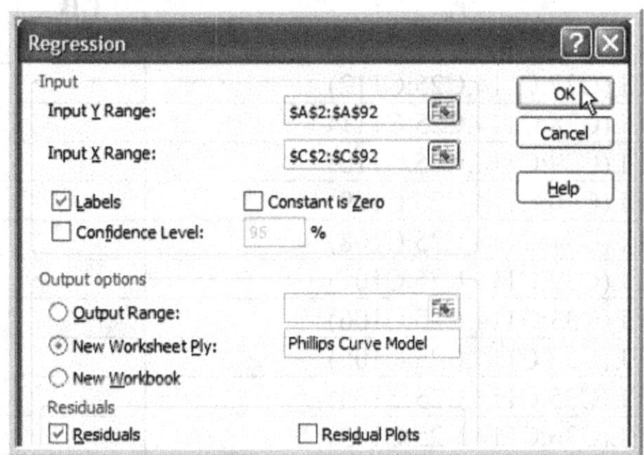

The result is (see also p. 352 in *Principles of Econometrics, 4e*):

	A	B	C	D	E	F	G	H	I
1	SUMMARY OUTPUT								
2									
3	*Regression Statistics*								
4	Multiple R	0.23822694							
5	R Square	0.056752075							
6	Adjusted R Square	0.046033348							
7	Standard Error	0.621988587							
8	Observations	90							
9									
10	ANOVA								
11		*df*	*SS*	*MS*	*F*	*Significance F*			
12	Regression	1	2.048346334	2.048346334	5.294665865	0.023753914			
13	Residual	88	34.04454256	0.386869802					
14	Total	89	36.09288889						
15									
16		*Coefficients*	*Standard Error*	*t Stat*	*P-value*	*Lower 95%*	*Upper 95%*	*Lower 95.0%*	*Upper 95.0%*
17	Intercept	0.777621257	0.065824943	11.81347414	7.53029E-20	0.646808019	0.908434496	0.646808019	0.908434496
18	du	-0.527863847	0.229404873	-2.301014095	0.023753914	-0.983757818	-0.071969877	-0.983757818	-0.071969877
19									
20									
21									
22	RESIDUAL OUTPUT								
23									
24	*Observation*	*Predicted 2*	*Residuals*						
25	1	0.830407642	0.669592358						
26	2	0.883194027	0.816805973						
27	3	0.830407642	0.969592358						

9.2.2c Correlogram for Residuals

In cells **E22:F34** and **G22:H23** of your **Phillips Curve Model** worksheet enter the following column labels and formulas.

	E	F	G	H
22	**lag**	**r_k**	**LB**	**UB**
23	**1**	=CORREL(C26:C114,C25:C113)	=-P2	=1.96/SQRT($B$8)
24	**2**	=CORREL(C27:C114,C25:C112)		
25	**3**	=CORREL(C28:C114,C25:C111)		
26	**4**	=CORREL(C29:C114,C25:C110)		
27	**5**	=CORREL(C30:C114,C25:C109)		
28	**6**	=CORREL(C31:C114,C25:C108)		
29	**7**	=CORREL(C32:C114,C25:C107)		
30	**8**	=CORREL(C33:C114,C25:C106)		
31	**9**	=CORREL(C34:C114,C25:C105)		
32	**10**	=CORREL(C35:C114,C25:C104)		
33	**11**	=CORREL(C36:C114,C25:C103)		
34	**12**	=CORREL(C37:C114,C25:C102)		

Copy the content of cells **G23:H23** to cells **G24:H34**. Here is how your table should look (see also reported correlations up to five lags on p. 353 in *Principles of Econometrics, 4e*):

	E	F	G	H
22	lag	r_k	LB	UB
23	1	0.552909832	-0.20660214	0.20660214
24	2	0.464008771	-0.226321306	0.226321306
25	3	0.44840179	-0.226321306	0.226321306
26	4	0.446943916	-0.226321306	0.226321306
27	5	0.366734168	-0.226321306	0.226321306

Again, note that your Excel results differ slightly from the one reported in *Principles of Econometrics, 4e* (see Section 9.2.1b for more details on that).

Proceed as in Section 9.2.1b to get the following correlogram for residuals (see also Figure 9.8 p. 353 in *Principles of Econometrics, 4e*):

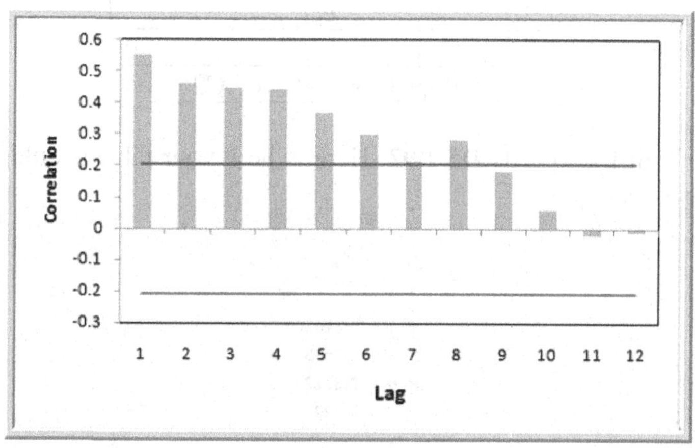

9.3 LAGRANGE MULTIPLIER TESTS FOR SERIALLY CORRELATED ERRORS

9.3.1 *t*-Test Version

Reconsider the Phillips curve model (9.4), restated below in a general form:

$$y_t = \beta_1 + \beta_2 x_t + e_t \tag{9.5}$$

Assume the error e_t follows a first-order autoregressive AR(1) model:

$$e_t = \rho e_{t-1} + v_t \tag{9.6}$$

Substituting (9.6) into (9.5) yields:

$$y_t = \beta_1 + \beta_2 x_t + \rho e_{t-1} + v_t \tag{9.7}$$

One way to test the null hypothesis $H_0 : \rho = 0$ is to use a *t*- or *F*-test to test the significance of the coefficient of $\hat{e}_{t-1}$ in (9.8):

$$y_t = \beta_1 + \beta_2 x_t + \rho \hat{e}_{t-1} + v_t \tag{9.8}$$

where $\hat{e}_{t-1}$'s are the lagged least squares residuals from the Phillips curve model (9.4).

The estimation of (9.8) requires a value for $\hat{e}_0$. Two commons way for overcoming the unavailability of $\hat{e}_0$ are (i) to delete the first observation and hence use a total of 89 observations, and (ii) set $\hat{e}_0 = 0$ and use all 90 observations.

Below, we walk you through the *t*-test for (ii) only.

In cells **D2:D4** of your **phillips_aus data** worksheet, enter the following column label, value and formula.

	D
1	e_{t-1}
2	0
3	='Phillips Curve Model'!C25

Copy the content of cell **D4** to cells **D5:D92**. Here is how your table should look (only the first five values are shown below):

	D
2	e_{t-1}
3	0
4	0.816806
5	0.969592
6	0.811233
7	0.922379

In the **Regression** dialog box, the **Input Y Range** should be **A2:A92**, and the **Input X Range** should be **C2:D92**. Check the box next to **Labels**. Select **New Worksheet Ply** and name it **t-test Version of LM Test.** Finally select **OK**.

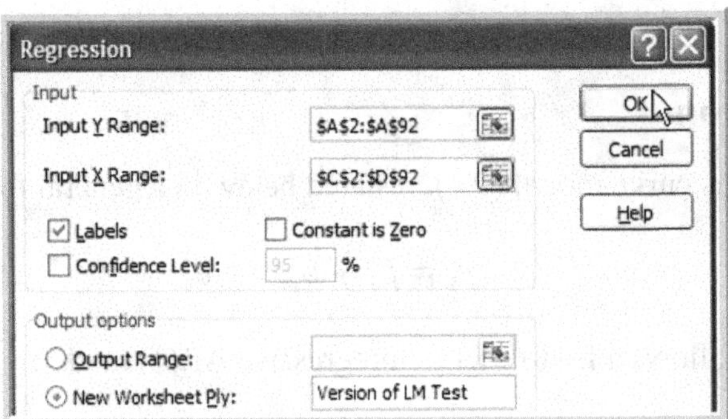

The result of the *t*-test is highlighted below (see also p. 354 in *Principles of Econometrics, 4e*):

	A	B	C	D	E	F	G	H	I
16		*Coefficients*	*Standard Error*	*t Stat*	*P-value*	*Lower 95%*	*Upper 95%*	*Lower 95.0%*	*Upper 95.0%*
17	Intercept	0.775458153	0.055128803	14.06629771	3.98583E-24	0.665883691	0.885032616	0.665883691	0.885032616
18	du	-0.679358279	0.193670737	-3.50780034	0.000717437	-1.064299833	-0.294416725	-1.064299833	-0.294416725
19	et-1	0.558783928	0.090096701	6.202046518	1.82193E-08	0.379706983	0.737860872	0.379706983	0.737860872

9.3.2 $T \times R^2$ Version

The $T \times R^2$ version of the Lagrange multiplier test is the one we worked with in Section 8.2.2a.

Consider the following auxiliary regression:

$$\hat{e}_t = \gamma_1 + \gamma_2 x_t + \rho \hat{e}_{t-1} + v_t \qquad (9.9)$$

where $\hat{e}_t$'s are the least squares residuals and $\hat{e}_{t-1}$'s the *lagged* least squares residuals from model the Phillips curve model (9.4).

Once again, the estimation of (9.9) requires a value for $\hat{e}_0$. Two commons way for overcoming the unavailability of $\hat{e}_0$ are (iii) to delete the first observation and hence use a total of 89 observations, and (iv) set $\hat{e}_0 = 0$ and use all 90 observations.

Below, we walk you alternative (iv) only.

Go back to your **phillips_aus data** worksheet. From there go to the **Regression** dialog box. The **Input Y Range** should be **C24:C114** *from the **Phillips Curve Model** worksheet*. The **Input X Range** should be **C2:D92** *from the **phillips_aus data** worksheet*. Check the box next to **Labels**. Select **New Worksheet Ply** and name it **Auxiliary Regression**. Finally select **OK**.

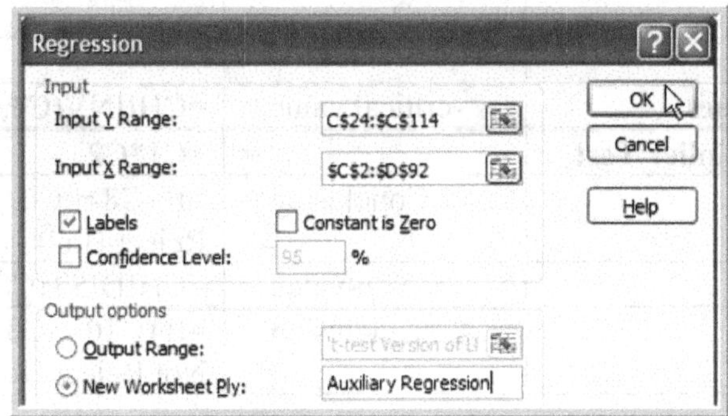

The results we are going to use for the Lagrange multiplier test are highlighted below:

	A	B	C	D	E	F
1	SUMMARY OUTPUT					
2						
3	*Regression Statistics*					
4	Multiple R	0.55369814				
5	R Square	0.30658163				
6	Adjusted R Square	0.290640978				
7	Standard Error	0.520908923				
8	Observations	90				
9						
10	ANOVA					
11		*df*	*SS*	*MS*	*F*	*Significance F*
12	Regression	2	10.43743135	5.218715674	19.23269051	1.21143E-07
13	Residual	87	23.60711121	0.271346106		
14	Total	89	34.04454256			

Insert a new worksheet by selecting the **Insert Worksheet** tab at the bottom of your screen. Rename it **Lagrange Multiplier Test**.

In it copy the Lagrange multiplier test template you created in Chapter 8.

The degrees of freedom for the Lagrange multiplier test are equal to the number of hypotheses being tested or number of parameters in the null hypothesis. When used to test for heteroskedasticity based on the variance function (Section 8.2.2a), the degrees of freedom also corresponded to the number of parameters in the auxiliary regression minus one. This is not the case anymore. We make the appropriate modifications to our template to reflect that.

Additionally, we replace the following reference: **[POE Chapter 8.xlsx]Variance Function** by **Auxiliary Regression**.

	A	B	C
1	**Data Input**	N =	='Auxiliary Regression'!B8
2		R^2 =	='Auxiliary Regression'!B5
3		α =	
4		m =	
5			
6	**Computed Values**	χ^2-critical value =	=CHIINV(C3,C4)
8	**Lagrange Multiplier Test**	χ^2 =	=C1*C2
9		Conclusion =	=IF(C8>=C6,"Reject Ho","Do Not Reject Ho")
10		*p*-value =	=CHIDIST(C8,C4)
11		Conclusion =	=IF(C10<=C3,"Reject Ho","Do Not Reject Ho")

At $\alpha = 0.05$, and with $m = 1$, the result of the test is (see also p. 355 in *Principles of Econometrics, 4e*):

	A	B	C
1	**Data Input**	N =	90
2		R^2 =	0.306582
3		α =	0.05
4		m =	1
5			
6	**Computed Values**	χ^2-critical value =	3.841459
7			
8		χ^2 =	27.59235
9	**Lagrange Multiplier Test**	Conclusion =	Reject Ho
10		*p*-value =	1.5E-07
11		Conclusion =	Reject Ho

9.4 ESTIMATION WITH SERIALLY CORRELATED ERRORS

9.4.1 Generalized Least Squares Estimation of an AR(1) Error Model

9.4.1a The Prais-Winsten Estimator

Reconsider the Phillips curve model (9.4) where the error e_t is assumed to follow a first-order autoregressive AR(1) model (9.6). The following Phillips curve model (9.10) has an error term v_t that is homoskedastic and uncorrelated over time (see Appendix 9C pp. 397-399 in *Principles of Econometrics, 4e* for more details):

$$y_t^* = \beta_1 x_{t1}^* + \beta_2 x_{t2}^* + v_t \tag{9.10}$$

where $y_t^* = y_t - \hat{\rho} y_{t-1}$, $x_{t1}^* = 1 - \hat{\rho}$, $x_{t2}^* = x_t - \hat{\rho} x_{t-1}$ for $t = 2, 3, \ldots, T$. Note, for $t = 1$: $y_1^* = \sqrt{1-\hat{\rho}^2} y_1$, $x_{11}^* = \sqrt{1-\hat{\rho}^2}$ and $x_{12}^* = \sqrt{1-\hat{\rho}^2} x_1$. Finally, $\hat{\rho}$ is the least squares estimate of (9.11):

$$\hat{e}_t = \rho \hat{e}_{t-1} + v_t \tag{9.11}$$

where $\hat{e}_t$'s are the least squares residuals from the Phillips curve model (9.4).

The process of first estimating model (9.4), second using the least squares residuals $\hat{e}_t$'s from (9.4) to estimate model (9.11), and third using the least squares estimate $\hat{\rho}$ of (9.11) to transform the dependent and independent variables and estimate model (9.10), is similar to what we have done in Section 8.5.

Note that both models (9.10) *and* (9.11) *do not have an intercept.*

Getting an Estimate $\hat{\rho}$ of the Autocorrelation Coefficient

We already went through the first step of the process and estimated model (9.4) in Section 9.2.2.b. The data we need to estimate (9.11) are in our **Phillips Curve Model** worksheet. From there, go to the **Regression** dialog box. The **Input Y Range** should be **C26:C114**, and the **Input X Range** should be **D4:D92** from the **phillips_aus data** worksheet. Uncheck the box next to **Labels**. Check the box next to **Constant is Zero**. Select **New Worksheet Ply** and name it **AR(1) Error Model**. Finally select **OK**.

Note that we are losing one observation as there is no $t - 1 = 0$ residual value corresponding to the first $t = 1$ residual value.

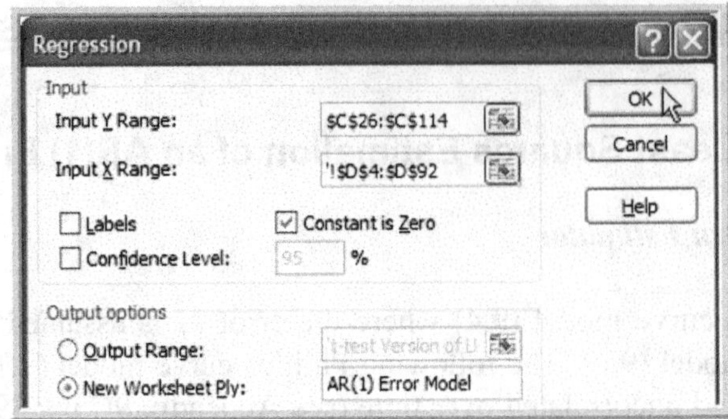

The result is:

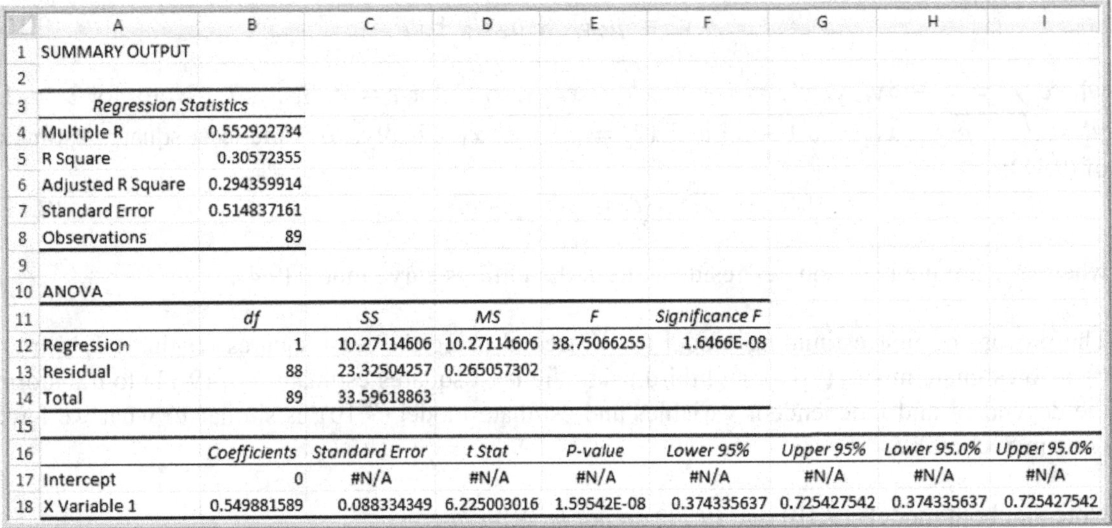

	A	B	C	D	E	F	G	H	I
1	SUMMARY OUTPUT								
2									
3	*Regression Statistics*								
4	Multiple R	0.552922734							
5	R Square	0.30572355							
6	Adjusted R Square	0.294359914							
7	Standard Error	0.514837161							
8	Observations	89							
9									
10	ANOVA								
11		*df*	*SS*	*MS*	*F*	*Significance F*			
12	Regression	1	10.27114606	10.27114606	38.75066255	1.6466E-08			
13	Residual	88	23.32504257	0.265057302					
14	Total	89	33.59618863						
15									
16		*Coefficients*	*Standard Error*	*t Stat*	*P-value*	*Lower 95%*	*Upper 95%*	*Lower 95.0%*	*Upper 95.0%*
17	Intercept	0	#N/A	#N/A	#N/A	#N/A	#N/A	#N/A	#N/A
18	X Variable 1	0.549881589	0.088334349	6.225003016	1.59542E-08	0.374335637	0.725427542	0.374335637	0.725427542

<u>*Getting the GLS Estimates for b_1 and b_2*</u>

Go back to your **phillips_aus data** worksheet. In cells **F1:G1**, and **I1:K3**, enter the following column labels and formulas.

	F	G
1	**ρ-hat =**	='AR(1) Error Model'!B18

	I	J	K
2	**y***	**x_1***	**x_2***
3	=SQRT(1-G1^2)*A3	=SQRT(1-G1^2)	=SQRT(1-G1^2)*C3
4	=A4-$G$1*A3	=1-$G$1	=C4-$G$1*C3

Copy the content of cells **I4:K4** to cells **I4:K92**. Here is how your table should look (only the first five values are shown below):

	F	G	H	I	J	K
1	ρ-hat =	0.549882				
2				y*	x_1*	x_2*
3				1.25286393	0.835243	-0.08352426
4				0.87517762	0.450118	-0.14501184
5				0.8652013	0.450118	0.009976318
6				0.81021314	0.450118	-0.34501184
7				0.71021314	0.450118	0.219952636

In the **Regression** dialog box, the **Input Y Range** should be **I2:I92**, and the **Input X Range** should be **J2:K92**. Check the boxes next to **Labels** *and* **Constant is Zero**. Select **New Worksheet Ply** and name it **Prais-Winsten estimates**. Finally select **OK**.

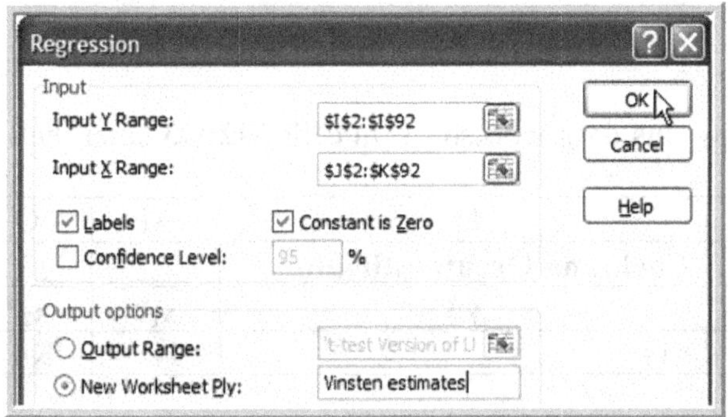

The result is:

	A	B	C	D	E	F	G	H	I
2									
3	*Regression Statistics*								
4	Multiple R	0.615057872							
5	R Square	0.378296186							
6	Adjusted R Square	0.359867734							
7	Standard Error	0.516781698							
8	Observations	90							
9									
10	ANOVA								
11		*df*	*SS*	*MS*	*F*	*Significance F*			
12	Regression	2	14.30030669	7.150153344	26.77325088	8.68792E-10			
13	Residual	88	23.50157241	0.267063323					
14	Total	90	37.8018791						
15									
16		*Coefficients*	*Standard Error*	*t Stat*	*P-value*	*Lower 95%*	*Upper 95%*	*Lower 95.0%*	*Upper 95.0%*
17	Intercept	0	#N/A	#N/A	#N/A	#N/A	#N/A	#N/A	#N/A
18	x1*	0.785837716	0.119563257	6.572568664	3.37831E-09	0.548230872	1.02344456	0.548230872	1.02344456
19	x2*	-0.699426866	0.242804756	-2.880614353	0.004984369	-1.181950288	-0.216903445	-1.181950288	-0.216903445

Note that these results do not match those in equation (9.45) in *Principles of Econometrics, 4e*, p. 362. What we have described is a simple two-step estimation process sometimes called the Prais-Winsten estimator. However, there are advantages to "iterating" this procedure, as we describe in the following section.

9.4.1b The Cochrane-Orcutt Estimator

Reconsider the GLS model (9.10). To estimate it, another option is to *not* include a transformation for the first observation as we did for the Prais-Winsten estimator, and proceed with the estimation on the basis of $T - 1$ observations only. We then repeat the GLS estimation process outlined in Section 9.4.1a until the least squares estimate b_1 and b_2 from model (9.10) do not change in value. This iterative procedure is known as the Cochrane-Orcutt estimator. Below we walk you through the first two iterations of this process.

Note that the omission of the first observation is not, in general, a good strategy. It simplifies the calculations, however, so we will use this trick. You might want to test your understanding by extending the iterative process we describe below to include the first observation.

First Iteration

Go back to your **phillips_aus data** worksheet. In cells **M2:O3** enter the following column labels and formulas.

	M	M	O
2	**Cochrane-Orcutt estimator**		
3	**y***	**x_1***	**x_2***
4	=I4	=J4	=K4

Copy the content of cells **M4:O4** to cells **M5:O92**. Here is how your table should look (only the first five values are shown below):

	M	N	O
2	**Cochrane-Orcutt estimator**		
3	**y***	**x_1***	**x_2***
4	0.875177616	0.450118	-0.145012
5	0.865201298	0.450118	0.009976
6	0.810213139	0.450118	-0.345012
7	0.710213139	0.450118	0.219953
8	0.965201298	0.450118	-0.6

In the **Regression** dialog box, the **Input Y Range** should be **M3:M92**, and the **Input X Range** should be **N3:O92**. Check the boxes next to **Labels** *and* **Constant is Zero**. Select **New Worksheet Ply** and name it **Cochrane-Orcutt estimates**. Finally select **OK**.

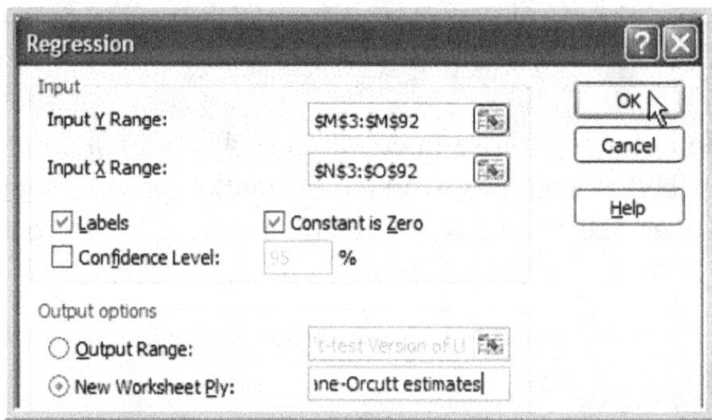

The result is:

	A	B	C	D	E	F	G	H	I
1	SUMMARY OUTPUT								
2									
3	*Regression Statistics*								
4	Multiple R	0.599724987							
5	R Square	0.359670061							
6	Adjusted R Square	0.340815693							
7	Standard Error	0.516404118							
8	Observations	89							
9									
10	ANOVA								
11		*df*	*SS*	*MS*	*F*	*Significance F*			
12	Regression	2	13.03164155	6.515820774	24.4337281	3.95754E-09			
13	Residual	87	23.20056952	0.266673213					
14	Total	89	36.23221107						
15									
16		*Coefficients*	*Standard Error*	*t Stat*	*P-value*	*Lower 95%*	*Upper 95%*	*Lower 95.0%*	*Upper 95.0%*
17	Intercept	0	#N/A	#N/A	#N/A	#N/A	#N/A	#N/A	#N/A
18	x1*	0.761084089	0.121726533	6.252409164	1.45899E-08	0.519139429	1.003028749	0.519139429	1.003028749
19	x2*	-0.691678828	0.242736933	-2.849499748	0.005465372	-1.174144756	-0.209212901	-1.174144756	-0.209212901

Second Iteration

Go back to your **phillips_aus data** worksheet. In cells **Q1:R2**, and **T3:U4**, enter the following column labels and formulas.

	Q	R	T	U
1	**b_1 =**	='Cochrane-Orcutt estimates'!B18		
2	**b_2 =**	='Cochrane-Orcutt estimates'!B19		
3			**e-hat$_t$**	**e-hat$_{t-1}$**
4			=A4-$R$1-$R$2*C4	=A3-$R$1-$R$2*C3

Copy the content of cells **T4:U4** to cells **T5:U92**. Here is how your table should look (only the first five values are shown below):

	Q	R	S	T	U
1	**b_1** = 0.761084				
2	**b_2** = -0.691679				
3				**e-hat$_t$**	**e-hat$_{t-1}$**
4				0.80058015	0.66974803
5				0.96974803	0.80058015
6				0.76224438	0.96974803
7				0.93891591	0.76224438
8				0.72390861	0.93891591

In the **Regression** dialog box, the **Input Y Range** should be **T3:T92**, and the **Input X Range** should be **U3:U92**. Check the boxes next to **Labels** *and* **Constant is Zero**. Select **Output Range** and specify it to be cell **A1** in your **AR(1) Model** worksheet: you can place your cursor in the **Output Range** window and move it to that cell to do that, or type **'AR(1) Model'!A1** in **the Output Range** window. Finally, select **OK**.

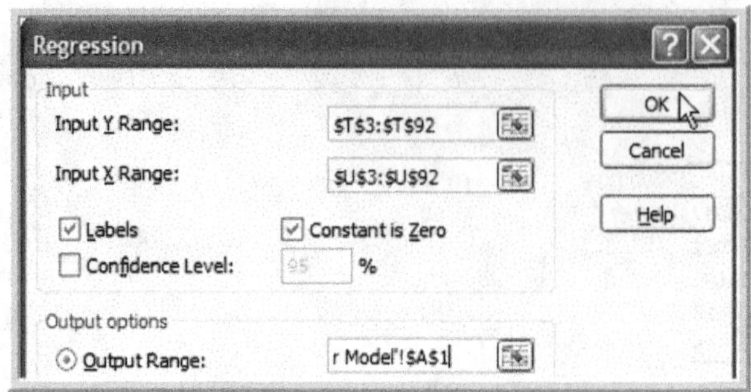

Excel informs you that the output range will overwrite existing data. Do select **OK** to overwrite the data in the specified range.

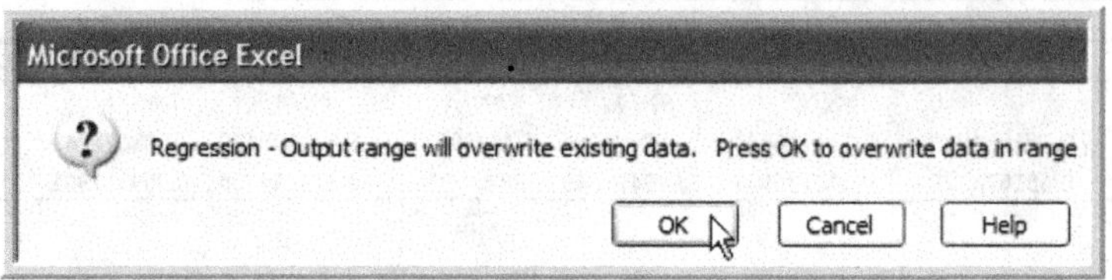

The result is:

	A	B	C	D	E	F	G	H	I
1	SUMMARY OUTPUT								
2									
3	*Regression Statistics*								
4	Multiple R	0.560169089							
5	R Square	0.313789408							
6	Adjusted R Square	0.302425772							
7	Standard Error	0.513441029							
8	Observations	89							
9									
10	ANOVA								
11		*df*	*SS*	*MS*	*F*	*Significance F*			
12	Regression	1	10.60827273	10.60827273	40.24051548	9.74557E-09			
13	Residual	88	23.19870879	0.263621691					
14	Total	89	33.80698151						
15									
16		*Coefficients*	*Standard Error*	*t Stat*	*P-value*	*Lower 95%*	*Upper 95%*	*Lower 95.0%*	*Upper 95.0%*
17	Intercept	0	#N/A	#N/A	#N/A	#N/A	#N/A	#N/A	#N/A
18	e-hatt-1	0.557261979	0.087847144	6.343541241	9.42502E-09	0.382684245	0.731839714	0.382684245	0.731839714

Go back to your **phillips_aus data** worksheet. Notice that in cell **G1** your ρ-hat value has been updated, and so have your transformed dependent and independent variables in columns **M-O**.

In the **Regression** dialog box, the **Input Y Range** should be **M3:M92**, and the **Input X Range** should be **N3:O92**. Check the boxes next to **Labels** *and* **Constant is Zero**. Select **Output Range** and specify it to be cell **A1** in your **Cochrane-Orcutt estimates** worksheet: you can place your cursor in the **Output Range** window and move it to that cell to do that, or type **'Cochrane-Orcutt estimates'!A1** in **the Output Range** window. Finally, select **OK**.

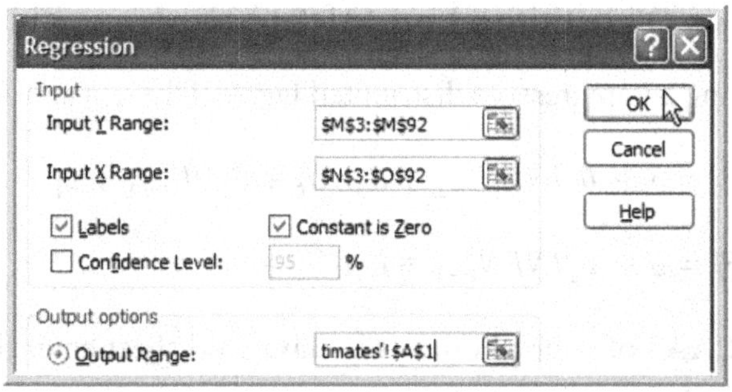

Regression

Input

Input Y Range: $M$3:$M$92

Input X Range: $N$3:$O$92

☑ Labels ☑ Constant is Zero

☐ Confidence Level: 95 %

Output options

⦿ Output Range: timates'!$A$1

OK Cancel Help

Excel informs you that the output range will overwrite existing data. Do select **OK** to overwrite the data in the specified range. The result is:

	A	B	C	D	E	F	G	H	I
1	SUMMARY OUTPUT								
2									
3	*Regression Statistics*								
4	Multiple R	0.594570371							
5	R Square	0.353513926							
6	Adjusted R Square	0.334588798							
7	Standard Error	0.516383048							
8	Observations	89							
9									
10	ANOVA								
11		*df*	*SS*	*MS*	*F*	*Significance F*			
12	Regression	2	12.6855867	6.34279335	23.78683218	5.99014E-09			
13	Residual	87	23.19867637	0.266651452					
14	Total	89	35.88426307						
15									
16		*Coefficients*	*Standard Error*	*t Stat*	*P-value*	*Lower 95%*	*Upper 95%*	*Lower 95.0%*	*Upper 95.0%*
17	Intercept	0	#N/A	#N/A	#N/A	#N/A	#N/A	#N/A	#N/A
18	x1*	0.760875315	0.123746111	6.148680627	2.30397E-08	0.514916525	1.006834105	0.514916525	1.006834105
19	x2*	-0.69434112	0.242933141	-2.858157253	0.005331068	-1.177197033	-0.211485206	-1.177197033	-0.211485206

We have run two additional iterations. The third and fourth iterations give identical estimates at the fourth decimal place level of precision. We can thus say that after a total of four iterations, we obtain the following stable estimates (see also p. 362 in *Principles of Econometrics, 4e*):

$$\begin{aligned} \widehat{INF} &= 0.7609 - 0.6944DU + e_t \\ (se) &\quad (0.1238)\ (0.2429) \end{aligned} \tag{9.12}$$

$$\begin{aligned} e_t &= 0.557e_{t-1} + v_t \\ (se) &\quad (0.088) \end{aligned} \tag{9.13}$$

The table below reports the Cochrane-Orcutt estimates obtained for each iteration:

Iteration	**1**	**2**	**3**	**4**
$\hat{\rho} =$	0.5499	0.5573	0.5574	0.5574
$b_1 =$	+0.76108	+0.76087	+0.76087	+0.76087
$b_2 =$	−0.69168	−0.69434	−0.69439	−0.69439

9.4.2 Autoregressive Distributed Lag (ARDL) Model

We consider the following autoregressive distributed lag ARDL(1,1) and ARDL (1,0) models:

$$INF_t = \delta + \theta_1 INFN_{t-1} + \delta_0 DU_t + \delta_1 DU_{t-1} + v_t \tag{9.14}$$

$$INF_t = \delta + \theta_1 INFN_{t-1} + \delta_0 DU_t + v_t \tag{9.15}$$

In cells **W3:Y4** and **Z2:AA3** of your **phillips_aus data** worksheet enter the following labels and formulas.

	W	X	Y	Z	AA
2				**inf_{t-1}**	**du_t**
3	**inf_{t-1}**	**du_t**	**du_{t-1}**	=A2	=C3
4	=A3	=C4	=C3		

Copy the content of cells **W4:Y4** to cells **W5:Y92** and the content of cells **Z3:AA3** to cells **Z4:AA92**. Here is how your table should look (only the first five values are shown below):

	W	X	Y	Z	AA
2				inf_{t-1}	du_t
3	inf_{t-1}	du_t	du_{t-1}	2	-0.1
4	1.5	-0.2	-0.1	1.5	-0.2
5	1.7	-0.1	-0.2	1.7	-0.1
6	1.8	-0.4	-0.1	1.8	-0.4
7	1.8	0	-0.4	1.8	0
8	1.7	-0.6	0	1.7	-0.6

In the **Regression** dialog box, the **Input Y Range** should be **A3:A92**, and the **Input X Range** should be **W3:Y92**. Check the box next to **Labels**. Select **New Worksheet Ply** and name it **ARDL(1,1) Phillips Curve Model**. Finally select **OK**.

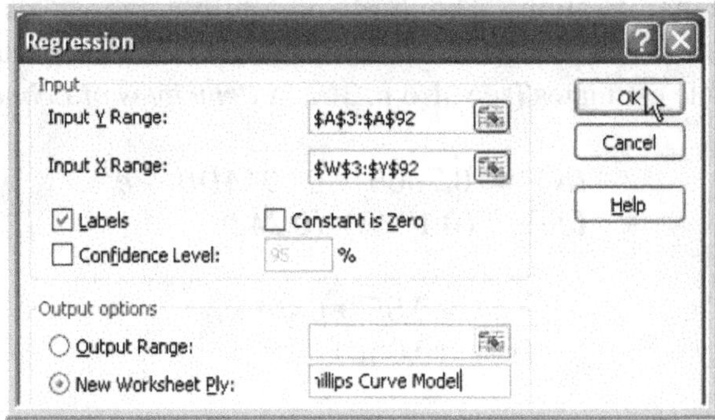

The result is (see also p. 364 and p. 365 in *Principles of Econometrics, 4e*):

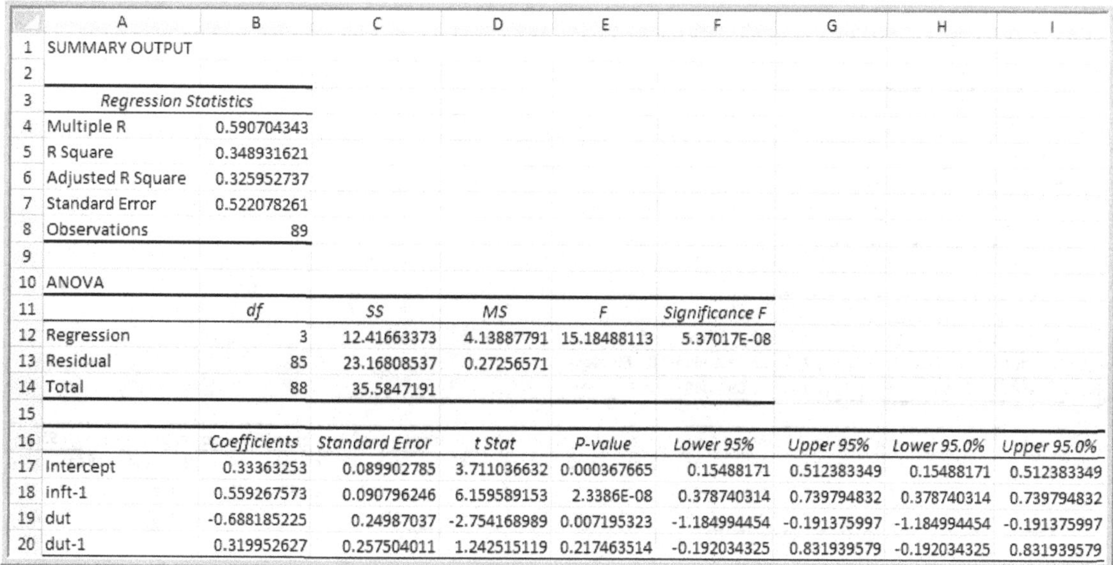

	A	B	C	D	E	F	G	H	I
1	SUMMARY OUTPUT								
2									
3	*Regression Statistics*								
4	Multiple R	0.590704343							
5	R Square	0.348931621							
6	Adjusted R Square	0.325952737							
7	Standard Error	0.522078261							
8	Observations	89							
9									
10	ANOVA								
11		*df*	*SS*	*MS*	*F*	*Significance F*			
12	Regression	3	12.41663373	4.13887791	15.18488113	5.37017E-08			
13	Residual	85	23.16808537	0.27256571					
14	Total	88	35.5847191						
15									
16		*Coefficients*	*Standard Error*	*t Stat*	*P-value*	*Lower 95%*	*Upper 95%*	*Lower 95.0%*	*Upper 95.0%*
17	Intercept	0.33363253	0.089902785	3.711036632	0.000367665	0.15488171	0.512383349	0.15488171	0.512383349
18	inft-1	0.559267573	0.090796246	6.159589153	2.3386E-08	0.378740314	0.739794832	0.378740314	0.739794832
19	dut	-0.688185225	0.24987037	-2.754168989	0.007195323	-1.184994454	-0.191375997	-1.184994454	-0.191375997
20	dut-1	0.319952627	0.257504011	1.242515119	0.217463514	-0.192034325	0.831939579	-0.192034325	0.831939579

Go back to your **phillips_aus data** worksheet.

In the **Regression** dialog box, the **Input Y Range** should be **A3:A92**, and the **Input X Range** should be **Z2:AA92**. Check the box next to **Labels**. Select **New Worksheet Ply** and name it **ARDL(1,0) Phillips Curve Model**. Finally select **OK**.

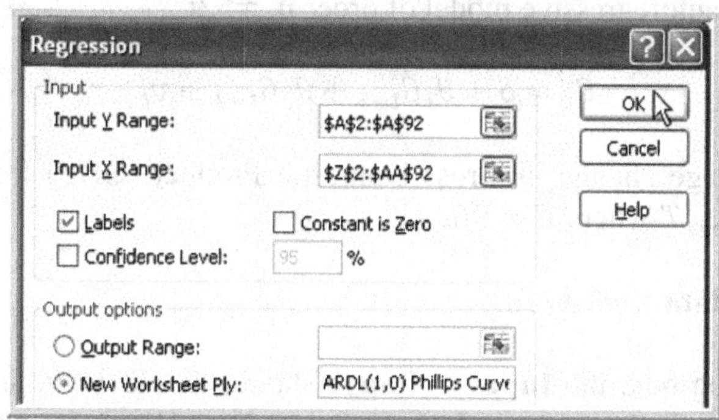

The result is (see also p. 364 and p. 365 in *Principles of Econometrics, 4e*):

	A	B	C	D	E	F	G	H	I
1	SUMMARY OUTPUT								
2									
3	*Regression Statistics*								
4	Multiple R	0.588552275							
5	R Square	0.346393781							
6	Adjusted R Square	0.33136835							
7	Standard Error	0.520726026							
8	Observations	90							
9									
10	ANOVA								
11		*df*	*SS*	*MS*	*F*	*Significance F*			
12	Regression	2	12.50235224	6.25117612	23.05383428	9.25238E-09			
13	Residual	87	23.59053665	0.271155594					
14	Total	89	36.09288889						
15									
16		*Coefficients*	*Standard Error*	*t Stat*	*P-value*	*Lower 95%*	*Upper 95%*	*Lower 95.0%*	*Upper 95.0%*
17	Intercept	0.35479511	0.087602333	4.050064624	0.00011085	0.180675991	0.528914229	0.180675991	0.528914229
18	inft-1	0.528247247	0.085075626	6.209149071	1.7658E-08	0.359150231	0.697344263	0.359150231	0.697344263
19	dut	-0.490864743	0.192149138	-2.554602891	0.012370485	-0.872781953	-0.108947533	-0.872781953	-0.108947533

9.5 FORECASTING

9.5.1 Using an Autoregressive Model

Consider the following autoregressive model of order $p = 2$:

$$G_t = \delta + \theta_1 G_{t-1} + \theta_2 G_{t-2} + v_t \tag{9.16}$$

where G is the percentage change in Gross Domestic Product (GDP) from quarter 2, 1985 to quarter 3, 2009; $t = 1, \ldots, T$ where $T = 96$.

Go back to your **okun data** worksheet.

In the **Regression** dialog box, the **Input Y Range** should be **H3:H99**, and the **Input X Range** should be **I4:J99**. Check the box next to **Labels**. Select **New Worksheet Ply** and name it **AR(2) Model**. Finally select **OK**.

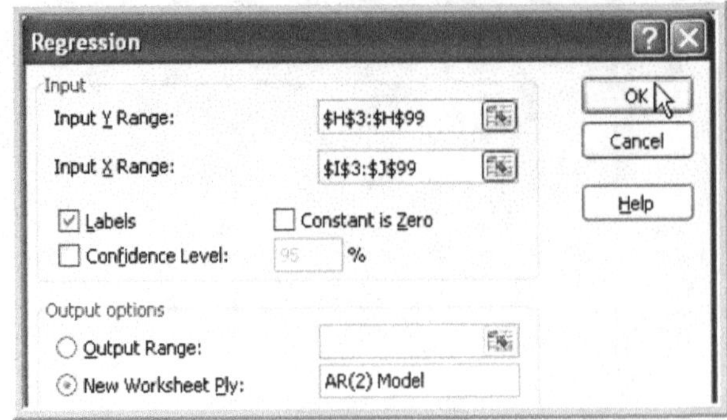

The result is (see also p. 371 in *Principles of Econometrics, 4e*):

	A	B	C	D	E	F	G	H	I
1	SUMMARY OUTPUT								
2									
3	*Regression Statistics*								
4	Multiple R	0.539149511							
5	R Square	0.290682195							
6	Adjusted R Square	0.275428049							
7	Standard Error	0.552687512							
8	Observations	96							
9									
10	ANOVA								
11		*df*	*SS*	*MS*	*F*	*Significance F*			
12	Regression	2	11.64179165	5.820895823	19.05594643	1.15904E-07			
13	Residual	93	28.40810419	0.305463486					
14	Total	95	40.04989583						
15									
16		*Coefficients*	*Standard Error*	*t Stat*	*P-value*	*Lower 95%*	*Upper 95%*	*Lower 95.0%*	*Upper 95.0%*
17	Intercept	0.465726171	0.143257588	3.250970363	0.001602369	0.181245001	0.750207342	0.181245001	0.750207342
18	gt-1	0.377001484	0.100020955	3.769225007	0.000287355	0.178379695	0.575623273	0.178379695	0.575623273
19	gt-2	0.246239399	0.102868812	2.393722589	0.018686064	0.04196233	0.450516467	0.04196233	0.450516467

Once estimated, the AR(2) model in (9.16) can be used to forecast GDP growth into the future.

Let G_T be the last sample observation; the forecast for GDP growth 1 quarter into the future ($\hat{G}_{T+1}$), 2 quarters into the future ($\hat{G}_{T+2}$), and 3 quarters into the future ($\hat{G}_{T+3}$), are given by (for more details see pp. 372-373 in *Principles of Econometrics, 4e*):

$$\hat{G}_{T+1} = \hat{\delta} + \hat{\theta}_1 G_T + \hat{\theta}_2 G_{T-1} \tag{9.17}$$

$$\hat{G}_{T+2} = \hat{\delta} + \hat{\theta}_1 \hat{G}_{T+1} + \hat{\theta}_2 G_T \tag{9.18}$$

$$\hat{G}_{T+3} = \hat{\delta} + \hat{\theta}_1 \hat{G}_{T+2} + \hat{\theta}_2 \hat{G}_{T+1} \tag{9.19}$$

The estimates of standard error of forecast error for GDP growth 1 quarter into the future ($\hat{\sigma}_1$), 2 quarters into the future ($\hat{\sigma}_2$), and 3 quarters into the future ($\hat{\sigma}_3$), are given by (for more details see p. 374 in *Principles of Econometrics, 4e*):

$$\hat{\sigma}_1 = \hat{\sigma}_v \tag{9.20}$$

$$\hat{\sigma}_2 = \hat{\sigma}_v \sqrt{1 + \hat{\theta}_1^2} \tag{9.21}$$

$$\hat{\sigma}_3 = \hat{\sigma}_v \sqrt{\left(\hat{\theta}_1^2 + \hat{\theta}_2\right)^2 + \hat{\theta}_1^2 + 1} \tag{9.22}$$

where $\hat{\sigma}_v$ is the estimated standard error of the regression model (9.16).

Finally, the lower limit (LL) and upper limit (UL) of a forecast interval for G_{T+j} are given by:

$$LL = \hat{G}_{T+j} - t_c \hat{\sigma}_j \tag{9.23}$$

$$UL = \hat{G}_{T+j} + t_c \hat{\sigma}_j \tag{9.24}$$

where t_c is the $100(1 - \alpha/2)$th percentile from the *t*-distribution with $T - K$ degrees of freedom, and K is the number of parameters in the autoregressive model (9.16).

Below we create a forecast interval template, similar to the prediction interval template we created in Section 4.1.

Insert a new worksheet by selecting the **Insert Worksheet** tab at the bottom of your screen. Rename it **Forecast Interval**.

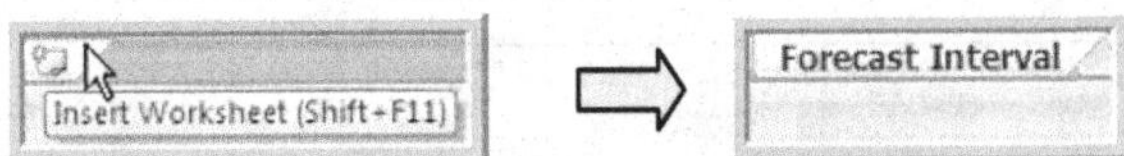

Create the following template to construct forecast intervals. In the bordering columns and rows you will find the numbers of the equations and the formatting options used, if any, in the template.

	A	B	C	
1	**Data Input**	Sample Size T =	='AR(2) Model'!B8	
2		Confidence Level =		*percentage 0 decimal place*
3		K =	='AR(2) Model'!B12+1	
4		σ-hat$_v$ =	='AR(2) Model'!B7	
5		δ-hat =	='AR(2) Model'!B17	
6		θ$_1$-hat =	='AR(2) Model'!B18	
7		θ$_2$-hat =	='AR(2) Model'!B19	
8		y_{T-1} =	='okun data'!H98	
9		y_T =	='okun data'!H99	
10				
11	**Computed Values**	α =	=1-C2	
12		df or m =	=C1-C3	
13		t_c =	=TINV(C11,C12)	
14				
15			**Forecast**	
16		y-hat$_{T+1}$ =	=C5+C6*C9+C7*C8	*(9.17)*
17		y-hat$_{T+2}$ =	=C5+C6*C16+C7*C9	*(9.18)*
18		y-hat$_{T+3}$ =	=C5+C6*C17+C7*C16	*(9.19)*

		D	E	F
14			**Forecast**	**Interval**
15		**σ-hat$_j$**	**Lower Limit**	**Upper Limit**
16	*(9.20)*	=C4	=C16-C13*D16	=C16+C13*D16
17	*(9.21)*	=C4*SQRT(1+C6^2)	=C17-C13*D17	=C17+C13*D17
18	*(9.22)*	=C4*SQRT((C6^2+C7)^2+C6^2+1)	=C18-C13*D18	=C18+C13*D18
			(9.23)	*(9.24)*

Here are the results you should get (see also Table 9.7 p. 374 in *Principles of Econometrics, 4e*):

	A	B	C	D	E	F
1	**Data Input**	Sample Size T =	96			
2		Confidence Level =	95%			
3		K =	3			
4		σ-hat$_v$ =	0.55268751			
5		δ-hat =	0.46572617			
6		θ_1-hat =	0.37700148			
7		θ_2-hat =	0.2462394			
8		y_{T-1} =	-0.2			
9		y_T =	0.8			
10						
11	**Computed Values**	α =	0.05			
12		df or m =	93			
13		t_c =	1.98580177			
14					**Forecast Interval**	
15			**Forecast**	**σ-hat$_j$**	**Lower Limit**	**Upper Limit**
16		y-hat$_{T-1}$ =	0.71807948	0.552687512	-0.37944836	1.815607318
17		y-hat$_{T-2}$ =	0.93343472	0.590659841	-0.239498637	2.106368076
18		y-hat$_{T-3}$ =	0.99445191	0.628452365	-0.253529912	2.242433722

9.5.2 Using an Exponential Smoothing Model

Go back to your **okun data** worksheet.

In cells **R1:U5**, enter the following labels and formulas.

	R	S	T	U
1	**T=**	=COUNT(A2:A99)		
2	**T/2=**	=S1/2	**ghat α =0.38**	**ghat α =0.8**
3	**ghat$_1$=**	=AVERAGE(A2:A50)	=S4*A2+(1-S4)*S3	=S5*A2+(1-S5)*S3
4	**α=**	0.8	=$S$4*A3+(1-$S$4)*T3	=$S$5*A3+(1-$S$5)*U3
5	**α=**	0.38		

Copy the content of cells **T4:U4** to cells **T5:U99**. Here is how your table should look (only the first five values are shown below):

	R	S	T	U
1	T=	98		
2	T/2=	49	**ghat α=0.38**	**ghat α=0.8**
3	ghat$_1$=	1.428776	1.4077551	1.42404082
4	α=	0.8	1.88155102	1.64290531
5	α=	0.38	1.4963102	1.55060129
6			1.49926204	1.5313728
7			1.01985241	1.29145114

Select the **Insert** tab located next to the **Home** tab. Select **T2:T99**. In the **Charts** group of commands select **Line**, and **Line** again.

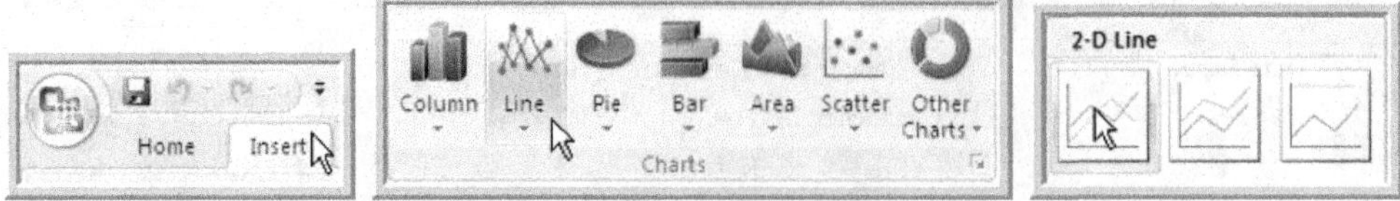

After adding the US GDP series (actual, cells **A3:A99**) and editing, the result is (see also Figure 9.12(a) p. 377 in *Principles of Econometrics, 4e*):

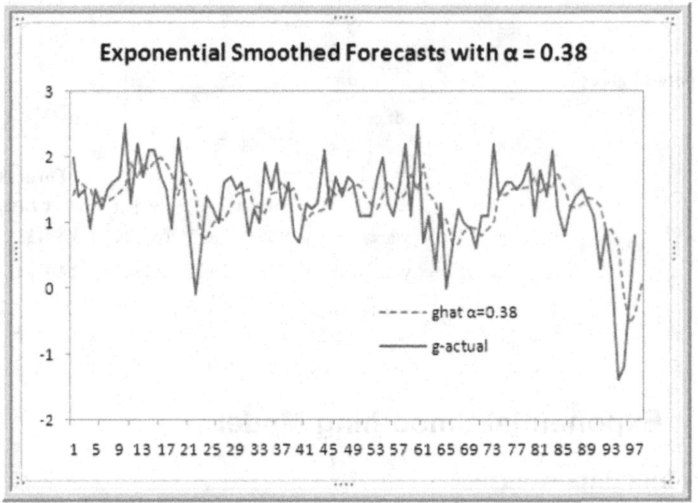

To plot the change in the US GDP series select cells **A3:A99**. After editing, the result is (see also Figure 9.12(b) p. 377 in *Principles of Econometrics, 4e*):

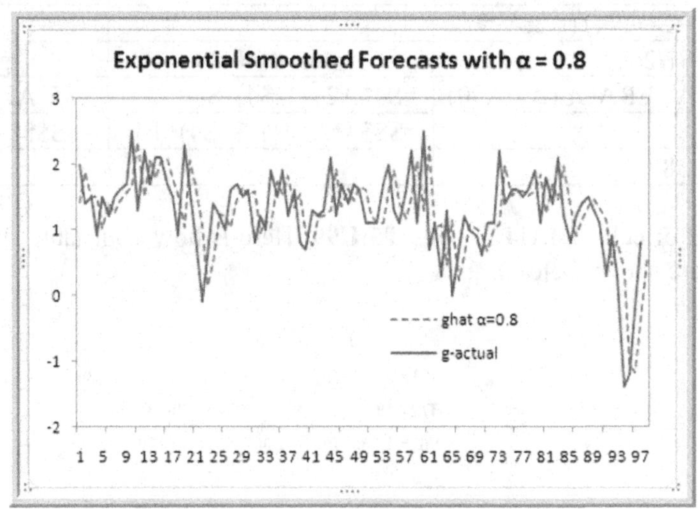

9.6 MULTIPLIER ANALYSIS

We consider the following ARDL(1,1) model to describe Okun's law:

$$DU_t = \delta + \theta_1 DU_{t-1} + \delta_0 G_t + \delta_1 G_{t-1} + v_t \tag{9.25}$$

In cells **W3:Y4** of your **kun data** worksheet enter the following labels and formulas.

	W	X	Y
3	du_{t-1}	g_t	g_{t-1}
4	=C3	=A4	=A3

Copy the content of cells **W4:Y4** to cells **W5:Y99**. Here is how your table should look (only the first five values are shown below):

	W	X	Y
3	du_{t-1}	g_t	g_{t-1}
4	-0.1	1.4	2
5	-0.2	1.5	1.4
6	0	0.9	1.5
7	0.2	1.5	0.9
8	-0.2	1.2	1.5

In the **Regression** dialog box, the **Input Y Range** should be **C3:C99**, and the **Input X Range** should be **W3:Y99**. Check the box next to **Labels**. Select **New Worksheet Ply** and name it **ARDL(1,1) Okun's Law Model**. Finally select **OK**.

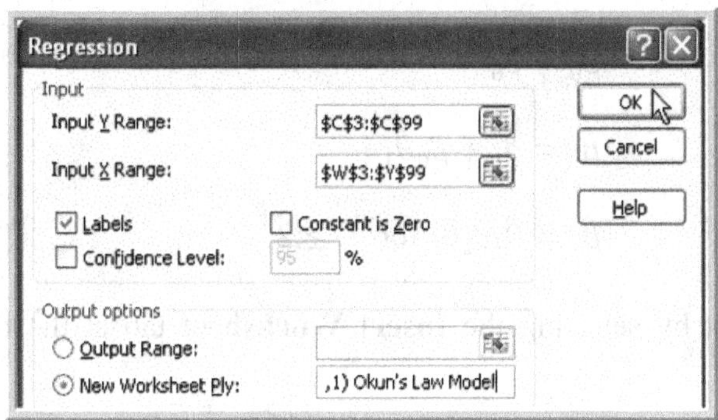

The result is (see also p. 381 is *Principles of Econometrics, 4e*):

	A	B	C	D	E	F	G	H	I
1	SUMMARY OUTPUT								
2									
3	*Regression Statistics*								
4	Multiple R	0.833126945							
5	R Square	0.694100506							
6	Adjusted R Square	0.684125523							
7	Standard Error	0.162277406							
8	Observations	96							
9									
10	ANOVA								
11		*df*	*SS*	*MS*	*F*	*Significance F*			
12	Regression	3	5.497276008	1.832425336	69.58412576	1.40186E-23			
13	Residual	92	2.422723992	0.026333956					
14	Total	95	7.92						
15									
16		*Coefficients*	*Standard Error*	*t Stat*	*P-value*	*Lower 95%*	*Upper 95%*	*Lower 95.0%*	*Upper 95.0%*
17	Intercept	0.378010424	0.0578398	6.535472545	3.47005E-09	0.263135591	0.492885256	0.263135591	0.492885256
18	dut-1	0.35011576	0.08457296	4.139807316	7.69455E-05	0.182146564	0.518084955	0.182146564	0.518084955
19	gt	-0.184084286	0.030698429	-5.996537631	3.9124E-08	-0.245054014	-0.123114557	-0.245054014	-0.123114557
20	gt-1	-0.099155204	0.036824428	-2.692647516	0.008423035	-0.172291695	-0.026018714	-0.172291695	-0.026018714

Estimates from (9.25) can be used to compute estimates of the impact multiplier and the delay multipliers for the first 7 quarters (see pp. 66-72 in *Principles of Econometrics, 4e* for more details):

$$\hat{\beta}_0 = \hat{\delta}_0 \tag{9.26}$$

$$\hat{\beta}_1 = \hat{\delta}_1 + \hat{\beta}_0\hat{\theta}_1 \tag{9.27}$$

$$\hat{\beta}_j = \hat{\beta}_{j-1}\hat{\theta}_1 \text{ for } j \geq 2 \tag{9.28}$$

Insert a new worksheet by selecting the **Insert Worksheet** tab at the bottom of your screen. Rename it **Multipliers**.

Create the following table to compute the lag weights. In the last column you will find the numbers of the equations used in the table.

	A	B	C	
1	**Data Input**	δ_0-hat =	='ARDL(1,1) Okun's Law Model'!B19	
2		δ_1-hat =	='ARDL(1,1) Okun's Law Model'!B20	
3		θ_1-hat =	='ARDL(1,1) Okun's Law Model'!B18	
4				
5	**Computed Values**	**j**	**B_j-hat**	
6		0	=C1	*(9.26)*
7		1	=C2+C6*C3	*(9.27)*
8		2	=C7*$C$3	*(9.28)*

Copy the content of cell **C8** to cells **C9:C13**.

The result is (see also p. 381 in *Principles of Econometrics, 4e*):

	A	B	C
1	**Data Input**	δ_0**-hat =**	-0.184084286
2		δ_1**-hat =**	-0.099155204
3		θ_1**-hat =**	0.35011576
4			
5	**Computed Values**	**j**	B_j**-hat**
6		0	-0.184084286
7		1	-0.163606014
8		2	-0.057281044
9		3	-0.020054996
10		4	-0.00702157
11		5	-0.002458362
12		6	-0.000860711
13		7	-0.000301349

Select cells **B5:C13**. Go to the **Insert** tab to the left of your tab list. Select the **Scatter** button in the **Charts** group of commands, and select **Scatter with Straight Lines** on the menu of **Scatter** chart type.

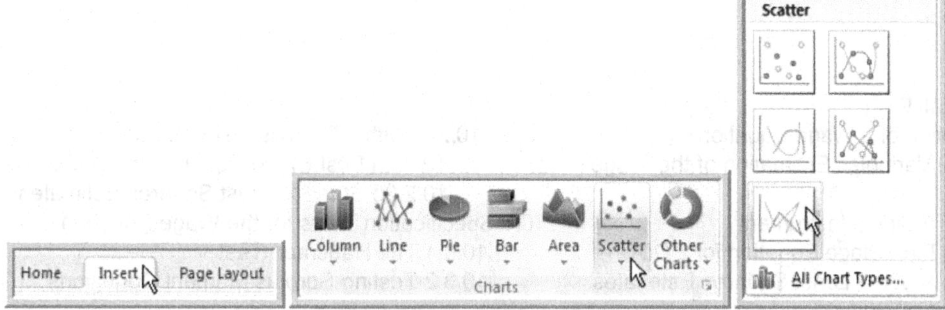

After editing, the result is (see also Figure 9.13 p. 381 in *Principles of Econometrics, 4e*):

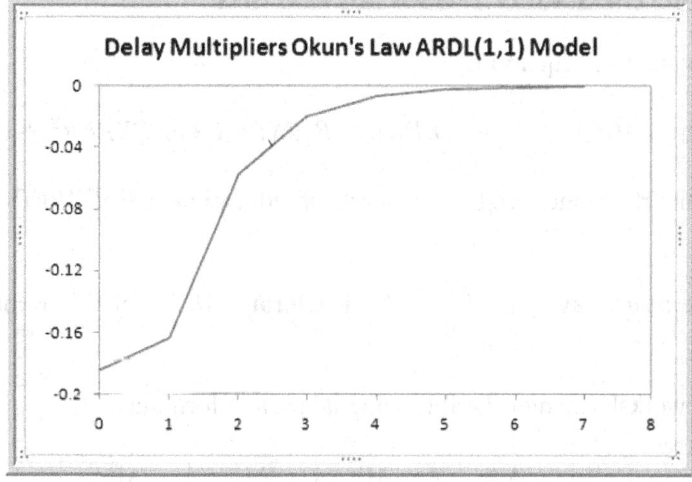

CHAPTER 10

Random Regressors and Moment-Based Estimation

CHAPTER OUTLINE

10.1 OLS ESTIMATION OF A WAGE EQUATION

Consider the following wage equation:

$$\ln(WAGE) = \beta_1 + \beta_2 EDUC + \beta_3 EXPER + \beta_4 EXPER^2 + e \qquad (10.1)$$

where $WAGE$ is hourly wage, $EDUC$ is years of education and $EXPER$ is years of work experience.

Open the Excel file ***mroz***. Save your file as **POE Chapter 10** Excel file. Rename sheet 1 **mroz data**.

In your **mroz data** worksheet enter the following labels and formulas.

	AA	AB	AC	AD
1	**ln(wage)**	**educ**	**exper**	**exper²**
2	=ln(M2)	=L2	=Y2	=AC2^2

The data set includes information on working and non-working women. **lfp** is a dummy variable which identifies labor force participation: it is set to 1 if a woman is in the labor force and 0 otherwise (you can find this variable in column **G**). We will use data on working women only – which span from row **2** to row **429** only.

Copy the content of cell **AA2:AD2** to cells **AD3:AD429**. Here is how your table should look (only the first five values are shown below):

	AA	AB	AC	AD
1	**ln(wage)**	**educ**	**exper**	**exper²**
2	1.210154	12	14	196
3	0.328512	12	5	25
4	1.514138	12	15	225
5	0.092123	12	6	36
6	1.524272	14	7	49

In the **Regression** dialog box, the **Input Y Range** should be **AA1:AA429**, and the **Input X Range** should be **AB1:AD429**. Check the box next to **Labels**. Select **New Worksheet Ply** and name it **OLS Wage Equation**. Finally select **OK**.

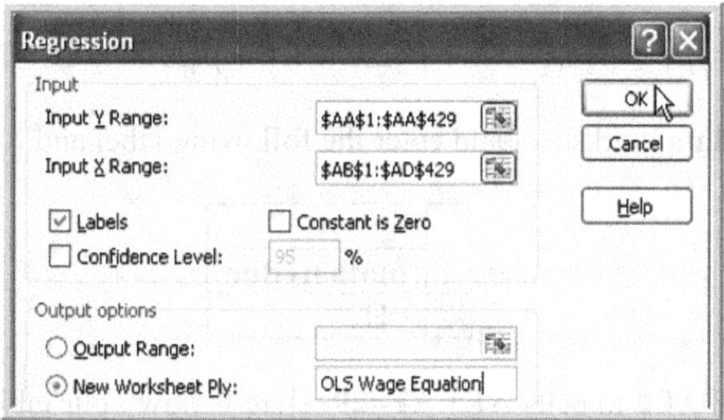

The regression analysis results are (see also p. 407 in *Principles of Econometrics, 4e*):

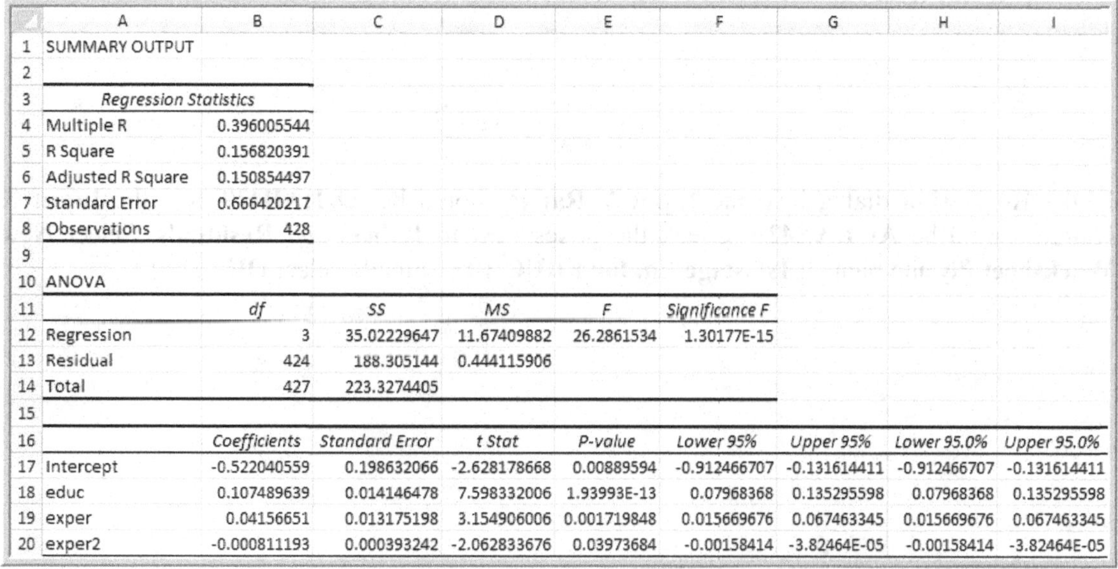

	A	B	C	D	E	F	G	H	I
1	SUMMARY OUTPUT								
2									
3	*Regression Statistics*								
4	Multiple R	0.396005544							
5	R Square	0.156820391							
6	Adjusted R Square	0.150854497							
7	Standard Error	0.666420217							
8	Observations	428							
9									
10	ANOVA								
11		*df*	*SS*	*MS*	*F*	*Significance F*			
12	Regression	3	35.02229647	11.67409882	26.2861534	1.30177E-15			
13	Residual	424	188.305144	0.444115906					
14	Total	427	223.3274405						
15									
16		*Coefficients*	*Standard Error*	*t Stat*	*P-value*	*Lower 95%*	*Upper 95%*	*Lower 95.0%*	*Upper 95.0%*
17	Intercept	-0.522040559	0.198632066	-2.628178668	0.00889594	-0.912466707	-0.131614411	-0.912466707	-0.131614411
18	educ	0.107489639	0.014146478	7.598332006	1.93993E-13	0.07968368	0.135295598	0.07968368	0.135295598
19	exper	0.04156651	0.013175198	3.154906006	0.001719848	0.015669676	0.067463345	0.015669676	0.067463345
20	exper2	-0.000811193	0.000393242	-2.062833676	0.03973684	-0.00158414	-3.82464E-05	-0.00158414	-3.82464E-05

10.2 INSTRUMENTAL VARIABLES ESTIMATION BASED ON THE 2*SLS* ESTIMATION PROCEDURE: ONE INSTRUMENT

The instrumental variables estimators, derived using the method of moments, are also called two-stage least squares (2*SLS*) estimators, because they can be obtained using two least squares regressions.

10.2.1 With a Single Instrument

10.2.1a First Stage Equation for EDUC

In the case of a multiple linear regression model with one instrument, the first stage equation has the random regressor or endogenous variable as the dependent variable, and the instrumental variable *plus* all the exogenous variables as the explanatory variables.

Let $MOTHEREDUC$ be our instrumental variable; the first stage equation for $EDUC$ is:

$$EDUC = \beta_1 + \beta_2 EXPER + \beta_3 EXPER^2 + \beta_4 MOTHEREDUC + v \tag{10.2}$$

Go back to your **mroz data** worksheet and enter the following label and formula.

	AE
1	**mothereduc**
2	=U2

Copy the content of cell **AE2** to cells **AE3:AE429**. Here is how your table should look (only the first five values are shown below):

	AE
1	**mothereduc**
2	12
3	7
4	12
5	7
6	12

In the **Regression** dialog box, the **Input Y Range** should be **AB1:AB429**, and the **Input X Range** should be **AC1:AE429**. Check the boxes next to **Labels** *and* **Residuals**. Select **New Worksheet Ply** and name it **1st Stage Eq. for EDUC 1 IV**. Finally select **OK**.

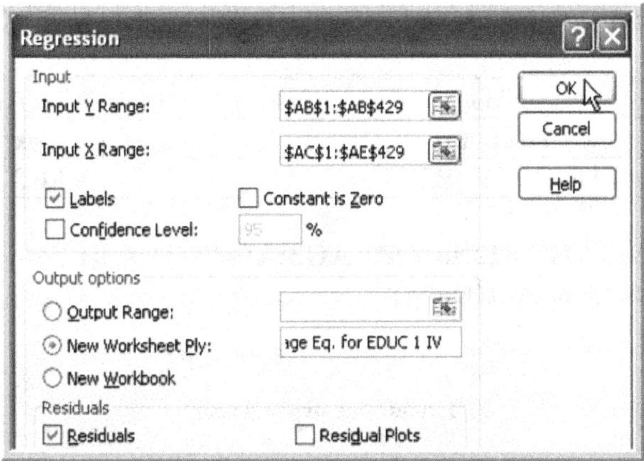

The result is (see also p. 415 in *Principles of Econometrics, 4e*):

	A	B	C	D	E	F	G	H	I
1	SUMMARY OUTPUT								
2									
3	*Regression Statistics*								
4	Multiple R	0.390760937							
5	R Square	0.15269411							
6	Adjusted R Square	0.146699021							
7	Standard Error	2.111099613							
8	Observations	428							
9									
10	ANOVA								
11		*df*	*SS*	*MS*	*F*	*Significance F*			
12	Regression	3	340.5378336	113.5126112	25.46986611	3.61726E-15			
13	Residual	424	1889.658428	4.456741576					
14	Total	427	2230.196262						
15									
16		*Coefficients*	*Standard Error*	*t Stat*	*P-value*	*Lower 95%*	*Upper 95%*	*Lower 95.0%*	*Upper 95.0%*
17	Intercept	9.77510269	0.423888615	23.06054547	7.57423E-77	8.941917986	10.60828739	8.941917986	10.60828739
18	exper	0.0488615	0.04166926	1.172603007	0.241613422	-0.033042541	0.130765541	-0.033042541	0.130765541
19	exper2	-0.001281065	0.001244906	-1.029045855	0.304044787	-0.00372802	0.00116589	-0.00372802	0.00116589
20	mothereduc	0.267690809	0.031129797	8.599182717	1.56823E-16	0.206502871	0.328878747	0.206502871	0.328878747
21									
22									
23									
24	RESIDUAL OUTPUT								
25									
26	*Observation*	*Predicted educ*	*Residuals*						
27	1	13.42036467	-1.420364665						
28	2	11.86121923	0.13878077						
29	3	13.43207528	-1.432075281						

10.2.1b Stage 2 Least Squares Estimates

In stage 2, we obtain the predicted values of our endogenous variable, in this case $\widehat{EDUC}$, from the estimated first stage equation (10.2) and insert them in the original linear regression model (10.1) to replace the $EDUC$ values. Then, we estimate the resulting equation (10.3) by least squares:

$$\ln(WAGE) = \beta_1 + \beta_2\widehat{EDUC} + \beta_3 EXPER + \beta_4 EXPER^2 + e \qquad (10.3)$$

where $\widehat{EDUC}$ are the predicted years of education from the estimated first stage equation (10.2).

Go back to your **mroz data** worksheet and enter the following labels and formulas.

	AG	AH	AI
1	**educ-hat**	**exper**	**exper^2**
2	='1st Stage Eq. for EDUC 1 IV'!B27	=AC2	=AH2^2

Copy the content of cells **AG2:AI2** to cells **AG3:AI429**. Here is how your table should look (only the first five values are shown below):

	AG	AH	AI
1	**educ-hat**	**exper**	**exper^2**
2	13.42036	14	196
3	11.86122	5	25
4	13.43208	15	225
5	11.89599	6	36
6	13.26665	7	49

In the **Regression** dialog box, the **Input Y Range** should be **AA1:AA429**, and the **Input X Range** should be **AG1:AI429**. Check the box next to **Labels**. <u>Uncheck</u> the box next to **Residuals**. Select **New Worksheet Ply** and name it **Stage 2 LS Estimates 1 IV**. Finally select **OK**.

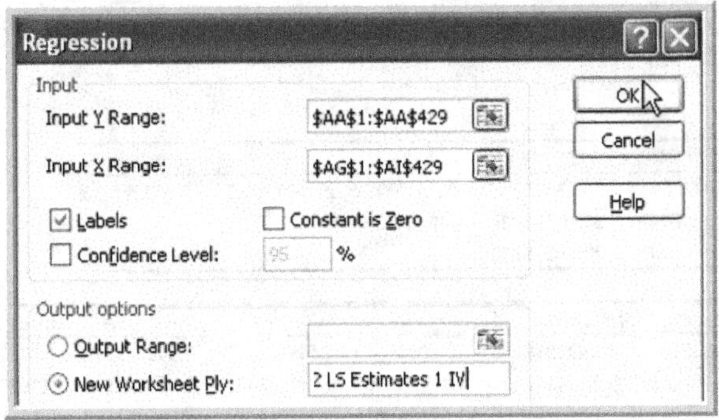

The result is (see also p. 415 in *Principles of Econometrics, 4e*):

	A	B	C	D	E	F	G	H	I
1	SUMMARY OUTPUT								
2									
3	*Regression Statistics*								
4	Multiple R	0.213515069							
5	R Square	0.045588685							
6	Adjusted R Square	0.038835775							
7	Standard Error	0.709015788							
8	Observations	428							
9									
10	ANOVA								
11		*df*	*SS*	*MS*	*F*	*Significance F*			
12	Regression	3	10.18120431	3.393734769	6.750968574	0.000186088			
13	Residual	424	213.1462361	0.502703387					
14	Total	427	223.3274405						
15									
16		*Coefficients*	*Standard Error*	*t Stat*	*P-value*	*Lower 95%*	*Upper 95%*	*Lower 95.0%*	*Upper 95.0%*
17	Intercept	0.198186077	0.493342657	0.401720942	0.688091816	-0.771515728	1.167887883	-0.771515728	1.167887883
18	educ-hat	0.049262951	0.039056201	1.261334918	0.207881726	-0.027504928	0.126030829	-0.027504928	0.126030829
19	exper	0.044855849	0.014164402	3.166801504	0.001652599	0.01701466	0.072697038	0.01701466	0.072697038
20	exper2	-0.000922076	0.000423969	-2.174867599	0.030192089	-0.001755419	-8.87337E-05	-0.001755419	-8.87337E-05

Note that while using this two-stage least squares approach yields proper instrumental variables estimates, the accompanying standard errors are not correct (see also p. 412 in *Principles of Econometrics, 4e*).

The correct standard error of the instrumental variable estimator of β_k is estimated using equation (10.4) below:

$$\widehat{se_{IV}(\hat{\beta}_k)} = \frac{\hat{\sigma}_{IV}}{\hat{\sigma}_{stage\ 2\ LS}} \widehat{se_{stage\ 2\ LS}(\hat{\beta}_k)} \qquad (10.4)$$

where

$$\hat{\sigma}_{IV} = \sqrt{\frac{\sum \hat{e}_{IV}^2}{N-K}} \qquad (10.5)$$

<u>*and*</u>

$$\hat{e}_{IV} = ln(WAGE)_i - \hat{\beta}_1 - \hat{\beta}_2 EDUC_i - \hat{\beta}_3 EXPER_i - \hat{\beta}_4 EXPER_i^2 \qquad (10.6)$$

In equation (10.6), $\hat{\beta}_1$, $\hat{\beta}_2$, $\hat{\beta}_3$ and $\hat{\beta}_4$ are the least squares estimates from equation (10.3).

Go back to your **mroz data** worksheet and enter the following labels and formulas. In the last column, you will find the numbers of the equations used, if any.

	AK	AL
1	**wage equation IV estimates using 2 SLS, 1 instrument**	
2	**β1-hat$_{IV}$ = β1-hat$_{stage\ 2\ LS}$ =**	='Stage 2 LS Estimates 1 IV'!B17
3	**β2-hat$_{IV}$ = β2-hat$_{stage\ 2\ LS}$ =**	='Stage 2 LS Estimates 1 IV'!B18
4	**β3-hat$_{IV}$ = β3-hat$_{stage\ 2\ LS}$ =**	='Stage 2 LS Estimates 1 IV'!B19
5	**β4-hat$_{IV}$ = β4-hat$_{stage\ 2\ LS}$ =**	='Stage 2 LS Estimates 1 IV'!B20

	AN	
1	**e-hat$_{IV}$^{2}**	
2	=(AA2-$AL$2-$AL$3*AB2-$AL$4*AC2-$AL$5*AD2)^2	*(10.6)*^{2}

Copy the content of cell **AN2** to cells **AN3:AN429**.

	AK	AL	
7	**N =**	='Stage 2 LS Estimates 1 IV'!B8	
8	**K =**	='Stage 2 LS Estimates 1 IV'!B12+1	
9	**σ-hat$_{stage\ 2\ LS}$ =**	='Stage 2 LS Estimates 1 IV'!B7	
10	**se(β$_1$-hat)$_{stage\ 2\ LS}$ =**	='Stage 2 LS Estimates 1 IV'!C17	
11	**se(β$_2$-hat)$_{stage\ 2\ LS}$ =**	='Stage 2 LS Estimates 1 IV'!C18	
12	**se(β$_3$-hat)$_{stage\ 2\ LS}$ =**	='Stage 2 LS Estimates 1 IV'!C19	
13	**se(β$_4$-hat)$_{stage\ 2\ LS}$ =**	='Stage 2 LS Estimates 1 IV'!C20	
14	**σ-hat$_{IV}$ =**	=SQRT(SUM(AN2:AN429)/(AL7-AL8))	*(10.5)*
15	**se(β$_1$-hat)$_{IV}$ =**	=(AL14/AL9)*AL10	*(10.4)*
16	**se(β$_2$-hat)$_{IV}$ =**	=(AL14/AL9)*AL11	*(10.4)*
17	**se(β$_3$-hat)$_{IV}$ =**	=(AL14/AL9)*AL12	*(10.4)*
18	**se(β$_4$-hat)$_{IV}$ =**	=(AL14/AL9)*AL13	*(10.4)*

The result is (see also standard errors estimates on p. 415 in *Principles of Econometrics, 4e*):

	AK	AL	AM	AN
1	**wage equation IV estimates using 2 SLS, 1 instrument**			**e-hat$_{IV}$^{2}**
2	**β$_1$-hatIV = β$_1$-hatstage 2 LS =**	0.19818608		0.000699
3	**β$_2$-hatIV = β$_2$-hatstage 2 LS =**	0.04926295		0.438319
4	**β$_3$-hatIV = β$_3$-hatstage 2 LS =**	0.04485585		0.067302
5	**β$_4$-hatIV = β$_4$-hatstage 2 LS =**	-0.00092208		0.870785
6				0.135126
7	**N =**	428		0.084702
8	**K =**	4		0.565539
9	**σ-hat$_{stage\ 2\ LS}$ =**	0.70901579		0.688703
10	**se(β$_1$-hat)$_{stage\ 2\ LS}$ =**	0.49334266		0.336899
11	**se(β$_2$-hat)$_{stage\ 2\ LS}$ =**	0.0390562		0.048497
12	**se(β$_3$-hat)$_{stage\ 2\ LS}$ =**	0.0141644		0.021671
13	**se(β$_4$-hat)$_{stage\ 2\ LS}$ =**	0.00042397		0.113528
14	**σ-hat$_{IV}$ =**	0.67960355		0.003068
15	**se(β$_1$-hat)$_{IV}$ =**	0.47287723		0.174914
16	**se(β$_2$-hat)$_{IV}$ =**	0.03743603		0.141433
17	**se(β$_3$-hat)$_{IV}$ =**	0.01357682		0.594541
18	**se(β$_4$-hat)$_{IV}$ =**	0.00040638		0.022506

10.2.2 With a Surplus Instrument

10.2.2a First Stage Equation for EDUC

In the case of the multiple linear regression model with two instruments, the reduced form equation has the random regressor or endogenous variable as the dependent variable, and the two instrumental variables *plus* all the exogenous variables as explanatory variables. In Section 10.2.1 we used "mother's education" as an instrument; let us add "father's education" as an additional instrumental variable. The first stage equation for $EDUC$ is:

$$EDUC = \beta_1 + \beta_2 EXPER + \beta_3 EXPER^2 + \beta_4 MOTHEREDUC + \beta_5 FATHEREDUC + v \quad (10.7)$$

Go back to your **mroz data** worksheet and enter the following label and formula.

	AF
1	**fathereduc**
2	=V2

Copy the content of cell **AF2** to cells **AF3:AF429**. Here is how your table should look (only the first five values are shown below):

	AF
1	**fathereduc**
2	7
3	7
4	7
5	7
6	14

In the **Regression** dialog box, the **Input Y Range** should be **AB1:AB429**, and the **Input X Range** should be **AC1:AF429**. Check the boxes next to **Labels** *and* **Residuals**. Select **New Worksheet Ply** and name it **1st Stage Eq. for EDUC 2 IV**. Finally select **OK**.

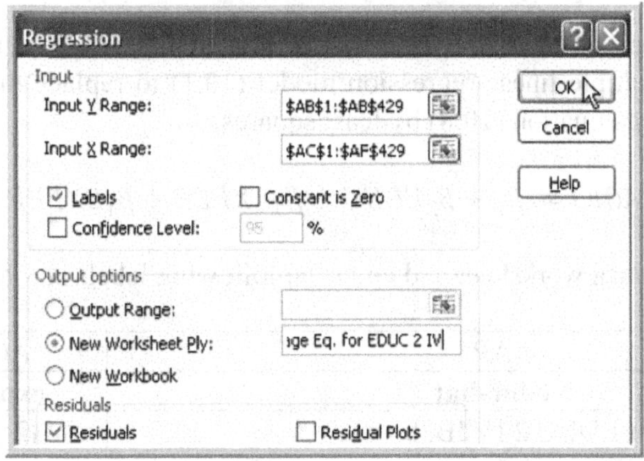

The result is (see also Table 10.1 p. 416 in *Principles of Econometrics, 4e*):

	A	B	C	D	E	F	G	H	I
1	SUMMARY OUTPUT								
2									
3	*Regression Statistics*								
4	Multiple R	0.459859354							
5	R Square	0.211470625							
6	Adjusted R Square	0.204014083							
7	Standard Error	2.038967467							
8	Observations	428							
9									
10	ANOVA								
11		*df*	*SS*	*MS*	*F*	*Significance F*			
12	Regression	4	471.6209982	117.9052496	28.36041288	6.87297E-21			
13	Residual	423	1758.575263	4.15738833					
14	Total	427	2230.196262						
15									
16		*Coefficients*	*Standard Error*	*t Stat*	*P-value*	*Lower 95%*	*Upper 95%*	*Lower 95.0%*	*Upper 95.0%*
17	Intercept	9.10264011	0.426561367	21.33957927	4.09847E-69	8.264196239	9.941083981	8.264196239	9.941083981
18	exper	0.045225423	0.040250712	1.123593117	0.261822938	-0.033890891	0.124341737	-0.033890891	0.124341737
19	exper2	-0.001009091	0.001203345	-0.838571743	0.402183285	-0.003374371	0.001356189	-0.003374371	0.001356189
20	mothereduc	0.157597033	0.035894116	4.390609167	1.42984E-05	0.087043993	0.228150073	0.087043993	0.228150073
21	fathereduc	0.18954841	0.033756467	5.615173276	3.56151E-08	0.123197107	0.255899714	0.123197107	0.255899714
22									
23									
24									
25	RESIDUAL OUTPUT								
26									
27	*Observation*	*Predicted educ*	*Residuals*						
28	1	12.75601747	-0.756017473						
29	2	11.73355805	0.266441947						
30	3	12.77197926	-0.771979259						

10.2.2b Stage 2 Least Squares Estimates

We obtain the predicted values $\widehat{EDUC}$ from the estimated first stage equation (10.7) and insert them in the original multiple linear regression model (10.1) to replace the $EDUC$ values. Then, we estimate the resulting equation (10.8) by least squares.

$$\ln(WAGE) = \beta_1 + \beta_2\widehat{EDUC} + \beta_3 EXPER + \beta_4 EXPER^2 + e \tag{10.8}$$

Go back to your **mroz data** worksheet and enter the following labels and formulas.

	AP	AQ	AR
1	**educ-hat**	**exper**	**exper²**
2	='1st Stage Eq. for EDUC 2 IV'!B28	=AH2	=AQ2^2

Copy the content of cell **AP2:AR2** to cells **AP3:AR429**. Here is how your table should look (only the first five values are shown below):

	AP	AQ	AR
1	**educ-hat**	**exper**	**exper²**
2	12.7560175	14	196
3	11.7335581	5	25
4	12.7719793	15	225
5	11.7676835	6	36
6	13.9146148	7	49

In the **Regression** dialog box, the **Input Y Range** should be **AA1:AA429**, and the **Input X Range** should be **AP1:AR429**. Check the box next to **Labels**. _Uncheck_ the box next to **Residuals**. Select **New Worksheet Ply** and name it **Stage 2 LS Estimates 2 IV**. Finally select **OK**.

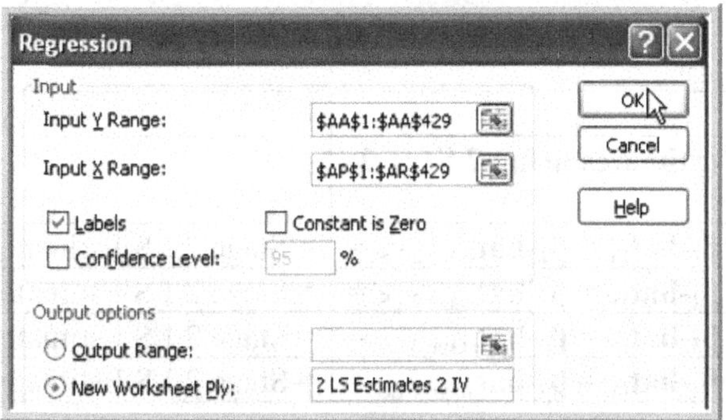

The result is (see also p. 416 in *Principles of Econometrics, 4e*):

	A	B	C	D	E	F	G	H	I
1	SUMMARY OUTPUT								
2									
3	*Regression Statistics*								
4	Multiple R	0.223120224							
5	R Square	0.049782634							
6	Adjusted R Square	0.043059398							
7	Standard Error	0.707456266							
8	Observations	428							
9									
10	ANOVA								
11		*df*	*SS*	*MS*	*F*	*Significance F*			
12	Regression	3	11.11782834	3.705942779	7.404564396	7.61541E-05			
13	Residual	424	212.2096121	0.500494368					
14	Total	427	223.3274405						
15									
16		*Coefficients*	*Standard Error*	*t Stat*	*P-value*	*Lower 95%*	*Upper 95%*	*Lower 95.0%*	*Upper 95.0%*
17	Intercept	0.048100303	0.419756475	0.114590972	0.908823579	-0.776962371	0.873162976	-0.776962371	0.873162976
18	educ-hat	0.061396628	0.032962356	1.862628638	0.0632059	-0.003393342	0.126186598	-0.003393342	0.126186598
19	exper	0.044170394	0.01408437	3.136128625	0.001831158	0.016486515	0.071854274	0.016486515	0.071854274
20	exper2	-0.00089897	0.00042118	-2.134407756	0.033382382	-0.00172683	-7.11091E-05	-0.00172683	-7.11091E-05

While using the two-stage least squares approach yields proper instrumental variables estimates, the accompanying standard errors are not correct. The correct standard error of the instrumental variable estimator of β_k is estimated using equations (10.4)-(10.6) restated next:

$$\widehat{se_{IV}(\hat{\beta}_k)} = \frac{\hat{\sigma}_{IV}}{\hat{\sigma}_{stage\ 2\ LS}} \widehat{se_{stage\ 2\ LS}(\hat{\beta}_k)} \tag{10.4}$$

where
$$\hat{\sigma}_{IV} = \sqrt{\frac{\sum \hat{e}_{IV}^2}{N-K}} \tag{10.5}$$

and
$$\hat{e}_{IV} = ln(WAGE)_i - \hat{\beta}_1 - \hat{\beta}_2 EDUC_i - \hat{\beta}_3 EXPER_i - \hat{\beta}_4 EXPER_i^2 \tag{10.6}$$

In equation (10.6), $\hat{\beta}_1$, $\hat{\beta}_2$, $\hat{\beta}_3$ and $\hat{\beta}_4$ are the least squares estimates from equation (10.8).

Go back to your **mroz data** worksheet and enter the following labels and formulas. In the last column, you will find the numbers of the equations used, if any. This is identical to what you have done in Section 10.2.1b except for the fact that you now retrieve the information needed from your **Stage 2 LS Estimates 2 IV** worksheet instead of your **Stage 2 LS Estimates 1 IV** worksheet.

	AT	AU
1	**wage equation IV estimates using 2 SLS, 2 instruments**	
2	**β_1-hat$_{IV}$ = β_1-hat$_{stage\ 2\ LS}$ =**	='Stage 2 LS Estimates 2 IV'!B17
3	**β_2-hat$_{IV}$ = β_2-hat$_{stage\ 2\ LS}$ =**	='Stage 2 LS Estimates 2 IV'!B18
4	**β_3-hat$_{IV}$ = β_3-hat$_{stage\ 2\ LS}$ =**	='Stage 2 LS Estimates 2 IV'!B19
5	**β_4-hat$_{IV}$ = β_4-hat$_{stage\ 2\ LS}$ =**	='Stage 2 LS Estimates 2 IV'!B20

	AW	
1	**e-hat$_{IV}^2$**	
2	=(AA2-$AU$2-$AU$3*AB2-$AU$4*AC2-$AU$5*AD2)^2	*(10.6)*^{2}

Copy the content of cell **AW2** to cells **AW3:AW429**.

	AT	AU	
7	**N =**	='Stage 2 LS Estimates 2 IV'!B8	
8	**K =**	='Stage 2 LS Estimates 2 IV'!B12+1	
9	**σ-hat$_{stage\ 2\ LS}$ =**	='Stage 2 LS Estimates 2 IV'!B7	
10	**se(β_1-hat)$_{stage\ 2\ LS}$ =**	='Stage 2 LS Estimates 2 IV'!C17	
11	**se(β_2-hat)$_{stage\ 2\ LS}$ =**	='Stage 2 LS Estimates 2 IV'!C18	
12	**se(β_3-hat)$_{stage\ 2\ LS}$ =**	='Stage 2 LS Estimates 2 IV'!C19	
13	**se(β_4-hat)$_{stage\ 2\ LS}$ =**	='Stage 2 LS Estimates 2 IV'!C20	
14	**σ-hat$_{IV}$ =**	=SQRT(SUM(AW2:AW429)/(AU7-AU8))	*(10.5)*
15	**se(β_1-hat)$_{IV}$ =**	=(AU14/AU9)*AU10	*(10.4)*
16	**se(β_2-hat)$_{IV}$ =**	=(AU14/AU9)*AU11	*(10.4)*
17	**se(β_3-hat)$_{IV}$ =**	=(AU14/AU9)*AU12	*(10.4)*
18	**se(β_4-hat)$_{IV}$ =**	=(AU14/AU9)*AU13	*(10.4)*

The result is (see also p. 416 in *Principles of Econometrics, 4e*):

	AT	AU	AV	AW
1	wage equation IV estimates using 2 SLS, 1 instrument			e-hat$_{IV}{}^2$
2	β_1-hatIV = β_1-hatstage 2 LS =	0.0481003		0.000285
3	β_2-hatIV = β_2-hatstage 2 LS =	0.06139663		0.428665
4	β_3-hatIV = β_3-hatstage 2 LS =	0.04417039		0.072356
5	β_4-hatIV = β_4-hatstage 2 LS =	-0.00089897		0.856358
6				0.123535
7	N =	428		0.085834
8	K =	4		0.507961
9	σ-hat$_{stage\ 2\ LS}$ =	0.70745627		0.68898
10	se(β_1-hat)$_{stage\ 2\ LS}$ =	0.41975647		0.328107
11	se(β_2-hat)$_{stage\ 2\ LS}$ =	0.03296236		0.052398
12	se(β_3-hat)$_{stage\ 2\ LS}$ =	0.01408437		0.024578
13	se(β_4-hat)$_{stage\ 2\ LS}$ =	0.00042118		0.128609
14	σ-hat$_{IV}$ =	0.6747117		0.002591
15	se(β_1-hat)$_{IV}$ =	0.40032808		0.167018
16	se(β_2-hat)$_{IV}$ =	0.0314367		0.16655
17	se(β_3-hat)$_{IV}$ =	0.01343248		0.562728
18	se(β_4-hat)$_{IV}$ =	0.00040169		0.019901

10.3 SPECIFICATION TESTS FOR THE WAGE EQUATION

10.3.1 The Hausman Test

Let us revisit the first stage equation (10.7) from Section 10.2.2a:

$$EDUC = \beta_1 + \beta_2 EXPER + \beta_3 EXPER^2 + \beta_4 MOTHEREDUC + \beta_5 FATHEREDUC + v \quad (10.7)$$

We obtain the residuals $\hat{v}$ from the estimated reduced form equation (10.7) and insert $\hat{v}$ in the original wage equation (10.1) as an additional explanatory variable. We estimate the resulting equation (10.9) by least squares:

$$\ln(WAGE) = \beta_1 + \beta_2 EDUC + \beta_3 EXPER + \beta_4 EXPER^2 + \delta\hat{v} + e \quad (10.9)$$

Go back to your **mroz data** worksheet and enter the following labels and formulas.

	AY	AZ	BA	BB
1	**educ**	**exper**	**exper^2**	**v-hat**
2	=AB2	=AC2	=AZ2^2	='1st Stage Eq. for EDUC 2 IV'!C28

Copy the content of cell **AY2:BB2** to cells **AY3:BB429**. Here is how your table should look (only the first five values are shown below):

	AY	AZ	BA	BB
1	**educ**	**exper**	**exper²**	**v-hat**
2	12	14	196	-0.756017
3	12	5	25	0.266442
4	12	15	225	-0.771979
5	12	6	36	0.232317
6	14	7	49	0.085385

In the **Regression** dialog box, the **Input Y Range** should be **AA1:AA429**, and the **Input X Range** should be **AY1:BB429**. Check the box next to **Labels**. Select **New Worksheet Ply** and name it **Hausman Test for Wage Equation**. Finally select **OK**.

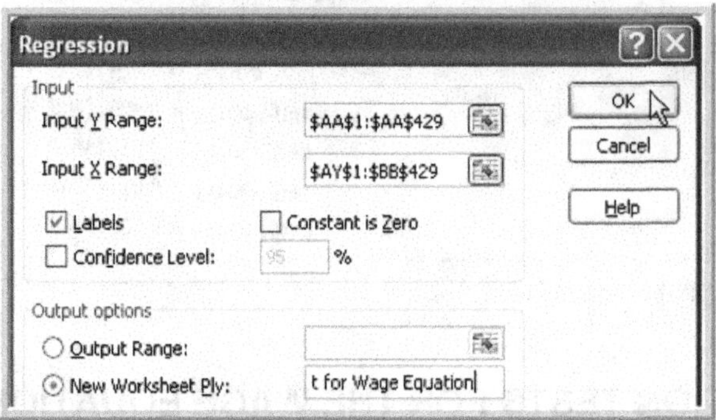

The result is (see also Table 10.2 on p. 422 of *Principles of Econometrics, 4e*):

	A	B	C	D	E	F	G	H	I
16		*Coefficients*	*Standard Error*	*t Stat*	*P-value*	*Lower 95%*	*Upper 95%*	*Lower 95.0%*	*Upper 95.0%*
17	Intercept	0.048100303	0.394575257	0.121904001	0.903032937	-0.727472056	0.823672661	-0.727472056	0.823672661
18	educ	0.061396628	0.030984942	1.981498884	0.048182345	0.000493	0.122300256	0.000493	0.122300256
19	exper	0.044170394	0.013239447	3.336271785	0.000924074	0.018147097	0.070193692	0.018147097	0.070193692
20	exper2	-0.00089897	0.000395913	-2.27062255	0.023671908	-0.001677172	-0.000120767	-0.001677172	-0.000120767
21	v-hat	0.058166612	0.034807276	1.671104998	0.095440554	-0.010250148	0.126583373	-0.010250148	0.126583373

We have outlined the *p*-value of the *t*-test of interest to us in the above table. The coefficient of the reduced form residuals is significant at the **10%** level of significance using a two-tail test. While this is not strong evidence of the endogeneity of education, it is sufficient cause for concern to consider using instrumental variables estimation.

10.3.2 Testing Surplus Moment Conditions

For the wage equation (10.1), restated below, if we use $MOTHEREDUC$ and $FATHEREDUC$ as instruments there is one surplus moment condition.

$$\ln(WAGE) = \beta_1 + \beta_2 EDUC + \beta_3 EXPER + \beta_4 EXPER^2 + e \qquad (10.1)$$

We obtain the residuals $\hat{e}_{IV}$ from the *IV* estimates for equation (10.1), as we did in Section 10.2.2:

$$\hat{e}_{IV} = ln(WAGE)_i - \hat{\beta}_1 - \hat{\beta}_2 EDUC_i - \hat{\beta}_3 EXPER_i - \hat{\beta}_4 EXPER_i^2 \qquad (10.6)$$

We then regress the residuals $\hat{e}_{IV}$ on all available exogenous and instrumental variables. In other words, we estimate the following equation:

$$\hat{e}_{IV} = \beta_1 + \beta_2 EXPER + \beta_3 EXPER^2 + \beta_4 MOTHEREDUC + \beta_5 FATHEREDUC + e \qquad (10.10)$$

Finally we use the R^2 from the estimated equation (10.10) and run a Lagrange multiplier test.

Go back to your **mroz data** worksheet and enter the following label and formula.

	BD
1	**e-hat$_{IV}$**
2	=AA2-$AU$2 -$AU$3*AY2-$AU$4*AZ2-$AU$5*BA2

Copy the content of cell **BD2** to cells **BD3:BD429**. Here is how your table should look (only the first five values are shown below):

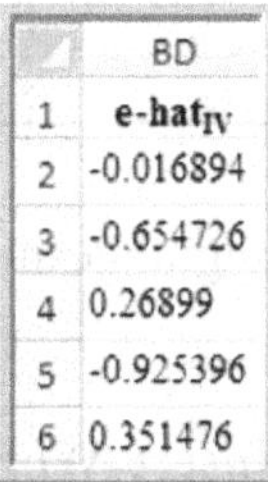

	BD
1	**e-hat$_{IV}$**
2	-0.016894
3	-0.654726
4	0.26899
5	-0.925396
6	0.351476

In the **Regression** dialog box, the **Input Y Range** should be **BD1:BD429**, and the **Input X Range** should be **AC1:AF429**. Check the box next to **Labels**. Select **New Worksheet ply** and name it **IV Residuals Regression**. Finally select **OK**.

The result is:

	A	B	C	D	E	F	G	H	I
1	SUMMARY OUTPUT								
2									
3	*Regression Statistics*								
4	Multiple R	0.029721113							
5	R Square	0.000883345							
6	Adjusted R Square	-0.008564567							
7	Standard Error	0.675210346							
8	Observations	428							
9									
10	ANOVA								
11		*df*	*SS*	*MS*	*F*	*Significance F*			
12	Regression	4	0.170503174	0.042625794	0.093496273	0.984495193			
13	Residual	423	192.8495118	0.455909011					
14	Total	427	193.0200149						
15									
16		*Coefficients*	*Standard Error*	*t Stat*	*P-value*	*Lower 95%*	*Upper 95%*	*Lower 95.0%*	*Upper 95.0%*
17	Intercept	0.010964064	0.141257108	0.077617785	0.938168795	-0.266689202	0.28861733	-0.266689202	0.28861733
18	exper	-1.83348E-05	0.013329147	-0.001375539	0.998903127	-0.026217945	0.026181276	-0.026217945	0.026181276
19	exper2	7.34139E-07	0.000398491	0.001842295	0.998530931	-0.000782536	0.000784004	-0.000782536	0.000784004
20	mothereduc	-0.006606533	0.011886447	-0.555803878	0.578638784	-0.029970389	0.016757323	-0.029970389	0.016757323
21	fathereduc	0.005782258	0.011178558	0.517263334	0.605242715	-0.01619018	0.027754696	-0.01619018	0.027754696

The results we are going to use for the Lagrange multiplier test are highlighted in the above summary output.

Insert a new worksheet by selecting the **Insert Worksheet** tab at the bottom of your screen. Rename it **Lagrange Multiplier Test.**

In it copy the Lagrange multiplier test template you created in Chapter 9.

We replace the following reference: **[POE Chapter 9.xlsx]Auxiliary Regression** by **IV Residuals Regression**.

	A	B	C
1	**Data Input**	N =	='IV Residuals Regression'!B8
2		R^2 =	='IV Residuals Regression'!B5
3		α =	
4		m =	
5			
6	**Computed Values**	χ^2-critical value =	=CHIINV(C3,C4)
8	**Lagrange Multiplier Test**	χ^2 =	=C1*C2
9		Conclusion =	=IF(C8>=C6,"Reject Ho","Do Not Reject Ho")
10		*p*-value =	=CHIDIST(C8,C4)
11		Conclusion =	=IF(C10<=C3,"Reject Ho","Do Not Reject Ho")

At $\alpha = 0.05$, and with $m = 1$, the result of the test, found in the **Lagrange Multiplier Test** worksheet is (see also pp. 422-423 in *Principles of Econometrics, 4e*):

	A	B	C	D
1	**Data Input**	N =	428	
2		R^2 =	0.000883	
3		α =	0.05	
4		m =	1	
5				
6	**Computed Values**	χ^2-critical value =	3.841459	
7				
8	**Lagrange Multiplier Test**	χ^2 =	0.378071	
9		Conclusion =	Do Not Reject Ho	
10		p-value =	0.538637	
11		Conclusion =	Do Not Reject Ho	

Note that the difference between the χ^2-statistic value reported above and the one reported on p. 422 of *Principles of Econometrics, 4e* is due to rounding number differences.

CHAPTER 11

Simultaneous Equations Models

CHAPTER OUTLINE

In this chapter, we estimate simultaneous equation models where there are two or more dependent variables that need to be estimated jointly. Ordinary least squares estimation is not possible when we are dealing with more than one equation. For example, to explain both price and quantity of a good, we need both supply and demand equations which work together to determine price and quantity *jointly*.

11.1 SUPPLY AND DEMAND MODEL FOR TRUFFLES

Consider the following supply and demand model for truffles:

$$\text{Demand:} \quad Q_i = \alpha_1 + \alpha_2 P_i + \alpha_3 PS_i + \alpha_4 DI_i + e_i^d \qquad (11.1)$$

$$\text{Supply:} \quad Q_i = \beta_1 + \beta_2 P_i + \beta_3 PF_i + e_i^s \qquad (11.2)$$

where Q is the quantity of truffles traded in a particular French market-place, indexed by i and measured in ounces. P is the market price of truffles and PS is the market price of a substitute for real truffles, both are measured in \$ per ounce. DI is per capita monthly disposable income of local residents, measured in \$1,000, and PF is the hourly rental rate (\$) for a truffle-finding pig.

11.1.1 The Reduced Form Equations

Consider the following reduced form equations for the supply and demand model for truffles:

$$Q_i = \pi_{11} + \pi_{21}PS_i + \pi_{31}DI_i + \pi_{41}PF_i + v_{i1} \tag{11.3}$$

$$P_i = \pi_{12} + \pi_{22}PS_i + \pi_{32}DI_i + \pi_{42}PF_i + v_{i2} \tag{11.4}$$

Open the Excel file ***truffles***. Save your file as **POE Chapter 11**. Rename sheet 1 **truffles data**.

11.1.1a Reduced Form Equation for Q

We first estimate the reduced form equation for Q (equation (11.3)).

In the **Regression** dialog box, the **Input Y Range** should be **B1:B31**, and the **Input X Range** should be **C1:E31**. Check the box next to **Labels**. Select **New Worksheet Ply** and name it **Truffles Reduced Form Eq. for Q**. Finally select **OK**.

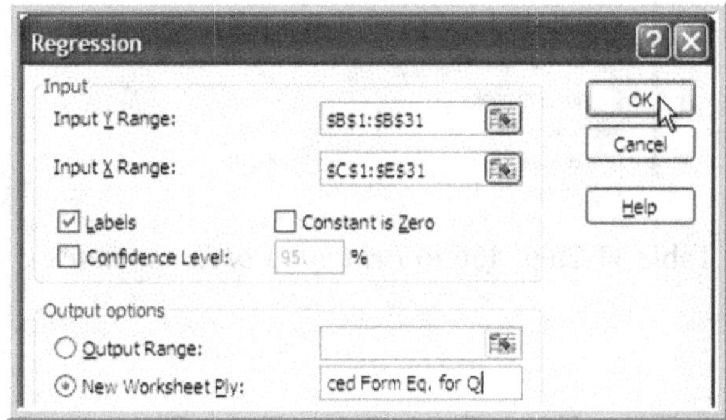

The result is (see also Table 11.2a p. 456 in *Principles of Econometrics, 4e*):

	A	B	C	D	E	F	G	H	I
1	SUMMARY OUTPUT								
2									
3	*Regression Statistics*								
4	Multiple R	0.835096462							
5	R Square	0.697386101							
6	Adjusted R Square	0.662469112							
7	Standard Error	2.680084498							
8	Observations	30							
9									
10	ANOVA								
11		*df*	*SS*	*MS*	*F*	*Significance F*			
12	Regression	3	430.3826319	143.4608773	19.97268759	6.33171E-07			
13	Residual	26	186.7541758	7.182852916					
14	Total	29	617.1368077						
15									
16		*Coefficients*	*Standard Error*	*t Stat*	*P-value*	*Lower 95%*	*Upper 95%*	*Lower 95.0%*	*Upper 95.0%*
17	Intercept	7.895100328	3.243421325	2.434188944	0.022099332	1.228152378	14.56204828	1.228152378	14.56204828
18	ps	0.656402011	0.142537596	4.605114937	9.53266E-05	0.36341179	0.949392232	0.36341179	0.949392232
19	di	2.167156078	0.700473729	3.093843477	0.004680802	0.727311721	3.607000435	0.727311721	3.607000435
20	pf	-0.506982392	0.121261645	-4.180896549	0.000291281	-0.75623927	-0.257725514	-0.75623927	-0.257725514

11.1.1b Reduced Form Equation for P

Next, we estimate the reduced form equation for *P* (equation (11.4)).

Go back to your **truffles data** worksheet.

In the **Regression** dialog box, the **Input Y Range** should be **A1:A31**, and the **Input X Range** should be **C1:E31**. Check the boxes next to **Labels** *and* **Residuals**. Select **New Worksheet Ply** and name it **Truffles Reduced Form Eq. for P**. Finally select **OK**.

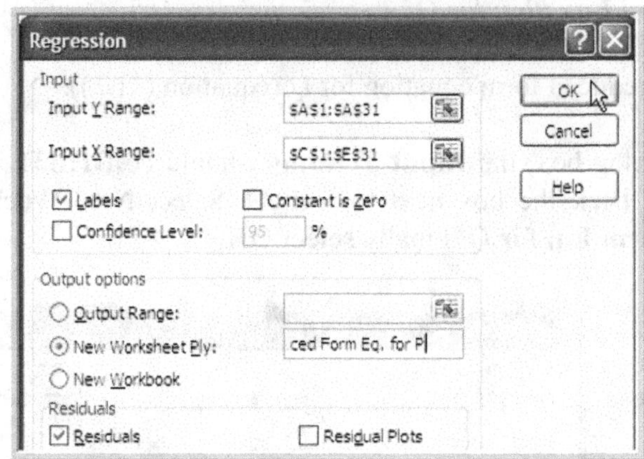

The result is (see also Table 11.2b p. 456 in *Principles of Econometrics, 4e*):

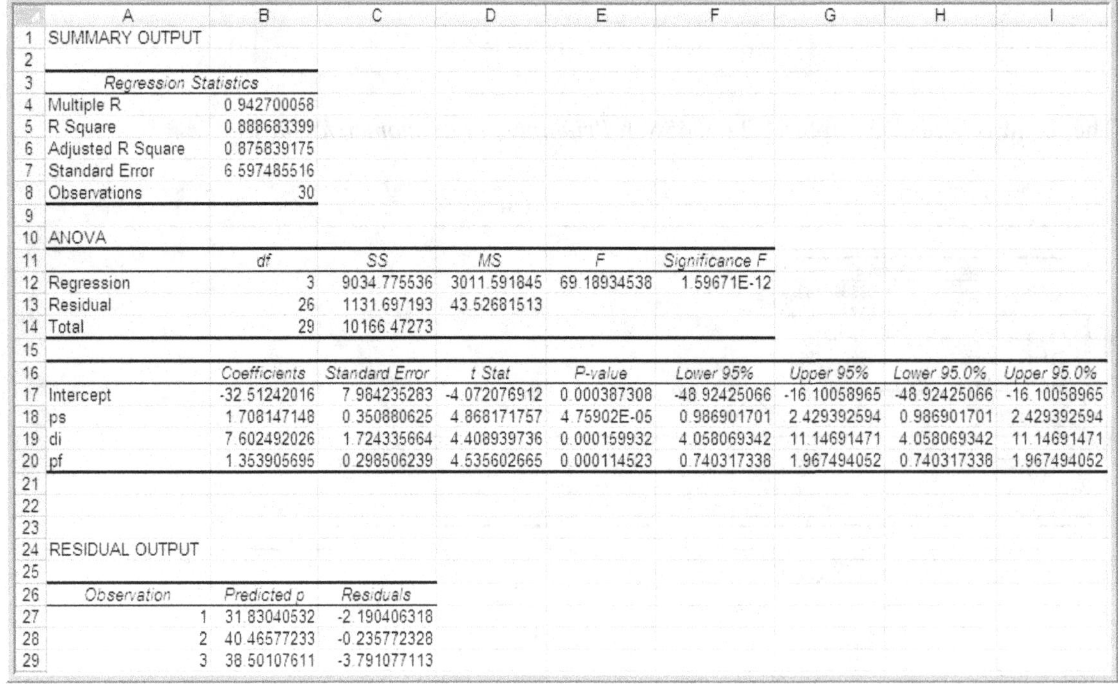

	A	B	C	D	E	F	G	H	I
1	SUMMARY OUTPUT								
2									
3	*Regression Statistics*								
4	Multiple R	0.942700058							
5	R Square	0.888683399							
6	Adjusted R Square	0.875839175							
7	Standard Error	6.597485516							
8	Observations	30							
9									
10	ANOVA								
11		*df*	*SS*	*MS*	*F*	*Significance F*			
12	Regression	3	9034.775536	3011.591845	69.18934538	1.59671E-12			
13	Residual	26	1131.697193	43.52681513					
14	Total	29	10166.47273						
15									
16		*Coefficients*	*Standard Error*	*t Stat*	*P-value*	*Lower 95%*	*Upper 95%*	*Lower 95.0%*	*Upper 95.0%*
17	Intercept	-32.51242016	7.984235283	-4.072076912	0.000387308	-48.92425066	-16.10058965	-48.92425066	-16.10058965
18	ps	1.708147148	0.350880625	4.868171757	4.75902E-05	0.986901701	2.429392594	0.986901701	2.429392594
19	di	7.602492026	1.724335664	4.408939736	0.000159932	4.058069342	11.14691471	4.058069342	11.14691471
20	pf	1.353905695	0.298506239	4.535602665	0.000114523	0.740317338	1.967494052	0.740317338	1.967494052
21									
22									
23									
24	RESIDUAL OUTPUT								
25									
26	*Observation*	*Predicted p*	*Residuals*						
27	1	31.83040532	-2.190406318						
28	2	40.46577233	-0.235772328						
29	3	38.50107611	-3.791077113						

11.1.2 The Structural Equations or Stage 2 Least Squares Estimates

We obtain the predicted values $\hat{P}_i$ from the estimated reduced form equation (11.4) and insert them in the structural demand and supply equations (11.1) and (11.2) to replace the P_i values. Then, we estimate the resulting equations (11.5) and (11.6) by least squares:

$$\text{Demand:} \quad Q_i = \alpha_1 + \alpha_2 \hat{P}_i + \alpha_3 PS_i + \alpha_4 DI_i + e_i^d \tag{11.5}$$

$$\text{Supply:} \quad Q_i = \beta_1 + \beta_2 \hat{P}_i + \beta_3 PF_i + e_i^s \tag{11.6}$$

11.1.2a 2SLS Estimates for Truffle Demand

Go back to your **truffles data** worksheet and enter the following labels and formulas.

	G	H	I
1	**p-hat**	**ps**	**di**
2	='Truffles Reduced Form Eq. for P'!B27	=C2	=D2

Copy the content of cells **G2:I2** to cells **G3:I31**. Here is how your table should look (only the first five values are shown below):

	G	H	I
1	p-hat	ps	di
2	31.83041	19.97	2.103
3	40.46577	18.04	2.043
4	38.50108	22.36	1.87
5	39.03302	20.87	1.525
6	40.44901	19.79	2.709

In the **Regression** dialog box, the **Input Y Range** should be **B1:B31**, and the **Input X Range** should be **G1:I31**. Check the box next to **Labels**. <u>*Uncheck*</u> the box next to **Residuals**. Select **New Worksheet Ply** and name it **Stage 2 LS Demand for Truffles**. Finally select **OK**.

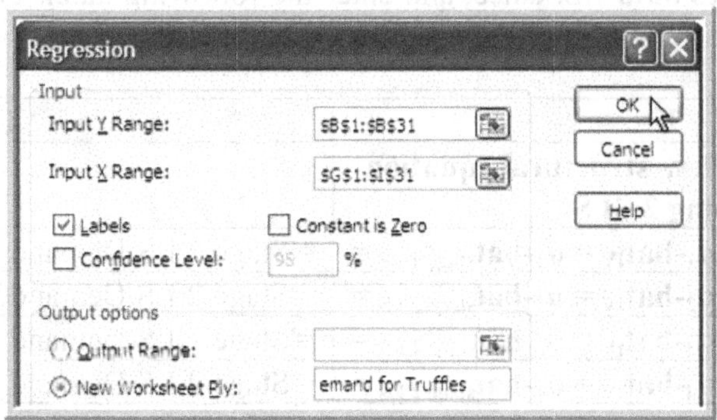

The result is (see also Table 11.3a on p. 456 in *Principles of Econometrics, 4e*):

	A	B	C	D	E	F	G	H	I
1	SUMMARY OUTPUT								
2									
3	*Regression Statistics*								
4	Multiple R	0.835096462							
5	R Square	0.697386101							
6	Adjusted R Square	0.662469112							
7	Standard Error	2.680084498							
8	Observations	30							
9									
10	ANOVA								
11		*df*	*SS*	*MS*	*F*	*Significance F*			
12	Regression	3	430.3826319	143.4608773	19.97268759	6.33171E-07			
13	Residual	26	186.7541758	7.182852916					
14	Total	29	617.1368077						
15									
16		*Coefficients*	*Standard Error*	*t Stat*	*P-value*	*Lower 95%*	*Upper 95%*	*Lower 95.0%*	*Upper 95.0%*
17	Intercept	-4.279473279	3.013833748	-1.41994338	0.167504529	-10.47449721	1.915550652	-10.47449721	1.915550652
18	p-hat	-0.374459162	0.089564321	-4.180896549	0.000291281	-0.558561259	-0.190357065	-0.558561259	-0.190357065
19	ps	1.296033361	0.193094429	6.711914817	4.02707E-07	0.899122081	1.69294464	0.899122081	1.69294464
20	di	5.013978871	1.241414409	4.038924337	0.000422352	2.462215032	7.56574271	2.462215032	7.56574271

Note that while using this two-stage least squares approach yields proper variables estimates, the accompanying standard errors are not correct. The correct standard error of the variable estimator of α_k is estimated using equations (10.4) and (10.5) restated below:

$$\widehat{se_{CORRECT}}(\hat{\alpha}_k) = \widehat{se_{IV}}(\hat{\alpha}_k) = \frac{\hat{\sigma}_{IV}}{\hat{\sigma}_{stage\ 2\ LS}} \widehat{se_{stage\ 2\ LS}}(\hat{\alpha}_k) \tag{10.4}$$

where

$$\hat{\sigma}_{IV} = \sqrt{\frac{\sum \hat{e}_{IV}^2}{N-K}} \tag{10.5}$$

<u>*and*</u>

$$\hat{e}_{IV} = \hat{e}_{IV}^d = Q_i - \hat{\alpha}_1 - \hat{\alpha}_2 P_i - \hat{\alpha}_3 PS_i - \hat{\alpha}_4 DI_i \tag{11.7}$$

where $\hat{\alpha}_1$, $\hat{\alpha}_2$, $\hat{\alpha}_3$ and $\hat{\alpha}_4$ are the least squares estimates from equation (11.5).

Go back to your **truffles data** worksheet and enter the following labels and formulas. In the last column, you will find the numbers of the equations used, if any.

	K	L
1	**Demand for Truffles, structural equation or IV estimates using 2 SLS**	
2	**α_1-hat$_{IV}$ = α_1-hat$_{stage\ 2\ LS}$ =**	='Stage 2 LS Demand for Truffles!B17
3	**α_2-hat$_{IV}$ = α_2-hat$_{stage\ 2\ LS}$ =**	='Stage 2 LS Demand for Truffles'!B18
4	**α_3-hat$_{IV}$ = α_3-hat$_{stage\ 2\ LS}$ =**	='Stage 2 LS Demand for Truffles'!B19
5	**α_4-hat$_{IV}$ = α_4-hat$_{stage\ 2\ LS}$ =**	='Stage 2 LS Demand for Truffles'!B20

	N
1	**e-hat$_{IV}^2$**
2	=(B2-$L$2-$L$3*A2-$L$4*C2-$L$5*D2)^2

Copy the content of cell **N2** to cells **N3:N31**.

	K	L	
7	**N =**	='Stage 2 LS Demand for Truffles'!B8	
8	**K =**	='Stage 2 LS Demand for Truffles'!B12+1	
9	**σ-hat$_{\text{stage 2 LS}}$ =**	='Stage 2 LS Demand for Truffles'!B7	
10	**se(α_1-hat)$_{\text{stage 2 LS}}$ =**	='Stage 2 LS Demand for Truffles'!C17	
11	**se(α_2-hat)$_{\text{stage 2 LS}}$ =**	='Stage 2 LS Demand for Truffles'!C18	
12	**se(α_3-hat)$_{\text{stage 2 LS}}$ =**	='Stage 2 LS Demand for Truffles'!C19	
13	**se(α_4-hat)$_{\text{stage 2 LS}}$ =**	='Stage 2 LS Demand for Truffles'!C20	
14	**σ-hat$_{\text{IV}}$ =**	=SQRT(SUM(N2:N31)/(L7-L8))	*(10.5)*
15	**se(α_1-hat)$_{\text{IV}}$ =**	=(L14/L9)*L10	*(10.4)*
16	**se(α_2-hat)$_{\text{IV}}$ =**	=(L14/L9)*L11	*(10.4)*
17	**se(α_3-hat)$_{\text{IV}}$ =**	=(L14/L9)*L12	*(10.4)*
18	**se(α_4-hat)$_{\text{IV}}$ =**	=(L14/L9)*L13	*(10.4)*

The result is (see also standard errors estimates in Table 11.3a on p. 456 of *Principles of Econometrics, 4e*):

	K	L	M	N
1	**Demand for Truffles, structural equation or IV estimates using 2 SLS**			**e-hat$_{\text{IV}}^2$**
2	**α_1-hat$_{\text{IV}}$ = α_1-hat$_{\text{stage 2 LS}}$ =**	-4.27947		1.340364
3	**α_2-hat$_{\text{IV}}$ = α_2-hat$_{\text{stage 2 LS}}$ =**	-0.37446		1.537691
4	**α3-hat$_{\text{IV}}$ = α_3-hat$_{\text{stage 2 LS}}$ =**	1.296033		2.156481
5	**α_4-hat$_{\text{IV}}$ = α_4-hat$_{\text{stage 2 LS}}$ =**	5.013979		4.967461
6				57.50169
7	**N =**	30		65.8819
8	**K =**	4		23.92123
9	**σ-hat$_{\text{stage 2 LS}}$ =**	2.680084		12.05736
10	**se(α_1-hat)$_{\text{stage 2 LS}}$ =**	3.013834		17.75874
11	**se(α_2-hat)$_{\text{stage 2 LS}}$ =**	0.089564		7.303551
12	**se(α_3-hat)$_{\text{stage 2 LS}}$ =**	0.193094		30.53484
13	**se(α_4-hat)$_{\text{stage 2 LS}}$ =**	1.241414		5.98552
14	**σ-hat$_{\text{IV}}$ =**	4.92996		6.781699
15	**se(α_1-hat)$_{\text{IV}}$ =**	5.543885		0.616516
16	**se(α_2-hat)$_{\text{IV}}$ =**	0.164752		3.568511
17	**se(α_3-hat)$_{\text{IV}}$ =**	0.355193		13.7012
18	**se(α_4-hat)$_{\text{IV}}$ =**	2.283556		32.17105

11.1.2b 2SLS Estimates for Truffle Supply

In your **truffles data** worksheet, enter the following labels and formulas.

	P	Q
1	**p-hat**	**pf**
2	=G2	=E2

Copy the content of cells **P2:Q2** to cells **P3:Q31**. Here is how your table should look (only the first five values are shown below):

	P	Q
1	**p-hat**	**pf**
2	31.83041	10.52
3	40.46577	19.67
4	38.50108	13.74
5	39.03302	17.95
6	40.44901	13.71

In the **Regression** dialog box, the **Input Y Range** should be **B1:B31**, and the **Input X Range** should be **P1:Q31**. Check the box next to **Labels**. Select **New Worksheet Ply** and name it **Stage 2 LS Supply for Truffles**. Finally select **OK**.

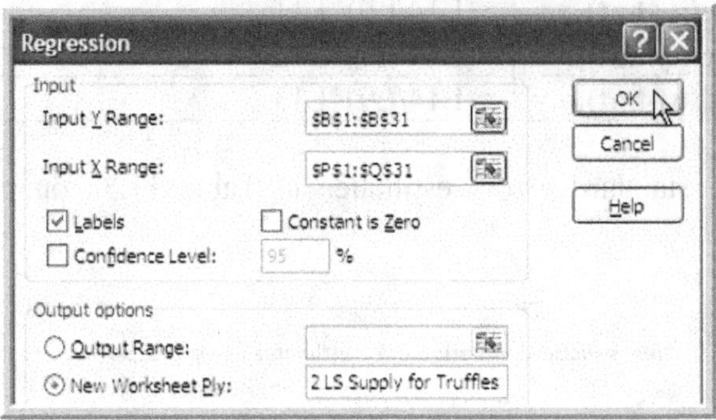

The result is (see also Table 11.3b on p. 457 in *Principles of Econometrics, 4e*):

	A	B	C	D	E	F	G	H	I
1	SUMMARY OUTPUT								
2									
3	*Regression Statistics*								
4	Multiple R	0.832088491							
5	R Square	0.692371257							
6	Adjusted R Square	0.669503943							
7	Standard Error	2.651687234							
8	Observations	30							
9									
10	ANOVA								
11		*df*	*SS*	*MS*	*F*	*Significance F*			
12	Regression	2	427.2877876	213.6438938	30.38406587	1.22564E-07			
13	Residual	27	189.8490201	7.031445189					
14	Total	29	617.1368077						
15									
16		*Coefficients*	*Standard Error*	*t Stat*	*P-value*	*Lower 95%*	*Upper 95%*	*Lower 95.0%*	*Upper 95.0%*
17	Intercept	20.03280279	2.165698376	9.250042857	7.35757E-10	15.58915682	24.47644875	15.58915682	24.47644875
18	p-hat	0.337981554	0.04412361	7.659879835	3.07433E-08	0.247447384	0.428515723	0.247447384	0.428515723
19	pf	-1.000909364	0.146127429	-6.849565273	2.33394E-07	-1.300738079	-0.701080649	-1.300738079	-0.701080649

Again, note that while using this two-stage least squares approach yields proper variables estimates, the accompanying standard errors are not correct. The correct standard error of the variable estimator of β_k is estimated using equations (10.4) and (10.5) restated below:

$$\widehat{se_{CORRECT}}(\hat{\beta}_k) = \widehat{se_{IV}}(\hat{\beta}_k) = \frac{\hat{\sigma}_{IV}}{\hat{\sigma}_{stage\ 2\ LS}} \widehat{se_{stage\ 2\ LS}}(\hat{\beta}_k) \tag{10.4}$$

where

$$\hat{\sigma}_{IV} = \sqrt{\frac{\sum \hat{e}_{IV}^2}{N-K}} \tag{10.5}$$

<u>and</u> $$\hat{e}_{IV} = \hat{e}_{IV}^{s} = Q_i - \hat{\beta}_1 - \hat{\beta}_2 P_i - \hat{\beta}_3 PF_i \qquad (11.8)$$

where $\hat{\beta}_1$, $\hat{\beta}_2$ and $\hat{\beta}_3$ are the least squares estimates from equation (11.6).

Go back to your **truffles data** worksheet and enter the following labels and formulas. In the last column, you will find the numbers of the equations used, if any.

	S	T
1	**Supply for Truffles, structural equation or IV estimates using 2 SLS**	
2	**β1-hat$_{IV}$ = β1-hat$_{stage\ 2\ LS}$ =**	='Stage 2 LS Supply for Truffles!B17
3	**β2-hat$_{IV}$ = β2-hat$_{stage\ 2\ LS}$ =**	='Stage 2 LS Supply for Truffles'!B18
4	**β3-hat$_{IV}$ = β3-hat$_{stage\ 2\ LS}$ =**	='Stage 2 LS Supply for Truffles'!B19

	V
1	**e-hat$_{IV}^2$**
2	=(B2-$T$2-$T$3*A2-$T$4*E2)^2

Copy the content of cell **V2** to cells **V3:V31**.

	S	T	
6	**N =**	='Stage 2 LS Supply for Truffles'!B8	
7	**K =**	='Stage 2 LS Supply for Truffles'!B12+1	
8	**σ-hat$_{stage\ 2\ LS}$=**	='Stage 2 LS Supply for Truffles'!B7	
9	**se(β1-hat)$_{stage\ 2\ LS}$ =**	='Stage 2 LS Supply for Truffles'!C17	
10	**se(β2-hat)$_{stage\ 2\ LS}$ =**	='Stage 2 LS Supply for Truffles'!C18	
11	**se(β3-hat)$_{stage\ 2\ LS}$ =**	='Stage 2 LS Supply for Truffles'!C19	
12	**σ-hat$_{IV}$ =**	=SQRT(SUM(V2:V31)/(T6-T7))	*(10.5)*
13	**se(β1-hat)$_{IV}$ =**	=(T12/T8)*T9	*(10.4)*
14	**se(β2-hat)$_{IV}$ =**	=(T12/T8)*T10	*(10.4)*
15	**se(β3-hat)$_{IV}$ =**	=(T12/T8)*T11	*(10.4)*

The result is (see also standard errors estimates in Table 11.3b on p. 457 of *Principles of Econometrics, 4e*):

	S	T	U	V
1	**Supply for Truffles, structural equation or IV estimates using 2 SLS**			**e-hat$_{IV}^2$**
2	**β1-hat$_{IV}$ = β1-hat$_{stage\ 2\ LS}$ =**	20.0328		0.136153
3	**β2-hat$_{IV}$ = β2-hat$_{stage\ 2\ LS}$ =**	0.337982		0.813440
4	**β3-hat$_{IV}$ = β3-hat$_{stage\ 2\ LS}$ =**	-1.00091		2.554734
5				1.125603
6	**N =**	30		3.234284
7	**K =**	3		2.921237
8	**σ-hat$_{stage\ 2\ LS}$ =**	2.651687		0.666898
9	**se(β1-hat)$_{stage\ 2\ LS}$ =**	2.165698		0.01213
10	**se(β2-hat)$_{stage\ 2\ LS}$ =**	0.044124		0.14584
11	**se(β3-hat)$_{stage\ 2\ LS}$ =**	0.146127		0.416504
12	**σ-hat$_{IV}$ =**	1.497585		0.062899
13	**se(β1-hat)$_{IV}$ =**	1.223115		0.507988
14	**se(β2-hat)$_{IV}$ =**	0.02492		0.653581
15	**se(β3-hat)$_{IV}$ =**	0.082528		4.571835

11.2 SUPPLY AND DEMAND MODEL FOR THE FULTON FISH MARKET

Consider the following supply and demand model for the Fulton fish market:

$$\text{Demand:} \quad ln(QUAN_t) = \begin{array}{l} \alpha_1 + \alpha_2 ln(PRICE_t) + \alpha_3 MON_t \\ +\alpha_4 TUE_t + \alpha_5 WED_t + \alpha_6 THU_t + e_t^d \end{array} \tag{11.9}$$

$$\text{Supply:} \quad ln(QUAN_t) = \beta_1 + \beta_2 ln(PRICE_t) + \beta_3 STORMY_t + e_t^s \tag{11.10}$$

where $QUAN$ is the quantity of fish sold, in pounds, and $PRICE$ is the average daily price per pound. The subscript "t" is used to index daily observations collected over the period December 2, 1991 to May 8, 1992. MON, TUE, WED, THU are dummy variables for the days of the week; they capture the day-to-day shifts in demand. $STORMY$ is a dummy variable indicating stormy weather during the previous 3 days; this variable is important in the supply equation because stormy weather makes fishing more difficult, reducing the supply of fish brought to market.

11.2.1 The Reduced Form Equations

Consider the following reduced form equations for the supply and demand model for the Fulton fish market:

$$ln(QUAN_t) = \begin{array}{l} \pi_{11} + \pi_{21} MON_t + \pi_{31} TUE_t + \pi_{41} WED_t \\ + \pi_{51} THU_t + \pi_{61} STORMY_t + v_{t1} \end{array} \tag{11.11}$$

$$ln(PRICE_t) = \begin{array}{l} \pi_{12} + \pi_{22} MON_t + \pi_{32} TUE_t + \pi_{42} WED_t \\ + \pi_{52} THU_t + \pi_{62} STORMY_t + v_{t2} \end{array} \tag{11.12}$$

Open the Excel file ***fultonfish***. Excel opens the data set in Sheet 1 of a new Excel file. Since we would like to save all our work from Chapter 11 in one file, create a new worksheet in your **POE Chapter 11** Excel file, rename it **fultonfish data**, and in it, copy the data set you just opened.

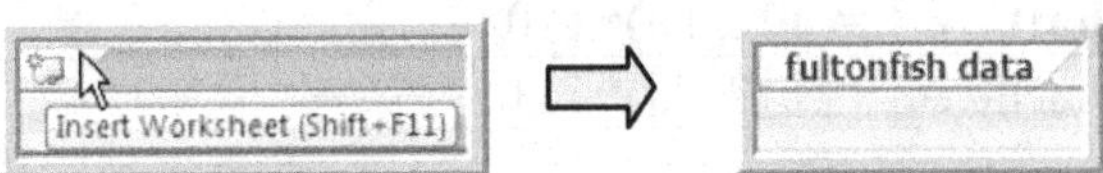

11.2.1a Reduced Form Equation for lnQ

We first estimate the reduced form equation for $ln(QUAN)$ (equation (11.11)).

In the **Regression** dialog box, the **Input Y Range** should be **D1:D112**, and the **Input X Range** should be **E1:I112**. Check the box next to **Labels**. Select **New Worksheet Ply** and name it **Fish Reduced Form Eq. for lnQ**. Finally select **OK**.

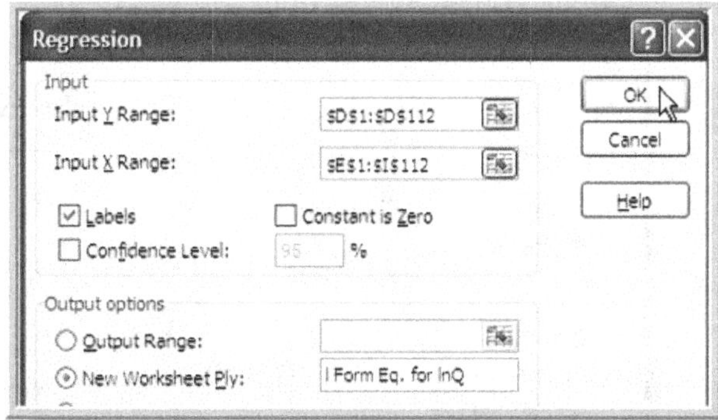

The result is (see also Table 11.4a p. 459 in *Principles of Econometrics, 4e*):

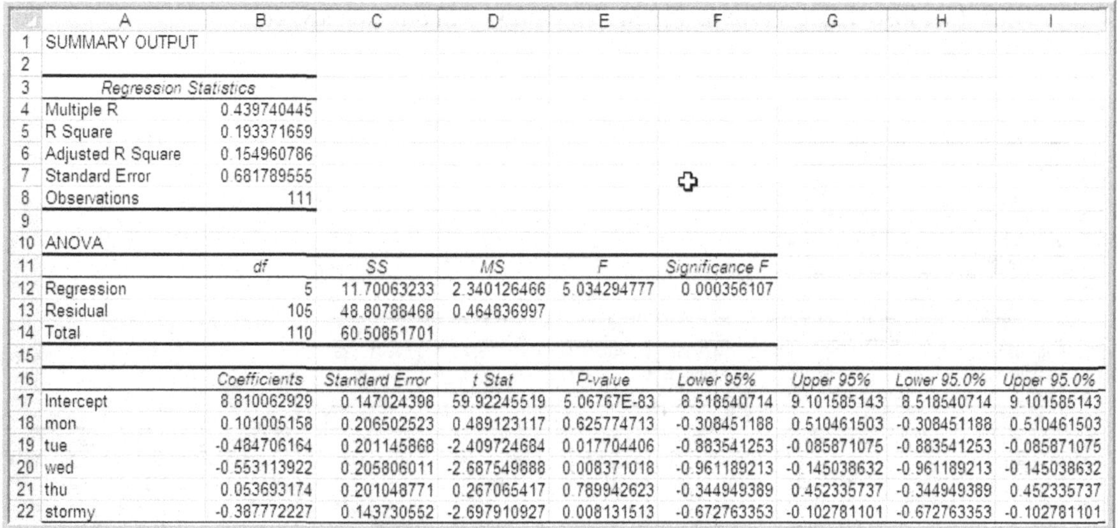

	A	B	C	D	E	F	G	H	I
1	SUMMARY OUTPUT								
2									
3	*Regression Statistics*								
4	Multiple R	0.439740445							
5	R Square	0.193371659							
6	Adjusted R Square	0.154960786							
7	Standard Error	0.681789555							
8	Observations	111							
9									
10	ANOVA								
11		*df*	*SS*	*MS*	*F*	*Significance F*			
12	Regression	5	11.70063233	2.340126466	5.034294777	0.000356107			
13	Residual	105	48.80788468	0.464836997					
14	Total	110	60.50851701						
15									
16		*Coefficients*	*Standard Error*	*t Stat*	*P-value*	*Lower 95%*	*Upper 95%*	*Lower 95.0%*	*Upper 95.0%*
17	Intercept	8.810062929	0.147024398	59.92245519	5.06767E-83	8.518540714	9.101585143	8.518540714	9.101585143
18	mon	0.101005158	0.206502523	0.489123117	0.625774713	-0.308451188	0.510461503	-0.308451188	0.510461503
19	tue	-0.484706164	0.201145868	-2.409724684	0.017704406	-0.883541253	-0.085871075	-0.883541253	-0.085871075
20	wed	-0.553113922	0.205806011	-2.687549888	0.008371018	-0.961189213	-0.145038632	-0.961189213	-0.145038632
21	thu	0.053693174	0.201048771	0.267065417	0.789942623	-0.344949389	0.452335737	-0.344949389	0.452335737
22	stormy	-0.387772227	0.143730552	-2.697910927	0.008131513	-0.672763353	-0.102781101	-0.672763353	-0.102781101

11.2.1b Reduced Form Equation for lnP

Next, we estimate the reduced form equation for $ln(PRICE)$ (equation (11.12)).

Go back to your **fultonfish data** worksheet.

In the **Regression** dialog box, the **Input Y Range** should be **B1:B112**, and the **Input X Range** should be **E1:I112**. Check the boxes next to **Labels** *and* **Residuals**. Select **New Worksheet Ply** and name it **Fish Reduced Form Eq. for lnP**. Finally select **OK**.

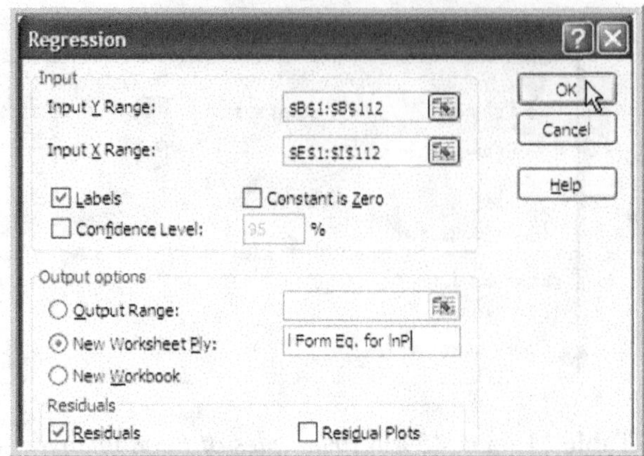

The result is (see also Table 11.4b p. 459 in *Principles of Econometrics, 4e*):

	A	B	C	D	E	F	G	H	I
1	SUMMARY OUTPUT								
2									
3	*Regression Statistics*								
4	Multiple R	0.422952792							
5	R Square	0.178889065							
6	Adjusted R Square	0.139788544							
7	Standard Error	0.354235114							
8	Observations	111							
9									
10	ANOVA								
11		*df*	*SS*	*MS*	*F*	*Significance F*			
12	Regression	5	2.870479668	0.574095934	4.575106963	0.000815588			
13	Residual	105	13.1756642	0.125482516					
14	Total	110	16.04614387						
15									
16		*Coefficients*	*Standard Error*	*t Stat*	*P-value*	*Lower 95%*	*Upper 95%*	*Lower 95.0%*	*Upper 95.0%*
17	Intercept	-0.271705457	0.076388974	-3.55686747	0.000564633	-0.423170677	-0.120240237	-0.423170677	-0.120240237
18	mon	-0.11292248	0.107291824	-1.052479825	0.294995532	-0.325662341	0.099817381	-0.325662341	0.099817381
19	tue	-0.04114933	0.104508685	-0.393740767	0.694570871	-0.24837074	0.166072081	-0.24837074	0.166072081
20	wed	-0.011824968	0.10692994	-0.110586129	0.912155647	-0.223847279	0.200197343	-0.223847279	0.200197343
21	thu	0.049645652	0.104458236	0.475267953	0.635583179	-0.157475728	0.256767033	-0.157475728	0.256767033
22	stormy	0.346405584	0.074677601	4.638681183	1.01527E-05	0.1983337	0.494477468	0.1983337	0.494477468
23									
24									
25									
26	RESIDUAL OUTPUT								
27									
28	*Observation*	*Predicted lprice*	*Residuals*						
29	1	-0.038222353	-0.392560647						
30	2	0.033550798	-0.033550798						
31	3	-0.283530425	0.355851425						

Next, we use the results of the estimated reduced form equation for $ln(PRICE)$ to test the significance of the daily dummy variables.

Equation (11.12), restated below, is our *unrestricted* model (for a review of the *F*-test, see Section 6.1):

$$ln(PRICE_t) = \begin{array}{l} \pi_{12} + \pi_{22}MON_t + \pi_{32}TUE_t + \pi_{42}WED_t \\ + \pi_{52}THU_t + \pi_{62}STORMY_t + v_{t2} \end{array} \tag{11.12}$$

Our *restricted* model is equation (11.13) below:

$$ln(PRICE_t) = \pi_{12} + \pi_{62}STORMY_t + v_{t2} \tag{11.13}$$

Go back to your **fultonfish data** worksheet. In the **Regression** dialog box, the **Input Y Range** should be **B1:B112**, and the **Input X Range** should be **I1:I112**. Check the box next to **Labels**. *Uncheck* the box next to **Residuals**. Select **New Worksheet Ply** and name it **Restricted Model**. Finally select **OK**.

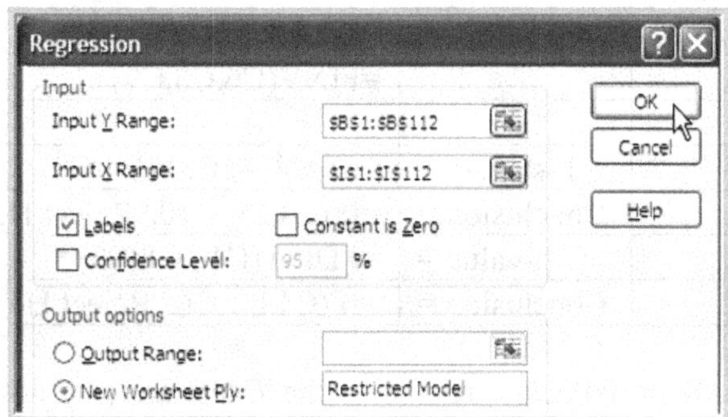

The result is:

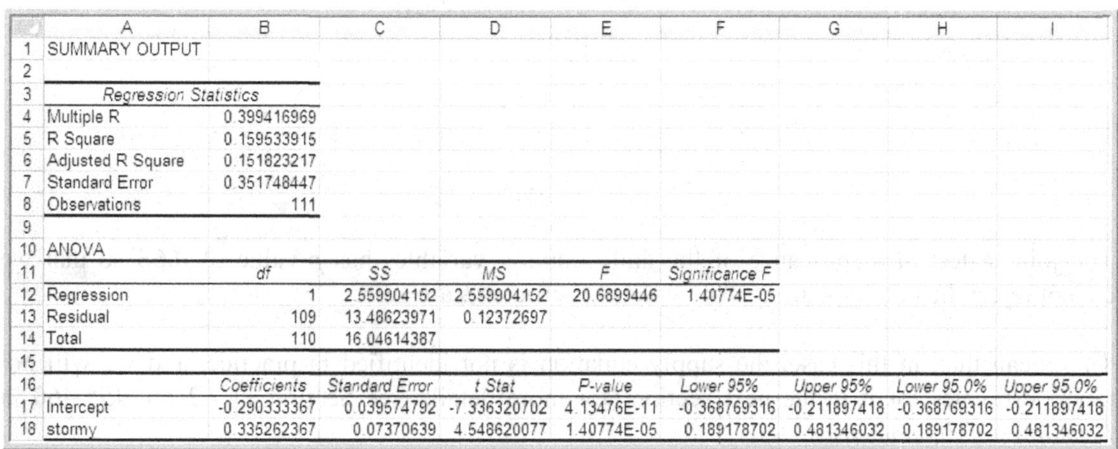

	A	B	C	D	E	F	G	H	I
1	SUMMARY OUTPUT								
2									
3	Regression Statistics								
4	Multiple R	0.399416969							
5	R Square	0.159533915							
6	Adjusted R Square	0.151823217							
7	Standard Error	0.351748447							
8	Observations	111							
9									
10	ANOVA								
11		df	SS	MS	F	Significance F			
12	Regression	1	2.559904152	2.559904152	20.6899446	1.40774E-05			
13	Residual	109	13.48623971	0.12372697					
14	Total	110	16.04614387						
15									
16		Coefficients	Standard Error	t Stat	P-value	Lower 95%	Upper 95%	Lower 95.0%	Upper 95.0%
17	Intercept	-0.290333367	0.039574792	-7.336320702	4.13476E-11	-0.368769316	-0.211897418	-0.368769316	-0.211897418
18	stormy	0.335262367	0.07370639	4.548620077	1.40774E-05	0.189178702	0.481346032	0.189178702	0.481346032

Insert a new worksheet by selecting the **Insert Worksheet** tab at the bottom of your screen. Rename it **F-test**.

In it copy the *F*-test template you created in Chapter 6.

Replace the following reference: **[POE Chapter 6.xlsx]Unrestricted Model** by **Fish Reduced Form Eq. for lnP**. Also delete references to **POE Chapter 6** attached to the **Restricted Model** references to obtain the following modified template:

	A	B	C
1	**Data Input**	J =	
2		N =	='Fish Reduced Form Eq. for lnP'!B8
3		K =	='Fish Reduced Form Eq. for lnP'!B12+1
4		SSE_U =	='Fish Reduced Form Eq. for lnP'!C13
5		SSE_R =	='Restricted Model'!C13

	A	B	C
6		α =	
7			
8	**Computed Values**	m_1 =	=C1
9		m_2 =	=C2-C3
10		F_c=	=FINV(C6,C8,C9)
11			
12	**F-test**	F-statistic=	=((C5-C4)/C8)/(C4/C9)
13		Conclusion =	=IF(C12>=C10,"Reject Ho","Do Not Reject Ho")
14		p-value =	=FDIST(C12,C8,C9)
15		Conclusion =	=IF(C14<=C6,"Reject Ho","Do Not Reject Ho")

With 4 restrictions, at $\alpha = 0.05$, the results of the *F*-test are (see also p. 460 of *Principles of Econometrics, 4e*):

	A	B	C
1	Data Input	J =	4
2		N =	111
3		K =	6
4		SSE_U =	13.17566
5		SSE_R =	13.48624
6		α =	0.05

	A	B	C	D
8	Computed Values	m_1 =	4	
9		m_2 =	105	
10		Fc =	2.45821	
11				
12	F-test	F-statistic =	0.618763	
13		Conclusion =	Do Not Reject Ho	
14		p-value =	0.65011	
15		Conclusion =	Do Not Reject Ho	

The joint *F*-test of significance of the daily dummy variables has *p*-value of 0.65 so that we cannot reject the null hypothesis that all these coefficients are zero.

This mean that, in this case, the supply equation is not identified in practice, and we will not report estimates for it in the next section (for more details, see Section 11.7.2 pp. 458-460 in *Principles of Econometrics, 4e*).

11.2.2 The Structural Equations or Stage 2 Least Squares Estimates

We obtain the predicted values $ln(\widehat{PRICE_t})$ from the estimated reduced form equation (11.12) and insert them in the structural demand equation (11.9) to replace the $ln(PRICE_t)$ values.

Then, we estimate the resulting equation (11.14) by least squares:

$$\text{Demand:} \quad ln(QUAN_t) = \begin{array}{c} \alpha_1 + \alpha_2 ln(\widehat{PRICE_t}) + \alpha_3 MON_t \\ +\alpha_4 TUE_t + \alpha_5 WED_t + \alpha_6 THU_t + e_t^d \end{array} \tag{11.14}$$

11.2.2a 2SLS Estimates for Fulton Fish Demand

Go back to your **fultonfish data** worksheet and enter the following labels and formulas.

	Q	R	S	T	U
1	**lnp-hat**	**mon**	**tue**	**wed**	**thu**
2	='Fish Reduced Form Eq. for lnP'!B29	=E2	=F2	=G2	=H2

Copy the content of cells **Q2:U2** to cells **Q3:U112**. Here is how your table should look (only the first five values are shown below):

	Q	R	S	T	U
1	**lnp-hat**	**mon**	**tue**	**wed**	**thu**
2	-0.03822	1	0	0	0
3	0.033551	0	1	0	0
4	-0.28353	0	0	1	0
5	0.124346	0	0	0	1
6	0.0747	0	0	0	0

In the **Regression** dialog box, the **Input Y Range** should be **D1:D112**, and the **Input X Range** should be **Q1:U112**. Check the box next to **Labels**. Select **New Worksheet Ply** and name it **Stage 2 LS Demand for Fish**. Finally select **OK**.

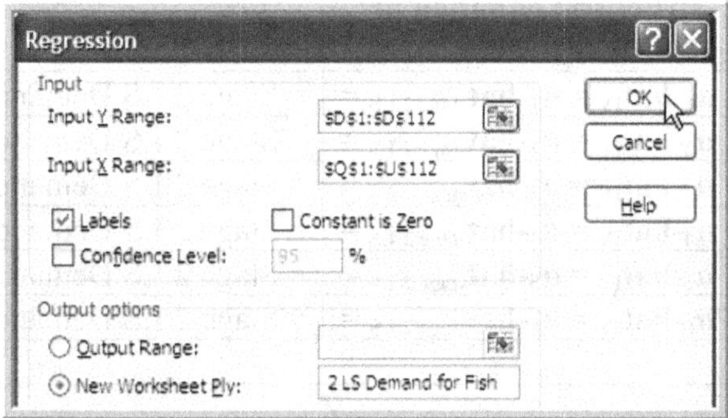

The result is (see also Table 11.5 on p. 460 in *Principles of Econometrics, 4e*):

	A	B	C	D	E	F	G	H	I
1	SUMMARY OUTPUT								
2									
3	*Regression Statistics*								
4	Multiple R	0.439740445							
5	R Square	0.193371659							
6	Adjusted R Square	0.154960786							
7	Standard Error	0.681789555							
8	Observations	111							
9									
10	ANOVA								
11		*df*	*SS*	*MS*	*F*	*Significance F*			
12	Regression	5	11.70063233	2.340126466	5.034294777	0.000356107			
13	Residual	105	48.80788468	0.464836997					
14	Total	110	60.50851701						
15									
16		*Coefficients*	*Standard Error*	*t Stat*	*P-value*	*Lower 95%*	*Upper 95%*	*Lower 95.0%*	*Upper 95.0%*
17	Intercept	8.505911279	0.160846266	52.88224267	1.66981E-77	8.186982854	8.824839703	8.186982854	8.824839703
18	lnp-hat	-1.11941679	0.414919848	-2.697910927	0.008131513	-1.942126178	-0.296707403	-1.942126178	-0.296707403
19	mon	-0.025402162	0.20780713	-0.122100211	0.902905096	-0.437623755	0.38681943	-0.437623755	0.38681943
20	tue	-0.530769415	0.201339958	-2.636185187	0.009655531	-0.929989347	-0.131549482	-0.929989347	-0.131549482
21	wed	-0.56635099	0.205942487	-2.750044429	0.007018196	-0.974696888	-0.158005092	-0.974696888	-0.158005092
22	thu	0.109267351	0.202101276	0.54065641	0.589889505	-0.291462135	0.509996836	-0.291462135	0.509996836

While using this two-stage least squares approach yields proper variables estimates, the accompanying standard errors are not correct. The correct standard error of the variable estimator of α_k is estimated using equations (10.4) and (10.5) restated below:

$$\widehat{se_{CORRECT}}(\hat{\alpha}_k) = \widehat{se_{IV}}(\hat{\alpha}_k) = \frac{\hat{\sigma}_{IV}}{\hat{\sigma}_{stage\ 2\ LS}} \widehat{se_{stage\ 2\ LS}}(\hat{\alpha}_k) \tag{10.4}$$

where $$\hat{\sigma}_{IV} = \sqrt{\frac{\sum \hat{e}_{IV}^2}{N-K}} \tag{10.5}$$

and $$\hat{e}_{IV} = \hat{e}_{IV}^d = \begin{array}{l} ln(QUAN_t) - \hat{\alpha}_1 - \hat{\alpha}_2 ln(PRICE_t) - \hat{\alpha}_3 MON_t \\ - \hat{\alpha}_4 TUE_t - \hat{\alpha}_5 WED_t - \hat{\alpha}_6 THU_t \end{array} \tag{11.15}$$

where $\hat{\alpha}_1$, $\hat{\alpha}_2$, $\hat{\alpha}_3$, $\hat{\alpha}_4$, $\hat{\alpha}_5$ and $\hat{\alpha}_6$ are the least squares estimates from equation (11.14).

Go back to your **fultonfish data** worksheet and enter the following labels and formulas. In the last column, you will find the numbers of the equations used, if any.

	W	X
1	**Demand for Fish, structural equation or IV estimates using 2 SLS**	
2	**α_1-hat$_{IV}$ = α_1-hat$_{stage\ 2\ LS}$ =**	='Stage 2 LS Demand for Fish'!B17
3	**α_2-hat$_{IV}$ = α_2-hat$_{stage\ 2\ LS}$ =**	='Stage 2 LS Demand for Fish'!B18
4	**α_3-hat$_{IV}$ = α_3-hat$_{stage\ 2\ LS}$ =**	='Stage 2 LS Demand for Fish'!B19
5	**α_4-hat$_{IV}$ = α_4-hat$_{stage\ 2\ LS}$ =**	='Stage 2 LS Demand for Fish'!B20
6	**α_5-hat$_{IV}$ = α_5-hat$_{stage\ 2\ LS}$ =**	='Stage 2 LS Demand for Fish'!B21
7	**α_6-hat$_{IV}$ = α_6-hat$_{stage\ 2\ LS}$ =**	='Stage 2 LS Demand for Fish'!B22

	Z
1	**e-hat$_{IV}^2$**
2	=(D2-$X$2-$X$3*B2-$X$4*E2-$X$5*F2-$X$6*G2-$X$7*H2)^2

Copy the content of cell **Z2** to cells **Z3:Z112**.

	W	X	
9	**N =**	='Stage 2 LS Demand for Fish'!B8	
10	**K =**	='Stage 2 LS Demand for Fish'!B12+1	
11	**σ-hat$_{stage\ 2\ LS}$ =**	='Stage 2 LS Demand for Fish'!B7	
12	**se(α_1-hat)$_{stage\ 2\ LS}$ =**	='Stage 2 LS Demand for Fish'!C17	
13	**se(α_2-hat)$_{stage\ 2\ LS}$ =**	='Stage 2 LS Demand for Fish'!C18	
14	**se(α_3-hat)$_{stage\ 2\ LS}$ =**	='Stage 2 LS Demand for Fish'!C19	
15	**se(α_4-hat)$_{stage\ 2\ LS}$ =**	='Stage 2 LS Demand for Fish'!C20	
16	**se(α_5-hat)$_{stage\ 2\ LS}$ =**	='Stage 2 LS Demand for Fish'!C21	
17	**se(α_6-hat)$_{stage\ 2\ LS}$ =**	='Stage 2 LS Demand for Fish'!C22	
18	**σ-hat$_{IV}$ =**	=SQRT(SUM(Z2:Z112)/(X9-X10))	*(10.5)*
19	**se(α_1-hat)$_{IV}$ =**	=(X18/X11)*X12	*(10.4)*
20	**se(α_2-hat)$_{IV}$ =**	=(X18/X11)*X13	*(10.4)*
21	**se(α_3-hat)$_{IV}$ =**	=(X18/X11)*X14	*(10.4)*
22	**se(α_4-hat)$_{IV}$ =**	=(X18/X11)*X15	*(10.4)*
23	**se(α_5-hat)$_{IV}$ =**	=(X18/X11)*X16	*(10.4)*
24	**se(α_6-hat)$_{IV}$ =**	=(X18/X11)*X17	*(10.4)*

The result is (see also standard errors estimates in Table 11.5 on p. 460 of *Principles of Econometrics*, *4e*):

	W	X	Y	Z
1	**Demand for Fish, structural equation or IV estimates using 2 SLS**			**e-hat$_{IV}^2$**
2	**α_1-hat$_{IV}$ = α_1-hat$_{stage\ 2\ LS}$ =**	8.505911		0.001004
3	**α_2-hat$_{IV}$ = α_2-hat$_{stage\ 2\ LS}$ =**	-1.11942		0.071866
4	**α_3-hat$_{IV}$ = α_3-hat$_{stage\ 2\ LS}$ =**	-0.0254		0.241662
5	**α_4-hat$_{IV}$ = α_4-hat$_{stage\ 2\ LS}$ =**	-0.53077		0.101396
6	**α_5-hat$_{IV}$ = α_5-hat$_{stage\ 2\ LS}$ =**	-0.56635		0.006722
7	**α_6-hat$_{IV}$ = α_6-hat$_{stage\ 2\ LS}$ =**	0.109267		0.347619
8				0.665611
9	**N =**	111		0.766534
10	**K =**	6		0.192356
11	**σ-hat$_{stage\ 2\ LS}$ =**	0.68179		0.10285
12	**se(α_1-hat)$_{stage\ 2\ LS}$ =**	0.160846		0.004693
13	**se(α_2-hat)$_{stage\ 2\ LS}$ =**	0.41492		0.334898
14	**se(α_3-hat)$_{stage\ 2\ LS}$ =**	0.207897		0.715987
15	**se(α_4-hat)$_{stage\ 2\ LS}$ =**	0.20134		0.502584
16	**se(α_6-hat)$_{stage\ 2\ LS}$ =**	0.205942		0.186604
17	**se(α_5-hat)$_{stage\ 2\ LS}$ =**	0.202101		0.328638
18	**σ-hat$_{IV}$ =**	0.704342		0.00283
19	**se(α_1-hat)$_{IV}$ =**	0.166167		2.762907
20	**se(α_2-hat)$_{IV}$ =**	0.428645		0.323631
21	**se(α_3-hat)$_{IV}$ =**	0.214774		1.000532
22	**se(α_4-hat)$_{IV}$ =**	0.208		0.305589
23	**se(α_5-hat)$_{IV}$ =**	0.212755		0.002431
24	**se(α_6-hat)$_{IV}$ =**	0.208787		0.522244

CHAPTER 12

Nonstationary Time-Series Data and Cointegration

CHAPTER OUTLINE

12.1 STATIONARY AND NONSTATIONARY VARIABLES

12.1.1 US Economic Time Series

Open the Excel file ***usa***. Save your file as **POE Chapter 12**. Rename sheet 1 **usa data**.

Below we plot the time series of some important economic variables for the US economy as in Figure 12.1 on p. 476 of *Principles of Econometrics, 4e*.

In cells **E2:H3**, enter the following labels and formulas.

	E	F	G	H
2	**Δgdp**	**Δinf**	**ΔF**	**ΔB**
3	=A3-A2	=B3-B2	=C3-C2	D3-D2

Copy the content of cells **E3:H3** to cells **E4:H105**. Here is how your table should look (only the first five values are shown below):

	E	F	G	H
2	Δgdp	Δinf	ΔF	ΔB
3	98.9	0.56	0.87	1.45
4	69.7	0.8	0.83	0
5	58	0.68	-2.12	-1.54
6	83.2	-1	-0.79	-0.42
7	58.5	-1.27	-0.56	-0.92

Select the **Insert** tab located next to the **Home** tab. Select **A1:A105**. In the **Charts** group of commands select **Line**, and **Line** again.

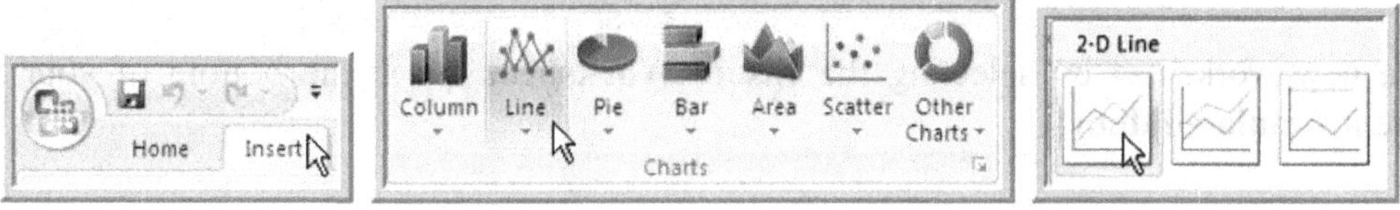

After editing, the result is (see also Figure 12.1(a) p. 476 in *Principles of Econometrics, 4e*):

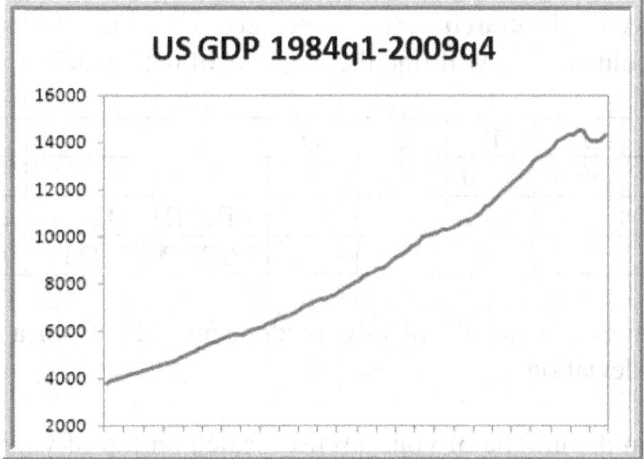

To plot the change in the US GDP series select cells **E2:E105**. After editing, the result is (see also Figure 12.1(b) p. 476 in *Principles of Econometrics, 4e*):

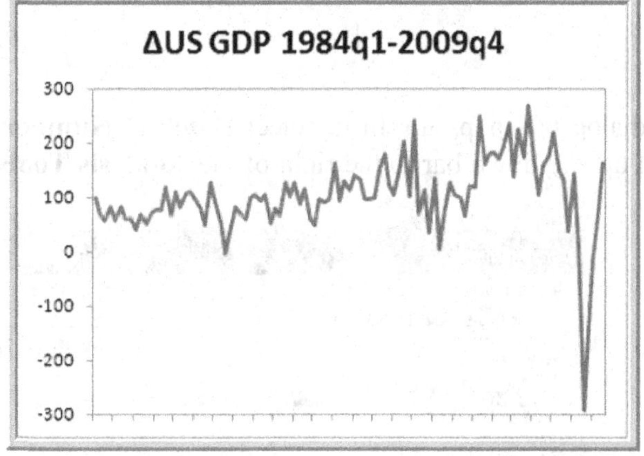

You can proceed similarly to replicate any of the other plots from Figure 12.1 p. 476 of *Principles of Econometrics, 4e*.

12.1.2 Simulated Data

Consider the following autoregressive model of order 1 (AR(1) model):

$$y_t = \rho y_{t-1} + v_t \tag{12.1}$$

where $\rho = 0.7$ and v_t are independent $N(0, 1)$ random errors.

Below, we generate our v_t and y_t values, similarly to the way we generated random samples in Sections 6.6.2, 3.1.4 and 2.4.4.

Insert a new worksheet by selecting the **Insert Worksheet** tab at the bottom of your screen. Rename it **simulated data**.

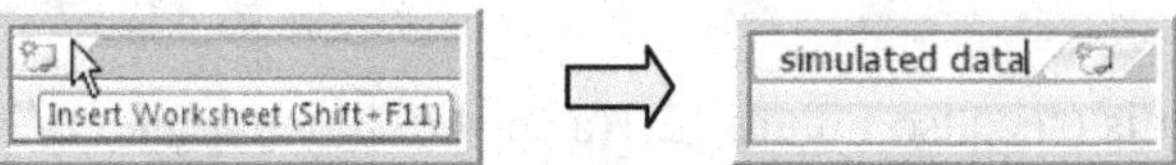

In cells **A1:E3** of your **simulated data** worksheet, enter the following labels, values and formulas. In the last column, you will find the numbers of the equations used, if any.

	A	B	C	D	E	
1	**y_0 =**	0		**v_t**	**y_t**	
2	**ρ =**	0.7			=B2*B1+D2	*(12.1)*
3					=$B$2*E2+D3	*(12.1)*

In column **D**, we generate a sample of 500 random numbers from a normal distribution with mean 0 and standard deviation 1.

Select the **Data** tab, in the middle of your tab list located on top of your screen. On the **Analysis** group of commands, to the far right, select **Data Analysis**.

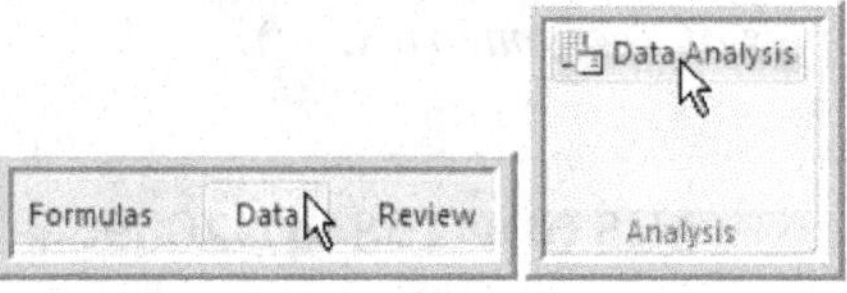

The **Data Analysis** dialog box pops up. In it, select **Random Number Generation** (you might need to use the scroll up and down bar to the right of the **Analysis Tools** window to find it), then select **OK**.

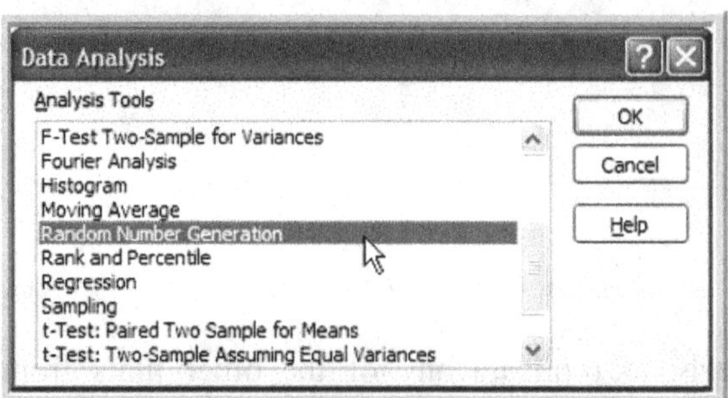

A **Random Number Generation** dialog box pops up. We need to generate one set of random numbers for our random errors, so we specify **1** in the **Number of Variables** window. We would like to generate 500 random numbers, so we specify **500** in the **Number of Random Numbers** window. We select **Normal** in the **Distribution** window; the selected **Parameters** should be **Mean** equal to **0**, and **Standard deviation** equal to **1**. Select **Output Range** and specify it to be **D2:D501**. Finally, select **OK.**

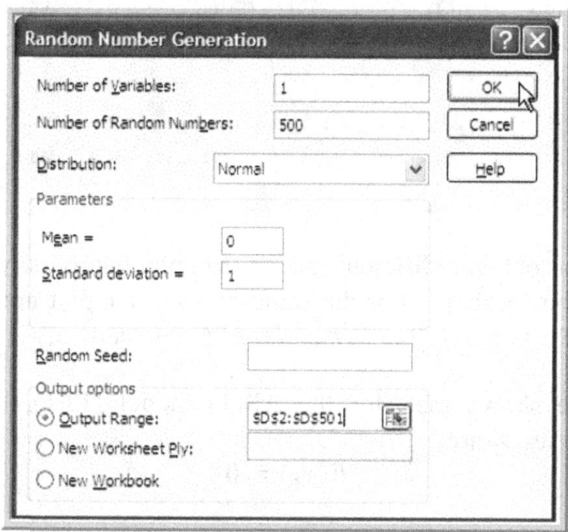

After you copy the content of cell **E3** to cells **E4:E501**, here is how your table should look (only the first five values are shown below):

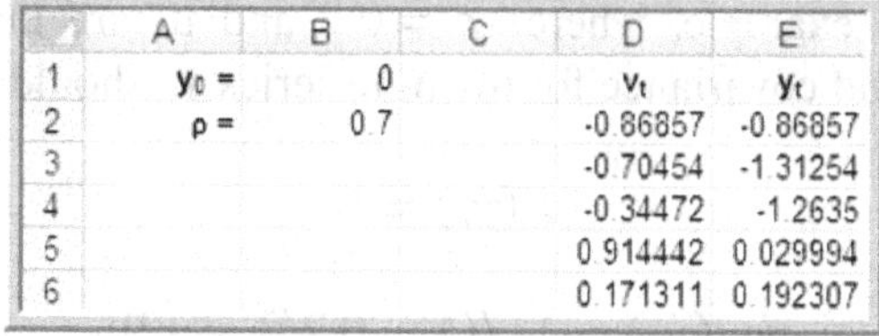

	A	B	C	D	E
1	y_0 =	0		v_t	y_t
2	ρ =	0.7		-0.86857	-0.86857
3				-0.70454	-1.31254
4				-0.34472	-1.2635
5				0.914442	0.029994
6				0.171311	0.192307

Note: you will obtain a different random sample than the one we obtained, so your v_t and y_t values should be slightly different than the ones reported above.

Select the **Insert** tab located next to the **Home** tab. Select **E1:E501**. In the **Charts** group of commands select **Line**, and **Line** again.

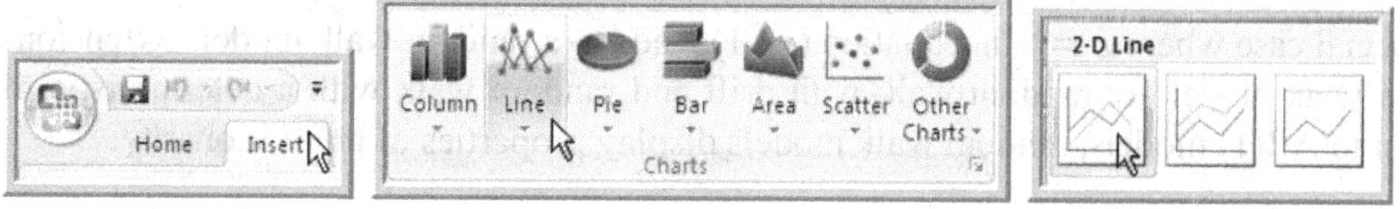

After editing, the result is (see also Figure 12.2(a) p. 479 in *Principles of Econometrics, 4e*):

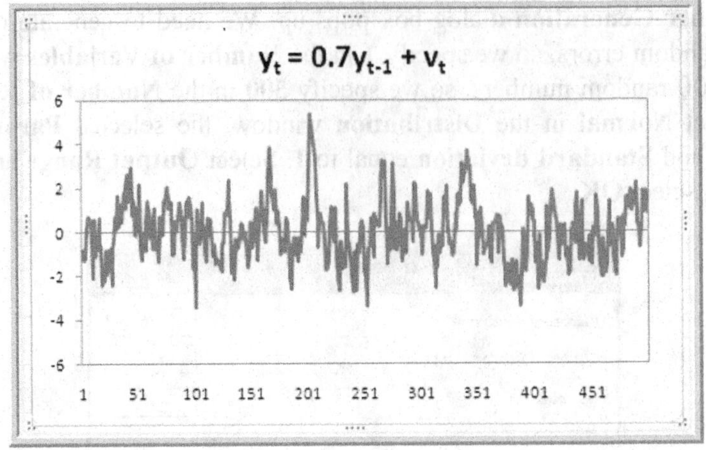

Again note that since you obtain a different random sample than ours, your plot will be slightly different than the one shown above. For the same reason, our plot and yours are also slightly different than Figure 12.2(a) on p. 479 of *Principles of Econometrics, 4e*.

Algebraically, it can be shown that, for the AR(1) model (12.1), the mean, variance and covariance of the time series y_t are:

$$E(y_t) = 0 \tag{12.2}$$

$$var(y_t) = \sigma_v^2/(1-\rho^2) \tag{12.3}$$

$$cov(y_t, y_{t+s}) = \sigma_v^2\rho^s/(1-\rho^2) \tag{12.4}$$

Let $s = 3$. For our specific example, where $\rho = 0.7$ and v_t are independent $N(0,1)$ random errors, the mean, variance and covariance for the time series y_t should then be:

$$E(y_t) = 0 \tag{12.5}$$

$$var(y_t) = 1^2/(1-0.7^2) = 1.96 \tag{12.6}$$

$$cov(y_t, y_{t+3}) = 1^2 0.7^3/(1-0.7^2) = 0.67 \tag{12.7}$$

The AR(1) model in (12.1) is a classic example of a stationary process with a zero mean. AR(1) models fluctuating around a nonzero mean and AR(1) models fluctuating around a linear trend are extensions to (12.1).

The special case where $\rho = 1$ in equation (12.1) leads to a random walk model. Extensions of the random walk model are random walk with drift and random walk with a deterministic trend. In contrast to AR(1) models, random walk models display properties of nonstationarity.

Examples of all those models are illustrated in Figures 12.2(b)-(f) on p. 479 of *Principles of Econometrics, 4e*. You too can consider all those additional models by proceeding as we did above.

12.2 SPURIOUS REGRESSIONS

Two independent random walks series, rw_1 and rw_2, were generated similarly to the way we generated our AR(1) time series in Section 12.1.2. The data set is named ***spurious***.

Open the Excel file ***spurious***. Excel opens the data set in Sheet 1 of a new Excel file. Since we would like to save all our work from Chapter 12 in one file, create a new worksheet in your **POE Chapter 12** Excel file, rename it **spurious data**, and in it, copy the data set you just opened.

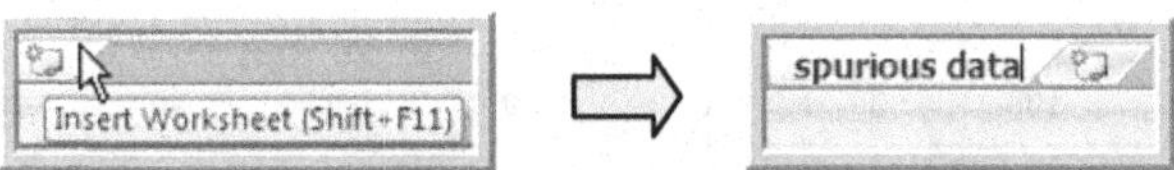

Select the **Insert** tab located next to the **Home** tab. Select **A1:B701**. In the **Charts** group of commands select **Line**, and **Line** again.

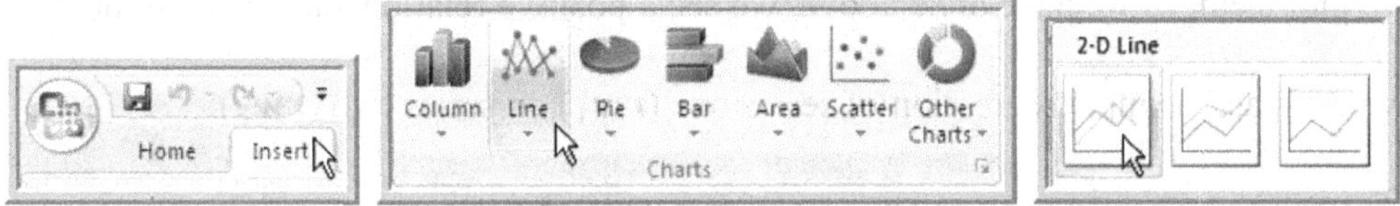

After editing, the result is (see also Figure 12.3(a) p. 483 in *Principles of Econometrics, 4e*):

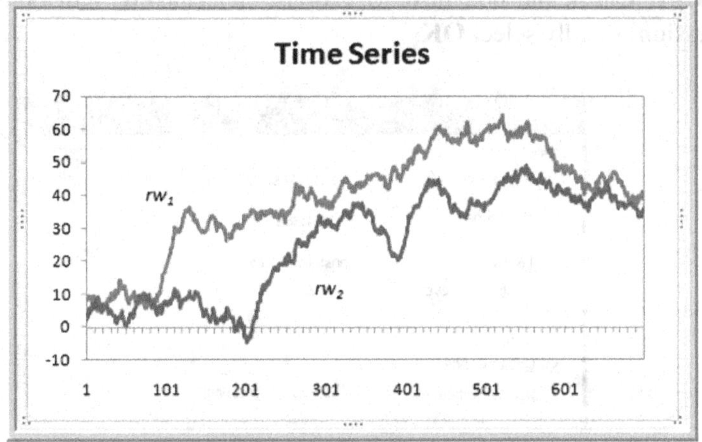

Select the **Insert** tab located next to the **Home** tab. Select **A1:B701**. <u>*This time*</u>, in the **Charts** group of commands select **Scatter**, and **Scatter with only Markers**.

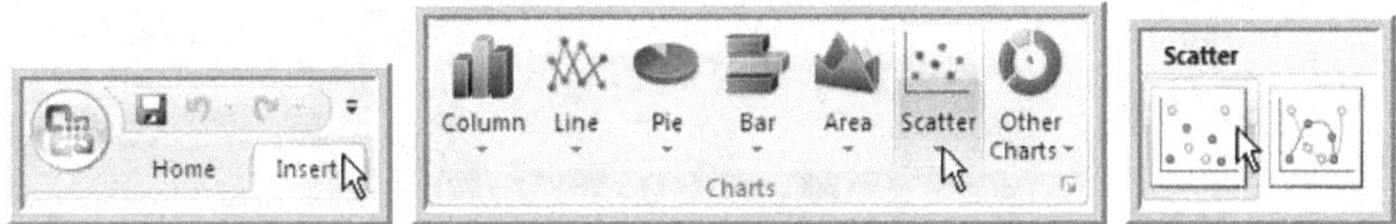

After editing (refer back to Section 2.1 if needed), the result is (see also Figure 12.3(b) p. 483 in *Principles of Econometrics, 4e*):

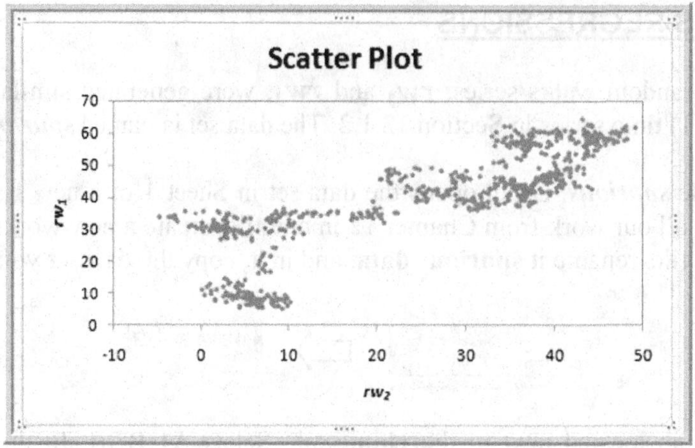

These time series were generated independently and, in truth, have no relation to one another, yet when we plot them, as we have done above, we see a positive relationship between them.

Next, we estimate a simple regression of series one ($\boldsymbol{rw_1}$) on series two ($\boldsymbol{rw_2}$):

$$rw_{1t} = \beta_1 + \beta_2 rw_{2t} + e_t \tag{12.8}$$

In the **Regression** dialog box, the **Input Y Range** should be **A1:A701**, and the **Input X Range** should be **B1:B701**. Check the box next to **Labels**. Select **New Worksheet Ply** and name it **Spurious Regression**. Finally select **OK**.

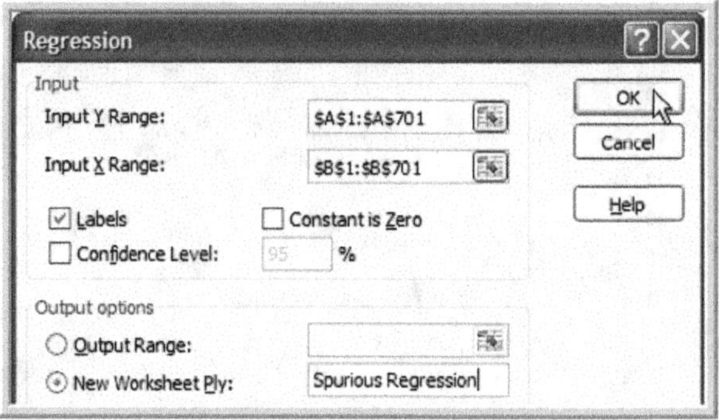

The result is (see also p. 482 in *Principles of Econometrics, 4e*):

	A	B	C	D	E	F	G	H	I
1	SUMMARY OUTPUT								
2									
3	*Regression Statistics*								
4	Multiple R	0.83960906							
5	R Square	0.704943374							
6	Adjusted R Square	0.704520657							
7	Standard Error	8.557267989							
8	Observations	700							
9									
10	ANOVA								
11		*df*	*SS*	*MS*	*F*	*Significance F*			
12	Regression	1	122116.5568	122116.5568	1667.647606	3.5686E-187			
13	Residual	698	51112.33113	73.22683543					
14	Total	699	173228.8879						
15									
16		*Coefficients*	*Standard Error*	*t Stat*	*P-value*	*Lower 95%*	*Upper 95%*	*Lower 95.0%*	*Upper 95.0%*
17	Intercept	17.81804111	0.620477603	28.71665477	2.4603E-120	16.59981498	19.03626723	16.59981498	19.03626723
18	rw2	0.84204116	0.020619645	40.83684128	3.5686E-187	0.801557201	0.88252512	0.801557201	0.88252512

This result suggests that the simple linear regression model fits the data well ($R^2 = 0.70$), and the estimated slope is highly significant (tiny p-value). These results are, however, completely meaningless, or spurious. The apparent significance of the relationship is false.

12.3 UNIT ROOT TESTS FOR STATIONARITY

The Federal Funds rate (F_t) and the 3-year Bond rate (B_t) series exhibit wandering behavior, so we suspect that they may be nonstationary variables. In addition, the series fluctuate around a nonzero mean, so the appropriate Dickey-Fuller test equation is the one that includes a constant term. Finally, following the procedures described in Sections 9.3 and 9.4 of *Principles of Econometrics, 4e*, we find that the inclusion of one lagged difference term is sufficient to eliminate autocorrelation in the residuals in both cases. The extended test equations are thus as follows:

$$\Delta F_t = \alpha + \gamma F_{t-1} + a_1 \Delta F_{t-1} + v_t \tag{12.9}$$

where $\Delta F_t = F_t - F_{t-1}$ and $\Delta F_{t-1} = F_{t-1} - F_{t-2}$.

$$\Delta B_t = \alpha + \gamma B_{t-1} + a_1 \Delta B_{t-1} + v_t \tag{12.10}$$

where $\Delta B_t = B_t - B_{t-1}$ and $\Delta B_{t-1} = B_{t-1} - B_{t-2}$.

The null and alternative hypotheses of the unit root test for stationarity are:

$$H_0: \gamma = 0$$

$$H_1: \gamma < 0$$

where the null hypothesis is that the series is nonstationary.

Go back to your **usa data** worksheet. In cells **J3:P4** enter the following labels and formulas.

	J	K	L	M	N	O	P
3	ΔF_t	F_{t-1}	ΔF_{t-1}		ΔB_t	B_{t-1}	ΔB_{t-1}
4	=C4-C3	=C3	=C3-C2		=D4-D3	=D3	=D3-D2

Copy the content of cells **J4:L4** to cells **J5:L105**, and the content of cells **N4:P4** to cells **N5:N105**. Here is how your table should look (only the first five values are shown below):

	J	K	L	M	N	O	P
3	ΔF_t	F_{t-1}	ΔF_{t-1}		ΔB_t	B_{t-1}	ΔB_{t-1}
4	0.83	10.56	0.87		0	12.64	1.45
5	-2.12	11.39	0.83		-1.54	12.64	0
6	-0.79	9.27	-2.12		-0.42	11.1	-1.54
7	-0.56	8.48	-0.79		-0.92	10.68	-0.42
8	-0.02	7.92	-0.56		-0.47	9.76	-0.92

In the **Regression** dialog box, the **Input Y Range** should be **J3:J105**, and the **Input X Range** should be **K3:L105**. Check the box next to **Labels**. Select **New Worksheet Ply** and name it **Dickey-Fuller Test for F**. Finally select **OK**.

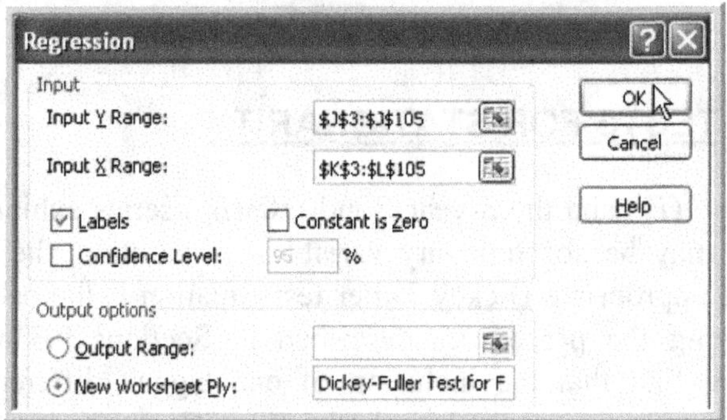

The result of estimated equation (12.9) is (see also p. 487 in *Principles of Econometrics, 4e*):

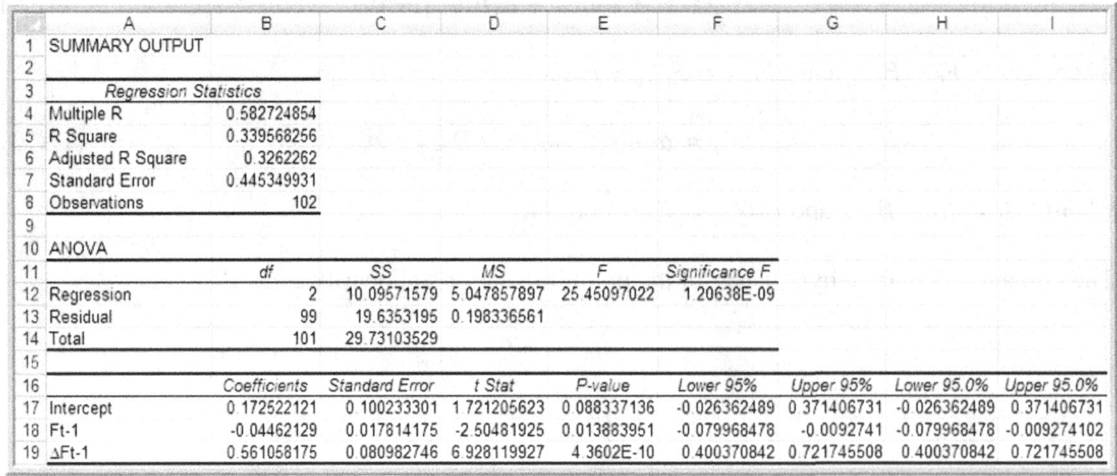

SUMMARY OUTPUT

Regression Statistics	
Multiple R	0.582724854
R Square	0.339568256
Adjusted R Square	0.3262262
Standard Error	0.445349931
Observations	102

ANOVA

	df	*SS*	*MS*	*F*	*Significance F*
Regression	2	10.09571579	5.047857897	25.45097022	1.20638E-09
Residual	99	19.6353195	0.198336561		
Total	101	29.73103529			

	Coefficients	*Standard Error*	*t Stat*	*P-value*	*Lower 95%*	*Upper 95%*	*Lower 95.0%*	*Upper 95.0%*
Intercept	0.172522121	0.100233301	1.721205623	0.088337136	-0.026362489	0.371406731	-0.026362489	0.371406731
Ft-1	-0.04462129	0.017814175	-2.50481925	0.013883951	-0.079968478	-0.0092741	-0.079968478	-0.009274102
ΔFt-1	0.561058175	0.080982746	6.928119927	4.3602E-10	0.400370842	0.721745508	0.400370842	0.721745508

The t-statistic (also referred to as τ-statistic in the context of a Dickey-Fuller testing procedure—for more details on that refer to Section 12.3 of *Principles of Econometrics, 4e*) is −2.505, and the 5% critical value for *tau*, τ_c, is −2.86 (value found in Table 12.2 on p. 486 of *Principles of*

Econometrics, 4e). In this case since $-2.505 > -2.86$, we do not reject the null hypothesis that the series is nonstationary. In other words, there is insufficient evidence to suggest that F_t is stationary.

Go back to your **usa data** worksheet.

In the **Regression** dialog box, the **Input Y Range** should be **N3:N105**, and the **Input X Range** should be **O3:P105**. Check the box next to **Labels**. Select **New Worksheet Ply** and name it **Dickey-Fuller Test for B**. Finally select **OK**.

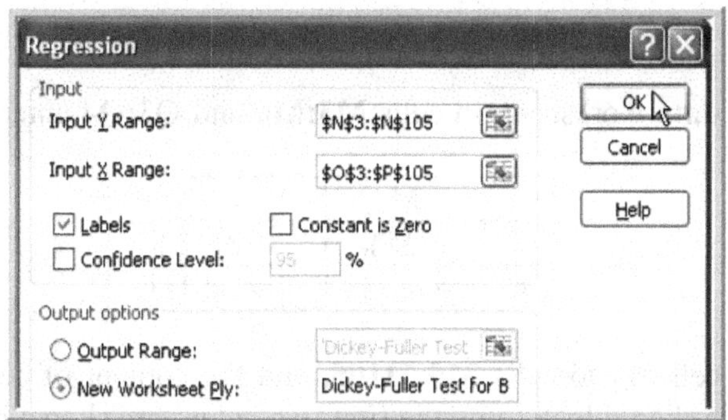

The result of estimated equation (12.10) is (see also p. 487 in *Principles of Econometrics, 4e*):

	A	B	C	D	E	F	G	H	I
1	SUMMARY OUTPUT								
2									
3	*Regression Statistics*								
4	Multiple R	0.379402286							
5	R Square	0.143946095							
6	Adjusted R Square	0.126652077							
7	Standard Error	0.502618036							
8	Observations	102							
9									
10	ANOVA								
11		*df*	*SS*	*MS*	*F*	*Significance F*			
12	Regression	2	4.205427073	2.102713537	8.323461466	0.000455832			
13	Residual	99	25.0098641	0.25262489					
14	Total	101	29.21529118						
15									
16		*Coefficients*	*Standard Error*	*t Stat*	*P-value*	*Lower 95%*	*Upper 95%*	*Lower 95.0%*	*Upper 95.0%*
17	Intercept	0.23687297	0.129173089	1.833764081	0.069693252	-0.019434455	0.493180396	-0.01943446	0.493180396
18	Bt-1	-0.056241169	0.020808115	-2.702847917	0.008091462	-0.097528982	-0.01495336	-0.09752898	-0.014953357
19	ΔBt-1	0.290307786	0.089606852	3.239794507	0.001629198	0.112508357	0.468107216	0.112508357	0.468107216

The *t*-statistic (also referred to as τ-statistic in the context of a Dickey-Fuller testing procedure) is -2.703, and the 5% critical value for *tau*, τ_c, is -2.86 (value found in Table 12.2 on p. 486 of *Principles of Econometrics, 4e*). In this case again, since $-2.703 > -2.86$, we do not reject the null hypothesis that the series is nonstationary. In other words, there is insufficient evidence to suggest that B_t is stationary.

Since we found insufficient evidence to suggest that F_t and B_t are stationary, we are interested to determine whether these series can be made stationary by taking their first difference. If we can establish that this is the case, then these series would be integrated of order 1, or I(1). In general, the order of integration of a series is the minimum number of times it must be differenced to make it stationary.

Because the series ΔF_t and ΔG_t appear to fluctuate around zero, to test the first difference of the Federal Funds rate ($\Delta F_t = F_t - F_{t-1}$) and the first difference of the Bond rate ($\Delta B_t = B_t - B_{t-1}$) for stationarity, we use the following test equations:

$$\Delta(\Delta F_t) = \gamma \Delta F_{t-1} + v_t \qquad (12.11)$$

where $\Delta(\Delta F_t) = \Delta F_t - \Delta F_{t-1}$ and $\Delta F_t = F_t - F_{t-1}$.

$$\Delta(\Delta B_t) = \gamma \Delta B_{t-1} + v_t \qquad (12.12)$$

where $\Delta(\Delta B_t) = \Delta B_t - \Delta B_{t-1}$ and $\Delta B_t = B_t - B_{t-1}$.

Go back to your **usa data** worksheet. In cells **M3:M4** and **Q3:Q4** enter the following labels and formulas.

	M	Q
3	**Δ(ΔF)ₜ**	**Δ(ΔB)ₜ**
4	=G4-G3	=H4-H3

Copy the content of cell **M4** to cells **M5:M105**, and the content of cell **Q4** to cells **Q5:Q105**. Here is how your table should look (only the first five values are shown below):

	M
3	Δ(ΔF)ₜ
4	-0.04
5	-2.95
6	1.33
7	0.23
8	0.54

	Q
3	Δ(ΔB)ₜ
4	-1.45
5	-1.54
6	1.12
7	-0.5
8	0.45

In the **Regression** dialog box, the **Input Y Range** should be **M3:M105**, and the **Input X Range** should be **L3:L105**. Check the boxes next to **Labels** *and* ***Constant is Zero***. Select **New Worksheet Ply** and name it **Dickey-Fuller Test for changeF**. Finally select **OK**.

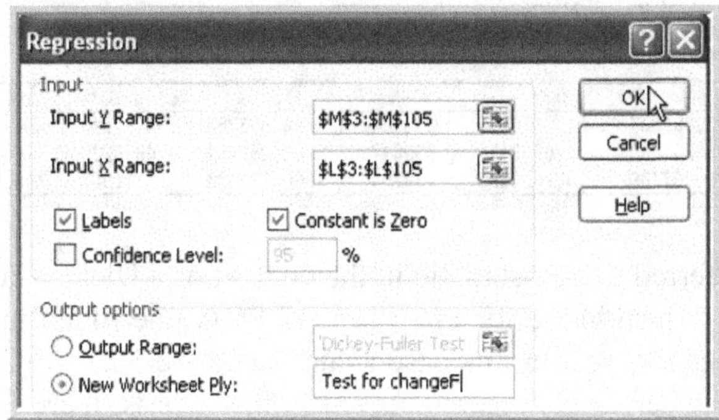

The result of estimated equation (12.11) is (see also p. 488 in *Principles of Econometrics, 4e*):

	A	B	C	D	E	F	G	H	I
1	SUMMARY OUTPUT								
2									
3	*Regression Statistics*								
4	Multiple R	0.47920942							
5	R Square	0.229641668							
6	Adjusted R Square	0.219740678							
7	Standard Error	0.457601805							
8	Observations	102							
9									
10	ANOVA								
11		*df*	*SS*	*MS*	*F*	*Significance F*			
12	Regression	1	6.304559392	6.304559392	30.10781804	3.09269E-07			
13	Residual	101	21.14934061	0.209399412					
14	Total	102	27.4539						
15									
16		*Coefficients*	*Standard Error*	*t Stat*	*P-value*	*Lower 95%*	*Upper 95%*	*Lower 95.0%*	*Upper 95.0%*
17	Intercept	0	#N/A	#N/A	#N/A	#N/A	#N/A	#N/A	#N/A
18	ΔFt-1	-0.446986047	0.081461861	-5.487059143	3.0409E-07	-0.60858446	-0.285387633	-0.60858446	-0.285387633

The *t*-statistic (also referred to as τ-statistic in the context of a Dickey-Fuller testing procedure) is -5.487, and the 5% critical value for *tau*, τ_c, is -1.94 (value found in Table 12.2 on p. 486 of *Principles of Econometrics, 4e*). In this case since $-5.487 < -1.94$, we do reject the null hypothesis that the series ΔF_t is nonstationary and accept the alternative that it is stationary.

Go back to your **usa data** worksheet.

In the **Regression** dialog box, the **Input Y Range** should be **Q3:Q105**, and the **Input X Range** should be **P3:P105**. Check the boxes next to **Labels** *and* **Constant is Zero**. Select **New Worksheet Ply** and name it **Dickey-Fuller Test for changeB**. Finally select **OK**.

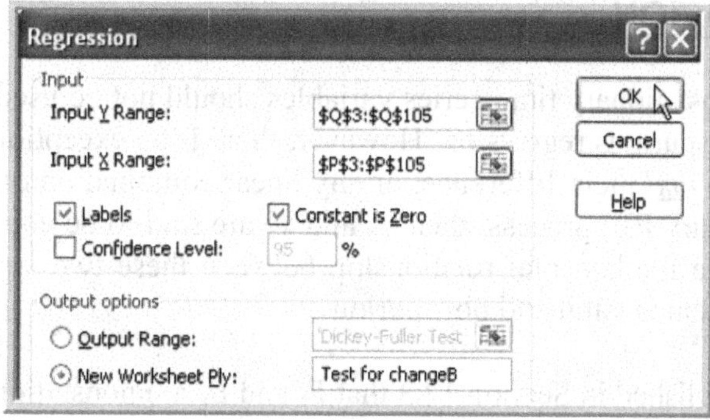

The result of estimated equation (12.12) is (see also p. 488 in *Principles of Econometrics, 4e*):

	A	B	C	D	E	F	G	H	I
1	SUMMARY OUTPUT								
2									
3	*Regression Statistics*								
4	Multiple R	0.606293811							
5	R Square	0.367592185							
6	Adjusted R Square	0.357691195							
7	Standard Error	0.522402752							
8	Observations	102							
9									
10	ANOVA								
11		*df*	*SS*	*MS*	*F*	*Significance F*			
12	Regression	1	16.02143188	16.02143188	58.70707139	1.20231E-11			
13	Residual	101	27.56336812	0.272904635					
14	Total	102	43.5848						
15									
16		*Coefficients*	*Standard Error*	*t Stat*	*P-value*	*Lower 95%*	*Upper 95%*	*Lower 95.0%*	*Upper 95.0%*
17	Intercept	0	#N/A	#N/A	#N/A	#N/A	#N/A	#N/A	#N/A
18	ΔBt-1	-0.70179559	0.091593663	-7.662053993	1.14657E-11	-0.883492774	-0.520098406	-0.883492774	-0.520098406

The *t*-statistic (also referred to as τ-statistic in the context of a Dickey-Fuller testing procedure) is -7.662, and the 5% critical value for *tau*, $\tau_{c,}$ is -1.94 (value found in Table 12.2 on p. 486 of *Principles of Econometrics, 4e*). In this case since $-7.662 < -1.94$, we do reject the null hypothesis that the series ΔB_t is nonstationary and accept the alternative that it is stationary.

These results imply that while the Federal Funds rate (F_t) and the Bond rate (B_t) are nonstationary, their first differences, ΔF_t and ΔB_t , are stationary. We say that the series F_t and B_t are integrated of order 1, I(1).

12.4 COINTEGRATION

As a general rule, nonstationary time-series variables should not be used in regression models, to avoid the problem of spurious regression. However, there is an exception to this rule. If y_t and x_t are nonstationary I(1) *and* their difference, or any linear combination of them, such as $e_t = y_t - \beta_1 - \beta_2 x_t$ is a stationary I(0) process, then y_t and x_t are said to be cointegrated. In other words, in this case, there is a fundamental relationship between these two variables, and an estimated regression between them is valid and not spurious.

We have already established in Section 12.3 that F_t and B_t are nonstationary. Now, we would like to test whether these series are cointegrated. The test for cointegration is a test of the stationarity of the residuals $\hat{e}_t = B_t - b_1 - b_2 F_t$, where b_1 and b_2 are the least squares estimates of the regression of B_t on F_t.

Below we first estimate the regression of B_t on F_t:

$$B_t = \beta_1 + \beta_2 F_t + e_t \tag{12.13}$$

Go back to your **usa data** worksheet.

In the **Regression** dialog box, the **Input Y Range** should be **D1:D105**, and the **Input X Range** should be **C1:C105**. Check the boxes next to **Labels** and **Residuals**; *uncheck* the box next to **Constant is Zero**. Select **New Worksheet Ply** and name it **Regression of B on F**. Finally select **OK**.

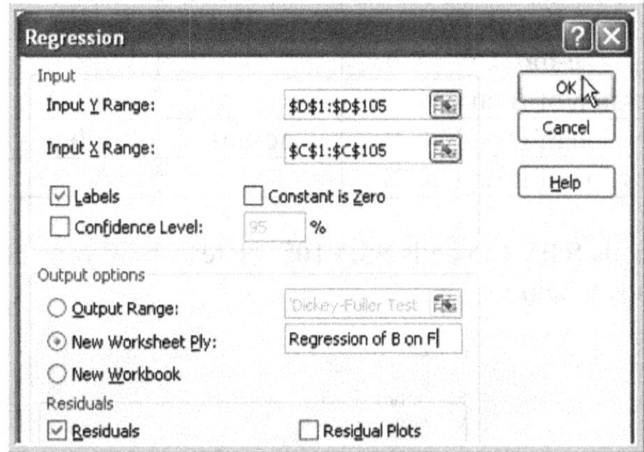

The result of estimated equation (12.13) is (see also p. 489 in *Principles of Econometrics, 4e*):

	A	B	C	D	E	F	G	H	I
1	SUMMARY OUTPUT								
2									
3	*Regression Statistics*								
4	Multiple R	0.945824892							
5	R Square	0.894584726							
6	Adjusted R Square	0.893551243							
7	Standard Error	0.810180169							
8	Observations	104							
9									
10	ANOVA								
11		*df*	*SS*	*MS*	*F*	*Significance F*			
12	Regression	1	568.1739601	568.1739601	865.6017148	1.22562E-51			
13	Residual	102	66.95197449	0.656391907					
14	Total	103	635.1259346						
15									
16		*Coefficients*	*Standard Error*	*t Stat*	*P-value*	*Lower 95%*	*Upper 95%*	*Lower 95.0%*	*Upper 95.0%*
17	Intercept	1.139829659	0.174083328	6.547609544	2.39926E-09	0.794536213	1.485123105	0.794536213	1.485123105
18	F	0.914411397	0.031080112	29.42111002	1.22562E-51	0.852764144	0.976058651	0.852764144	0.976058651
19									
20									
21									
22	RESIDUAL OUTPUT								
23									
24	*Observation*	*Predicted B*	*Residuals*						
25	1	10.0004761	1.189523901						
26	2	10.79601401	1.843985985						
27	3	11.55497547	1.085024526						

The test for stationarity of the residuals is based on the test equation (12.14) which follows. This is the augmented Dickey-Fuller version of the test equation (12.7) found on p. 489 of *Principles of Econometrics, 4e*. It includes one lagged term Δe_{t-1} to correct for autocorrelation.

$$\Delta\hat{e}_t = \gamma\hat{e}_{t-1} + a_1\Delta\hat{e}_{t-1} + v_t \tag{12.14}$$

where $\Delta\hat{e}_t = \hat{e}_t - \hat{e}_{t-1}$ and $\Delta\hat{e}_{t-1} = \hat{e}_{t-1} - \hat{e}_{t-2}$.

Go back to your **usa data** worksheet.

In cells **S1:V4** enter the following labels and formulas.

	S	T	U	V
1	**e-hat$_t$**			
2	='Regression of B on F'!C25			
3	='Regression of B on F'!C26	**Δe-hat$_t$**	**e-hat$_{t-1}$**	**Δe-hat$_{t-1}$**
4	='Regression of B on F'!C27	=S4-S3	=S3	=S3-S2

Copy the content of cells **S4:V4** to cells **S5:V105**. Here is how your table should look (only the first five values are shown below):

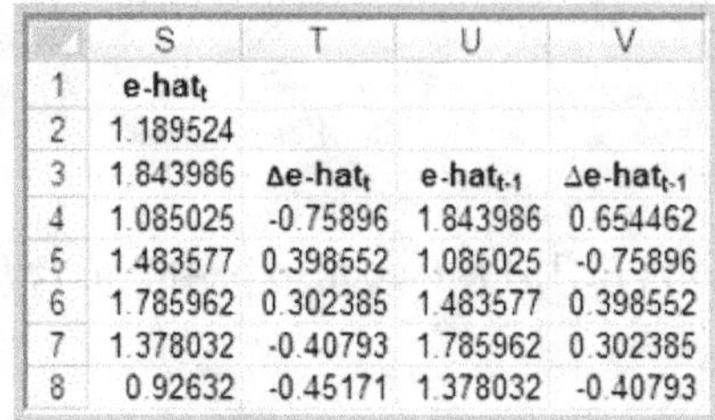

	S	T	U	V
1	e-hat$_t$			
2	1.189524			
3	1.843986	Δe-hat$_t$	e-hat$_{t-1}$	Δe-hat$_{t-1}$
4	1.085025	-0.75896	1.843986	0.654462
5	1.483577	0.398552	1.085025	-0.75896
6	1.785962	0.302385	1.483577	0.398552
7	1.378032	-0.40793	1.785962	0.302385
8	0.92632	-0.45171	1.378032	-0.40793

In the **Regression** dialog box, the **Input Y Range** should be **T3:D105**, and the **Input X Range** should be **U3:V105**. Check the boxes next to **Labels** _and_ **Constant is Zero**; _uncheck_ the box next to **Residuals**. Select **New Worksheet Ply** and name it **Cointegration Test**. Finally select **OK**.

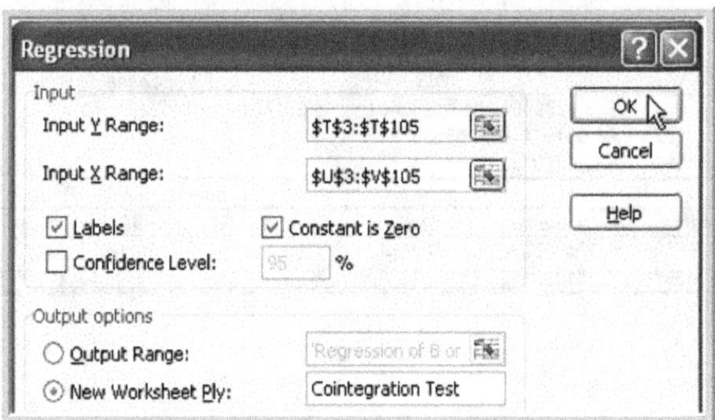

The result of estimated equation (12.14) is (see also p. 489 in *Principles of Econometrics*, *4e*):

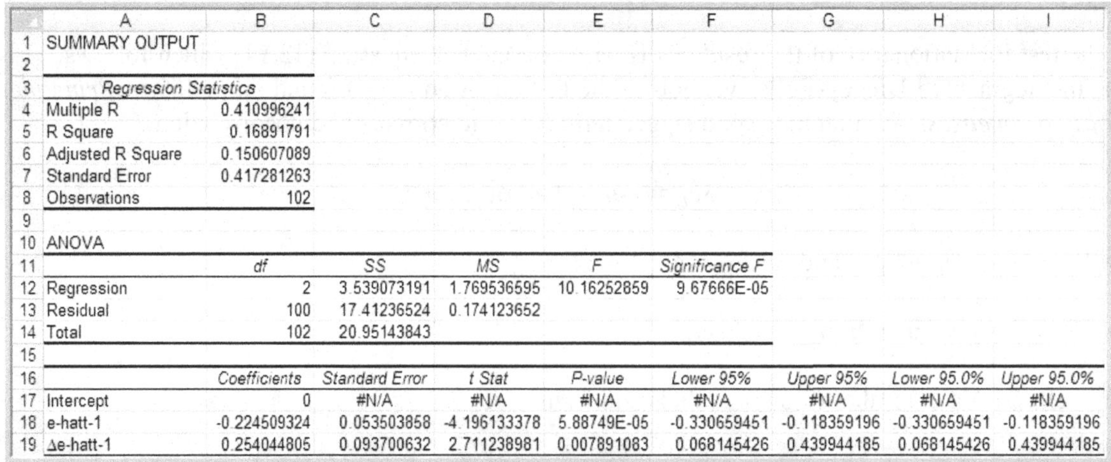

	A	B	C	D	E	F	G	H	I
1	SUMMARY OUTPUT								
2									
3	*Regression Statistics*								
4	Multiple R	0.410996241							
5	R Square	0.16891791							
6	Adjusted R Square	0.150607089							
7	Standard Error	0.417281263							
8	Observations	102							
9									
10	ANOVA								
11		*df*	*SS*	*MS*	*F*	*Significance F*			
12	Regression	2	3.539073191	1.769536595	10.16252859	9.67666E-05			
13	Residual	100	17.41236524	0.174123652					
14	Total	102	20.95143843						
15									
16		*Coefficients*	*Standard Error*	*t Stat*	*P-value*	*Lower 95%*	*Upper 95%*	*Lower 95.0%*	*Upper 95.0%*
17	Intercept	0	#N/A	#N/A	#N/A	#N/A	#N/A	#N/A	#N/A
18	e-hatt-1	-0.224509324	0.053503858	-4.196133378	5.88749E-05	-0.330659451	-0.118359196	-0.330659451	-0.118359196
19	Δe-hatt-1	0.254044805	0.093700632	2.711238981	0.007891083	0.068145426	0.439944185	0.068145426	0.439944185

The *t*-statistic (also referred to as τ-statistic in the context of a Dickey-Fuller testing procedure) is -4.196, and the 5% critical value for *tau*, τ_c, is -3.37 (value found in Table 12.4 on p. 489 of *Principles of Econometrics*, *4e*). In this case since $-4.196 < -3.37$, we do reject the null hypothesis that the residuals are nonstationary and accept the alternative that they are stationary. This implies that the Bond rate and the Federal Funds rate are cointegrated. In other words, the regression relationship between them, estimated above, is valid.

CHAPTER 13

Vector Error Correction and Vector Autoregressive Models

CHAPTER OUTLINE

13.1 ESTIMATING A VEC MODEL

Open the Excel file ***gdp***. Save your file as **POE Chapter 13**. Rename sheet 1 **gdp data**.

Insert a new column to the left of the column labeled **usa**. In your new cells **A1:A5**, enter the following label and values.

	A
1	**q*-year**
2	q1-1970
3	q2-1970
4	q3-1970
5	q4-1970

Select cells **A2:A5**, move your cursor to the lower right corner of your selection until it turns into a skinny cross as shown below; left-click, hold it and drag it down to cell **A125**.

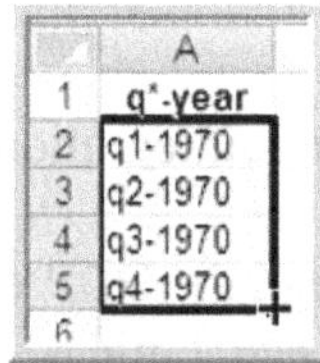

Excel recognizes the series and automatically completes it for you. Here is how your table should look (only the *last* five values are shown below):

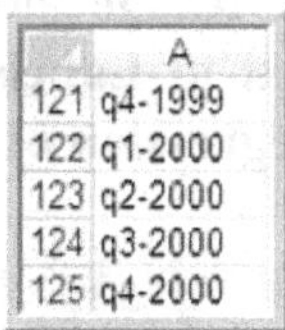

	A
121	q4-1999
122	q1-2000
123	q2-2000
124	q3-2000
125	q4-2000

Next, we plot the time series of the quarterly real GDP of Australia and the United States for the sample period 1970 to 2000.

Select the **Insert** tab located next to the **Home** tab. Select **A1:C125**. In the **Charts** group of commands select **Line**, and **Line** again.

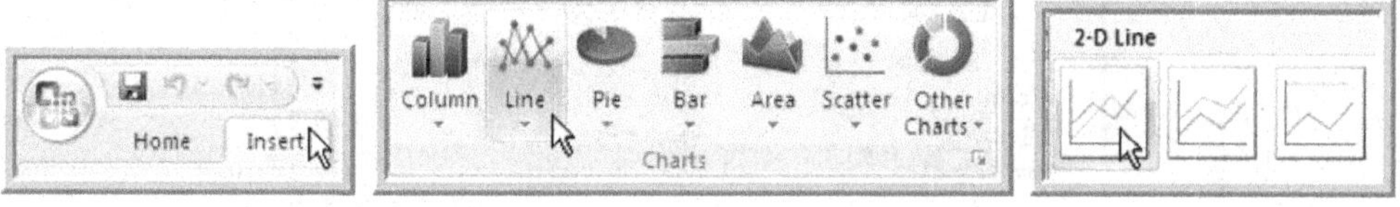

After editing, the result is (see also Figure 13.1 p. 502 in *Principles of Econometrics, 4e*):

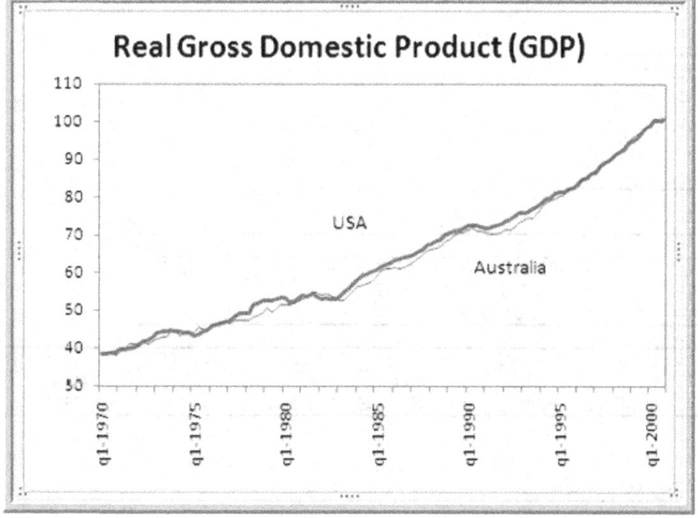

It appears from the figure above that both series are nonstationary and possibly cointegrated. Formal unit root test of the series have confirmed that they are indeed nonstationary.

13.1.1 Test for Cointegration

We proceed as in Section 12.4 to check for cointegration.

We first estimate the regression of Australia's GDP (A) on the United States' GDP (U)—the intercept term is omitted because it has no economic meaning:

$$A_t = \beta_2 U_t + e_t \tag{13.1}$$

In the **Regression** dialog box, the **Input Y Range** should be **C1:C125**, and the **Input X Range** should be **B1:B125**. Check the boxes next to **Labels** *and* **Constant is Zero,** *and* **Residuals.** Select **New Worksheet Ply** and name it **Regression of ausGDP on usaGDP**. Finally select **OK.**

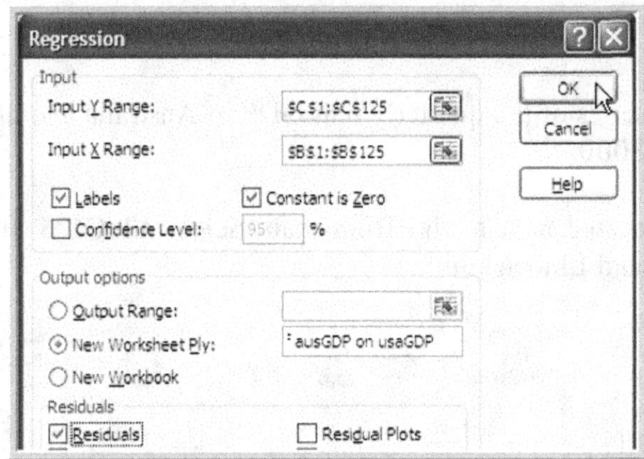

The result of the estimated equation (13.1) is (see also p. 502 in *Principles of Econometrics, 4e*):

	A	B	C	D	E	F	G	H	I
1	SUMMARY OUTPUT								
2									
3	*Regression Statistics*								
4	Multiple R	0.999826204							
5	R Square	0.999652439							
6	Adjusted R Square	0.991522358							
7	Standard Error	1.219374742							
8	Observations	124							
9									
10	ANOVA								
11		*df*	*SS*	*MS*	*F*	*Significance F*			
12	Regression	1	526014.2115	526014.2115	353771.6996	4.4122E-213			
13	Residual	123	182.8855956	1.486874761					
14	Total	124	526197.0971						
15									
16		*Coefficients*	*Standard Error*	*t Stat*	*P-value*	*Lower 95%*	*Upper 95%*	*Lower 95.0%*	*Upper 95.0%*
17	Intercept	0	#N/A	#N/A	#N/A	#N/A	#N/A	#N/A	#N/A
18	usa	0.985349542	0.001656642	594.7871045	1.3477E-214	0.98207032	0.988628764	0.98207032	0.988628764
19									
20									
21									
22	RESIDUAL OUTPUT								
23									
24	*Observation*	*Predicted aus*	*Residuals*						
25	1	37.73997333	0.49552667						
26	2	37.8112141	0.943885899						
27	3	38.14652559	0.624073405						

Select the **Insert** tab located next to the **Home** tab. Select cells **C25:C148** from your **Regression of ausGDP on usaGDP** worksheet. In the **Charts** group of commands select **Line**, and **Line** again.

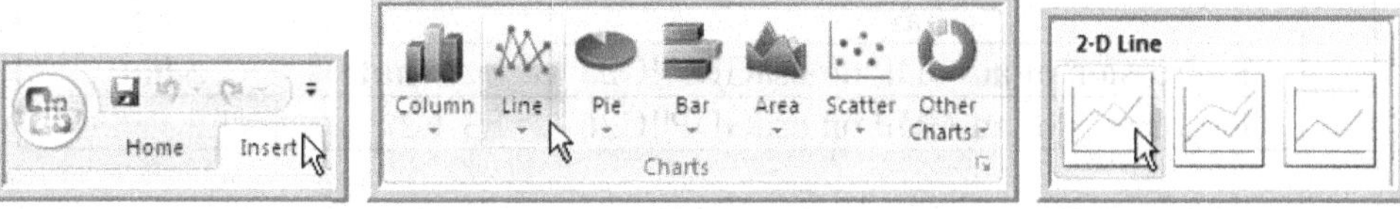

After editing, the result is (see also Figure 13.2 p. 502 in *Principles of Econometrics, 4e*):

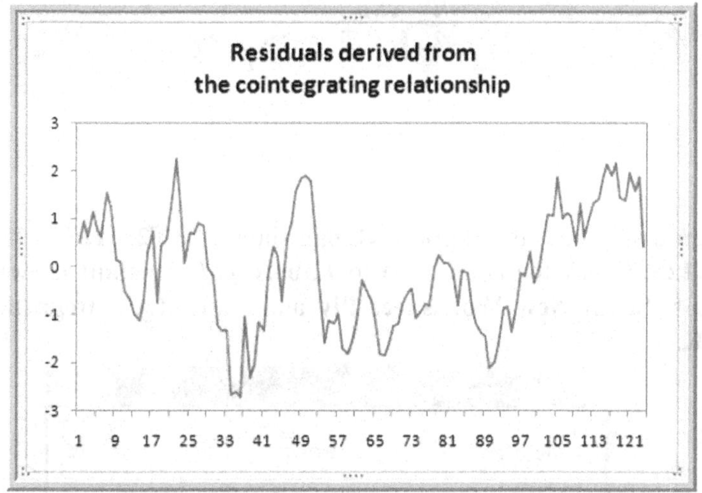

To compute the first order autocorrelation use the CORREL function as you have done in Chapter 9. In cells **E24:E25** of your **Regression of ausGDP on usaGDP** worksheet, enter the following label and formula.

	E
24	$\mathbf{r_1}$
25	=CORREL(C26:C148,C25:C147)

The result is:

	E
24	r_1
25	0.871647553

Again, note that your Excel results differ slightly from the one reported in *Principles of Econometrics, 4e* (see Section 9.2.1b for more details on that).

The test for stationarity of the residuals is based on the Dickey-Fuller test equation (12.7) found on p. 489 of *Principles of Econometrics, 4e*. It is restated below:

$$\Delta\hat{e}_t = \gamma\hat{e}_{t-1} + v_t \tag{13.2}$$

where $\Delta\hat{e}_t = \hat{e}_t - \hat{e}_{t-1}$.

Go back to your **gdp data** worksheet.

In cells **E1:G3** enter the following labels and formulas.

	E	F	G
1	**e-hat$_t$**		
2	='Regression of ausGDP on usaGDP'!C25	**Δe-hat$_t$**	**e-hat$_{t-1}$**
3	='Regression of ausGDP on usaGDP'!C26	=E3-E2	=E2

Copy the content of cells **E3:G3** to cells **E4:G125**. Here is how your table should look (only the first five values are shown below):

	E	F	G
1	e-hat$_t$		
2	0.495527	Δe-hat$_t$	e-hat$_{t-1}$
3	0.943886	0.448359	0.495527
4	0.624073	-0.31981	0.943886
5	1.156798	0.532725	0.624073
6	0.777263	-0.37954	1.156798
7	0.636521	-0.14074	0.777263

In the **Regression** dialog box, the **Input Y Range** should be **F2:F125**, and the **Input X Range** should be **G2:G125**. Check the boxes next to **Labels** *and* **Constant is Zero**; *uncheck* the box next to **Residuals**. Select **New Worksheet Ply** and name it **Cointegration Test for GDPs**. Finally select **OK**.

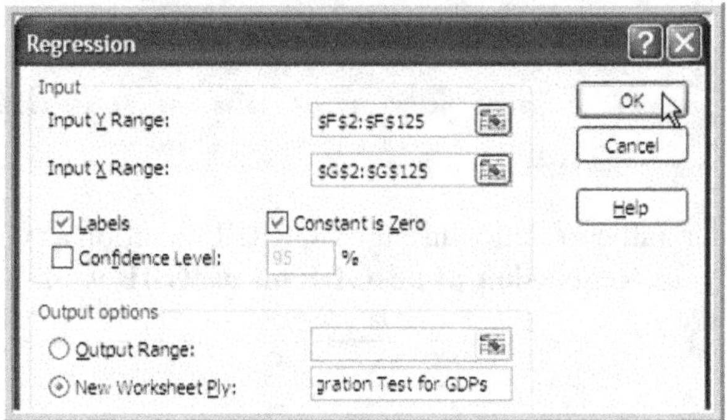

The result of estimated equation (13.2) is (see also p. 502 in *Principles of Econometrics, 4e*):

	A	B	C	D	E	F	G	H	I
1	SUMMARY OUTPUT								
2									
3	*Regression Statistics*								
4	Multiple R	0.253071206							
5	R Square	0.064045035							
6	Adjusted R Square	0.055848314							
7	Standard Error	0.598499617							
8	Observations	123							
9									
10	ANOVA								
11		*df*	*SS*	*MS*	*F*	*Significance F*			
12	Regression	1	2.990323011	2.990323011	8.34815202	0.004576407			
13	Residual	122	43.70061859	0.358201792					
14	Total	123	46.6909416						
15									
16		*Coefficients*	*Standard Error*	*t Stat*	*P-value*	*Lower 95%*	*Upper 95%*	*Lower 95.0%*	*Upper 95.0%*
17	Intercept	0	#N/A	#N/A	#N/A	#N/A	#N/A	#N/A	#N/A
18	e-hatt-1	-0.127936484	0.044279146	-2.889316878	0.004570296	-0.215591475	-0.040281493	-0.215591475	-0.040281493

The *t*-statistic (also referred to as τ-statistic in the context of a Dickey-Fuller testing procedure) is -2.889, and the 5% critical value for *tau*, $\tau_{c,}$ is -2.76 (value found in Table 12.4 on p. 489 of *Principles of Econometrics, 4e*). In this case since $-2.889 < -2.76$, we do reject the null hypothesis that the residuals are nonstationary and accept the alternative that they are stationary. This implies that Australia's GDP and the United States' GDP are cointegrated. In other words, the regression relationship between them, estimated above, is valid.

According to the estimated equation (13.1), if the United States' GDP increases by one unit, the GDP of Australia would increase by 0.985 of a unit. But the Australian economy may not respond fully by this amount within the quarter. To ascertain how much it will respond within a quarter, we estimate the vector error correction model.

13.1.2 The VEC Model

The vector error correction model (VEC model) for Australia's GDP (A_t) and the United States' GDP (U_t) is as follows:

$$\Delta A_t = \alpha_{10} + \alpha_{11}\hat{e}_{t-1} + v_t^A \qquad (13.3)$$

$$\Delta U_t = \alpha_{20} + \alpha_{21}\hat{e}_{t-1} + v_t^U \qquad (13.4)$$

where $\hat{e}_{t-1}$ are the lagged residuals from estimated equation (13.1).

Go back to your **gdp data** worksheet.

In cells **I2:J3** enter the following labels and formulas.

	I	J
2	**Δusa**	**Δaus**
3	=B3-B2	=C3-C2

Copy the content of cells **I3:J3** to cells **I4:J125**. Here is how your table should look (only the first five values are shown below):

	I	J
2	Δusa	Δaus
3	0.0723	0.5196
4	0.340297	0.015499
5	-0.4146	0.124199
6	1.062401	0.667301
7	0.222099	0.078103

In the **Regression** dialog box, the **Input Y Range** should be **J2:J125**, and the **Input X Range** should be **G2:G125**. Check the box next to **Labels**; <u>*uncheck*</u> the box next to **Constant is Zero.** Select **New Worksheet Ply** and name it **VEC Model Eq. for ausGDP**. Finally select **OK**.

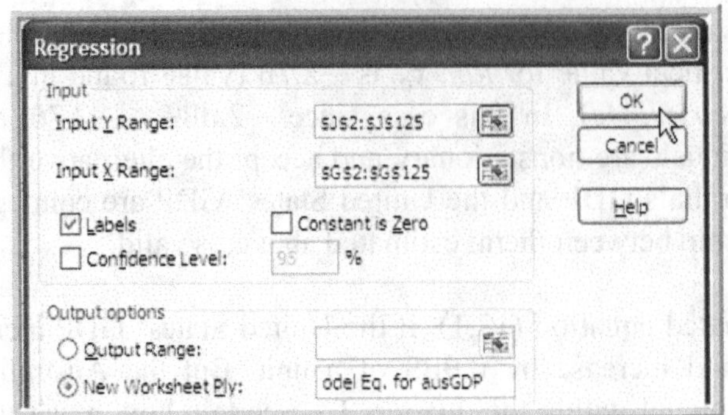

The result of estimated equation (13.3) is (see also p. 503 in *Principles of Econometrics, 4e*):

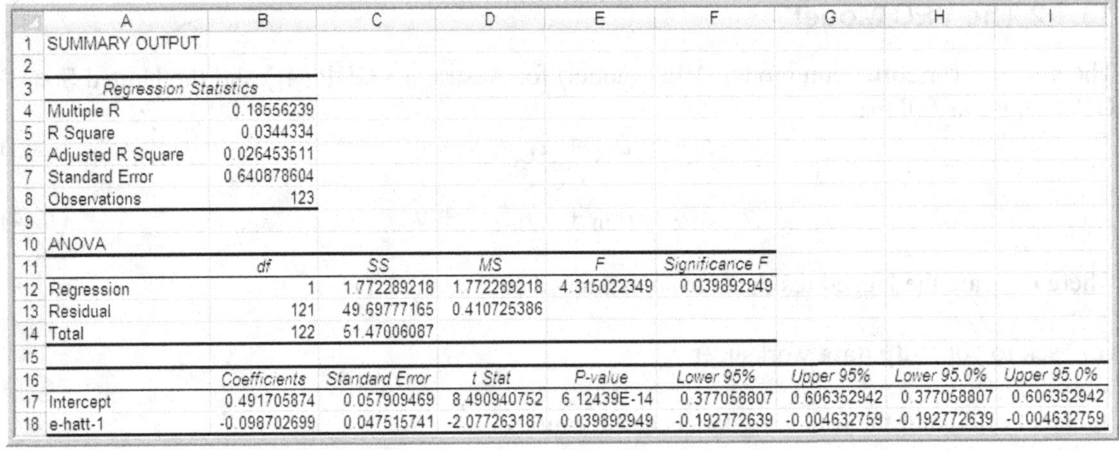

	A	B	C	D	E	F	G	H	I
1	SUMMARY OUTPUT								
2									
3	*Regression Statistics*								
4	Multiple R	0.18556239							
5	R Square	0.0344334							
6	Adjusted R Square	0.026453511							
7	Standard Error	0.640878604							
8	Observations	123							
9									
10	ANOVA								
11		*df*	*SS*	*MS*	*F*	*Significance F*			
12	Regression	1	1.772289218	1.772289218	4.315022349	0.039892949			
13	Residual	121	49.69777165	0.410725386					
14	Total	122	51.47006087						
15									
16		*Coefficients*	*Standard Error*	*t Stat*	*P-value*	*Lower 95%*	*Upper 95%*	*Lower 95.0%*	*Upper 95.0%*
17	Intercept	0.491705874	0.057909469	8.490940752	6.12439E-14	0.377058807	0.606352942	0.377058807	0.606352942
18	e-hatt-1	-0.098702699	0.047515741	-2.077263187	0.039892949	-0.192772639	-0.004632759	-0.192772639	-0.004632759

Go back to your **gdp data** worksheet.

In the **Regression** dialog box, the **Input Y Range** should be **I2:I125**, and the **Input X Range** should be **G2:G125**. Check the box next to **Labels**; <u>uncheck</u> the box next to **Constant is Zero**. Select **New Worksheet Ply** and name it **VEC Model Eq. for usaGDP**. Finally select **OK**.

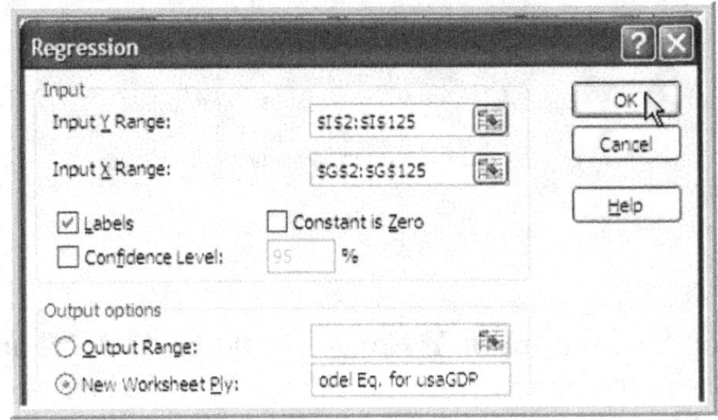

The result of estimated equation (13.4) is (see also p. 503 in *Principles of Econometrics, 4e*):

	A	B	C	D	E	F	G	H	I
1	SUMMARY OUTPUT								
2									
3	*Regression Statistics*								
4	Multiple R	0.071619325							
5	R Square	0.005129328							
6	Adjusted R Square	-0.003092744							
7	Standard Error	0.516568014							
8	Observations	123							
9									
10	ANOVA								
11		*df*	*SS*	*MS*	*F*	*Significance F*			
12	Regression	1	0.166469321	0.166469321	0.623848573	0.431165838			
13	Residual	121	32.2879441	0.266842513					
14	Total	122	32.45441342						
15									
16		*Coefficients*	*Standard Error*	*t Stat*	*P-value*	*Lower 95%*	*Upper 95%*	*Lower 95.0%*	*Upper 95.0%*
17	Intercept	0.509884284	0.046676827	10.92371351	9.50767E-20	0.417475195	0.602293373	0.417475195	0.602293373
18	e-hatt-1	0.030250241	0.038299159	0.789840853	0.431165838	-0.045573046	0.106073527	-0.045573046	0.106073527

13.2 ESTIMATING A VAR MODEL

Open the Excel file ***fred***. Excel opens the data set in Sheet 1 of a new Excel file. Since we would like to save all our work from Chapter 13 in one file, create a new worksheet in your **POE Chapter 13** Excel file, rename it **fred data**, and in it, copy the data set you just opened.

Insert a new column to the left of the column labeled **A**. In your new cells **A1:A5**, enter the following label and values.

	A
1	**q*-year**
2	q1-1960
3	q2-1960
4	q3-1960
5	q4-1960

Select cells **A2:A5**, move your cursor to the lower right corner of your selection until it turns into a skinny cross as shown below; left-click, hold it and drag it down to cell **A201**.

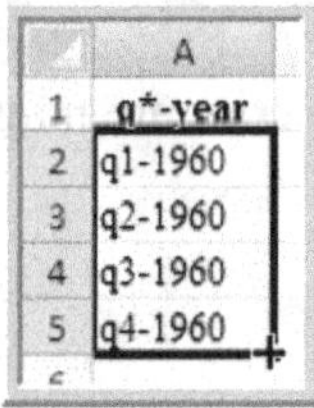

Excel recognizes the series and automatically completes it for you. Here is how your table should look (only the *last* five values are shown below):

	A
197	q4-2008
198	q1-2009
199	q2-2009
200	q3-2009
201	q4-2009

Next, we plot the time series of the quarterly log of Real Personal Disposable Income (denoted as Y or ly in your Excel file) and log of Real Personal Consumption Expenditure (denoted as C or lc in your Excel file) for the US economy over the period $1960{:}1$ to $2009{:}4$.

Select the **Insert** tab located next to the **Home** tab. Select **A1:C201**. In the **Charts** group of commands select **Line**, and **Line** again.

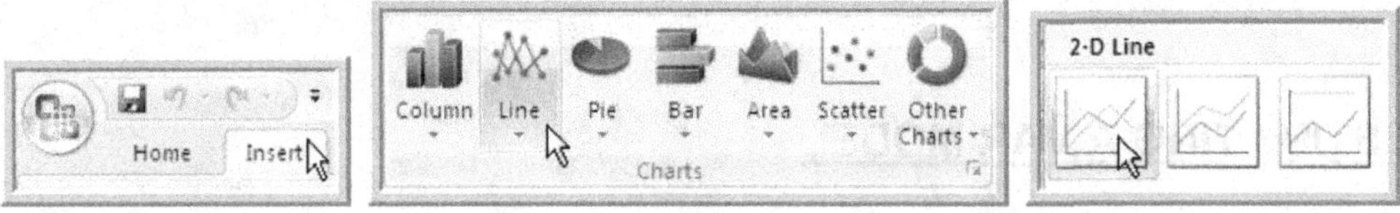

After editing, the result is (see also Figure 13.3 p. 504 in *Principles of Econometrics, 4e*):

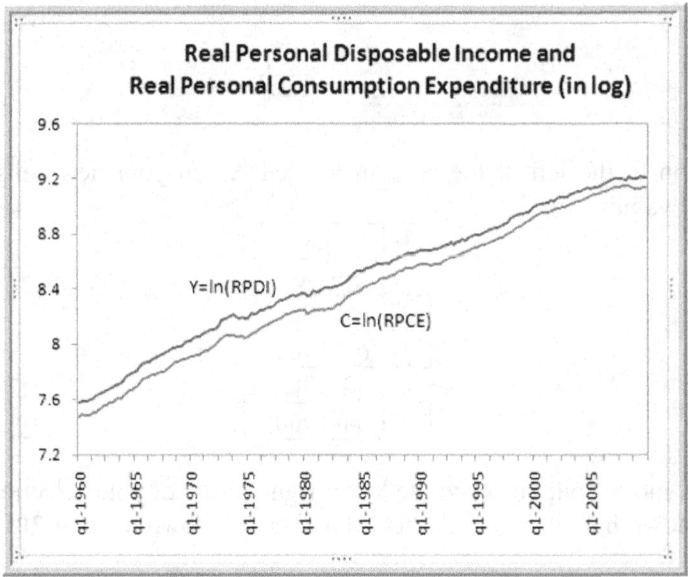

It appears from the figure above that both series are nonstationary.

13.2.1 Test for Cointegration

We proceed as in Section 12.4 to check for cointegration.

We first estimate the regression of the log of Real Personal Consumption Expenditure (C) on the log of Real Personal Disposable Income (Y) for the US economy:

$$C_t = \beta_1 + \beta_2 Y_t + e_t \tag{13.5}$$

In the **Regression** dialog box, the **Input Y Range** should be **B1:B201**, and the **Input X Range** should be **C1:C201**. Check the boxes next to **Labels** *and* **Residuals**. Select **New Worksheet Ply** and name it **Regression of C on Y**. Finally select **OK**.

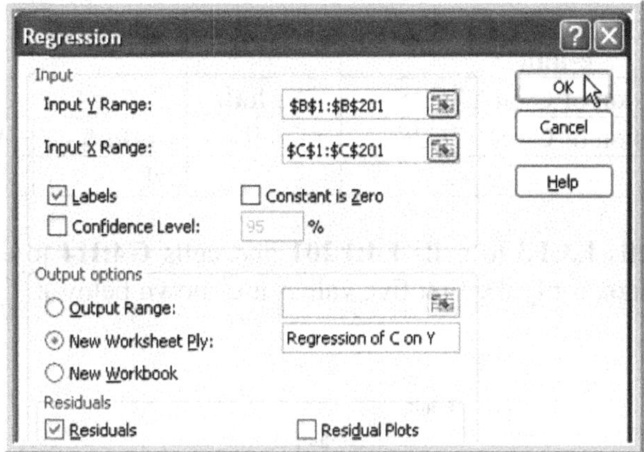

The result of the estimated equation (13.5) is (see also p. 503 in *Principles of Econometrics*, *4e*):

	A	B	C	D	E	F	G	H	I
1	SUMMARY OUTPUT								
2									
3	*Regression Statistics*								
4	Multiple R	0.999198794							
5	R Square	0.998398229							
6	Adjusted R Square	0.998390139							
7	Standard Error	0.019680429							
8	Observations	200							
9									
10	ANOVA								
11		*df*	*SS*	*MS*	*F*	*Significance F*			
12	Regression	1	47.80108067	47.80108067	123415.1893	1.0206E-278			
13	Residual	198	0.076689215	0.000387319					
14	Total	199	47.87776988						
15									
16		*Coefficients*	*Standard Error*	*t Stat*	*P-value*	*Lower 95%*	*Upper 95%*	*Lower 95.0%*	*Upper 95.0%*
17	Intercept	-0.404162766	0.02505341	-16.1320464	6.24675E-38	-0.453568527	-0.354757006	-0.453568527	-0.354757006
18	ly	1.035287621	0.002946977	351.3049804	1.0206E-278	1.029476131	1.04109911	1.029476131	1.04109911
19									
20									
21									
22	RESIDUAL OUTPUT								
23									
24	*Observation*	*Predicted lc*	*Residuals*						
25	1	7.441661973	0.037355027						
26	2	7.447258738	0.044331262						
27	3	7.448153227	0.039468773						

The test for stationarity of the residuals is based on the Dickey-Fuller test equation (12.7) found on p. 489 of *Principles of Econometrics*, *4e*. It is restated below (and includes the extra term $\Delta\hat{e}_{t-1}$):

$$\Delta\hat{e}_t = \gamma\hat{e}_{t-1} + \Delta\hat{e}_{t-1} + v_t \tag{13.6}$$

where $\Delta\hat{e}_t = \hat{e}_t - \hat{e}_{t-1}$.

Go back to your **fred data** worksheet.

In cells **E1:H4** enter the following labels and formulas.

	E	F	G	H
1	**e-hat$_t$**			
2	='Regression of C on Y'!C25	**Δe-hat$_t$**		
3	='Regression of C on Y'!C26	=E3-E2	**e-hat$_{t-1}$**	**Δe-hat$_{t-1}$**
4			=E3	=F3

Copy the content of cells **E3:F3** to cells **E4:F201** and cells **G4:H4** to cells **G5:H201**. Here is how your table should look (only the first five values are shown below):

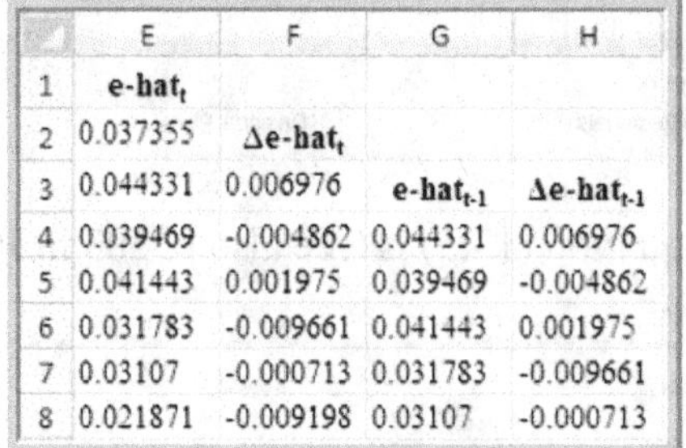

	E	F	G	H
1	**e-hat$_t$**			
2	0.037355	**Δe-hat$_t$**		
3	0.044331	0.006976	**e-hat$_{t-1}$**	**Δe-hat$_{t-1}$**
4	0.039469	-0.004862	0.044331	0.006976
5	0.041443	0.001975	0.039469	-0.004862
6	0.031783	-0.009661	0.041443	0.001975
7	0.03107	-0.000713	0.031783	-0.009661
8	0.021871	-0.009198	0.03107	-0.000713

In the **Regression** dialog box, the **Input Y Range** should be **F3:F181**, and the **Input X Range** should be **G3:H201**. Check the boxes next to **Labels** *and* **Constant is Zero**; *uncheck* the box next to **Residuals**. Select **New Worksheet Ply** and name it **Cointegration Test for C and Y.** Finally select **OK**.

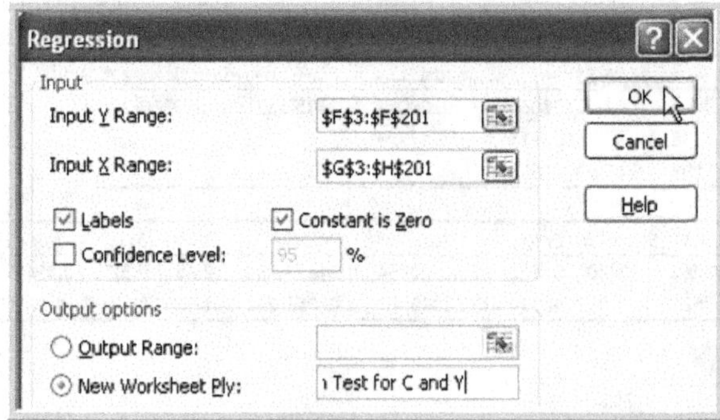

The result of estimated equation (13.6) is (see also p. 503 in *Principles of Econometrics, 4e*):

	A	B	C	D	E	F	G	H	I
1	SUMMARY OUTPUT								
2									
3	*Regression Statistics*								
4	Multiple R	0.388877197							
5	R Square	0.151225474							
6	Adjusted R Square	0.141792951							
7	Standard Error	0.008189208							
8	Observations	198							
9									
10	ANOVA								
11		*df*	*SS*	*MS*	*F*	*Significance F*			
12	Regression	2	0.002341922	0.001170961	17.46058112	1.05786E-07			
13	Residual	196	0.013144373	6.70631E-05					
14	Total	198	0.015486295						
15									
16		*Coefficients*	*Standard Error*	*t Stat*	*P-value*	*Lower 95%*	*Upper 95%*	*Lower 95.0%*	*Upper 95.0%*
17	Intercept	0	#N/A	#N/A	#N/A	#N/A	#N/A	#N/A	#N/A
18	e-hatt-1	-0.087647619	0.030508415	-2.87289975	0.004515395	-0.147814521	-0.027480717	-0.147814521	-0.027480717
19	Δe-hatt-1	-0.299406355	0.067160619	-4.45806428	1.39045E-05	-0.431856576	-0.166956134	-0.431856576	-0.166956134

The t-statistic (also referred to as τ-statistic in the context of a Dickey-Fuller testing procedure) is -2.873, and the 5% critical value for *tau*, τ_c, is -3.37 (value found in Table 12.4 on p. 489 of *Principles of Econometrics, 4e*). In this case since $-2.873 > -3.37$, it indicates that the errors are nonstationary and hence the relationship between C (i.e., ln(*RPCE*)) and Y (i.e., ln(*RPDI*)) is spurious. That is, we have no cointegration. Thus we do not apply a VEC model to examine the dynamic relationship between the log of Real Personal Disposable Income Y and the log of Real Personal Consumption Expenditure C. Instead we estimate a VAR model for the set of I(0) variables $\{\Delta Y_t, \Delta C_t\}$.

13.2.2 The VAR Model

The vector autoregressive model (VAR model) for the log of US Real Personal Disposable Income (Y_t) and the log of US Real Personal Consumption Expenditure (C_t) is as follows. For illustrative purposes, the order of the lag in this example has been restricted to 1.

$$\Delta Y_t = \beta_{10} + \beta_{11}\Delta Y_{t-1} + \beta_{12}\Delta C_{t-1} + v_t^{\Delta Y} \tag{13.7}$$

$$\Delta C_t = \beta_{20} + \beta_{21}\Delta Y_{t-1} + \beta_{22}\Delta C_{t-1} + v_t^{\Delta C} \tag{13.8}$$

where $\Delta Y_t = Y_t - Y_{t-1}$, $\Delta Y_{t-1} = Y_{t-1} - Y_{t-2}$, $\Delta C_t = C_t - C_{t-1}$ and $\Delta C_{t-1} = C_{t-1} - C_{t-2}$.

Go back to your **fred data** worksheet.

In cells **I3:L4** enter the following labels and formulas.

	I	J	K	L
3	ΔC_t	ΔY_t	ΔC_{t-1}	ΔY_{t-1}
4	=B4-B3	=C4-C3	=B3-B2	=C3-C2

Copy the content of cells **I4:L4** to cells **I5:L201**. Here is how your table should look (only the first five values are shown below):

	I	J	K	L
3	ΔC_t	ΔY_t	ΔC_{t-1}	ΔY_{t-1}
4	-0.003968	0.000864	0.012573	0.005406
5	0.001343	-0.00061	-0.003968	0.000864
6	-0.00028	0.009061	0.001343	-0.00061
7	0.01477	0.014955	-0.00028	0.009061
8	0.004839	0.013559	0.01477	0.014955

In the **Regression** dialog box, the **Input Y Range** should be **J3:J201**, and the **Input X Range** should be **K3:L201**. Check the box next to **Labels**; *uncheck* the box next to **Constant is Zero**. Select **New Worksheet Ply** and name it **VAR Model Eq. for Y**. Finally select **OK**.

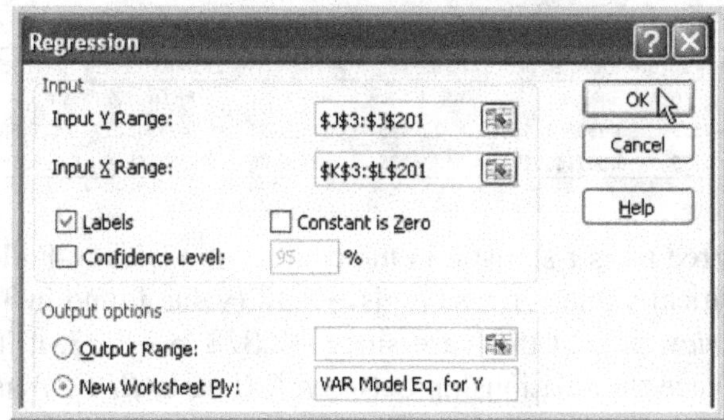

The result of estimated equation (13.7) is (see also p. 504 in *Principles of Econometrics, 4e*):

	A	B	C	D	E	F	G	H	I
1	SUMMARY OUTPUT								
2									
3	*Regression Statistics*								
4	Multiple R	0.334387691							
5	R Square	0.111815128							
6	Adjusted R Square	0.10270554							
7	Standard Error	0.008561528							
8	Observations	198							
9									
10	ANOVA								
11		*df*	*SS*	*MS*	*F*	*Significance F*			
12	Regression	2	0.001799428	0.000899714	12.27444346	9.52969E-06			
13	Residual	195	0.014293454	7.32998E-05					
14	Total	197	0.016092881						
15									
16		*Coefficients*	*Standard Error*	*t Stat*	*P-value*	*Lower 95%*	*Upper 95%*	*Lower 95.0%*	*Upper 95.0%*
17	Intercept	0.006036673	0.000986078	6.121903131	4.98959E-09	0.004091927	0.00798142	0.004091927	0.00798142
18	ΔCt-1	0.475427604	0.097326409	4.884877702	2.15226E-06	0.283480071	0.667375137	0.283480071	0.667375137
19	ΔYt-1	-0.217167947	0.075172994	-2.888909094	0.004303069	-0.365424427	-0.068911466	-0.365424427	-0.068911466

Go back to your **fred data** worksheet.

In the **Regression** dialog box, the **Input Y Range** should be **I3:I201**, and the **Input X Range** should be **K3:L201**. Check the box next to **Labels**; *uncheck* the box next to **Constant is Zero**. Select **New Worksheet Ply** and name it **VAR Model Eq. for C**. Finally select **OK**.

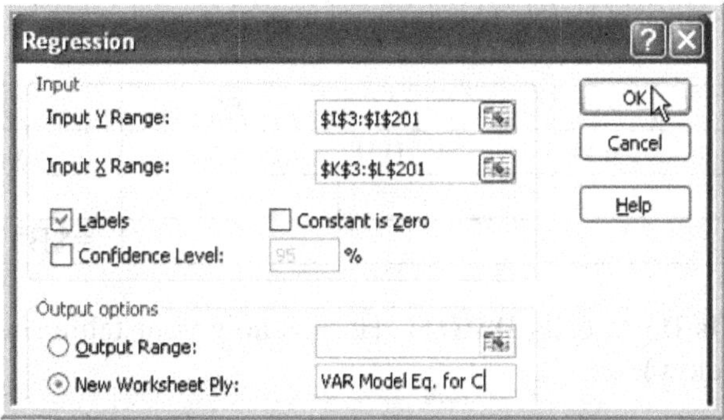

The result of estimated equation (13.8) is (see also p. 504 in *Principles of Econometrics, 4e*):

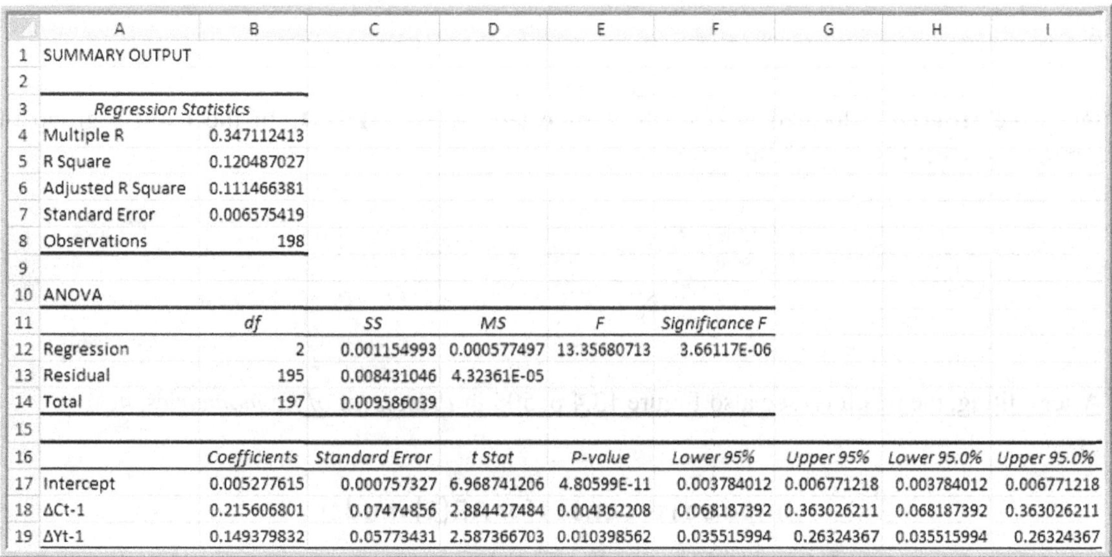

	A	B	C	D	E	F	G	H	I
1	SUMMARY OUTPUT								
2									
3	*Regression Statistics*								
4	Multiple R	0.347112413							
5	R Square	0.120487027							
6	Adjusted R Square	0.111466381							
7	Standard Error	0.006575419							
8	Observations	198							
9									
10	ANOVA								
11		*df*	*SS*	*MS*	*F*	*Significance F*			
12	Regression	2	0.001154993	0.000577497	13.35680713	3.66117E-06			
13	Residual	195	0.008431046	4.32361E-05					
14	Total	197	0.009586039						
15									
16		*Coefficients*	*Standard Error*	*t Stat*	*P-value*	*Lower 95%*	*Upper 95%*	*Lower 95.0%*	*Upper 95.0%*
17	Intercept	0.005277615	0.000757327	6.968741206	4.80599E-11	0.003784012	0.006771218	0.003784012	0.006771218
18	ΔCt-1	0.215606801	0.07474856	2.884427484	0.004362208	0.068187392	0.363026211	0.068187392	0.363026211
19	ΔYt-1	0.149379832	0.05773431	2.587366703	0.010398562	0.035515994	0.26324367	0.035515994	0.26324367

13.3 IMPULSE RESPONSES FUNCTIONS

13.3.1 The Univariate Case

Consider the following autoregressive model of order 1 (AR(1) model):

$$y_t = \rho y_{t-1} + v_t \tag{13.9}$$

where $\rho = 0.9$, $y_0 = 0$, $v_1 = 1$ and $v_t = 0$ for $t > 1$. Note: because $y_0 = 0$ and $v_1 = 1$, $y_1 = 1$; because $v_t = 0$ for $t > 1$, $y_t = \rho y_{t-1}$ for $t > 1$.

Insert a new worksheet by selecting the **Insert Worksheet** tab at the bottom of your screen. Rename it **simulated data**.

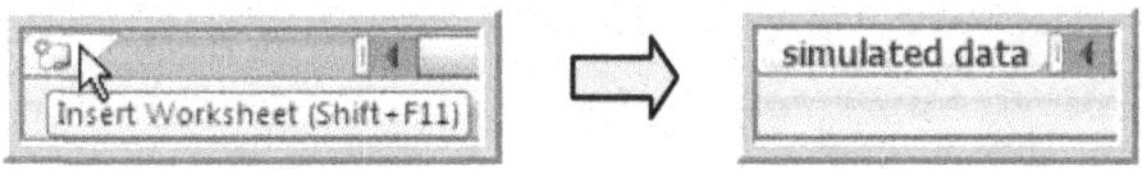

In cells **A1:D3** enter the following labels, values and formula.

	A	B	C	D
1	ρ =	0.9		y_t
2				1
3				=$B$1*D2

Copy the content of cells **D3** to cells **D4:D31**. Here is how your table should look (only the first five values are shown below):

	A	B	C	D
1	ρ =	0.9		y_t
2				1
3				0.9
4				0.81
5				0.729
6				0.6561

Select the **Insert** tab located next to the **Home** tab. Select **D1:D31**. In the **Charts** group of commands select **Line**, and **Line** again.

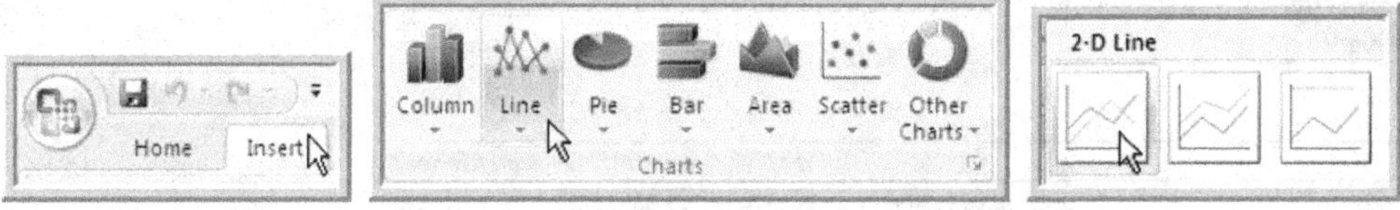

After editing, the result is (see also Figure 13.4 p. 505 in *Principles of Econometrics, 4e*):

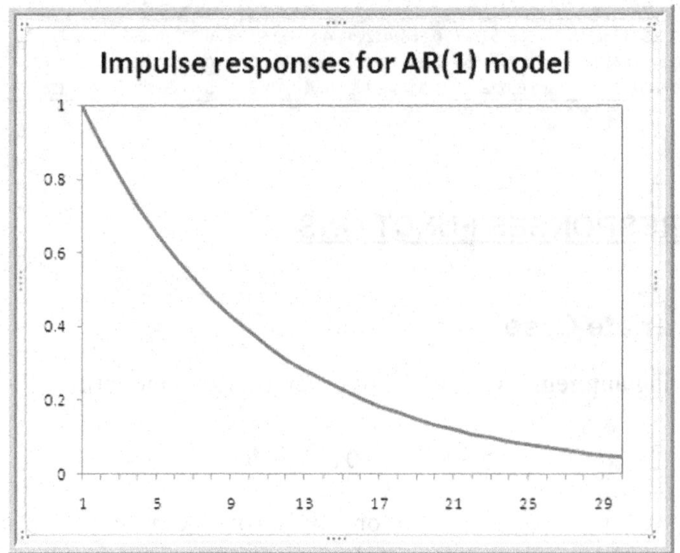

13.3.2 The Bivariate Case

Consider the following bivariate VAR system of stationary variables:

$$y_t = \delta_{10} + \delta_{11}y_{t-1} + \delta_{12}x_{t-1} + v_t^y \tag{13.10}$$

$$x_t = \delta_{20} + \delta_{21}y_{t-1} + \delta_{22}x_{t-1} + v_t^x \tag{13.11}$$

where the errors v_t^y and v_t^x are independent of each other (contemporaneously uncorrelated); $v^y \sim N(0, \sigma_y^2)$ and $v^x \sim N(0, \sigma_x^2)$.

In this case, there are two possible shocks to the system—one to y and the other to x. Thus we are interested in four impulse responses functions—the effect of a shock to y on the time-paths of y and x, and the effect of a shock to x on the time-paths of y and x.

First, let us consider what happens when there is a one standard deviation shock to y, so that $v_1^y = \sigma_y$ and $v_t^y = 0$ for $t > 1$; assume $v_t^x = 0$ for all t.

We further assume the following numerical values: $y_0 = x_0 = 0$, $\sigma_y = 1$, $\delta_{10} = \delta_{20} = 0$, $\delta_{11} = 0.7$ and $\delta_{12} = 0.2$, $\delta_{21} = 0.3$ and $\delta_{22} = 0.6$.

Note: this implies $y_1 = 1$ and $x_1 = 0$. For $t > 1$, y_t and x_t are given by equations (13.12) and (13.13):

$$y_t = \delta_{10} + \delta_{11}y_{t-1} + \delta_{12}x_{t-1} \tag{13.12}$$

$$x_t = \delta_{20} + \delta_{21}y_{t-1} + \delta_{22}x_{t-1} \tag{13.13}$$

In cells **F1:G6** enter the following labels and values.

	F	G
1	**δ_{10} =**	0
2	**δ_{11} =**	0.7
3	**δ_{12} =**	0.2
4	**δ_{20} =**	0
5	**δ_{21} =**	0.3
6	**δ_{22} =**	0.6

In cells **I1:K3** enter the following labels, values and formulas. In the last row, you will find the numbers of the equations used, if any.

	I	J	K
1	**Shock to y:**	**y_t**	**x_t**
2		1	0
3		=$G$1+$G$2*J2+$G$3*K2	=$G$4+$G$5*J2+$G$6*K2
		(13.12)	*(13.13)*

Copy the content of cells **J3:K3** to cells **J4:K31**. Here is how your table should look (only the first five values are shown below):

	F	G	H	I	J	K
1	δ_{10} =	0		Shock to y:	y_t	x_t
2	δ_{11} =	0.7			1	0
3	δ_{12} =	0.2			0.7	0.3
4	δ_{20} =	0			0.55	0.39
5	δ_{21} =	0.3			0.463	0.399
6	δ_{22} =	0.6			0.4039	0.3783

Select the **Insert** tab located next to the **Home** tab. Select **J1:J31**. In the **Charts** group of commands select **Line**, and **Line** again.

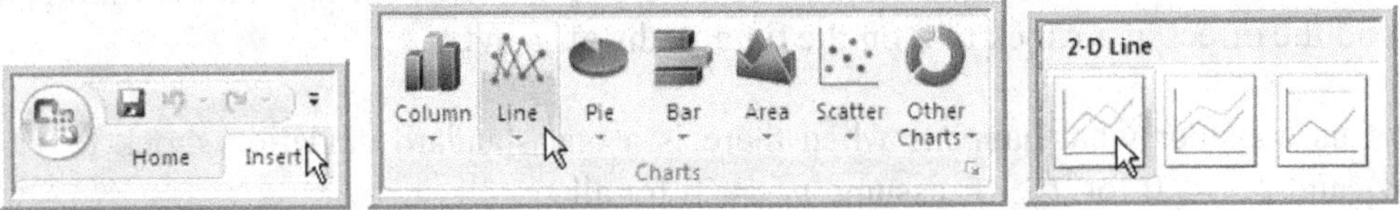

After editing, the result is (see also Figure 13.5 p. 507 in *Principles of Econometrics, 4e*). We also show the response of x to y, plotted by selecting cells **K1:K31**.

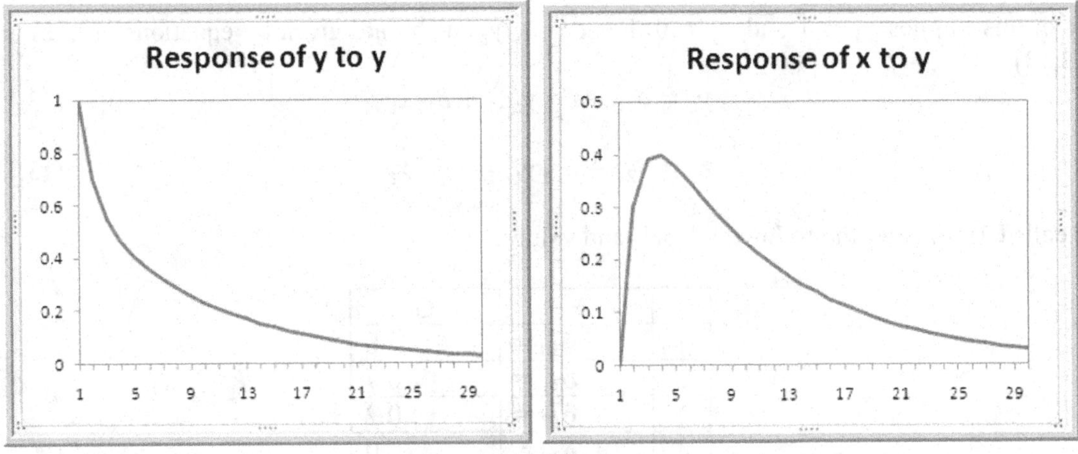

Note that the figures above looks slightly different from the ones found in *Principles of Econometrics, 4e*. The difference is explained by the fact that in the above figures we did not plot the y_0 and x_0 values, but started instead with y_1 and x_1.

Next, let us consider what happens when there is a one standard deviation shock to x, so that $v_1^x = \sigma_x$ and $v_t^x = 0$ for $t > 1$; assume $v_t^y = 0$ for all t.

We further assume the following numerical value: $\sigma_x = 2$. Note: this implies $y_1 = 0$ and $x_1 = 2$. For $t > 1$, y_t and x_t are given by equations (13.12) and (13.13) restated below:

$$y_t = \delta_{10} + \delta_{11} y_{t-1} + \delta_{12} x_{t-1} \tag{13.12}$$

$$x_t = \delta_{20} + \delta_{21} y_{t-1} + \delta_{22} x_{t-1} \tag{13.13}$$

In cells **M1:O3** enter the following labels, values and formulas. In the last row, you will find the numbers of the equations used, if any.

	M	N	O
1	**Shock to x:**	y_t	x_t
2		0	2
3		=$G$1+$G$2*N2+$G$3*O2	=$G$4+$G$5*N2+$G$6*O2
		(13.12)	*(13.13)*

Copy the content of cells **N3:O3** to cells **N4:O31**. Here is how your table should look (only the first five values are shown below):

	M	N	O
1	Shock to x:	y_t	x_t
2		0	2
3		0.4	1.2
4		0.52	0.84
5		0.532	0.66
6		0.5044	0.5556

We plot the response of y to x by selecting cells **N1:N31**, and the response of x to x by selecting cells **O1:O31**. After editing, the result is (see also Figure 13.5 p. 507 in *Principles of Econometrics, 4e*):

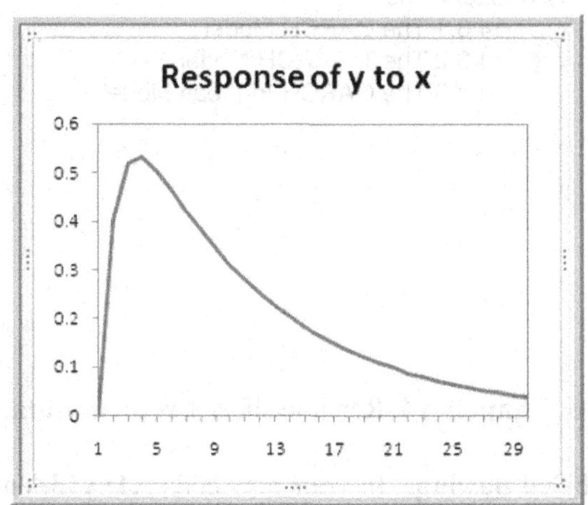

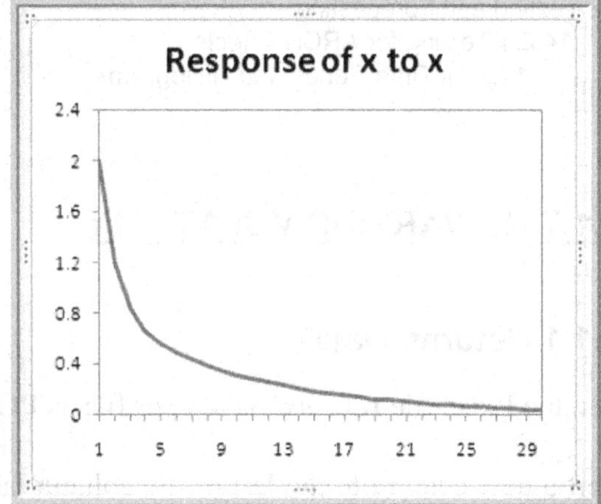

CHAPTER 14

Time-Varying Volatility and ARCH Models

CHAPTER OUTLINE

14.1 TIME-VARYING VOLATILITY

14.1.1 Returns Data

Open the Excel file ***returns***. Save your file as **POE Chapter 14**. Rename sheet 1 **returns data**.

Insert a new column to the left of the column labeled **nasdaq**. In your new cells **A1:A13**, enter the following label and values.

	A
1	**m*-year**
2	m1-1988
3	m2-1988
4	m3-1988
5	m4-1988
6	m5-1988
7	m6-1988

	A
8	m7-1988
9	m8-1988
10	m9-1988
11	m10-1988
12	m11-1988
13	m12-1988

Select cells **A2:A13**, move your cursor to the lower right corner of your selection until it turns into a skinny cross as shown below, left-click, hold it and drag it down to cell **A272**.

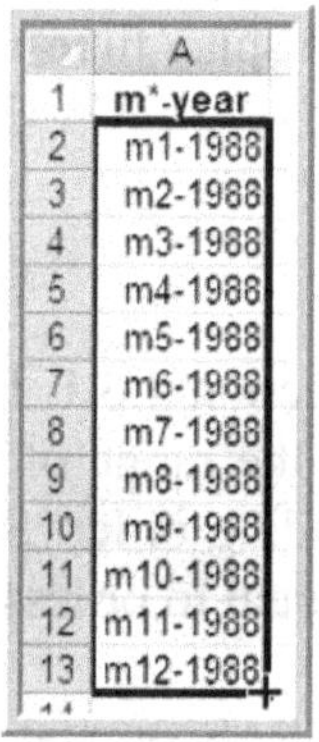

	A
1	m*-year
2	m1-1988
3	m2-1988
4	m3-1988
5	m4-1988
6	m5-1988
7	m6-1988
8	m7-1988
9	m8-1988
10	m9-1988
11	m10-1988
12	m11-1988
13	m12-1988

Excel recognizes the series and automatically completes it for you. Here is how your table should look (only the <u>*last*</u> five values are shown below):

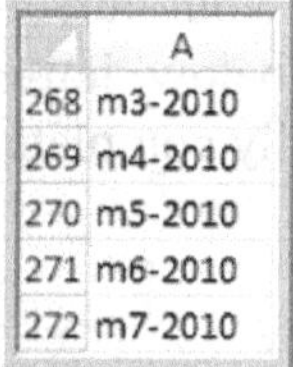

	A
268	m3-2010
269	m4-2010
270	m5-2010
271	m6-2010
272	m7-2010

Next, we plot the time series of the monthly returns to the United States Nasdaq stock price index ($NASDAQ$).

Select the **Insert** tab located next to the **Home** tab. Select **A1:B272**. In the **Charts** group of commands select **Line**, and **Line** again.

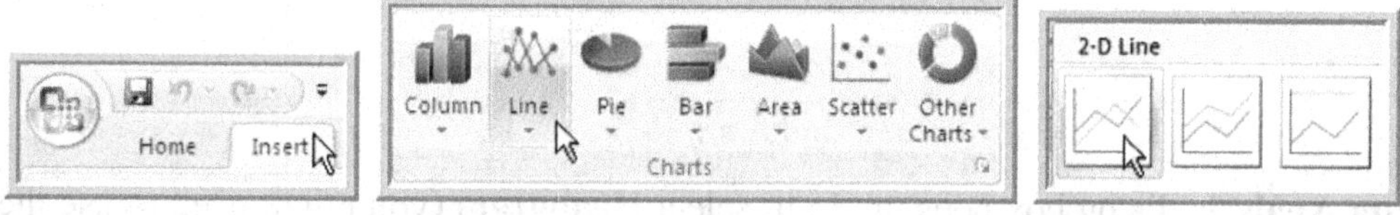

After editing, the result is (see also Figure 14.1(a) p. 520 in *Principles of Econometrics, 4e*):

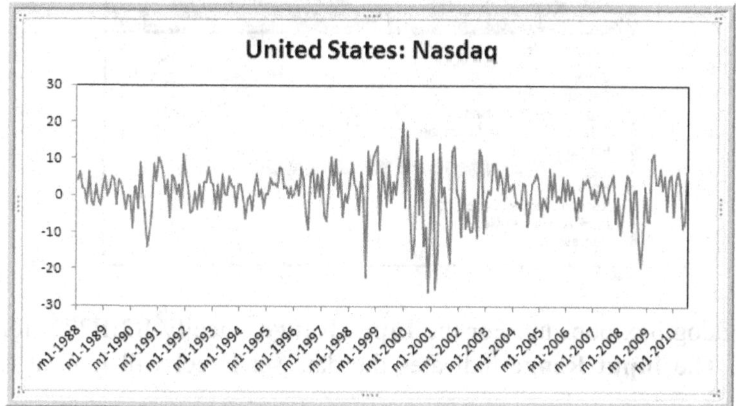

The values of this series change rapidly from period to period in an apparently unpredictable manner; we say the series is volatile. Furthermore, there are periods when large changes are followed by further large changes and periods when small changes are followed by further small changes. In this case, the series is said to display time-varying volatility as well as "clustering" of changes.

Next, we plot a histogram of the returns.

We proceed as we have done before in Section 4.6.1. First, we create a **BIN** column. In cell **G1**, type **BIN**. The bin values will determine the range of values for each column of the histogram. The bin values have to be given in ascending order. Starting with the lowest bin value, a value will be counted in a particular bin if it is equal to or less than the bin value.

Note that econometric packages such as SAS or Stata automate the choice of the number and width of bins. Thus the figures they produce might differ slightly from ours.

Fill in the bin values as shown below. Note that all you need to do is enter the first two values: **– 30** and **– 27.5**, select cells **G2:G3**, move your cursor to the lower right corner of your selection until it turns into a skinny cross as shown below, left-click, hold it and drag it down to cell **G26**: Excel recognizes the series and automatically completes it for you.

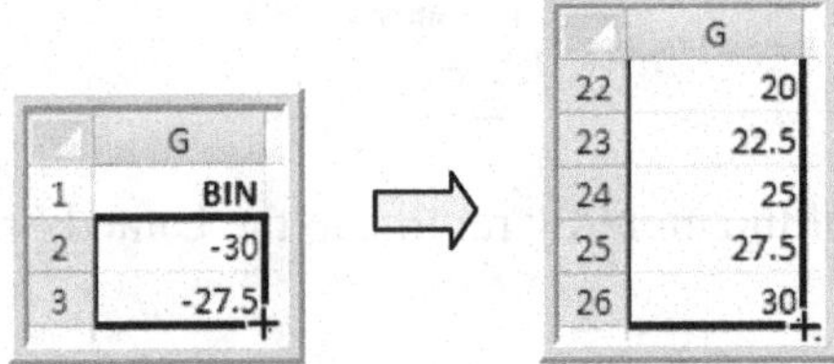

Select the **Data** tab, in the middle of your tab list. On the **Analysis** group of commands to the far right of the ribbon, select **Data analysis**.

The **Data Analysis** dialog box pops up. In it, select **Histogram** (you might need to use the scroll up and down bar to the right of the **Analysis Tools** window to find it), then select **OK**.

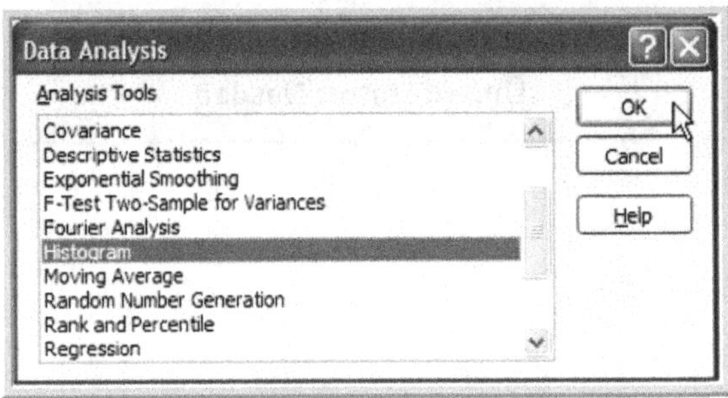

An **Histogram** dialog box pops up. For the **Input Range**, specify **B2:B272**; for the **Bin Range**, specify **G2:G26**. The **Input Range** indicates the data set Excel will look at to determine how many values are counted in each bin of the **Bin Range**. Check the **New Worksheet Ply** option and name it **US Nasdaq Histogram**; check the box next to **Chart Output**. Finally, select **OK**.

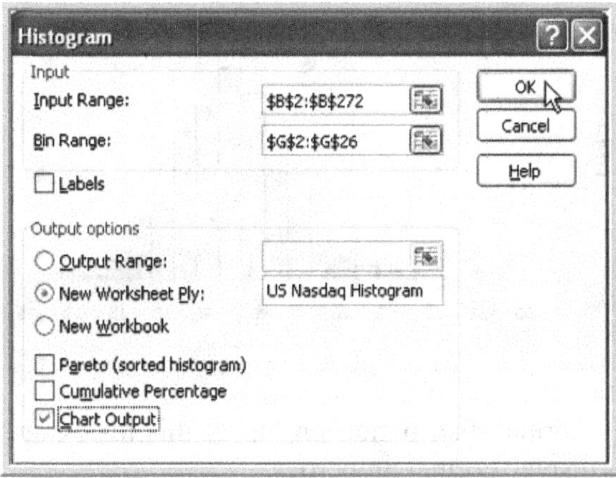

Select the columns in your chart area, right-click and select **Format Data Series**. The **Series Options** tab of the **Format Data Series** dialog box should be open. Select the **Gap Width** button and move it to the far left, towards **No Gap**. Select **Close**.

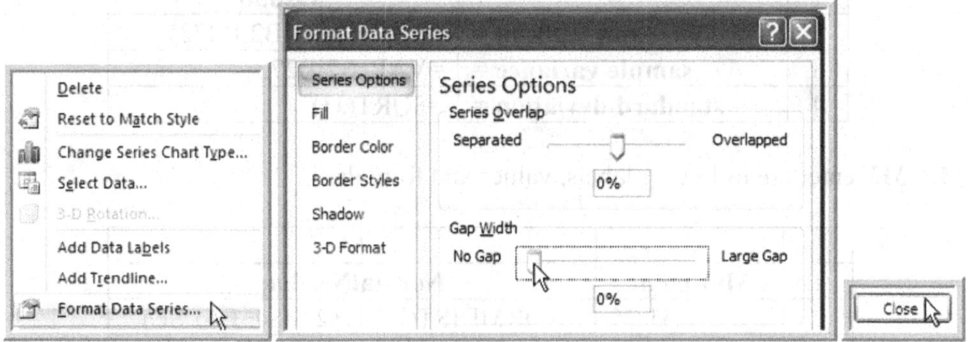

Go to the **Border Color** tab and select **Solid line**, choose a different **Color** if you would like. Select **Close**.

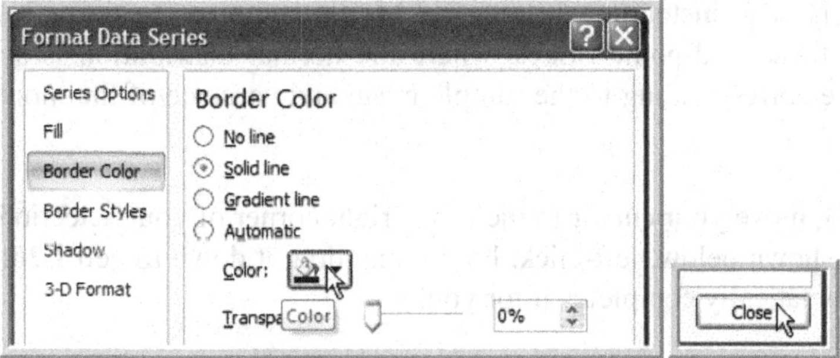

Finally, delete the **Legend**, and increase the size of the **Chart area** (see Section 2.3.4 for more details on that). After editing, the result is (see Figure 14.2(a) p. 521 in *Principles of Econometrics, 4e*):

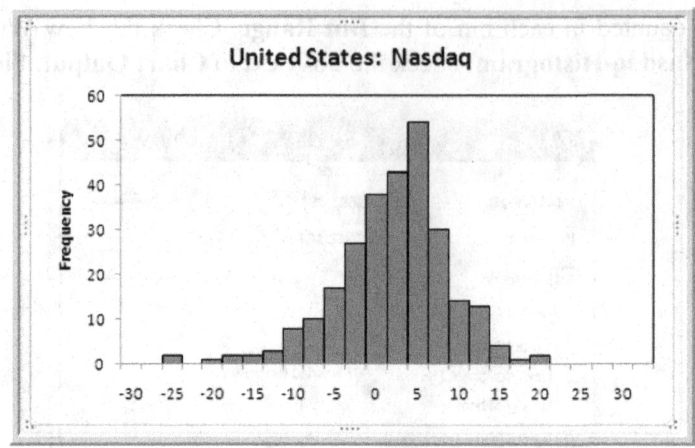

We would like to draw a normal distribution on top of this histogram so we can better assess whether or not the returns display normal properties.

Go back to your **returns data** worksheet. In cells **I1:J4**, enter the following labels and formulas.

	I	J
1		**Nasdaq**
2	**sample mean =**	=AVERAGE(B2:B272)
3	**sample variance =**	=VAR(B2:B272)
4	**standard deviation =**	=SQRT(J3)

In cells **L1:M3**, enter the following labels, values and formula.

	L	M
1	**Mid-point**	**NormalNasdaq**
2	-31.25	=NORMDIST(L2,$J$2,$J$4, FALSE)
3	-28.75	

In **column L**, we specify the mid-point or mid-value of the bins or class intervals we used to construct the US Nasdaq histogram. In **column M**, we compute the normal distribution values corresponding to those mid-point values, where the normal distribution is specified to have a mean and variance corresponding to the sample mean and variance of the monthly returns of US Nasdaq.

Select cells **L2:L3**, move your cursor to the lower right corner of your selection until it turns into a skinny cross as shown below, left-click, hold it and drag it down to cell **L26**: Excel recognizes the series and automatically completes it for you.

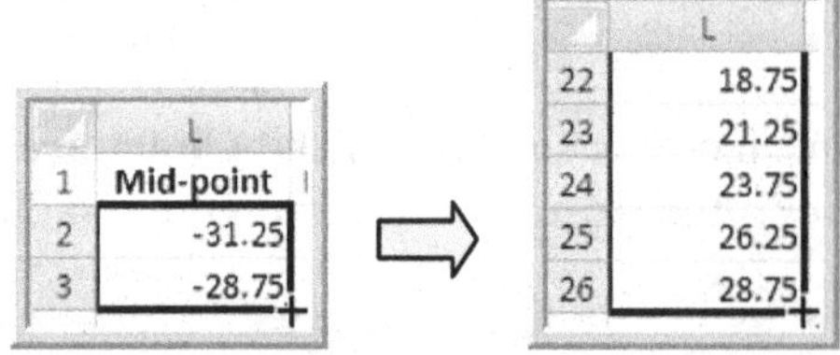

Copy cell **M2** to cells **M3:M26**. Here is how your table should look (only the first five values are shown below):

	I	J	K	L	M
1		nasdaq		Mid-point	NormalNasdaq
2	sample mean =	0.708548		-31.25	9.62135E-07
3	sample variance =	46.35319		-28.75	5.0411E-06
4	standard deviation =	6.808318		-26.25	2.30812E-05
5				-23.75	9.2349E-05
6				-21.25	0.000322886

Go back to your **US Nasdaq Histogram** worksheet. Select the histogram, right-click and choose **Select Data** on the list of options that pops up. In the **Select Data Source** dialog box, select **Add**. In the **Edit Series** dialog box, specify the **Series values** to be **M2:M26** from the **returns data** worksheet. Finally select **OK**. The **Select Data Source** dialog box reappears again. Select **OK** one more time.

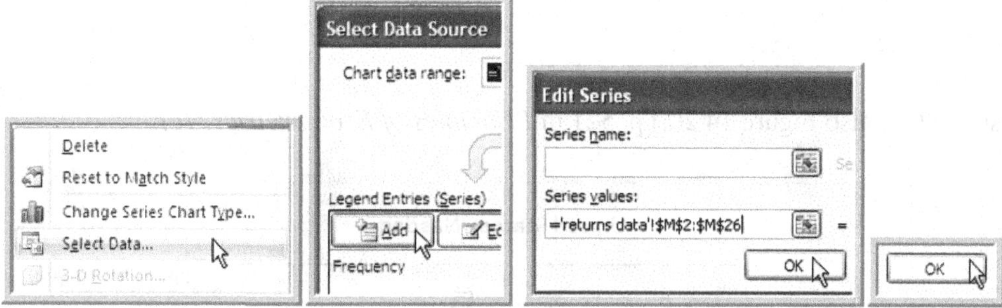

The series you just added is barely visible, at the bottom of your plot area. Select it, right-click and select **Change Series Chart Type**. In the **Change Chart Type** dialog box, select **Line**. In the list of **Line** charts, select **Line** again. Finally select **OK**.

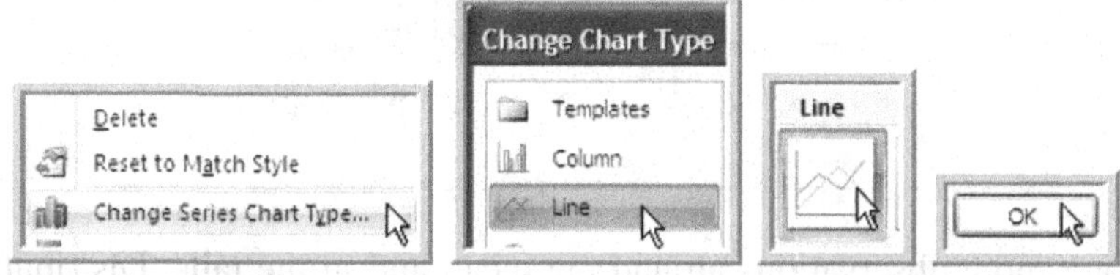

Your series is now is little bit more visible, still at the bottom of your plot area. Select it again, right-click and select **Format Data Series** this time. In the **Series Options**, select **Secondary Axis**.

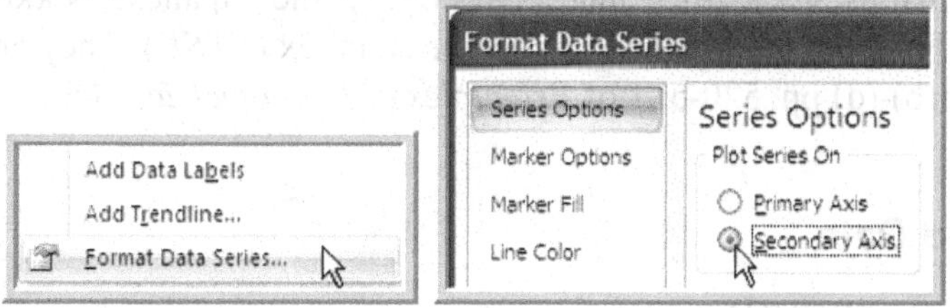

In the **Line Style** options, select **Smoothed Line**. Finally, select **Close**.

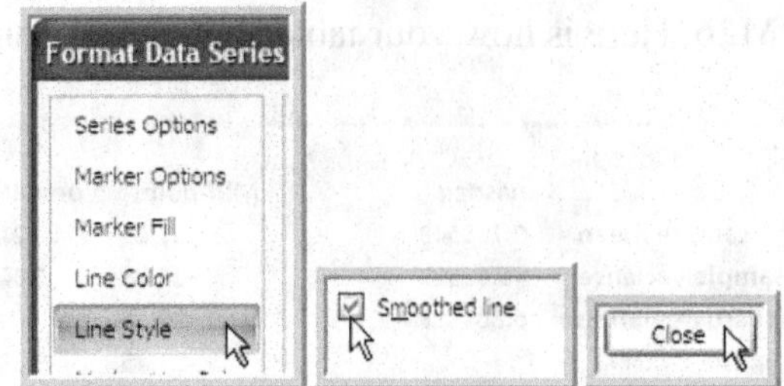

Select the right-vertical axis, right click and select **Format Axis**. Select the **Axis Options** tab, specify **Fixed Minimum** at 0.0 and **Fixed Maximum** at 0.09. Finally select **Close.**

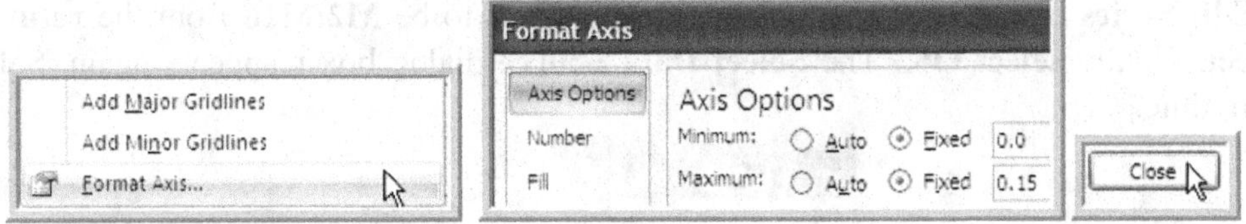

The result is (see also Figure 14.2(a) p. 521 in *Principles of Econometrics, 4e*):

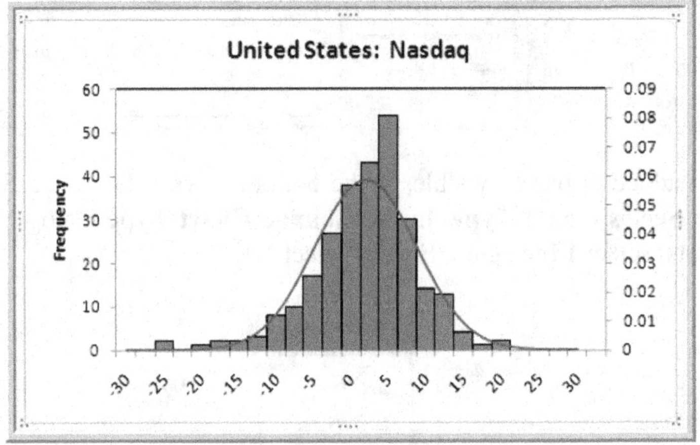

Note that there are more observations around the mean and in the tails. Distributions with these properties—more peaked around the mean and relatively fat tails—are said to be leptokurtic.

You can proceed similarly to plot the time series and histograms of the monthly returns to the Australian All Ordinaries stock price index (*ALLODS*), the Japanese Nikkei stock price index (*NIKKEI*), and the United Kingdom FTSE stock price index (*FTSE*). They are shown on Figures 14.1(b)-(d) and 14.2(b)-(d) pp. 520-521 of *Principles of Econometrics, 4e*.

14.1.2 Simulated Data

Consider the following ARCH(1) model:

$$y_t = \beta_0 + e_t \tag{14.1a}$$

$$e_t | I_{t-1} \sim N(0, h_t) \tag{14.1b}$$

$$h_t = \alpha_0 + \alpha_1 e_{t-1}^2, \alpha_0 > 0, 0 \leq \alpha_1 < 1 \tag{14.1c}$$

where $\beta_0 = 0$, $\alpha_0 = 1$ and $\alpha_1 = 0$. Note: these values imply $h_t = 1$, which means that $var(e_t|I_{t-1})$ is constant and not time varying.

Insert a new worksheet by selecting the **Insert Worksheet** tab at the bottom of your screen. Rename it **simulated data**.

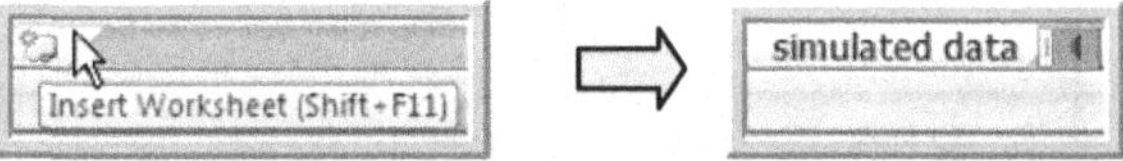

In cells **A1:E3** enter the following labels, values and formula.

	A	B	C	D	E
1	$\beta_0 =$	0		e_t	y_t
2	$\alpha_0 =$	1			=$B$1+D2
3	$\alpha_1 =$	0			

In column **D**, we generate a sample of 200 random numbers from a normal distribution with mean 0 and standard deviation 1.

Select the **Data** tab, in the middle of your tab list located on top of your screen. On the **Analysis** group of commands, to the far right, select **Data Analysis.** The **Data Analysis** dialog box pops up. In it, select **Random Number Generation** (you might need to use the scroll up and down bar to the right of the **Analysis Tools** window to find it), then select **OK.**

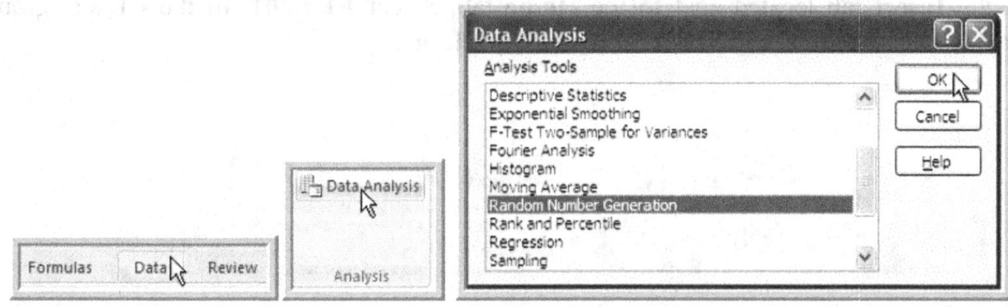

A **Random Number Generation** dialog box pops up. We need to generate one set of random numbers for our random errors, so we specify **1** in the **Number of Variables** window. We would like to generate 200 random numbers, so we specify **200** in the **Number of Random Numbers** window. We select **Normal** in the **Distribution** window; the selected **Parameters** should be **Mean** equal to **0**, and **Standard deviation** equal to **1**. Select **Output Range** and specify it to be **D2:D201**. Finally, we select **OK**.

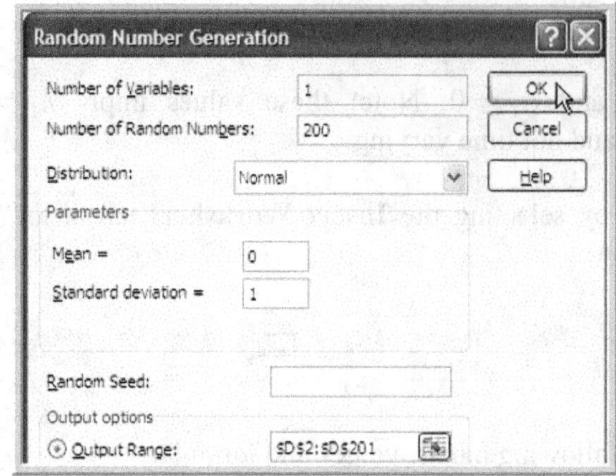

After you copy the content of cell **E2** to cells **E3:E201**, here is how your table should look (only the first five values are shown below):

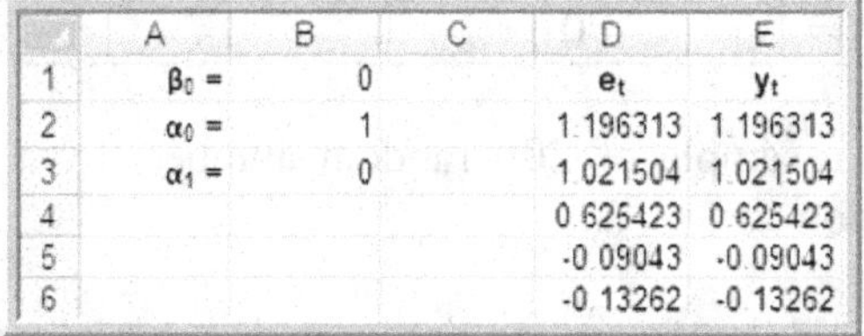

	A	B	C	D	E
1	β_0 =	0		e_t	y_t
2	α_0 =	1		1.196313	1.196313
3	α_1 =	0		1.021504	1.021504
4				0.625423	0.625423
5				-0.09043	-0.09043
6				-0.13262	-0.13262

Note: you will obtain a different random sample than the ones we obtained, so your e_t and y_t values should be slightly different than the ones reported above.

Select the **Insert** tab located next to the **Home** tab. Select **E1:E201**. In the **Charts** group of commands select **Scatter**, and **Scatter with Smooth Lines**.

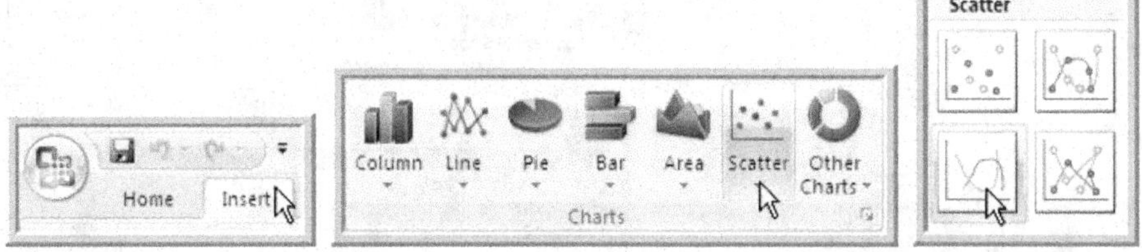

After editing, the result is (see also Figure 14.3(a) p. 522 in *Principles of Econometrics, 4e*):

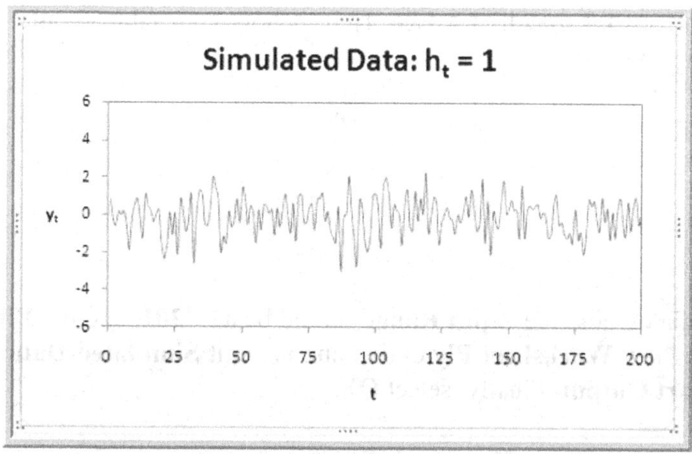

Next, we standardize the simulated data we just generated. That is for each observation we subtract the sample mean and divide by the sample standard deviation.

In cells **G1:J3**, enter the following labels and formulas.

	G	H	I	J
1		y_t		**standardized y_t**
2	**sample mean =**	=AVERAGE(E2:E201)		=(E2-$H$2)/$H$4
3	**sample variance =**	=VAR(E2:E201)		
4	**standard deviation =**	=SQRT(H3)		

After you copy the content of cell **J2** to cells **J3:J201**, here is how your table should look (only the first five values are shown below):

	G	H	I	J
1		y_t		standardized y_t
2	sample mean =	0.005703		1.309547877
3	sample variance =	0.826602		1.117275611
4	sample standard deviation =	0.909177		0.681628202
5				-0.105734753
6				-0.152135987

Remember that your numbers our going to be different than ours since you are working with a different random sample.

To plot the histogram of the standardized y_t, we proceed as we have done in Section 14.1.1.

In cells **L1:L3**, enter the following label, value and formula.

	L
1	**BIN**
2	-4
3	=L2+1/3

Copy the content of cell **L3** to cells **L4:L26**. Here is how your table should look (only the first five values are shown below):

	L
1	BIN
2	-4
3	-3.66667
4	-3.33333
5	-3
6	-2.66667

In the **Histogram** dialog box, the **Input Range** should be **J2:J201**, and the **Bin Range** should be **L2:L26**. Check the **New Worksheet Ply** option and name it **Simulated Data Histogram**; check the box next to **Chart Output**. Finally, select **OK**.

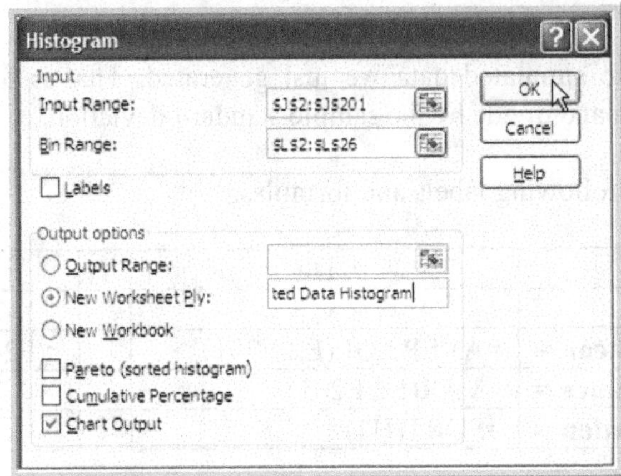

Select the columns in your chart area, right-click and select **Format Data Series**. The **Series Options** tab of the **Format Data Series** dialog box should be open. Select the **Gap Width** button and move it to the far left, towards **No Gap**. In the **Border Color** tab, select **Solid line**, and change the **Color** to black. Finally select **Close**.

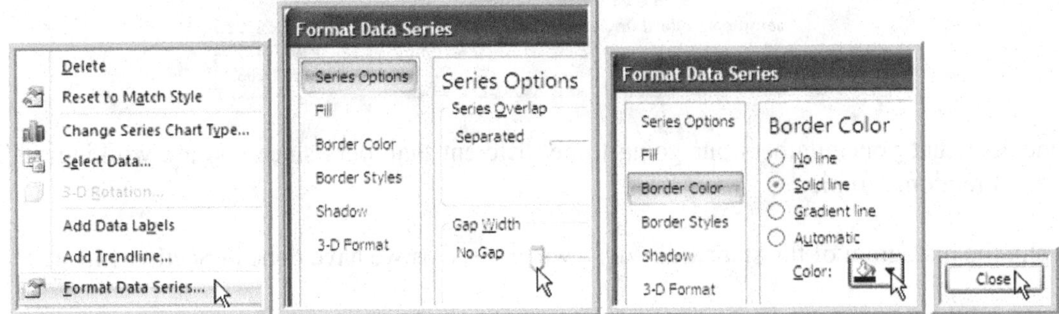

After editing, the result is (see Figure 14.4(a) p. 522 in *Principles of Econometrics, 4e*):

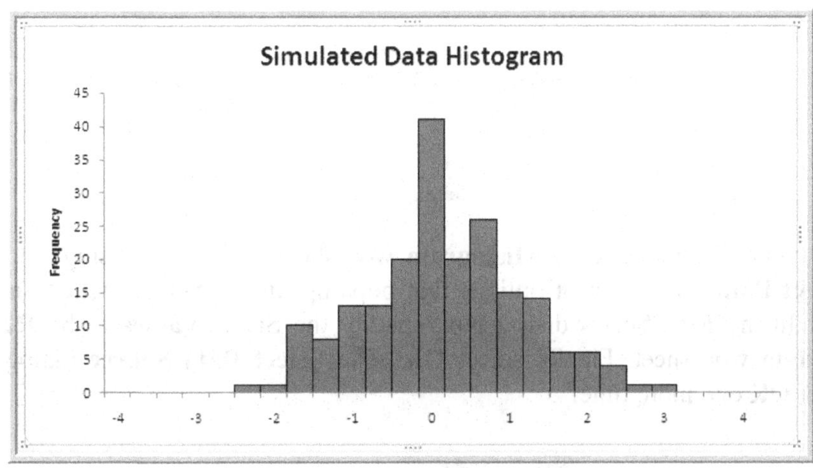

Note: we obtain a different histogram than the one illustrated in Figure 14.4(a) since ours is based on a different random sample. Yours will be different than ours and that of the textbook for the same reason.

We would like to draw a normal distribution on top of this histogram so we can better assess whether or not the ARCH(1) model with constant variance display normal properties.

Go back to your **simulated data** worksheet. In cells **N1:O3**, enter the following labels and formulas.

	N	O
1		**standardized y_t**
2	**sample mean =**	=AVERAGE(J2:J201)
3	**sample variance =**	=VAR(J2:J201)
4	**standard deviation =**	=SQRT(O3)

You should find that the sample mean of the standardized y_t is 0 and the variance is 1.

In cells **Q1:R3**, enter the following labels and formulas.

	Q	R
1	**Mid-point**	**StandardNormal**
2	=L2-0.5*(L3-L2)	=NORMDIST(Q2,0,1, FALSE)
3	=(L2+L3)/2	

In **column L**, we specify the mid-point or mid-value of the bins or class intervals we used to construct the simulated data histogram. In **column M**, we compute the normal distribution values corresponding to those mid-point values, where the normal distribution is specified to have a mean 0 and variance 1.

Copy the content of cell **Q3** to cells **Q4:Q26**, and copy the content of cell **R2** to cells **R3:R26**.

Here is how your table should look (only the first five values are shown below):

	N	O	P	Q	R
1		standardized y_t		Mid-point	Standard Normal
2	sample mean =	-2.77556E-18		-4.166667	6.7763E-05
3	sample variance =	1		-3.833333	0.00025707
4	sample standard deviation =	1		-3.5	0.000872683
5				-3.166667	0.002650976
6				-2.833333	0.0072061

Go back to your **Simulated Data Histogram** worksheet. Select the histogram, right-click and choose **Select Data** on the list of options that pops up. In the **Select Data Source** dialog box, select **Add**. In the **Edit Series** dialog box, specify the **Series values** to be **R2:R26** from the **simulated data** worksheet. Finally select **OK**. The **Select Data Source** dialog box reappears again. Select **OK** one more time.

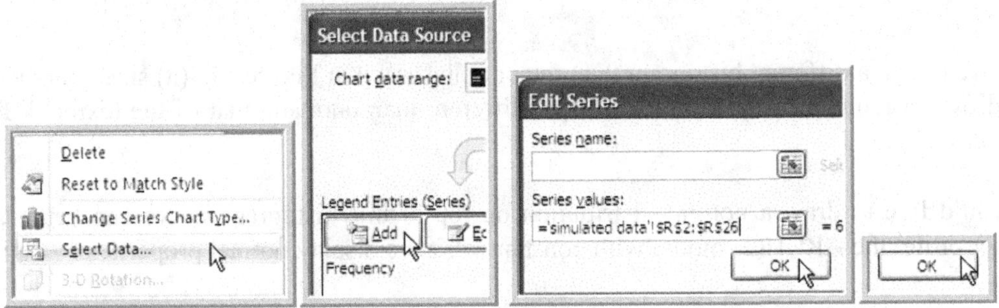

The series you just added is barely visible, at the bottom of your plot area. Select it, right-click and select **Change Series Chart Type**. In the **Change Chart Type** dialog box, select **Line**. In the list of **Line** charts, select **Line** again. Finally select **OK**.

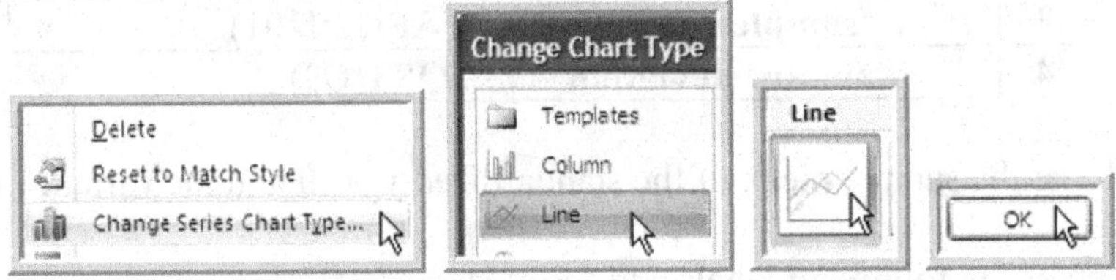

Your series is now a little bit more visible, still at the bottom of your plot area. Select it again, right-click and select **Format Data Series** this time. In the **Series Options**, select **Secondary Axis**.

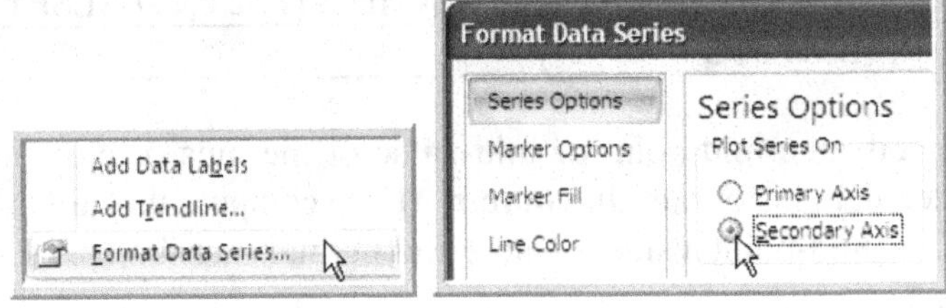

In the **Line Style** options, select **Smoothed Line**. Finally, select **Close**.

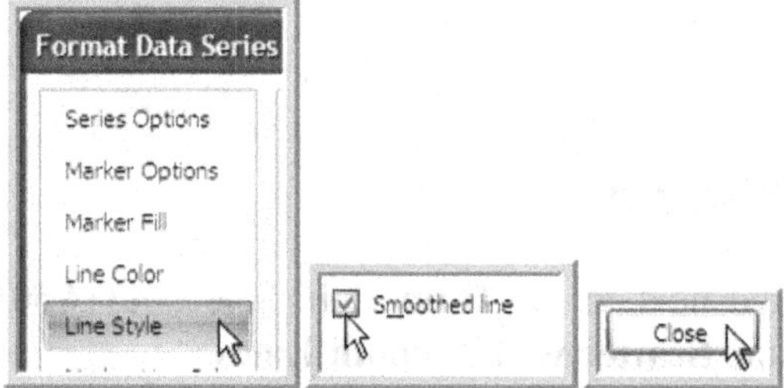

Select the right-vertical axis, right click and select **Format Axis**. Select the **Axis Options** tab, specify **Fixed Minimum** at 0.0 and **Fixed Maximum** at 0.85. Finally select **Close**.

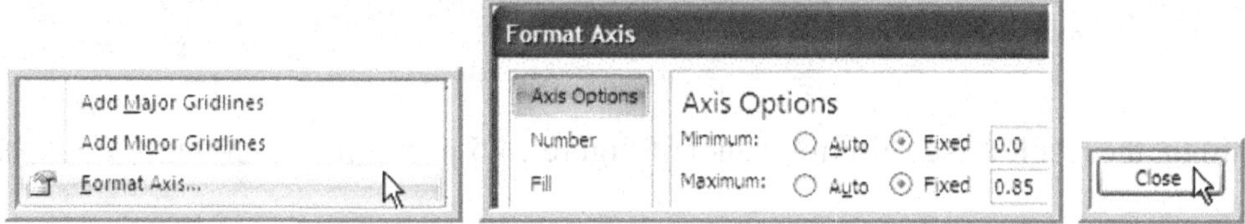

The result is (see also Figure 14.4(a) p. 522 in *Principles of Econometrics, 4e*):

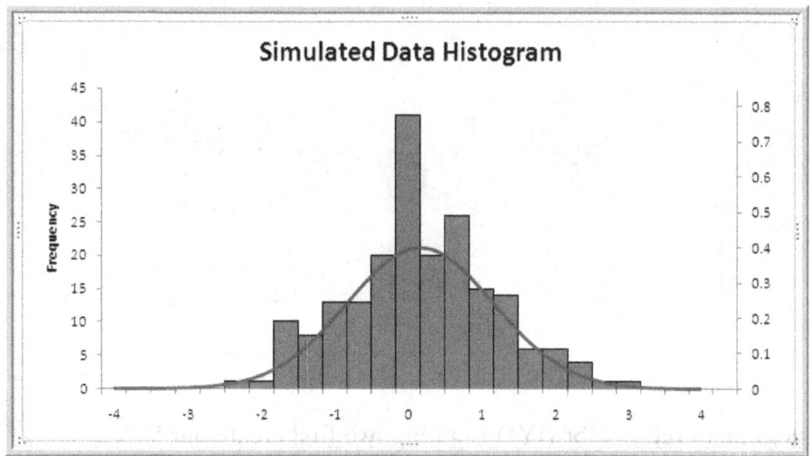

The bottom panels in Figures 14.3 and 14.4 of *Principles of Econometrics, 4e* (p. 522) illustrates the case of a time-varying variance. It is would be much more complicated to generate such a series in Excel; we will not investigate this problem at this point.

14.2 TESTING AND FORECASTING

14.2.1 Testing for ARCH Effects

Open the Excel file ***byd***. Excel opens the data set in Sheet 1 of a new Excel file. Since we would like to save all our work from Chapter 14 in one file, create a new worksheet in your **POE Chapter 14** Excel file, rename it **byd data**, and in it, copy the data set you just opened.

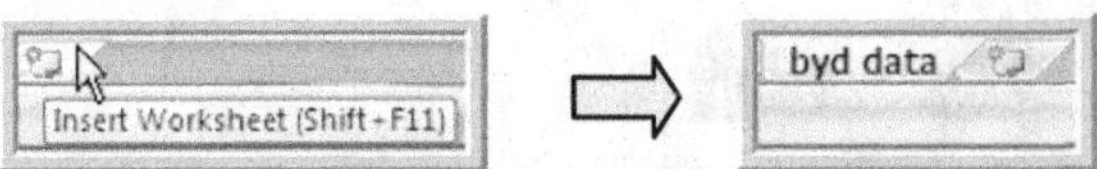

14.2.1a Times Series and Histogram

Select the **Insert** tab located next to the **Home** tab. Select **A1:A501**. In the **Charts** group of commands select **Scatter**, and **Scatter with Smooth Lines.**

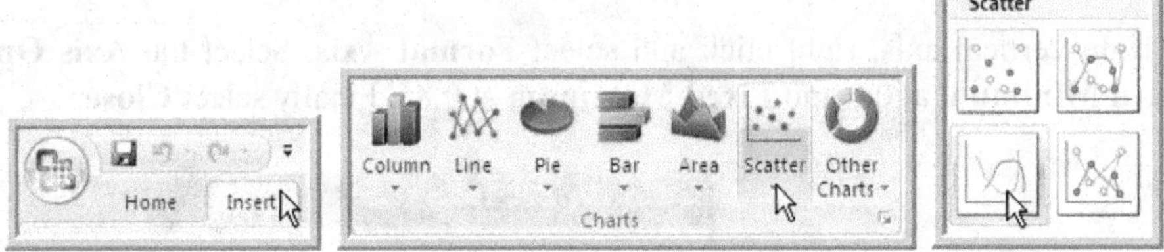

After editing, the result is (see also top panel of Figure 14.5 p. 524 in *Principles of Econometrics, 4e*):

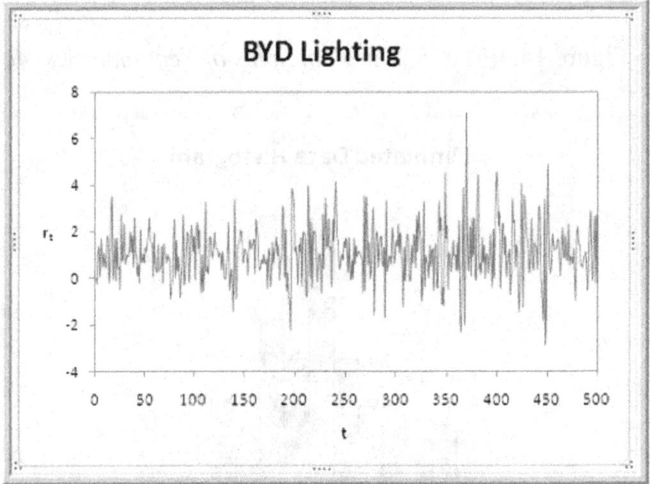

To plot the histogram of returns for BYD Lighting, we first create our BIN column.

In cells **D1:D3**, enter the following label and values.

	D
1	**BIN**
2	-8
3	-7.5

Select cells **D2:D3**, move your cursor to the lower right corner of your selection until it turns into a skinny cross as shown below, left-click, hold it and drag it down to cell **D34**: Excel recognizes the series and automatically completes it for you.

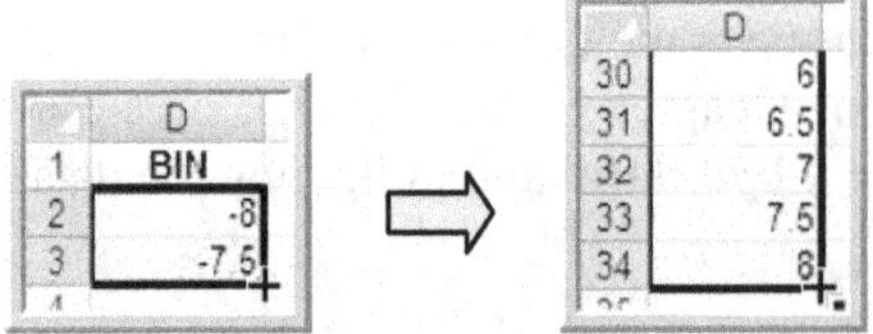

In the **Histogram** dialog box pops up, the **Input Range** should be **A2:A501**, and the **Bin Range** should be **D2:D34**. Check the **New Worksheet Ply** option and name it **BYD Lighting Histogram**; check the box next to **Chart Output**. Finally, select **OK**.

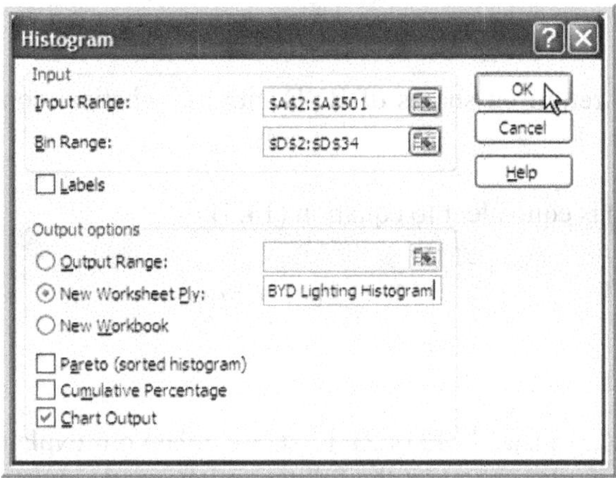

Select the columns in your chart area, right-click and select **Format Data Series**. The **Series Options** tab of the **Format Data Series** dialog box should be open. Select the **Gap Width** button and move it to the far left, towards **No Gap**. In the **Border Color** tab, select **Solid line**, and change the **Color** to black. Finally select **Close**.

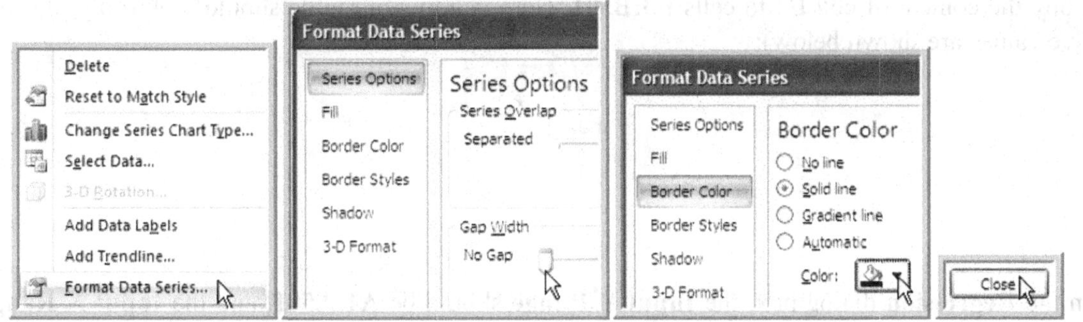

After editing, the result is (see lower panel of Figure 14.5 p. 524 in *Principles of Econometrics, 4e*):

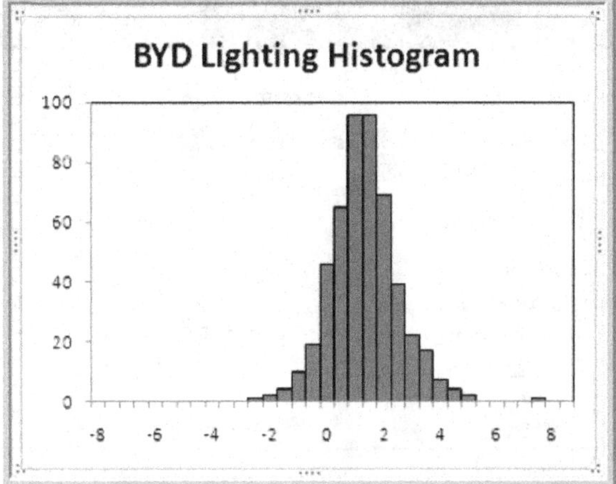

14.2.1b Lagrange Multiplier Test

We first estimate the following mean equation:

$$r_t = \beta_0 + e_t \tag{14.2}$$

where r_t is the monthly return on shares of BYD, the hypothetical company BrightenYourDay Lighting.

Note that equation (14.2) is equivalent to equation (14.3):

$$r_t = \beta_0 x_t + e_t \tag{14.3}$$

where $x_t = 1$ for all t's.

We estimate equation (14.3) instead of (14.2). First, we create our explanatory variable x. In cells **B1:B2** of your **byd data** worksheet, enter the following label and value.

	B
1	x
2	1

Copy the content of cell **B2** to cells **B3:B501**. Here is how your table should look (only the first five values are shown below):

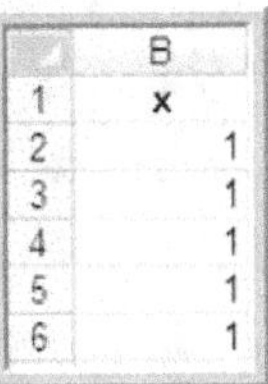

	B
1	x
2	1
3	1
4	1
5	1
6	1

In the **Regression** dialog box, the **Input Y Range** should be **A1:A501**, and the **Input X Range** should be **B1:B501**. Check the boxes next to **Labels** *and* **Constant is Zero** *and* **Residuals**. Select **New Worksheet Ply** and name it **Mean Equation for BYD**. Finally select **OK**.

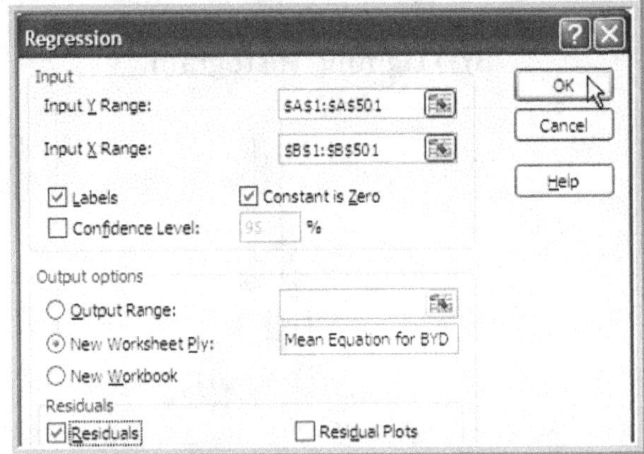

The result is:

	A	B	C	D	E	F	G	H	I
1	SUMMARY OUTPUT								
2									
3	*Regression Statistics*								
4	Multiple R	0.673382652							
5	R Square	0.453444196							
6	Adjusted R Square	0.451440188							
7	Standard Error	1.185024524							
8	Observations	500							
9									
10	ANOVA								
11		*df*	*SS*	*MS*	*F*	*Significance F*			
12	Regression	1	581.3592124	581.3592124	413.9900305	1.97762E-67			
13	Residual	499	700.7372778	1.404283122					
14	Total	500	1282.09649						
15									
16		*Coefficients*	*Standard Error*	*t Stat*	*P-value*	*Lower 95%*	*Upper 95%*	*Lower 95.0%*	*Upper 95.0%*
17	Intercept	0	#N/A	#N/A	#N/A	#N/A	#N/A	#N/A	#N/A
18	x	1.07829422	0.052995908	20.34674496	1.83308E-67	0.974171607	1.182416833	0.974171607	1.182416833
19									
20									
21									
22	RESIDUAL OUTPUT								
23									
24	*Observation*	*Predicted r*	*Residuals*						
25	1	1.07829422	-1.07829422						
26	2	1.07829422	-1.30548722						
27	3	1.07829422	0.27254878						

A Lagrange multiplier (*LM*) test (used previously in Sections 9.3.2 and 8.2.2a) is used to test for the presence of ARCH effects.

To test for first-order ARCH, we first consider the following auxiliary regression:

$$\hat{e}_t^2 = \gamma_0 + \gamma_1 \hat{e}_{t-1}^2 + v_t \tag{14.4}$$

where $\hat{e}_t^2$ are the squared residuals and $\hat{e}_{t-1}^2$ are the *lagged* squared residuals from model (14.2) or (14.3).

The null and alternative hypotheses for a test of the presence of ARCH effects based on the auxiliary regression (14.4) are: $H_0\colon \gamma_1 = 0$ and $H_1\colon \gamma_1 \neq 0$.

When H_0 is true, there are no ARCH effects, and the sample size $(T - q)$, where q is the order of the lag, multiplied by the R^2 goodness-of-fit statistic from (14.4) has a chi-square distribution with $m = S - 1$ degrees of freedom, where S is the number of parameters in (14.4)—note that: $m = S - 1 = q$.

$$\chi^2 = (T - q) \times R^2 \sim \chi^2_{(m=S-1=q)} \tag{14.5}$$

In cells **D25:E26** of your **Mean Equation for BYD** worksheet, enter the following labels and formulas:

	D	E
25	**Residuals$_t^2$**	**Residuals$_{t-1}^2$**
26	=C26^2	=C25^2

Copy the content of cell **D26:E26** to cells **D27:E524**. Here is how your table should look (only the first five values are shown below):

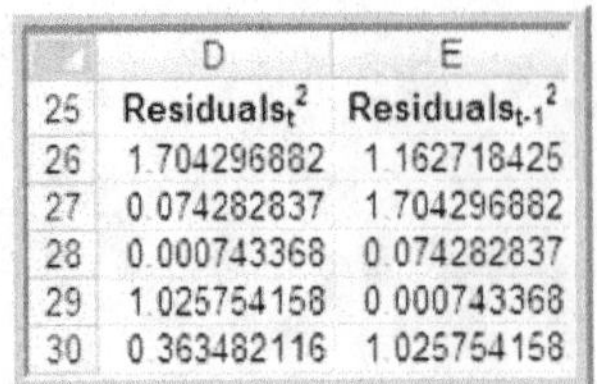

	D	E
25	$Residuals_t^2$	$Residuals_{t-1}^2$
26	1.704296882	1.162718425
27	0.074282837	1.704296882
28	0.000743368	0.074282837
29	1.025754158	0.000743368
30	0.363482116	1.025754158

In the **Regression** dialog box, the **Input Y Range** should be **D25:D524**, and the **Input X Range** should be **E25:E524**. Check the box next to **Labels**. <u>Uncheck</u> the boxes next to **Constant is Zero** <u>*and*</u> **Residuals**. Select **New Worksheet Ply** and name it **Auxiliary Regression**. Finally select **OK**.

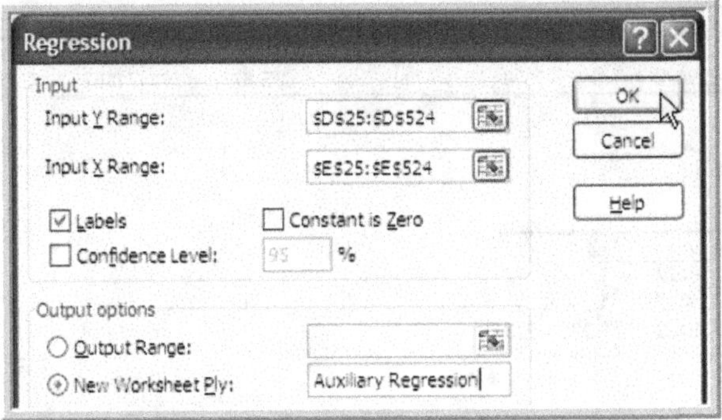

The result is (see also p. 523 in *Principles of Econometrics, 4e*):

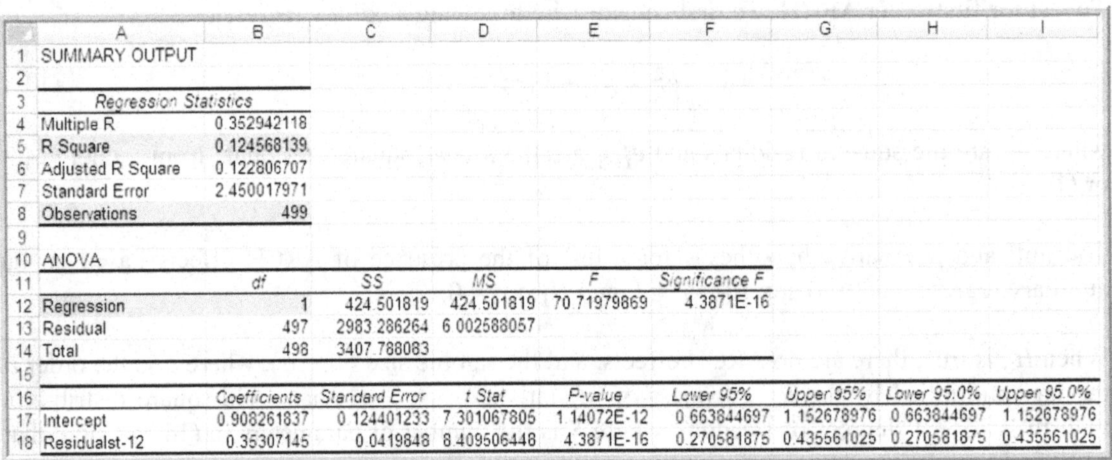

	A	B	C	D	E	F	G	H	I
1	SUMMARY OUTPUT								
2									
3	*Regression Statistics*								
4	Multiple R	0.352942118							
5	R Square	0.124568139							
6	Adjusted R Square	0.122806707							
7	Standard Error	2.450017971							
8	Observations	499							
9									
10	ANOVA								
11		*df*	*SS*	*MS*	*F*	*Significance F*			
12	Regression	1	424.501819	424.501819	70.71979869	4.3871E-16			
13	Residual	497	2983.286264	6.002588057					
14	Total	498	3407.788083						
15									
16		*Coefficients*	*Standard Error*	*t Stat*	*P-value*	*Lower 95%*	*Upper 95%*	*Lower 95.0%*	*Upper 95.0%*
17	Intercept	0.908261837	0.124401233	7.301067805	1.14072E-12	0.663844697	1.152678976	0.663844697	1.152678976
18	Residualst-12	0.35307145	0.0419848	8.409506448	4.3871E-16	0.270581875	0.435561025	0.270581875	0.435561025

The results we are going to use for the Lagrange multiplier test are highlighted in the above table.

Insert a new worksheet by selecting the **Insert Worksheet** tab at the bottom of your screen. Rename it **Lagrange Multiplier Test**.

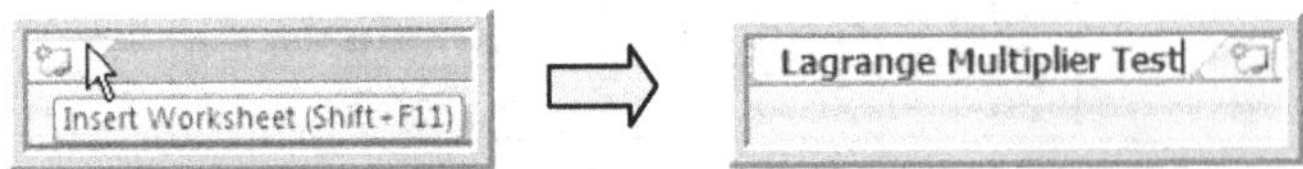

In it copy the Lagrange multiplier test template you created in Chapter 8.

Replace the following reference: **[POE Chapter 8.xlsx]Variance Function** by **Auxiliary Regression**.

	A	B	C
1	**Data Input**	N =	='Auxiliary Regression'!B8
2		S =	='Auxiliary Regression'!B12+1
3		R^2 =	='Auxiliary Regression'!B5
4		α =	
5			
6	**Computed Values**	m =	=C2-1
7		χ^2-critical value =	=CHIINV(C4,C6)
8			
9	**Lagrange Multiplier Test**	χ^2 =	=C1*C3
10		Conclusion =	=IF(C9>=C7,"Reject Ho","Do Not Reject Ho")
11		*p*-value =	=CHIDIST(C9,C6)
12		Conclusion =	=IF(C11<=C4,"Reject Ho","Do Not Reject Ho")

At $\alpha = 0.05$, the result of the test is (see also p. 524 in *Principles of Econometrics, 4e*):

	A	B	C
1	Data Input	N =	499
2		S =	2
3		R^2 =	0.124568
4		α =	0.05
5			
6	Computed Values	m =	1
7		χ^2-critical value =	3.841459
8			
9	Lagrange Multiplier Test	χ^2 =	62.1595
10		Conclusion =	Reject Ho
11		*p*-value =	3.17E-15
12		Conclusion =	Reject Ho

The value of the Lagrange multiplier statistic reported in *Principles of Econometrics, 4e*, p. 524, is $LM = (T-1)R^2 = 499 \times 0.124 = 61.876$. Our calculation is slightly different because more decimal places are used for R^2.

14.2.2 Forecasting Volatility

Equation (14.6) shows the results from estimating an ARCH(1) model applied to the monthly returns from buying shares in the company BrightenYourDayLighting. These results are obtained using econometrics software such as EViews, Stata or GRETL—computer manuals for those can be found at http://www.principlesofeconometrics.com/. The estimated mean of the series is described in (14.6a) while the estimated variance is given in (14.6b):

$$\hat{r}_t = \hat{\beta}_0 = 1.063 \tag{14.6a}$$

$$\hat{h}_t = \hat{\alpha}_0 + \hat{\alpha}_1 \hat{e}_{t-1}^2 = 0.642 + 0.569\hat{e}_{t-1}^2 \tag{14.6b}$$

We can use the estimated model to forecast next period's return r_{t+1} and the conditional volatility h_{t+1}. For our case study of investing in BrightenYourDayLighting, the forecast return and volatility are:

$$\hat{r}_{t+1} = \hat{\beta}_0 = 1.063 \tag{14.7a}$$

$$\hat{h}_{t+1} = \hat{\alpha}_0 + \hat{\alpha}_1\left(r_t - \hat{\beta}_0\right)^2 = 0.642 + 0.569(r_t - 1.063)^2 \tag{14.7b}$$

Go back to your **byd data** worksheet.

In cells **F1:I4** enter the following labels, values and formula. In the last column, you will find the numbers of the equations used, if any.

	F	G	H	I	
1	**ARCH(1)**				
2	**β_0-hat =**	1.063		**h_{t+1}-hat**	
3	**α_0-hat =**	0.642		=$G$3+$G$4*((A2-$G$2)^2)	*(14.7b)*
4	**α_1-hat =**	0.569			

Copy the content of cell **I3** to cells **I4:I501**. Here is how your table should look (only the first five values are shown below):

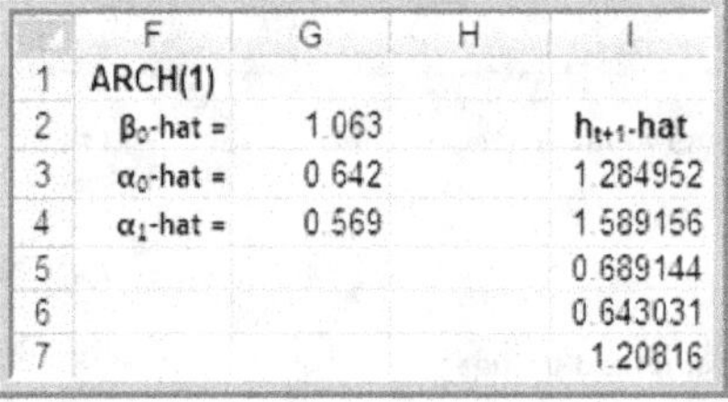

	F	G	H	I
1	ARCH(1)			
2	β_0-hat =	1.063		h_{t+1}-hat
3	α_0-hat =	0.642		1.284952
4	α_1-hat =	0.569		1.589156
5				0.689144
6				0.643031
7				1.20816

Select the **Insert** tab located next to the **Home** tab. Select **I2:I501**. In the **Charts** group of commands select **Scatter**, and **Scatter with Smooth Lines**.

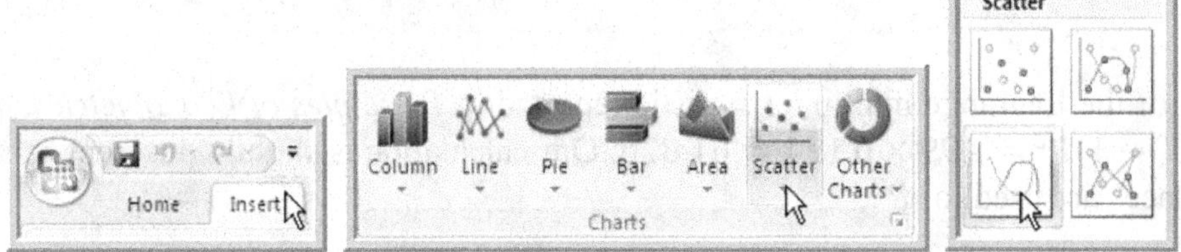

After editing, the result is (see also Figure 14.6 p. 525 in *Principles of Econometrics, 4e*):

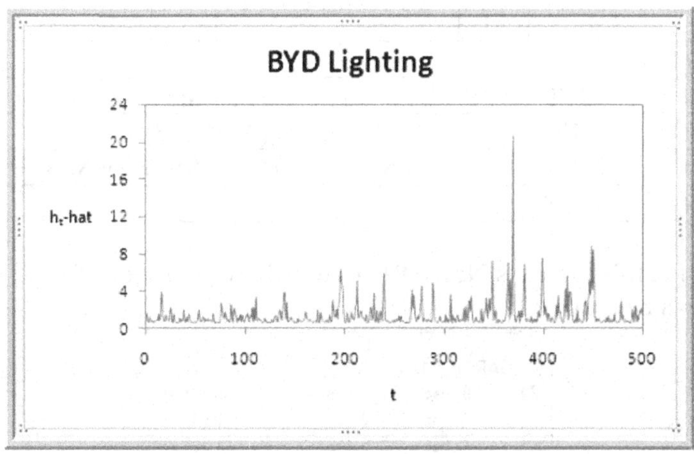

14.3 EXTENSIONS

14.3.1 The GARCH Model

The GARCH model, or generalized ARCH model, allows capturing long lagged effects with few parameters. The general GARCH(p,q) model has p lagged h terms and q lagged e^2 terms. The conditional variance function of a GARCH(1,1) model is given by :

$$h_t = \delta + \alpha_1 e_{t-1}^2 + \beta_1 h_{t-1} \tag{14.8}$$

where $\alpha_1 + \beta_1 < 1$.

The returns to shares in our BrightenYourDayLighting example have been reestimated under the new GARCH(1,1) model:

$$\hat{r}_t = 1.049 \tag{14.9a}$$

$$\hat{h}_t = 0.401 + 0.492\hat{e}_{t-1}^2 + 0.238\hat{h}_{t-1} \tag{14.9b}$$

We use the estimated GARCH(1,1) model to forecast next period's return r_{t+1} and the conditional volatility h_{t+1}:

$$\hat{r}_{t+1} = \hat{\beta}_0 = 1.049 \tag{14.10a}$$

$$\hat{h}_{t+1} = \hat{\delta} + \hat{\alpha}_1\left(r_t - \hat{\beta}_0\right)^2 + \hat{\beta}_1\hat{h}_t = 0.401 + 0.492(r_t - 1.049)^2 + 0.238\hat{h}_t \tag{14.10b}$$

In cells **K1:N5** enter the following labels, values and formulas. In the last column, you will find the numbers of the equations used, if any. Note that for our first $\hat{h}_{t+1}$ value, there is no $\hat{h}_t$ value available, hence the shortened version of equation (14.10b) in cell **N3**.

	K	L	M	N	
1	**GARCH(1)**				
2	**β_0-hat =**	1.049		**h_{t+1}-hat**	
3	**δ-hat =**	0.401		=$L$3+$L$4*((A2-$L$2)^2)	*(14.10b)*
4	**α_1-hat =**	0.492		=$L$3+$L$4*((A3-$L$2)^2)+$L$5*N3	*(14.10b)*
5	**β_1-hat =**	0.238			

Copy the content of cell **N4** to cells **N5:N501**. Here is how your table should look (only the first five values are shown below):

	K	L	M	N
1	GARCH(1,1)			
2	β_0-hat =	1.049		h_{t+1}-hat
3	δ-hat =	0.401		0.942397
4	α_1-hat =	0.492		1.426595
5	β_1-hat =	0.238		0.785355
6				0.589488
7				1.017197

Select the **Insert** tab located next to the **Home** tab. Select **N2:N501**. In the **Charts** group of commands select **Scatter**, and **Scatter with Smooth Lines**.

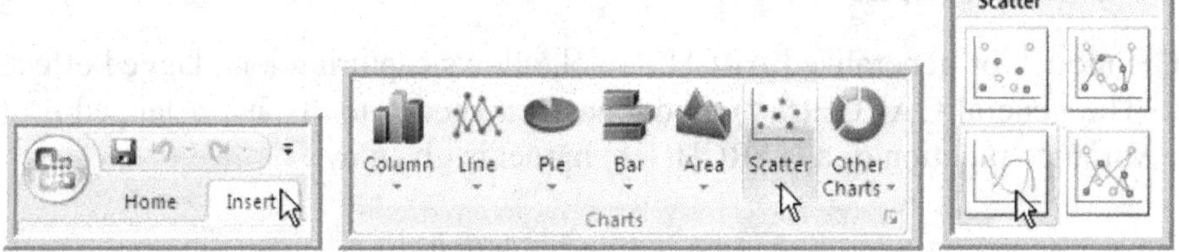

After editing, the result is (see also Figure 14.7b p. 527 in *Principles of Econometrics, 4e*):

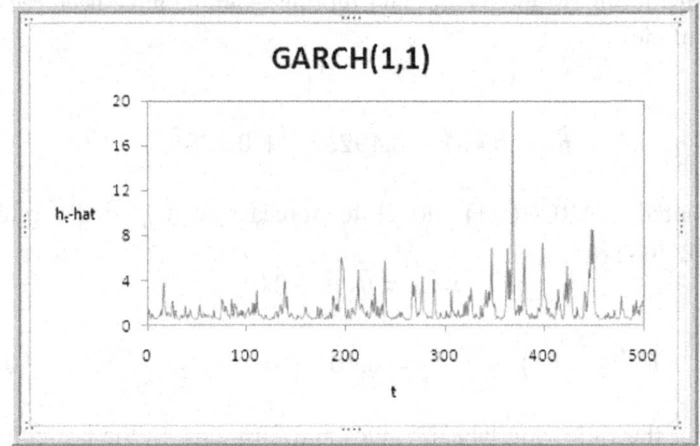

14.3.2 The T-GARCH Model

In the T-GARCH version of the model, the specification of the conditional variance is:

$$h_t = \delta + \alpha_1 e_{t-1}^2 + \gamma d_{t-1} e_{t-1}^2 + \beta_1 h_{t-1} \tag{14.11}$$

$$d_t = \begin{cases} 1 & e_t < 0 \\ 0 & e_t \geq 0 \end{cases}$$

The returns to shares in our BrightenYourDayLighting example have been re-estimated with a T-GARCH(1,1) specification:

$$\hat{r}_t = 0.994 \tag{14.12a}$$

$$\hat{h}_t = 0.356 + 0.263\hat{e}_{t-1}^2 + 0.492 d_{t-1}\hat{e}_{t-1}^2 + 0.287\hat{h}_{t-1} \tag{14.12b}$$

We use the estimated T-GARCH(1,1) model to forecast the conditional volatility.

In cells **P1:U6** enter the following labels, values and formulas. In the last column, you will find the numbers of the equations used, if any. Note that for our first $\hat{h}_t$ value, there is no $\hat{h}_{t-1}$ value available, hence the shortened version of equation (14.12b) in cell **U3**.

	P	Q	R	S
1	**T-GARCH(1,1)**			**e_t**
2	**β_0-hat =**	0.994		=A2-$Q$2
3	**δ-hat =**	0.356		
4	**α_1-hat =**	0.263		
5	**γ-hat =**	0.492		
6	**β_1-hat =**	0.287		

	T	U	
1	**d_t**		
2	=IF(S2<0,"1","0")	**h_t-hat**	
3		=$Q$3+$Q$4*(S2^2)+$Q$5*T2*(S2^2)	*(14.12b)*
4		=$Q$3+$Q$4*(S3^2)+$Q$5*T3*(S3^2)+$Q$6*U3	*(14.12b)*

Copy the content of cells **S2:T2** to cells **S3:T501** and copy the content of cell **U4** to cells **U5:U501**. Here is how your table should look (only the first five values are shown below):

	P	Q	R	S	T	U
1	T-GARCH(1,1)			e_t	d_t	
2	β_0-hat =	0.994		-0.994	1	h_t-hat
3	δ-hat =	0.356		-1.22119	1	1.101967
4	α_1-hat =	0.263		0.356843	0	1.798205
5	γ-hat =	0.492		0.111559	0	0.905575
6	β_1-hat =	0.287		-0.9285	1	0.619173
7				0.687189	0	1.184599

Select the **Insert** tab located next to the **Home** tab. Select **U2:U501**. In the **Charts** group of commands select **Scatter**, and **Scatter with Smooth Lines.**

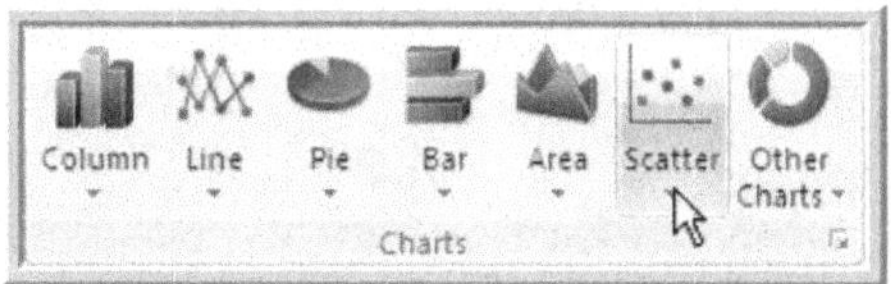

After editing, the result is (see also Figure 14.7d p. 527 in *Principles of Econometrics, 4e*):

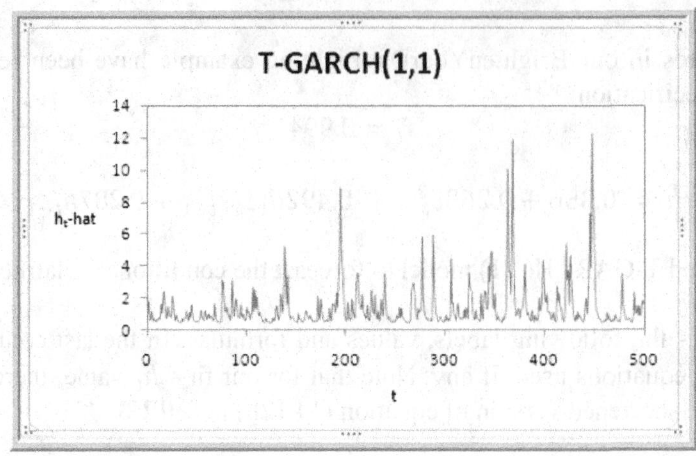

14.3.3 The GARCH-In-Mean Model

The aim of a GARCH-in-mean model is to use risk to explain returns. The equations of a T-GARCH-in-mean model are shown below:

$$y_t = \beta_0 + \theta h_t + e_t \tag{14.13a}$$

$$e_t | I_{t-1} \sim N(0, h_t) \tag{14.13b}$$

$$h_t = \delta + \alpha_1 e_{t-1}^2 + \gamma d_{t-1} e_{t-1}^2 + \beta_1 h_{t-1},\ \delta > 0,\ 0 \le \alpha_1 < 1,\ 0 \le \beta_1 < 1$$

$$d_t = \begin{cases} 1 & e_t < 0 \\ 0 & e_t \ge 0 \end{cases} \tag{14.13c}$$

The returns to shares in our BrightenYourDayLighting example have been reestimated as a T-GARCH-in-mean model. The results are:

$$\hat{r}_t = 0.818 + 0.196 h_t \tag{14.14a}$$

$$\hat{h}_t = 0.370 + 0.295\hat{e}_{t-1}^2 + 0.321 d_{t-1}\hat{e}_{t-1}^2 + 0.278\hat{h}_{t-1} \tag{14.14b}$$

We use the estimated GARCH-in-mean model to forecast conditional return and volatility.

In cells **W1:AC7** enter the following labels, values and formulas. In the last row, you will find the numbers of the equations used, if any. Note that for our first $\hat{h}_t$ value, there is no $\hat{h}_{t-1}$ value available, hence the shortened version of equation (14.14b) in cell **AC3**.

	W	X	Y	Z	AA
1	**GARCH-in-mean**			$\mathbf{e_t}$	$\mathbf{d_t}$
2	**β_0-hat =**	0.818		=A2-$X$2	=IF(Z2<0,"1","0")
3	**θ =**	0.196		=A3-$X$2-$X$3*AC3	
4	**δ-hat =**	0.370			
5	**α_1-hat =**	0.295			
6	**γ-hat =**	0.321			
7	**β_1-hat =**	0.278			

	AB	AC
1		
2	**E(r$_t$)**	**h$_t$-hat**
3	=$X$2+$X$3*AC3	=$X$4+$X$5*(Z2^2)+$X$6*AA2*(Z2^2)
4		=$X$4+$X$5*(Z3^2)+$X$6*AA3*(Z3^2)+$X$7*AC3
	(14.14a)	*(14.14b)*

Copy the content of cell **Z3** to cells **Z4:Z501**, copy the content of cell **AA2** to cells **AA3:AA501**, copy the content of cell **AB3** to cells **AB4:AB501**, and copy the content of cell **AC4** to cells **AC5:AC501**. Here is how your table should look (only the first five values are shown below):

	W	X	Y	Z	AA	AB	AC
1	GARCH-in-mean			e_t	d_t		
2	β_0-hat =	0.818		-0.818	1	E(r$_t$)	h$_t$-hat
3	θ =	0.196		-1.1985	1	0.971307	0.78218
4	δ-hat =	0.37		0.244278	0	1.106565	1.47227
5	α_1-hat =	0.295		0.131368	0	0.974191	0.796894
6	γ-hat =	0.321		-0.86944	1	0.934939	0.596628
7	β_1-hat =	0.278		0.666892	0	1.014297	1.001513

Select the **Insert** tab located next to the **Home** tab. Select **AB2:AB501**. In the **Charts** group of commands select **Scatter**, and **Scatter with Smooth Lines**.

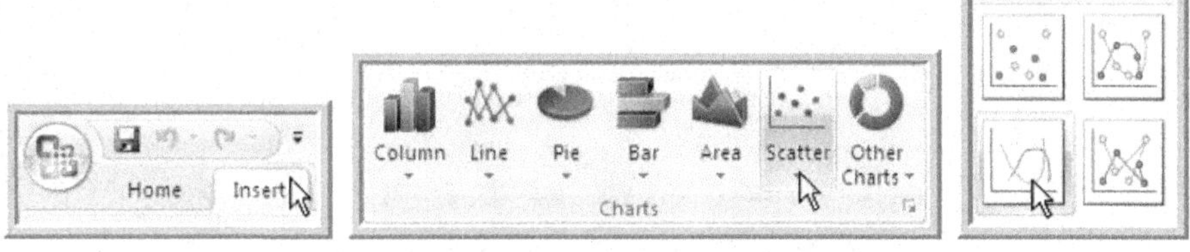

After editing, the result is (see also Figure 14.7e p. 527 in *Principles of Econometrics, 4e*):

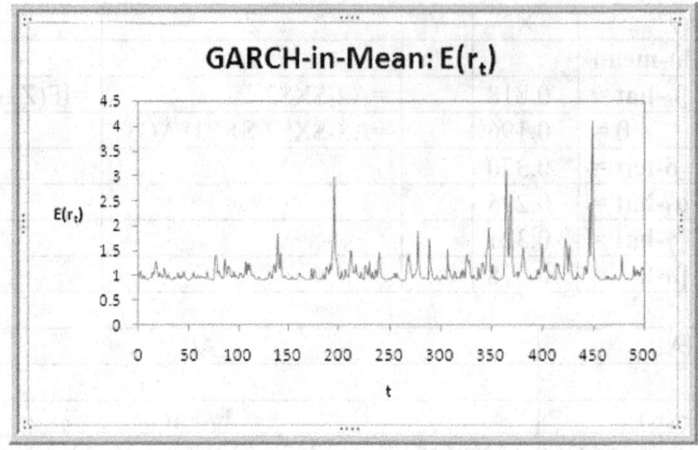

Select cells **AC2:AC501** and plot a **Scatter with Smooth Lines** again.

After editing, the result is (see also Figure 14.7f p. 527 in *Principles of Econometrics, 4e*):

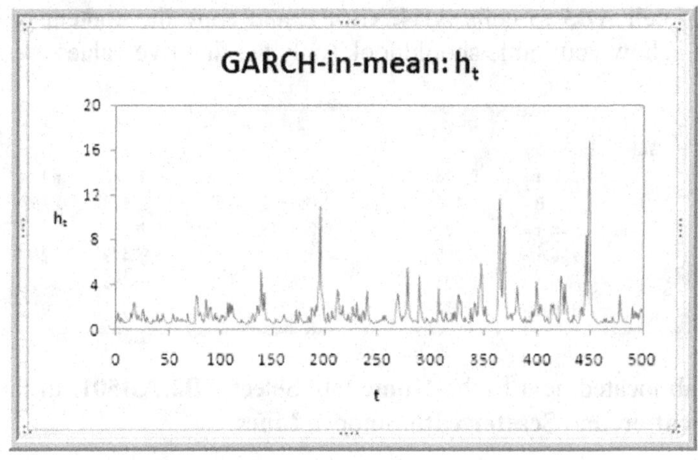

CHAPTER 15

Panel Data Models

Chapter Outline

15.1 POOLED LEAST SQUARES ESTIMATES OF WAGE EQUATION

Open the Excel file ***nls_panel***. Save your file as **POE Chapter 15**. Rename sheet 1 **nls panel data**. The **nls panel data** contains information on a sample of $N = 716$ women who were interviewed over $T = 5$ years: 1982, 1983, 1985, 1987 and 1988.

We consider the following wage equation:

$$ln(WAGE)_{it} = \begin{array}{l}\beta_1 + \beta_2 EDUC_{it} + \beta_3 EXPER_{it} + \beta_4 EXPER_{it}^2 + \beta_5 TENURE_{it} \\ + \beta_6 TENURE_{it}^2 + \beta_7 BLACK_i + \beta_8 SOUTH_{it} + \beta_9 UNION_{it} + e_{it}\end{array} \quad (15.1)$$

where $EDUC$ measures years of education. $EXPER$ measures total labor force experience, and its square is measured by $EXPER^2$. $TENURE$ measures tenure in current job, and its square is measured by $TENURE^2$. $BLACK$, $SOUTH$ and $UNION$ are indicator variables.

In cells **T1:AB2**, enter the following labels and formulas.

	T	U	V	W	X	Y	Z	AA	AB
1	**lnwage**	**educ**	**exper**	**exper2**	**tenure**	**tenure2**	**black**	**south**	**Union**
2	=C2	=F2	=O2	=P2	=Q2	=R2	=M2	=L2	=N2

Copy the content of cells **T2:AB2** to cells **T3:AB3581**. Here is how your table should look (only the first five values are shown below):

	T	U	V	W	X	Y	Z	AA	AB
1	lnwage	educ	exper	exper2	tenure	tenure2	black	south	union
2	1.808289	12	7.666667	58.77777	7.666667	58.77777	1	0	1
3	1.863417	12	8.583333	73.67361	8.583333	73.67361	1	0	1
4	1.789367	12	10.17949	103.622	1.833333	3.361111	1	0	1
5	1.84653	12	12.17949	148.3399	3.75	14.0625	1	0	1
6	1.856449	12	13.62179	185.5533	5.25	27.5625	1	0	1

In the **Regression** dialog box, the **Input Y Range** should be **T1:T3581**, and the **Input X Range** should be **U1:AB3581**. Check the box next to **Labels** *and* **Residuals**. Select **New Worksheet Ply** and name it **Pooled LS Wage Equation**. Finally select **OK**.

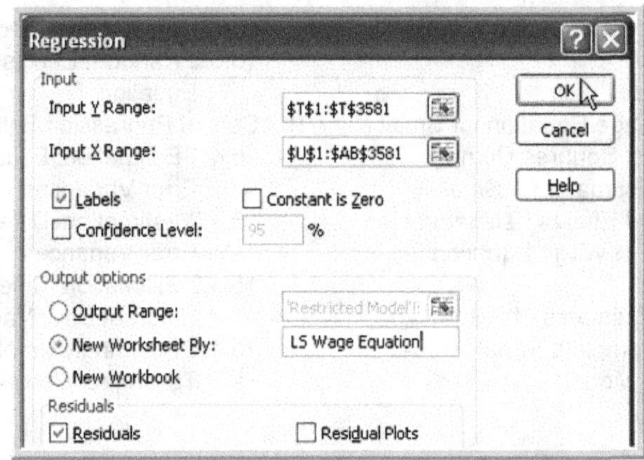

The result is (see also Table 15.2 p. 543 in *Principles of Econometrics, 4e*):

	A	B	C	D	E	F	G	H	I
1	SUMMARY OUTPUT								
2									
3	*Regression Statistics*								
4	Multiple R	0.570601352							
5	R Square	0.325585903							
6	Adjusted R Square	0.324075034							
7	Standard Error	0.38197492							
8	Observations	3580							
9									
10	ANOVA								
11		*df*	*SS*	*MS*	*F*	*Significance F*			
12	Regression	8	251.5350441	31.44188051	215.495803	1.1658E-298			
13	Residual	3571	521.0261811	0.145904839					
14	Total	3579	772.5612252						
15									
16		*Coefficients*	*Standard Error*	*t Stat*	*P-value*	*Lower 95%*	*Upper 95%*	*Lower 95.0%*	*Upper 95.0%*
17	Intercept	0.476600026	0.05615585	8.487094854	3.0622E-17	0.366499268	0.586700784	0.366499268	0.586700784
18	educ	0.071448792	0.002689392	26.56689212	4.5664E-142	0.066175893	0.076721691	0.066175893	0.076721691
19	exper	0.055685059	0.00860716	6.469620676	1.11606E-10	0.038809616	0.072560501	0.038809616	0.072560501
20	exper2	-0.001147538	0.000361287	-3.176250628	0.001504632	-0.001855887	-0.000439188	-0.001855887	-0.000439188
21	tenure	0.014960011	0.004407276	3.394389488	0.000695317	0.006318981	0.023601042	0.006318981	0.023601042
22	tenure2	-0.000486042	0.000257704	-1.886045622	0.059369878	-0.000991304	1.92203E-05	-0.000991304	1.92203E-05
23	black	-0.116713867	0.015715895	-7.426485425	1.3874E-13	-0.147526899	-0.085900835	-0.147526899	-0.085900835
24	south	-0.106002565	0.014200829	-7.464533577	1.04458E-13	-0.133845115	-0.078160016	-0.133845115	-0.078160016
25	union	0.132243201	0.014961608	8.838836333	1.48971E-18	0.102909047	0.161577355	0.102909047	0.161577355
26									
27									
28									
29	RESIDUAL OUTPUT								
30									
31	*Observation*	*Predicted lnwage*	*Residuals*						
32	1	1.79510891	0.01318009						
33	2	1.835533305	0.027883695						
34	3	1.823243235	-0.033876235						

15.2 THE FIXED EFFECTS MODEL

15.2.1 Estimates of Wage Equation for Small *N*

15.2.1a The Least Squares Dummy Variable Estimator for Small N

Again, we consider a wage equation model, but this time we are working with $N = 10$ women, over the same period of $T = 5$ years. Furthermore, we assume that all behavioral differences between individuals and over time are captured by the intercept. Assuming equal variances of the error terms across individuals, this model can follow the dummy variable format of (15. 2):

$$\begin{aligned} ln(WAGE)_{it} = \beta_{1,1}D_{1i} + \beta_{1,2}D_{2i} + \cdots + \beta_{1,10}D_{10i} + \beta_2 EXPER_{it} \\ + \beta_3 EXPER_{it}^2 + \beta_4 TENURE_{it} + \beta_5 TENURE_{it}^2 \\ + \beta_6 UNION_{it} + e_{it} \end{aligned} \quad (15.2)$$

where D_{ki}, $k = 1, \ldots, 10$ are 10 dummy variables defined as: $D_{ki} = \begin{cases} 1 & i = k \\ 0 & otherwise \end{cases}$.

In cells **AD1:AR2**, enter the following labels and formulas:

	AD	AE	AF	AG	AH
1	**d1**	**d2**	**d3**	**d4**	**d5**
2	=IF(A2=1,1,0)	=IF(A2=2,1,0)	=IF(A2=3,1,0)	=IF(A2=4,1,0)	=IF(A2=5,1,0)

	AI	AJ	AK	AL	AM
1	**d6**	**d7**	**d8**	**d9**	**d10**
2	=IF(A2=6,1,0)	=IF(A2=7,1,0)	=IF(A2=8,1,0)	=IF(A2=9,1,0)	=IF(A2=10,1,0)

	AN	AO	AP	AQ	AR
1	**exper**	**exper2**	**tenure**	**tenure2**	**union**
2	=O2	=P2	=Q2	=R2	=N2

Below cells **AD1:AM1**, we assign values to the dummy variables. In cell **AD2**, Excel is instructed to look at the value contained in cell **A2**. If this value is equal to **1**, i.e. if we are looking at information regarding individual **1**, then the dummy variable **d1** is assigned the value **1**, and **0** otherwise. In cell **AE2**, Excel is again instructed to look at the value contained in cell **A2**. This time, if this value is equal to **2**, i.e. if we are looking at information regarding individual **2**, then the dummy variable **d2** is assigned the value **1**, and **0** otherwise. 1's and 0's are assigned similarly to dummy variables **d3-d10** (for more details on the IF function, see Section 3.1.4e).

Copy the content of cells **AD2:AR2** to cells **AD3:AR51**. Here is how your table should look (only the first five values are shown below):

	AD	AE	AF	AG	AH	AI	AJ	AK	AL	AM	AN	AO	AP	AQ	AR
1	d1	d2	d3	d4	d5	d6	d7	d8	d9	d10	exper	exper2	tenure	tenure2	union
2	1	0	0	0	0	0	0	0	0	0	7.666667	58.77777	7.666667	58.77777	1
3	1	0	0	0	0	0	0	0	0	0	8.583333	73.67361	8.583333	73.67361	1
4	1	0	0	0	0	0	0	0	0	0	10.17949	103.622	1.833333	3.361111	1
5	1	0	0	0	0	0	0	0	0	0	12.17949	148.3399	3.75	14.0625	1
6	1	0	0	0	0	0	0	0	0	0	13.62179	185.5533	5.25	27.5625	1

In the **Regression** dialog box, the **Input Y Range** should be **C1:C51**, and the **Input X Range** should be **AD1:AR51**. Check the boxes next to **Labels** *and* **Constant is Zero**. Select **New Worksheet Ply** and name it **LS Dummy Variable Wage Equation**. Finally select **OK**.

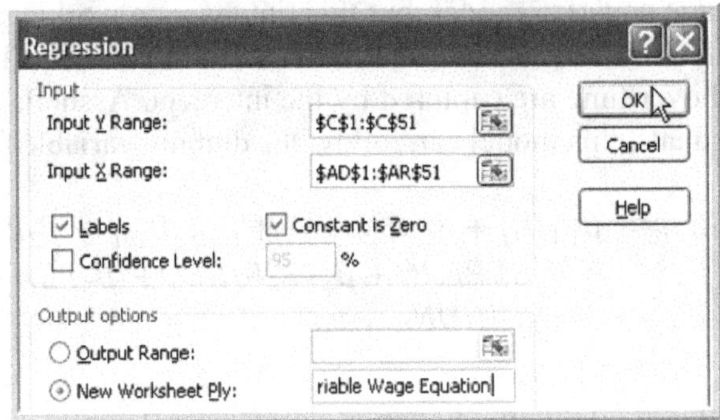

The result is (see also Table 15.3 p. 545 in *Principles of Econometrics, 4e*):

	A	B	C	D	E	F	G	H	I
1	SUMMARY OUTPUT								
2									
3	*Regression Statistics*								
4	Multiple R	0.994617953							
5	R Square	0.989264872							
6	Adjusted R Square	0.956399393							
7	Standard Error	0.276053302							
8	Observations	50							
9									
10	ANOVA								
11		*df*	*SS*	*MS*	*F*	*Significance F*			
12	Regression	15	245.787227	16.38581513	215.0216335	3.64051E-29			
13	Residual	35	2.667189903	0.076205426					
14	Total	50	248.4544169						
15									
16		*Coefficients*	*Standard Error*	*t Stat*	*P-value*	*Lower 95%*	*Upper 95%*	*Lower 95.0%*	*Upper 95.0%*
17	Intercept	0	#N/A	#N/A	#N/A	#N/A	#N/A	#N/A	#N/A
18	d1	0.151905392	1.096745764	0.138505565	0.890634719	-2.074606865	2.378417649	-2.074606865	2.378417649
19	d2	0.186894325	1.071484875	0.174425537	0.862536102	-1.988335601	2.362124252	-1.988335601	2.362124252
20	d3	-0.06304245	1.35091707	-0.04666641	0.963044365	-2.805549888	2.679464987	-2.805549888	2.679464987
21	d4	0.185625866	1.343498368	0.138166052	0.89090105	-2.541820806	2.913072537	-2.541820806	2.913072537
22	d5	0.938986547	1.097780248	0.855350193	0.398174997	-1.289625824	3.167598918	-1.289625824	3.167598918
23	d6	0.794484529	1.111771459	0.714611373	0.479588711	-1.462531509	3.051500567	-1.462531509	3.051500567
24	d7	0.581198727	1.235914274	0.470258124	0.64108787	-1.927840623	3.090238078	-1.927840623	3.090238078
25	d8	0.537924881	1.097498134	0.4901374	0.627095226	-1.690114767	2.76596453	-1.690114767	2.76596453
26	d9	0.418334011	1.084048857	0.385899592	0.701906832	-1.782402154	2.619070176	-1.782402154	2.619070176
27	d10	0.614557865	1.090176696	0.563723172	0.576536971	-1.598618475	2.827734205	-1.598618475	2.827734205
28	exper	0.237998541	0.187756613	1.267590719	0.213312844	-0.143167646	0.619164727	-0.143167646	0.619164727
29	exper2	-0.008188168	0.007904819	-1.035845053	0.307378566	-0.024235804	0.007859468	-0.024235804	0.007859468
30	tenure	-0.01235005	0.034143325	-0.361711998	0.719741906	-0.081664684	0.056964583	-0.081664684	0.056964583
31	tenure2	0.00229615	0.002688457	0.854077425	0.398870183	-0.003161707	0.007754008	-0.003161707	0.007754008
32	union	0.113543476	0.150862842	0.752627185	0.45670644	-0.192724374	0.419811327	-0.192724374	0.419811327

We test the following hypothesis using an *F*-test:

$$\begin{aligned} &H_0: \beta_{1,1} = \beta_{1,2} = \cdots = \beta_{1,10} \\ &H_1: \text{the } \beta_{1,i} \text{ are not all equal} \end{aligned} \tag{15.3}$$

Our unrestricted model is equation (15.2). In the restricted model, equation (15.4) below, all the intercept parameters are equal.

$$\begin{aligned} ln(WAGE)_{it} = \beta_1 + \beta_2 EXPER_{it} + \beta_3 EXPER_{it}^2 + \beta_4 TENURE_{it} \\ + \beta_5 TENURE_{it}^2 + \beta_6 UNION_{it} + e_{it} \end{aligned} \tag{15.4}$$

Go back to your **nls panel data** worksheet.

In the **Regression** dialog box, the **Input Y Range** should be **C1:C51**, and the **Input X Range** should be **AN1:AR51**. Check the box next to **Labels.** <u>*Uncheck*</u> the box next to **Constant is Zero**. Select **New Worksheet Ply** and name it **Restricted Model**. Finally select **OK**.

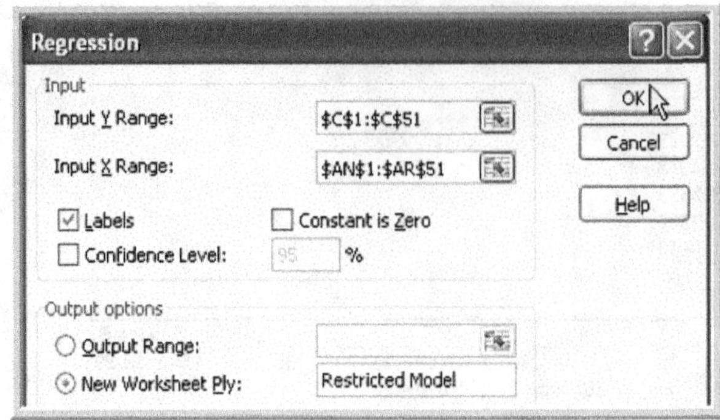

The result of this pooled regression model is (see also Table 15.4 p. 546 in *Principles of Econometrics, 4e*):

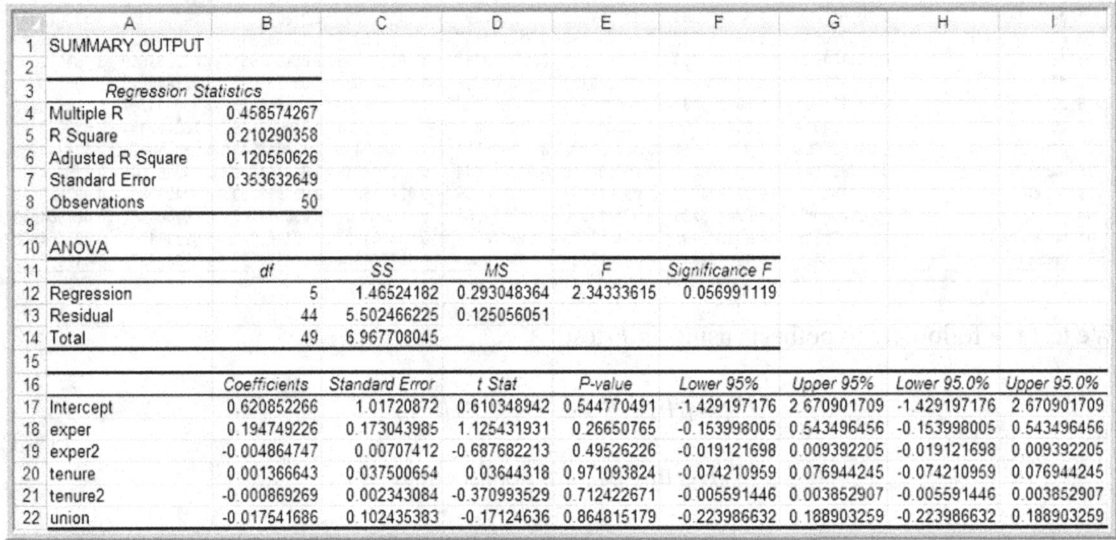

	A	B	C	D	E	F	G	H	I
1	SUMMARY OUTPUT								
2									
3	*Regression Statistics*								
4	Multiple R	0.458574267							
5	R Square	0.210290358							
6	Adjusted R Square	0.120550626							
7	Standard Error	0.353632649							
8	Observations	50							
9									
10	ANOVA								
11		*df*	*SS*	*MS*	*F*	*Significance F*			
12	Regression	5	1.46524182	0.293048364	2.34333615	0.056991119			
13	Residual	44	5.502466225	0.125056051					
14	Total	49	6.967708045						
15									
16		*Coefficients*	*Standard Error*	*t Stat*	*P-value*	*Lower 95%*	*Upper 95%*	*Lower 95.0%*	*Upper 95.0%*
17	Intercept	0.620852266	1.01720872	0.610348942	0.544770491	-1.429197176	2.670901709	-1.429197176	2.670901709
18	exper	0.194749226	0.173043985	1.125431931	0.26650765	-0.153998005	0.543496456	-0.153998005	0.543496456
19	exper2	-0.004864747	0.00707412	-0.687682213	0.49526226	-0.019121698	0.009392205	-0.019121698	0.009392205
20	tenure	0.001366643	0.037500654	0.03644318	0.971093824	-0.074210959	0.076944245	-0.074210959	0.076944245
21	tenure2	-0.000869269	0.002343084	-0.370993529	0.712422671	-0.005591446	0.003852907	-0.005591446	0.003852907
22	union	-0.017541686	0.102435383	-0.17124636	0.864815179	-0.223986632	0.188903259	-0.223986632	0.188903259

Insert a new worksheet by selecting the **Insert Worksheet** tab at the bottom of your screen. Rename it **F-test**.

In it copy the F-test template you created in Chapter 6.

Replace the references to **[POE Chapter 6.xlsx]Unrestricted Model** by **LS Dummy Variable Wage Equation**, and delete all other references to **[POE Chapter 6.xlsx]**. Also, in cell **B2**, change the notation for the total number of observations from **N** to **NT**, which corresponds to the number of cross-sectional units (N) times the number of time periods (T) of the panel data. Finally, since our **LS Dummy Variable Wage Equation** model does not have an intercept, the total number of parameters K in the model corresponds to the regression degrees of freedom in the summary output: delete the **+1** in cell **C3** of your template.

	A	B	C
1	**Data Input**	J =	
2		NT =	='LS Dummy Variable Wage Equation'!B8
3		K =	='LS Dummy Variable Wage Equation'!B12
4		SSE_U =	='LS Dummy Variable Wage Equatioin'!C13
5		SSE_R =	='Restricted Model'!C13
6		α =	
8	**Computed Values**	m_1 =	=C1
9		m_2 =	=C2-C3
10		F_c=	=FINV(C6,C8,C9)
12	**F-test**	F-statistic=	=((C5-C4)/C8)/(C4/C9)
13		Conclusion =	=IF(C12>=C10,"Reject Ho","Do Not Reject Ho")
14		p-value =	=FDIST(C12,C8,C9)
15		Conclusion =	=IF(C14<=C6,"Reject Ho","Do Not Reject Ho")

With 9 joint null hypotheses, at $\alpha = 0.05$, the results of the *F*-test are (see also p. 546 of *Principles of Econometrics, 4e*):

	A	B	C
1	Data Input	J =	9
2		N =	50
3		K =	15
4		SSE_U =	2.66719
5		SSE_R =	5.502466
6		α =	0.05

	A	B	C
8	Computed Values	m_1 =	9
9		m_2 =	35
10		Fc =	2.160829
11			
12	F-test	F-statistic =	4.133967
13		Conclusion =	Reject Ho
14		p-value =	0.001084
15		Conclusion =	Reject Ho

15.2.1b The Fixed Effects Estimator: Estimates of Wage Equation for N = 10

We consider the following wage equation:

$$\ln(\widetilde{WAGE})_{it} = \begin{matrix} \beta_2\widetilde{EXPER}_{it} + \beta_3\widetilde{EXPER}^2_{it} + \beta_4\widetilde{TENURE}_{it} \\ +\beta_5\widetilde{TENURE}^2_{it} + \beta_6\widetilde{UNION}_{it} + \tilde{e}_{it} \end{matrix} \qquad (15.5)$$

where variables are in deviation from the mean form.

Go back to your **nls panel data** worksheet where we will first transform our data in deviation from the mean form.

In cells **AT1:AY2**, enter the following labels and formulas.

	AT	AU	AV	AW	AX	AY
1	**lnwage**	**exper**	**exper2**	**tenure**	**tenure2**	**union**
2	=C2	=O2	=P2	=Q2	=R2	=N2

Copy the content of cells **AT2:AY2** to cells **AT3:AY51**.

The result is:

	AT	AU	AV	AW	AX	AY
1	lnwage	exper	exper2	tenure	tenure2	union
2	1.808289	7.666667	58.77777	7.666667	58.77777	1
3	1.863417	8.583333	73.67361	8.583333	73.67361	1
4	1.789367	10.17949	103.622	1.833333	3.361111	1
5	1.84653	12.17949	148.3399	3.75	14.0625	1
6	1.856449	13.62179	185.5533	5.25	27.5625	1

In cells **BA1:BA6** and **BB1:BF1**, enter the following labels and formulas.

	BA
1	**lnwagebar**
2	=AVERAGE(AT2:AT6)
3	=AVERAGE(AT2:AT6)
4	=AVERAGE(AT2:AT6)
5	=AVERAGE(AT2:AT6)
6	=AVERAGE(AT2:AT6)

	BB	BC	BD
1	**experbar**	**exper2bar**	**tenurebar**

	BE	BF
1	**tenure2bar**	**unionbar**

Copy the content of cells **BA2:BA6** to cells **BB2:BF6**.

The result is:

	BA	BB	BC	BD	BE	BF
1	lnwagebar	experbar	exper2bar	tenurebar	tenure2bar	unionbar
2	1.8328104	10.44615	113.99332	5.4166666	35.4874978	1
3	1.8328104	10.44615	113.99332	5.4166666	35.4874978	1
4	1.8328104	10.44615	113.99332	5.4166666	35.4874978	1
5	1.8328104	10.44615	113.99332	5.4166666	35.4874978	1
6	1.8328104	10.44615	113.99332	5.4166666	35.4874978	1

Select cells **BA2:BF6**, move your cursor to the lower right corner of your selection until it turns into a skinny cross as shown below; left-click, hold it and drag it down to cell **BF51**.

	BA	BB	BC	BD	BE	BF
1	lnwagebar	experbar	exper2bar	tenurebar	tenure2bar	unionbar
2	1.8328104	10.44615	113.99332	5.4166666	35.4874978	1
3	1.8328104	10.44615	113.99332	5.4166666	35.4874978	1
4	1.8328104	10.44615	113.99332	5.4166666	35.4874978	1
5	1.8328104	10.44615	113.99332	5.4166666	35.4874978	1
6	1.8328104	10.44615	113.99332	5.4166666	35.4874978	1
7						

Here is how your table should look (only the *last* five values are shown below):

	BA	BB	BC	BD	BE	BF
47	2.276607	13.19102	179.63768	2.1333334	8.647222	0
48	2.276607	13.19102	179.63768	2.1333334	8.647222	0
49	2.276607	13.19102	179.63768	2.1333334	8.647222	0
50	2.276607	13.19102	179.63768	2.1333334	8.647222	0
51	2.276607	13.19102	179.63768	2.1333334	8.647222	0

In cells **BH1:BM2**, enter the following labels and formula.

	BH	BI	BJ	BK	BL	BM
1	**lnwaged**	**experd**	**exper2d**	**tenured**	**tenure2d**	**uniond**
2	=AT2-BA2					

Copy the content of cell **BH2** to cells **BI2:BM2** and then copy the content of cells **BH2:BM2** to cells **BH3:BM51**. Here is how your table should look (only the first five values are shown below):

	BH	BI	BJ	BK	BL	BM
1	**lnwaged**	**experd**	**exper2d**	**tenured**	**tenure2d**	**uniond**
2	-0.02452	-2.77949	-55.2155	2.25	23.29027	0
3	0.030607	-1.86282	-40.3197	3.166666	38.18611	0
4	-0.04344	-0.26666	-10.3713	-3.58333	-32.1264	0
5	0.01372	1.733336	34.34659	-1.66667	-21.425	0
6	0.023639	3.175636	71.55998	-0.16667	-7.925	0

In the **Regression** dialog box, the **Input Y Range** should be **BH1:BH51**, and the **Input X Range** should be **BI1:BM51**. Check the boxes next to **Labels** *and* **Constant is Zero**. Select **New Worksheet Ply** and name it **Fixed Effects Wage Equation**. Finally select **OK**.

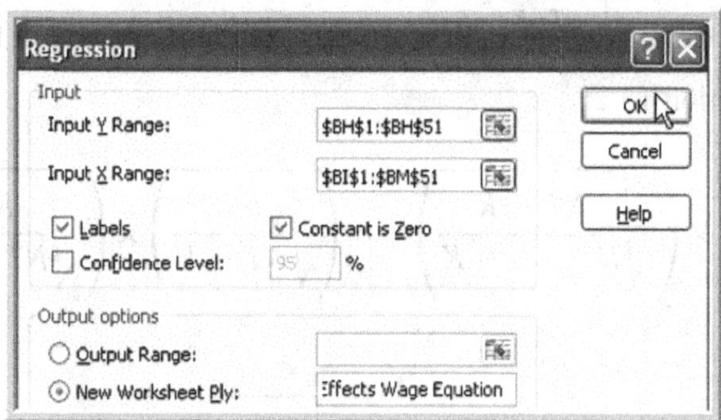

The result is (see also Table 15.6 p.549 in *Principles of Econometrics, 4e*):

	A	B	C	D	E	F	G	H	I
1	SUMMARY OUTPUT								
2									
3	*Regression Statistics*								
4	Multiple R	0.470143855							
5	R Square	0.221035244							
6	Adjusted R Square	0.129571711							
7	Standard Error	0.243456129							
8	Observations	50							
9									
10	ANOVA								
11		*df*	*SS*	*MS*	*F*	*Significance F*			
12	Regression	5	0.756828814	0.151365763	2.553796157	0.041012102			
13	Residual	45	2.667189903	0.059270887					
14	Total	50	3.424018716						
15									
16		*Coefficients*	*Standard Error*	*t Stat*	*P-value*	*Lower 95%*	*Upper 95%*	*Lower 95.0%*	*Upper 95.0%*
17	Intercept	0	#N/A	#N/A	#N/A	#N/A	#N/A	#N/A	#N/A
18	experd	0.237998541	0.165585769	1.437312775	0.157546605	-0.095508312	0.571505393	-0.095508312	0.571505393
19	exper2d	-0.008188168	0.006971395	-1.174537889	0.246357791	-0.022229278	0.005852943	-0.022229278	0.005852943
20	tenured	-0.01235005	0.030111582	-0.410142854	0.683647332	-0.072997889	0.048297788	-0.072997889	0.048297788
21	tenure2d	0.00229615	0.002370996	0.968432772	0.338004699	-0.002479281	0.007071581	-0.002479281	0.007071581
22	uniond	0.113543476	0.133048521	0.853399012	0.397957987	-0.154429997	0.38151695	-0.154429997	0.38151695

Note that the least squares residuals from (15.5), $SSE = 2.66719$, are the same as the least squares residuals from (15.2). Furthermore, the least squares estimates of the β_k parameters from (15.5), shown in the above table, are identical to the least squares estimates from the dummy variable fixed effects model (15.2) shown in Section 15.2. The standard errors of those coefficients estimates are slightly different though. This is because the estimate of the error variance above uses $\hat{\sigma}^2_{e,WRONG} = \frac{SSE}{NT-K}$ when it should use $\hat{\sigma}^2_{e,CORRECT} = \frac{SSE}{NT-N-K}$. The calculation of $\hat{\sigma}^2_{e,WRONG}$ ignores the loss of $N = 10$ degrees of freedom from correcting the variables by their sample means. So, if we multiply the standard errors estimates of the coefficients, from the above table, by the correction factor $\sqrt{\frac{NT-K}{NT-N-K}}$, the resulting standard errors will be correct and identical to those obtained in Section 15.2:

$$\left(\hat{\sigma}_{e,WRONG}\right) \times \left(\sqrt{\frac{NT-K}{NT-N-K}}\right) = \left(\sqrt{\frac{SSE}{NT-K}}\right) \times \left(\sqrt{\frac{NT-K}{NT-N-K}}\right) \qquad (15.6)$$

$$= \sqrt{\frac{SSE}{NT-N-K}} = \hat{\sigma}_{e,CORRECT}$$

With $N = 10$, $T = 5$ and $K = 5$, the correction factor for the standard error estimates from the table above is:

$$\sqrt{\frac{NT-K}{NT-N-K}} = \sqrt{\frac{45}{35}} \qquad (15.7)$$

We use (15.7) below.

Select cells **D16:D22**, right click and select **Insert** in the menu of options that pops up. In the **Insert** window, select **Shift cells right** and then **OK**.

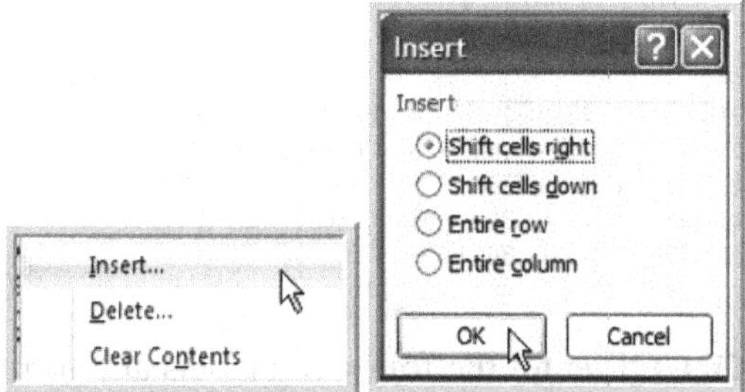

In your new cells **D16:D18**, enter the following label and formula:

	D
16	*Correct SE*
17	
18	=SQRT(45/35)*C18

Copy the content of cell **D18** to cell **D19:D22**. The result is:

	A	B	C	D
16		*Coefficients*	*Standard Error*	*Correct SE*
17	Intercept	0	#N/A	
18	experd	0.237998541	0.165585769	0.187756613
19	exper2d	-0.008188168	0.006971395	0.007904819
20	tenured	-0.01235005	0.030111582	0.034143325
21	tenure2d	0.00229615	0.002370996	0.002688457
22	uniond	0.113543476	0.133048521	0.150862842

Note that the subsequent *t*-statistics, *p*-values and confidence intervals estimates would need correction as well.

15.2.2 Fixed Effects Estimates of Wage Equation from Complete Panel

We consider the following wage equation:

$$\ln(\widetilde{WAGE})_{it} = \begin{array}{l} \beta_2\widetilde{EXPER}_{it} + \beta_3\widetilde{EXPER}^2_{it} + \beta_4\widetilde{TENURE}_{it} \\ +\beta_5\widetilde{TENURE}^2_{it} + \beta_6\widetilde{SOUTH}_{it} + \beta_7\widetilde{UNION}_{it} + \tilde{e}_{it} \end{array} \tag{15.8}$$

where variables are in deviation from the mean form.

Go back to your **nls panel data** worksheet where we will transform our data in deviation from the mean form.

In cells **BO1:BU2**, enter the following labels and formulas.

	BO	BP	BQ	BR	BS	BT	BU
1	**lnwage**	**exper**	**exper2**	**tenure**	**tenure2**	**south**	**union**
2	=C2	=O2	=P2	=Q2	=R2	=L2	=N2

Copy the content of cells **BO2:BU2** to cells **BU3:BU3581**.

The result is:

	BO	BP	BQ	BR	BS	BT	BU
3577	1.609438	12.4359	154.6516	3.083333	9.506944	1	0
3578	1.459441	13.4359	180.5233	4.083333	16.67361	1	0
3579	1.427116	15.4359	238.2669	6.083333	37.00695	1	0
3580	1.494368	17.4359	304.0105	8.166667	66.69445	1	0
3581	1.341422	18.85897	355.6609	9.583333	91.84027	1	0

In cells **BW1:BW6** and **BX1:CC1**, enter the following labels and formulas.

	BW
1	**lnwagebar**
2	=AVERAGE(BO2: BO6)
3	=AVERAGE(BO2: BO6)
4	=AVERAGE(BO2: BO6)
5	=AVERAGE(BO2: BO6)
6	=AVERAGE(BO2: BO6)

	BX	BY	BZ
1	**experbar**	**exper2bar**	**tenurebar**

	CA	CB	CC
1	**tenure2bar**	**southbar**	**unionbar**

Copy the content of cells **BW2:BW6** to cells **BX2:CC6**.

The result is:

	BW	BX	BY	BZ	CA	CB	CC
1	**lnwagebar**	**experbar**	**exper2bar**	**tenurebar**	**tenure2bar**	**southbar**	**unionbar**
2	1.8328104	10.44615	113.99332	5.4166666	35.4874978	0	1
3	1.8328104	10.44615	113.99332	5.4166666	35.4874978	0	1
4	1.8328104	10.44615	113.99332	5.4166666	35.4874978	0	1
5	1.8328104	10.44615	113.99332	5.4166666	35.4874978	0	1
6	1.8328104	10.44615	113.99332	5.4166666	35.4874978	0	1

Select cells **BW2:CC6**, move your cursor to the lower right corner of your selection until it turns into a skinny cross as shown below; left-click, hold it and drag it down to cell **CC3581**.

	BW	BX	BY	BZ	CA	CB	CC
1	**lnwagebar**	**experbar**	**exper2bar**	**tenurebar**	**tenure2bar**	**southbar**	**unionbar**
2	1.8328104	10.44615	113.99332	5.4166666	35.4874978	0	1
3	1.8328104	10.44615	113.99332	5.4166666	35.4874978	0	1
4	1.8328104	10.44615	113.99332	5.4166666	35.4874978	0	1
5	1.8328104	10.44615	113.99332	5.4166666	35.4874978	0	1
6	1.8328104	10.44615	113.99332	5.4166666	35.4874978	0	1
7							

Here is how your table should look (only the *last* five values are shown below):

	BW	BX	BY	BZ	CA	CB	CC
3577	1.466357	15.52051	246.62264	6.1999998	44.3444452	1	0
3578	1.466357	15.52051	246.62264	6.1999998	44.3444452	1	0
3579	1.466357	15.52051	246.62264	6.1999998	44.3444452	1	0
3580	1.466357	15.52051	246.62264	6.1999998	44.3444452	1	0
3581	1.466357	15.52051	246.62264	6.1999998	44.3444452	1	0

In cells **CE1:CK2**, enter the following labels and formula.

	CE	CF	CG	CH	CI	CJ	CK
1	**Lnwaged**	**experd**	**exper2d**	**tenured**	**tenure2d**	**southd**	**uniond**
2	=BO2-BW2						

Copy the content of cell **CE2** to cells **CF2:CK2** and then copy the content of cells **CE2:CK2** to cells **CE3: CK3581**. Here is how your table should look (only the first five values are shown below):

	CE	CF	CG	CH	CI	CJ	CK
3577	0.143081	-3.08461	-91.971	-3.11667	-34.8375	0	0
3578	-0.00692	-2.08461	-66.0993	-2.11667	-27.6708	0	0
3579	-0.03924	-0.08461	-8.35573	-0.11667	-7.3375	0	0
3580	0.028011	1.915386	57.38786	1.966667	22.35	0	0
3581	-0.12494	3.338457	109.0383	3.383333	47.49583	0	0

In the **Regression** dialog box, the **Input Y Range** should be **CE1:CE3581**, and the **Input X Range** should be **CF1:CK3581**. Check the boxes next to **Labels** *and* **Constant is Zero**. Select **New Worksheet Ply** and name it **Fixed Effects Wage Equation All**. Finally select **OK**.

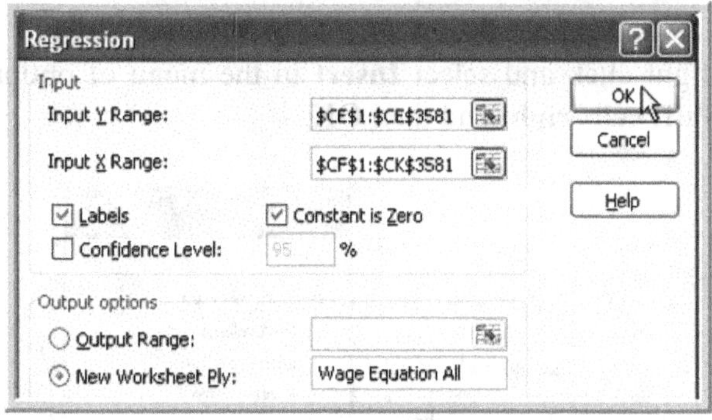

The result is (see also Table 15.7 p. 350 in *Principles of Econometrics, 4e*):

	A	B	C	D	E	F	G	H	I
1	SUMMARY OUTPUT								
2									
3	*Regression Statistics*								
4	Multiple R	0.378119087							
5	R Square	0.142974044							
6	Adjusted R Square	0.141495272							
7	Standard Error	0.174475408							
8	Observations	3580							
9									
10	ANOVA								
11		*df*	*SS*	*MS*	*F*	*Significance F*			
12	Regression	6	18.15040072	3.025066787	99.37257027	6.026E-116			
13	Residual	3574	108.7985212	0.030441668					
14	Total	3580	126.948922						
15									
16		*Coefficients*	*Standard Error*	*t Stat*	*P-value*	*Lower 95%*	*Upper 95%*	*Lower 95.0%*	*Upper 95.0%*
17	Intercept	0	#N/A	#N/A	#N/A	#N/A	#N/A	#N/A	#N/A
18	experd	0.041083173	0.005919878	6.939868298	4.64003E-12	0.029476495	0.052689851	0.029476495	0.052689851
19	exper2d	-0.000409052	0.000244425	-1.673525633	0.094311373	-0.000888279	7.0175E-05	-0.000888279	7.0175E-05
20	tenured	0.013908943	0.002931175	4.745176192	2.16481E-06	0.008161999	0.019655887	0.008161999	0.019655887
21	tenure2d	-0.000896227	0.000184088	-4.868462433	1.17338E-06	-0.001257155	-0.000535298	-0.001257155	-0.000535298
22	southd	-0.016322397	0.032325859	-0.504933131	0.613636935	-0.079701378	0.047056584	-0.079701378	0.047056584
23	uniond	0.063697234	0.01274631	4.997307672	6.09248E-07	0.038706463	0.088688006	0.038706463	0.088688006

With $N = 716$, $T = 5$ degrees of freedom and $K = 6$, the correction factor for the standard error estimates from the table above is:

$$\sqrt{\frac{NT - K}{NT - N - K}} = \sqrt{\frac{3580 - 6}{3580 - 716 - 6}} = \sqrt{\frac{3574}{2858}} \tag{15.9}$$

We use (15.9) below.

Select cells **D16:D23**, right click and select **Insert** in the menu of options that pops up. In the **Insert** window, select **Shift cells right** and then **OK**.

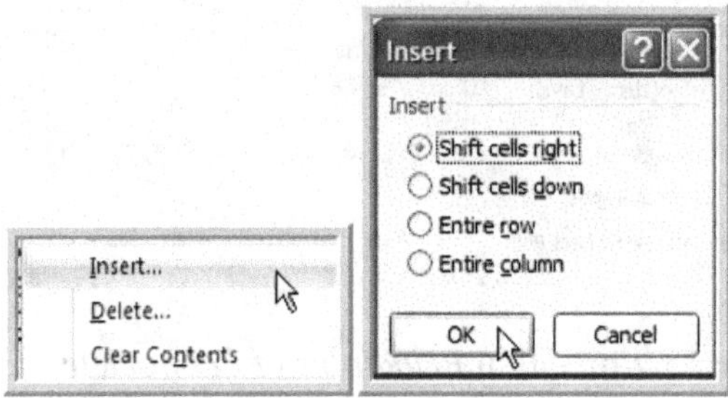

In your new cells **D16:D23**, enter the following label and formula:

	D
16	*Correct SE*
17	
18	=SQRT(3574/2858)*C18

Copy the content of cell **D18** to cell **D19:D23**. The result is:

	A	B	C	D
16		Coefficients	Standard Error	Correct SE
17	Intercept	0	#N/A	
18	experd	0.041083173	0.005919878	0.006620014
19	exper2d	-0.000409052	0.000244425	0.000273333
20	tenured	0.013908943	0.002931175	0.003277841
21	tenure2d	-0.000896227	0.000184088	0.00020586
22	southd	-0.016322397	0.032325859	0.036148995
23	uniond	0.063697234	0.01274631	0.0142538

Note that the subsequent t-statistics, p-values and confidence intervals estimates would need correction as well.

Next, we test the following hypothesis using an F-test:

$$H_0: \beta_{1,1} = \beta_{1,2} = \cdots = \beta_{1,N}$$
$$H_1: \text{the } \beta_{1,i} \text{ are not all equal} \tag{15.10}$$

where $N = 716$.

Our unrestricted model is equation (15.8). In the restricted model, equation (15.11) below, all the intercept parameters are equal.

$$ln(WAGE)_{it} = \begin{array}{l} \beta_1 + \beta_2 EXPER_{it} + \beta_3 EXPER_{it}^2 + \beta_4 TENURE_{it} \\ +\beta_5 TENURE_{it}^2 + \beta_6 SOUTH_{it} + \beta_7 UNION_{it} + e_{it} \end{array} \tag{15.11}$$

Go back to your **nls panel data** worksheet.

In the **Regression** dialog box, the **Input Y Range** should be **BO1:BO3581**, and the **Input X Range** should be **BP1:BU3581**. Check the box next to **Labels.** <u>Uncheck</u> the box next to **Constant is Zero**. Select **Output Range** and specify it to be **A1** in your **Restricted Model** worksheet. Finally select **OK**.

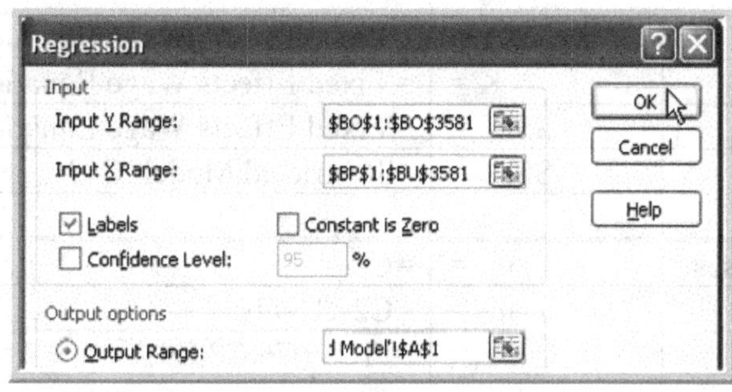

Excel informs you that the output range will overwrite existing data. Do select **OK** to overwrite the data in the specified range.

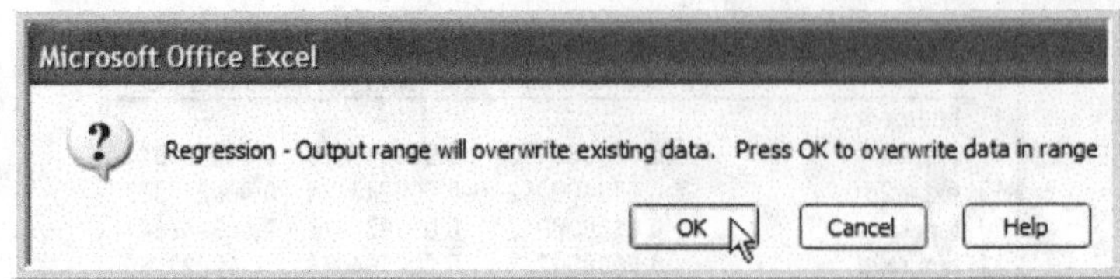

The result is:

	A	B	C	D	E	F	G	H	I
1	SUMMARY OUTPUT								
2									
3	*Regression Statistics*								
4	Multiple R	0.408141951							
5	R Square	0.166579852							
6	Adjusted R Square	0.165180322							
7	Standard Error	0.424504153							
8	Observations	3580							
9									
10	ANOVA								
11		*df*	*SS*	*MS*	*F*	*Significance F*			
12	Regression	6	128.6931345	21.44885575	119.0255624	1.8746E-137			
13	Residual	3573	643.8680907	0.180203776					
14	Total	3579	772.5612252						
15									
16		*Coefficients*	*Standard Error*	*t Stat*	*P-value*	*Lower 95%*	*Upper 95%*	*Lower 95.0%*	*Upper 95.0%*
17	Intercept	1.284930375	0.052094637	24.66530998	3.5454E-124	1.182792166	1.387068585	1.182792166	1.387068585
18	exper	0.078366738	0.009511456	8.239194458	2.40618E-16	0.059718309	0.097015166	0.059718309	0.097015166
19	exper2	-0.002009946	0.000399301	-5.033658213	5.04964E-07	-0.002792827	-0.001227065	-0.002792827	-0.001227065
20	tenure	0.012062145	0.004896715	2.463313468	0.013812755	0.002461507	0.021662783	0.002461507	0.021662783
21	tenure2	-0.000243385	0.000286174	-0.85048033	0.39511508	-0.000804466	0.000317695	-0.000804466	0.000317695
22	south	-0.195957455	0.014523639	-13.4923107	1.67616E-40	-0.22443291	-0.167481999	-0.22443291	-0.167481999
23	union	0.10977422	0.016355781	6.711646547	2.22914E-11	0.077706616	0.141841823	0.077706616	0.141841823

In your **F-test** worksheet replace the reference **LS Dummy Variable Wage Equation** by **Fixed Effects Wage Equation All**. Also, the denominator degrees of freedom, m_2, in cell **C9**, needs to be corrected to account for the loss of $N = 716$ degrees of freedom from correcting the variables by their sample means.

	A	B	C
1	**Data Input**	J =	
2		NT =	='Fixed Effects Wage Equation All'!B8
3		K =	='Fixed Effects Wage Equation All'!B12
4		SSE_U =	='Fixed Effects Wage Equation All'!C13
5		SSE_R =	='Restricted Model'!C13
6		α =	
8	**Computed Values**	m_1 =	=C1
9		m_2 =	=C2-C3-716
10		F_c=	=FINV(C6,C8,C9)
12	**F-test**	F-statistic=	=((C5-C4)/C8)/(C4/C9)
13		Conclusion =	=IF(C12>=C10,"Reject Ho","Do Not Reject Ho")
14		p-value =	=FDIST(C12,C8,C9)
15		Conclusion =	=IF(C14<=C6,"Reject Ho","Do Not Reject Ho")

With 715 joint null hypotheses, at $\alpha = 0.01$, the results of the F-test are:

	A	B	C
1	**Data Input**	J =	715
2		N =	3580
3		K =	6
4		SSE_U =	108.7985
5		SSE_R =	643.8681
6		α =	0.01

	A	B	C
8	**Computed Values**	m_1 =	715
9		m_2 =	2858
10		Fc =	1.144628
11			
12	F-test	F-statistic =	19.65819
13		Conclusion =	Reject Ho
14		p-value =	0
15		Conclusion =	Reject Ho

Thus we reject the null hypothesis of no fixed effect differences between these women; it is proper to include individual effects in the model.

15.3 THE RANDOM EFFECTS MODEL

15.3.1 Testing for Random Effects

In the random effects model we again assume that all individual differences are captured by the intercept parameters, but we also recognize that the individuals in our sample were randomly selected, and thus we treat the individual differences as random rather than fixed, as we did in the fixed effects dummy variable model.

Below we re-consider the wage equation of Section 15.2.2 and treat individual differences between the 716 women as random effects:

$$\begin{aligned} ln(WAGE)_{it} = \; & \bar{\beta}_1 + \beta_2 EDUC_i + \beta_3 EXPER_{it} + \beta_4 EXPER_{it}^2 + \beta_5 TENURE_{it} \\ & + \beta_6 TENURE_{it}^2 + \beta_7 BLACK_i + \beta_8 SOUTH_{it} + \beta_9 UNION_{it} + v_{it} \end{aligned} \qquad (15.12)$$

where $\bar{\beta}_1$ is a fixed population parameter. $v_{it} = e_{it} + u_i$, where u_i are random individual differences or random effects. The component u_i that is common to all time periods implies that the errors v_{it} are correlated over time for a given individual, but otherwise uncorrelated. The correlation is given by:

$$\rho = corr(v_{it}, v_{is}) = \frac{cov(v_{it}, v_{is})}{\sqrt{var(v_{it})var(v_{is})}} = \frac{\sigma_u^2}{\sigma_u^2 + \sigma_e^2} \qquad (15.13)$$

We test for the presence of random effects by testing the null hypothesis $H_0\colon \sigma_u^2 = 0$ against the alternative hypothesis $H_1\colon \sigma_u^2 > 0$. If the null hypothesis is true, i.e. there are no random effects, then the Lagrange multiplier test statistic (15.14) is distributed as a $\chi^2_{(1)}$ random variable in large samples:

$$LM = \frac{NT}{2(T-1)}\left\{\frac{\sum_{i=1}^{N}(\sum_{t=1}^{T}\hat{e}_{it})^2}{\sum_{i=1}^{N}\sum_{t=1}^{T}\hat{e}_{it}^2} - 1\right\}^2 \qquad (15.14)$$

where $\hat{e}_{i,t}$ are estimated residuals from model (15.15) below—which (15.12) reduces to when there is no need for a random effects model:

$$\begin{aligned} ln(WAGE)_{it} = \; & \bar{\beta}_1 + \beta_2 EDUC_i + \beta_3 EXPER_{it} + \beta_4 EXPER_{it}^2 + \beta_5 TENURE_{it} \\ & + \beta_6 TENURE_{it}^2 + \beta_7 BLACK_i + \beta_8 SOUTH_{it} + \beta_9 UNION_{it} + e_{it} \end{aligned} \qquad (15.15)$$

You will recognize model (15.5) as model (15.1) from Section 15.1.

Go back to your **nls panel data** worksheet.

Insert four columns to the left of column **C** labeled **lwage**.

In your new cells **C1:F2**, enter the following labels and formulas:

	C	D	E	F
1	**e-hat$_{it}$**	**∑e-hat$_{it}$over$_t$**	**(∑e-hat$_{it}$over$_t$)^2**	**e-hat$^2_{it}$**
2	='Pooled LS Wage Equation'!C32	=SUM(C2:C6)	=D2^2	=C2^2

Copy the content of cell **C2** to cells **C3:C3581** and the content of cell **F2** to cells **F3:F3581**. Here is how your table should look (only the first five values are shown below):

	C	F
1	**e-hat$_{it}$**	**e-hat$^2_{it}$**
2	0.01318	0.000174
3	0.027884	0.000778
4	-0.03388	0.001148
5	-0.06024	0.003629
6	-0.10381	0.010777

Select cells **D2:E6**, move your cursor to the lower right corner of your selection until it turns into a skinny cross as shown below; left-click, hold it and drag it down to cell **E3581**.

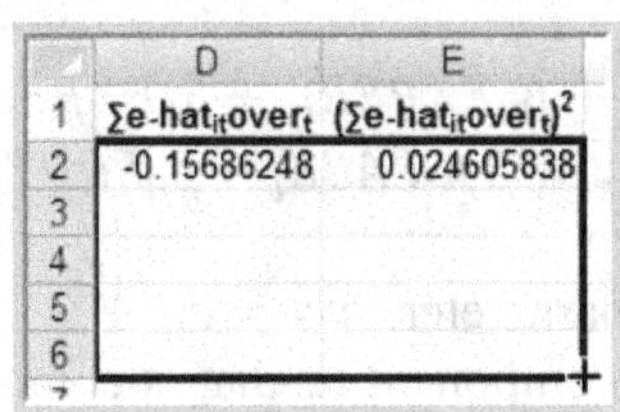

	D	E
1	∑e-hat$_{it}$over$_t$	(∑e-hat$_{it}$over$_t$)^2
2	-0.15686248	0.024605838
3		
4		
5		
6		

Here is how your table should look (only the *last* five values are shown below):

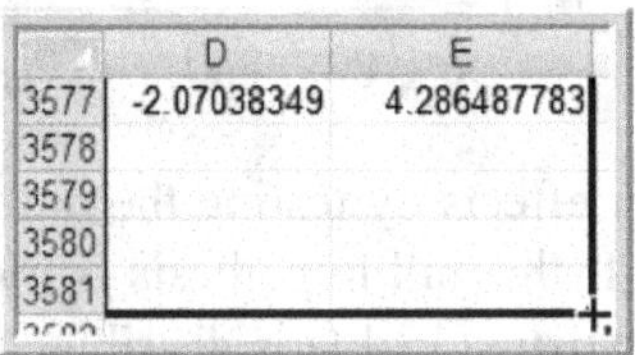

	D	E
3577	-2.07038349	4.286487783
3578		
3579		
3580		
3581		

Insert a new worksheet by selecting the **Insert Worksheet** tab at the bottom of your screen. Rename it **Lagrange Multiplier Test**.

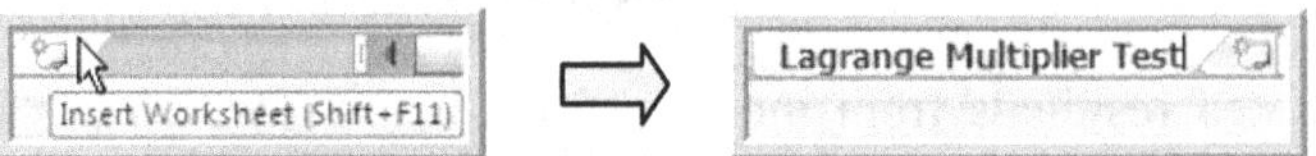

In it copy the simplified Lagrange multiplier test template you created in Chapter 9.

In cell **B2**, replace $\mathbf{R^2}$ by **T**. Delete the content of cells **C1:C2**. In cell **C8**, we enter the formula for the Lagrange multiplier statistic given by equation (15.14).

	A	B	C
1	**Data Input**	N =	
2		T =	
3		α =	
4		m =	
5			
6	**Computed Values**	χ^2-critical value =	=CHIINV(C3,C4)
8	**Lagrange Multiplier Test**	χ^2 =	=SQRT((C1*C2)/(2*(C2-1)))*((SUM('nls panel data'!E2:E3581)/SUM('nls panel data'!F2:F3581))-1)
9		Conclusion =	=IF(C8>=C6,"Reject Ho","Do Not Reject Ho")
10		*p*-value =	=CHIDIST(C8,C4)
11		Conclusion =	=IF(C10<=C3,"Reject Ho","Do Not Reject Ho")

At $\alpha = 0.05$, with $T = 5$, $N = 716$ and $m = 1$, the result of the test is (see also p. 556 in *Principles of Econometrics, 4e*):

	A	B	C
1	**Data Input**	N =	716
2		T =	5
3		α =	0.05
4		m =	1
5			
6	**Computed Values**	χ^2-critical value =	3.841459
7			
8	**Lagrange Multiplier Test**	χ^2 =	62.12314
9		Conclusion =	Reject Ho
10		*p*-value =	3.23E-15
11		Conclusion =	Reject Ho

15.3.2 Random Effects Estimation of the Wage Equation

Estimation of the random effects model is done via generalized least squares (GLS). As was the case when we had heteroskedasticity or autocorrelation, we obtain the GLS estimator in the random effects model by applying least squares to a transformed model. The transformed model is:

$$ln(WAGE)^*_{i,t} = \begin{array}{l} \beta_1 X^*_{1,it} + \beta_2 EDUC^*_{it} + \beta_3 EXPER^*_{it} + \beta_4 EXPER^{*2}_{it} + \beta_5 TENURE^*_{it} \\ + \beta_6 TENURE^{*2}_{it} + \beta_7 BLACK^*_{it} + \beta_8 SOUTH^*_{it} + \beta_9 UNION^*_{it} + v^*_{it} \end{array} \quad (15.16)$$

where the transformed variables are: $X^*_{1,it} = 1 - \alpha$ and $X^*_{it} = X_{it} - \alpha\bar{X}_i$ for all other variables.

The transformation parameter α is defined as:

$$\alpha = 1 - \frac{\sigma_e}{\sqrt{T\sigma_u^2 + \sigma_e^2}} \quad (15.17)$$

Least squares is applied to (15.16) with σ_e^2 and σ_u^2 replaced by $\hat{\sigma}_e^2$ and $\hat{\sigma}_u^2$ in (15.17).

Below we first get estimates of $\hat{\sigma}_e^2$ and $\hat{\sigma}_u^2$.

The regression error variance σ_e^2 comes from the fixed effects wage equation estimated in Section 15.2.2 and re-stated below:

$$\ln(\widetilde{WAGE})_{it} = \begin{array}{l} \beta_2 \widetilde{EXPER}_{it} + \beta_3 \widetilde{EXPER}^2_{it} + \beta_4 \widetilde{TENURE}_{it} \\ +\beta_5 \widetilde{TENURE}^2_{it} + \beta_6 \widetilde{SOUTH}_{it} + \beta_7 \widetilde{UNION}_{it} + \tilde{e}_{it} \end{array} \tag{15.18}$$

where variables are in deviation from the mean form.

The wage equation (15.18) is referred to as the deviation (DV) regression as it uses variables in deviation from the mean form.

Re-consider the following correction factor, used in Section 15.2.2:

$$\sqrt{\frac{NT - K_{DV}}{NT - N - K_{DV}}} \tag{15.19}$$

A consistent estimator of σ_e^2 is obtained by multiplying the estimate of the error variance from (15.18) by the correction factor (15.19)—see also Appendix 15B p. 583 in *Principles of Econometrics, 4e*):

$$\hat{\sigma}_{eDV,WRONG} \times \left(\sqrt{\frac{NT - K_{DV}}{NT - N - K_{DV}}}\right) = \sqrt{\frac{SSE_{DV}}{NT - K_{DV}}} \times \left(\sqrt{\frac{NT - K_{DV}}{NT - N - K_{DV}}}\right)$$

$$= \sqrt{\frac{SSE_{DV}}{NT - N - K_{DV}}} = \hat{\sigma}_{eDV,CORRECT}$$

where $\hat{\sigma}_{eDV,WRONG}$ is the estimated standard error of the regression, SSE_{DV} are the least squares residuals and K_{DV} is the number of parameters from model (15.18); $K_{DV} = 6$, because they are all slope parameters. K_{DV} is also referred as K_{slopes}.

With $= 716$, $T = 5$ and $K_{DV} = 6$, the correction factor is:

$$\sqrt{\frac{NT - K_{DV}}{NT - N - K_{DV}}} = \sqrt{\frac{3580 - 6}{3580 - 716 - 6}} = \sqrt{\frac{3574}{2858}} \tag{15.20}$$

We use (15.20) below.

Go back to your **Fixed Effects Wage Equation All** worksheet.

In cells **C6:C7**, enter the following label and formula.

	C
6	*Correct SE*
7	=SQRT(3574/2858)*B7

The result is (see also p. 557 in *Principles of Econometrics, 4e*):

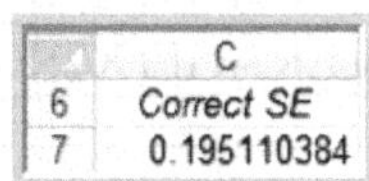

	C
6	*Correct SE*
7	0.195110384

Next, we obtain an estimate of σ_u^2 by getting the regression error variance of the following model:

$$\overline{ln(WAGE)}_i = \begin{array}{l} \beta_1 + \beta_2\overline{EDUC}_i + \beta_3\overline{EXPER}_i + \beta_4\overline{EXPER_i^2} + \beta_5\overline{TENURE}_i \\ + \beta_6\overline{TENURE_i^2} + \beta_7\overline{BLACK}_i + \beta_8\overline{SOUTH}_i + \beta_9\overline{UNION}_i \\ +u_i + \bar{e}_i \end{array} \quad (15.21)$$

where $\bar{x}_i$ are time-averaged observations: $\bar{x}_i = \sum_{t=1}^{T} x_{i,t}$ and $v_i = u_i + \bar{e}_i$.

Equation (15.21) is referred to as the between estimator (BE) regression as it uses variation between individuals as a basis for estimating the regression parameters.

The estimate of the error variance from (15.21) is given by:

$$\widehat{var(u_i + \bar{e}_i)} = \sigma_u^2 + \frac{\sigma_e^2}{T} = \frac{SSE_{BE}}{N - K_{BE}} = \hat{\sigma}_v^2 \quad (15.22)$$

where $\hat{\sigma}_v^2$ is the mean square residual, SSE_{BE} are the least squares residuals and K_{BE} is the number of parameters from model (15.21); $K_{BE} = 9$, the intercept and 8 slope parameters.

With estimate (15.22) in hand, we can estimate σ_u^2 as (see also Appendix 15B p. 583 in *Principles of Econometrics, 4e*):

$$\begin{aligned} \hat{\sigma}_u^2 = \widehat{\sigma_u^2 + \frac{\sigma_e^2}{T}} - \frac{\hat{\sigma}_2^2}{T} &= \frac{SSE_{BE}}{N - K_{BE}} - \frac{1}{T}\left(\frac{SSE_{DV}}{NT - N - K_{slopes}}\right) \\ &= \hat{\sigma}_v^2 - \frac{1}{T}\hat{\sigma}_{eDV,CORRECT} \end{aligned} \quad (15.23)$$

where $T = 5$ years.

Go back to your **nls panel data** worksheet.

In cells **CQ1:CQ6** and **CR1:CX1**, enter the following labels and formulas.

	CQ
1	**Lnwagebar**
2	=AVERAGE(X2:X6)
3	=AVERAGE(X2:X6)
4	=AVERAGE(X2:X6)
5	=AVERAGE(X2:X6)
6	=AVERAGE(X2:X6)

	CR	CS	CT	CU
1	**educbar**	**experbar**	**exper2bar**	**tenurebar**

	CV	CW	CX	CY
1	**tenure2bar**	**blackbar**	**southbar**	**unionbar**

Copy the content of cells **CQ2:CQ6** to cells **CR2:CY6**.

Here is how your table should look (only the first five values are shown below):

	CQ	CR	CS	CT	CU	CV	CW	CX	CY
1	**lnwagebar**	**educbar**	**experbar**	**exper2bar**	**tenurebar**	**tenure2bar**	**blackbar**	**southbar**	**unionbar**
2	1.8328104	12	10.44615	113.99332	5.4166666	35.4874978	1	0	1
3	1.8328104	12	10.44615	113.99332	5.4166666	35.4874978	1	0	1
4	1.8328104	12	10.44615	113.99332	5.4166666	35.4874978	1	0	1
5	1.8328104	12	10.44615	113.99332	5.4166666	35.4874978	1	0	1
6	1.8328104	12	10.44615	113.99332	5.4166666	35.4874978	1	0	1

Select cells **CQ2:CY6**, move your cursor to the lower right corner of your selection until it turns into a skinny cross as shown below; left-click, hold it and drag it down to cell **CY3581**.

	CQ	CR	CS	CT	CU	CV	CW	CX	CY
1	**lnwagebar**	**educbar**	**experbar**	**exper2bar**	**tenurebar**	**tenure2bar**	**blackbar**	**southbar**	**unionbar**
2	1.8328104	12	10.44615	113.99332	5.4166666	35.4874978	1	0	1
3	1.8328104	12	10.44615	113.99332	5.4166666	35.4874978	1	0	1
4	1.8328104	12	10.44615	113.99332	5.4166666	35.4874978	1	0	1
5	1.8328104	12	10.44615	113.99332	5.4166666	35.4874978	1	0	1
6	1.8328104	12	10.44615	113.99332	5.4166666	35.4874978	1	0	1

Here is how your table should look (only the *last* five values are shown):

	CQ	CR	CS	CT	CU	CV	CW	CX	CY
3577	1.466357	12	15.52051	246.62264	6.1999998	44.3444452	0	1	0
3578	1.466357	12	15.52051	246.62264	6.1999998	44.3444452	0	1	0
3579	1.466357	12	15.52051	246.62264	6.1999998	44.3444452	0	1	0
3580	1.466357	12	15.52051	246.62264	6.1999998	44.3444452	0	1	0
3581	1.466357	12	15.52051	246.62264	6.1999998	44.3444452	0	1	0

Select cells **CQ1:CY3581**. Right-click, select **Copy**.

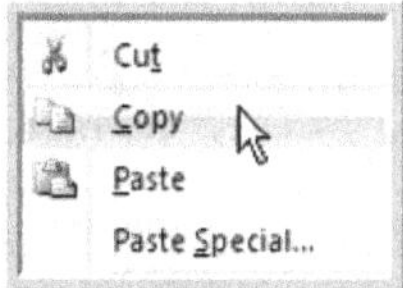

Place your cursor in cell **DA1**. Right-click, select **Paste Special**. In the **Paste Special** dialog box that pops up, select **Values**. Finally, select **OK**.

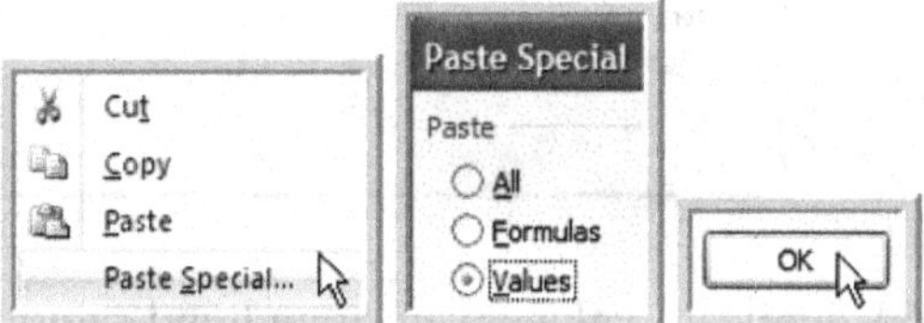

Here is how your table should look (only the first five values are shown below):

	DA	DB	DC	DD	DE	DF	DG	DH	DI
1	lnwagebar	educbar	experbar	exper2bar	tenurebar	tenure2bar	blackbar	southbar	unionbar
2	1.83281	12	10.44615	113.9933	5.416667	35.4875	1	0	1
3	1.83281	12	10.44615	113.9933	5.416667	35.4875	1	0	1
4	1.83281	12	10.44615	113.9933	5.416667	35.4875	1	0	1
5	1.83281	12	10.44615	113.9933	5.416667	35.4875	1	0	1
6	1.83281	12	10.44615	113.9933	5.416667	35.4875	1	0	1

Go to the **Insert** tab, at the upper left corner of your screen. In the **Tables** group of commands, select **Table**. A **Create Table** dialog box pops up. **The data for your table** are found in cells **DA1:DI3581**. Select **My table has headers**. Finally, select **OK**.

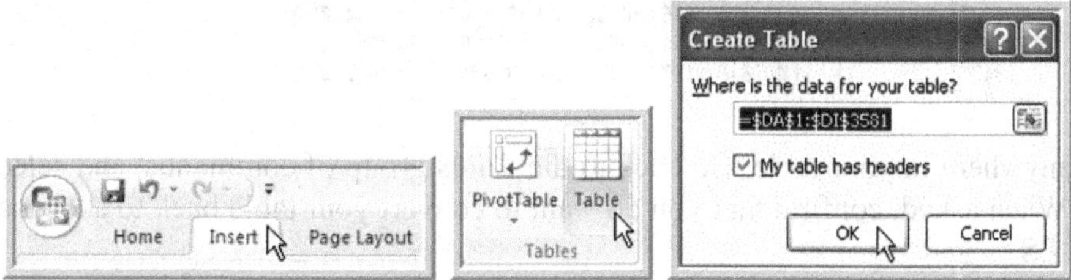

Here is how your table should look (only the first five values are shown):

	DA	DB	DC	DD	DE	DF	DG	DH	DI
1	lnwageba	educba	experba	exper2ba	tenureba	tenure2ba	blackba	southba	unionba
2	1.8328104	12	10.446154	113.993317	5.4166666	35.4874978	1	0	1
3	1.8328104	12	10.446154	113.993317	5.4166666	35.4874978	1	0	1
4	1.8328104	12	10.446154	113.993317	5.4166666	35.4874978	1	0	1
5	1.8328104	12	10.446154	113.993317	5.4166666	35.4874978	1	0	1
6	1.8328104	12	10.446154	113.993317	5.4166666	35.4874978	1	0	1

Table Tools and its **Design** tab show up. In the **Tools** group of commands of the **Design** tab, select **Remove Duplicates**. This will delete duplicated rows across selected columns. All columns of your table should be selected. If not, select the **Select All** button. Finally, select **OK**.

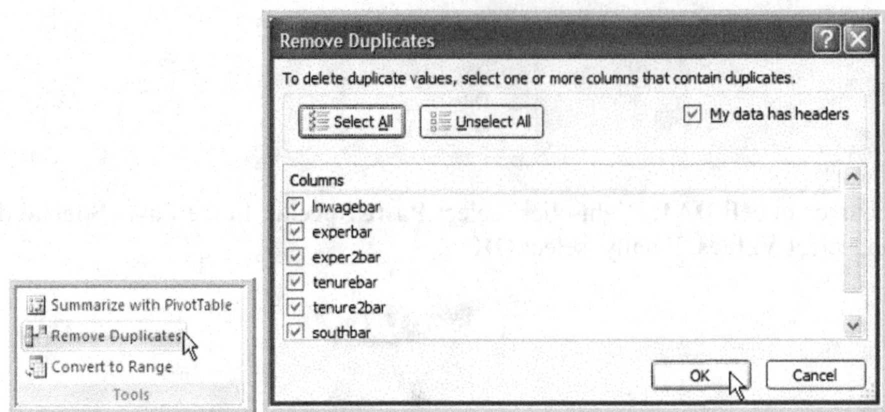

Excel informs you that 2864 duplicate values were found and removed, and 716 unique values remain. Those are the 716 time-averaged observations we need to run model (15.21). Select **OK**.

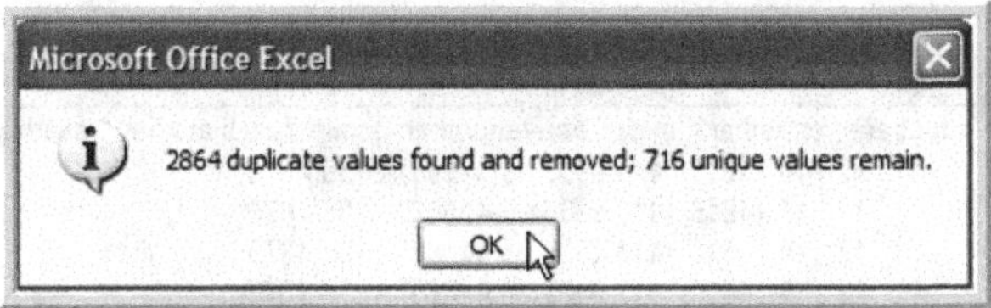

Here is how your table should look (only the first five values are shown below):

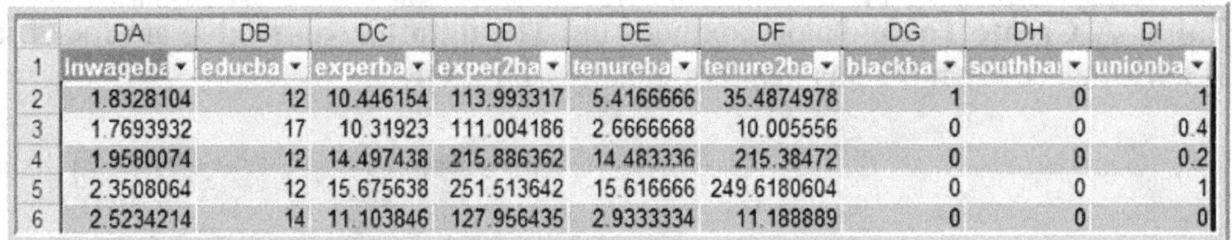

	DA	DB	DC	DD	DE	DF	DG	DH	DI
1	lnwageba	educba	experba	exper2ba	tenureba	tenure2ba	blackba	southba	unionba
2	1.8328104	12	10.446154	113.993317	5.4166666	35.4874978	1	0	1
3	1.7693932	17	10.31923	111.004186	2.6666668	10.005556	0	0	0.4
4	1.9580074	12	14.497438	215.886362	14.483336	215.38472	0	0	0.2
5	2.3508064	12	15.675638	251.513642	15.616666	249.6180604	0	0	1
6	2.5234214	14	11.103846	127.956435	2.9333334	11.188889	0	0	0

Left-click anywhere in your table. Go back to the **Tools** group of commands, and select **Convert to Range**. When asked, confirm that you do want to convert your table back to a normal range by selecting **YES**.

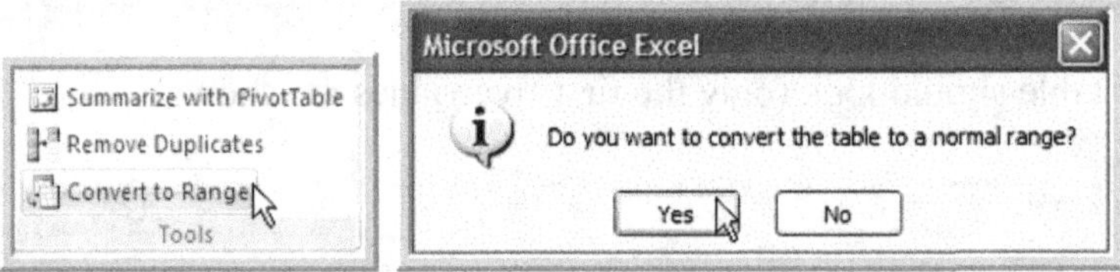

Here is how your table should look (only the first five values are shown below):

	DA	DB	DC	DD	DE	DF	DG	DH	DI
1	lnwagebar	educbar	experbar	exper2bar	tenurebar	tenure2bar	blackbar	southbar	unionbar
2	1.8328104	12	10.446154	113.993317	5.4166666	35.4874978	1	0	1
3	1.7693932	17	10.31923	111.004186	2.6666668	10.005556	0	0	0.4
4	1.9580074	12	14.497438	215.886362	14.483336	215.38472	0	0	0.2
5	2.3508064	12	15.675638	251.513642	15.616666	249.6180604	0	0	1
6	2.5234214	14	11.103846	127.956435	2.9333334	11.188889	0	0	0

In the **Regression** dialog box, the **Input Y Range** should be **DA1:DA717**, and the **Input X Range** should be **DB1:DI717**. Check the box next to **Labels**. Select **New Worksheet Ply** and name it **Between Wage Equation**. Finally select **OK**.

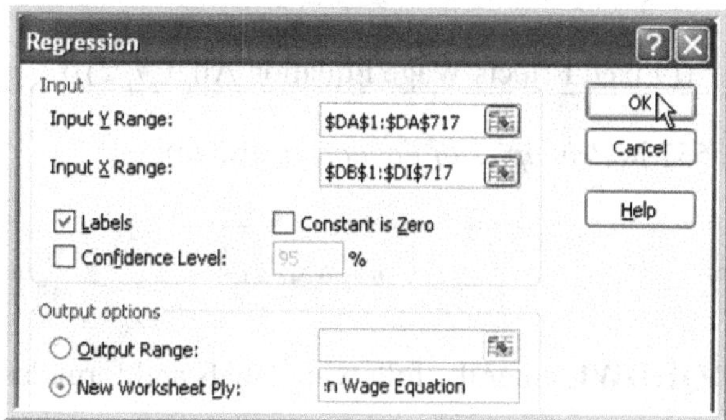

The result is:

	A	B	C	D	E	F	G	H	I
1	SUMMARY OUTPUT								
2									
3	*Regression Statistics*								
4	Multiple R	0.604539637							
5	R Square	0.365468173							
6	Adjusted R Square	0.35828818							
7	Standard Error	0.340422217							
8	Observations	716							
9									
10	ANOVA								
11		*df*	*SS*	*MS*	*F*	*Significance F*			
12	Regression	8	47.19014976	5.89876872	50.90091369	5.45243E-65			
13	Residual	707	81.93231089	0.115887286					
14	Total	715	129.1224606						
15									
16		*Coefficients*	*Standard Error*	*t Stat*	*P-value*	*Lower 95%*	*Upper 95%*	*Lower 95.0%*	*Upper 95.0%*
17	Intercept	0.416688577	0.135761818	3.069261906	0.002227968	0.150144005	0.68323315	0.150144005	0.68323315
18	educbar	0.070772317	0.005387371	13.13670748	1.98558E-35	0.060195157	0.081349478	0.060195157	0.081349478
19	experbar	0.066192432	0.023455392	2.822056097	0.004905678	0.020141874	0.112242989	0.020141874	0.112242989
20	exper2bar	-0.001606476	0.000999826	-1.606754494	0.108554728	-0.00356946	0.000356509	-0.00356946	0.000356509
21	tenurebar	0.016558044	0.012201636	1.357034712	0.175203258	-0.007397734	0.040513822	-0.007397734	0.040513822
22	tenure2bar	-0.000494785	0.000702808	-0.70401177	0.481657249	-0.001874627	0.000885056	-0.001874627	0.000885056
23	blackbar	-0.121550603	0.031660135	-3.839231961	0.000134485	-0.183709738	-0.059391468	-0.183709738	-0.059391468
24	southbar	-0.105317325	0.029100454	-3.619095589	0.000316717	-0.162450975	-0.048183676	-0.162450975	-0.048183676
25	unionbar	0.155735498	0.035460749	4.391771186	1.29639E-05	0.086114522	0.225356474	0.086114522	0.225356474

In cells **D3:E3**, enter the following label and formula.

	D	E
3	**σ^2_u-hat =**	=D13-((1/5)*(('Fixed Effects Wage Equation All'!C7)^2))

The result is (see also p. 557 in *Principles of Econometrics, 4e*):

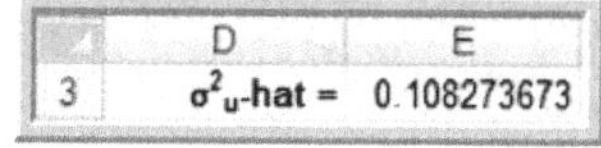

We now have the ingredients we need for our transformation parameter α and thus for estimating model (15.16).

Go back to your **nls panel data** worksheet.

In cells **DK1:DL1,** enter the following label and formula.

	DK	DL
1	α =	=1-('Fixed Effects Wage Equation All'!C7/ SQRT((5*'Between Wage Equation'!E3) +('Fixed Effects Wage Equation All'!C7^2)))

The result is (see also p. 557 in *Principles of Econometrics, 4e*):

	DK	DL
1	α =	0.743683

In cells **DN1:DP2** and **DQ1:DW1**, enter the following labels and formulas.

	DN	DO	DP
1	**lnwage***	**x1***	**educ***
2	=X2-$DL$1*CQ2	=1-$DL$1	=Y2-$DL$1*CR2

	DQ	DR	DS	DT	DU	DV	DW
1	**exper***	**exper2***	**tenure***	**tenure2***	**black***	**south***	**union***

Copy the content of cell **DP2** to cells **DQ2:DW2**, and then copy the content of cells **DN2:DW2** to cells **DN3:DW3581**.

Here is how your table should look (only the first five values are shown below):

	DN	DO	DP	DQ	DR	DS	DT	DU	DV	DW
1	lnwage*	x1*	educ*	exper*	exper2*	tenure*	tenure2*	black*	south*	union*
2	0.445259	0.256317	3.075805	-0.10196	-25.9971	3.638384	32.38632	0.256317	0	0.256317
3	0.500387	0.256317	3.075805	0.814706	-11.1013	4.55505	47.28216	0.256317	0	0.256317
4	0.426337	0.256317	3.075805	2.410863	18.84712	-2.19495	-23.0303	0.256317	0	0.256317
5	0.4835	0.256317	3.075805	4.410863	63.56502	-0.27828	-12.3289	0.256317	0	0.256317
6	0.493419	0.256317	3.075805	5.853163	100.7784	1.221717	1.171053	0.256317	0	0.256317

In the **Regression** dialog box, the **Input Y Range** should be **DN1:DN3581**, and the **Input X Range** should be **DO1:DW3581**. Check the boxes next to **Labels** *and* to **Constant is Zero.** Select **New Worksheet Ply** and name it **Random Effects Wage Equation**. Finally select **OK.**

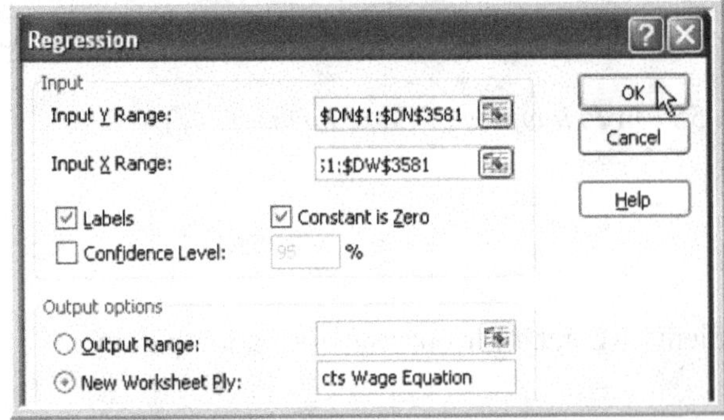

The result is (see also Table 15.9 p. 556 in *Principles of Econometrics, 4e*):

	A	B	C	D	E	F	G	H	I
1	SUMMARY OUTPUT								
2									
3	*Regression Statistics*								
4	Multiple R	0.931719736							
5	R Square	0.868101666							
6	Adjusted R Square	0.867526145							
7	Standard Error	0.195504389							
8	Observations	3580							
9									
10	ANOVA								
11		*df*	*SS*	*MS*	*F*	*Significance F*			
12	Regression	9	898.3263827	99.81404252	2611.431402	0			
13	Residual	3571	136.4906409	0.038221966					
14	Total	3580	1034.817024						
15									
16		*Coefficients*	*Standard Error*	*t Stat*	*P-value*	*Lower 95%*	*Upper 95%*	*Lower 95.0%*	*Upper 95.0%*
17	Intercept	0	#N/A	#N/A	#N/A	#N/A	#N/A	#N/A	#N/A
18	x1*	0.5339294	0.079882787	6.683910526	2.68878E-11	0.377308934	0.690549866	0.377308934	0.690549866
19	educ*	0.073253564	0.005330756	13.74168457	6.53774E-42	0.062801933	0.083705196	0.062801933	0.083705196
20	exper*	0.043616994	0.006357584	6.860623854	8.04754E-12	0.031152133	0.056081854	0.031152133	0.056081854
21	exper2*	-0.000560959	0.000262608	-2.136113712	0.032737953	-0.001075835	-4.60837E-05	-0.001075835	-4.60837E-05
22	tenure*	0.014154128	0.003166561	4.469874232	8.06962E-06	0.007945679	0.020362576	0.007945679	0.020362576
23	tenure2*	-0.000755342	0.000194726	-3.878999975	0.000106777	-0.001137128	-0.000373557	-0.001137128	-0.000373557
24	black*	-0.116736587	0.030208705	-3.864335975	0.000113371	-0.175964635	-0.057508539	-0.175964635	-0.057508539
25	south*	-0.081811707	0.02241094	-3.650525396	0.000265453	-0.125751234	-0.037872179	-0.125751234	-0.037872179
26	union*	0.080235324	0.013213209	6.072356904	1.39249E-09	0.054329129	0.106141518	0.054329129	0.106141518

15.4 SETS OF REGRESSION EQUATIONS

Open the Excel file ***grunfeld2***. Excel opens the data set in Sheet 1 of a new Excel file. Since we would like to save all our work from Chapter 15 in one file, create a new worksheet in your **POE Chapter 15** Excel file, rename it **grunfeld2 data**, and in it, copy the data set you just opened.

We consider a model for describing gross firm investment for $N = 2$ firms, General Electric (GE) and Westinghouse (WE), over a period of $T = 20$ years.

15.4.1 Estimation: Equal Coefficients, Equal Error Variances

If we assume that these two firms have similar investment behavior over time, their investment equation can be specified as:

$$INV_{it} = \beta_1 + \beta_2 V_{it} + \beta_3 K_{it} + e_{it} \tag{15.24}$$

where $t = 1, \ldots, 20$; $i = GE$ or WE; and $var(e_{GE,t}) = \sigma_{GE}^2 = \sigma_{WE}^2 = var(e_{WE,t})$.

INV_{it} denotes gross firm investment, for the ith firm in the tth period of time. V_{it} denotes the stock market value of firm i at the beginning of year t, and is used as a proxy for expected profits. K_{it} denotes the actual capital stock of firm i at the beginning of the year t, and is used as a proxy for permanent desired capital stock.

If, in addition, we assume the errors are uncorrelated, both over time for each firm and between firms, then equation (15.24) can estimated with the General Electric and Westinghouse data pooled together using the least squares regression technique, as in Section 15.1 for our wage equation example.

In cells **G1:I1**, enter the following labels.

	G	H	I
1	**inv**	**v**	**k**

Copy the content of cells **A2:C21** to cells **G2:I21**, and the content of cells **D2:F21** to cells **G22:I41**. Here is how your table should look (only the first five values are shown below):

	G	H	I
1	**inv**	**v**	**k**
2	33.1	1170.6	97.8
3	45	2015.8	104.4
4	77.2	2803.3	118
5	44.6	2039.7	156.2
6	48.1	2256.2	172.6

In the **Regression** dialog box, the **Input Y Range** should be **G1:G41**, and the **Input X Range** should be **H1:L41**. Check the box next to **Labels**. Select **New Worksheet Ply** and name it **Pooled LS Investment Model**. Finally select **OK**.

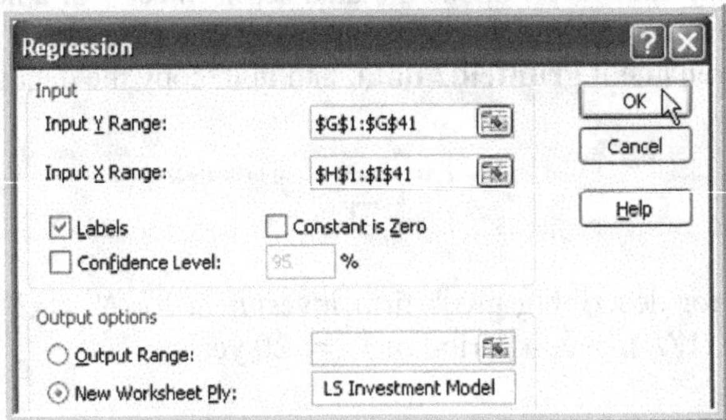

The result is (see also Table 15.11 p. 564 in *Principles of Econometrics, 4e*):

	A	B	C	D	E	F	G	H	I
1	SUMMARY OUTPUT								
2									
3	*Regression Statistics*								
4	Multiple R	0.899873334							
5	R Square	0.809772017							
6	Adjusted R Square	0.799489423							
7	Standard Error	21.1577108							
8	Observations	40							
9									
10	ANOVA								
11		*df*	*SS*	*MS*	*F*	*Significance F*			
12	Regression	2	70506.221	35253.1105	78.75172745	4.64063E-14			
13	Residual	37	16563.00288	447.6487265					
14	Total	39	87069.22388						
15									
16		*Coefficients*	*Standard Error*	*t Stat*	*P-value*	*Lower 95%*	*Upper 95%*	*Lower 95.0%*	*Upper 95.0%*
17	Intercept	17.87200128	7.024080507	2.544390154	0.015252924	3.639862407	32.10414015	3.639862407	32.10414015
18	v	0.015192638	0.006196238	2.451913329	0.019050853	0.002637868	0.027747409	0.002637868	0.027747409
19	k	0.143579159	0.018600986	7.718900416	3.19392E-09	0.105889981	0.181268336	0.105889981	0.181268336

15.4.2 Estimation: Different Coefficients, Equal Error Variances

Using the indicator (dummy) variable format from Chapter 7:

$$INV_{it} = \beta_{1,GE} + \delta_1 D_i + \beta_{2,GE} V_{it} + \delta_2 (D_i \times V_{it}) + \beta_{3,GE} K_{it} + \delta_3 (D_i \times K_{it}) + e_{it} \quad (15.25)$$

where $var(e_{GE,t}) = var(e_{WE,t})$, and D_i is a dummy variable equal to 1 for Westinghouse observations and 0 for General Electric observations.

Equation (15.25) is estimated using the pooled set of General Electric and Westinghouse data.

Go back to your **grunfeld2 data** worksheet.

Insert a column to the left of the column labeled **v** and one to the left of the column labeled **k**.

In your new cells **H1:L2**, enter the following labels and formulas for the dummy variables.

	H	I	J	K	L
1	**d**		**dxv**		**dxk**
2			=H2*I2		=H2*K2

Enter value **0** in cells **H2:H21**, and value **1** in cells **H22:H41**. Copy the content of cell **J2** to cells **J3:J41**, and the content of cell **L2** to cells **L3:L41**. Here is how your table should look (only the first five values are shown below):

	H	I	J	K	L
1	d	v	dxv	k	dxk
2	0	1170.6	0	97.8	0
3	0	2015.8	0	104.4	0
4	0	2803.3	0	118	0
5	0	2039.7	0	156.2	0
6	0	2256.2	0	172.6	0

In the **Regression** dialog box, the **Input Y Range** should be **G1:G41**, and the **Input X Range** should be **H1:L41**. Check the box next to **Labels**. Select **New Worksheet Ply** and name it **Dummy Variable Model**. Finally select **OK**.

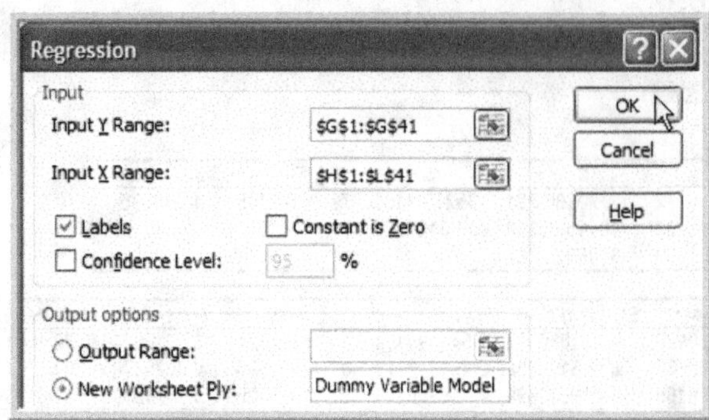

The result is (see also Table 15.12 p. 565 in *Principles of Econometrics, 4e*):

	A	B	C	D	E	F	G	H	I
1	SUMMARY OUTPUT								
2									
3	*Regression Statistics*								
4	Multiple R	0.909857235							
5	R Square	0.827840188							
6	Adjusted R Square	0.802522568							
7	Standard Error	20.99707349							
8	Observations	40							
9									
10	ANOVA								
11		*df*	*SS*	*MS*	*F*	*Significance F*			
12	Regression	5	72079.40264	14415.88053	32.69818434	4.607E-12			
13	Residual	34	14989.82123	440.8770951					
14	Total	39	87069.22388						
15									
16		*Coefficients*	*Standard Error*	*t Stat*	*P-value*	*Lower 95%*	*Upper 95%*	*Lower 95.0%*	*Upper 95.0%*
17	Intercept	-9.956308498	23.62636432	-0.421406712	0.676110456	-57.97085739	38.05824039	-57.97085739	38.05824039
18	d	9.446920615	28.80535028	0.327957151	0.744955164	-49.092594	67.98643523	-49.092594	67.98643523
19	v	0.026551189	0.011722048	2.265064058	0.029996268	0.002729122	0.050373257	0.002729122	0.050373257
20	dxv	0.02634293	0.034352676	0.766837801	0.448470172	-0.043470106	0.096155966	-0.043470106	0.096155966
21	k	0.151693875	0.019356449	7.836865036	4.01578E-09	0.112356839	0.191030911	0.112356839	0.191030911
22	dxk	-0.05928736	0.116946429	-0.506961693	0.615454094	-0.296951096	0.178376377	-0.296951096	0.178376377

15.4.3 Estimation: Different Coefficients, Different Error Variances

If we assume that these two firms have distinct investment behaviors, fixed over time, their separate regressions can be specified as:

$$INV_{it} = \beta_{1,i} + \beta_{2,i}V_{it} + \beta_{3,i}K_{it} + e_{it} \tag{15.26}$$

where $t = 1, \ldots, 20$; $i = GE$ or WE; and $var(e_{GE,t}) = \sigma_{GE}^2 \neq \sigma_{WE}^2 = var(e_{WE,t})$.

If, in addition, we assume there is no contemporaneous correlation, then equation (15.26) can be estimated twice, first with General Electric data, and then with Westinghouse data, using the least square regression technique. Equation (15.26) equivalently as the set of equations (15.2a) and (15.2b):

$$INV_{GE,t} = \beta_{1,GE} + \beta_{2,GE}V_{GE,t} + \beta_{3,GE}K_{GE,t} + e_{GE,t} \quad (15.26a)$$

$$INV_{WE,t} = \beta_{1,WE} + \beta_{2,WE}V_{WE,t} + \beta_{3,WE}K_{WE,t} + e_{WE,t} \quad (15.26b)$$

Note that the dummy variable format equation (15.25) becomes equations (15.27a) and (15.27b):

$$INV_{GE,t} = \beta_{1,GE} + \beta_{2,GE}V_{GE,t} + \beta_{3,GE}K_{GE,t} + e_{GE,t} \quad (15.27a)$$

$$INV_{WE,t} = (\beta_{1,GE} + \delta_1) + (\beta_{2,GE} + \delta_2)V_{WE,t} + (\beta_{3,GE} + \delta_3)K_{WE,t} + e_{WE,t} \quad (15.27b)$$

The least squares estimates of $\beta_{k,GE}$ from (15.26a) will be equal to the least squares estimates of $\beta_{k,GE}$ from (15.27a), $k = 1, 2, 3$. The least squares estimates of $\beta_{k,WE}$ from (15.26b) will be equal to the least squares estimates of $(\beta_{k,WE} + \delta_k)$ from (15.27b), $k = 1, 2, 3$. The difference will be in the standard errors, due to the fact that model (15.26) allows for error variances that differ for the two firms, while model (15.25) assumes that the variance of the error term is constant across firms.

Go back to your **grunfeld2 data** worksheet.

In the **Regression** dialog box, the **Input Y Range** should be **A1:A21**, and the **Input X Range** should be **B1:C21**. Check the boxes next to **Labels** *and* **Residuals**. Select **New Worksheet Ply** and name it **GE Investment Equation.** Finally select **OK.**

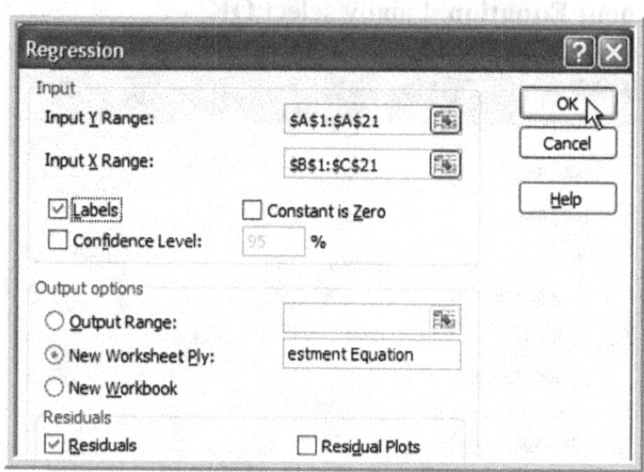

The result is (see also Table 15.13 p. 566 in *Principles of Econometrics, 4e*):

	A	B	C	D	E	F	G	H	I
1	SUMMARY OUTPUT								
2									
3	*Regression Statistics*								
4	Multiple R	0.839825405							
5	R Square	0.70530671							
6	Adjusted R Square	0.670636911							
7	Standard Error	27.88272414							
8	Observations	20							
9									
10	ANOVA								
11		*df*	*SS*	*MS*	*F*	*Significance F*			
12	Regression	2	31632.0322	15816.0161	20.34354783	3.08779E-05			
13	Residual	17	13216.58719	777.4463053					
14	Total	19	44848.61939						
15									
16		*Coefficients*	*Standard Error*	*t Stat*	*P-value*	*Lower 95%*	*Upper 95%*	*Lower 95.0%*	*Upper 95.0%*
17	Intercept	-9.956308498	31.37424837	-0.317340144	0.754849882	-76.15018584	56.23756885	-76.15018584	56.23756885
18	v_ge	0.026551189	0.015566104	1.705705521	0.106265091	-0.006290419	0.059392797	-0.006290419	0.059392797
19	k_ge	0.151693875	0.025704083	5.901547865	1.74208E-05	0.097463001	0.205924748	0.097463001	0.205924748
20									
21									
22									
23	RESIDUAL OUTPUT								
24									
25	*Observation*	*Predicted inv_ge*	*Residuals*						
26	1	35.96017445	-2.860176453						
27	2	59.40242101	-14.40242101						
28	3	82.37451897	-5.174521973						

Go back to your **grunfeld2 data** worksheet.

In the **Regression** dialog box, the **Input Y Range** should be **D1:D21**, and the **Input X Range** should be **E1:F21**. Check the boxes next to **Labels** *and* **Residuals**. Select **New Worksheet Ply** and name it **WE Investment Equation**. Finally select **OK**.

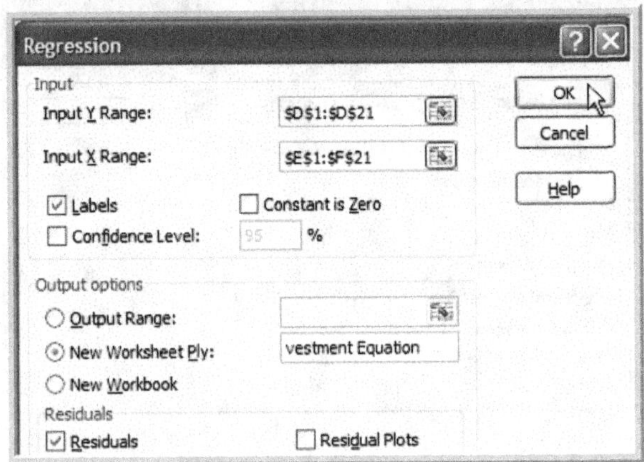

The result is (see also Table 15.13 p. 566 in *Principles of Econometrics, 4e*):

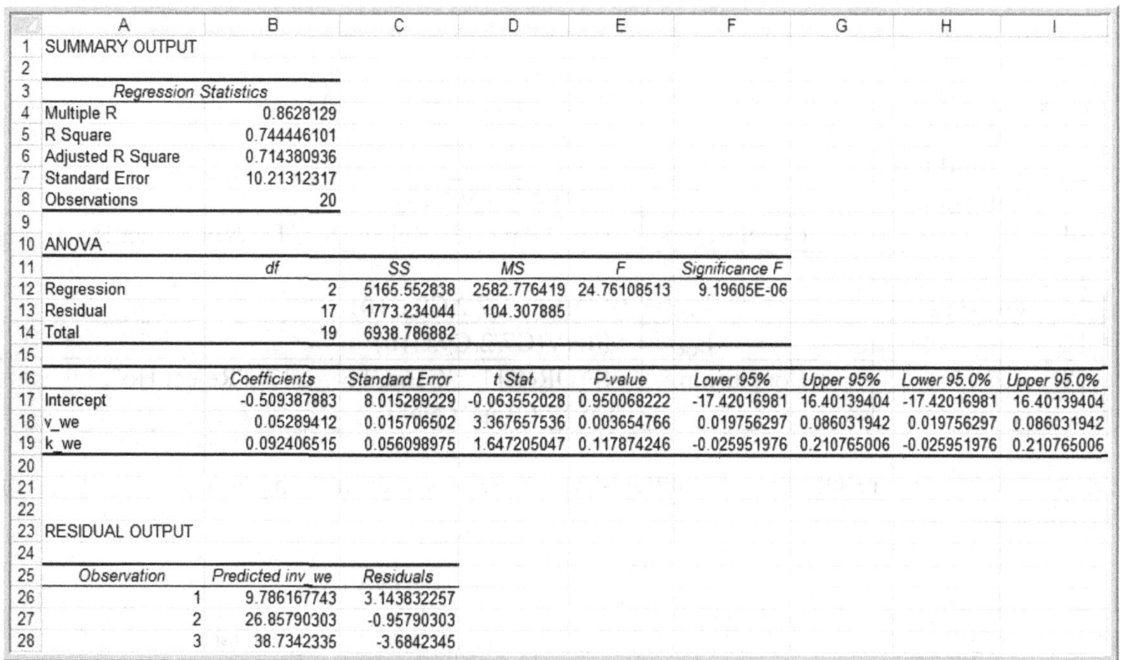

	A	B	C	D	E	F	G	H	I
1	SUMMARY OUTPUT								
2									
3	*Regression Statistics*								
4	Multiple R	0.8628129							
5	R Square	0.744446101							
6	Adjusted R Square	0.714380936							
7	Standard Error	10.21312317							
8	Observations	20							
9									
10	ANOVA								
11		*df*	*SS*	*MS*	*F*	*Significance F*			
12	Regression	2	5165.552838	2582.776419	24.76108513	9.19605E-06			
13	Residual	17	1773.234044	104.307885					
14	Total	19	6938.786882						
15									
16		*Coefficients*	*Standard Error*	*t Stat*	*P-value*	*Lower 95%*	*Upper 95%*	*Lower 95.0%*	*Upper 95.0%*
17	Intercept	-0.509387883	8.015289229	-0.063552028	0.950068222	-17.42016981	16.40139404	-17.42016981	16.40139404
18	v_we	0.05289412	0.015706502	3.367657536	0.003654766	0.019756297	0.086031942	0.019756297	0.086031942
19	k_we	0.092406515	0.056098975	1.647205047	0.117874246	-0.025951976	0.210765006	-0.025951976	0.210765006
20									
21									
22									
23	RESIDUAL OUTPUT								
24									
25	*Observation*	*Predicted inv_we*	*Residuals*						
26	1	9.786167743	3.143832257						
27	2	26.85790303	-0.95790303						
28	3	38.7342335	-3.6842345						

Below we use the Goldfeld-Quandt test to test the null hypothesis $H_0: \sigma^2_{GE} = \sigma^2_{WE}$.

Insert a new worksheet by selecting the **Insert Worksheet** tab at the bottom of your screen. Rename it **Goldfeld-Quandt Test.**

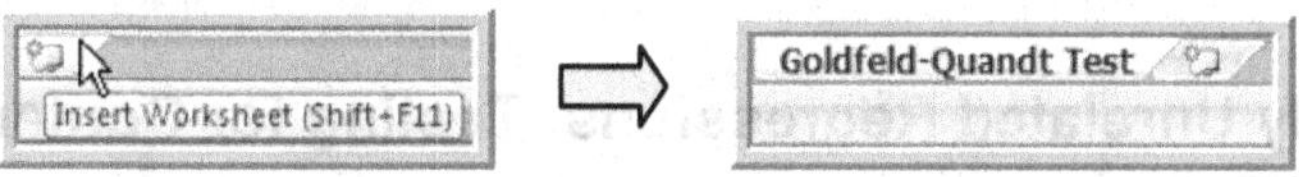

In it copy the Goldfeld-Quandt test template you created in Chapter 8.

Replace the following reference: **[POE Chapter 8.xlsx]Subsample 1 Model** by **GE Investment Equation**, and replace: **[POE Chapter 8.xlsx]Subsample 2 Model** by **WE Investment Equation.**

	A	B	C
1	**Data Input**	$N_1 =$	='GE Investment Equation'!B8
2		$K_1 =$	='GE Investment Equation'!B12+1
3		MS Residual 1 =	='GE Investment Equation'!D13
4		$N_2 =$	='WE Investment Equation'!B8
5		$K_2 =$	='WE Investment Equation'!B12+1
6		MS Residual 2 =	='WE Investment Equation'!D13
7		$\alpha =$	
8			
9	**Computed Values**	$m_1 =$	=C1-C2
10		$m_2 =$	=C4-C5
11		F-statistic =	=C3/C6

	A	B	C
12	**Goldfeld-Quandt test**		
13	**Right-tail**	F_c=	=FINV(C7,C9,C10)
14		Conclusion =	=IF(C11>=C13,"Reject Ho","Do Not Reject Ho")
15			
16	**Two-tail**	F_{Lc}=	=FINV(1-C7/2,C9,C10)
17		F_{Uc}=	=FINV(C7/2,C9,C10)
18		Conclusion =	=IF(OR(C11<=C16,C11>=C17),"Reject Ho", "Do Not Reject Ho")

At $\alpha = 0.05$, the result of the Goldfeld-Quandt test is (see also p. 566 in *Principles of Econometrics, 4e*):

	A	B	C
1	**Data Input**	N_1 =	20
2		K_1 =	3
3		MS Residual 1 =	777.4463
4		N_2 =	20
5		K_2 =	3
6		MS Residual 2 =	104.3079
7		α =	0.05

	A	B	C
9	**Computed Values**	m_1 =	17
10		m_2 =	17
11		F-statistic =	7.45338
12	**Goldfeld-Quandt test**		
13	**Right-tail**	F_c =	2.271893
14		Conclusion =	Reject Ho
15			
16	**Two-tail**	F_{Lc} =	0.374069
17		F_{Uc} =	2.6733
18		Conclusion =	Reject Ho

15.4.4 Seemingly Unrelated Regressions: Testing for Contemporaneous Correlation

Again, we consider a model for describing gross firm investment for General Electric (GE) and Westinghouse (WE), over a period of $T = 20$ years. These two firms have distinct investment behaviors that are fixed over time.

This time we assume that the variances of the error terms are different across firms, (15.28), *and* the error terms across firms, at the same point in time, are correlated, (15.29):

$$var(e_{GE,t}) = \sigma_{GE}^2 \neq \sigma_{WE}^2 = var(e_{WE,t}) \tag{15.28}$$

$$cov(e_{GE,t}, e_{WE,t}) = \sigma_{GE,WE} \neq 0 \tag{15.29}$$

Correlation like (15.29) is called contemporaneous correlation, and to be accounted for, a dummy variable model, not separate investment equations, has to be estimated. As we saw in Section 15.4.2, a dummy variable model like (15.25) implies that $var(e_{GE,t}) = var(e_{WE,t})$. So, the dummy variable model will have to (1) correct for the heteroskedasticity implied by (15.28) *and* (2) account for the contemporaneous correlation between the errors of GE and WE implied by (15.29). This is what a seemingly unrelated regressions (SUR) model does.

We would like to test whether or not $\sigma_{GE,WE} = 0$ to determine if we need a SUR model. To carry out such a test we compute the squared correlation:

$$r_{GE,WE}^2 = \frac{\hat{\sigma}_{GE,WE}^2}{\hat{\sigma}_{GE}^2 \hat{\sigma}_{WE}^2} \tag{15.30}$$

where $\hat{\sigma}_{GE}^2$ and $\hat{\sigma}_{WE}^2$ are the mean square residuals from the GE and WE investment equations.

The estimated covariance is computed from (see also p. 567 in *Principles of Econometrics, 4e*):

$$\hat{\sigma}_{GE,WE} = \frac{1}{17}\sum_{t=1}^{20} \hat{e}_{GE,t}\hat{e}_{WE,t} \tag{15.31}$$

Go back to your **grunfeld2** data worksheet.

In cells **N1:O5**, enter the following labels and formulas. In the last column, you will find the numbers of the equations used, if any.

	N	O	
1	**σ-hat$_{GE,WE}$ =**	=(1/17)*SUMPRODUCT('GE Investment Equation'!C26:C45, 'WE Investment Equation'!C26:C45)	*(15.31)*
2	**σ²-hat$_{GE}$ =**	='GE Investment Equation'!D13	
3	**σ²-hat$_{WE}$ =**	='WE Investment Equation'!D13	
4	**r²$_{GE,WE}$ =**	=(O1^2)/(O2*O3)	*(15.30)*
5	**r$_{GE,WE}$ =**	=SQRT(O4)	

The result is (see also p. 569 in *Principles of Econometrics, 4e*):

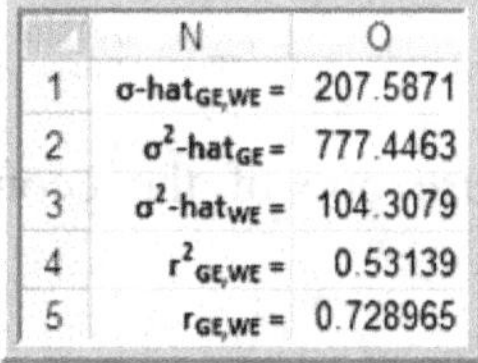

	N	O
1	σ-hat$_{GE,WE}$ =	207.5871
2	σ²-hat$_{GE}$ =	777.4463
3	σ²-hat$_{WE}$ =	104.3079
4	r²$_{GE,WE}$ =	0.53139
5	r$_{GE,WE}$ =	0.728965

The correlation $r_{GE,WE} = 0.729$ indicates a strong contemporaneous correlation between errors of the GE and WE investment equations. To check the statistical significance of $r_{GE,WE}^2$, we can test the null hypothesis $H_0: \sigma_{GE,WE} = 0$. If $\sigma_{GE,WE} = 0$, then $LM = Tr_{GE,WE}^2$ is a Lagrange multiplier test statistic that is distributed as a $\chi_{(1)}^2$ random variable in large samples.

Insert a new worksheet by selecting the **Insert Worksheet** tab at the bottom of your screen. Rename it **Lagrange Multiplier Test simple**.

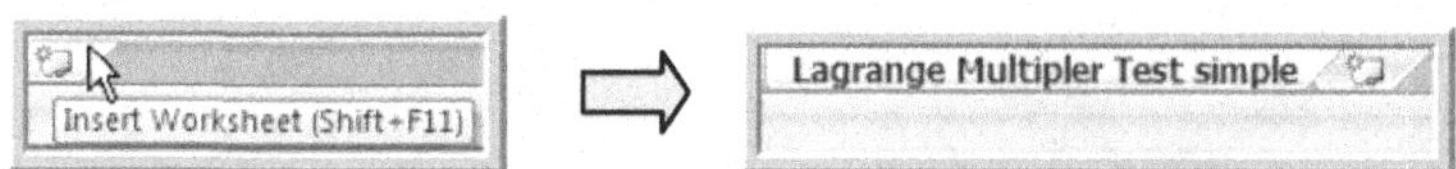

In it copy the simplified Lagrange multiplier test template you created in Chapter 9.

In cell **B1**, replace **N** by **T**. In cell **B2**, rcplace $\mathbf{R^2}$ by $\mathbf{r^2_{GE,WE}}$. Delete the content of cells **C1:C2**. In cell **C2**, we get the value of $\mathbf{r^2_{GE,WE}}$ from our **grunfeld2 data** worksheet, as shown in the table below.

	A	B	C
1	**Data Input**	T =	
2		$r^2_{GE,WE}$ =	='grunfeld2 data'!O4
3		α =	
4		m =	
5			
6	**Computed Values**	χ^2-critical value =	=CHIINV(C3,C4)
8	**Lagrange Multiplier Test**	χ^2 =	=C1*C2
9		Conclusion =	=IF(C8>=C6,"Reject Ho","Do Not Reject Ho")
10		*p*-value =	=CHIDIST(C8,C4)
11		Conclusion =	=IF(C10<=C3,"Reject Ho","Do Not Reject Ho")

At $\alpha = 0.05$, with $T = 20$ and $m = 1$, the result of the test is (see also p. 569 in *Principles of Econometrics, 4e*):

	A	B	C
1	**Data Input**	T =	20
2		$r^2_{GE,WE}$ =	0.53139
3		α =	0.05
4		m =	1
5			
6	**Computed Values**	χ^2-critical value =	3.841459
7			
8	**Lagrange Multiplier Test**	χ^2 =	10.6278
9		Conclusion =	Reject Ho
10		*p*-value =	0.001114
11		Conclusion =	Reject Ho

To implement the SUR estimation use one of the econometric software programs listed at www.principlesofeconometrics.com.

CHAPTER 16

Qualitative and Limited Dependent Variable Models

CHAPTER OUTLINE

16.1 LEAST SQUARES FITTED LINEAR PROBABILITY MODEL

Open the Excel file ***transport***. Save your file as **POE Chapter 16**. Rename sheet 1 **transport data**.

We consider a model for explaining individuals' choices between driving (private transportation) and taking the bus (public transportation) when commuting to work, assuming that these are the only two alternatives:

$$y = \beta_1 + \beta_2 x + e \tag{16.1}$$

where the dependent variable y is a dummy variable representing an individual's choice:

$$y = \begin{cases} 1 & \text{individual drives to work} \\ 0 & \text{individual takes bus to work} \end{cases} \tag{16.2}$$

and the explanatory variable x is defined as:

$$x = (\text{commuting time by bus} - \text{commuting time by car}) \tag{16.3}$$

If the probability that an individual drives to work is p, then $P[y = 1] = p$. It follows that the probability that a person uses public transportation is $P[y = 0] = 1 - p$. The probability function for such a binary random variable is:

$$f(y) = p^y(1-p)^{1-y}, y = 0, 1 \tag{16.4}$$

where p is the probability that y takes the value 1. This discrete random variable has expected value $E[y] = p$ and variance $var(y) = p(1-p)$.

A priori we expect that as x increases, and commuting time by bus increases relative to commuting time by car, an individual would be more inclined to drive. That is, we expect a positive relationship between x and p, the probability that an individual will drive to work:

$$E(y) = p = \beta_1 + \beta_2 x \tag{16.5}$$

In the **Regression** dialog box, the **Input Y Range** should be **D1:D22**, and the **Input X Range** should be **C1:C22**. Check the boxes next to **Labels** *and* **Residuals**. Select **New Worksheet Ply** and name it **LS Linear Probability Model**. Finally select **OK**.

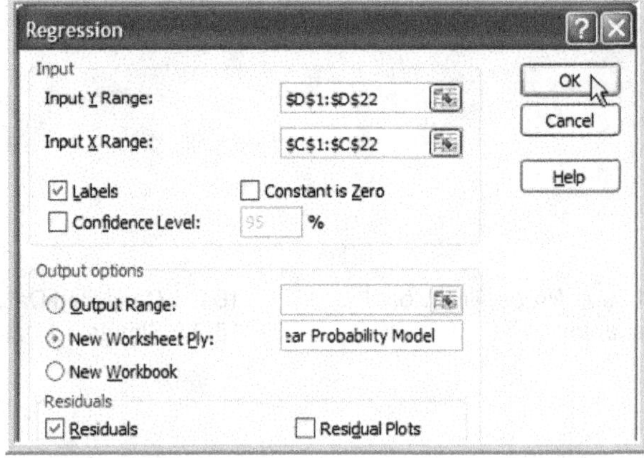

The result is:

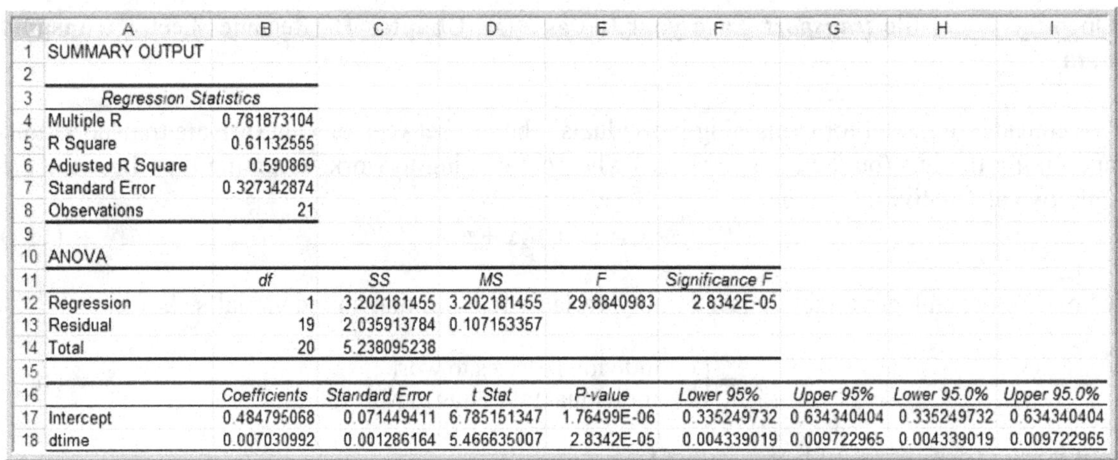

	A	B	C	D	E	F	G	H	I
1	SUMMARY OUTPUT								
2									
3	*Regression Statistics*								
4	Multiple R	0.781873104							
5	R Square	0.61132555							
6	Adjusted R Square	0.590869							
7	Standard Error	0.327342874							
8	Observations	21							
9									
10	ANOVA								
11		*df*	*SS*	*MS*	*F*	*Significance F*			
12	Regression	1	3.202181455	3.202181455	29.8840983	2.8342E-05			
13	Residual	19	2.035913784	0.107153357					
14	Total	20	5.238095238						
15									
16		*Coefficients*	*Standard Error*	*t Stat*	*P-value*	*Lower 95%*	*Upper 95%*	*Lower 95.0%*	*Upper 95.0%*
17	Intercept	0.484795068	0.071449411	6.785151347	1.76499E-06	0.335249732	0.634340404	0.335249732	0.634340404
18	dtime	0.007030992	0.001286164	5.466635007	2.8342E-05	0.004339019	0.009722965	0.004339019	0.009722965

We are particularly interested in the predicted probabilities of automobile transportation being chosen. As outlined below, by using least squares to estimate model (16.1), we obtain values of $\hat{p}$ that are less than 0 or greater than 1—values that do not make sense as probabilities.

	A	B	C
22	RESIDUAL OUTPUT		
23			
24	*Observation*	*Predicted auto*	*Residuals*
25	1	0.143791971	-0.143791971
26	2	0.656351265	-0.656351265
27	3	1.066961201	-0.066961201
28	4	0.311832673	-0.311832673
29	5	0.262615731	-0.262615731
30	6	1.124615311	-0.124615311
31	7	0.851109721	0.148890279
32	8	-0.131822882	0.131822882
33	9	0.365268209	-0.365268209
34	10	0.122698996	-0.122698996
35	11	-0.152915857	0.152915857
36	12	0.945325023	0.054674977
37	13	0.175431434	0.824568566
38	14	0.435578126	-0.435578126
39	15	0.847594225	0.152405775
40	16	0.712599213	0.287400787
41	17	0.050279789	-0.050279789
42	18	0.723848785	0.276151215
43	19	0.680959736	0.319040264
44	20	-0.02776424	0.02776424
45	21	0.835641567	0.164358433

The underlying feature that causes this problem is that the linear probability model (16.1) implicitly assumes that as x increases the probability of driving increases at a constant rate. However, since $0 \le p \le 1$, a constant rate of increase is impossible. To overcome this problem a nonlinear probit or logit model must be used. These estimation options are available in econometric software packages such as those listed at www.principlesofeconometrics.com.

16.2 LIMITED DEPENDENT VARIABLES

16.2.1 Censored Data

Open the Excel file ***mroz***. Excel opens the data set in Sheet 1 of a new Excel file. Since we would like to save all our work from Chapter 16 in one file, create a new worksheet in your **POE Chapter 16** Excel file, rename it **mroz data**, and in it, copy the data set you just opened.

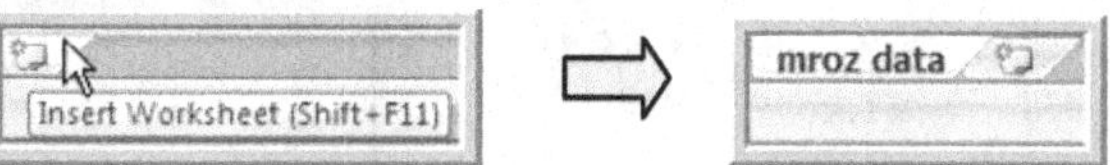

To plot the histogram of the wife's hours of work in 1975 (*hours*), we proceed as we have done previously in Chapters 4 and 14.

In cells **AA1:AA3**, enter the following label and values.

	AA
1	**BIN**
2	0
3	200

Select cells **AA2:AA3**, move your cursor to the lower right corner of your selection until it turns into a skinny cross as shown below; left-click, hold it and drag it down to cell **AA27**: Excel recognizes the series and automatically completes it for you.

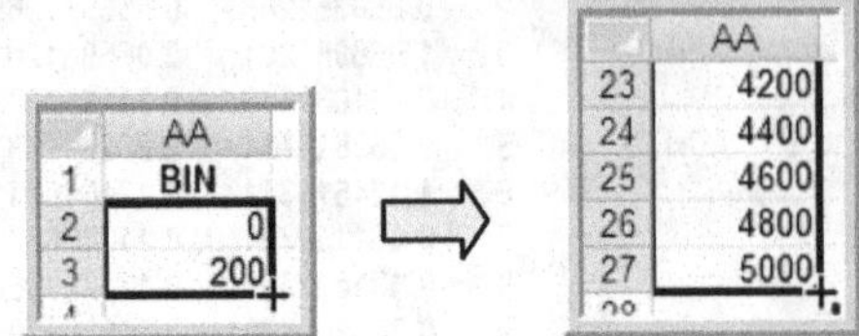

In the **Histogram** dialog box, the **Input Range** should be **H2:H754**, and the **Bin Range** should be **AA2:AA27**. Check the **New Worksheet Ply** option and name it **Censored Data Histogram**; check the box next to **Chart Output**. Finally, select **OK**.

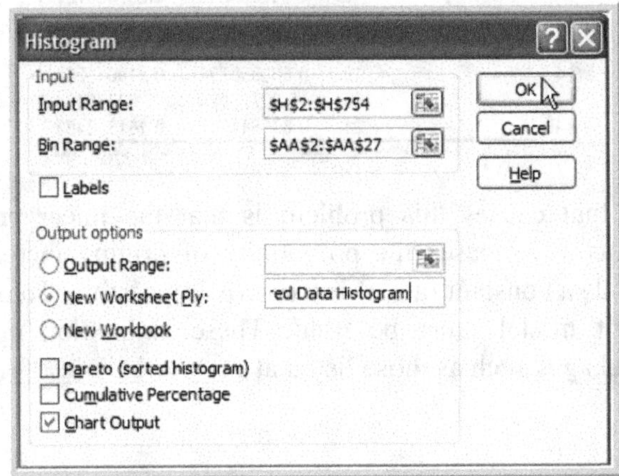

Select the columns in your chart area, right-click and select **Format Data Series**. The **Series Options** tab of the **Format Data Series** dialog box should be open. Select the **Gap Width** button and move it to the far left, towards **No Gap**. In the **Border Color** tab, select **Solid line**, and change the **Color** to black. Finally select **Close**.

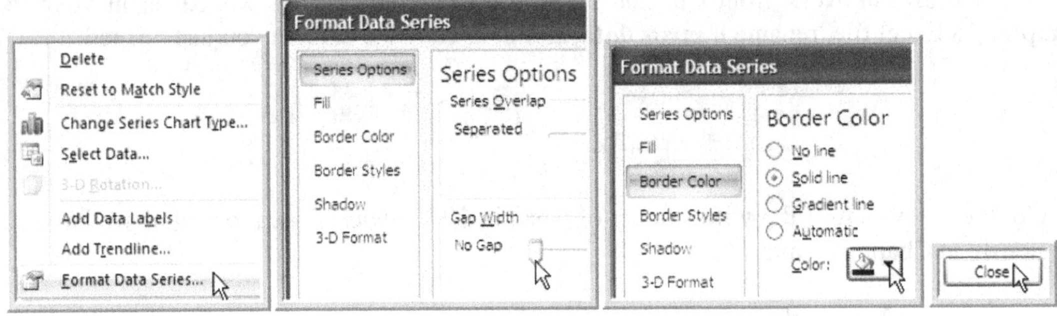

After editing, the result is (see Figure 16.3 p. 614 in *Principles of Econometrics, 4e*):

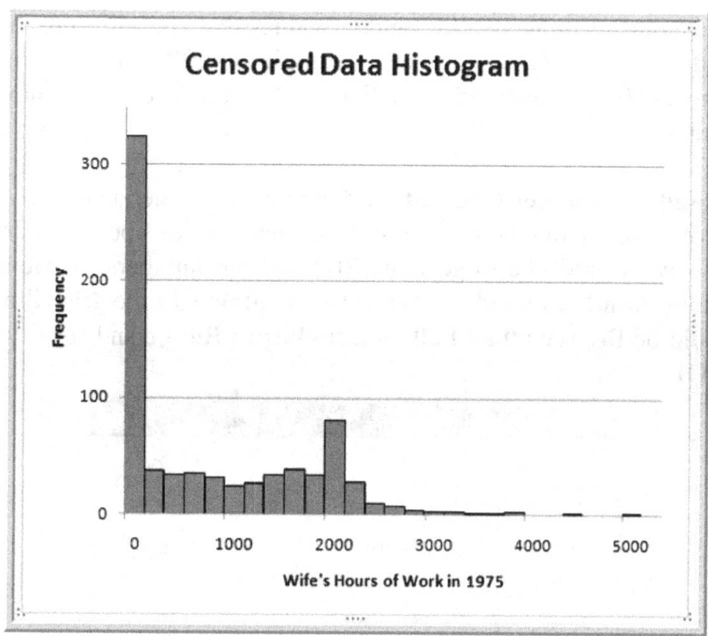

The histogram shows the large fraction of women who did not enter the labor force. This is an example of censored data, meaning that a substantial fraction of the observations on the dependent variable take a limit value—which is zero in the case of market hours worked by married women.

16.2.2 Simulated Data

Consider the following index or latent variable model:

$$y_i^* = -9 + x_i + e_i \tag{16.6}$$

where x_i are uniformly distributed over the interval $[0,20]$ and e_i are normally distributed with mean 0 and standard deviation 4.

The observed y_i are defined as:

$$y_i = \begin{cases} 0 & \text{if } y_i^* \le 0 \\ y_i^* & \text{if } y_i^* > 0 \end{cases} \tag{16.7}$$

Insert a new worksheet by selecting the **Insert Worksheet** tab at the bottom of your screen. Rename it **simulated data**.

In cells **A1:E2** enter the following labels and formulas.

	A	B	C	D	E
1	**y***	**x**	**e**	**y**	**E(y*)**
2	=-9+B2+C2			=IF(A2<=0,0,A2)	=-9+B2

In column **B** we generate a sample of 200 random values that are uniformly distributed over the interval [0,20] and in column **C** we generate a sample of 200 random values from a normal distribution with mean 0 and standard deviation 4. We proceed as we have done before in Chapters 14, 12 and 3.

We first use the **Random Number Generation** dialog box to generate our x values. We need to generate one set of random numbers for our x values, so we specify **1** in the **Number of Variables** window. We would like to generate 200 random numbers, so we specify **200** in the **Number of Random Numbers** window. We select **Uniform** in the **Distribution** window; the selected range should be **Between 0 and 20**. Select **Output Range** and specify it to be **B2:B201**. Finally, we select **OK**.

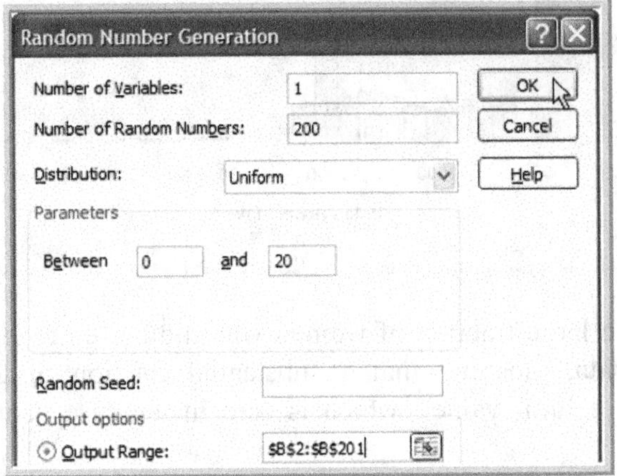

Next, we use the **Random Number Generation** dialog box to generate our e values. We need to generate one set of random numbers for our e values, so we specify **1** in the **Number of Variables** window. We would like to generate 200 random numbers, so we specify **200** in the **Number of Random Numbers** window. We select **Normal** in the **Distribution** window; the selected **Parameters** should be **Mean** equal to **0**, and **Standard deviation** equal to **4**. Select **Output Range** and specify it to be **C2:C201**. Finally, we select **OK**.

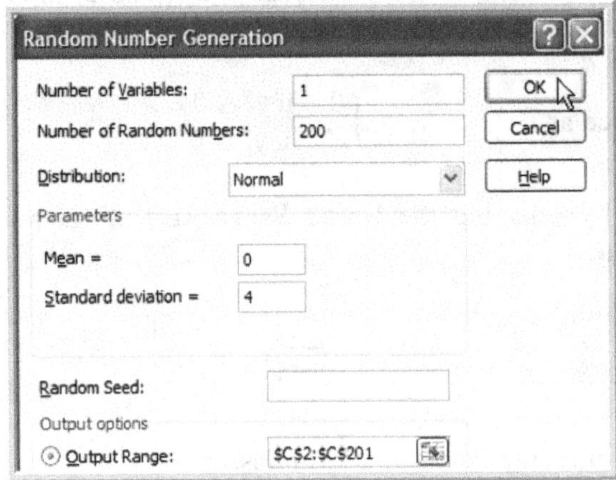

After you copy the content of cell **A2** to cells **A3:A201**, and the content of cells **D2:E2** to cells **D3:E201**, here is how your table should look (only the first five values are shown below):

	A	B	C	D	E
1	y*	x	e	y	E(y*)
2	1.780206	8.465224	2.314982	1.780206	-0.53478
3	11.94971	15.71398	5.235725	11.94971	6.713981
4	13.0952	14.20209	7.893104	13.0952	5.202094
5	-7.16142	5.369427	-3.53085	0	-3.63057
6	14.77688	19.96582	3.811065	14.77688	10.96582

Note: you will obtain different random samples than the ones we obtained for x and e, so your y^*, y and $E(y^*)$ values should also be different than the ones reported above.

Next, we plot the uncensored sample data and the latent regression function as we have done before, in Chapter 2 for example. We choose a **Scatter with only Markers** chart type for the uncensored sample data series, where the x-axis values are **B2:B201** and the y-axis values are **A2:A201**. The latent regression function is plotted using a **Scatter with Smooth Lines** chart type, where the x-axis values are **B2:B201** and the y-axis values are **E2:E201**.

The result is (see also Figure 16.4 p. 616 in *Principles of Econometrics, 4e*):

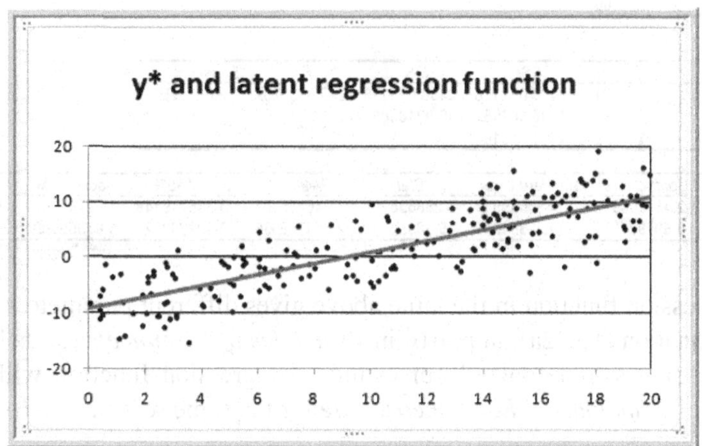

The latent or uncensored data y^* are scattered along the latent regression function. If we observed these data we could estimate the parameters using the least squares principle, by fitting a line through the center of the data.

However, we do not observe all the latent data. What we can do is estimate the parameters of our regression, using the least squares principles, by fitting a line through the center of the *observed* or *censored* data—which is what we do next.

In the **Regression** dialog box, the **Input Y Range** should be **D1:D201**, and the **Input X Range** should be **B1:B201**. Check the box next to **Labels**. *Uncheck* the box next to **Residuals**. Select **New Worksheet Ply** and name it **LS Fitted Censored Data Model**. Finally select **OK**.

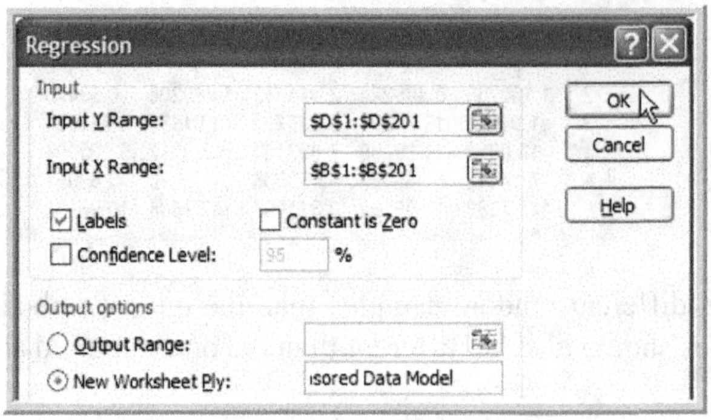

Regression	
Input	
Input Y Range:	$D$1:$D$201
Input X Range:	$B$1:$B$201
☑ Labels	☐ Constant is Zero
☐ Confidence Level:	95 %
Output options	
○ Output Range:	
⦿ New Worksheet Ply:	ısored Data Model

OK · Cancel · Help

The result is:

	A	B	C	D	E	F	G	H	I
1	SUMMARY OUTPUT								
2									
3	*Regression Statistics*								
4	Multiple R	0.742330341							
5	R Square	0.551054335							
6	Adjusted R Square	0.548786933							
7	Standard Error	3.167307796							
8	Observations	200							
9									
10	ANOVA								
11		*df*	*SS*	*MS*	*F*	*Significance F*			
12	Regression	1	2438.071126	2438.071126	243.0333267	2.80475E-36			
13	Residual	198	1986.304057	10.03183867					
14	Total	199	4424.375184						
15									
16		*Coefficients*	*Standard Error*	*t Stat*	*P-value*	*Lower 95%*	*Upper 95%*	*Lower 95.0%*	*Upper 95.0%*
17	Intercept	-2.451600913	0.463559917	-5.288638697	3.24646E-07	-3.365749149	-1.537452677	-3.365749149	-1.537452677
18	x	0.597924573	0.038354249	15.58952619	2.80475E-36	0.522289325	0.673559821	0.522289325	0.673559821

The estimated regression function in the table above gives different parameters estimates than the ones reported in equation (16.32a) on p. 616 in *Principles of Econometrics, 4e* because it is based on a different censored sample data. Your estimated regression function will also be different than ours and that of *Principles of Econometrics, 4e* for the same reason.

Go back to your **simulated data** worksheet.

In cells **F1:F2** enter the following label and formula.

	F
1	**LS Fitted**
2	='LS Fitted Censored Data Model'!$B$17+ 'LS Fitted Censored Data Model'!$B$18*'simulated data'!B2

Copy the content of cell **F2** to cells **F3:F201**.

After you copy the content of cell **F2** to cells **F3:F201**, here is how your table should look (only the first five values are shown below):

	F
1	LS Fitted
2	2.609965
3	6.944174
4	6.04018
5	0.758911
6	9.486453

Note: since you are working with different random samples than the ones we are working with, your **LS fitted** values should also be different than the ones reported above.

Next, we plot the *censored* sample data, its least squares fitted regression function, as well as the latent regression function we plotted earlier. We choose a **Scatter with only Markers** chart type for the censored sample data series, where the *x*-axis values are **B2:B201** and the *y*-axis values are **D2:D201**. The regression functions are plotted using a **Scatter with Smooth Lines** chart type. For the least squares fitted regression function, based on the censored sample data, the *x*-axis values are **B2:B201** and the *y*-axis values are **F2:F201**. For the latent regression function, as plotted earlier, the *x*-axis values are **B2:B201** and the *y*-axis values are **E2:E201**.

The result is (see also Figure 16.5 p. 617 in *Principles of Econometrics, 4e*):

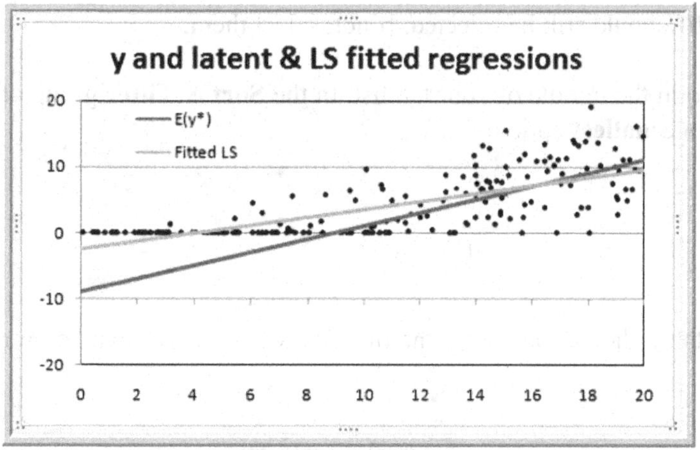

Note that the least squares principle fails to estimate $\beta_1 = -9$ and $\beta_2 = 1$ because the observed data do not fall along the underlying regression function $E(y^*) = \beta_1 + \beta_2 x = -9 + x$.

Finally, we can estimate the parameters of our regression, using the least squares principles, by fitting a line through the center of only the *positive* sample data—which is what we do next.

In cells **H1:I2** enter the following labels and formulas.

	H	I
1	y	x
2	=D2	=B2

Copy the content of cells **H2:I2** to cells **H3:I201**.

Copy the content of cells **H1:I1** to cells **K1:L1**.

Next, select cells **H2:I201**. Right-click, select **Copy**. Place your cursor in cell **K2**. Right-click, select **Paste Special**. In the **Paste Special** dialog box that pops up, select **Values**. Finally, select **OK**.

Here is how your table should look (only the first five values are shown below):

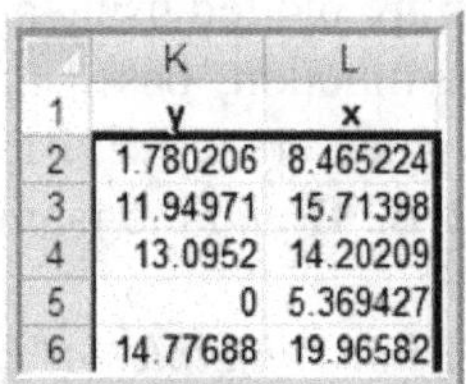

	K	L
1	y	x
2	1.780206	8.465224
3	11.94971	15.71398
4	13.0952	14.20209
5	0	5.369427
6	14.77688	19.96582

Your cells **K2:L201** should still be selected. If not, select them.

Select the **Data** tab in the middle of your tab list. In the **Sort & Filter** group of commands, select the **Sort Largest to Smallest** option.

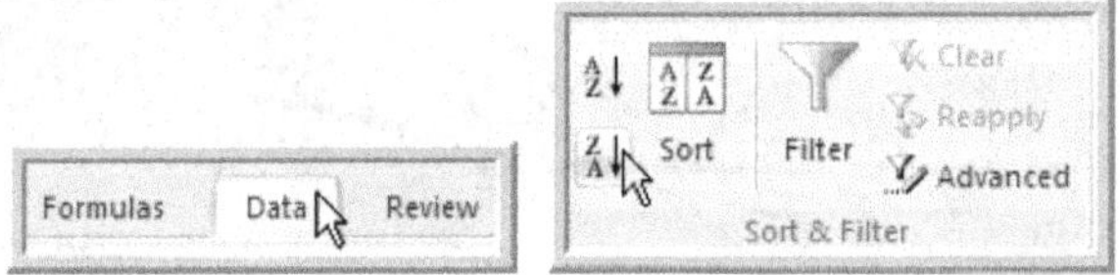

Here is how your table should look (only the first five values are shown below):

	K	L
1	y	x
2	19.15563	18.06635
3	16.17665	19.72045
4	15.50975	15.03769
5	15.0975	17.97296
6	14.77688	19.96582

In the **Regression** dialog box, select only your *positive* y-values in column **K** and their corresponding x-values in column **L**. Our **Input Y Range** is **K1:K112**, and our **Input X Range** is **L1:L112**; yours will be different because you have a different sample of data. Check the box next to **Labels**. Select **New Worksheet Ply** and name it **LS Fitted Positive Data Model**. Finally select **OK**.

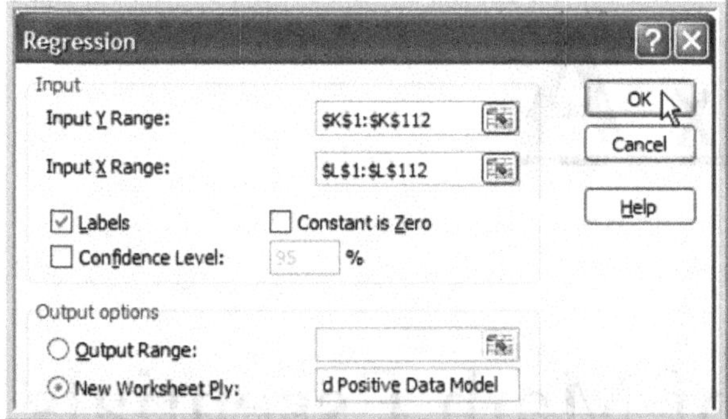

The result is:

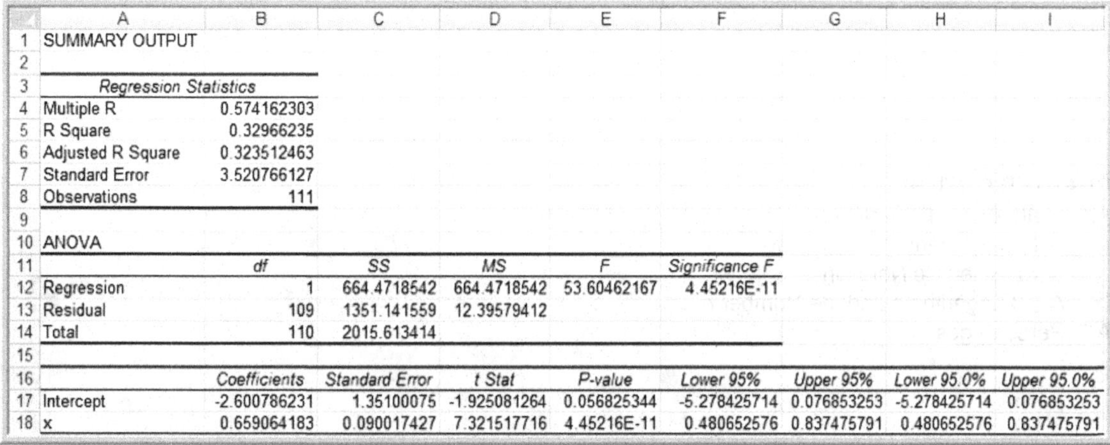

	A	B	C	D	E	F	G	H	I
1	SUMMARY OUTPUT								
2									
3	*Regression Statistics*								
4	Multiple R	0.574162303							
5	R Square	0.32966235							
6	Adjusted R Square	0.323512463							
7	Standard Error	3.520766127							
8	Observations	111							
9									
10	ANOVA								
11		*df*	*SS*	*MS*	*F*	*Significance F*			
12	Regression	1	664.4718542	664.4718542	53.60462167	4.45216E-11			
13	Residual	109	1351.141559	12.39579412					
14	Total	110	2015.613414						
15									
16		*Coefficients*	*Standard Error*	*t Stat*	*P-value*	*Lower 95%*	*Upper 95%*	*Lower 95.0%*	*Upper 95.0%*
17	Intercept	-2.600786231	1.35100075	-1.925081264	0.056825344	-5.278425714	0.076853253	-5.278425714	0.076853253
18	x	0.659064183	0.090017427	7.321517716	4.45216E-11	0.480652576	0.837475791	0.480652576	0.837475791

Again, the estimated regression function in the table above gives different parameters estimates than the ones reported in equation (16.32b) on p. 616 in *Principles of Econometrics, 4e* because it is based on a different positive sample data. Your estimated regression function will also be different than ours and that of *Principles of Econometrics, 4e* for the same reason.

Note that once again the least squares principle fails to estimate $\beta_1 = -9$ and $\beta_2 = 1$. If the dependent variable is censored, having a lower limit and/or an upper limit, then the least squares estimators of the regression parameters are biased and inconsistent. In this case we can apply an alternative estimation procedure, which is called Tobit in honor of James Tobin, winner of the 1981 Nobel Prize in Economics, who first studied this model. The Tobit estimation procedure is available in standard econometric software.

APPENDIX A

Review of Math Essentials

CHAPTER OUTLINE

A.1 MATHEMATICAL OPERATIONS

If you have not done so, read Chapter 1 in this manual. Do it now.

The basic **arithmetic operations** are described in Section 1.3.1. Here we explain the use of some Excel functions that may help in computations. Open Excel and save the workbook as **Appendix A**. Rename **Sheet 1** as **math functions**. In cell **A1** type the label **x** to name the column. Enter the values **1,5** , **−3, 3** in cells **A2:A5**.

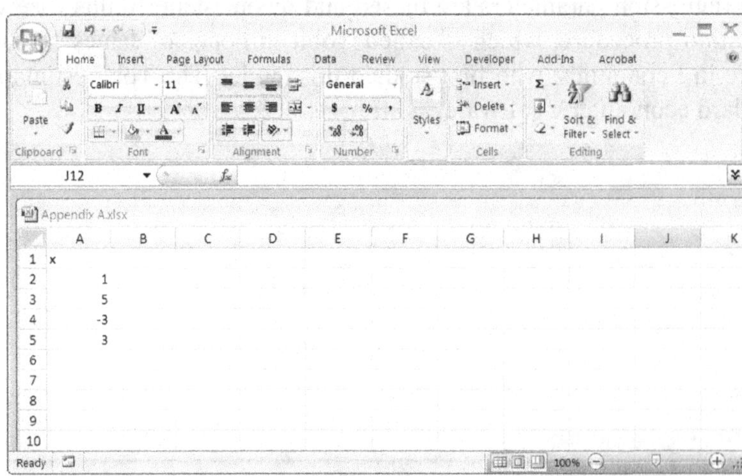

Many mathematical functions are built into Excel. These are easy to access with a few clicks. Suppose we want to find the sum $\sum_{i=1}^{4} x_i$. In cell **A8** type the label **sum x**. Click in cell **B8** to make it the **Active cell**. Locate the **Insert Function** icon, to the left of the **formula bar**.

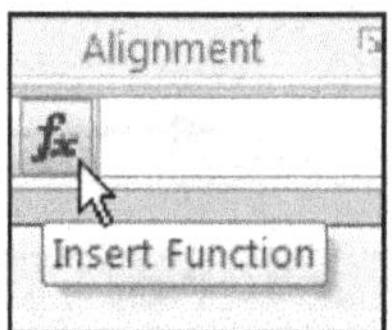

A click opens a dialog box. In the search box you can enter the term you are seeking. Type **sum** and click **Go**. The recommended function is called **SUM**. The command format is shown below the function window, and the very important **Help on this function** link is given in the lower left corner.

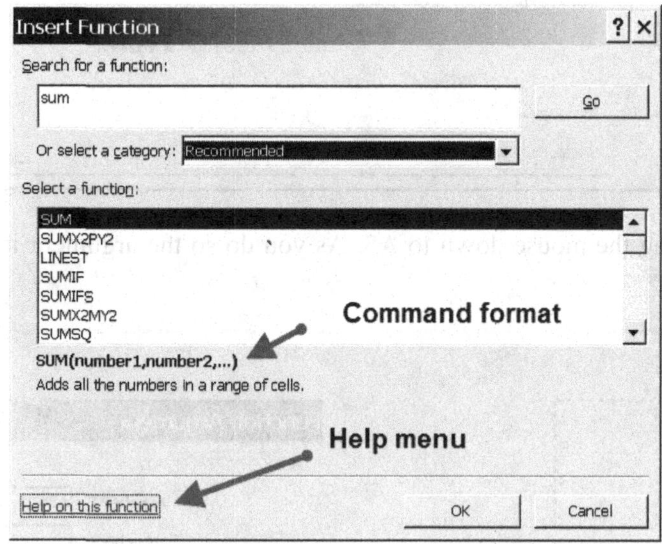

Click on **OK**.

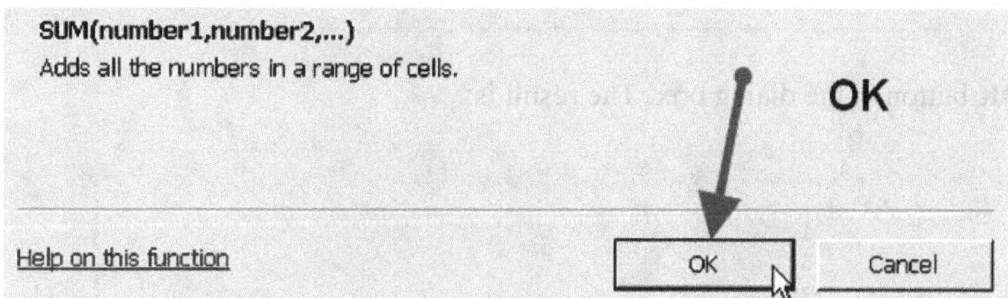

Several changes occur. First, in the **formula bar** "=SUM()" appears—the summation command is awaiting a range of values to add up. In the active cell **B8** the command is mirrored.

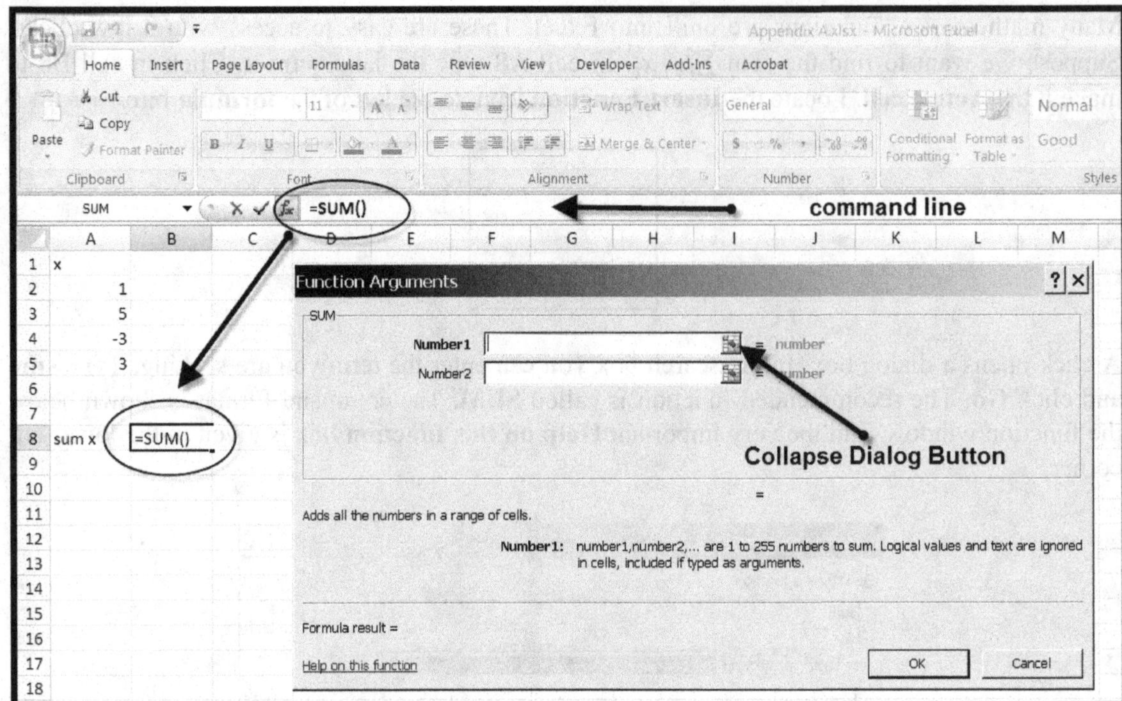

Click on **A2** and drag the mouse down to **A5**. As you do so the argument in the **SUM** function changes to **A2:A5**.

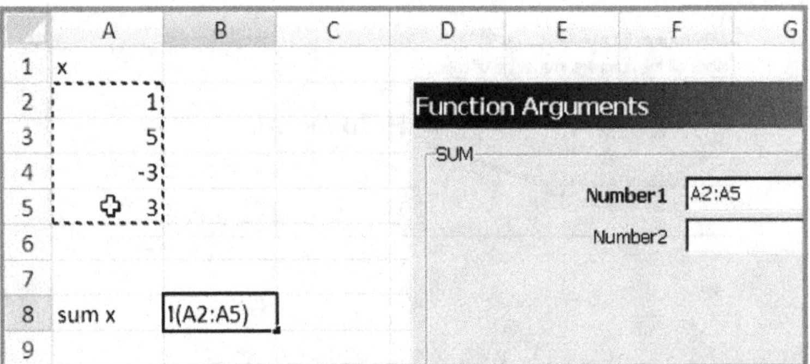

Click the **OK** button in the dialog box. The result is:

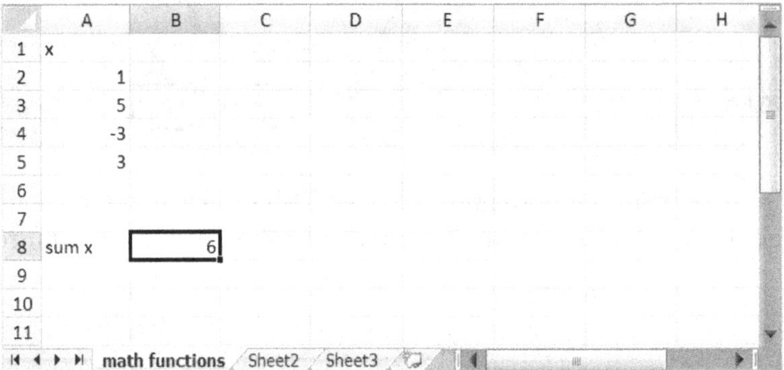

If the **Function Argument** dialog box happens to be in the way of numbers you want to select, click on the oddly but aptly named **collapse dialog button**. It will temporarily reduce the dialog box and allow you to drag it out of the way. After you are done selecting data click the **restore button** to return the dialog box to full size.

A more direct approach is to type a formula, beginning with an equal sign in an active cell. To illustrate compute $\sum_{i=1}^{4} x_i^2$. In cell **A9** enter **sum x^2** where the caret is a way to indicate a power. In cell **B9** enter **=sum** and a drop down list of functions appears.

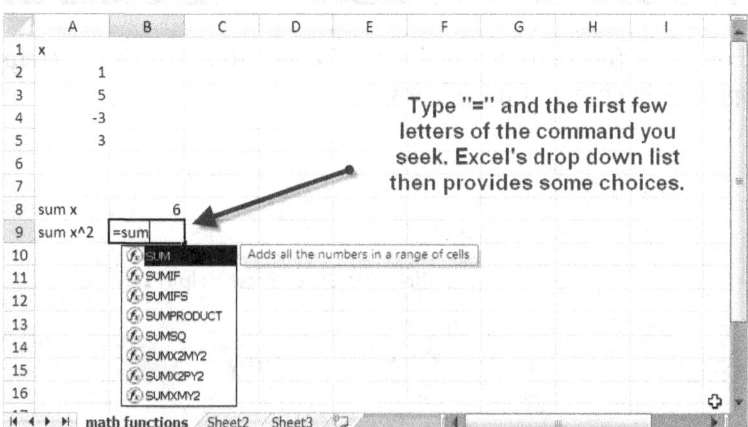

Select **SUMSQ** and a definition is provided.

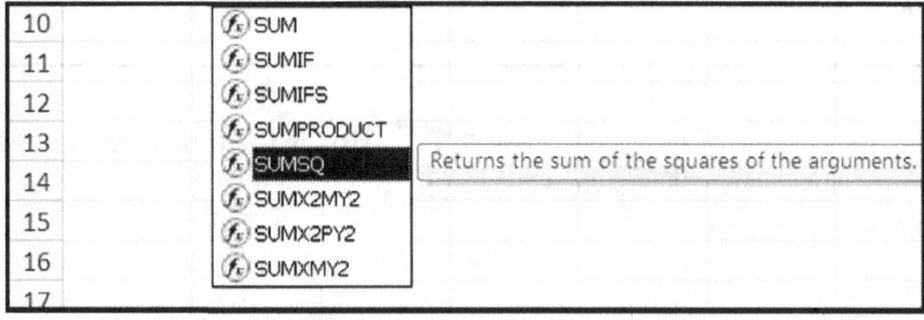

Double-click **SUMSQ** and the function enters **B9**. Specify the function arguments by filling in the range **A2:A5**. Don't forget the closing parenthesis. Then press **Enter** to obtain the sum of squared values.

SUM | =SUMSQ(A2:A5)

	A	B	C	D	E
1	x				
2	1				
3	5				
4	-3				
5	3				
6					
7					
8	sum x	6			
9	sum x^2	=SUMSQ(A2:A5)			
10					

	A	B
1	x	
2		1
3		5
4		-3
5		3
6		
7		
8	sum x	6
9	sum x^2	44
10		

The trick is to know what functions are available. The key tool here is the **Help** button that will be found in the upper right corner of the window.

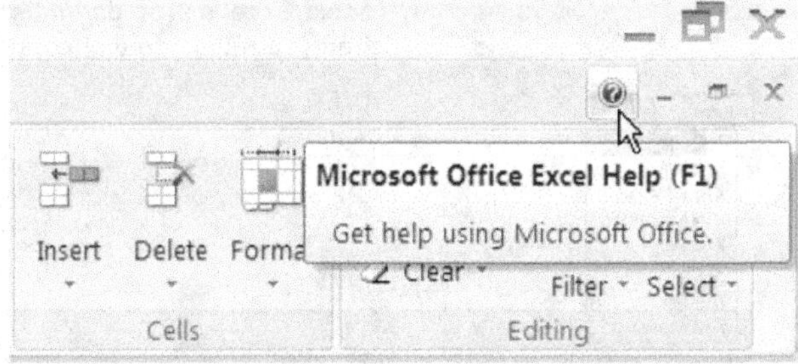

In the resulting **Help** window you can find resources for functions and many other tasks. If you do not see what you are seeking, enter a short phrase or keyword into the **Search** window and press **Enter.**

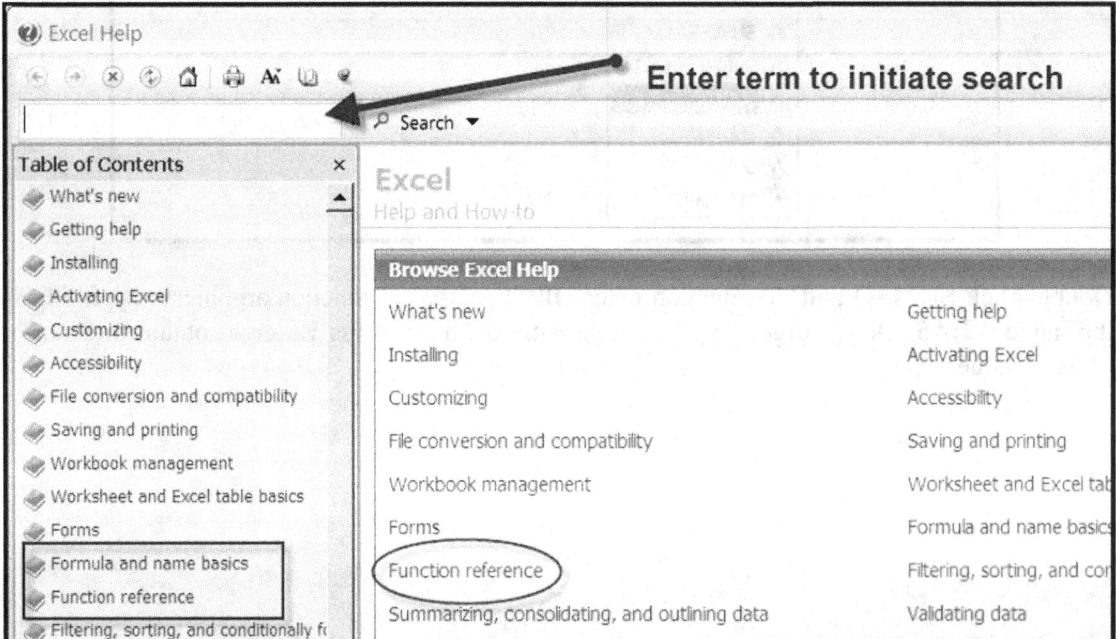

Click on **Function reference**. There are sections for **Math and trigonometry** and **Statistical** functions.

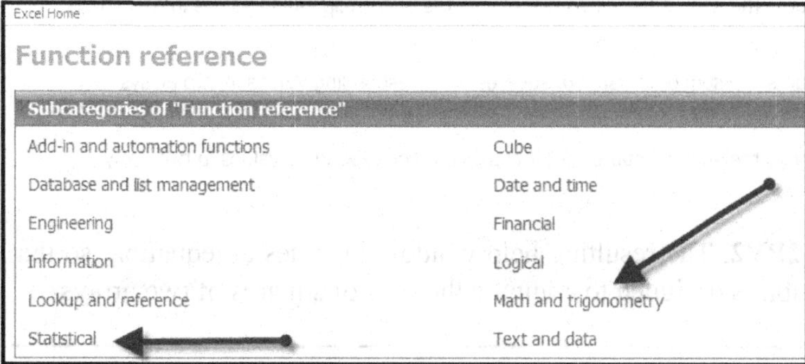

Click on **Math and trigonometry**.

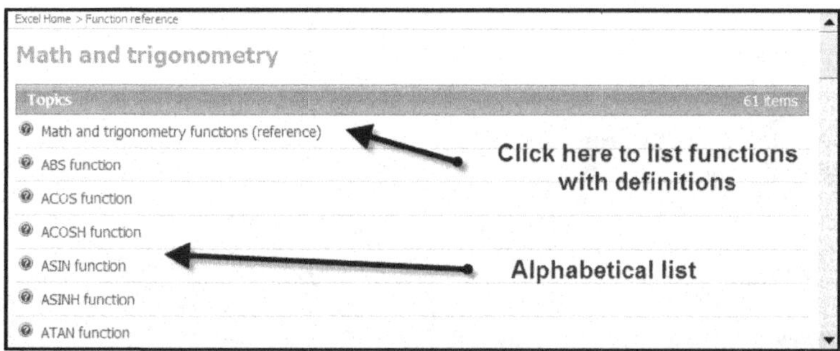

Click on **Math and trigonometry functions (reference)**. Below is a very abbreviated list (copied directly from the Excel **Help)** of some useful functions.

Function	Description
ABS	Returns the absolute value of a number
EXP	Returns *e* raised to the power of a given number
LN	Returns the natural logarithm of a number
PI	Returns the value of pi
POWER	Returns the result of a number raised to a power
ROUND	Rounds a number to a specified number of digits
SQRT	Returns a positive square root
SUM	Adds its arguments

SUMSQ	Returns the sum of the squares of the arguments
SUMX2MY2	Returns the sum of the difference of squares of corresponding values in two arrays
SUMX2PY2	Returns the sum of the sum of squares of corresponding values in two arrays
SUMXMY2	Returns the sum of squares of differences of corresponding values in two arrays

Click on **SUMX2PY2**. The resulting help window includes an equation, so that you can quickly see that the function is designed to compute the sum of squares of two arrays.

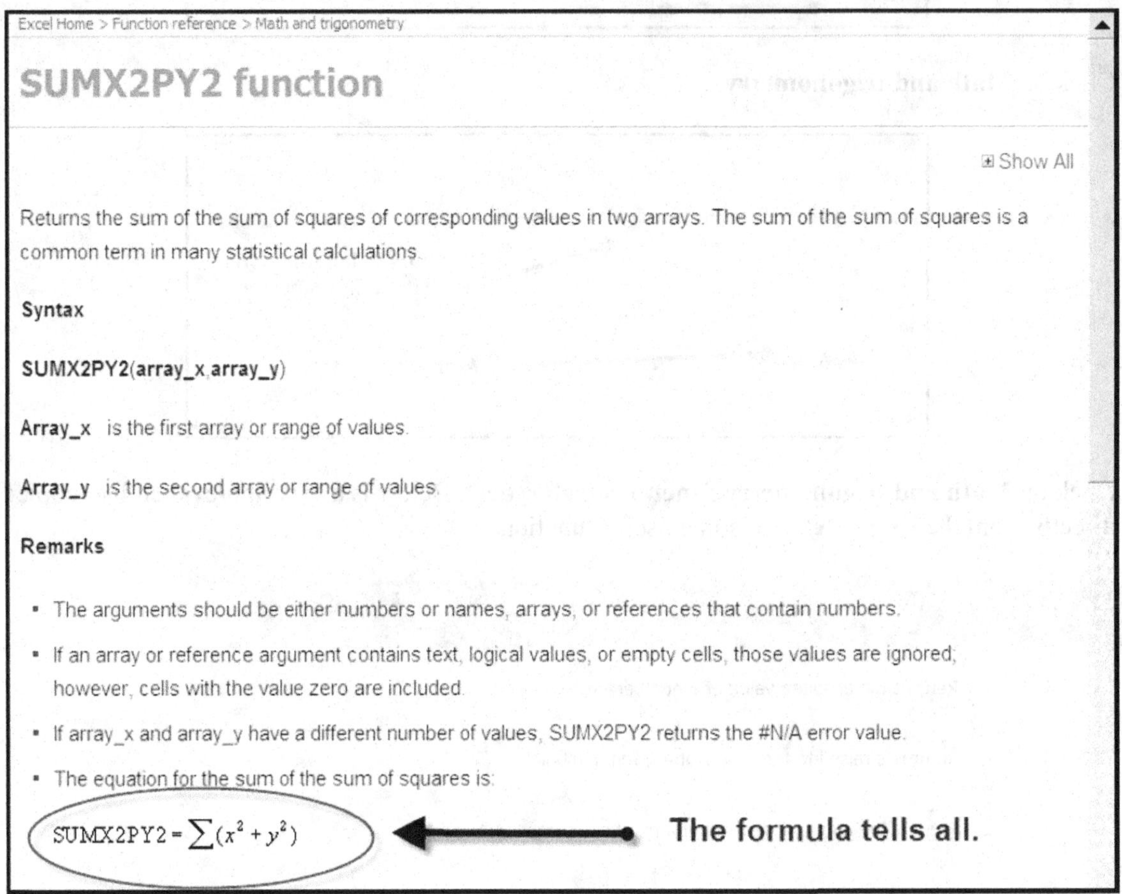

Excel Home > Function reference > Math and trigonometry

SUMX2PY2 function

Show All

Returns the sum of the sum of squares of corresponding values in two arrays. The sum of the sum of squares is a common term in many statistical calculations.

Syntax

SUMX2PY2(array_x,array_y)

Array_x is the first array or range of values.

Array_y is the second array or range of values.

Remarks

- The arguments should be either numbers or names, arrays, or references that contain numbers.
- If an array or reference argument contains text, logical values, or empty cells, those values are ignored; however, cells with the value zero are included.
- If array_x and array_y have a different number of values, SUMX2PY2 returns the #N/A error value.
- The equation for the sum of the sum of squares is:

$$\text{SUMX2PY2} = \sum (x^2 + y^2)$$

A.1.1 Exponents

The notation x^n means take x to the nth power (see p. 635 in *Principles of Econometrics, 4e*). The function **POWER** achieves this in Excel. We will use this function to raise each value in the array **x** to the power -3. Note that $x^{-3} = 1/x^3$ as long as x is not zero.

Close the Excel help window. In cell **B1** enter **x^-3**. In **B2** enter **=POWER(A2,-3)** and press **Enter**. Select cell **B2**. Move the cursor to the lower right corner of **B2** until it turns into a skinny cross. Drag the cross down to cell **B5** and release. Cells **B2:B5** contain the calculated values.

	A	B	C
1	x	x^-3	
2	1	1	
3	5		
4	-3		
5	3		

	A	B	C
1	x	x^-3	
2	1	1	
3	5	0.008	
4	-3	-0.03704	
5	3	0.037037	
6			

Instead of using the power function we could have entered **=A2^-3** into cell **B2** and pressed **Enter**, then dragged the formula down to achieve the same result.

A.1.2 Scientific Notation

Very large or very small numbers can be expressed as a number between 1 and 10 times a power of 10. For example, 0.00000034 is $3.4 \times 10^{-7} = 3.4\text{E} - 7$. In cell **A10** enter **small x** and in **B10** enter **.00000034**. Right-click on the cell **B10** and select **Format Cells** from the menu.

	A	B
1	x	x^-3
2	1	1
3	5	0.008
4	-3	-0.037037
5	3	0.03703704
6		
7		
8	sum x	6
9	sum x^2	44
10	small x	0.00000034
11		

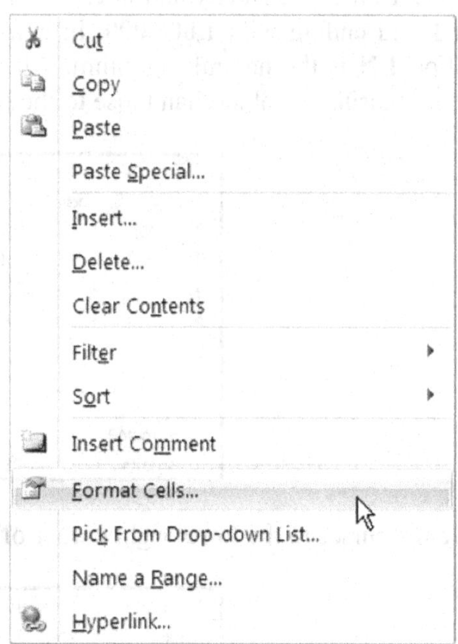

Select **Scientific** with **2 Decimal places** and then **OK**, the number is now represented in scientific notation.

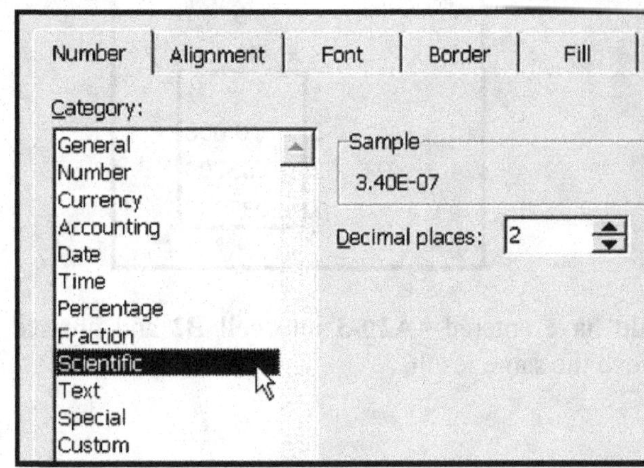

	A	B
1	x	x^-3
2	1	1
3	5	0.008
4	-3	-0.037037
5	3	0.03703704
6		
7		
8	sum x	6
9	sum x^2	44
10	small x	3.40E-07
11		

A.1.3 Logarithms and the Number e

In cell **D1** enter the label **y** and in **E1** enter the label **ln(y)**. In **D2:D8** enter powers of 10 starting with **1** and ending with **1,000,000**. In cell **E2** enter the formula **=ln(D2)** and press **Enter**. The function **LN** is the natural logarithm. All the logarithms in *Principles of Econometrics*, *4e* are natural logarithms, rather than those to the base 10, or some other base.

	A	B	C	D	E
1	x	x^-3		y	ln(y)
2	1	1		1	=ln(D2)
3	5	0.008		10	
4	-3	-0.037037		100	
5	3	0.03703704		1000	
6				10000	
7				100000	
8	sum x	6		1000000	
9	sum x^2	44			
10	small x	3.40E-07			

Move the cursor to the lower right corner of **E2** and drag the formula down to **E8**.

	A	B	C	D	E
1	x	x^-3		y	ln(y)
2	1	1		1	0
3	5	0.008		10	2.302585
4	-3	-0.037037		100	4.60517
5	3	0.03703704		1000	6.907755
6				10000	9.21034
7				100000	11.51293
8	sum x	6		1000000	13.81551
9	sum x^2	44			
10	small x	3.40E-07			

Logarithms are very useful in econometrics. The properties of logarithms are discussed on p. 636 of *Principles of Econometrics, 4e*. For example $z = ln(y^{0.5}) = 0.5 \times ln(y)$. In cell **F1** enter the label **z=0.5ln(y)**. In cell **F2** enter the formula **=0.5*E2**. Copy the formula from cell **F2** down to cells **F3:F8**. Now that we have *z*, a variable in logarithmic form. Next, we would like to convert z back into a non-logarithmic form (this is called taking the **antilogarithm**). To do that we use the **exponential function**. In **G1** enter the label **exp(z)**. In **G2** enter the formula **=EXP(F2)**, and then press **Enter**. Copy that formula down to **G3:G8**. Now, compare columns **D** and **G**. The values in **G2:G8** are the square roots of the values in **D2:D8**. Of course we could have simply used the **SQRT** function to do this calculation, but the point here was to demonstrate operations with logarithms.

D	E	F
y	ln(y)	z=0.5ln(y)
1	0	0
10	2.302585	1.151293
100	4.60517	2.302585
1000	6.907755	3.453878
10000	9.21034	4.60517
100000	11.51293	5.756463
1000000	13.81551	6.907755

D	E	F	G
y	ln(y)	z=0.5ln(y)	exp(z)
1	0	0	1
10	2.302585	1.151293	3.162278
100	4.60517	2.302585	10
1000	6.907755	3.453878	31.62278
10000	9.21034	4.60517	100
100000	11.51293	5.756463	316.2278
1000000	13.81551	6.907755	1000

To illustrate another point, in cell **I1** enter the label **x**, again. Excel doesn't mind. In cells **I2** and **I3** enter the values **1** and **2**. Highlight these two cells and drag the sequence down to **I11**. You will find you have the sequence of numbers **1** through **10**. In **J1** enter the label **y=.03*EXP(x)**, then in **J2** enter the formula **=.03*EXP(I2)** then press **Enter**. Copy the formula from cell **J2** to cells **J3:J11**. The values you obtain quickly go from being small to much larger.

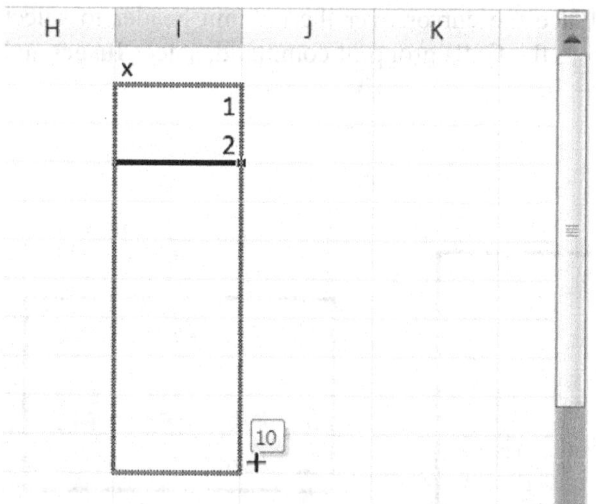

I	J
x	y=.03exp(x)
1	0.081548
2	0.221672
3	0.602566
4	1.637945
5	4.452395
6	12.10286
7	32.89899
8	89.42874
9	243.0925
10	660.794

Highlight **I1:J11** (all the cells from these two columns, including labels). Click on the ribbon tab **Insert** and then select **Scatter** charts.

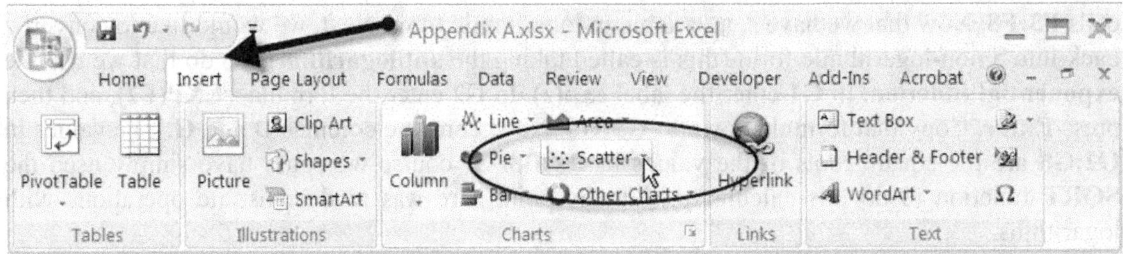

From the drop down menu choose the one showing curvy lines. A graph is superimposed showing the plotted relationship with a title (since you included the header row with text labels in your cells selection).

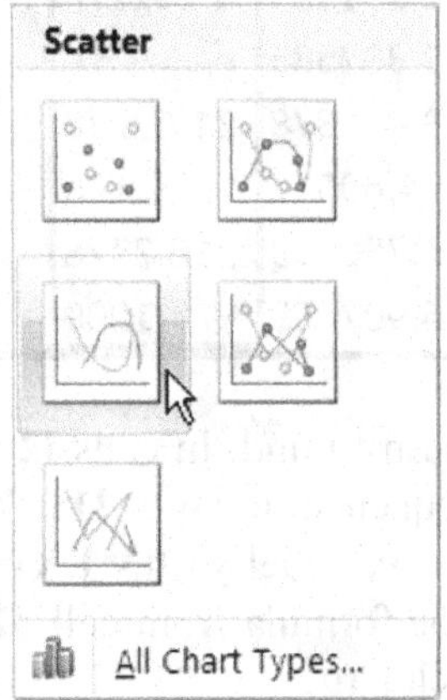

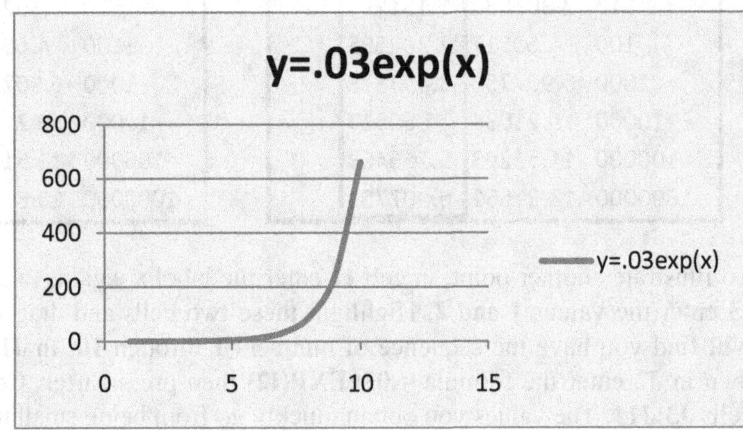

Select the figure and drag it off to the side. Place the cursor over the column header to select column **J**. Select the **Home** tab. Once there, go to the **Cells** group of command, select **Insert** and then **Insert Sheet Columns.**

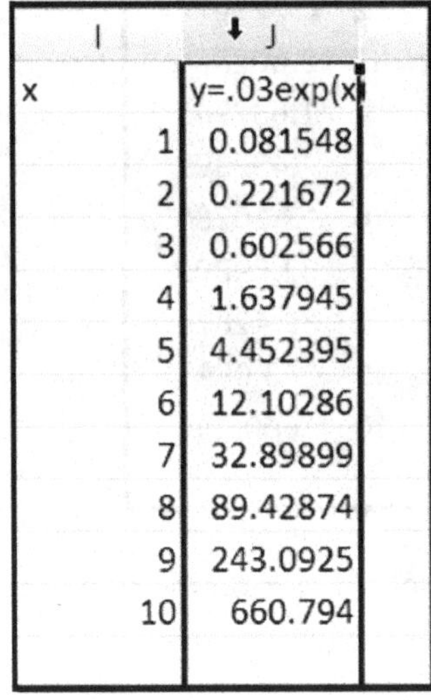

I	J
x	y=.03exp(x
1	0.081548
2	0.221672
3	0.602566
4	1.637945
5	4.452395
6	12.10286
7	32.89899
8	89.42874
9	243.0925
10	660.794

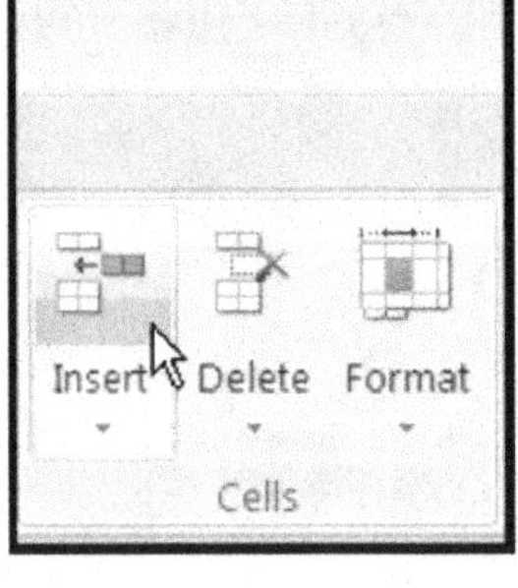

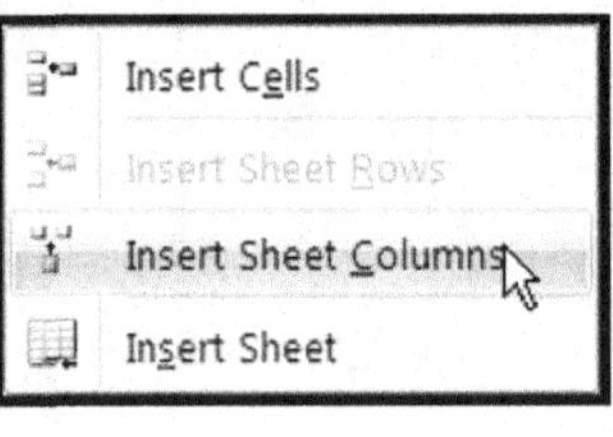

Now column **J** is empty and column **K** contains the **y** values. In the new **J1** enter the label **ln(y)**, in **J2** enter the formula **=ln(K2)**, then press **Enter**. Copy the formula from cell **J2** to cells **J3:J11**. Now graph the relationship between **x** and **ln(y)**. As you can see it is a straight line.

I	J	K
x	ln(y)	y=.03exp(x)
1	-2.50656	0.081548455
2	-1.50656	0.221671683
3	-0.50656	0.602566108
4	0.493442	1.637944501
5	1.493442	4.452394773
6	2.493442	12.1028638
7	3.493442	32.89899475
8	4.493442	89.42873961
9	5.493442	243.0925178
10	6.493442	660.7939738

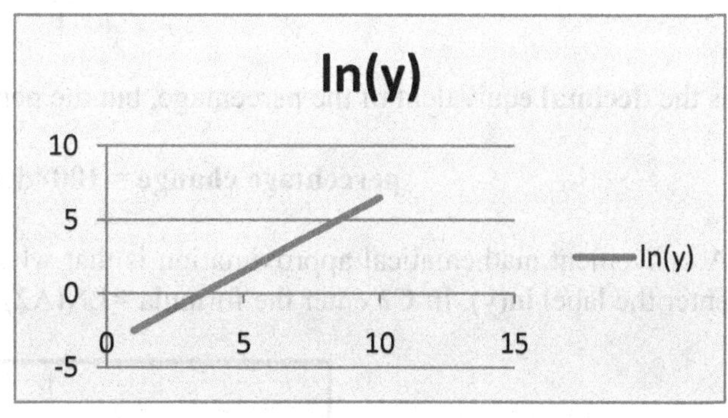

For econometric analysis the ability to convert "curved" relationships to straight lines is sometimes very important.

A.2 PERCENTAGES

While we have understood percentages since grade school, let us consider them again. In particular we should keep the distinction between a percentage change and its decimal form clear. In the **Appendix A** workbook label a new worksheet **percentages**. In **A1** enter the label **y**. In **A2:A7** enter values **1.01, 1.05, 1.10, 1.15, 1.20,** and **1.25**. If the y-value changes from y_0 to y_1 then the **percentage change** is

$$\%\Delta y = \frac{y_1 - y_0}{y_0} \times 100$$

For each of the values in **A2:A7** compute the percentage change from the value $y_0 = 1$. This choice of y_0 value implies that the percentage change equation becomes: $\%\Delta y = (y_1 - 1) \times 100$.

In **B1** enter the label **pct chg**. In **B2** enter the formula **=100*(A2-1)**, then press **Enter**. Place your cursor on the lower right corner of **B2** to form a skinny cross, then drag it down to **B7**.

	A	B
1	y	pct chg
2	1.01	=100*(A2-1)
3	1.05	
4	1.10	
5	1.15	
6	1.20	
7	1.25	

	A	B
1	y	pct chg
2	1.01	1
3	1.05	
4	1.10	
5	1.15	
6	1.20	
7	1.25	

	A	B
1	y	pct chg
2	1.01	1
3	1.05	5
4	1.10	10
5	1.15	15
6	1.20	20
7	1.25	25

There is a 10% percentage change from $y_0 = 1$ to $y_1 = 1.10$. The following value:

$$\frac{y_1 - y_0}{y_0} = \frac{1.10-1}{1} = .10$$

is the **decimal** equivalent of the percentage, but the percentage itself is multiplied by 100:

percentage change = 100×decimal equivalent.

A convenient mathematical approximation is that when x is "small", then $ln(1+x) \cong x$. In **C1** enter the label **ln(y)**. In **C2** enter the formula **=LN(A2)**. Copy this formula to **C3:C7**.

	A	B	C
1	y	pct chg	ln(y)
2	1.01	1	0.00995
3	1.05	5	0.04879
4	1.10	10	0.09531
5	1.15	15	0.139762
6	1.20	20	0.182322
7	1.25	25	0.223144

You can see that the approximation works pretty well for the first few cases. In *Principles of Econometrics, 4e*, p. 638, it is shown that this trick with logarithms can be used to approximate percentage changes when the change is small.

$$\%\Delta y \cong 100\left(ln(y_1) - ln(y_0)\right)$$

Use this approximation to compute the percentage changes in column **D**. In **D1** enter the label **approx pct chg**. Since $y_0 = 1$, $ln(y_o) = 0$, and the approximate percentage changes equation reduces to: $\%\Delta y \cong \left(ln(y_1)\right)$. In **D2** enter the formula **=100*(LN(A2))**, press **Enter**. Drag this formula down to **D3:D7**.

	A	B	C	D
1	y	pct chg	ln(y)	approx pct chg
2	1.01	1	0.00995	=100*(LN(A2))
3	1.05	5	0.04879	
4	1.10	10	0.09531	
5	1.15	15	0.139762	
6	1.20	20	0.182322	
7	1.25	25	0.223144	

The default in Excel is to report many decimals.

	A	B	C	D
1	y	pct chg	ln(y)	approx pct chg
2	1.01	1	0.00995	0.995033085
3	1.05	5	0.04879	4.879016417
4	1.10	10	0.09531	9.53101798
5	1.15	15	0.139762	13.97619424
6	1.20	20	0.182322	18.23215568
7	1.25	25	0.223144	22.31435513

Highlight **C2:D7**, right-click and select **Format Cells**. Choose the **Number** format with **4** Decimal places. Click **OK**.

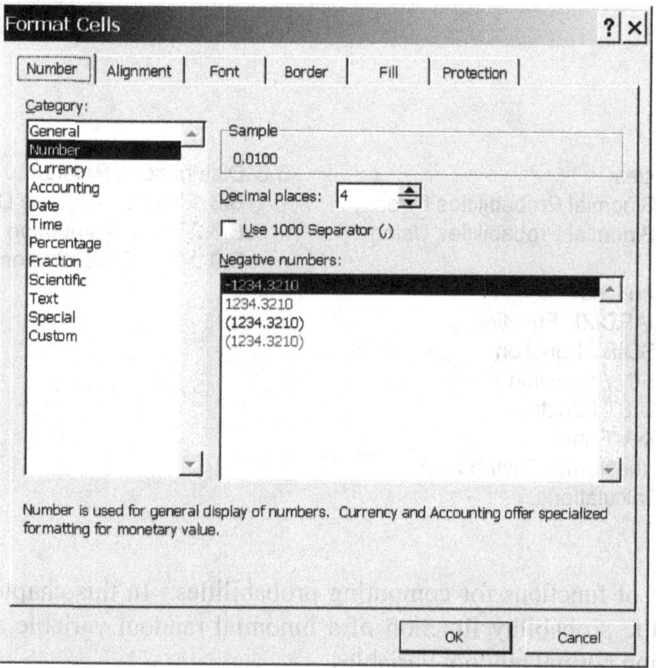

Compare the results in columns **B** and **D**. For the first few values of y the approximation is pretty good, but when $y = 1.10$ the approximation error is already ½%.

	A	B	C	D
1	y	pct chg	ln(y)	approx pct chg
2	1.01	1	0.0100	0.9950
3	1.05	5	0.0488	4.8790
4	1.10	10	0.0953	9.5310
5	1.15	15	0.1398	13.9762
6	1.20	20	0.1823	18.2322
7	1.25	25	0.2231	22.3144

Use the approximation $\%\Delta y \cong 100\big(ln(y_1) - ln(y_0)\big)$ only for small changes in y.

APPENDIX B

Review of Probability Concepts

CHAPTER OUTLINE

Excel has a number of functions for computing probabilities. In this chapter we will show you how to work with the probability function of a binomial random variable and how to compute probabilities involving normal random variables.

B.1 BINOMIAL PROBABILITIES

A binomial experiment consists of a fixed number of trials, n. On each independent trial the outcome is success or failure, with the probability of success, p, being the same for each trial. The random variable X is the number of successes in n trials, so $x = 0, 1, \ldots, n$. For this discrete random variable, the probability that $X = x$ is given by the probability function:

$$P(X = x) = f(x) = \left(\frac{n!}{x!(n-x)!}\right) p^x (1-p)^{n-x}, x = 0, 1, \ldots, n$$

We can compute these probabilities two ways: the hard way and the easy way.

B.1.1 Computing Binomial Probabilities Directly

Excel has a number of mathematical functions that make computation of formulas straightforward. Assume there are $n = 5$ trials, that the probability of success is $p = 0.3$, and that we want the probability of $x = 3$ successes. What we must compute is:

$$P(X = 3) = f(3) = \left(\frac{5!}{3!\,(5-3)!}\right) 0.3^3(1 - 0.3)^{5-3}$$

Open Excel and name the workbook **Appendix B**. Rename Sheet 1 **binomial**. Make cell **A1** active by "clicking" it.

Eventually you will learn many shortcuts in Excel, but should you forget how to compute some mathematical or statistical quantity, there is an **Insert Function** f_x button to the right of the cell reference window.

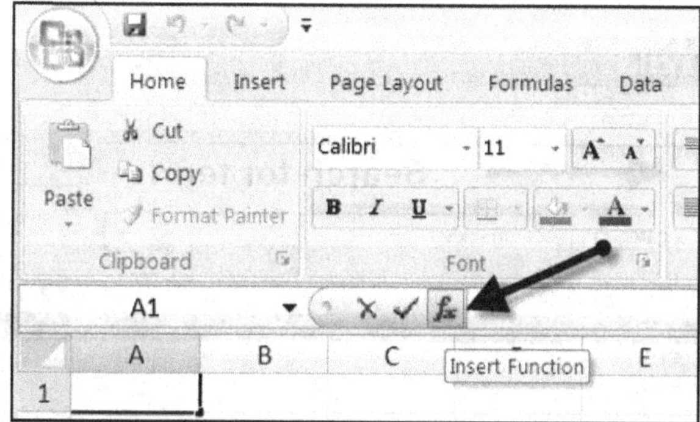

Click on the **Insert Function** button, select **Math & Trig** in the **Or select a category** window. Next, scroll down the list of functions in **Select a function** window. Select **FACT**; this function returns the factorial of a number.

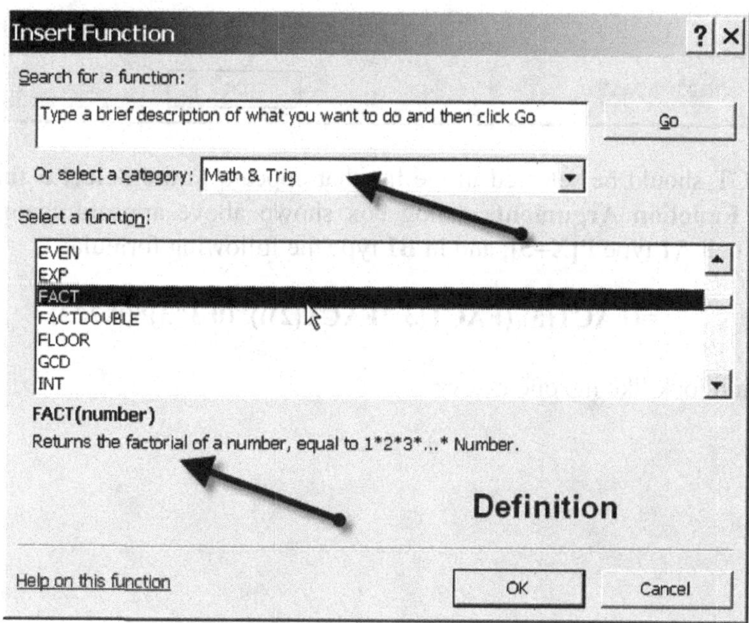

Click **OK**. Enter **5** in the **Number** window of the **Function Arguments** dialog box that opens up. Excel determines that 5! = 120. Click **Cancel**.

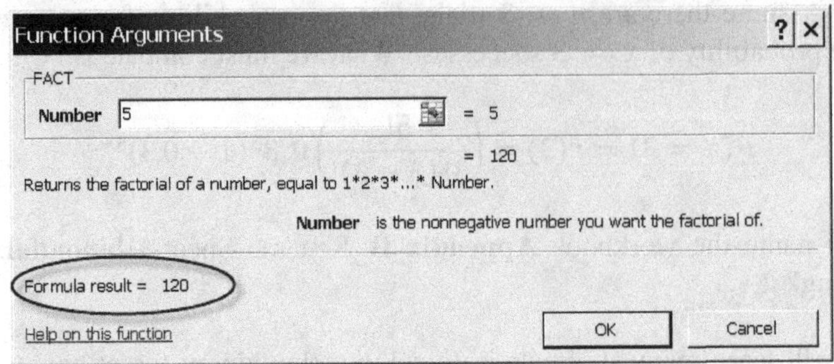

Your cell **A1** should still be active. Click on **Insert function** again. This time search for the term **factorial** and click **Go.**

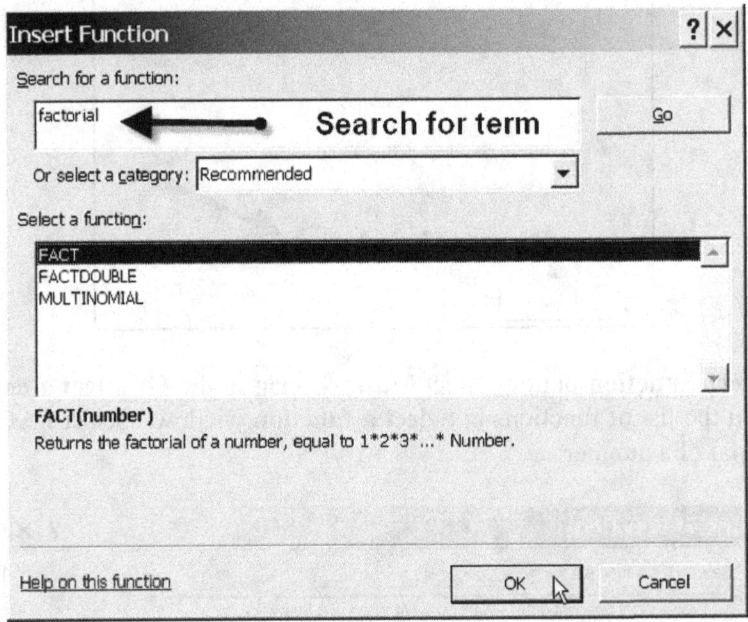

The funtion **FACT** should be selected in the list that appears in the **Select a function** window. Click **OK.** The **Function Arguments** dialog box shown above appears again. Click **Cancel.** Alternatively, in cell **A1** type **P[X=3]**, and in **B1** type the following formula:

=(FACT(5)/(FACT(3)*FACT(2)))*(0.3^3)*(0.7^2)

Your screen should look like the one below:

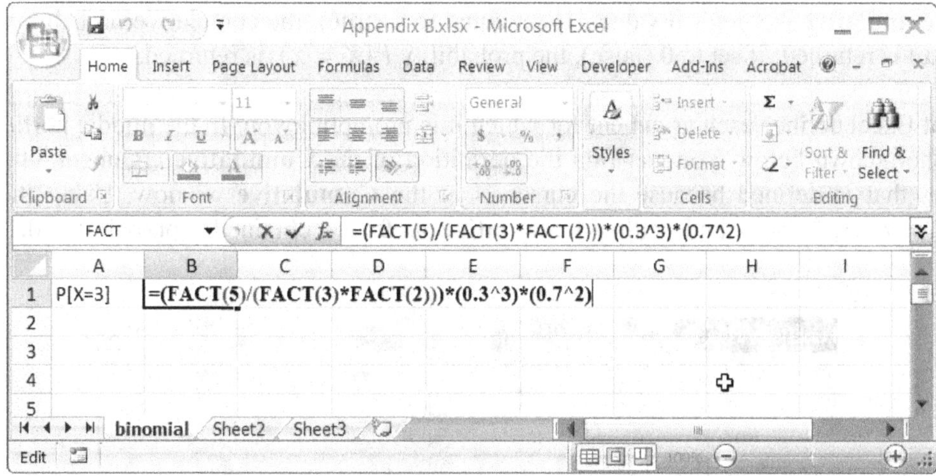

Note that we have used parentheses to group operations. Press **Enter**. The result is 0.1323.

B.1.2 Computing Binomial Probabilities Using BINOMDIST

Make cell **B6** active. Click on the **Insert Function** button. Select **Statistical** in the **Or select a category** window of the **Insert Function** dialog box. Next, scroll down the list of functions in the **Select a function** window, and select **BINOMDIST**. Select **OK**.

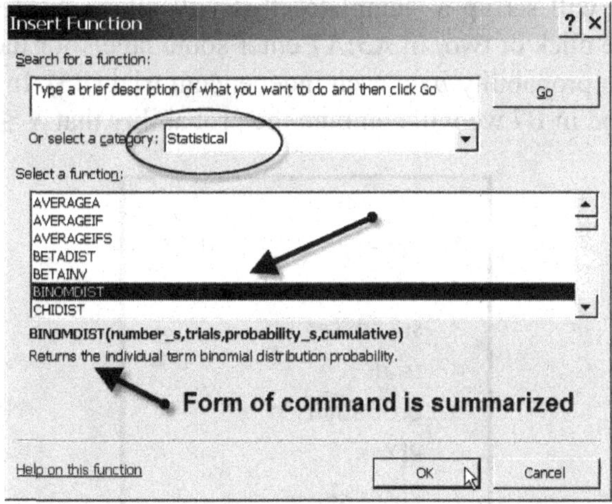

The **Function Arguments** dialog box pops up.

The Excel function **BINOMDIST** can be used to find either cumulative probability, $P(X \leq x)$ or the probability function, $P(X = x)$ for a Binomial random variable. Syntax for the function is:

BINOMDIST(number, trials, probability, cumulative)

where:

- **number** is the number of successes in n trials,
- **trials** is the number of independent trials (n),
- **probability** is p, the probability of success on any one trial,

- **cumulative** is a logical value. If set equal to 1 (true), the cumulative probability $P(X \leq x)$ is returned; if set to 0 (false), the probability $P(X = x)$ is returned.

Note that Excel defines each argument for which it is prompting you. In the middle portion of the screen shot shown below, you can find the definition of the **Cumulative** argument—this is the argument that is defined because the cursor is in the **Cumulative** window. Using the values $n = 5$, $p = .3$, $x = 3$ and setting **Cumulative** to **0**, we obtain the probability 0.1323, as above.

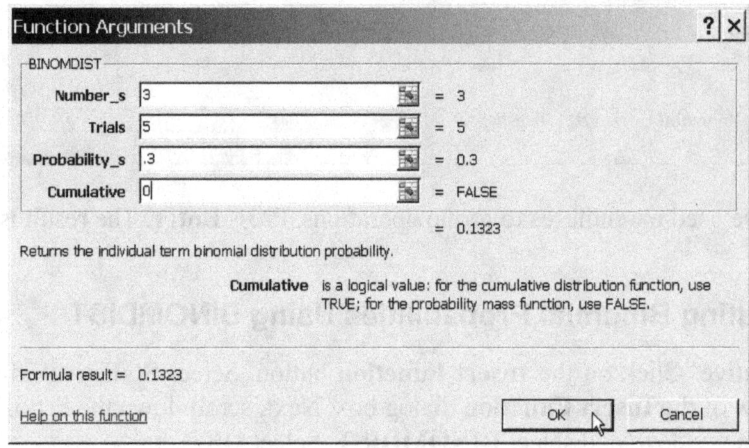

Press **Cancel**. Next, we will set up a "template" that will allow you to compute any binomial probability with a simple click or two. In **A3:A7** enter some labels for the number of successes x (**B3**) in n trials (**B4**) with probability p on each independent trial (**B5**). In **B6** we will compute the probability that $X = x$ and in **B7** we will compute the probability that $X \leq x$.

	A	B
1	P[X=3]	0.1323
2		
3	successes x	
4	trials n	
5	probability p	
6	P[X=x]	
7	P[X<=x]	
8		
9		
10		

binomial / Sheet2

Enter values $x = 3$, $n = 5$, and $p = 0.3$ in cells **B3:B5**.

Make cell **B6** active again. Access the **BINOMDIST** function via the **Insert Function** button as you have just done above or directly type the function in cell **B6**. Either way, this time around, instead of specifying the values of the arguments x, n and p, specify the locations (cell references) where Excel can find those values. Repeat the exercise in cell **B7**, but this time set the **Cumulative** to **1**.

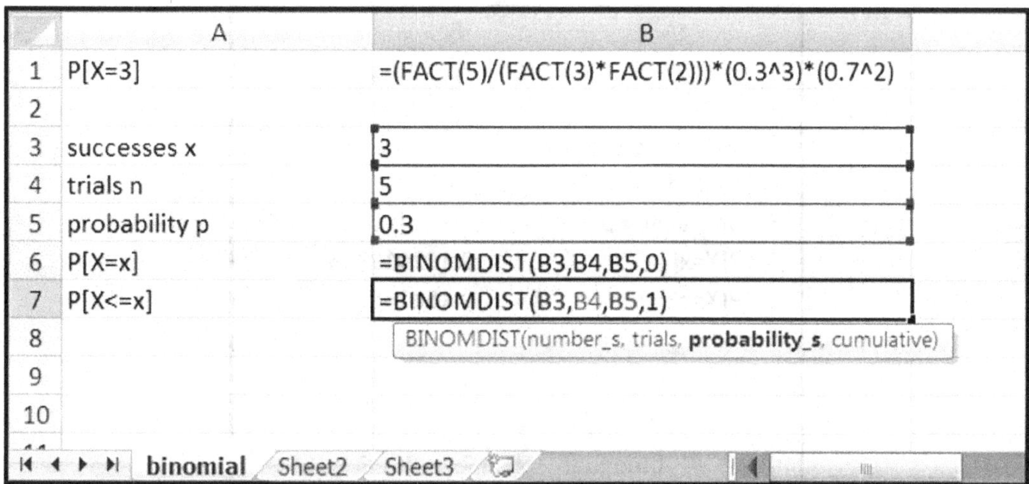

	A	B
1	P[X=3]	=(FACT(5)/(FACT(3)*FACT(2)))*(0.3^3)*(0.7^2)
2		
3	successes x	3
4	trials n	5
5	probability p	0.3
6	P[X=x]	=BINOMDIST(B3,B4,B5,0)
7	P[X<=x]	=BINOMDIST(B3,B4,B5,1)
8		BINOMDIST(number_s, trials, **probability_s**, cumulative)
9		
10		

In this book we will use "templates" a great deal. These templates are Excel pages with cells addresses in the formulas so that by changing a numerical value (say in **B3**) we can compute an alternative probability. It is very instructive to see the formulas to check on exactly the structure of the commands. Select the **Formulas** tab on the Excel ribbon, and then go to the **Formula Auditing** group of commands.

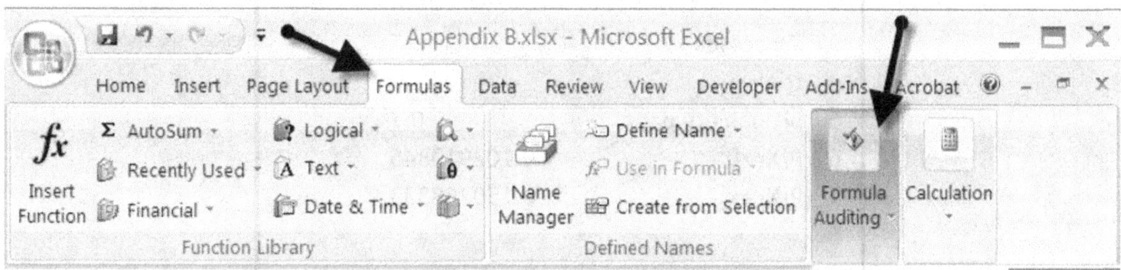

Select **Show Formulas**. You can switch between the numerical values, shown below, and the formulas shown above.

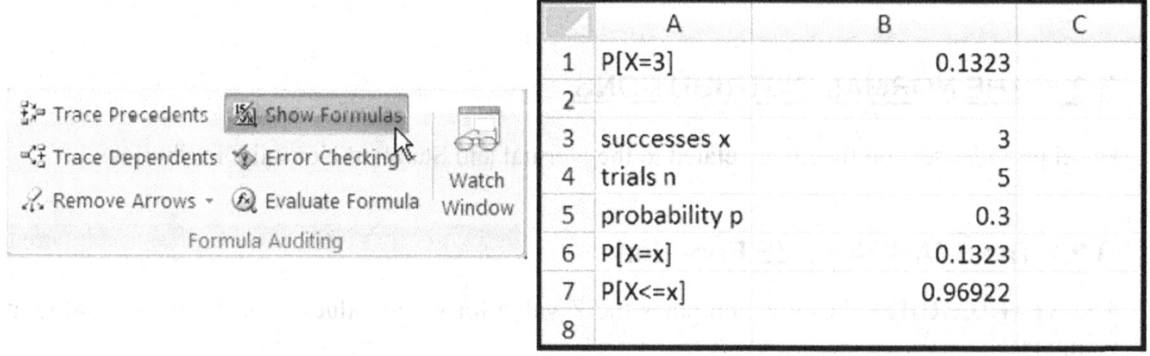

	A	B	C
1	P[X=3]	0.1323	
2			
3	successes x	3	
4	trials n	5	
5	probability p	0.3	
6	P[X=x]	0.1323	
7	P[X<=x]	0.96922	
8			

Next time you need to compute a binomial probability you can call up the function **BINOMDIST** or you can open your **Appendix B** workbook, go to the **binomial** worksheet and enter values into the template. For example, use the template to compute the probabilities for **5** successes, in **10** trials if the probability is **0.7**. Here are the results you should get:

	A	B	C
1	P[X=3]	0.1323	
2			
3	successes x	5	
4	trials n	10	
5	probability p	0.7	
6	P[X=x]	0.102919345	
7	P[X<=x]	0.150268333	
8			
9			
10			

binomial Sheet2 Sheet3

So that this template can be perfectly general, delete the entries in the first row and, in cell **A1**, enter the label **Computing binomial probabilities.** Save your workbook.

	A	B	C
1	Computing binomial probabilities		
2			
3	successes x	5	
4	trials n	10	
5	probability p	0.7	
6	P[X=x]	0.102919345	
7	P[X<=x]	0.150268333	
8			
9			
10			

binomial Sheet2 Sheet3

B.2 THE NORMAL DISTRIBUTIONS

Excel provides several functions related to the Normal and Standard Normal Distributions.

B.2.1 The STANDARDIZE Function

The **STANDARDIZE** function computes the Z value for given values of X, μ and σ. That is, it computes:

$$Z = \frac{X - \mu}{\sigma}$$

The format of this function is:

STANDARDIZE(X, μ, σ)

For example for $\mu = 3$ and $\sigma = 3$, if we wanted to find the Z value corresponding to $X = 6$, we would enter **=STANDARDIZE(6,3,3)** in a cell, and the value computed would be 1.0.

B.2.2 The NORMSDIST Function

The **NORMSDIST** function computes the area, or cumulative probability, less than a given Z value. Geometrically, the cumulative probability is the area under the standard normal probability density function to the left of the given value. In many statistics books the cumulative distribution function of a standard normal random variable is denoted by the special symbol Φ. Then,

$$P(Z \leq z) = \Phi(z)$$

Standard normal probabilities are contained in Table 1, Appendix E of *Principles of Econometrics, 4e*. ·

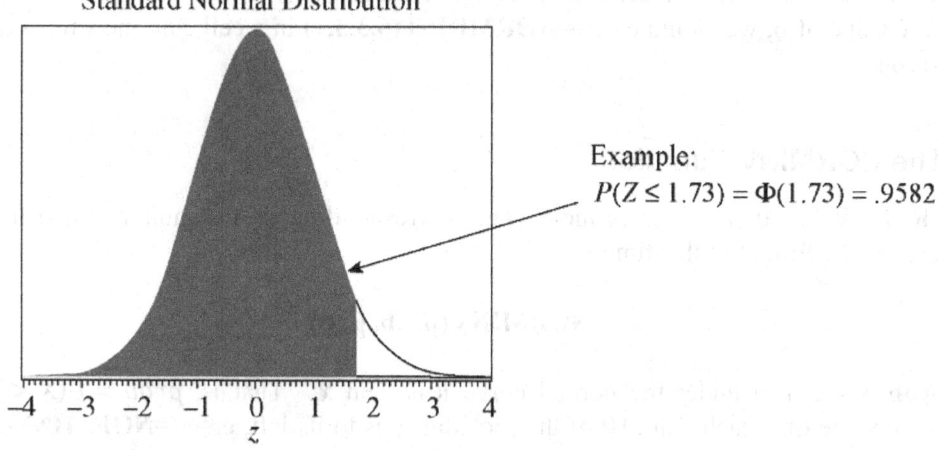

Instead of a table in the book we will use the function in Excel. The format of this function is:

NORMSDIST(Z)

If we wanted to find the area below a Z value of 1.0, we would enter **=NORMSDIST(1.0)** in a cell, and the value computed would be .8413.

B.2.3 The NORMSINV Function

The **NORMSINV** function computes the Z value, z_c, corresponding to a given cumulative area under the normal curve. The format of this function is:

NORMSINV(prob)

where **prob** is the area under the standard normal curve less than z_c. That is, $prob = P(Z < z_c)$. If we wanted to find the z_c value corresponding to a cumulative area of $.10$, we would enter **=NORMSINV(.10)** in a cell and the value computed would be -1.2815.

B.2.4 The NORMDIST Function

The **NORMDIST** function computes the area or probability less than a given X value, or the value of the normal *pdf* for given values of the distribution mean μ and standard deviation σ. The format of this function is:

NORMDIST(X, μ, σ, CUMULATIVE)

Let $X \sim N(\mu, \sigma^2)$. Then the function **NORMDIST** will compute:

$$P(X \leq x) \text{ if } \textbf{CUMULATIVE} = 1$$

$$f(x) = \frac{1}{\sqrt{2\pi\sigma^2}} exp\left[-\frac{(x-\mu)^2}{2\sigma^2}\right] \text{ if } \textbf{CUMULATIVE} = 0$$

CUMULATIVE is a logical value, which can be replaced by 1. If we wanted to find the area below an X value of 6, we would enter **=NORMDIST(6,3,3,1)** in a cell, and the value computed would be $.8413$.

B.2.5 The NORMINV Function

The **NORMINV** function computes the x value corresponding to a cumulative area under the normal curve. The format of this function is:

NORMINV(prob, μ, σ)

where **prob** is the area under the normal curve less than x. That is, $prob = P(X < x)$. To compute the value of x such that $.10$ of the probability is to its left, enter **=NORMINV(.10,3,3)** in a cell, yielding –0.8446.

B.2.6 A Template for Normal Distribution Probability Calculations

Rename your Sheet 2 **normal** and build a template for normal probabilities by entering the formulas shown below. The highlighted cells require user input. The formulas in the other cells do the computations.

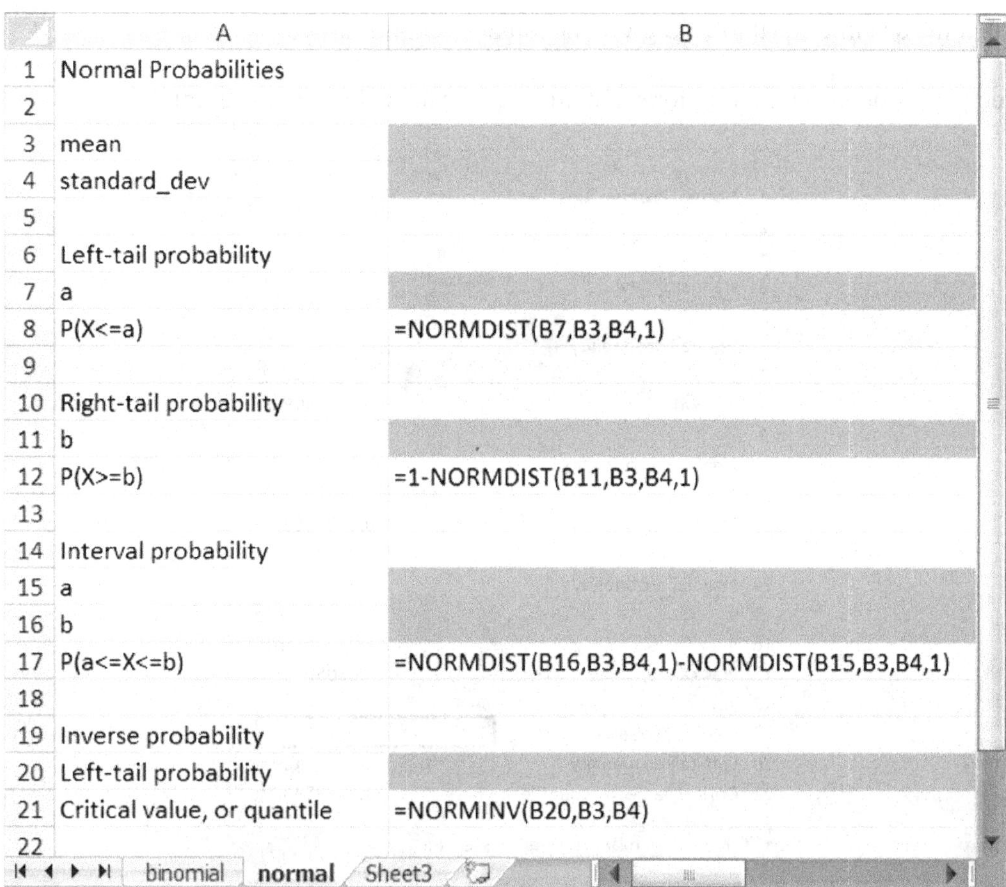

	A	B
1	Normal Probabilities	
2		
3	mean	
4	standard_dev	
5		
6	Left-tail probability	
7	a	
8	P(X<=a)	=NORMDIST(B7,B3,B4,1)
9		
10	Right-tail probability	
11	b	
12	P(X>=b)	=1-NORMDIST(B11,B3,B4,1)
13		
14	Interval probability	
15	a	
16	b	
17	P(a<=X<=b)	=NORMDIST(B16,B3,B4,1)-NORMDIST(B15,B3,B4,1)
18		
19	Inverse probability	
20	Left-tail probability	
21	Critical value, or quantile	=NORMINV(B20,B3,B4)
22		

Using $X \sim N(\mu = 3, \sigma^2 = 9)$, the above template would produce the following results:

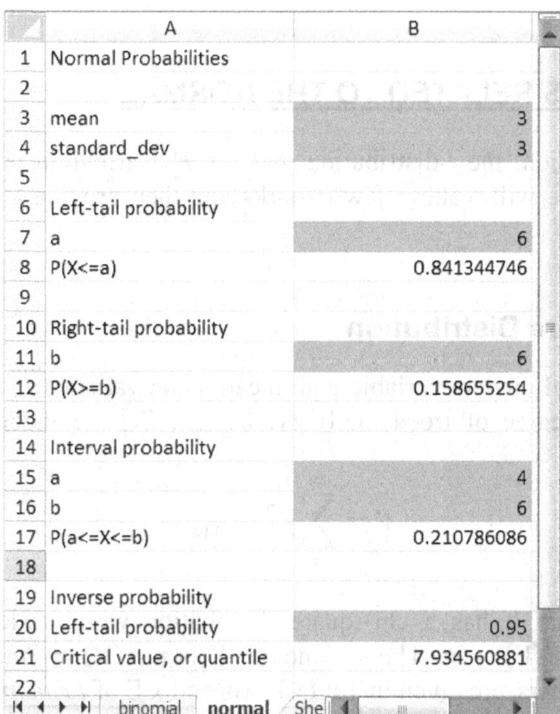

	A	B
1	Normal Probabilities	
2		
3	mean	3
4	standard_dev	3
5		
6	Left-tail probability	
7	a	6
8	P(X<=a)	0.841344746
9		
10	Right-tail probability	
11	b	6
12	P(X>=b)	0.158655254
13		
14	Interval probability	
15	a	4
16	b	6
17	P(a<=X<=b)	0.210786086
18		
19	Inverse probability	
20	Left-tail probability	0.95
21	Critical value, or quantile	7.934560881
22		

Note that the quantile equal to 7.93 gives the top 5% "cut off" value.

The template works equally well for standard normal calculations. For example,

	A	B
1	Normal Probabilities	
2		
3	mean	0
4	standard_dev	1
5		
6	Left-tail probability	
7	a	2
8	P(X<=a)	0.977249868
9		
10	Right-tail probability	
11	b	2
12	P(X>=b)	0.022750132
13		
14	Interval probability	
15	a	1.5
16	b	2.5
17	P(a<=X<=b)	0.060597536
18		
19	Inverse probability	
20	Left-tail probability	0.95
21	Critical value, or quantile	1.644853627
22		

binomial | normal | She

It might be a useful exercise for you to compute these normal probabilities using Table 1 in Appendix E of *Principles of Econometrics, 4e*.

B.3 DISTRIBUTIONS RELATED TO THE NORMAL

The chi-square distribution, the *t*-distribution and the *F*-distribution are related to the normal distribution. For each we will make a few remarks and then provide a template for probability calculations.

B.3.1 The Chi-Square Distribution

If Z_1 is a standard normal random variable with mean 0 and variance 1, then Z_1^2 has a chi-square distribution with one degree of freedom. If Z_1, Z_2, …, Z_m are independent $N(0,1)$ random variables then:

$$V = \sum_{i=1}^{m} Z_i^2 \sim \chi^2_{(m)}$$

This notation means that V has a chi-square distribution with m degrees of freedom. The expected value of V is $E(V) = m$. The variance of V is $var(V) = 2m$. The 90th, 95th and 99th percentiles, and some others, are given in Table 3, Appendix E of *Principles of Econometrics, 4e*.

The template we will create next will make calculations to answer the following two questions:

1. For any value $v > 0$ what is the probability that a chi-square random variable will be greater than v?
2. What is the "critical value" for the percentile p. That is, what is the value c such that $P(V \leq c) = p$.

To answer the first type of question we use the Excel function **CHIDIST**. The format of the function is:

CHIDIST(x, df)

Here **x** is the value of the chi-square variable and **df** is its degrees of freedom. The **CHIDIST** function returns the probability in the **right-tail** of the distribution, the probability that $V > x$. To calculate the probability that $V \leq x$, use the function 1−**CHIDIST**.

To answer the second question we use the function **CHIINV**. The format of the command is:

CHIINV(probability,df)

where **probability** is the **right-tail** probability and **df** is the degrees of freedom. To find the 95th percentile use the function **CHIINV(.05,df)**.

Rename Sheet 3 **chi-square** and create the following template.

	A	B
1	Chi-square probabilities	
2		
3	value	
4	df	
5		
6	P[V<=value]	=1-CHIDIST(B3,B4)
7	P[V>value]	=CHIDIST(B3,B4)
8		
9	Cumulative Percentile	
10	Critical value	=CHIINV(1-B9,B4)

The calculations are illustrated for a chi-square distribution with 5 degrees of freedom, for the value 7.7 below. We find that $P(\chi^2_{(5)} > 7.7) = 0.173563$, and that the 95th percentile value is 11.0705.

	A	B
1	Chi-square probabilities	
2		
3	value	7.7
4	df	5
5		
6	P[V<=value]	0.826437
7	P[V>value]	0.173563
8		
9	Cumulative Percentile	0.95
10	Critical value	11.0705
11		

B.3.2 The *t*-Distribution

A *t*-probability density function is bell-shaped and centered at zero, like the normal distribution. Its variance depends upon its **degrees of freedom** parameter m, and is equal to $m/(m-2)$. We denote the *t*-distribution with m degrees of freedom as $t_{(m)}$. As $m \to \infty$ the *t*-distribution converges to the standard normal $N(0,1)$. The function used to compute *t*-probabilities is **TDIST**. The function used to compute critical values is **TINV**.

The format of the **TDIST** function is:

TDIST(x, df, tails)

In this function **x** is the value of the *t*-random variable and $x > 0$. The **df** is the degrees of freedom parameter, and **tails** takes the value either 1 or 2.

TDIST(x, df, 1) computes $P(t_{(df)} > x)$, this is the **right-tail** probability.

TDIST(x, df, 2) computes $P(t_{(df)} < -x) + P(t_{(df)} > x)$, this is the **two-tail** probability.

To compute **left-tail** probabilities, for $x > 0$, $P(t_{(df)} < x)$ use **1−TDIST(x,df,1)**. To compute probabilities for negative **x** values we use the symmetry of the distribution. For example,

$$P(t_{(df)} < -x) = P(t_{(df)} > x) \text{ and } P(t_{(df)} > -x) = P(t_{(df)} < x)$$

Critical values are computed using **TINV** with format:

TINV(probability, df)

where **probability** is the **two-tail** probability. This function computes the value t_c such that $P(t_{(df)} < -t_c) + P(t_{(df)} > t_c) = probability$.

Insert a new sheet, name it **t-distribution**, and create the following template for basic probability calculations.

	A	B
1	t-distribution	
2		
3	df	
4		
5	value > 0	
6	P[t<=value]	=1-TDIST(B5,B3,1)
7	P[t>value]	=TDIST(B5,B3,1)
8		
9	value < 0	
10	P[t<=value]	=TDIST(-B9,B3,1)
11	P[t>value]	=1-TDIST(-B9,B5,1)
12		
13	cumulative percentile	
14	critical value	=TINV(2*(1-B13),B3)
15		

normal / chi-square / **t-distribution**

The calculations are illustrated below for a t-distribution with 5 degrees of freedom, a positive $t = 2.3$, a negative $t = -1.5$ and the 95th percentile.

	A	B	C
1	t-distribution		
2			
3	df	5	
4			
5	value > 0	2.3	
6	P[t<=value]	0.96511377	
7	P[t>value]	0.03488623	
8			
9	value < 0	-1.5	
10	P[t<=value]	0.09695184	
11	P[t>value]	0.86380344	
12			
13	cumulative percentile	0.95	
14	critical value	2.01504837	
15			

normal / chi-square / **t-distribution**

B.3.3 The *F*-Distribution

The F-distribution is used in a variety of hypothesis testing situations. Its shape is controlled by two **degrees of freedom** parameters called the **numerator degrees of freedom** and the **denominator degrees of freedom**. Probabilities are computed using the Excel function **FDIST**. Critical values are computed using **FINV**. The formats for these functions are:

FDIST(x, df1, df2)

This function computes the probability that an F-random variable, with numerator degrees of freedom **df1** and denominator degrees of freedom **df2,** is greater than **x,** $P(F > x)$.

The **FINV** function computes the critical value F_c so that $P(F > F_c) = \alpha$. The format of the function is:

FINV(probability, df1, df2)

Here **probability** is the right tail probability, and **df1** and **df2** are the numerator and denominator degrees of freedom.

Insert a new sheet, name it **F-distribution**, and create the following template to compute cumulative probabilities, right-tail probabilities and percentile critical values.

	A	B
1	F-distribution probabilities	
2		
3	value	
4	df_numerator	
5	df_denominator	
6		
7	P[F<=value]	=1-FDIST(B3,B4,B5)
8	P[F>value]	=FDIST(B3,B4,B5)
9		
10	cumulative percentile	
11	critical value	=FINV(1-B10,B4,B5)

normal / chi-square / t-distribution / **F-distribution**

To illustrate, let the numerator degrees of freedom equal 2, the denominator degrees of freedom equal 10 and the F-random variable value equal 3.2. Finally, let us find the 95th percentile value.

	A	B	C	D
1	F-distribution probabilities			
2				
3	value	3.2		
4	df_numerator	2		
5	df_denominator	10		
6				
7	P[F<=value]	0.915709		
8	P[F>value]	0.084291		
9				
10	cumulative percentile	0.95		
11	critical value	4.102821		

normal / chi-square / t-distribution / **F-distribution**

APPENDIX C

Review of Statistical Inference

CHAPTER OUTLINE

C.1 EXAMINING A SAMPLE OF DATA

When faced with a new set of data observations, or a data set, it is wise to "look" at the data graphically, and to look at its summary statistics. To illustrate open the Excel file ***hip***. You will find a single list of numbers with the label **y** in cell **A1**. Examining the definition file ***hip.def*** we find that the variable *y* is the hip width of 50 individuals; we also find some basic summary statistics that we will recompute. Save the workbook as **Appendix C.** Rename the worksheet ply **hlp data**.

Select the **Data** tab, in the middle of your tab list. On the **Analysis** group of commands to the far right of the ribbon, select **Data Analysis**.

If the **Data Analysis** tool does not appear on the ribbon, you need to load it first.

Select the **Office Button** in the upper left corner of your screen, **Excel Options** on the bottom of the **Office Button** tasks panel, **Add-Ins** in the **Excel Options** dialog box, **Excel Add-ins** in the **Manage** window at the bottom of the **Excel Options** dialog box, and then **Go**.

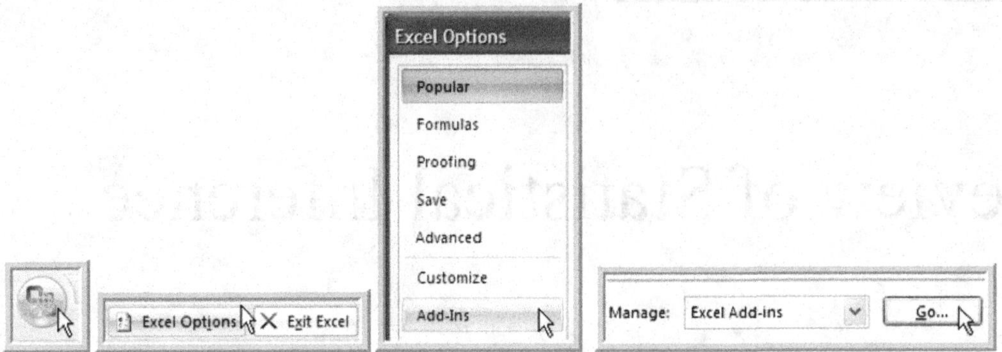

In the **Add-Ins** dialog box, check the box in front of **Analysis ToolPak**. Select **OK**.

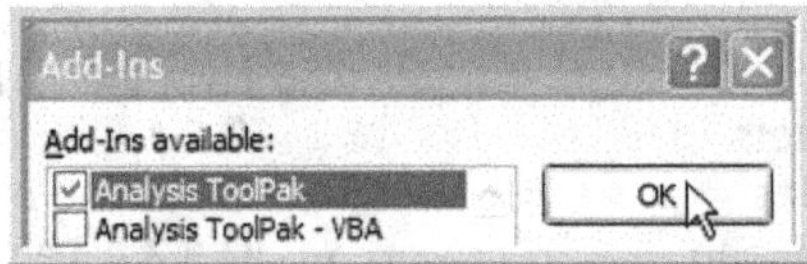

Now **Data Analysis** should be available on the **Analysis** group of commands. Select it. From the dialog box choose **Descriptive Statistics** and select **OK**.

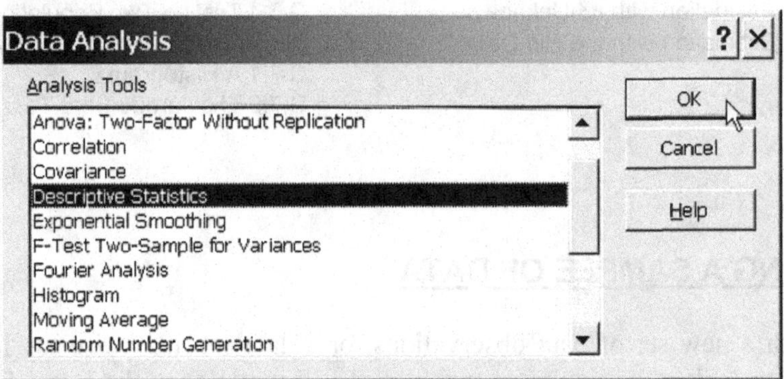

In the dialog box that results specify the input range of the data to be **A1:A51**, indicate that the data are in **Columns** and indicate that there is a **Label in** the **First Row**. Under **Output options** choose **New Worksheet Ply** and assign the name **hip data summary stats**. Finally, check the box next to **Summary statistics** so that the statistics will actually be transferred to the new worksheet. Select **OK**.

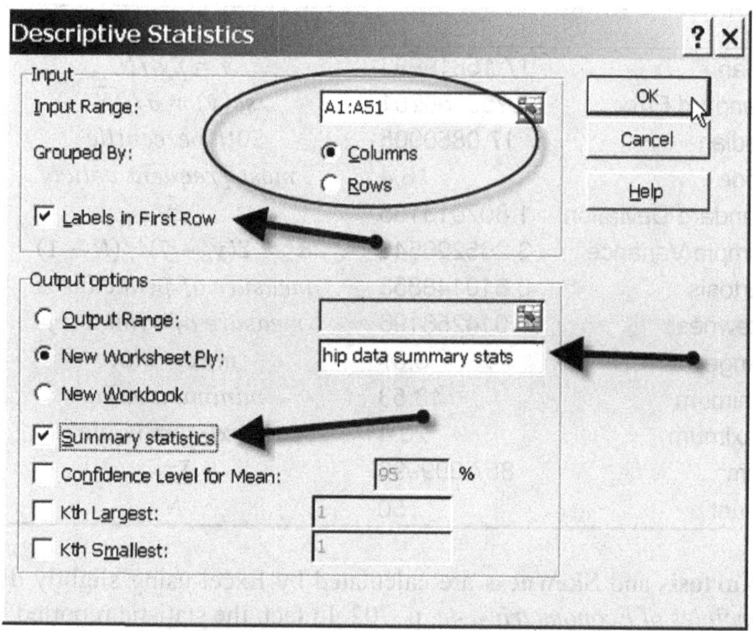

The summary statistics are pressed into two columns so that the labels are not visible, but it should be highlighted. Back in the **Home** tab, go to the **Cells** group of commands. Select **Format** and then **AutoFit Column Width**.

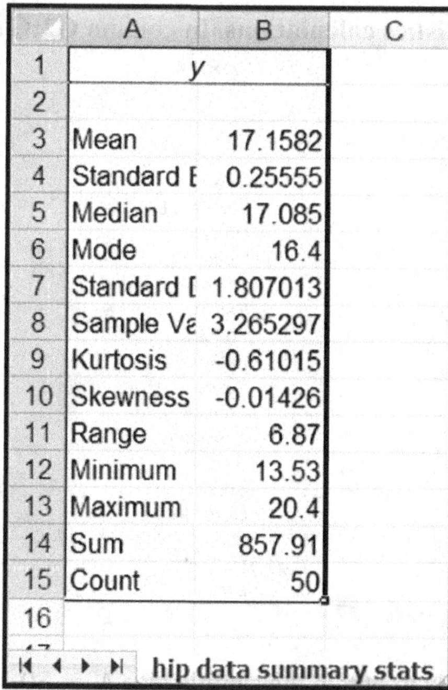

	A	B	C
1	y		
2			
3	Mean	17.1582	
4	Standard E	0.25555	
5	Median	17.085	
6	Mode	16.4	
7	Standard D	1.807013	
8	Sample Va	3.265297	
9	Kurtosis	-0.61015	
10	Skewness	-0.01426	
11	Range	6.87	
12	Minimum	13.53	
13	Maximum	20.4	
14	Sum	857.91	
15	Count	50	
16			

hip data summary stats

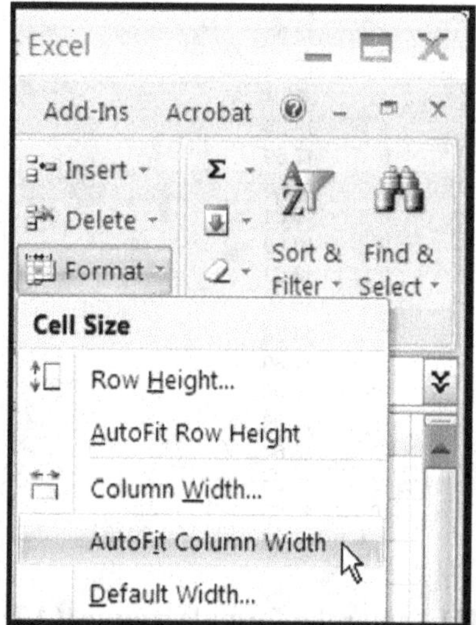

This makes the columns fully visible. The values reported and brief explanations are given next.

y		
Mean	17.15819992	$\bar{y} = \Sigma y_i / N$
Standard Error	0.255550251	$se(\bar{y}) = \hat{\sigma}/\sqrt{N}$
Median	17.0850005	$50th\ percentile$
Mode	16.4	$most\ frequent\ value$
Standard Deviation	1.807013155	$\hat{\sigma}$
Sample Variance	3.265296541	$\hat{\sigma}^2 = \Sigma(y_i - \bar{y})^2/(N-1)$
Kurtosis	-0.610148853	$measure\ of\ peakedness$
Skewness	-0.014256196	$measure\ of\ symmetry$
Range	6.87	$max - min$
Minimum	13.53	$minimum\ value$
Maximum	20.4	$maximum\ value$
Sum	857.909996	Σy_i
Count	50	N

The values of **Kurtosis** and **Skewness** are calculated by Excel using slightly different formulas than used in *Principles of Econometrics, 4e*, p. 702. In fact, the statistic reported by Excel is often called "excess" Kurtosis. It is a measure of Kurtosis minus 3, which is the Kurtosis value for the normal distribution. The formulas are equivalent in large samples, except for the minus 3. We will take this opportunity to show the calculations explicitly. The formulas are used in Section C.7.2 of this manual as part of a test for normality.

Copy the hip data to a new worksheet named **statistics calculations.** In column **G2:G18** enter the labels shown below.

	A	B	C	D	E	F	G
1	y						
2	14.96						Mean
3	17.34						Standard Error
4	16.4						Median
5	19.33						Mode
6	17.69						Standard Deviation
7	17.5						Sample Variance
8	15.84						Kurtosis
9	18.69						Skewness
10	18.63						Range
11	18.55						Minimum
12	14.76						Maximum
13	17.89						Sum
14	18.36						Count
15	17.59						Sigma tilde
16	16.64						Mu2
17	20.23						Mu3
18	16.98						Mu4

hip data summary stats / hip data / statist

- In **H14** enter the formula **=count(A2:A51)** to obtain the sample size $N = 50$.
- In **H2** enter the formula **=sum(A2:A51)/H14** to obtain the sample mean $\bar{y} = 17.1852$.
- In **B1** enter the label **y-ybar**. In **B2** enter the formula **=A2-$H$2**. Copy this formula to **B3:B51**.
- In **C1:E1** enter labels **(y-ybar)^2, (y-ybar)^3, (y-ybar)^4**. In **C2** enter **=B2^2**, in **D2** enter **=B2^3**, in **E2** enter **=B2^4**. This will create the square, cube and fourth power of the difference between the value of y and the sample mean $\bar{y}$.

- Highlight **C2:E2** and move your cursor to lower right corner of your selection until a skinny cross is formed. Left-click, hold it, and drag it down to cell **E51**.

	A	B	C	D	E
1	y	y-ybar	(y-ybar)^2	(y-ybar)^3	(y-ybar)^4
2	14.96	-2.1982	4.832083	-10.62188	23.34903
3	17.34	0.1818			
4	16.4	-0.7582			

The first five rows of the result are:

	A	B	C	D	E
1	y	y-ybar	(y-ybar)^2	(y-ybar)^3	(y-ybar)^4
2	14.96	-2.1982	4.832083	-10.62188	23.34903
3	17.34	0.1818	0.033051	0.006009	0.001092
4	16.4	-0.7582	0.574867	-0.435864	0.330472
5	19.33	2.1718	4.716716	10.24376	22.24741
6	17.69	0.531801	0.282812	0.1504	0.079983

hip data | **statistics calcul**

In cells **H2:H18** complete entering the formulas as shown below.

	G	H
1		
2	Mean	=SUM(A2:A51)/H14
3	Standard Error	=H6/SQRT(H14)
4	Median	=MEDIAN(A2:A51)
5	Mode	=MODE(A2:A51)
6	Standard Deviation	=SQRT(H7)
7	Sample Variance	=SUM(C2:C51)/(H14-1)
8	Kurtosis	=H18/(H15^4)
9	Skewness	=H17/(H15^3)
10	Range	=H12-H11
11	Minimum	=MIN(A2:A51)
12	Maximum	=MAX(A2:A51)
13	Sum	=SUM(A2:A51)
14	Count	=COUNT(A2:A51)
15	Sigma tilde	=SQRT(H16)
16	Mu2	=SUM(C2:C51)/H14
17	Mu3	=SUM(D2:D51)/H14
18	Mu4	=SUM(E2:E51)/H14

hip data | **statistics calculatio**

The numerical values are shown on the following page. Note that the values match Excel's descriptive statistics except for the **Skewness** and **Kurtosis**, which are computed using the formulas in the middle of p. 702 of *Principles of Econometrics*, *4e*. The value of excess Kurtosis = Kurtosis − 3 = −0.66847 which is close to the value Excel reports for Kurtosis automatically when computing descriptive statistics. In large samples, the calculation using our approach and that of Excel will converge to the same value.

	G	H
1		
2	Mean	17.15819992
3	Standard Error	0.255550251
4	Median	17.0850005
5	Mode	16.4
6	Standard Deviation	1.807013155
7	Sample Variance	3.265296541
8	Kurtosis	2.331534288
9	Skewness	-0.0138249
10	Range	6.87
11	Minimum	13.53
12	Maximum	20.4
13	Sum	857.909996
14	Count	50
15	Sigma tilde	1.788851757
16	Mu2	3.19999061
17	Mu3	-0.07913797
18	Mu4	23.874771

C.2 ESTIMATING POPULATION PARAMETERS

Consider a population of interest. We wish to examine a characteristic which we denote by the random variable Y. The population parameters $E(Y) = \mu$ and $var(Y) = \sigma^2$ provide summary information about the location of the center of the probability density function of Y and its spread. To estimate these parameters, assume we have a random sample $Y_1, Y_2, \ldots, Y_N$. The estimators of the population mean and variance are the sample mean $\bar{Y} = \sum Y_i/N$ and sample variance $\hat{\sigma}^2 = \sum(Y_i - \bar{Y})^2/(N-1)$. These estimators are random variables because their values change from one sample of values to another. In order to illustrate this we will carry out a "simulation" experiment, creating data such as that in Table C.2 of *Principles of Econometrics, 4e*, p. 696. We will create 10 samples of random data from a normal population with mean $\mu = 17$ and variance $\sigma^2 = 6.25$.

C.2.1 Creating Random Samples

Label a new worksheet **ten samples**. In cells **B1:K1** place the labels **h1**, …, **h10** as sample names of the random samples we draw next.

Select **Data Analysis** then **Random Number Generation**, and **OK**.

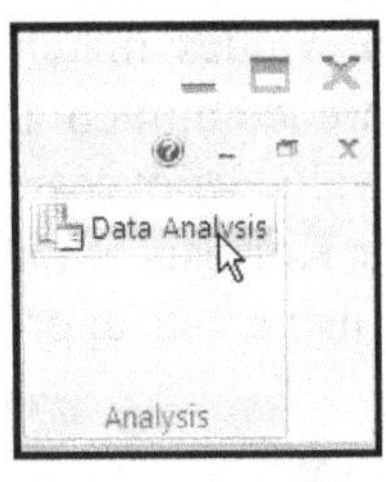

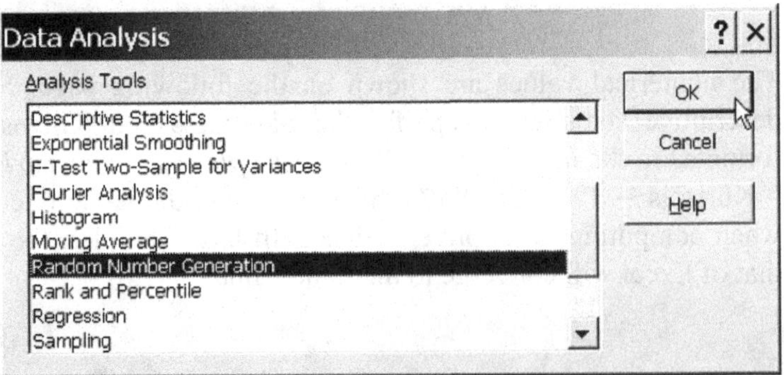

Create **10** samples of **40** observations each based on the normal distribution with **Mean** = **17** and **Standard deviation** = **2.5**. Recall that the standard deviation is the square root of the variance. For $\sigma^2 = 6.25$ this means $\sigma = \sqrt{6.25} = 2.5$. Creating numbers that behave randomly is a science, and how they are created is beyond the scope of this work. It is quite a fascinating subject and many web sites provide introductions. See, for example, http://www.random.org/ or visit Wikipedia http://en.wikipedia.org/wiki/Random_number. We specify a **Random Seed** = **12345**. The actual value of the seed does not matter, but odd numbers with 5 to 7 digits are frequently chosen. If you do not include a random seed value, Excel will create its own value based on the time and date. If you do not use a seed, each time you generate a set of random values you will obtain different values. This is an exciting possible approach, and one that we use at various points in this manual. However at this point we will use a seed value so that you can follow our steps and replicate our values. The values will be placed in the cells **B2:K41**. Select **OK**.

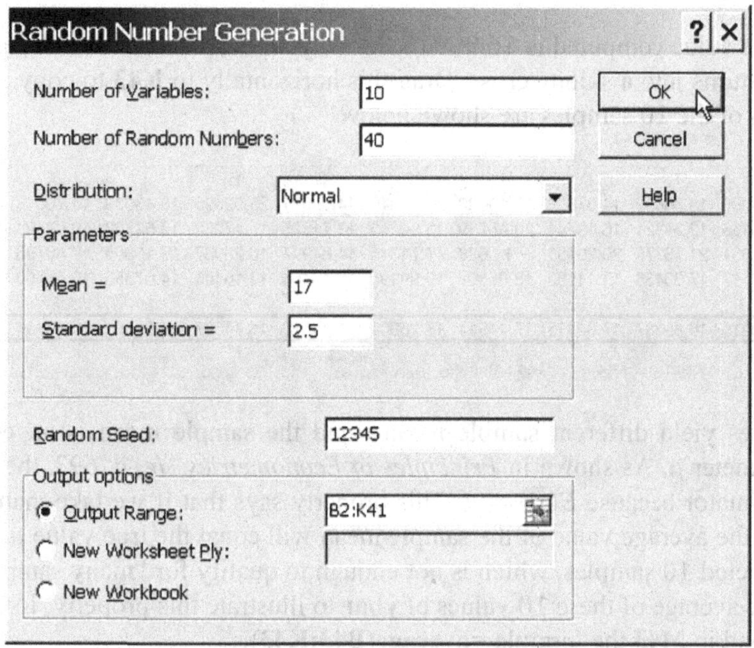

The 10 columns of numbers we obtain represent values we might have collected from a population. We have $N = 40$ observations in each sample. The first few rows should look as shown below.

	A	B	C	D	E	F	G	H	I	J	K
1		h1	h2	h3	h4	h5	h6	h7	h8	h9	h10
2		15.16482	17.53583	18.90207	18.13595	14.09114	18.41487	19.47136	14.5667	20.02987	18.41465
3		16.72703	16.69642	17.78928	18.05322	15.62357	16.55638	18.10234	15.77295	19.06652	14.06899
4		15.77338	15.34563	15.9641	16.78947	13.49482	15.83066	17.98444	13.92702	12.63854	19.53194
5		17.95701	13.20396	16.34176	21.68638	14.26905	18.24109	14.91513	17.87418	16.85045	19.76842
6		16.74914	16.52	18.19651	18.92167	16.2352	20.00413	12.78505	15.15303	13.63347	17.30609

hip data | statistics calculations | **ten samples**

C.2.2 Estimating a Population Mean

The values in sample **h1** are values of the random variable Y, namely $y_1, y_2, \ldots, y_{40}$. Using these 40 values we compute the sample mean $\bar{y} = \Sigma y_i/40$. In cell **A43** enter the label **ybar**. In **B43** enter the equation to calculate the sample mean, **=average(B2:B41)**.

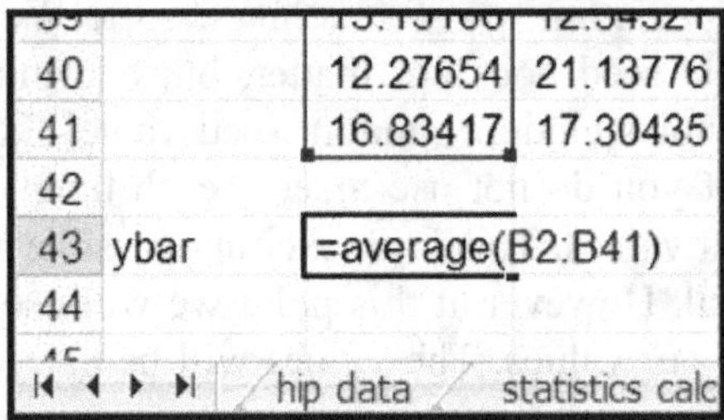

Press **Enter**. The value computed is 16.99915. Move your cursor to the lower right corner of the cell **B43** until it turns into a skinny cross. Drag this horizontally to **K43** to copy the formula. The sample averages of the 10 samples are shown below.

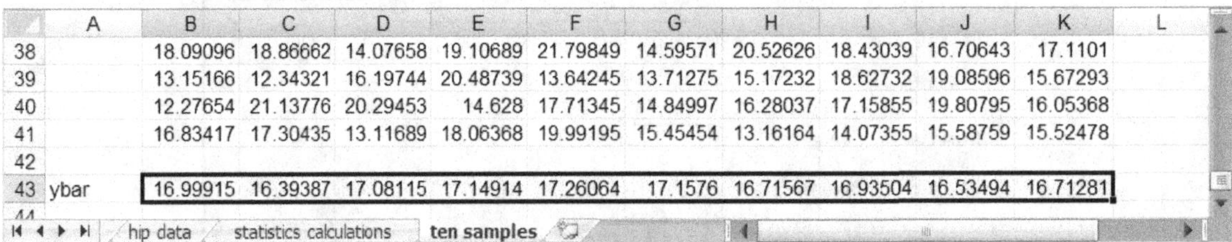

	A	B	C	D	E	F	G	H	I	J	K	L
38		18.09096	18.86662	14.07658	19.10689	21.79849	14.59571	20.52626	18.43039	16.70643	17.1101	
39		13.15166	12.34321	16.19744	20.48739	13.64245	13.71275	15.17232	18.62732	19.08596	15.67293	
40		12.27654	21.13776	20.29453	14.628	17.71345	14.84997	16.28037	17.15855	19.80795	16.05368	
41		16.83417	17.30435	13.11689	18.06368	19.99195	15.45454	13.16164	14.07355	15.58759	15.52478	
42												
43	ybar	16.99915	16.39387	17.08115	17.14914	17.26064	17.1576	16.71567	16.93504	16.53494	16.71281	

Different samples yield different sample means, and the sample mean is an **estimator** of the population parameter μ. As shown in *Principles of Econometrics, 4e*, p. 697, the sample mean is an unbiased estimator because $E(\bar{Y}) = \mu$. This property says that if we take many samples from this population, the average value of the sample mean will equal the true value μ. Our illustration has only constructed 10 samples, which is not enough to qualify for "many samples," but we can still compute the average of these 10 values of **ybar** to illustrate this property. In cell **M42** put the label **average**, and in **M43** the formula **=average(B43:K43)**.

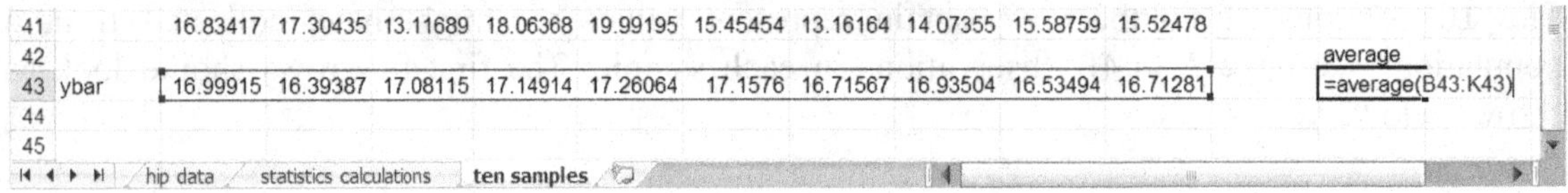

41		16.83417	17.30435	13.11689	18.06368	19.99195	15.45454	13.16164	14.07355	15.58759	15.52478	
42												average
43	ybar	16.99915	16.39387	17.08115	17.14914	17.26064	17.1576	16.71567	16.93504	16.53494	16.71281	=average(B43:K43)
44												
45												

Press **Enter**. The resulting average is 16.894. This is not $\mu = 17$. Repeating the experiment with 1000 samples, the average of the sample means is 16.9902, which is very close to the true mean 17.

C.2.3 Estimating a Population Variance

The estimator of σ^2 is $\hat{\sigma}^2 = \Sigma(y_i - \bar{y})^2/(N-1)$. This too is an unbiased estimator. For each of the 10 samples **h1-h10** compute the sample variance using the **var** function. Enter the label **sighat^2** in **A44**. In **B44** enter the formula **=var(B2:B41)**. Press **Enter**. Copy this formula across to **K44**.

In **M44** compute the average of the 10 variance estimates by entering the formula **=average(B44:K44)**. The result is shown below.

	A	B	C	D	E	F	G	H	I	J	K	L	M	N	O
40		12.27654	21.13776	20.29453	14.628	17.71345	14.84997	16.28037	17.15855	19.80795	16.05368				
41		16.83417	17.30435	13.11689	18.06368	19.99195	15.45454	13.16164	14.07355	15.58759	15.52478				
42													average		
43	ybar	16.99915	16.39387	17.08115	17.14914	17.26064	17.1576	16.71567	16.93504	16.53494	16.71281		16.894		
44	sighat^2	6.457193	5.74982	7.329992	3.713185	6.886413	7.62167	6.840028	5.797105	9.319506	5.741701		6.545661		
45															

hip data / statistics calculations / **ten samples**

The average of the 10 variance estimates is 6.545661. If we repeat this for 1000 samples, the average value of $\hat{\sigma}^2$ is 6.252163, which is very close to the true value 6.25.

C.2.4 Standard Error of the Sample Mean

The variance of the sample mean is $var(\bar{Y}) = \sigma^2/N = 6.25/40 = 0.15625$. This value indicates how much the sample mean $\bar{Y}$ varies from sample to sample. In the worksheet **ten samples**, label cell **N42 variance**. In **N43** enter the formula **=var(B43:K43)**. This is the sampling variation of $\bar{Y}$. In the 10 samples **h1-h10** the sampling variation is 0.084495. For 1000 samples we obtain a calculated variance of the sample mean of 0.144631. Sampling variation is harder to capture than the average value in a simulation experiment. In a larger number of samples the variance of $\bar{Y}$ will approach 0.15625.

The value of the variance of $\bar{Y}$ is usually unknown because σ^2 is unknown. The estimated variance is $\widehat{var}(\bar{Y}) = \hat{\sigma}^2/N$. The square root of $\widehat{var}(\bar{Y})$ is called the **standard error of the mean** or sometimes the **standard error of the estimate**. It can be referred to as $se(\bar{Y}) = \hat{\sigma}/\sqrt{N}$. The standard error of the mean is a very important component of hypothesis tests and confidence intervals. It is reported automatically when we use **Descriptive Statistics** in the **Data Analysis** tool. Let us add it to our **ten samples** worksheet. In cell **A45** enter the label **N**, for sample size. In **B45** enter the function **=count(B2:B41)** and press **Enter**. This counts the sample size $N = 40$. Copy this formula to **C45:K45**.

In **A46** enter the label **Std error**. In **B46** enter **=SQRT(B44/B45)**. Because **B44** contains the estimated variance, the command takes the square root of $\hat{\sigma}^2/N$, which is $se(\bar{Y}) = \hat{\sigma}/\sqrt{N}$. Copy this equation to **C46:K46**. The calculated values should look as shown below.

	A	B	C	D	E	F	G	H	I	J	K	L	M	N
43	ybar	16.99915	16.39387	17.08115	17.14914	17.26064	17.1576	16.71567	16.93504	16.53494	16.71281		16.894	0.084495
44	sighat^2	6.457193	5.74982	7.329992	3.713185	6.886413	7.62167	6.840028	5.797105	9.319506	5.741701		6.545661	
45	N	40	40	40	40	40	40	40	40	40	40			
46	Std error	0.401783	0.379138	0.428077	0.30468	0.414922	0.436511	0.413522	0.380694	0.482688	0.37887			
47														

hip data / statistics calculations / **ten samples**

C.3 THE CENTRAL LIMIT THEOREM

An amazing result in the theory of statistics is the central limit theorem. It says, if we take N random variables, $Y_1, Y_2, \ldots, Y_N$, that are statistically independent and identically distributed (no matter what that distribution might be), then the sample mean $\bar{Y}$ will have approximately a normal distribution with mean μ and variance σ^2/N. This is what in statistics is called a "large sample" or "asymptotic" result, which means that for the approximation to hold the sample size N must be large.

Specifically, the theorem (*Principles of Econometrics, 4e*, p. 699) is stated in terms of the standardized variable:

$$Z_N = \frac{\bar{Y} - \mu}{\sigma/\sqrt{N}} \overset{a}{\sim} N(0,1)$$

This standardized variable has an approximate standard normal distribution in large samples. To illustrate, we use one of the simplest but most useful distribution in statistics: a uniform random variable in the interval between 0 and 1. Create a new worksheet called **CLT**. Select **Data** and then **Data Analysis.** In the **Data Analysis** window choose **Random Number Generation**. We will create **1000** variables—these will be our samples. Each sample will consist of $N = \mathbf{10}$ values. The **Distribution** is **Uniform** between **0** and **1**, and we use a **Random Seed** = **12345** so that you can replicate our results. In the **Output Range** simply specify cell **A1**. Select **OK**.

We will not use column and row labels in this example (too many) so remember that each column is a sample of 10 observations, and the rows 1:10 are observation values from a uniform distribution between 0 and 1.

Random Number Generation
Number of Variables: 1000
Number of Random Numbers: 10
Distribution: Uniform
Parameters
Between 0 and 1
Random Seed: 12345
Output options
Output Range: A1
New Worksheet Ply:
New Workbook
OK
Cancel
Help

The result is 10 random numbers between 0 and 1 in columns **A** to **ALL**. In cell **A12** enter the formula **=average(A1:A10)**, and press **Enter**. This will compute the sample mean $\bar{Y}$ for the values in **A1:A10** that represents the first of 1000 samples. Next, you need to copy and paste this formula to cells **B12**: **ALL12** to compute the sample means for all the samples. The easiest way to do this in this case is first select **A12**, select **Copy**, select **B12**, press and hold down the **SHIFT** key, press the **CTRL** and **END** keys, and finally select **Paste**.

Remark: When faced with the task of copying formulas across large ranges Excel's keyboard shortcuts become very useful. Click on the **Help** button and search.

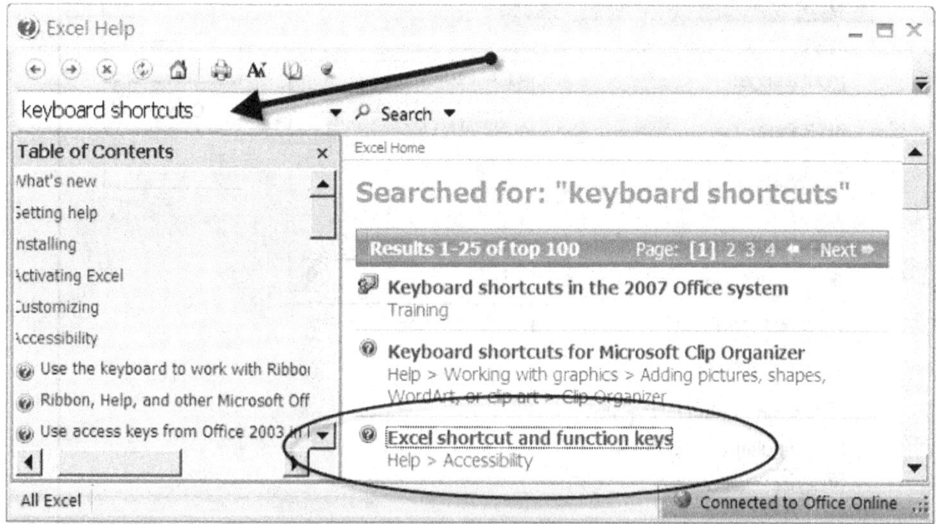

For selecting large areas the following are very useful.

- CTRL+ARROW KEY moves to the edge of the current data region in a worksheet.
- SHIFT+ARROW KEY extends the selection of cells by one cell.
- CTRL+SHIFT+ARROW KEY extends the selection of cells to the last nonblank cell in the same column or row as the active cell, or if the next cell is blank, extends the selection to the next nonblank cell.

The results for the first few columns are shown below. The values in row 12 are sample means.

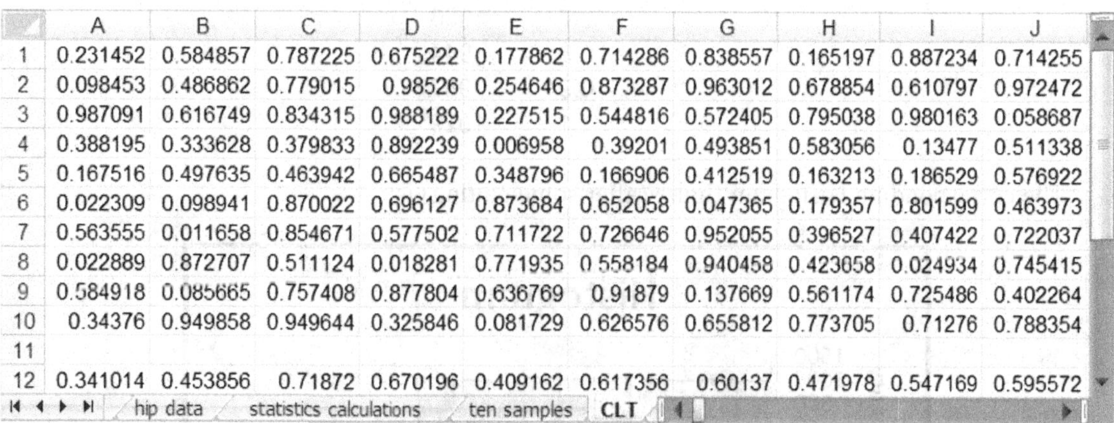

	A	B	C	D	E	F	G	H	I	J
1	0.231452	0.584857	0.787225	0.675222	0.177862	0.714286	0.838557	0.165197	0.887234	0.714255
2	0.098453	0.486862	0.779015	0.98526	0.254646	0.873287	0.963012	0.678854	0.610797	0.972472
3	0.987091	0.616749	0.834315	0.988189	0.227515	0.544816	0.572405	0.795038	0.980163	0.058687
4	0.388195	0.333628	0.379833	0.892239	0.006958	0.39201	0.493851	0.583056	0.13477	0.511338
5	0.167516	0.497635	0.463942	0.665487	0.348796	0.166906	0.412519	0.163213	0.186529	0.576922
6	0.022309	0.098941	0.870022	0.696127	0.873684	0.652058	0.047365	0.179357	0.801599	0.463973
7	0.563555	0.011658	0.854671	0.577502	0.711722	0.726646	0.952055	0.396527	0.407422	0.722037
8	0.022889	0.872707	0.511124	0.018281	0.771935	0.558184	0.940458	0.423058	0.024934	0.745415
9	0.584918	0.085665	0.757408	0.877804	0.636769	0.91879	0.137669	0.561174	0.725486	0.402264
10	0.34376	0.949858	0.949644	0.325846	0.081729	0.626576	0.655812	0.773705	0.71276	0.788354
11										
12	0.341014	0.453856	0.71872	0.670196	0.409162	0.617356	0.60137	0.471978	0.547169	0.595572

hip data / statistics calculations / ten samples / CLT

To display the shape of the uniform distribution, first enter the label **Bin** in cell **ALN1**. In **ALN2:ALN11** put the values **0.1**, **0.2**, ..., **1.0**. On the **Data** tab, select **Data Analysis**, **Histogram**, and then **OK**. Use the 10000 values in **A1:ALL10** to construct the histogram.

Specify the **Bin Range** to be **ALN2:ALN11** and the **Output Range** to be **ALN15**. Finally select **Chart Ouput** and then **OK**.

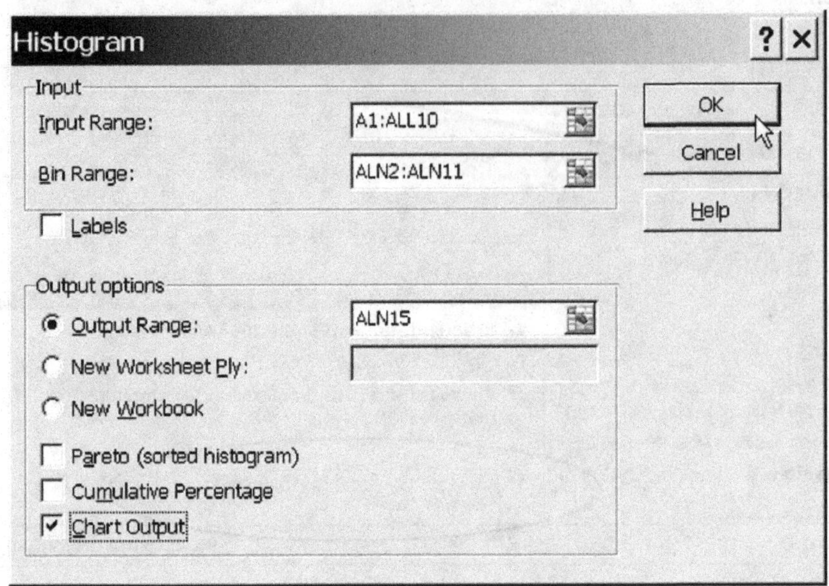

The distribution shows that the 10000 values are evenly spread over the interval [0, 1], with about 1000 values in each of the intervals of width 0.1.

Bin	*Frequency*
0.1	983
0.2	1002
0.3	975
0.4	1011
0.5	1030
0.6	1003
0.7	1036
0.8	944
0.9	987
1	1029

The corresponding Histogram figure (after some editing) is:

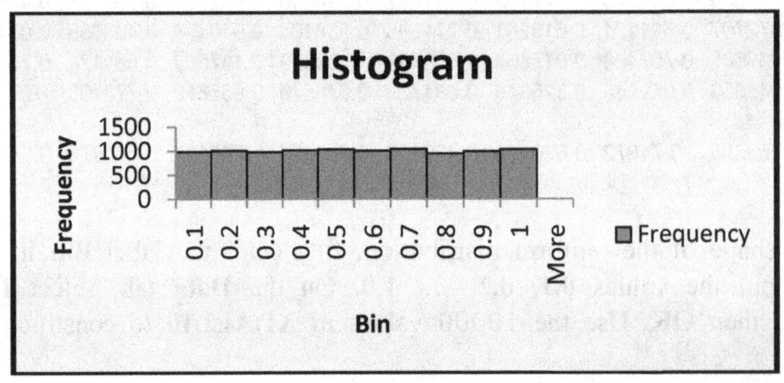

The uniform random variable U on the interval $[a\,,b]$ has mean $E(U)=(a+b)/2$ and variance $var(U)=(b-a)^2/12$. If U is on the interval $[0,1]$, it has mean $E(U)=0.5$ and variance $var(U)=1/12$. The central limit theorem says that the standardized $\bar{Y}$ variable is asymptotically standard normal distributed, which in this case is

$$Z_N=\frac{\bar{U}-0.5}{\sqrt{1/12/\sqrt{10}}}=\frac{\bar{U}-0.5}{\sqrt{1/(12\times 10)}}\overset{a}{\sim}N(0,1)$$

In cell **A13** enter the formula for the standardized variable, **=(A12-0.5)/SQRT(1/(12*10))**, and press **Enter**. Next you need to copy and paste this formula to **B13:ALL13**. An easy way to do this in this case is first select **A13**, select **Copy**, select **B13**, press the **F8** key, use your scroll bar at the bottom of your Excel window to get to the right of your table of data, select **ALL13**, and finally select **Paste**. The first few values are shown below.

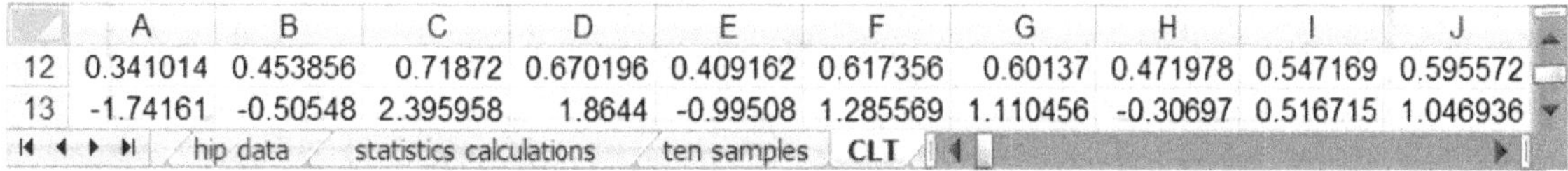

	A	B	C	D	E	F	G	H	I	J
12	0.341014	0.453856	0.71872	0.670196	0.409162	0.617356	0.60137	0.471978	0.547169	0.595572
13	-1.74161	-0.50548	2.395958	1.8644	-0.99508	1.285569	1.110456	-0.30697	0.516715	1.046936

hip data / statistics calculations / ten samples / CLT

Now we repeat the steps of constructing a histogram. In **A14** put the label **Bin**. In **A15:A30** put the values **−3.5, −3.0, −2.5, …, 4.0**. On the **Data** tab, select **Data Analysis** and then **Histogram**. Fill in the dialog box as shown below to chart all the standardized values in row 13. Finally select **OK**.

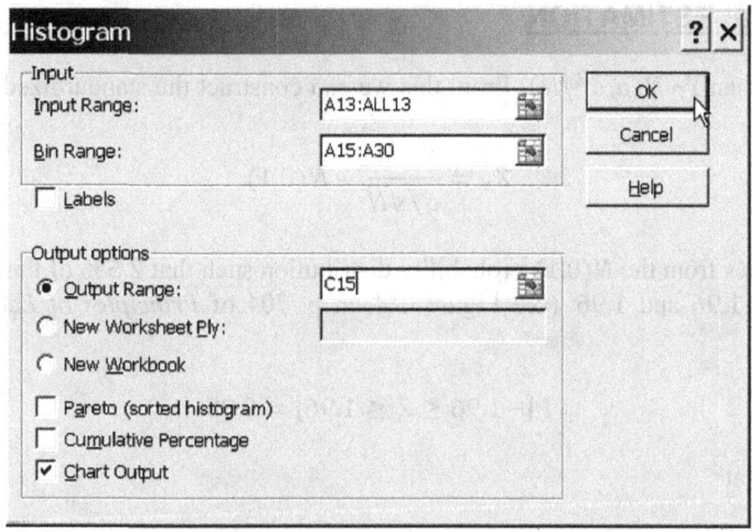

The resulting histogram show a bell shaped curve (we have eliminated the gaps) which is the characteristic of a normally distributed random variable. Note that it is centered at 0 and the range of values is -3 to 3, which you will see using Table 1 in Appendix E of *Principles of Econometrics*, *4e* is 0.9974 of the probability from a standard normal distribution.

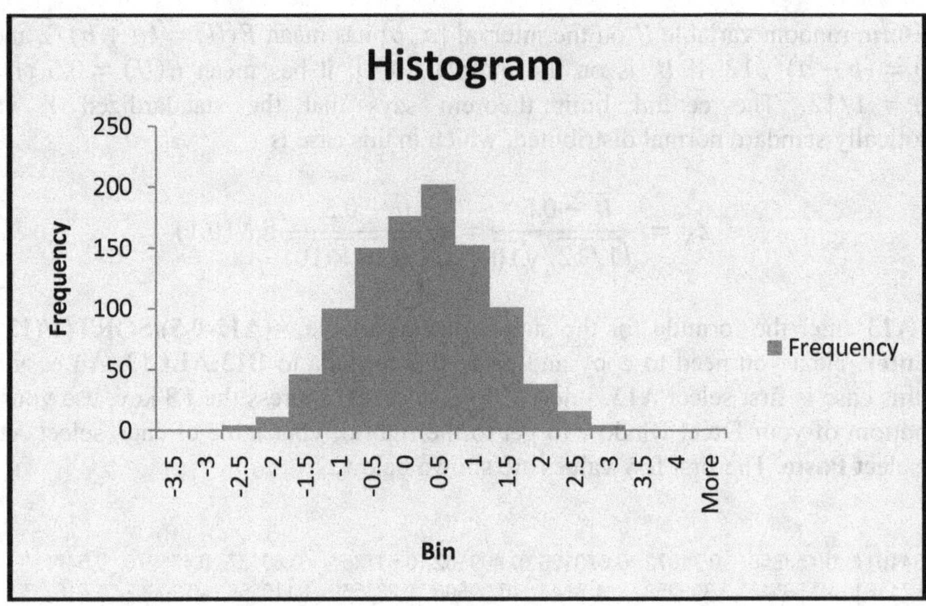

What we have shown is that if we take samples of 10 values from a uniform distribution, which is not bell shaped at all, then the standardized means, or averages, of these samples of 10 values has a probability distribution that is approximately normal.

C.4 INTERVAL ESTIMATION

If $Y \sim N(\mu, \sigma^2)$ then $\bar{Y} \sim N(\mu, \sigma^2/N)$. From this we can construct the standardized normal random variable :

$$Z_N = \frac{\bar{Y} - \mu}{\sigma/\sqrt{N}} \sim N(0,1)$$

The critical values from the $N(0,1)$ probability distribution such that 2.5% of the probability is in either tail are -1.96 and 1.96 (see Figure C.4 on p. 704 of *Principles of Econometrics, 4e*). Consequently:

$$P[-1.96 \leq Z \leq 1.96] = 0.95$$

which implies that:

$$P\left[\bar{Y} - 1.96\frac{\sigma}{\sqrt{N}} \leq \mu \leq \bar{Y} + 1.96\frac{\sigma}{\sqrt{N}}\right] = 0.95$$

In general, if $\Phi(z_c) = 1 - \alpha/2$, then the $100(1-\alpha)\%$ confidence interval estimator of μ is:

$$\bar{Y} \pm z_c \frac{\sigma}{\sqrt{N}}$$

It must be emphasized that a 95% interval estimator will contain the true population mean μ in 95% of *many repeated samples* of size N. To illustrate return to the **ten samples** worksheet. In cell **A48** put the label **LL** and in **A49** put the label **UL**. In **B48** enter the formula **=B43-1.96*SQRT(6.25/B45)** and in **B49** enter **=B43+1.96*SQRT(6.25/B45)**. These calculations find the lower and upper bounds of the interval estimate of μ given that σ is known. Copy **B48:B49** across to **K48:K49**.

	A	B	C	D	E	F	G	H	I	J	K
43	ybar	16.99914806	16.39386953	17.08114945	17.14914399	17.26063653	17.15759809	16.71567455	16.9350386	16.53493891	16.71280829
44	sighat^2	6.457193452	5.749819876	7.32999189	3.713185124	6.886413044	7.62167024	6.840028208	5.7971046	9.319505952	5.741700823
45	N	40	40	40	40	40	40	40	40	40	40
46	Std error	0.40178332	0.379137834	0.428076859	0.30467955	0.414922072	0.436510889	0.413522315	0.3806936	0.482687941	0.378870058
47											
48	LL	16.22439003	15.6191115	16.30639142	16.37438596	16.4858785	16.38284007	15.94091652	16.1602805	15.76018088	15.93805026
49	UL	17.77390609	17.16862756	17.85590748	17.92390201	18.03539455	17.93235612	17.49043257	17.7097966	17.30969693	17.48756632

statistics calculations | ten samples

Note that the intervals created move around because they are centered at the sample mean $\bar{Y}$ which varies from sample to sample. As it happens all 10 of the intervals we have created contain the true population mean $\mu = 17$. We can ask Excel to tell us this using some **logical functions**.

In cell **A50** enter the label **Cover**. In **A51** enter the label **Success**. In **B50** enter the formula **=AND(B48<=17,17<=B49)**. Press **Enter**. This logical function is TRUE if the value of 17 is between the upper and lower bounds, otherwise it is FALSE. In **B51** enter the formula **=IF(B50,1,0)**. If the result in **B50** is TRUE, then we assign the value 1; and if **B50** is false we assign a value of 0. In this way we can record whether our interval estimate successfully contains (or covers) the true parameter μ. Copy the formulas from **B50:B51** to **C50:K51**. The result is shown below.

	A	B	C	D	E	F	G	H	I	J	K
43	ybar	16.99914806	16.39386953	17.08114945	17.14914399	17.26063653	17.15759809	16.71567455	16.9350386	16.53493891	16.71280829
44	sighat^2	6.457193452	5.749819876	7.32999189	3.713185124	6.886413044	7.62167024	6.840028208	5.7971046	9.319505952	5.741700823
45	N	40	40	40	40	40	40	40	40	40	40
46	Std error	0.40178332	0.379137834	0.428076859	0.30467955	0.414922072	0.436510889	0.413522315	0.3806936	0.482687941	0.378870058
47											
48	LL	16.22439003	15.6191115	16.30639142	16.37438596	16.4858785	16.38284007	15.94091652	16.1602805	15.76018088	15.93805026
49	UL	17.77390609	17.16862756	17.85590748	17.92390201	18.03539455	17.93235612	17.49043257	17.7097966	17.30969693	17.48756632
50	cover	TRUE	TRUE	TRUE	TRUE	TRUE	TRUE	TRUE	TRUE	TRUE	TRUE
51	success	1	1	1	1	1	1	1	1	1	1

statistics calculations | ten samples

To further illustrate, create in a new worksheet 1000 samples of size 40 from a normal distribution with mean 17 and standard deviation 2.5.

Random Number Generation

Number of Variables: 1000

Number of Random Numbers: 40

Distribution: Normal

Parameters

Mean = 17

Standard deviation = 2.5

Random Seed: 12345

Output options

Output Range: $A$1

New Worksheet Ply: 1000 samples

New Workbook

OK

Cancel

Help

For our 1000 samples we obtained an average value of success of .961. This means that 96.1% of the 1000 interval estimates cover the true parameter $\mu = 17$, which is close to the expected 95%. If we had used more than 1000 samples to test this idea we would have gotten a success rate closer to 95%.

C.4.1 Interval Estimation With σ^2 Unknown

The interval estimation procedure described above depended upon specific knowledge of the value of $var(Y) = \sigma^2$. If the variance is not known we substitute the estimated sample variance $\hat{\sigma}^2 = \sum (Y_i - \bar{Y})^2/(N-1)$. When we do so, the standardized variable follows the *t*-distribution with $N - 1$ degrees of freedom.

$$t = \frac{\bar{Y} - \mu}{\hat{\sigma}/\sqrt{N}} = \frac{\bar{Y} - \mu}{se(\bar{Y})} \sim t_{(N-1)}$$

The confidence interval estimator is now:

$$\bar{Y} \pm t_c \frac{\hat{\sigma}}{\sqrt{N}}, \text{ or } \bar{Y} \pm t_c se(\bar{Y})$$

The critical value t_c is the $1 - \alpha/2$ percentile from the t-distribution with $N - 1$ degrees of freedom, or $t_{(N-1)}$.

Return now to the **ten samples** worksheet. Put the label **tc** in cell **A53**. In cell **B53** use the **Insert function** key and scroll to the statistical function **TINV**. This function returns the $1 - \alpha/2$ percentile. Given $\alpha = 0.05$ and degrees of freedom $N - 1 = 39$, we see that the critical value is $t_c = 2.02269$. Click **OK**.

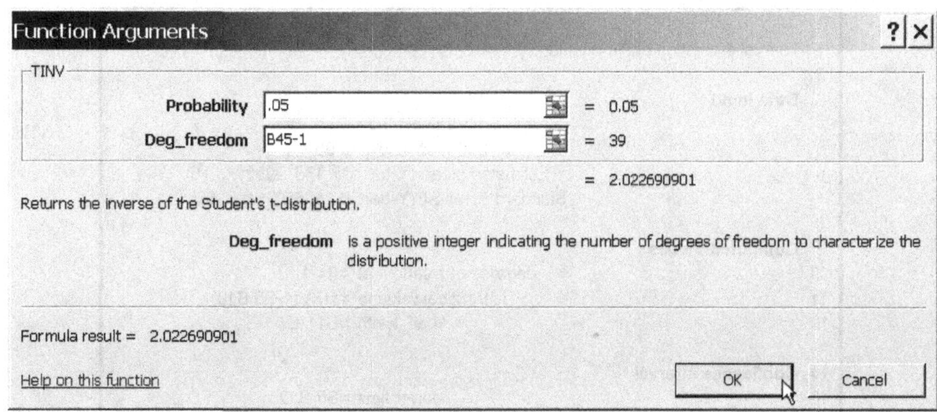

In **A54** enter the label **LL** and in **A55** enter **UL**. In **B54** enter the formula **=B43-B53*B46**, which computes $\bar{Y} - t_c se(\bar{Y})$. In **B55** enter **=B43+B53*B46**, which computes $\bar{Y} + t_c se(\bar{Y})$. Copy the content of **B53:B55** to **C53:K55**.

	A	B	C	D	E	F	G	H	I	J	K
43	ybar	16.99915	16.39387	17.08115	17.14914	17.26064	17.1576	16.71567	16.93504	16.53494	16.71281
44	sighat^2	6.457193	5.74982	7.329992	3.713185	6.886413	7.62167	6.840028	5.797105	9.319506	5.741701
45	N	40	40	40	40	40	40	40	40	40	40
46	Std error	0.401783	0.379138	0.428077	0.30468	0.414922	0.436511	0.413522	0.380694	0.482688	0.37887
47											
48	LL	16.22439	15.61911	16.30639	16.37439	16.48588	16.38284	15.94092	16.16028	15.76018	15.93805
49	UL	17.77391	17.16863	17.85591	17.9239	18.03539	17.93236	17.49043	17.7098	17.3097	17.48757
50	cover	TRUE	TRUE	TRUE	TRUE	TRUE	TRUE	TRUE	TRUE	TRUE	TRUE
51	success	1	1	1	1	1	1	1	1	1	1
52											
53	tc	2.022691	2.022691	2.022691	2.022691	2.022691	2.022691	2.022691	2.022691	2.022691	2.022691
54	LL	16.18646	15.62699	16.21528	16.53287	16.42138	16.27467	15.87925	16.16501	15.55861	15.94647
55	UL	17.81183	17.16075	17.94702	17.76542	18.0999	18.04052	17.5521	17.70506	17.51127	17.47915
56	cover	TRUE	TRUE	TRUE	TRUE	TRUE	TRUE	TRUE	TRUE	TRUE	TRUE
57	success	1	1	1	1	1	1	1	1	1	1

statistics calculations | **ten samples** | CLT | 1000 samples

The resulting 10 interval estimates for μ all cover the true parameter value $\mu = 17$, but note that now the center of the distribution *and* its width vary from sample to sample. The intervals are also slightly wider because the t-distribution critical value is larger than 1.96. In a large number of samples such intervals will cover the true parameter 95% of the time.

C.4.2 Interval Estimation With the Hip Data

Now we create a template for constructing interval estimates for the sample mean. Label a new worksheet **Interval Template**. Set up your template as shown below.

	A	B
1	Interval estimation of the population mean	
2		
3	**Data Input**	
4	Sample Size	50
5	Confidence level	0.95
6	Estimated mean (Y-bar)	17.15819992
7	Standard Error-SE(Y-bar)	0.255550251063506
8		
9	**Computed Values**	
10	degrees of freedom df	=B4-1
11	t-critical value tc	=TINV(1-B5,B10)
12	half_width	=B11*B7
13		
14	**Confidence Interval**	
15	lower limit	=B6-B12
16	upper limit	=B6+B12
17		

The values shown in the shaded area for the mean and standard error, under the section called **Data Input** can be copied and pasted from the **hip data summary stats** worksheet. For example, highlight the entry for **Mean**, then press both the **Ctrl** and **C keys** (Ctrl+C) to copy the number to the Windows clipboard. Return to the **Interval Template** and click on the target cell to make it active, then select **Paste** and **Paste Values** to transfer the numbers (or Ctrl+V).

The result is:

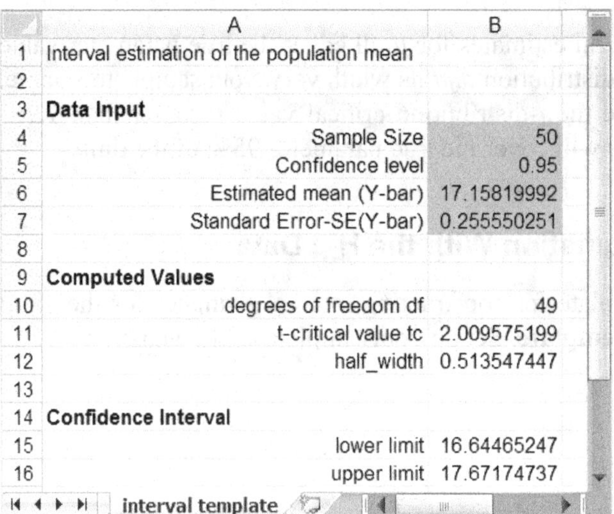

	A	B
1	Interval estimation of the population mean	
2		
3	**Data Input**	
4	Sample Size	50
5	Confidence level	0.95
6	Estimated mean (Y-bar)	17.15819992
7	Standard Error-SE(Y-bar)	0.255550251
8		
9	**Computed Values**	
10	degrees of freedom df	49
11	t-critical value tc	2.009575199
12	half_width	0.513547447
13		
14	**Confidence Interval**	
15	lower limit	16.64465247
16	upper limit	17.67174737

interval template

C.5 HYPOTHESIS TESTS ABOUT A POPULATION MEAN

Hypothesis tests about the population mean are based on the statistic:

$$t = \frac{\bar{Y} - \mu}{\hat{\sigma}/\sqrt{N}} = \frac{\bar{Y} - \mu}{se(\bar{Y})} \sim t_{(N-1)}$$

If the null hypothesis $H_0: \mu = c$ is true, then:

$$t = \frac{\bar{Y} - c}{\hat{\sigma}/\sqrt{N}} = \frac{\bar{Y} - c}{se(\bar{Y})} \sim t_{(N-1)}$$

The null hypothesis will be rejected if the value of the test statistic becomes too large or too small, depending upon the nature of the alternative hypothesis.

For the **right-tail** alternative hypothesis $H_1: \mu > c$, we reject the null hypothesis and accept the alternative if $t \geq t_c = t_{(1-\alpha,N-1)}$ where $t_{(1-\alpha,N-1)}$ is the $100(1-\alpha)$ percentile of the $t_{(N-1)}$ distribution. The value α is the level of significance of the test, and is the probability of rejecting the null hypothesis when it is true [Type I error]. In the figure below $m = N - 1$.

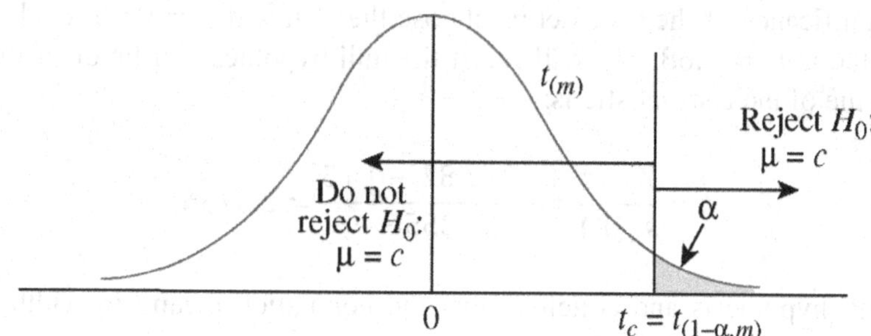

For the **left-tail** alternative hypothesis $H_1: \mu < c$, we reject the null hypothesis and accept the alternative if $t \leq t_c = t_{(\alpha,N-1)}$ where $t_{(\alpha,N-1)}$ is the 100α percentile of the $t_{(N-1)}$ distribution. The value α is the level of significance of the test, and is the probability of rejecting the null hypothesis when it is true [Type I error]. In the figure below $m = N - 1$.

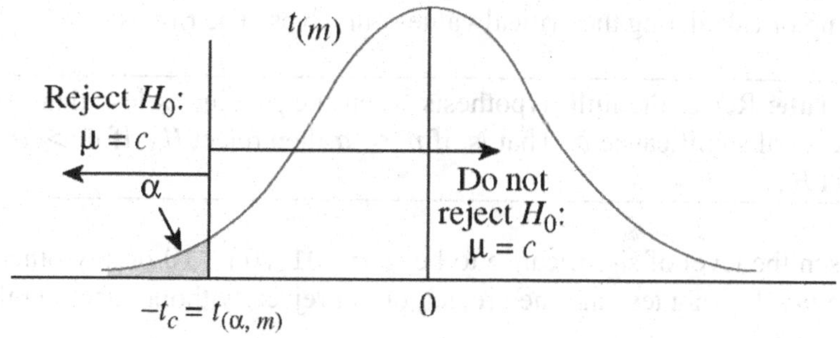

For the **two-tail** alternative hypothesis $H_1: \mu \neq c$, we reject the null hypothesis and accept the alternative if $t \leq -t_c = t_{(\alpha/2,N-1)}$ or if $t \geq t_c = t_{(1-\alpha/2,N-1)}$. The value α is the level of significance of the test, and is the probability of rejecting the null hypothesis when it is true [Type

I error]. The rejection regions each include $\alpha/2$ of the rejection probability. In the figure below $m = N - 1$.

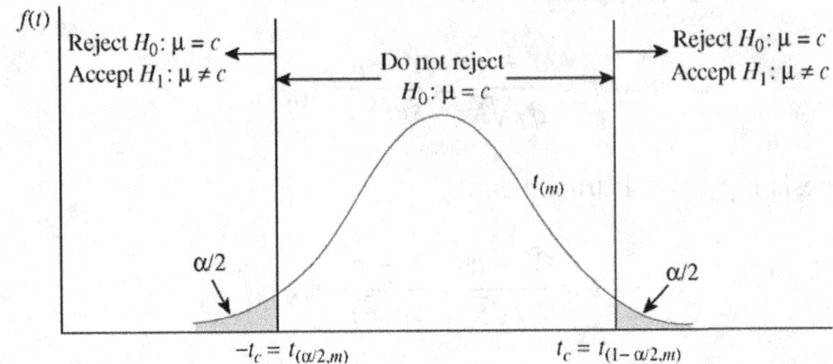

C.5.1 An Example

Using the hip data, let us test the null hypothesis $H_0{:}\mu = 16.5$ against the right-tail alternative hypothesis $H_1{:}\mu > 16.5$. For the hip data $N = 50$, and the degrees of freedom for the t-distribution are $N - 1 = 49$. We reject the null hypothesis and accept the alternative if $t \geq t_c = t_{(1-\alpha,N-1)}$ where $t_{(1-\alpha,N-1)}$ is the $100(1-\alpha)$ percentile of the $t_{(N-1)}$ distribution. The value α is the level of significance of the test. Let us choose the standard $\alpha = 0.05$ level of significance. The t-critical value is $t_c = 1.68$. We will reject the null hypothesis in favor of the alternative if $t \geq 1.68$. The value of the test statistic is:

$$t = \frac{\bar{Y} - c}{se(\bar{Y})} = \frac{17.1582 - 16.5}{.2556} = 2.5756$$

We reject the null hypothesis and conclude that the population mean hip width is greater than 16.5 inches.

C.5.2 The *p*-Value

The p-value is a number associated with a hypothesis. If we have the p-value of a test, p, we can determine the outcome of the test by comparing the p-value to the chosen level of significance, α, *without* looking up or calculating the critical values ourselves. The rule is:

> ***p*-value rule**: Reject the null hypothesis when the p-value is less than, or equal to, the level of significance α. That is, if $p \leq \alpha$ then reject H_0. If $p > \alpha$ then do not reject H_0.

If you have chosen the level of significance to be $\alpha = .01, .05, .10$ or any other value, you can compare it to the p-value of a test and then reject, or not reject, without checking the critical value t_c.

How the p-value is computed depends on the alternative. If t is the calculated value [not the critical value t_c] of the t-statistic with $N - 1$ degrees of freedom, then:

- if $H_1: \mu > c, p =$ probability to the right of t
- if $H_1: \mu < c, p =$ probability to the left of t
- if $H_1: \mu \neq c, p =$ *sum* of probabilities to the right of $|t|$ *and* to the left of $-|t|$

For the numerical example in the previous section the p-value is the area under the $t_{(49)}$ distribution to the right of 2.5756. This probability is 0.00654 and is smaller than $\alpha = 0.05$,. Following the p-value rule we reject the null hypothesis. In the next section we will build a testing template for each type of test.

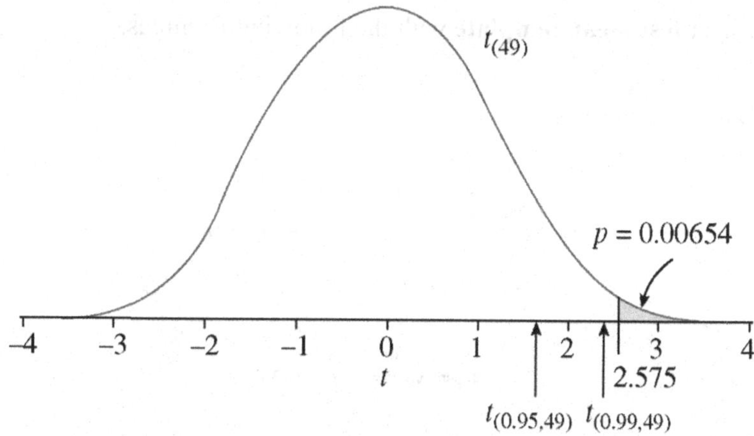

C.5.3 A Template for Hypothesis Tests

Insert a new sheet and rename it **test mean template**. To construct the template we will employ two primary functions related to the t-distribution: **TINV** that we have already used to find the critical value, and **TDIST**. We also use the logical operator **IF**.

The syntax for **TDIST** is $TDIST(x, m, tails)$ where $x > 0$ is the value at which the distribution is evaluated, and m is the degrees of freedom, and $tails$ is 1 or 2. If $tails = 1$, the function returns $TDIST = P(t_{(m)} > x)$. If $tails = 2$, the function returns $TDIST = P(t_{(m)} < -x) + P(t_{(m)} > x)$.

IF(logical_test, value_if_true, value_if_false) evaluates the condition "logical test" and returns either TRUE or FALSE. If the condition is TRUE then the function returns "value_if_true", and if the condition is FALSE the function returns "value_if_false".

Recall that for helpful descriptions such as that above you can click the question mark icon, and in the resulting Excel Help window you can type into the search box the term you seek help on.

Fill in your worksheet **test mean template** with the following formulas.

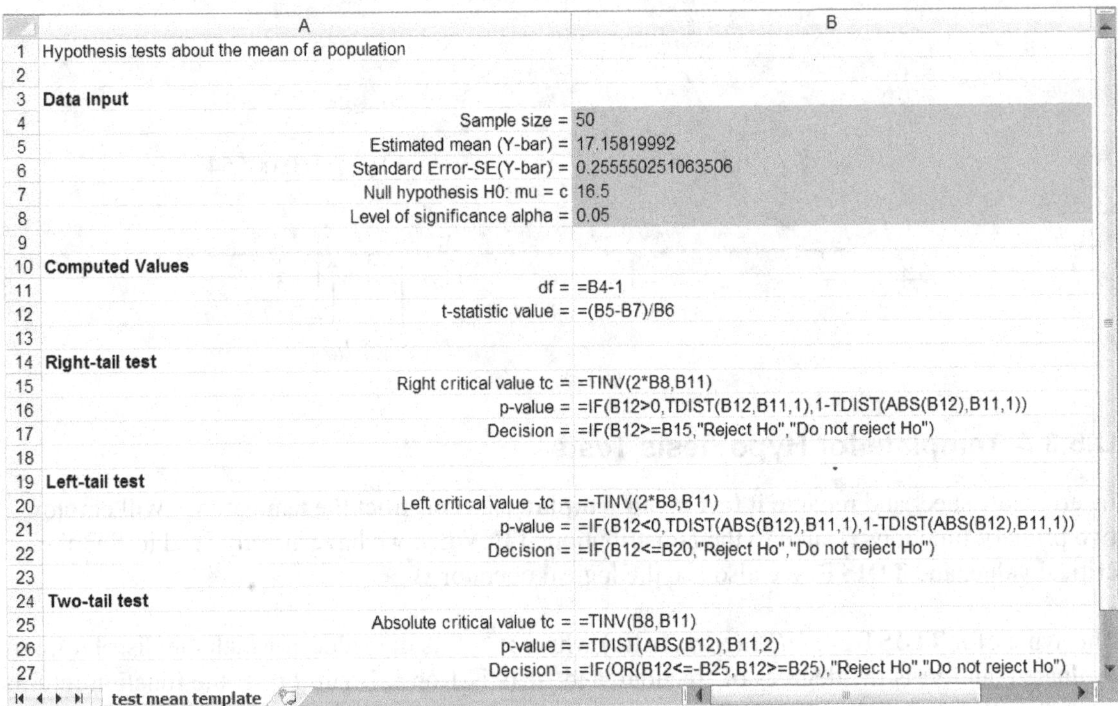

	A	B
1	Hypothesis tests about the mean of a population	
2		
3	**Data Input**	
4	Sample size =	50
5	Estimated mean (Y-bar) =	17.15819992
6	Standard Error-SE(Y-bar) =	0.255550251063506
7	Null hypothesis H0: mu = c	16.5
8	Level of significance alpha =	0.05
9		
10	**Computed Values**	
11	df =	=B4-1
12	t-statistic value =	=(B5-B7)/B6
13		
14	**Right-tail test**	
15	Right critical value tc =	=TINV(2*B8,B11)
16	p-value =	=IF(B12>0,TDIST(B12,B11,1),1-TDIST(ABS(B12),B11,1))
17	Decision =	=IF(B12>=B15,"Reject Ho","Do not reject Ho")
18		
19	**Left-tail test**	
20	Left critical value -tc =	=-TINV(2*B8,B11)
21	p-value =	=IF(B12<0,TDIST(ABS(B12),B11,1),1-TDIST(ABS(B12),B11,1))
22	Decision =	=IF(B12<=B20,"Reject Ho","Do not reject Ho")
23		
24	**Two-tail test**	
25	Absolute critical value tc =	=TINV(B8,B11)
26	p-value =	=TDIST(ABS(B12),B11,2)
27	Decision =	=IF(OR(B12<=-B25,B12>=B25),"Reject Ho","Do not reject Ho")

test mean template

In this template note that for *p*-value calculations we must first ascertain whether the calculated *t*-statistic is positive, or not. Recall that argument for the function $TDIST(x, m, tails)$ is $x > 0$. Thus the *p*-value command uses the logical *IF* statement to check on that. For example, for the right-tail test, the command is;

=IF(B12>0,TDIST(B12,B11,1),1-TDIST(ABS(B12),B11,1))

- If **B12>0** (the *t*-statistic > 0) is **TRUE**, then the *p*-value is **TDIST(B12,B11,1)** where **B12** is the *t*-statistic value and **B11** is the degrees of freedom $N-1$. This is $P(t_{(N-1)} > t)$.
- If **B12>0** (the *t*-statistic > 0) is **FALSE**, then the *p*-value is **1-TDIST(ABS(B12),B11,1)** where **B12** is the *t*-statistic value and **B11** is the degrees of freedom $N-1$. Here we use the symmetry of the *t*-distribution. The *p*-value for this right tail test is $P(t_{(N-1)} > -t)$ $= 1 - P(t_{(N-1)} > t)$ by symmetry. The *TDIST* function only computes probability values for positive values of the *t*-statistic. So we take the absolute value of the *t*-statistic

(which is negative based on the **IF** statement) to change its sign to positive and then use the fact that the total probability is "one".

The resulting values in the template are given below. Note that the *p*-value for the test $H_0: \mu = 17$ against the alternative $H_1: \mu > 17$ is 0.0065 , which is smaller than $\alpha = 0.05$. Based on the *p*-value rule (reject the null hypothesis when $p < \alpha$), we reject the hypothesis that $\mu = 17$ and accept the alternative that $\mu > 17$. Recall that μ is the population mean hip size for adults, and this result means we can conclude that the average hip size is now greater than 17 inches, at the 5% level of significance.

	A	B
1	Hypothesis tests about the mean of a population	
2		
3	**Data Input**	
4	Sample size =	50
5	Estimated mean (Y-bar) =	17.15819992
6	Standard Error-SE(Y-bar) =	0.255550251
7	Null hypothesis H0: mu = c	16.5
8	Level of significance alpha =	0.05
9		
10	**Computed Values**	
11	df =	49
12	t-statistic value =	2.575618366
13		
14	**Right-tail test**	
15	Right critical value tc =	1.676550893
16	p-value =	0.006536948
17	Decision =	Reject Ho
18		
19	**Left-tail test**	
20	Left critical value -tc =	-1.676550893
21	p-value =	0.993463052
22	Decision =	Do not reject Ho
23		
24	**Two-tail test**	
25	Absolute critical value tc =	2.009575199
26	p-value =	0.013073897
27	Decision =	Reject Ho

test mean template

C.6 OTHER USEFUL TESTS

C.6.1 Simulating Data

In this section we will carry out various tests. To illustrate we will use some randomly generated data from normal distributions. Label a new worksheet **three samples**. In **A1:C1** enter the labels **Y1, Y2, Y3**. In these columns we will create 3 samples of size $N = 20$ from the following distributions: $Y1 \sim N(0,1)$, $Y2 \sim N(1.5,1)$, $Y3 \sim (1.5,4)$. Select the **Data** tab and the **Data Analysis** button in the **Analysis** group of commands found in the far right of the Excel ribbon. Choose **Random Number Generation** from the menu. First create the $N(0,1)$ data values as shown below.

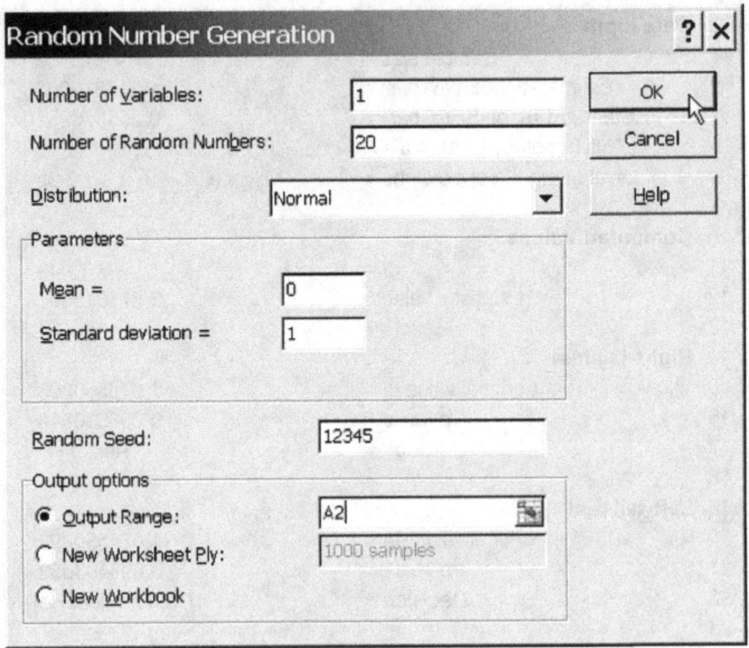

Then create the $N(1.5,1)$ values, starting in **B2** and using **Random Seed** 123. Because we will be using tests comparing one population to another, by using a different Random Seed we ensure that the populations are independent of each other.

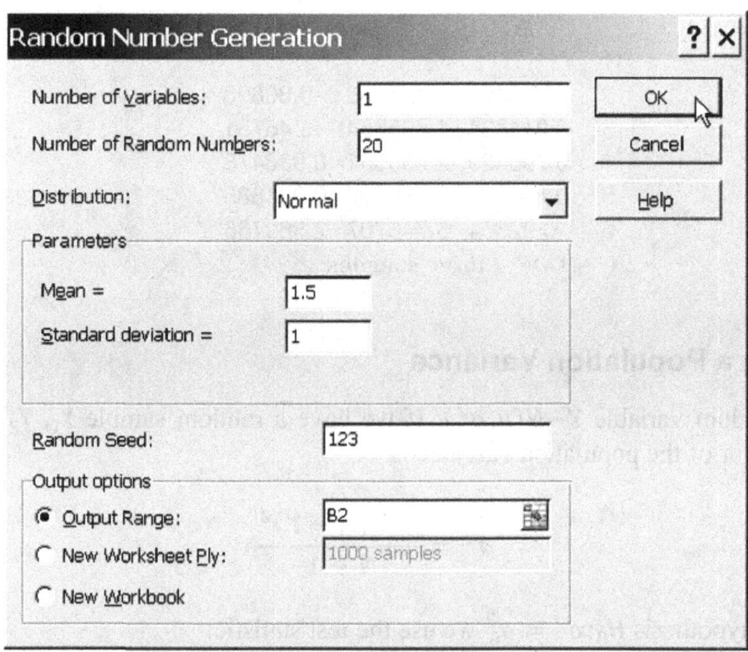

Finally create the $N(1.5,4)$ values using **Random Seed** 1234.

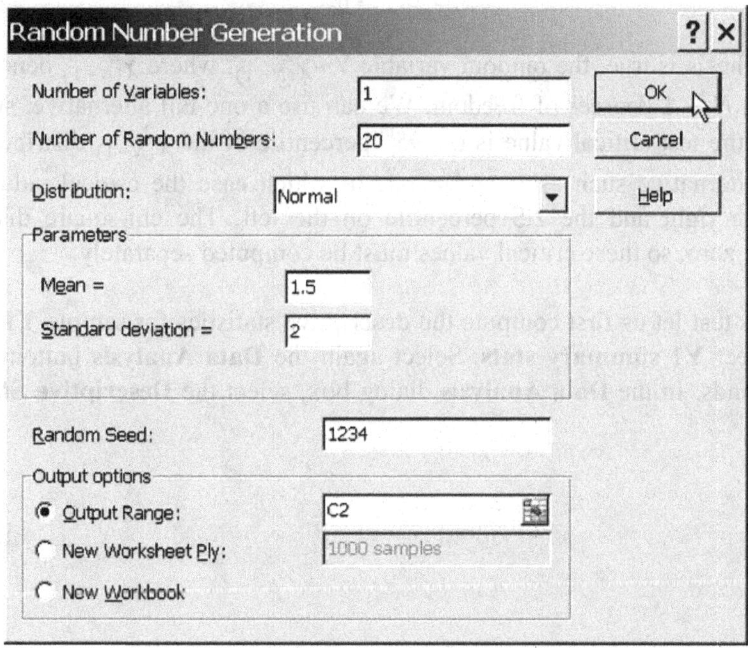

The first few values should look like as shown below.

	A	B	C	D
1	Y1	Y2	Y3	
2	-0.73407	-0.7136	-0.80898	
3	0.214334	1.705654	-3.46751	
4	0.796829	2.036561	0.938478	
5	0.454379	1.246432	0.257885	
6	-0.92354	3.746707	2.569766	

three samples

C.6.2 Testing a Population Variance

Suppose the random variable $Y \sim N(\mu, \sigma^2)$. If we have a random sample Y_1, Y_2, …, Y_N then an unbiased estimator of the population variance is:

$$\hat{\sigma}^2 = \frac{\sum_{i=1}^{N}(Y_i - \bar{Y})^2}{N-1}$$

To test the null hypothesis $H_0: \sigma^2 = \sigma_0^2$ we use the test statistic:

$$V = \frac{(N-1)\hat{\sigma}^2}{\sigma_0^2}$$

If the null hypothesis is true, the random variable $V \sim \chi^2_{(N-1)}$, where $\chi^2_{(N-1)}$ denotes a chi-square distribution with $N-1$ degrees of freedom. We can use a one-tail alternative, such as $H_1: \sigma^2 > \sigma_0^2$. In this case the test critical value is the 95th percentile of the $\chi^2_{(N-1)}$ distribution. Or we can use a two-tail alternative such as $H_1: \sigma^2 \neq \sigma_0^2$, in which case the critical values are the 97.5 percentile on the right and the 2.5 percentile on the left. The chi-square distribution is not symmetric about zero, so these critical values must be computed separately.

To carry out this test let us first compute the descriptive statistics for sample **Y1**, and store them into the worksheet **Y1 summary stats**. Select again the **Data Analysis** button in the **Analysis** group of commands. In the **Data Analysis** dialog box, select the **Descriptive Statistics** analysis tool.

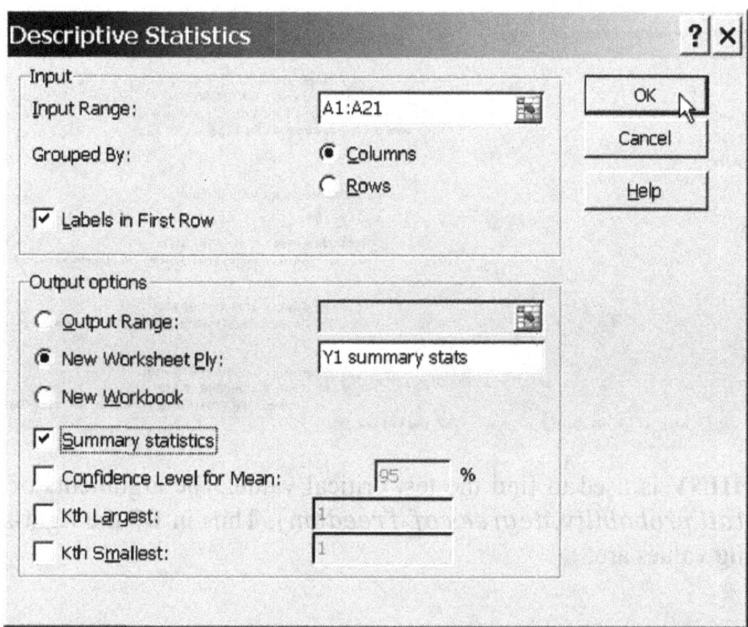

The results are shown below.

	A	B	C
1	*Y1*		
2			
3	Mean	0.077479399	
4	Standard Error	0.156646934	
5	Median	0.265023345	
6	Mode	#N/A	
7	Standard Deviation	0.700546384	
8	Sample Variance	0.490765237	
9	Kurtosis	-1.001298518	
10	Skewness	-0.291266209	
11	Range	2.384351774	
12	Minimum	-1.172402335	
13	Maximum	1.211949439	
14	Sum	1.549587978	
15	Count	20	
16			

Y1 summary stats

The **Sample Variance** is 0.490765. This is the statistic we have called $\hat{\sigma}^2$. Insert a new worksheet and rename it **test variance**. In it, build the following template. Copy and paste the value of the sample variance into the template.

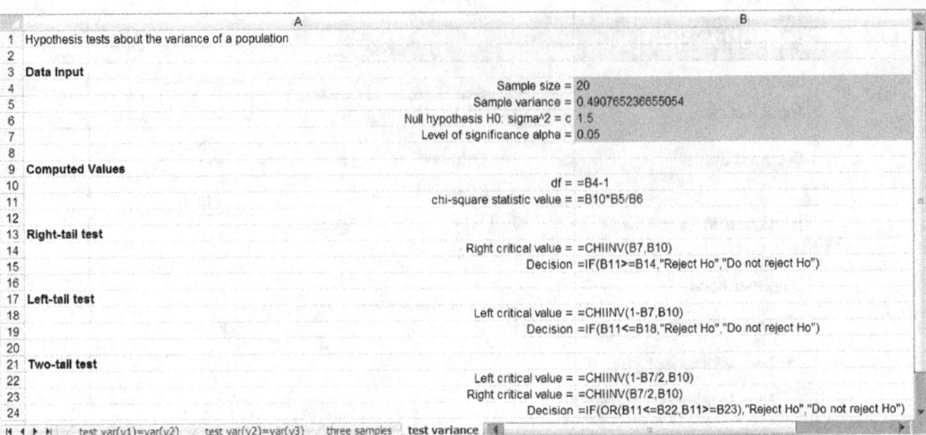

	A	B
1	Hypothesis tests about the variance of a population	
2		
3	**Data Input**	
4	Sample size =	20
5	Sample variance =	0.490765236655054
6	Null hypothesis H0: sigma^2 = c	1.5
7	Level of significance alpha =	0.05
8		
9	**Computed Values**	
10	df =	=B4-1
11	chi-square statistic value =	=B10*B5/B6
12		
13	**Right-tail test**	
14	Right critical value =	=CHIINV(B7,B10)
15	Decision	=IF(B11>=B14,"Reject Ho","Do not reject Ho")
16		
17	**Left-tail test**	
18	Left critical value =	=CHIINV(1-B7,B10)
19	Decision	=IF(B11<=B18,"Reject Ho","Do not reject Ho")
20		
21	**Two-tail test**	
22	Left critical value =	=CHIINV(1-B7/2,B10)
23	Right critical value =	=CHIINV(B7/2,B10)
24	Decision	=IF(OR(B11<=B22,B11>=B23),"Reject Ho","Do not reject Ho")

test var(y1)=var(y2) / test var(y2)=var(y3) / three samples / test variance

The function **CHIINV** is used to find the test critical value. The arguments of the function are $CHIINV(right\_tail\ probabiliy, degrees\ of\ freedom)$. Thus in **B7** the right-tail probability is 0.05. The resulting values are:

	A	B
1	Hypothesis tests about the variance of a population	
2		
3	**Data Input**	
4	Sample size =	20
5	Sample variance =	0.490765237
6	Null hypothesis H0: sigma^2 = c	1.5
7	Level of significance alpha =	0.05
8		
9	**Computed Values**	
10	df =	19
11	chi-square statistic value =	6.216359664
12		
13	**Right-tail test**	
14	Right critical value =	30.14352721
15	Decision	Do not reject Ho
16		
17	**Left-tail test**	
18	Left critical value =	10.11701315
19	Decision	Reject Ho
20		
21	**Two-tail test**	
22	Left critical value =	8.906516548
23	Right critical value =	32.85232686
24	Decision	Reject Ho

test variance / Jarque Bera Template

Thus, when testing $H_0: \sigma^2 = 1.5$ against the alternatives, at the 5% level of significance:

- $H_1: \sigma^2 > 1.5$: we do not have enough evidence to reject the null hypothesis,
- $H_1: \sigma^2 < 1.5$: we have enough evidence to reject the null hypothesis and conclude that the population variance is less than 1.5,

- $H_1: \sigma^2 \neq 1.5$: we have enough evidence to reject the null in favor of the alternative and conclude that the population variance is not 1.5.

C.6.3 Testing Two Population Means

If we have two populations $Y1 \sim N(\mu_1, \sigma_1^2)$ and $Y2 \sim N(\mu_2, \sigma_2^2)$ we may like to test the null hypothesis that the two populations have the same mean. This test is carried out differently if the two population variances are equal (**Case 1**) or unequal (**Case 2**). Recall that the **three samples** worksheet contains $N = 20$ observations from $Y1 \sim N(0,1)$, $Y2 \sim N(1.5,1)$, and $Y3 \sim (1.5,4)$. Let us first test that the means of populations $Y1$ and $Y2$ are equal. The test statistic formula is on p. 717 of *Principles of Econometrics, 4e*.

Go back to your **three samples** worksheet. Select the **Data** tab, and then the **Data Analysis** button on the **Analysis** group of commands. In the **Data Analysis** dialog box, select the **t-test: Two-Sample Assuming Equal Variances**.

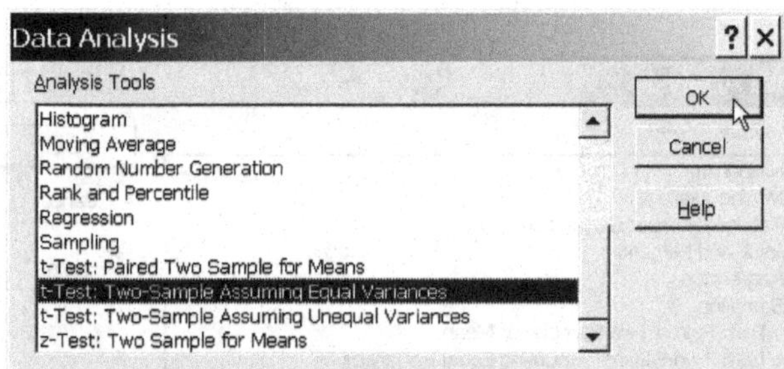

In the **t-Test** dialog box enter the data ranges, select **Labels**, use the 5% level of significance and output the results to a new worksheet. Since we are testing the null hypothesis that two populations have the same mean, we specify the **Hypothesized Mean Difference** to be **0**.

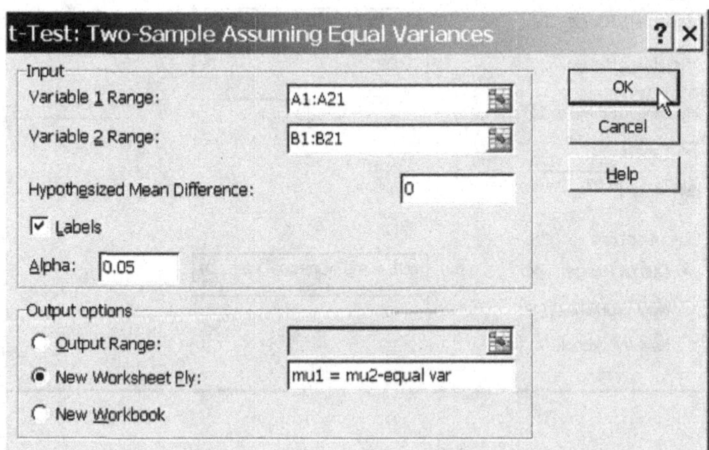

The result shows the calculated *t*-statistic as well as the one- and two-tail critical values and *p*-values. Note that the one-tail *p*-value is calculated from the left tail because the test statistic value is negative. If the test statistic value had been positive it would have computed the one-tail *p*-value from the right tail of the *t*-distribution.

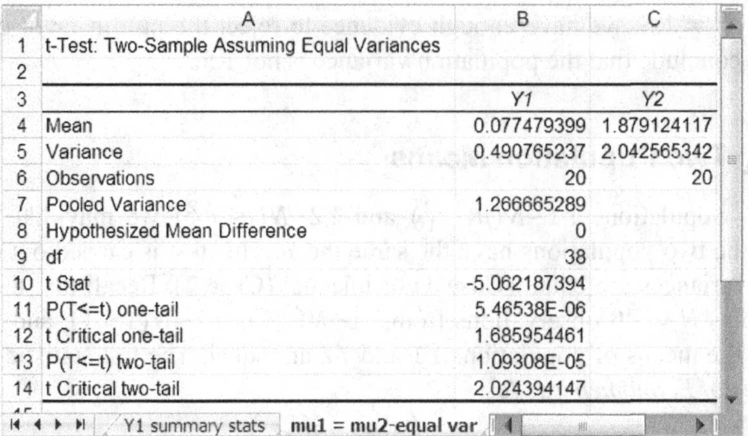

	A	B	C
1	t-Test: Two-Sample Assuming Equal Variances		
2			
3		*Y1*	*Y2*
4	Mean	0.077479399	1.879124117
5	Variance	0.490765237	2.042565342
6	Observations	20	20
7	Pooled Variance	1.266665289	
8	Hypothesized Mean Difference	0	
9	df	38	
10	t Stat	-5.062187394	
11	P(T<=t) one-tail	5.46538E-06	
12	t Critical one-tail	1.685954461	
13	P(T<=t) two-tail	1.09308E-05	
14	t Critical two-tail	2.024394147	

Y1 summary stats | mu1 = mu2-equal var

Go back to the **three samples** worksheet. Repeat the test using $Y1$ and $Y3$ and use the "unequal" variance test option. The test statistic and adjusted degrees of freedom for this test are given on pp. 717 and 718 of *Principles of Econometrics, 4e*.

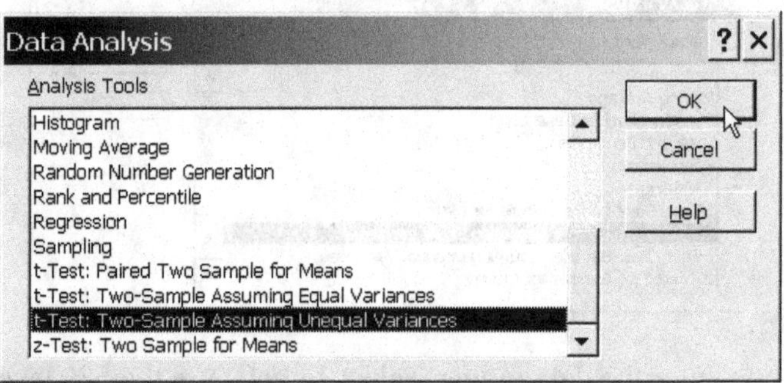

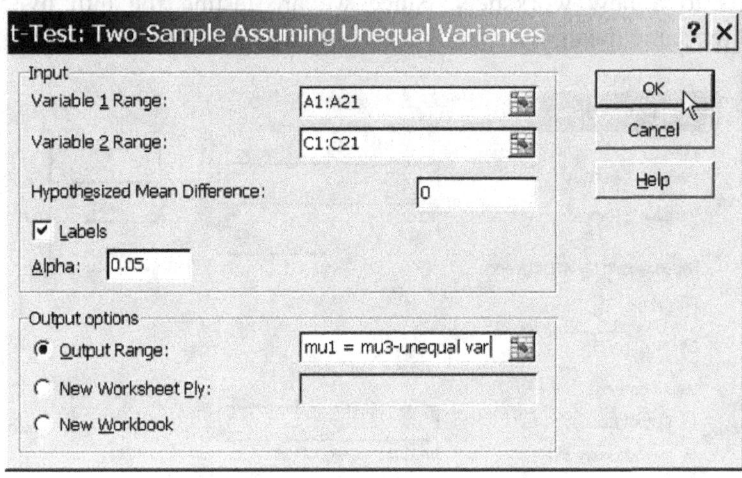

	A	B	C
1	t-Test: Two-Sample Assuming Unequal Variances		
2			
3		*Y1*	*Y3*
4	Mean	0.077479399	0.614201614
5	Variance	0.490765237	2.769870711
6	Observations	20	20
7	Hypothesized Mean Difference	0	
8	df	26	
9	t Stat	-1.329270642	
10	P(T<=t) one-tail	0.097652808	
11	t Critical one-tail	1.705617901	
12	P(T<=t) two-tail	0.195305617	
13	t Critical two-tail	2.055529418	

mu1 = mu3-unequal var / test v

Recall that $Y1 \sim N(0,1)$ and $Y3 \sim (1.5,4)$. We fail to reject the null hypothesis that the means are equal in this case. We commit a Type II error.

C.6.4 Testing Two Population Variances

Given two normal populations, we can test whether their variances are equal. Recall that the **three samples** we drew were from $1 \sim N(0,1)$,$Y2 \sim N(1.5,1)$ and $Y3 \sim (1.5,4)$. Let us first test the hypothesis that the variance of $Y2$ equals the variance of $Y1$. Go back to your **three samples** worksheet. Select the **Data** tab, and then the **Data Analysis** button on the **Analysis** group of commands. In the **Data Analysis** dialog box, select the **F-test Two-Sample for Variances**. This tool will carry out the F-test for equal variances shown on p. 718 of *Principles of Econometrics, 4e*.

In the dialog box, enter the range for $Y1$ first, and then enter the range for $Y2$. Which one is labeled **Variable 1** and which **Variable 2** does not matter for the outcome (p-value) of the test.

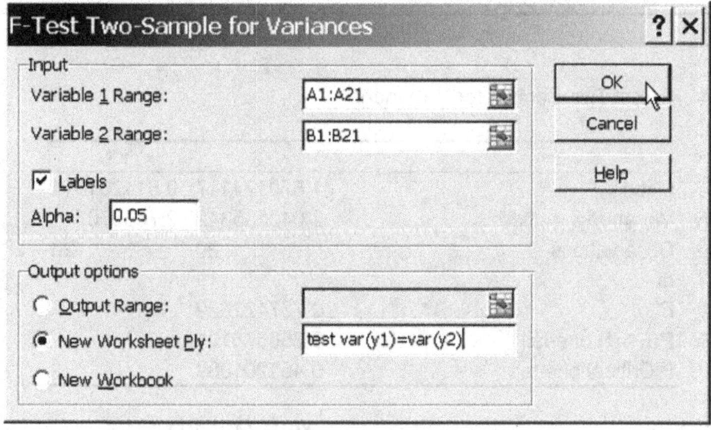

The test result shows the sample variances for $Y1$ and $Y2$, the value of the calculated F-statistic (0.2403) and the left-tail (since $F < 1$) critical value for a 5% test. The p-value is also reported, and based on this test we reject the equality of the population variances, even though we know them to be true. We commit a Type I error.

	A	B	C
1	F-Test Two-Sample for Variances		
2			
3		*Y1*	*Y2*
4	Mean	0.077479399	1.879124117
5	Variance	0.490765237	2.042565342
6	Observations	20	20
7	df	19	19
8	F	0.240269051	
9	P(F<=f) one-tail	0.001578898	
10	F Critical one-tail	0.461201089	
11			
12			

test var(y1)=var(y2) / three sample

Testing the variances of *Y*2 and *Y*3 we find ourselves unable to reject the hypothesis that the variances are equal, despite the fact that the null hypothesis is false. We commit a Type II error.

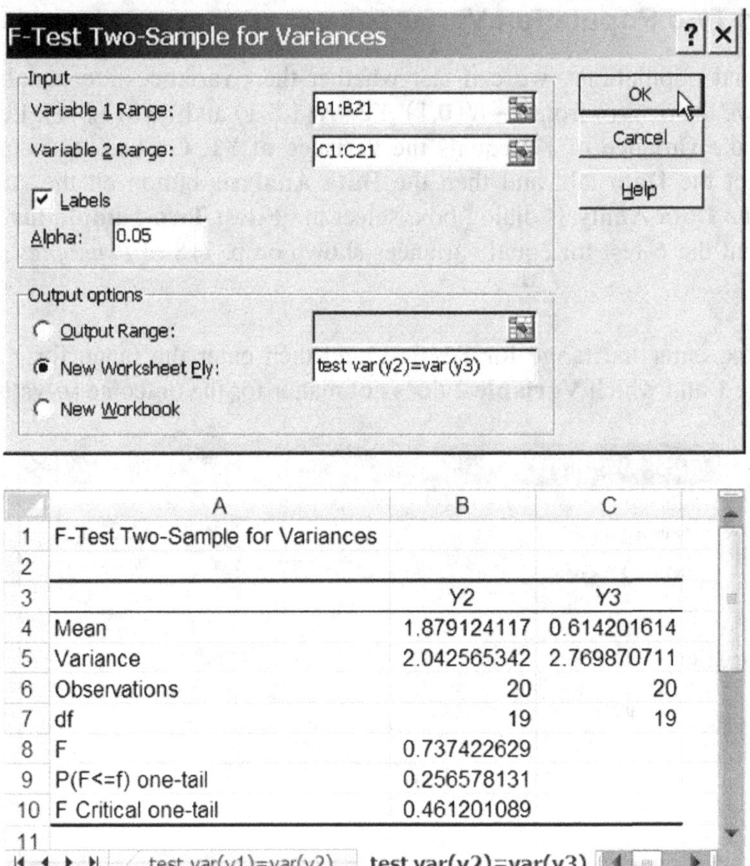

	A	B	C
1	F-Test Two-Sample for Variances		
2			
3		Y2	Y3
4	Mean	1.879124117	0.614201614
5	Variance	2.042565342	2.769870711
6	Observations	20	20
7	df	19	19
8	F	0.737422629	
9	P(F<=f) one-tail	0.256578131	
10	F Critical one-tail	0.461201089	
11			

test var(y1)=var(y2) / test var(y2)=var(y3)

C.7 TESTING POPULATION NORMALITY

Hypothesis tests and interval estimation procedures are based on the underlying normality of the population. If the population is not normal, the same procedures are used based on an appeal to the Central Limit Theorem, and assuming the sample is adequately large. If the population is normally distributed then no such worries exist. While there are many tests for normality we will suggest two. First, construct a histogram and look for a bell shape. Second, use the test proposed by Jarque and Bera.

C.7.1 A Histogram

Return to the worksheet **hip data**. For a histogram we must specify the "bins" into which the data will be placed. The worksheet **hip data summary statistics** contains the descriptive statistics (see Section C.1 of this workbook). The minimum hip width is 13.53 inches, and the maximum is 20.4. Specify the first bin to be "up to" 14 inches, and the last bin will be 20 "or more" inches. In cell **C1** enter the label **bin**. In **C2:C8** enter the values **14, 15, …, 20.**

Select the **Data** tab, and then the **Data Analysis** button on the **Analysis** group of commands. Select **Histogram** from the pull down list. Fill out the dialog box as shown below. Note that we have selected **Labels.** The **Output Range** is worksheet **hip data histogram**, and, most importantly, we want to **Chart Output**.

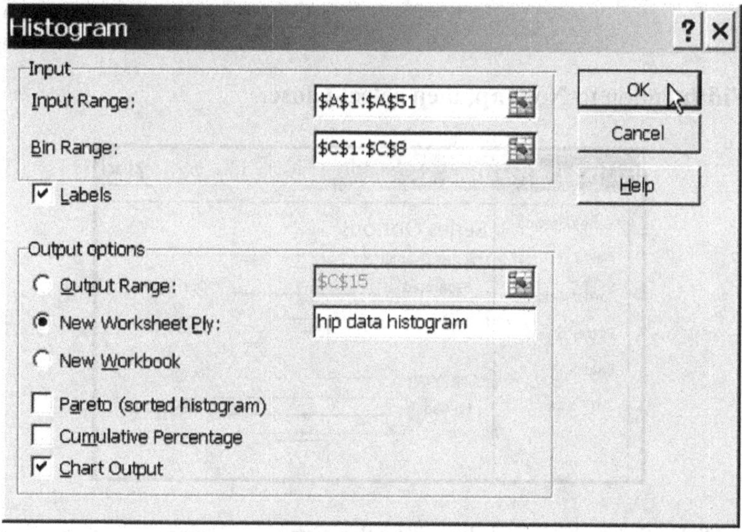

The resulting histogram is:

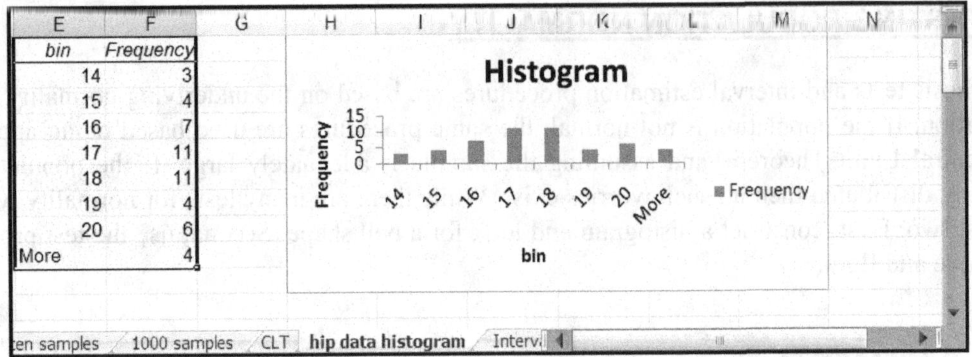

To beautify the histogram remove the spaces between the bars. Click inside the histogram until the bars have little circles surrounding them. **Right-click** and select **Format Data Series.**

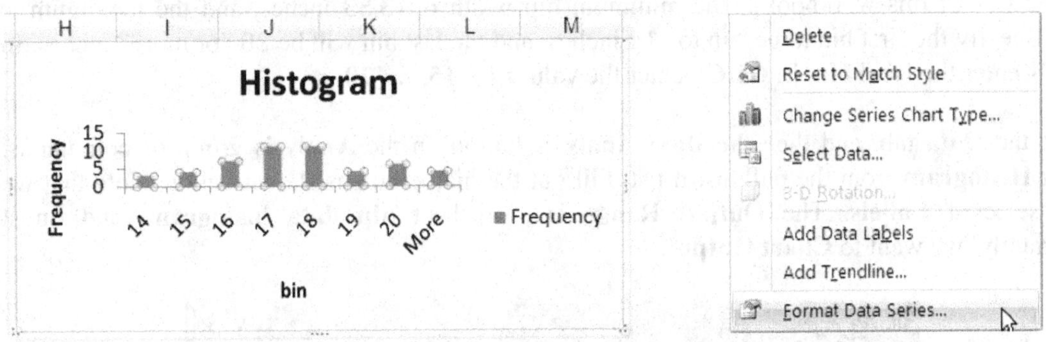

Slide the **Gap Width** button to **No Gap**, then select **Close.**

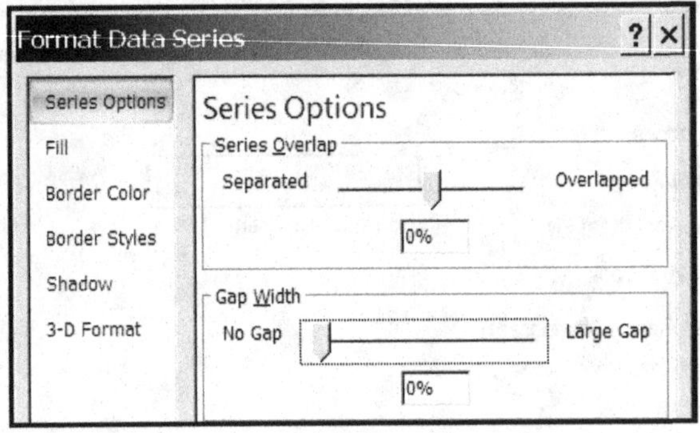

Select the corner of the figure box and drag it to the size you desire.

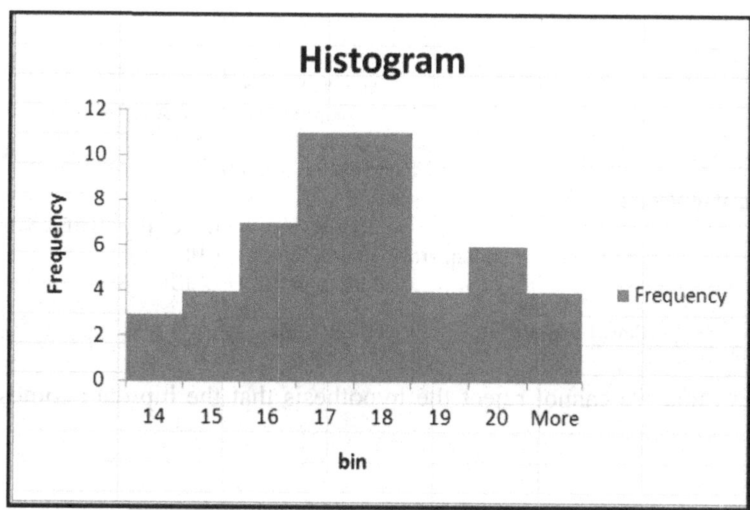

With only 50 data points, using too many bins can result in a figure with no shape. You should experiment with fewer bins of alternative sizes to see if you can improve the figure. Using one inch bins is logical.

C.7.2 The Jarque-Bera Test

The Jarque-Bera test for normality examines the **skewness** and **kurtosis** of the data (these terms are defined in Section C.1 of this manual). For a normal distribution the skewness is zero, and the "excess" kurtosis should be zero. The Jarque-Bera test statistic is:

$$JB = \frac{N}{6}\left(S^2 + \frac{(K-3)^2}{4}\right) \sim \chi^2_{(2)}$$

Using the formulas given in *Principles of Econometrics, 4e*, p. 702, the skewness and kurtosis coefficients are:

$$skewness = S = \frac{\tilde{\mu}_3}{\tilde{\sigma}^3} \quad \text{and} \quad kurtosis = K = \frac{\tilde{\mu}_4}{\tilde{\sigma}^4}$$

where:

$$\tilde{\sigma} = \sqrt{\frac{\Sigma(y_i - \bar{y})^2}{N}}\,, \qquad \tilde{\mu}_3 = \frac{\Sigma(y_i - \bar{y})^3}{N}\,, \qquad \tilde{\mu}_4 = \frac{\Sigma(y_i - \bar{y})^4}{N}$$

Use the results from the **statistics calculations** worksheet to make the following calculations. The critical value for this chi-square test will be obtained using the **CHIINV** function (see Section C.6.2 of this workbook) and the test *p*-value is obtained using **CHIDIST**. Enter the formulas shown below in a new worksheet called **Jarque Bera Template**.

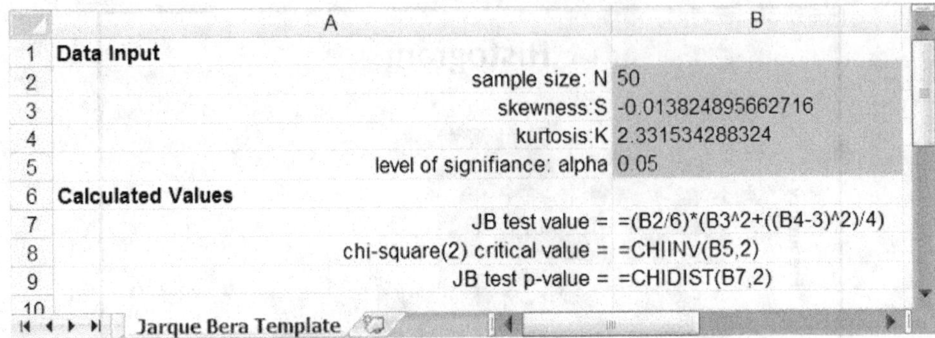

	A	B
1	**Data Input**	
2	sample size: N	50
3	skewness:S	-0.013824895662716
4	kurtosis:K	2.331534288324
5	level of signifiance: alpha	0.05
6	**Calculated Values**	
7	JB test value =	=(B2/6)*(B3^2+((B4-3)^2)/4)
8	chi-square(2) critical value =	=CHIINV(B5,2)
9	JB test p-value =	=CHIDIST(B7,2)
10		

Jarque Bera Template

The p-value shows that we cannot reject the hypothesis that the hip data comes from a normal distribution.

	A	B
1	**Data Input**	
2	sample size: N	50
3	skewness:S	-0.013824896
4	kurtosis:K	2.331534288
5	level of signifiance: alpha	0.05
6	**Calculated Values**	
7	JB test value =	0.932522747
8	chi-square(2) critical value =	5.991464547
9	JB test p-value =	0.627343294

Jarque Bera Template

INDEX